Pensions at a Glance 2011

RETIREMENT-INCOME SYSTEMS IN OECD AND G20 COUNTRIES

OECD

This work is published on the responsibility of the Secretary-General of the OECD. The opinions expressed and arguments employed herein do not necessarily reflect the official views of the Organisation or of the governments of its member countries.

Please cite this publication as:
OECD (2011), *Pensions at a Glance 2011: Retirement-income Systems in OECD and G20 Countries*, OECD Publishing.
http://dx.doi.org/10.1787/pension_glance-2011-en

ISBN 978-92-64-09523-6 (print)
ISBN 978-92-64-09628-8 (PDF)

The statistical data for Israel are supplied by and under the responsibility of the relevant Israeli authorities. The use of such data by the OECD is without prejudice to the status of the Golan Heights, East Jerusalem and Israeli settlements in the West Bank under the terms of international law.

Corrigenda to OECD publications may be found on line at: *www.oecd.org/publishing/corrigenda*.

Foreword

This fourth edition of Pensions at a Glance *provides an expanded range of indicators for comparing pension policies and the outcomes of these policies between OECD countries. The indicators are also, where possible, provided for new OECD member countries and the other major economies that are members of the G20. In Part I, five special chapters provide deeper analysis of the central issues of pensions, retirement and life expectancy.*

This report was prepared by the pensions team in the Social Policy Division of the OECD's Directorate for Employment, Labour and Social Affairs. The team comprises Edward Whitehouse, Anna Cristina D'Addio and Andrew Reilly. National officials – particularly delegates to the OECD Working Party on Social Policy and members of the OECD pension expert group – provided active and invaluable input to the report. For OECD countries, the results of the OECD pension models have been confirmed and validated by national authorities.

Chapter 1 in Part I on "Pensionable age and life expectancy, 1950-2050" was written by Edward Whitehouse. It is based on earlier work with Rafal Chomik of the Department of Work and Pensions in the United Kingdom while he was seconded to the OECD Secretariat. Anna Cristina D'Addio and Edward Whitehouse prepared Chapter 2 on "Trends in retirement and in working at older ages" and Chapter 3 "Pension incentives to retire". Anna D'Addio, Mark Keese (of the Employment Analysis and Policy Division of the OECD's Directorate for Employment, Labour and Social Affairs) and Edward Whitehouse wrote Chapter 4 "Helping older workers find and retain jobs". Edward Whitehouse was responsible for Chapter 5 "Linking pensions to life expectancy", the final special chapter in Part I.

The indicators related to private pensions were mainly provided by the OECD's private-pensions unit in the Directorate for Financial and Enterprise Affairs: Pablo Antolín, Stephanie Payet, Jean-Marc Salou and Juan Yermo.

The report has benefited from the commentary of many national officials and colleagues in the OECD Secretariat, notably John P. Martin, Monika Queisser, Stefano Scarpetta, Anne Sonnet and Fiona Stewart. It is a joint project co-financed by the European Commission and the OECD. The OECD pension models, that underpin the indicators of pension entitlements, use the APEX (Analysis of Pension Entitlements across Countries) models developed by Axia Economics.

Table of Contents

Part II

Pension-policy Indicators

Part III

Country Profiles

Editorial
Three Solutions to the Pensions Paradox

Pension policy has always involved balancing the *adequacy* of benefits with their *affordability*. This balancing act has got harder as a result of the recent economic and financial crisis. It adds to the existing and much greater challenge to pension systems arising from population ageing. Despite these short-term problems, it is important to remember that pensions are a long-term issue.

In the first instance, there is an obvious trade off between adequacy and sustainability: higher public pensions deliver larger incomes in old age but cost more. However, if public pensions are at risk of being inadequate, there will be pressure for *ad hoc* increases in pensions or supplementary retirement benefits to prevent old-age poverty.

Similarly, pension benefits can be too high, rendering the system financially unsustainable. If governments delay reforms, then the scale of adjustment to benefits needed in the medium or long term will be more sudden and painful. Greece, Hungary and Ireland have all had to accept substantial pension reforms as part of the fiscal consolidation required for international bail-outs. Such sudden changes make it very difficult for individuals to change their work, retirement and savings decisions to reflect the new financial realities.

How can governments maintain retirement-income adequacy without endangering financial sustainability? There are three main routes out of the dilemma.

The first is longer working lives. Half of OECD countries are already increasing statutory pension ages or will do so in the coming decades. Pension eligibility ages for men currently average 63 and, for women, 62. These will increase to nearly 65 by 2050 for both sexes on current plans. However, in all but five OECD countries, projected gains in life expectancy over the next four decades will outstrip prospective increases in pension ages. Thus, financial sustainability is not guaranteed unless pension ages are increased beyond current plans in most of the OECD.

As an alternative to higher pension ages, seven countries have introduced an automatic link between pension levels and life expectancy. But their effect is different: benefits will fall as people live longer. While stabilising the finances of the pension system, the adequacy of benefits may be jeopardised in the long term. It is surprising that the alternative approach of linking pension ages to life expectancy has been adopted by just a few countries. This policy would have the advantage of providing a clear signal of the need to work longer. And it would allow annual benefits to be maintained at a higher level than if people continued to draw their pensions at the same age as life expectancy increases.

Countries have also dismantled many of the incentives to retire early provided by their pension systems. But we still need to recognise that older workers face a range of barriers in finding and retaining jobs. Pension reforms need to be bolstered by action from government and employers on age discrimination, training opportunities for older workers and working conditions. The ongoing jobs crisis should not be used as an excuse to revert to failed past policies of pushing older workers off the unemployment rolls and into *de facto* early retirement, especially through long-term sickness or disability benefits. Keeping older workers in the labour force does not reduce job opportunities for the young.

The second way of achieving both adequacy and sustainability is to concentrate the efforts of public retirement provision on the most vulnerable. For example, three of the countries with the lowest rates of income poverty in old age – Canada, the Netherlands and New Zealand – spend only 4-5% of their national income on public pensions, well below the OECD average. In contrast, more than one in five older people in Greece and Spain are poor while public pension expenditure is relatively high. The key to explaining this pattern is greater *redistribution* within public provisions of retirement incomes. Of course, some countries would need to change the philosophy underlying their pension systems if they were to move in this direction, because it involves a weakening of the link between individual contributions and benefits. But this link is already being powerfully tested by demographic realities, which require public schemes to pay low implicit rates of return on contributions to maintain financial sustainability.

Indeed, many countries' reforms have increased redistribution in their retirement-income systems. Finland, France and Sweden, for example, protected low earners from the full force of benefit cuts. Australia and the United Kingdom have used some of the fiscal space created by higher pension ages to increase benefit levels, and these increases have been targeted on low-income retirees. In contrast, Austria, Germany and Japan have cut benefits across the board, including for low earners. And Hungary, Italy, Poland and the Slovak Republic have tightened the link between contributions and benefits, eliminating all or most redistribution.

The third solution is to encourage people to save for their own retirement to make up for reductions in public benefits that are already in the pipeline or are likely to be required. There have been some significant successes in this area. The KiwiSaver scheme in New Zealand, which automatically enrols people in private pensions unless they opt out, has rapidly expanded coverage of private pensions. The United Kingdom will follow this approach in 2012. The Riester pensions in Germany have also been widely taken up, notably among the young and low earners, groups that other countries have found hard to reach (although these plans rely on relatively generous fiscal incentives rather than automatic enrolment).

Public benefits are the cornerstone of old-age income support in OECD countries, accounting for 60% of old-age incomes on average. The remaining 40% is divided almost equally between private pensions and other savings on the one hand and income from working on the other. The public sector's role in providing incomes in old age will remain very important, but will diminish. Working longer and private pensions will inevitably have to fill the gap.

However, the financial crisis has sapped confidence in private pensions' ability to provide a secure retirement income. In some countries that substituted private pensions for part of public provision, recuperating contribution revenues that should go to private pension plans has proved an attractive way out of short-term fiscal problems. But reversal of these pension reforms, which sought to encourage more private provision for retirement, would be regrettable. Taking the long view, a *diversified* pension system – mixing public and private provision, and pay-as-you-go and pre-funding as sources of finances – is not only the most realistic prospect but the best policy.

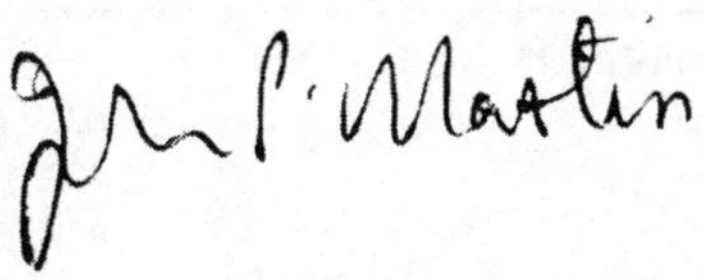

John P. Martin
Director
Employment, Labour and Social Affairs, OECD

Carolyn Ervin
Director
Financial and Enterprise Affairs, OECD

ISO Country Codes

OECD countries		OECD countries *(cont.)*	
Australia	AUS	New Zealand	NZL
Austria	AUT	Norway	NOR
Belgium	BEL	Poland	POL
Canada	CAN	Portugal	PRT
Chile	CHL	Slovak Republic	SVK
Czech Republic	CZE	Slovenia	SVN
Denmark	DNK	Spain	ESP
Estonia	EST	Sweden	SWE
Finland	FIN	Switzerland	CHE
France	FRA	Turkey	TUR
Germany	DEU	United Kingdom	GBR
Greece	GRC	United States	USA
Hungary	HUN		
Iceland	ISL	**OECD non-member countries**	
Ireland	IRL	Argentina	ARG
Israel	ISR	Brazil	BRA
Italy	ITA	China	CHN
Japan	JPN	India	IND
Korea	KOR	Indonesia	IDN
Luxembourg	LUX	Russian Federation	RUS
Mexico	MEX	Saudi Arabia	SAU
Netherlands	NLD	South Africa	ZAF

Pensions at a Glance 2011
Retirement-income Systems in OECD and G20 Countries

Executive Summary

Controversies over pension reforms in general – and increases in pension age in particular – have never been far from the news headlines since the previous edition of *Pensions at a Glance* was published in June 2009. It is appropriate, therefore, that the theme of this 2011 edition is pensions, retirement and life expectancy and the links between them.

"Pensionable age and life expectancy, 1950-2050" is the first of five special chapters of Part I. It shows that around half of OECD countries have already begun increasing pension ages or plan to do so in near the future. Pension ages will increase in 18 countries for women and 14 countries for men. By 2050, the average pensionable age in OECD countries will reach nearly 65 for both sexes. This represents an increase in 2010 of nearly 2.5 years for men and 4 years for women.

Life expectancy has seen a near-continuous increase in the latter half of the 20th century. The result was an increase in the length of time people spent in retirement. Between 1960 and 1993, life expectancy at national pension ages grew from an average of 13.4 to 16.5 years. For women, the increase in expected duration of retirement from 1960 was 4.8 years, to reach 21.6 years in 1993. In part, this reflected the trend to longer lives. But one-third of the growth was a result of falling pension ages: between 1950 and 2010, ten OECD countries reduced pensionable age for men at some point and 13 did so for women.

Most forecasts show continued growth in life expectancy in the future. On the basis of the United Nations projections, life expectancy at normal pension ages will increase further to 20.3 years for men and 24.5 years for women in 2050. This is despite the increases in pension age that are planned for the future. Indeed, only five countries have increased pension ages enough to stabilise the length of time spent in retirement in the coming four decades for both men and women, while a further four will do so for women alone.

This analysis looks only at normal pension ages. But most people in most OECD countries retire before the normal pension age. This is shown in Chapter 2 on "Trends in retirement and in working at older ages". The effective age at which people leave the labour market on average fell throughout the 1970s and 1980s. However, the long-term trend to earlier retirement ended for men in the mid-1990s and, for women, slightly later. Still, in 2002-07, the average age of leaving the labour market on OECD countries was 4-5 years lower than in the late 1960s, at about 63.5 years for men and 62.5 years for women. Simply to keep pace with the projected increase in life expectancy until 2050, effective retirement ages would need to increase to around 66.5 for men and nearly 66 for women. This is an indication of the scale of the challenge that governments face.

The policies that governments can pursue to extend working lives are the subject of the next two special chapters. The first of these looks at the "supply side", presenting information on incentives to work and retire embedded in pension system. The second looks at the "demand side", examining ways of ensuring that there are jobs for older workers.

There is overwhelming evidence that financial incentives affect retirement behaviour. "Pension incentives to retire", discussed in Chapter 3, therefore matters for reasons of economic efficiency. But they also matter for reasons of equity. People who work more and contribute more *should* have higher pensions. Equally, those who are forced to drop out of employment early, perhaps through no fault of their own, need to have a reasonable standard of living.

Improving incentives to retire has therefore been a central plank of most pension reforms: around half of OECD countries have taken action in this area. These changes include tighter qualifying conditions for early retirement, greater benefit penalties for early retirees and greater pension increments for people retiring after the normal pension age. Chapter 3 shows that these reforms have been effective, and that only a few OECD countries still have pension systems that strongly encourage early retirement. However, there remain ways in which most countries could further improve the financial incentives in their pension systems. Nine policy recommendations that would reward people for working longer are set out.

If there are barriers to working longer on the demand side, pension reforms designed to improve work incentives may be less effective. Chapter 4 looks at a range of policies with the aim of "Helping older workers find and retain jobs". On the part of employers, there are barriers in the form of ageist attitudes, particularly over the ability of older workers to adapt to change. Legislation against age discrimination and public-information campaigns have often (but not always) been effective. The high cost of employing older workers remains a problem in some countries. And employers sometimes use early retirement as a convenient way of adjusting the size of their workforces.

The employment opportunities for older workers can also be limited. Sometimes, their skills have become devalued and training remains targeted on younger workers. There is often a need for more help in finding jobs.

A recurring theme in the controversies over higher pension ages has been the claim that having more older workers in jobs reduces opportunities for younger workers. There is no evidence to support this view. Indeed, the employment rate of people in their early 20s is strongly and positively correlated with the employment rate of people in their late 50s. A survey of attitudes shows that more people are likely to support the view that older workers worsen the job prospects of youths in countries where the employment of either older or younger workers is relatively low.

Chapter 5 returns to the issues of pensions and life expectancy. Around half of OECD countries have elements in their mandatory retirement-income provision that provide an automatic link between pensions and a change in life expectancy. This represents a major shift in pension policy.

First, many have introduced mandatory defined-contribution schemes as a substitute for or in addition to public pension provision. Secondly, some have changed their pay-as-you-go public pension schemes into "notional accounts". Thirdly, a couple have a link between benefit levels or qualifying conditions for pensions and life expectancy. In addition to these changes, there has been a marked shift from defined-benefit to defined-contribution provision in voluntary, private pensions.

These changes have important implications for the way the cost of providing for pensions as life expectancy increases is shared. Increasingly, this will be borne by individual retirees in the form of lower benefits. Chapter 5 shows the degree of uncertainty inherent in projections of life expectancy and assesses policies "Linking pensions to life expectancy". It goes on to show how pension entitlements would be affected by slower or faster improvements in life expectancy than the central forecast.

Together, the five special chapters of Part I set out and evaluate the full range of policies that OECD countries have adopted to deal with growing pressure of population ageing on government budgets. Increases in pension age – the most visible and widely understood parameter of the pension system – have tended to grab the headlines. But these are only a small part of the story of pensions, retirement and life expectancy.

Part II of the report updates the "Indicators of pension policies" from the previous three editions of *Pensions at a Glance* and provides an extra 18 indicators compared with the previous edition. Furthermore, where possible the analysis has been extended to G20 countries that are not currently members of the OECD: Argentina, Brazil, China, India, Indonesia, The Russian Federation, Saudi Arabia and South Africa.

It begins with a look at the design of retirement-income systems, providing taxonomy to describe highly diverse retirement-income systems (Part II.1). The main parameters and rules of pension systems are presented to facilitate cross-country comparisons.

These parameters and rules are then used to model pension entitlements for men and women at different levels of earnings (Part II.2). While most of the indicators look at mandatory pension provision, there is also an analysis of typical voluntary private pensions in countries where these have broad coverage. Close attention is paid to the tax treatment of pensions and pensioners and how this affects living standards in retirement relative to when working.

The analysis of pension entitlements is forward looking, in the sense that it considers the value of benefits for workers entering the labour market today. The indicators in Part II.3 look at the financial position of people of pension age currently: at average incomes, sources of incomes and risk of poverty.

Having analysed the position of individuals, Part II.4 examines the finances of retirement-income systems as a whole. Here are data on public and private expenditure on pensions, contribution rates for mandatory pensions and aggregate contribution revenues for public pension schemes.

The background and context in which retirement-incomes systems must operate is presented in Part II.5. These indicators include demographic measures – such as life expectancy and fertility – and average earnings. Finally, Part II.6 offers information specifically about private pensions and public-pension reserve funds.

PART I

Policy Issues: Pensions, Retirement and Life Expectancy

An in-depth look at the questions pensions policy makers face today is provided in this part of the report. Pensions, retirement and life expectancy are the themes of the five chapters.

The first looks at pensionable ages, showing how these changed between 1950 and 2010. Around half of OECD countries are in the process of increasing pension ages or have already legislated increases for the future. This chapter also looks at how pension ages will develop between now and 2050 on current plans. By combining this information with projections of life expectancy, the implications for these changes for the length of time people spend in retirement is analysed.

The second chapter looks at retirement behaviour, showing how actual ages of labour-market exit compare with the normal pension ages presented in the first chapter. Data are presented on changes in work at older ages, showing a slowing or even a reversal of the trend to earlier retirement in some countries.

The financial incentives to retire or to remain in work at older ages embedded in pension systems have been shown to have an important effect on individuals' decisions. The third chapter looks at measures of retirement and work incentives and suggests policies to improve the situation.

Financial incentives alone are not enough to entrench a movement to working longer. The fourth chapter looks at measures that governments can take to help older workers find and retain jobs, such as combating ageism, building skills through training and dealing with the barriers to hiring older workers resulting from labour costs and employment-protection legislation.

Increasing pensionable ages, discussed in the first chapter, are one policy response to the continual growth in life expectancy. But many countries have gone further: pension plans that have an automatic link between pensions and life expectancy are discussed in the fifth and final chapter.

Pensions at a Glance 2011
Retirement-income Systems in OECD and G20 Countries

PART I

Chapter 1

Pensionable Age and Life Expectancy, 1950-2050

Around half of OECD countries have already begun increasing pension ages or plan to do so in the future: 18 countries for women and 14 countries for men. Recent increases in pensionable ages have often proved controversial because of their greater visibility to politicians and voters.

By 2050, the average pensionable age in OECD countries will reach nearly 65 for both sexes: an increase of nearly 2.5 years for men and 4 years for women on 2010. However, life expectancy is projected to grow faster than these increases in pension age. Life expectancy at pensionable age is forecast to increase by about 3 years for men and 2.5 years for women between 2010 and 2050.

Rapid ageing of the population around the world is a major challenge to affordability of pensions and financial sustainability of retirement-income systems. This problem has been reinforced by a long period during which increases in life expectancy were continually under-estimated by experts.[1]

This special chapter explores trends in one key parameter of the pension system: the age of eligibility for mandatory pension benefits.[2] The "retirement age" is the most visible parameter of the pension system. As such, it sends a clear signal for people in choosing when to cease work. Increases in pension age have often proved among the more contentious elements of pension reforms, compared with other, less visible, changes to retirement-income provision. The following section discusses some of the issues in defining pensionable age, which is not always as clear cut a concept as one might imagine.

Section 1.2 then presents a new dataset of the evolution of pension eligibility age covering a period of a century, looking back to 1950 and forwards to 2050. The main finding is that average pensionable age in OECD[3] countries dropped by nearly two years during the second half of the 20th century to 62.5 for men and 61.1 for women. Legislation already in place will increase it almost to 65 for both sexes by 2050.

The relationship between pension age and life expectancy – both observed in the past and forecast into the future – is examined in Section 1.3. The analysis shows how the expected duration of retirement has been, and is likely to be, affected by changes in pension age and by the near-continuous growth in life expectancy observed in the past. Between 1960 and the turn of the century, life expectancy after pensionable age is shown to have grown from 13.4 to 17.3 years for men and 16.8 to 22.1 years for women on average in OECD countries. However, life expectancy after normal pension age is projected to reach 20.3 and 24.6 years (for men and women respectively) in 2050, despite many OECD countries having already legislated for phased increases in the pension age in the future.

1.1. Defining "pensionable age"

Pensionable age is defined here as the age at which people can first draw full benefits (that is, without actuarial reduction for early retirement). Normal pension ages in most countries are clearly set out in legislation. However, it may be possible to retire earlier than the normal age without an "actuarial" reduction in pension benefits (to reflect the longer duration of benefit payment). Typically, this requires that certain contribution requirements are met (see the indicator of "Normal, early and late retirement" in Part II.1). Some countries do not have a "normal" pension age, instead defining a range of ages at which the pension may first be drawn. The definition adopted here is designed to be comparable between countries.

As in the rest of this report, a full career is defined as an individual starting work at age 20 and contributing in every year from that time. In countries where there are different retirement-income programmes for different groups of workers, the data relate to the main, national scheme for private-sector workers. The analysis does not take account of earlier retirement ages or more favourable treatment of, for example, public-sector employees or workers in specific hazardous or arduous occupations.[4] Where pension ages differ with women's marital status or the number of children that they have had, pension ages are shown for childless, unmarried women.[5]

Country-specific issues when it comes to defining pension age are addressed in detail in Box 1.1, which explains the reasoning behind the approach adopted here.

Box 1.1. **Defining pensionable age: Country-specific issues**

Recent reforms in ***France*** gradually increased the number of covered years for a full benefit from 37.5 years to 40 years in 2008 and 41 years in 2012. (Note that this volume was prepared before the increase in the standard pension age from 60 to 62 was legislated.) Assuming individuals start work at age 20, pensionable age as defined here will move from 60 to 61 in 2012 on the OECD measure (from 20 + 40 to 20 + 41 years). (Again, a further phased increase in the number of contribution years to 42 has been agreed since the detailed analysis was prepared.)

A similar difficulty arising with analysis of ***Turkey***: the abolition of the standard retirement age in 1969 meant that the sole constraint on receipt of a full pension was the required 25 years of contributions. Pensionable age for Turkey during the 1970s and 80s was around age 45 (20 + 25 years) on the standard assumption of entry at age 20. This will change in the future as the standard retirement age has been reinstated and will be gradually increased.

The standard retirement age in ***Hungary*** was 62 for men and 58 for women in 2002 (reaching a unisex age of 62 in 2009). However, a full pension was accessible as early as 60 for men (with a minimum of 38 covered years) and 55 for women (with 37 years of contributions). Recent reforms have tightened the rules for early retirement. For men born after 1950 and women after 1958, early retirement without reduction will no longer be allowed. Consequently the pensionable age (as defined here) and standard retirement age will coincide for these cohorts.

Similarly, the statutory retirement age in ***Belgium*** is 65 but actuarially unreduced benefits are available from age 60 with 35 years' contributions. Also, in ***Greece*** the normal pension age is 65 but unreduced benefits are now paid from any age with 37 years of contributions, giving a pensionable age of 57 (20 + 37) on the definition used here. The recent reform, however, will restrict access to early retirement to age 60 in the future.

The phased increase in the statutory pension age – from 65 to 67 beginning in 2035 – in ***Germany*** will open up a difference between this and the OECD definition of pensionable age. It will still be possible to claim a full pension after the reform with 45 years of contributions. Thus, pensionable age on the OECD definition will remain at 65 (that is, 20 + 45 years).

In ***Italy***, statutory pension ages in the long term will be 65 for men but 60 for women. However, the notional-accounts scheme means that benefits for women retiring at age 60 will be actuarially reduced to reflect the longer expected duration over which the benefit will be paid compared with drawing the pension from age 65. The earlier statutory pension age for women of age 60 is treated here as preferential access to early retirement and not as a difference in pensionable age. The normal pension age will be increased in line with life expectancy from 2015. But it will still be possible to retire at any age with 40 years of contribution.

In most cases, the pensionable age applies to all individuals at a particular point in time. Where the phasing-in of changes in pension ages affects different date-of-birth cohorts differently, it is easy to convert these into the ages that particular people will reach pension age. In others – ***Italy*** and ***Turkey***, for example – different conditions apply depending on the number of years of contributions achieved at a certain date or the age of first entry into the pension system. Following the conventions outlined above, the relevant pension age has been computed for individuals with a full contribution history from age 20.

The final question is how to deal with countries that do not set a normal pension age in their main schemes. In ***Finland*** and ***Sweden***, for example, there is no fixed age for public, earnings-related benefits. However, access to resource-tested schemes – the national and guarantee pensions respectively – is restricted to age 65 and above. This is used as pensionable age here.

1.2. Trends in pensionable ages over a century

Figures 1.1 and 1.2 and Tables 1.1 and 1.2 show the development of pensionable ages in OECD countries over time. The data begin in 1949, by which time all OECD countries bar Korea and Turkey already had some sort of public, retirement-income provision in place. Historical trends in pension ages from 1949 to 2010 and future pension ages on current plans up to 2050 together give a century of pensionable ages for 30 OECD countries.

Up to 2010, pension ages were constant for both men and women in only six countries: Finland, Iceland, Mexico, the Netherlands, Spain and the United Kingdom. Pension ages for men remained the same (while those for women changed) in Australia, Austria, Belgium, Hungary, Portugal and Switzerland. Only in Poland did the pension age for women remain unchanged while that for men was raised.

Looking forward, 11 OECD countries plan to increase pension ages for both men and women: Australia, the Czech Republic, Denmark, France, Greece, Hungary, Italy, Korea, Turkey, the United Kingdom and the United States.[6] A further two – Austria and the Slovak Republic – will increase pensionable ages for women to equalise those of men during that period. Switzerland will increase women's pension age but it will still be one year below men's. These changes have already been legislated but will be phased in over the coming years.

Figure 1.1 shows the time series of pensionable ages for men, country-by-country. (The data underlying the charts is given in Table 1.1). The charts group the countries into five different time series patterns. By far the most common pattern – illustrated in Panels A and B at the top of Figure 1.1 – is for an increase in pension age over time. For example, Australia, the United Kingdom and the United States had pension ages for men of age 65 for much of the period since 1950. But increases to 67 or 68 are now underway or are planned for the future. Poland increased its pensionable age from 60 to 65 for men: the Czech Republic and Hungary are in the process of following suit.

The left-hand side of the middle row of Figure 1.1 (Panel C) confirms that, for men, there has been no change in pension age since 1950, nor is any currently planned in the period 2010-50, in nine OECD countries. This is the second most common pattern of pensionable ages over time. Most stick at 65 over this period, but Iceland has retained a pension age of 67 while Belgium provides full-career workers with early retirement at age 60 without reduction in benefits.

The right-hand chart in this middle row (Panel D) shows the pattern for five countries that reduced the pension age in the past. In Canada, Ireland and Norway, for example, pensionable age was as high as age 70 in the earlier part of the period studied. The other reductions were from 67 to 65 in Sweden and from 65 to 60 in Luxembourg (for unreduced early-retirement benefits). Declines in pension age typically took place many years ago, with the most recent being completed by the early 1990s.

The penultimate group of countries – at the bottom, left-hand side of Figure 1.1 (Panel E) – show a U-shaped pension age for men over time. This is the result of a reduction in the past, followed by a period of no change, and now a reversal of earlier declines that is already being phased in or has been announced. For example, France cut pensionable age from 65 to 60 in the 1980s. However, the increase in the contribution requirement for a full benefit to 41 years from 2012 raises the OECD measure of pensionable age above 60. New Zealand cut pension age from 65 to 60 some time ago, only to return quickly to 65 around the turn of the century. The most striking development was in Turkey: the statutory retirement age of 60 was abolished and replaced with a requirement of around 25 years'

Figure 1.1. **Pensionable age in OECD countries, men, 1950-2050**

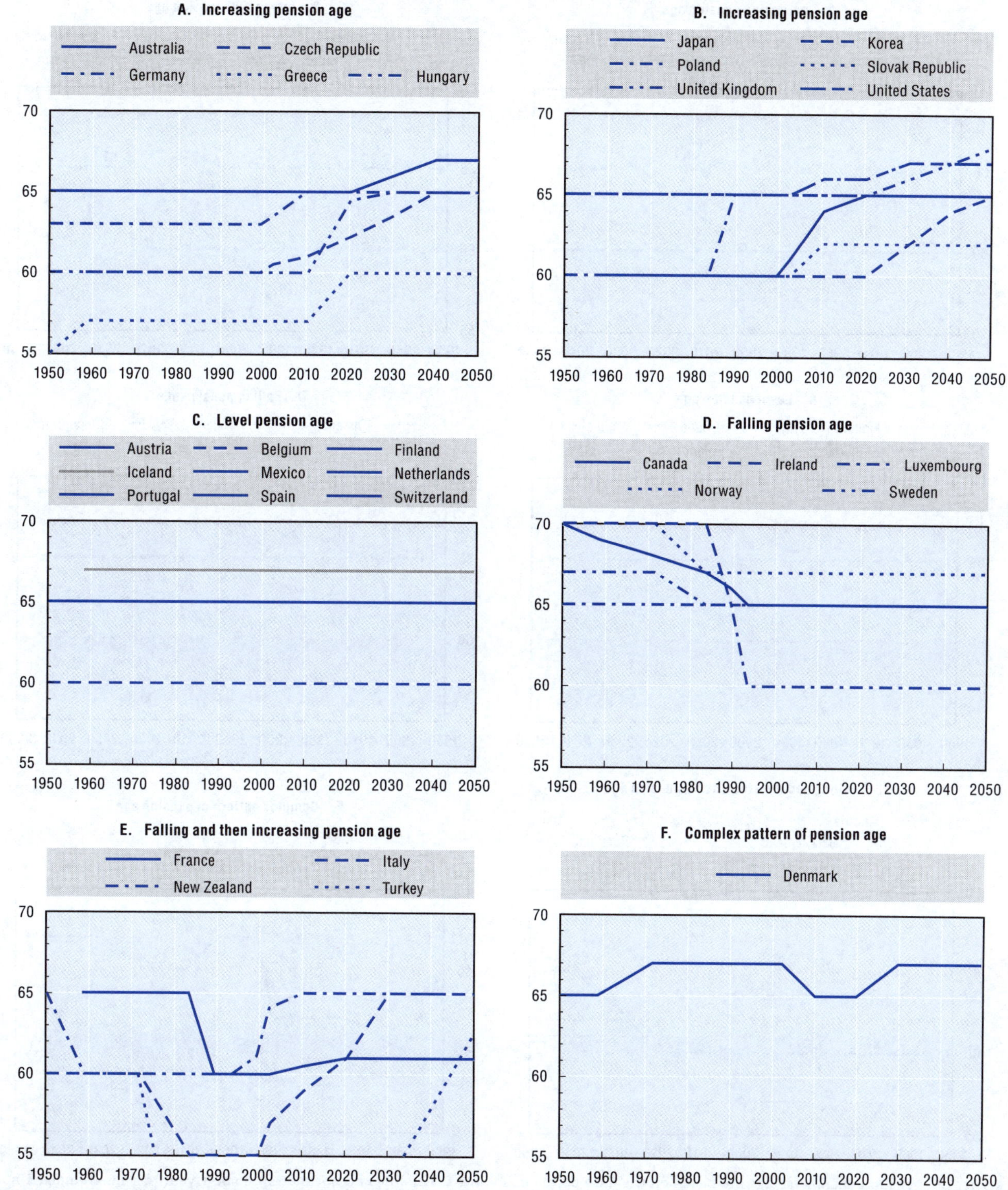

Note: Changes in pensionable age are based on the data points in Table 1.1. The lines do not therefore show year-to-year changes. Data for Turkey when the pension age is less than 55 are not shown.

Source: National officials, OECD calculations and Turner (2007).

StatLink http://dx.doi.org/10.1787/888932370151

Figure 1.2. **Pensionable age in OECD countries, women, 1950-2050**

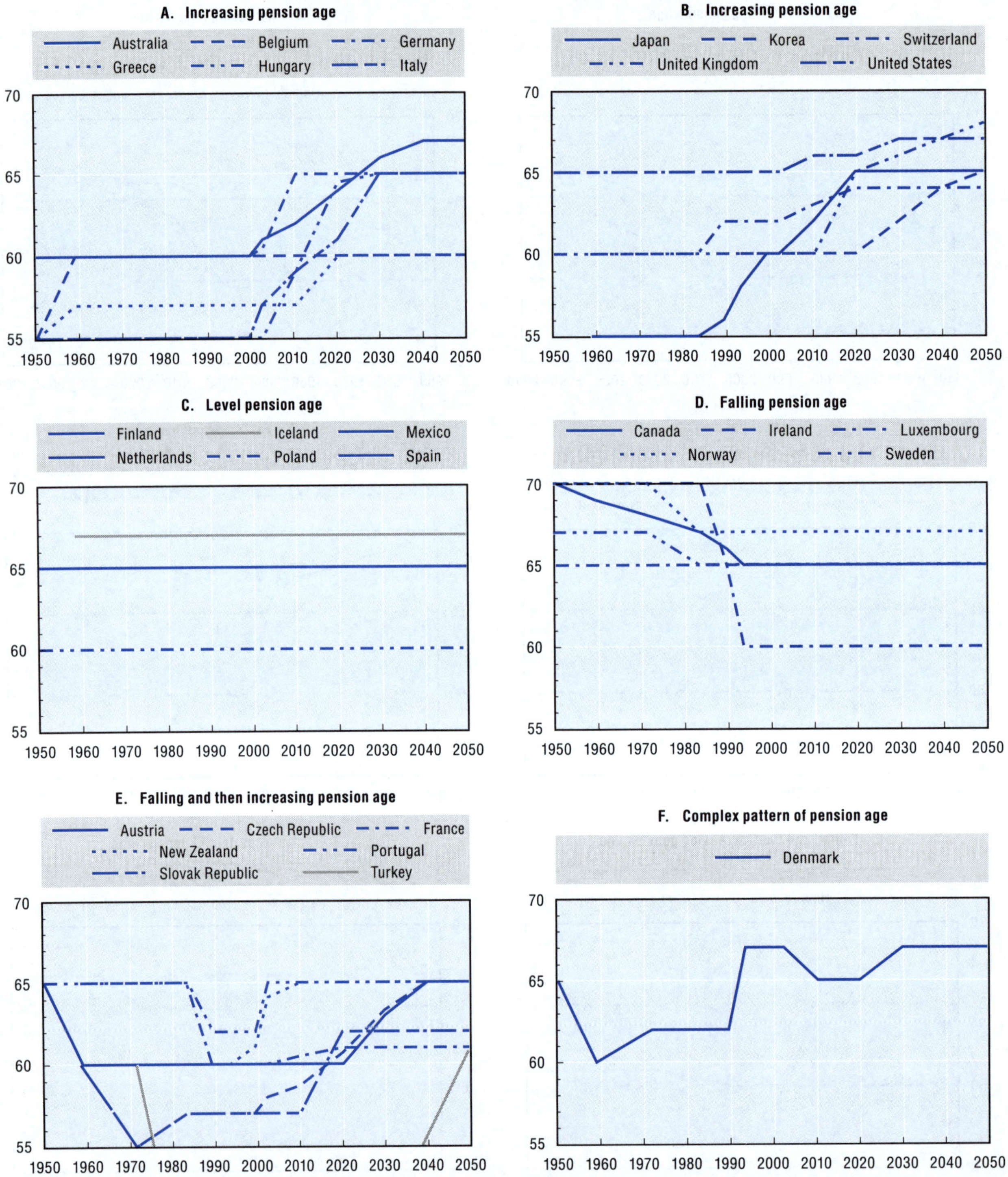

Note: Changes in pensionable age are based on the data points in Table 1.1. The lines do not therefore show year-to-year changes. Data for Turkey when the pension age is less than 55 are not shown.

Source: National officials, OECD calculations and Turner (2007).

StatLink http://dx.doi.org/10.1787/888932370170

Table 1.1. **Men's pensionable age in OECD countries, 1949-2050**

	1949	1958	1971	1983	1989	1993	1999	2002	2010	2020	2030	2040	2050
Australia	65.0	65.0	65.0	65.0	65.0	65.0	65.0	65.0	65.0	65.0	66.0	67.0	67.0
Austria	65.0	65.0	65.0	65.0	65.0	65.0	65.0	65.0	65.0	65.0	65.0	65.0	65.0
Belgium	60.0	60.0	60.0	60.0	60.0	60.0	60.0	60.0	60.0	60.0	60.0	60.0	60.0
Canada	70.0	69.0	68.0	67.0	66.0	65.0	65.0	65.0	65.0	65.0	65.0	65.0	65.0
Czech Republic		60.0	60.0	60.0	60.0	60.0	60.0	60.5	61.0	62.2	63.5	65.0	65.0
Denmark	65.0	65.0	67.0	67.0	67.0	67.0	67.0	67.0	65.0	65.0	67.0	67.0	67.0
Finland		65.0	65.0	65.0	65.0	65.0	65.0	65.0	65.0	65.0	65.0	65.0	65.0
France		65.0	65.0	65.0	60.0	60.0	60.0	60.0	60.5	61.0	61.0	61.0	61.0
Germany	63.0	63.0	63.0	63.0	63.0	63.0	63.0	63.5	65.0	65.0	65.0	65.0	65.0
Greece	55.0	57.0	57.0	57.0	57.0	57.0	57.0	57.0	57.0	60.0	60.0	60.0	60.0
Hungary	60.0	60.0	60.0	60.0	60.0	60.0	60.0	60.0	60.0	64.5	65.0	65.0	65.0
Iceland		67.0	67.0	67.0	67.0	67.0	67.0	67.0	67.0	67.0	67.0	67.0	67.0
Ireland	70.0	70.0	70.0	70.0	65.0	65.0	65.0	65.0	65.0	65.0	65.0	65.0	65.0
Italy	60.0	60.0	60.0	55.0	55.0	55.0	55.0	57.0	59.0	61.0	65.0	65.0	65.0
Japan		60.0	60.0	60.0	60.0	60.0	60.0	61.0	64.0	65.0	65.0	65.0	65.0
Korea						60.0	60.0	60.0	60.0	60.0	62.0	64.0	65.0
Luxembourg	65.0	65.0	65.0	65.0	65.0	60.0	60.0	60.0	60.0	60.0	60.0	60.0	60.0
Mexico		65.0	65.0	65.0	65.0	65.0	65.0	65.0	65.0	65.0	65.0	65.0	65.0
Netherlands	65.0	65.0	65.0	65.0	65.0	65.0	65.0	65.0	65.0	65.0	65.0	65.0	65.0
New Zealand	65.0	60.0	60.0	60.0	60.0	60.0	61.1	64.1	65.0	65.0	65.0	65.0	65.0
Norway	70.0	70.0	70.0	67.0	67.0	67.0	67.0	67.0	67.0	67.0	67.0	67.0	67.0
Poland	60.0	60.0	60.0	60.0	65.0	65.0	65.0	65.0	65.0	65.0	65.0	65.0	65.0
Portugal	65.0	65.0	65.0	65.0	65.0	65.0	65.0	65.0	65.0	65.0	65.0	65.0	65.0
Slovak Republic		60.0	60.0	60.0	60.0	60.0	60.0	60.0	62.0	62.0	62.0	62.0	62.0
Spain	65.0	65.0	65.0	65.0	65.0	65.0	65.0	65.0	65.0	65.0	65.0	65.0	65.0
Sweden	67.0	67.0	67.0	67.0	65.0	65.0	65.0	65.0	65.0	65.0	65.0	65.0	65.0
Switzerland		65.0	65.0	65.0	65.0	65.0	65.0	65.0	65.0	65.0	65.0	65.0	65.0
Turkey		60.0	45.0	45.0	45.0	45.0	45.0	44.0	44.9	48.6	53.1	57.7	62.3
United Kingdom	65.0	65.0	65.0	65.0	65.0	65.0	65.0	65.0	65.0	65.0	66.0	67.0	68.0
United States	65.0	65.0	65.0	65.0	65.0	65.0	65.0	65.0	66.0	66.0	67.0	67.0	67.0
Average	**64.3**	**63.9**	**63.8**	**62.9**	**62.7**	**62.4**	**62.4**	**62.6**	**62.9**	**63.5**	**64.1**	**64.4**	**64.6**

Note: Germany refers to West Germany for the period 1949-2002. Czechoslovakian data are used for the Czech and Slovak Republics where appropriate. Where there is more than one value per calendar year, these have been averaged. The recent amendment, in the United Kingdom, to the rate of increase in pension age is not reflected in the table.
Source: National officials, OECD calculations and Turner (2007).

StatLink http://dx.doi.org/10.1787/888932372089

contributions to receive a full pension, which translates into a pension age of 44-45 on the OECD definition. (This pensionable age is such an outlier that it is not shown in the chart for much of the time.)

Finally, Denmark is shown alone in the bottom right of Figure 1.1 (Panel F). It is unique in increasing pension age from 65 to 67, cutting it back to 65 and then increasing it again to 67 by 2027. Denmark will link pension age to life expectancy after 2027, but the impact of this policy is not shown.[7]

Figure 1.1 illustrates significant differences in the pace at which pension ages changed. Falls in pension ages were generally rapid (Panels D and E of Figure 1.1). Increases in pensionable age, in contrast, have tended to be phased in more gradually. For example, the Italian reform only affected workers who had been in the system for 18 years or less; the new system will only be fully in place once labour-market entrants of 1995 and beyond have retired. Under reforms in Turkey, the new retirement age of 65 will only be reached for

Table 1.2. **Women's pensionable age in OECD countries, 1949-2050**

	1949	1958	1971	1983	1989	1993	1999	2002	2010	2020	2030	2040	2050
Australia	**60.0**	**60.0**	**60.0**	**60.0**	**60.0**	**60.0**	**60.0**	**61.0**	**62.0**	**64.0**	66.0	67.0	67.0
Austria	65.0	**60.0**	**60.0**	**60.0**	**60.0**	**60.0**	**60.0**	**60.0**	**60.0**	**60.0**	**63.0**	65.0	65.0
Belgium	**55.0**	60.0	60.0	60.0	60.0	60.0	60.0	60.0	60.0	60.0	60.0	60.0	60.0
Canada	70.0	69.0	68.0	67.0	66.0	65.0	65.0	65.0	65.0	65.0	65.0	65.0	65.0
Czech Republic		60.0	**55.0**	**57.0**	**57.0**	**57.0**	**57.0**	**58.0**	**58.7**	**60.7**	**63.3**	65.0	65.0
Denmark	65.0	**60.0**	**62.0**	**62.0**	**62.0**	67.0	67.0	67.0	65.0	65.0	67.0	67.0	67.0
Finland		65.0	65.0	65.0	65.0	65.0	65.0	65.0	65.0	65.0	65.0	65.0	65.0
France		65.0	65.0	65.0	60.0	60.0	60.0	60.0	60.5	61.0	61.0	61.0	61.0
Germany	**60.0**	**60.0**	**60.0**	**60.0**	**60.0**	**60.0**	**60.0**	**60.5**	65.0	65.0	65.0	65.0	65.0
Greece	55.0	57.0	57.0	57.0	57.0	57.0	57.0	57.0	57.0	60.0	60.0	60.0	60.0
Hungary	**55.0**	**55.0**	**55.0**	**55.0**	**55.0**	**55.0**	**55.0**	**55.0**	**59.0**	64.5	65.0	65.0	65.0
Iceland		67.0	67.0	67.0	67.0	67.0	67.0	67.0	67.0	67.0	67.0	67.0	67.0
Ireland	70.0	70.0	70.0	70.0	65.0	65.0	65.0	65.0	65.0	65.0	65.0	65.0	65.0
Italy	**55.0**	**55.0**	**55.0**	55.0	55.0	55.0	55.0	57.0	59.0	61.0	65.0	65.0	65.0
Japan		**55.0**	**55.0**	**55.0**	**56.0**	**58.0**	**60.0**	**60.0**	**62.0**	65.0	65.0	65.0	65.0
Korea						60.0	60.0	60.0	60.0	60.0	62.0	64.0	65.0
Luxembourg	65.0	65.0	65.0	65.0	65.0	60.0	60.0	60.0	60.0	60.0	60.0	60.0	60.0
Mexico		65.0	65.0	65.0	65.0	65.0	65.0	65.0	65.0	65.0	65.0	65.0	65.0
Netherlands	65.0	65.0	65.0	65.0	65.0	65.0	65.0	65.0	65.0	65.0	65.0	65.0	65.0
New Zealand	65.0	60.0	60.0	60.0	60.0	60.0	61.1	64.1	65.0	65.0	65.0	65.0	65.0
Norway	70.0	70.0	70.0	67.0	67.0	67.0	67.0	67.0	67.0	67.0	67.0	67.0	67.0
Poland	60.0	60.0	60.0	60.0	**60.0**	**60.0**	**60.0**	**60.0**	**60.0**	**60.0**	**60.0**	**60.0**	**60.0**
Portugal	65.0	65.0	65.0	65.0	**62.0**	**62.0**	**62.0**	65.0	65.0	65.0	65.0	65.0	65.0
Slovak Republic		60.0	**55.0**	**57.0**	**57.0**	**57.0**	**57.0**	**57.0**	**57.0**	62.0	62.0	62.0	62.0
Spain	65.0	65.0	65.0	65.0	65.0	65.0	65.0	65.0	65.0	65.0	65.0	65.0	65.0
Sweden	67.0	67.0	67.0	65.0	65.0	65.0	65.0	65.0	65.0	65.0	65.0	65.0	65.0
Switzerland		**60.0**	**60.0**	**60.0**	**62.0**	**62.0**	**62.0**	**62.0**	**63.0**	**64.0**	**64.0**	**64.0**	**64.0**
Turkey			60.0	45.0	45.0	45.0	45.0	**40.0**	**41.0**	**45.2**	**50.4**	**55.6**	**60.8**
United Kingdom	**60.0**	**60.0**	**60.0**	**60.0**	**60.0**	**60.0**	**60.0**	**60.0**	**60.0**	65.0	66.0	67.0	68.0
United States	65.0	65.0	65.0	65.0	65.0	65.0	65.0	65.0	66.0	66.0	67.0	67.0	67.0
Average	**62.9**	**62.3**	**61.9**	**61.3**	**61.0**	**61.0**	**61.1**	**61.3**	**61.8**	**62.9**	**63.7**	**64.1**	**64.4**

Note: Data shown in **bold** type indicates that pension ages are different for women than men. Germany refers to West Germany for the period 1949-2002. Czechoslovakian data are used for the Czech and Slovak Republics where appropriate. Where there is more than one value per calendar year, these have been averaged. The recent amendment, in the United Kingdom, to the rate of increase in pension age is not reflected in the table.

Source: National officials, OECD calculations and Turner (2007).

StatLink http://dx.doi.org/10.1787/888932372108

people retiring after 2050, since an increase from age 60 to 65 will be phased in for labour-market entrants from 2008 onwards. In contrast, New Zealand and Poland increased pension ages much more rapidly.

Turning to women's pension ages, exactly one half of OECD countries have had at some time a different pension age for women from men. This is demonstrated in the detailed data of Table 1.2: where women's pension age is lower than men's – it is never higher – the data are shown in bold face. These cases account for 28% of the data points in Table 1.2.[8] The difference in pensionable age between the sexes is most commonly five years. It is never larger than five years and averages 3.8 years.

Figure 1.2 repeats the country-country time-series analysis of Figure 1.1, this time for women. Again, countries have been grouped into five time-series patterns.

The first row of Figure 1.2 (Panels A and B) shows the time series for 11 countries where women's pension ages were flat and then increased. Of these countries, only in Greece, Korea and the United States have women's pension ages always been the same as men's. In five other countries in this group, women's pensionable ages were below those for men and so have increased further. These comprise Australia, Germany, Hungary, Italy and the United Kingdom. In Belgium and Switzerland, women's pension ages have increased while men's remained the same. Finally, Japan increased pensionable ages for both sexes from 60 to 65, but the increase was a little earlier in time for men than for women.

In the second row of Figure 1.2 at the left-hand side (Panel C), both men's and women's pension ages have remained the same since 1950 and will remain the same until 2050 in Finland, Iceland, Mexico, the Netherlands and Spain. Only Poland, of this group, plans to maintain differential pension ages for women in the long term, with an increase in pension age for men from 60 to 65 while women's pension age remains at 60.

There have never been different pension ages for men and women in the five countries in Panel D. Women's pension age – as for men's – fell in the past but there are no current plans to increase it in the future.

Panel E shows seven countries where pension ages for women fell in the past and have, in most cases, since increased. Future increases are already legislated in Austria, the Czech and Slovak Republics, and Turkey to equalise pension ages between men and women and, in some cases, then increase pension age for both sexes. Portugal equalised pension ages between men and women in the past, while France and New Zealand have always had equal pension ages, with the same pattern of pension age over time applying to men and women. Finally, Panel F shows the more complex time series pattern of pension age in Denmark. Through the 1960s, 1970s and 1980s, pension age for women was below that for men.

1.3. Expected duration of retirement: Life expectancy at pensionable age

Reductions in pension age up to 1993 in many OECD countries came at the same time as rapid increases in life expectancy. In the early part of the 20th century, most of the gains in total life expectancy were due to lower mortality at younger ages: at birth, during childhood and at working age. But in the second half of the 20th century, mortality risk at retirement ages has also fallen significantly. Between 1960 and 2010, OECD-average life expectancy at age 65 increased by around 3.9 years for men and 5.4 years for women (Figure 1.3). Increases in life expectancy at age 60 were larger than at age 65.

The United Nations population division projects further increases in life expectancy between 2010 and 2050. These amount to 3.1 additional years for men and 3.6 years for women at age 65. As in the past, the lengthening of life expectancy at age 60 is greater, but by a smaller margin than observed between 1960 and 2010.

Data on national pension ages from Section 1.2 above are now combined with information on developments in mortality and life expectancy. The calculations give the number of years of additional years of life after normal pension age (on average[9]) between countries and over time. This concept is here called "expected retirement duration" for short. Since this illustrates the length of the period over which pension benefits must be paid, it is an important determinant of cost of paying for pensions.

Figure 1.3. **Life expectancy at age 60 and 65 by sex, OECD average, 1960-2050**

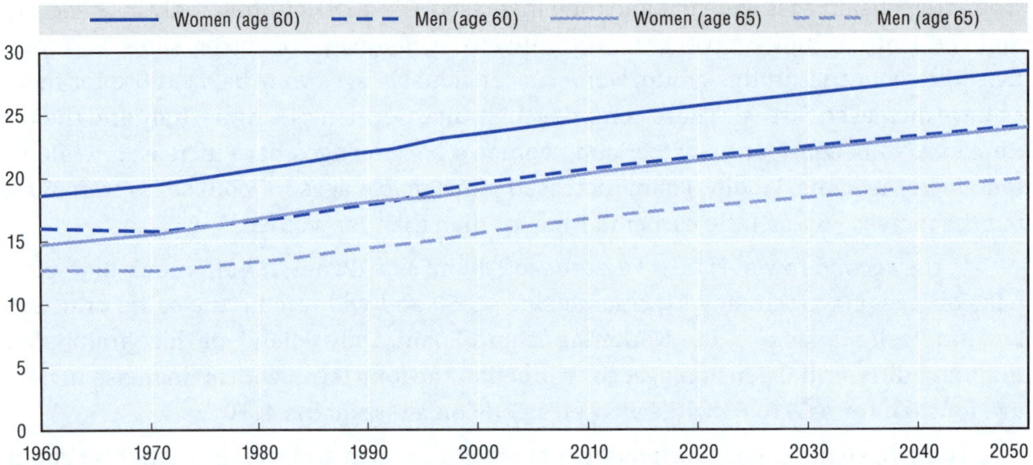

Source: Historical data on life expectancy from the *OECD Health Database 1960-95*. Recent data and projections of life expectancy in the future based on the *United Nations Population Division Database, World Population Prospects – The 2008 Revision.*

StatLink http://dx.doi.org/10.1787/888932370189

Tables 1.3 and 1.4 provide detailed national calculations for men and women respectively. In 2010, the period in retirement to death from normal pension age is 18.5 years on average for men. For women, the expected duration in retirement from normal pension age averages 23.3 years, nearly five years longer than for men. The longest retirement durations for men in 2010 – over 20 years – are found in seven countries where the pension age is age 60 or lower: Belgium, France, Greece, Italy, Korea, Luxembourg and Turkey. Long retirement durations for women in 2010 – above 25 years – are also found in countries with low pension ages, such as Austria, Belgium, France, Greece, Italy and Korea.

In contrast, retirement durations are the shortest for men in Poland and the Slovak Republic, reflecting the short life expectancy in these countries: at age 65, for example, life expectancy for men at age 65 is 14.4 and 13.8 years respectively, compared with an OECD average of 16.9 years and 18.8 years or more in Iceland, Japan and Switzerland. Other countries with short retirement durations for men in 2010 include those with pension ages already above age 67: Iceland and Norway. There are also short expected retirement durations for women in these countries plus the United States. However, different pension ages for the sexes in Hungary, Poland and the Slovak Republic mean that these do not feature among those with the shortest life expectancy at pension age for women (whereas they do for men). Moreover, life expectancy at age 60 or age 65 is closer to the OECD average for women than it is for men.

Figures 1.4 and 1.5 summarise the pattern in life expectancy at pensionable age over time for different countries, again for men and women separately. These figures group countries by the degree to which pension age has changed over the period from 1960 to 2050.

To explore the impact of life-expectancy changes over time, it is useful first to focus on the countries that saw no change in pension age over the period analysed. This group comprises nine countries for men, as shown in the bottom row of Figure 1.4 (Panels E and F). Average expected duration in retirement increased for these countries from 13.2 years for men in the 1960s to 17.8 years in 2010. With no future increase in pension age

Table 1.3. **Life expectancy after pensionable age in the OECD, 1958-2050, men**

	1958	1971	1983	1989	1993	1999	2002	2010	2020	2030	2040	2050
Australia	12.5	12.5	14.2	14.7	15.7	16.6	17.5	18.6	19.5	19.3	19.0	19.7
Austria	12.0	12.0	13.1	14.3	14.7	15.7	16.0	17.5	18.7	19.5	20.3	21.1
Belgium	15.3	15.3	16.6	17.6	18.1	19.2	19.4	21.1	22.3	23.1	24.0	24.8
Canada		10.7	12.8	14.4	15.8	16.3	17.1	18.3	19.1	19.9	20.7	21.4
Czech Republic	15.4	14.2	14.3	14.8	15.7	16.9	16.5	17.0	16.9	17.8	17.2	18.1
Denmark	13.7	11.7	11.9	12.2	12.0	13.0	13.4	16.4	17.1	15.8	16.5	17.2
Finland	11.5	11.4	13.0	13.9	14.1	15.2	15.5	16.8	17.6	18.3	19.1	19.8
France	12.5	13.0	14.2	18.8	19.4	20.2	20.5	21.7	22.4	23.3	24.0	24.8
Germany	14.2	14.1	15.2	16.0	16.5	17.6	17.2	17.0	17.9	18.7	19.5	20.3
Greece	19.9	20.7	21.6	22.4	22.7	23.1	22.7	24.0	21.8	22.5	23.3	24.1
Hungary	15.6	15.1	14.5	14.8	14.5	14.9	15.6	16.5	14.4	14.5	15.4	16.3
Iceland			13.5	14.0	14.7	14.9	15.8	16.8	17.5	18.3	19.1	19.8
Ireland	7.6	7.7	7.9	13.1	13.4	14.1	15.2	16.9	17.7	18.5	19.2	20.0
Italy		16.7	17.1	23.6	24.2	25.4	23.8	22.8	21.7	19.4	20.1	20.9
Japan	14.8	16.6	19.0	20.0	20.2	20.9	20.9	19.8	19.6	20.3	21.0	21.6
Korea					16.2	17.5	18.7	20.2	21.1	19.9	19.6	19.3
Luxembourg	12.5	11.4	12.9	13.8	17.8	19.0	19.2	20.8	22.1	23.0	23.8	24.6
Mexico	14.2	15.3	15.5	16.2	16.1	16.4	16.4	17.2	17.9	18.3	18.6	18.9
Netherlands	13.9	13.3	13.7	14.3	14.4	15.1	15.7	17.3	18.1	19.0	19.8	20.6
New Zealand		15.7	16.8	17.9	18.8	19.0	17.9	18.1	19.0	19.7	20.5	21.2
Norway	9.5	8.9	12.5	12.7	12.8	13.7	14.3	15.7	16.6	17.3	18.1	18.9
Poland	15.9	15.0	15.7	14.3	14.2	15.0	13.9	14.4	14.9	15.6	16.4	17.2
Portugal	12.4	11.8	13.4	14.3	14.2	15.0	15.5	16.3	17.1	17.8	18.5	19.2
Slovak Republic	16.6	15.5	15.3	15.3	16.1	15.9	16.1	14.9	15.7	16.6	17.6	18.6
Spain	13.1	13.7	14.9	15.6	15.9	16.2	16.6	17.9	19.0	19.9	20.6	21.4
Sweden	11.7	12.0	14.7	15.4	15.5	16.4	16.8	17.9	18.8	19.5	20.3	21.1
Switzerland	12.9	13.3	14.6	15.5	15.9	16.9	17.5	18.9	20.0	20.8	21.6	22.4
Turkey		14.6	29.2	29.9	30.5	31.1	31.5	31.1	28.4	24.5	21.0	22.5
United Kingdom	11.9	12.3	13.2	13.8	14.2	15.4	16.0	16.9	17.7	17.5	17.2	16.9
United States	12.8	13.2	14.4	15.0	15.3	16.1	16.7	16.8	17.3	16.8	17.2	17.7
Average	**13.4**	**13.5**	**15.0**	**16.2**	**16.7**	**17.4**	**17.7**	**18.5**	**18.9**	**19.2**	**19.6**	**20.3**

Note: Life-expectancy is calculated using data from 1960 for the pensionable ages applicable in 1958.
Source: Data on pensionable ages over time from Table 1.1. Historical data on life expectancy are taken from the *OECD Health Database* 1960-95. Recent data and projections of life expectancy in the future based on the *United Nations Population Division Database, World Population Prospects – The 2008 Revision.*

StatLink http://dx.doi.org/10.1787/888932372127

as on current plans, men's retirement duration in these countries will expand further to a projected 20.9 years in 2050. The equivalent analysis for the five countries where women's ages have not changed (Figure 1.5, Panel E), shows an increase from 15.5 years in 1960 to 20.8 years in 2010 and 24.1 years in 2050. This illustrates that a policy of "no change" on pension age does not, in practice, mean there are no changes: it means an ever extending average period in retirement and so a continual increase in pension costs.

Turning to the countries where pension ages have changed over time, the top rows for Figures 1.4 and 1.5 show countries with relatively large adjustments. The increase in pensionable ages in Italy will significantly reduce expected retirement duration: from a peak of over 25 years for men to around 20 years at the end of the forecast horizon. For women, expected retirement duration peaked at 30 years in 1999 and is projected to fall to 25.5 years in 2050.

Table 1.4. **Life expectancy after pensionable age in the OECD, 1958-2050, women**

	1958	1971	1983	1989	1993	1999	2002	2010	2020	2030	2040	2050
Australia	19.4	20.0	22.4	22.8	23.7	24.5	24.2	24.3	23.7	22.6	22.5	23.3
Austria	18.6	19.0	20.6	22.1	22.6	23.7	23.8	25.1	26.1	24.6	23.6	24.5
Belgium	18.5	19.3	21.1	22.5	23.1	23.9	23.6	25.8	27.0	28.0	28.9	29.8
Canada		14.5	17.2	18.7	19.9	20.1	20.4	21.4	22.3	23.1	24.0	24.8
Czech Republic	18.5	23.3	21.4	22.1	23.0	24.1	23.1	23.8	23.1	22.3	21.6	22.5
Denmark	19.3	18.6	19.6	19.9	15.6	16.1	16.6	19.8	20.8	19.6	20.3	21.0
Finland	13.7	14.4	17.5	17.8	18.0	19.5	19.3	21.0	22.0	22.9	23.8	24.7
France	15.6	16.8	18.4	24.0	24.6	25.3	25.4	26.5	26.9	27.8	28.7	29.5
Germany	18.1	19.0	20.8	21.8	22.5	23.7	23.3	20.7	21.7	22.6	23.5	24.4
Greece	21.5	22.5	23.7	25.2	25.6	26.1	25.3	27.1	25.3	26.3	27.4	28.3
Hungary	22.6	23.2	23.5	24.2	24.2	24.7	25.4	22.6	19.0	19.4	20.3	21.1
Iceland			16.5	17.0	17.0	17.2	18.3	19.2	20.2	21.1	22.0	22.9
Ireland	9.4	10.0	10.6	16.5	17.0	17.6	18.6	20.6	21.6	22.5	23.4	24.3
Italy		25.2	26.5	28.1	28.8	29.9	28.1	27.4	26.3	23.7	24.6	25.5
Japan	22.8	25.0	27.7	28.3	25.9	26.3	27.4	26.7	25.2	26.0	26.9	27.7
Korea					20.8	22.2	23.2	25.2	26.2	25.1	24.6	24.5
Luxembourg	14.5	14.7	16.8	17.8	22.9	24.2	23.7	24.9	25.9	26.8	27.7	28.6
Mexico	14.6	16.0	17.2	17.9	17.9	18.0	18.2	19.4	20.4	21.0	21.5	21.9
Netherlands	15.3	16.2	18.3	18.9	18.8	19.1	19.1	20.4	21.2	22.0	22.8	23.5
New Zealand		19.8	21.1	22.0	22.7	22.6	20.9	20.9	21.8	22.6	23.4	24.3
Norway	11.1	11.9	16.7	16.7	16.8	17.5	17.7	18.9	19.9	20.8	21.7	22.5
Poland	18.7	18.9	19.9	19.9	20.1	21.0	21.8	23.1	24.0	24.9	25.8	26.6
Portugal	14.5	14.2	16.5	19.8	19.8	20.8	18.8	20.2	21.2	22.1	22.9	23.6
Slovak Republic	18.4	23.7	22.3	22.8	23.7	23.6	23.8	24.9	21.0	22.0	23.0	23.9
Spain	15.3	16.3	18.2	19.2	19.8	20.3	20.6	21.8	22.8	23.6	24.4	25.1
Sweden	13.3	14.9	18.5	19.1	19.1	19.9	20.0	21.1	21.9	22.7	23.4	24.2
Switzerland	19.0	20.5	22.9	22.3	22.6	23.2	23.4	24.1	24.0	24.9	25.8	26.6
Turkey		16.0	30.8	31.9	32.5	33.1	37.2	36.9	34.7	30.9	27.2	23.2
United Kingdom	18.9	19.8	21.0	21.5	21.9	22.7	23.3	24.5	21.2	21.1	22.0	21.9
United States	15.8	17.1	18.6	18.8	18.9	19.1	19.1	19.3	20.2	20.1	21.0	21.9
Average	**17.0**	**18.2**	**20.2**	**21.4**	**21.7**	**22.3**	**22.5**	**23.3**	**23.2**	**23.4**	**23.9**	**24.6**

Note: Life-expectancy is calculated using data from 1960 for the pensionable ages applicable in 1958.

Source: Data on pensionable ages over time from Table 1.2. Historical data on life expectancy are taken from the OECD *Health Database 1960-95*. Recent data and projections of life expectancy in the future based on the *United Nations Population Division Database, World Population Prospects – The 2008 Revision*.

StatLink http://dx.doi.org/10.1787/888932372146

With the possibility of retiring at any age with 20-25 years of contributions, the expected duration of retirement in Turkey is way off the scale of the charts. For men, the peak value is 32 years and for women, 37 years (both occurring in 2002). This means that a woman with a full contribution history from age 20 could draw a pension for nearly twice as many years as the time she spent paying into the system. For men, the expected duration of drawing a pension could be nearly 30% longer than the period they spent contributing.

In some other cases where pension ages have been increased, the expected duration in retirement will remain broadly stable for significant periods. In Greece, for example, life expectancy at pensionable age for men is projected to remain in the range 22-24 years from 1993 to 2050. Similarly, in the Czech Republic, retirement duration for men is expected to be around 17 years from 1999 to 2040. A comparable pattern is observed for men in Hungary, Korea, New Zealand and Poland. In Australia and the United Kingdom, increases in pension age for women from 60 to 67 and 68 respectively are sufficient to ensure that expected duration of retirement in 2050 is about the same as it was in 1993.

Figure 1.4. **Life expectancy at pensionable age in OECD countries, men, 1950-2050**

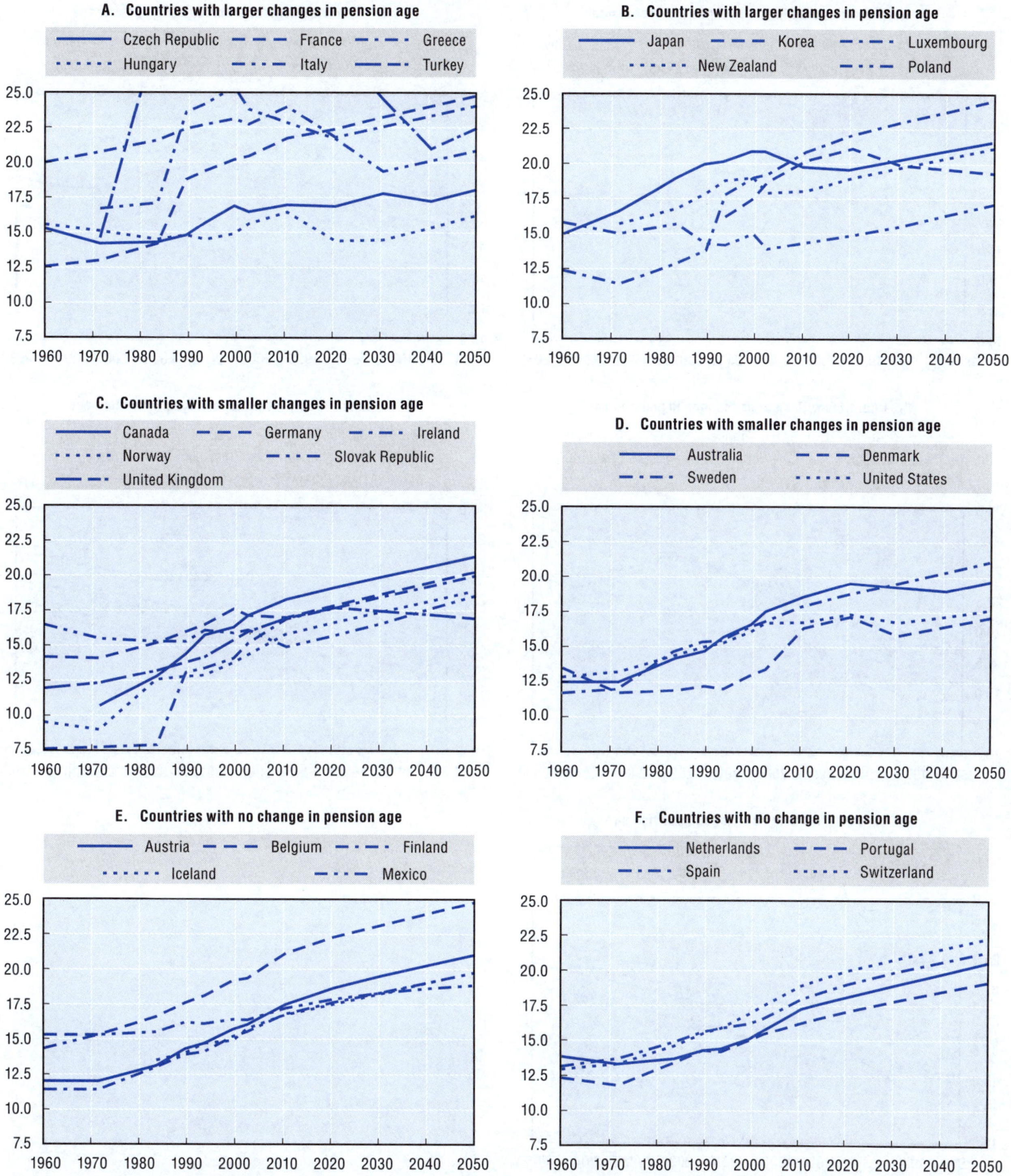

Note: Values have been capped at 25 years, which means that expected retirement duration in Turkey is off the scale.

Source: Data on pensionable ages over time from Table 1.1. Historical data on life expectancy are taken from the *OECD Health Database 1960-95*. Recent data and projections of life expectancy in the future based on the *United Nations Population Division Database, World Population Prospects – The 2008 Revision*.

StatLink http://dx.doi.org/10.1787/888932370208

Figure 1.5. **Life expectancy at pensionable age in OECD countries, women, 1950-2050**

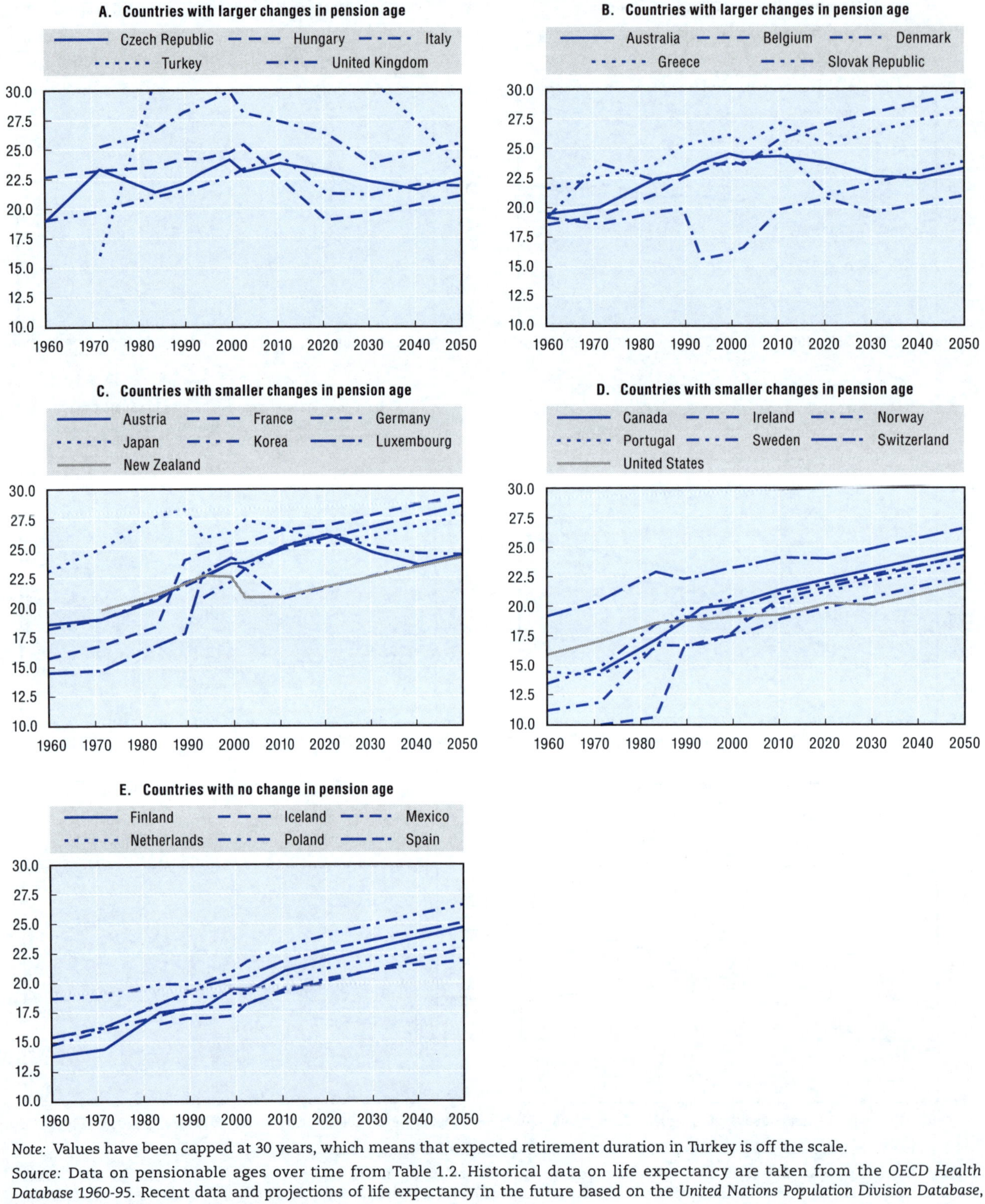

Note: Values have been capped at 30 years, which means that expected retirement duration in Turkey is off the scale.

Source: Data on pensionable ages over time from Table 1.2. Historical data on life expectancy are taken from the *OECD Health Database 1960-95*. Recent data and projections of life expectancy in the future based on the *United Nations Population Division Database, World Population Prospects – The 2008 Revision*.

StatLink http://dx.doi.org/10.1787/888932370227

However, men's pension age started at 65 in both countries. In the United Kingdom, expected duration of retirement for men is projected to fall to its 2010 level by 2050. But the increase in Australia for men is insufficient to prevent a continued increase in life expectancy at pensionable age.

1.4. Conclusions and policy implications

The pension age is the most visible parameter of the retirement-income system. It has an impact on the financial incentives to retire at different ages, which are analysed in more detail in Chapter 3 of Part I ("Pension incentives to retire"). As a signal, it can also have an important effect on people's retirement decisions.

The long-term survey of policy revealed a period of significant decline in pension ages in the latter half of the 20th century (Figure 1.6). Between 1950 and 2010, ten countries reduced pensionable age for men at some point and 13 did so for women. The average pension age in 30 OECD countries fell from 64.3 years in 1949 to a nadir of 62.4 years in 1993 for men, a drop of nearly two years. For women, the fall over the same period was also just below two years, from 62.9 to 61.0 years in 1993.

Figure 1.6. **Average pensionable age in OECD countries by sex, 1950-2050**

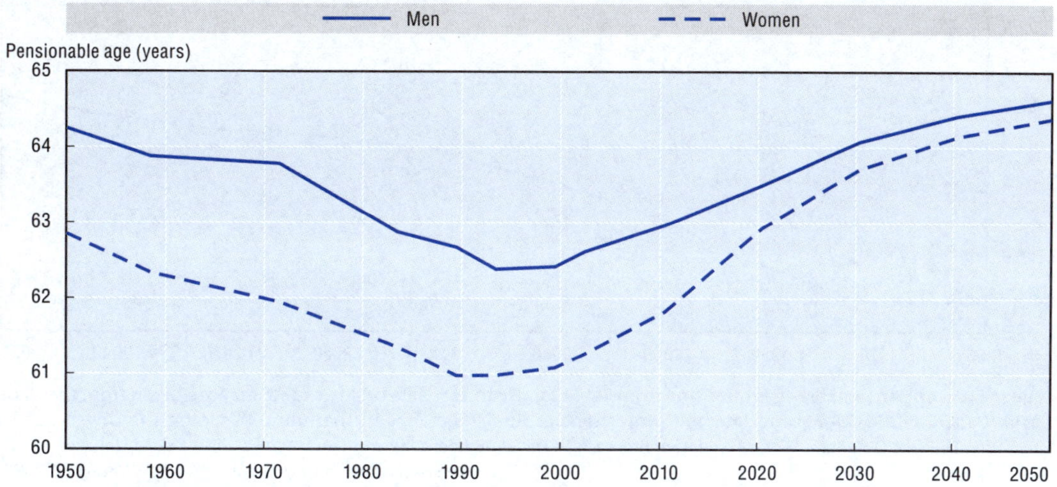

Source: National officials, OECD calculations and Turner (2007).

StatLink http://dx.doi.org/10.1787/888932370246

Beginning in the 1990s and after, governments started taking action to reverse the trend and put in place legislation that has already increased or will increase pensionable age up to 2050. From a low point in 1993, 14 countries have increased or plan to increase pension ages for men and 18 for women. Already by 2010, average pension ages have increased by 0.5 years for men and 0.8 years for women from the low point.

Looking forward, current plans will increase the average pensionable age to 64.6 years for men and 64.4 years for women in 2050. The slightly lower average pension age for women is because Poland and Switzerland still have legislation in place to keep differential ages in the long term and equalisation of men's and women's pension ages in Turkey will not be complete by 2050.

Despite these increases, it is noticeable that the average pension age for men will only reach the same level as 1950 by 2040. Increases in pension age are larger and often earlier for women than for men, reflecting the equalisation of pension ages between the sexes in 12 of the 15 countries that have had different pensionable ages at some point. However, even for women, the pensionable age will only reach the level it was in 1950 from 2020 onwards.

Life expectancy has seen a near-continuous increase in the latter half of the 20th century; and most estimates show continued growth in the future. Over the period from 1960 to the low-point for pension ages in 1993, the amount of time a man of pension age could expect to live grew from 13.4 to 16.7 years (Figure 1.7). Over 40% of the growth in expected retirement duration was a result of falling pension ages, with a small majority coming from longer life expectancy. For women, the increase in expected duration of retirement from 1960 was 4.7 years, to reach 21.7 years in 1993. For women, 70% of the growth was a result of longer life expectancy and 30% from lower pension ages.

Figure 1.7. **Life expectancy after pensionable age by sex, 1960-2050**

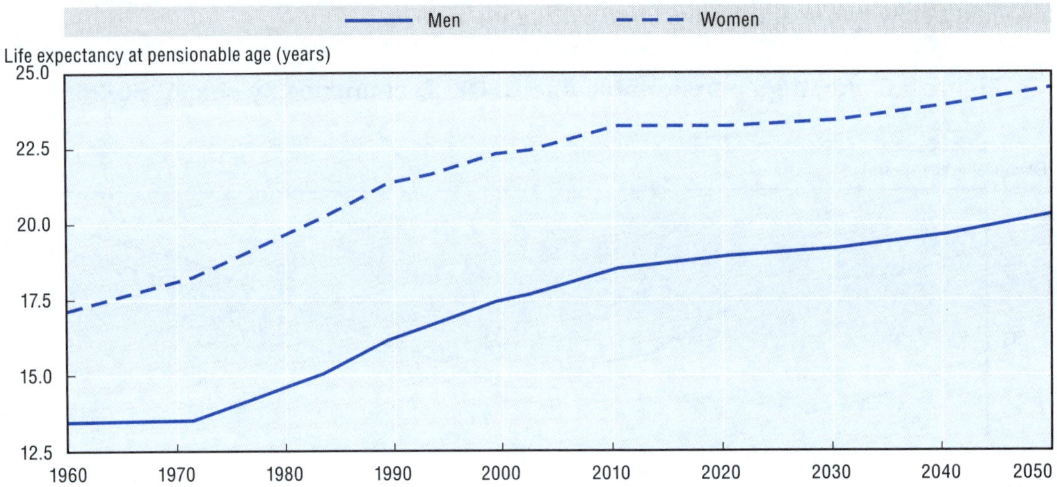

Source: Data on pensionable ages over time from Table 1.2. Historical data on life expectancy are taken from the OECD *Health Database 1960-95*. Recent data and projections of life expectancy in the future based on the *United Nations Population Division Database, World Population Prospects – The 2008 Revision.*

StatLink http://dx.doi.org/10.1787/888932370265

In the recent period of 1993-2010, the expected duration of retirement has increased more slowly than before: 1.6 additional years for women taking it to 23.3 years and 1.8 extra years for men, increasing to 18.5 years. The slower growth for women reflects the fact that pension ages increased more rapidly than men's over this period. If pension ages had not increased, expected retirement duration would have been 0.8 years longer for women and 0.4 years for men in 2010.

Looking forward to 2050, expected retirement duration in the coming four decades is projected to grow at a much slower rate than observed in the five decades from 1960 to 2010. On average in OECD countries, women in 2050 are projected to have a life expectancy of 24.6 years at pensionable age, compared with 20.3 years for men. Only five OECD countries – Hungary, Italy, Korea, Turkey and the United Kingdom – have increased pension ages sufficiently to stabilise or reduce the expected duration of retirement between 2010 and 2050 for both men and women. Australia, Austria and the Czech and Slovak Republics will do so for women alone (due to equalisation of pension ages).

In some countries, the debate about a later pensionable age has been framed not only in terms of sustainable pension-system finances but also higher pension levels for retirees than would otherwise be affordable. There is a trade-off between benefit levels and pension age. The terms of this trade-off can be demonstrated by using annuity rates to calculate pension replacement rates at different ages for a given budget constraint on the pension provider. Such a hypothetical scenario is illustrated in Figure 1.8 using the OECD pension models. It shows that delaying retirement by five years from age 65 allows for a pension replacement rate of 72%, compared with 60% at 65. (The rate of 60% was chosen because it is approximately the average replacement rate for people with mean earnings in OECD countries.) Conversely, earlier retirement means that the given budget needs to be spread over a longer period. In this case, retiring five years earlier, at age 60 would result in a replacement rate of 52%.

Figure 1.8. **The trade-off between the replacement rate and pensionable age**

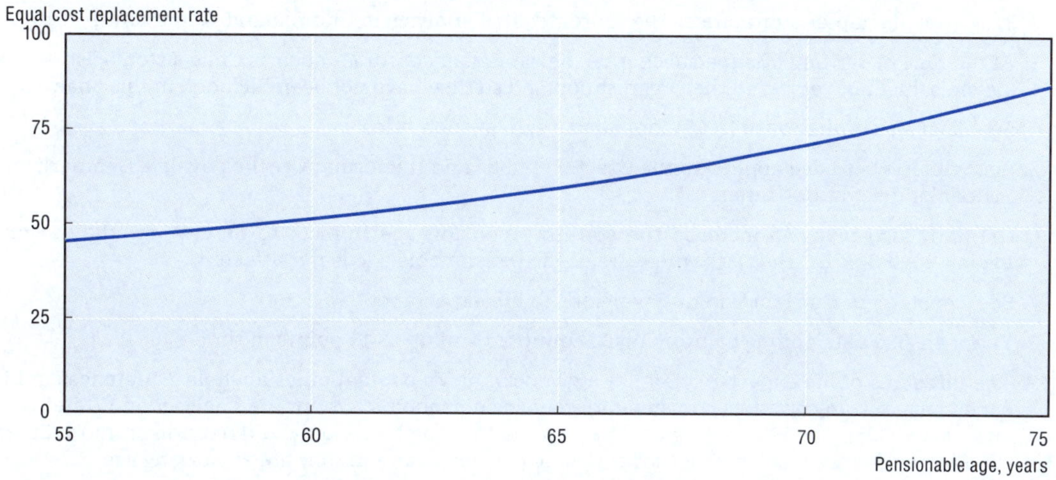

Source: OECD pension models. Annuity rates calculated from mortality data by age from the *United Nations Population Division Database, World Population Prospects – The 2008 Revision.*

StatLink http://dx.doi.org/10.1787/888932370284

Other reforms to pension systems should be borne in mind when interpreting the results presented above. First, around half of OECD countries have taken measures over the past decade, other than increases in pension age, to encourage people to work longer. These include tighter qualifying conditions for early retirement, larger pension decrements for early retirees and larger benefit increments for later retirement. These reforms are discussed in more detail in Chapter 3 in Part I on "Pension incentives to retire".[10] A second significant set of reforms are addressed in Chapter 5 in Part I on "Linking pensions to life expectancy". Most of these new pension schemes will automatically reduce benefits as life expectancy increases so that the lifetime value of pensions from these schemes will remain broadly constant. These changes can therefore be seen as a partial substitute for increases in pension age in ensuring retirement-income provision is financially sustainable.

What happens next? Almost half of OECD countries will increase pension ages over the coming four decades. But in many, the policy is a case of "running to stand still": in only a few will increases in pension age be sufficient to offset future growth in life expectancy, let alone claw-back some of the past extension of life. The expected duration of retirement in 2050 is projected to be 25 years for women and 20 years for men 7-8 years or 50% longer than it was in 1960.

In some countries, the pension-policy discourse is already suggesting the possibility of further increases in pension ages to mitigate the impact of continuing rises in life expectancy. For example, the former head of the pension-reform commission in the United Kingdom, Lord Turner, has floated the idea of a further increase in pension age to 70 beyond the increase to 68 already planned. In other countries, the debate over the future pension age has only just started, but if past experience is any guide, many are likely to follow those that have already announced increases in pension ages.

Notes

1. See the discussion in Whitehouse (2007).
2. This special chapter summarises the more detailed analysis in Chomik and Whitehouse (2010).
3. At the time of drafting this special chapter, new member countries, such as Chile, Estonia, Israel and Slovenia, had not yet joined the Organisation and so they have not been included in this analysis.
4. See Zaidi and Whitehouse (2009) for a discussion of such rules.
5. Such differences have applied to the Czech Republic and the former Czechoslovakia, Denmark and Switzerland at various times.
6. Germany also plans to increase the statutory pension age from 65 to 67, but, for the reasons explained in Box 1.1, the OECD measure of the pensionable age is not affected.
7. See Chapter 5 in Part I on "Linking pensions to life expectancy".
8. There are 390 data points, comprising 30 countries and up to 13 points in time.
9. The measures of life expectancy are for a given country's population as a whole. Differences in life expectancy within countries between different socio-economic groups are analysed in Whitehouse and Zaidi (2008). The key finding of that paper is that socio-economic differentials in mortality in OECD countries are much smaller for people of pension age than they are at working age.
10. See also Whitehouse *et al.* (2009), the chapters on pension reforms in OECD (2007, 2009) and Ebbinghaus (2006).

References

Chomik, R. and E.R. Whitehouse (2010), "Trends in Pension Eligibility Ages and Life Expectancy, 1950-2050", *Social, Employment and Migration Working Paper*, No. 105, OECD Publishing, Paris.

Ebbinghaus, B. (2006), *Reforming Early Retirement in Europe, Japan and the USA*, Oxford University Press, Oxford.

OECD (2005), *Pensions at a Glance: Public Policies across OECD Countries*, OECD Publishing, Paris.

OECD (2006), *Live Longer, Work Longer*, OECD Publishing, Paris.

OECD (2007a), *Pensions at a Glance: Public Policies across OECD Countries*, OECD Publishing, Paris.

OECD (2007b), "Public Sector Pensions and the Challenge of an Ageing Public Service", *Working Paper on Public Governance*, No. 2, OECD Publishing, Paris.

OECD (2008), *Employment Outlook*, OECD Publishing, Paris.

OECD (2009), *Pensions at a Glance: Retirement-Income Systems in OECD Countries*, OECD Publishing, Paris.

Palacios, R.J. and E.R. Whitehouse (2006), "Civil-service Pension Schemes Around the World", *Pension Reform Primer Series, Social Protection Discussion Paper*, No. 06/02, World Bank, Washington DC.

Queisser, M. and E.R. Whitehouse (2006), "Neutral or Fair? Actuarial Concepts and Pension-System Design", *Social, Employment and Migration Working Paper*, No. 40, OECD Publishing, Paris.

Turner, J. (2007), "Social Security Pensionable Ages in OECD Countries: 1949-2035", *International Social Security Review*, Vol. 60, No. 1, pp. 81-99.

Whitehouse, E.R. (2007), "Life-Expectancy Risk and Pensions: Who Bears the Burden?", *Social, Employment and Migration Working Paper*, No. 60, OECD Publishing, Paris.

Whitehouse, E.R. and A. Zaidi (2008), "Socio-Economic Differences in Mortality: Implications for Pension Policy", *Social, Employment and Migration Working Paper*, No. 71, OECD Publishing, Paris.

Whitehouse, E.R., A.C. D'Addio, R. Chomik and A. Reilly (2009), "Two Decades of Pension Reform: What has been Achieved and What Remains to be Done?", *Geneva Papers on Risk and Insurance*, Vol. 34, pp. 515-535.

Zaidi, A. and E.R. Whitehouse (2009), "Should Pension Systems Recognise Hazardous and Arduous Work?", *Social, Employment and Migration Working Paper*, No. 91, OECD Publishing, Paris.

Pensions at a Glance 2011
Retirement-income Systems in OECD and G20 Countries

PART I

Chapter 2

Trends in Retirement and in Working at Older Ages

This chapter examines labour-market behaviour of older workers, their pattern across countries and over time. There was a strong trend to early retirement throughout the 1970s and 1980s. However, this came to an end in the mid 1990s, and during the 2000s, the proportion of 50-64 years olds participating in the labour market has started to creep up.

A detailed analysis of pathways into retirement suggest that at least half of men use routes such as unemployment, sickness or disability benefits in half of countries. Women also often leave the labour market to care for family members.

Older workers appear to have fared relatively well in the economic downturn that followed the global financial crisis in most OECD countries. This contrasts with previous recessions, where older workers were often the first to lose their jobs and found it hardest to find new employment.

A decomposition of governments' long-term projections of the finance of the pension system shows that these are highly dependent on further increases in participation rates at older ages and effective retirement ages.

Increasing the age at which people retire has been a major objective of many recent pension reforms. This has been driven by the greying of the population in OECD countries, a well-known phenomenon that has been going on for six decades. In 1950, there were more than seven people of working age for every one of pension age. By 2047, there will be just two workers per pensioner.[1] As a result, public spending on old-age pensions and survivors' benefits has grown more rapidly than national income for at least 20 years, and this trend is expected to continue in nearly all countries over the next five decades.[2]

In the face of rapid population ageing, the long-run fall in effective retirement ages in most OECD countries needs to be reversed. There are some positive signs that this is beginning to happen, but how optimistic can we be that this will continue? What is the impact on older workers of the economic downturn in the wake of the global financial crisis?

This special chapter examines labour-force participation rates and their pattern across countries, age groups and time (Section 2.1). Sections 2.2 and 2.3 look in more detail at retirement behaviour, examining the effective of age of labour market exit and the different pathways people take into retirement. Section 2.4 takes a look at long-term projections of pension expenditure. Not only are governments seeking to reduce the growing burden on taxpayers and contributors to pay for pensions, but their forecasts are predicated on the assumption that people will work longer in the future. A brief summary is provided in Section 2.5.

2.1. Older workers: Labour-market participation

Older workers are less likely to be in employment than their prime aged counterparts (aged 25-50). Participation rates of older workers (age 50-64) in OECD countries averaged 63% in 2008, while those of prime aged workers averaged 75% in the same year. These averages hide large cross-country differences (Figure 2.1). Participation rates for older workers exceed 70% in seven countries, including Japan and the United States. At the other end of the spectrum, Belgium, Hungary, Italy, Poland and Turkey all have less than half of older workers active in the labour market.

Participation rates of older workers in most OECD countries were higher in 2008 than they were in 1970. In many cases, participation rates declined during the early part of the period 1970-2008, a trend that was later reversed, typically in the last decade or so. Germany, Iceland, the Netherlands and New Zealand saw the largest increases. In only five countries – France, Greece, Hungary, Poland and Turkey – were participation rates lower in 2008 than they were in 1970.

The main reason that the share of 50-64 year-olds that are active in the labour market has increased is growing labour-force participation of women. Between 1995 and 2008, for example, the participation rate for women aged 50-64 in OECD countries increased by around 11 percentage points on average, compared with just 4 points for men. Nevertheless, there

Figure 2.1. **Participation rates of 50-64 year-olds in 1970 and 2008**

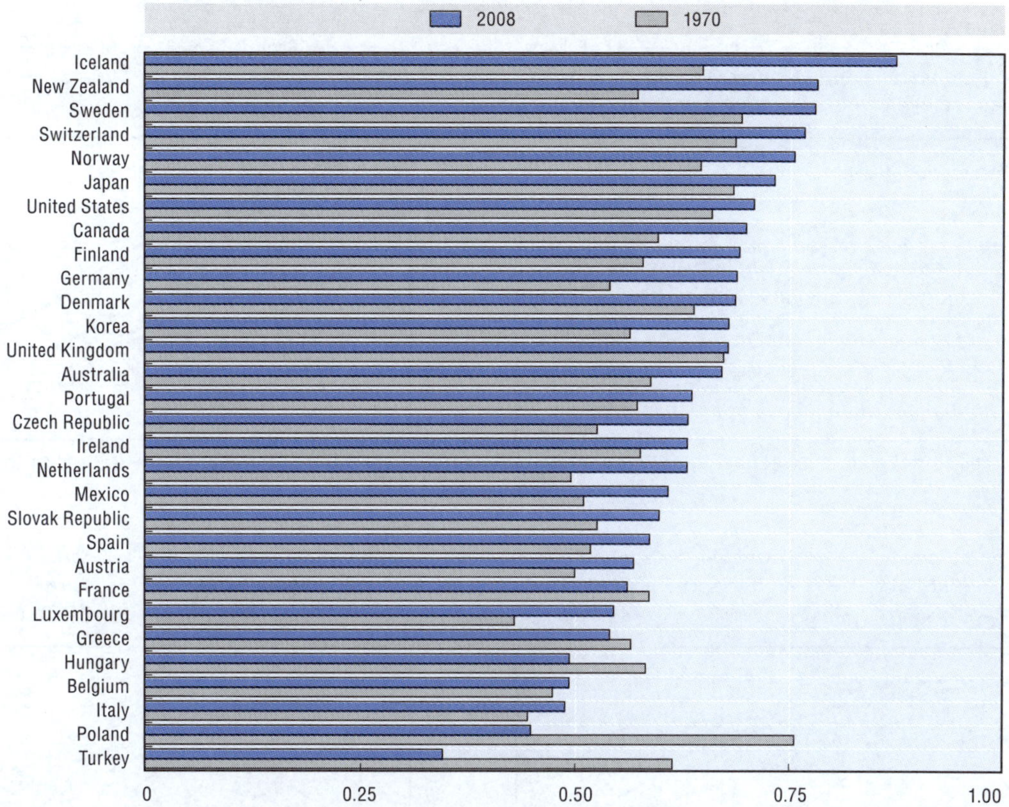

Source: D'Addio *et al.* (2010) based on *OECD Employment Database.*

StatLink http://dx.doi.org/10.1787/888932370303

remains a large difference between the sexes. On average in OECD countries, about 75% of older men were economically active in 2008, compared with just over 50% of women. The gap is particularly large in Greece, Ireland, Italy, Japan, Korea, Mexico, Poland, Spain and Turkey.

Differences in participation rates between OECD countries widen as people get older (Figure 2.2). For example, more than a half of 65-69 year-olds were still working in Iceland, Korea and Mexico; and between a quarter and a half of all persons in the same group were still working in Australia, Canada, Ireland, Japan, New Zealand, Norway, Portugal and the United States. But these proportions fall to less than one in ten in many European countries, such as Belgium, France, Germany, Hungary, Luxembourg, the Slovak Republic and Spain.

2.2. Retirement and labour-market exit

Most workers in most OECD countries leave the labour market before the standard pension eligibility age; in some cases, much earlier. Figure 2.3 shows the recent average effective age of withdrawal from the labour market, as well as pensionable, age in OECD countries for men and women.[3] Countries are ranked by men's effective age of labour-market exit. To mitigate the impact of cyclical variations, the exit age is measured here by taking the average age of exit from the labour force over a five-year period (2004-09).

In a limited number of OECD countries – such as Ireland, New Zealand and Sweden – labour-market exit occurs, on average, close to the pensionable age. But there are large differences elsewhere. Men leave the labour market, on average, later than the pensionable

Figure 2.2. **Labour-force participation rates by age, 2008**

Percentages

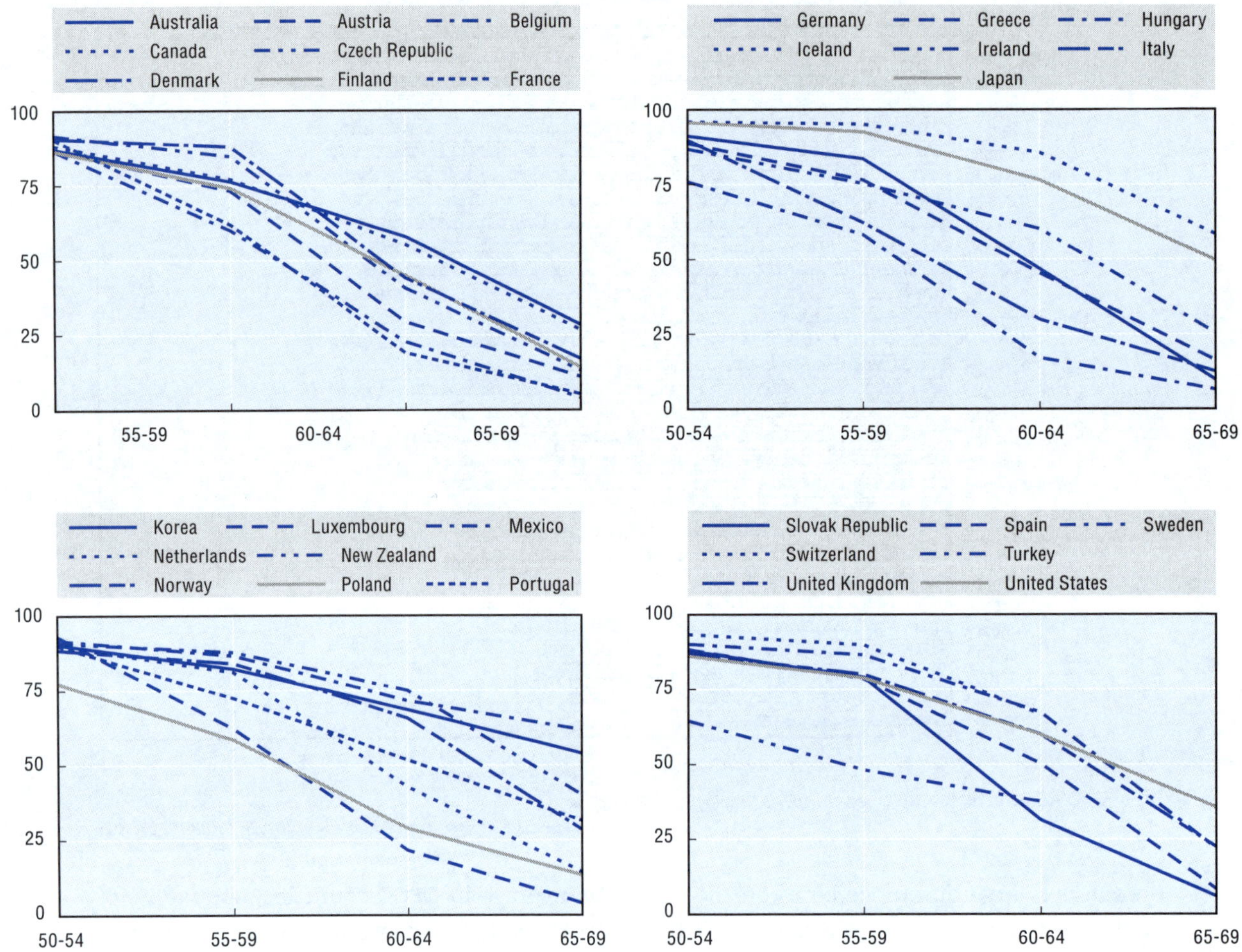

Source: D'Addio et al. (2010) based on OECD *Employment Database*.

StatLink http://dx.doi.org/10.1787/888932370322

age in 12 of the 30 countries shown. For women, late retirement is the norm in ten countries. People leave the labour market significantly earlier than normal pensionable age in Austria, Belgium, Finland, the Netherlands, Poland and Spain. In these countries, men retire on average 3-6 years earlier than the pensionable age.

Figure 2.4 shows how the effective retirement age for men and women in the OECD changed over time. The charts cover the period from 1965 to 2007, and show both the average figure and the range of observations for OECD countries. In almost all OECD countries, the effective retirement age has declined substantially since 1970. However, this has been reversed more recently. Over the past decade, the average flattened out followed by a small upturn. Nevertheless, the effective retirement age remains well below the levels of the 1960s and 1970s in OECD countries (except in Japan and Korea). For men, the average effective retirement age fell from 68.6 in the late 1960s to 63.5 in the five years to 2009. The average age of labour-market exit for women dropped from 66.7 to 62.3 over the same period.

Figure 2.3. **Average effective age of labour-market exit and normal pensionable age**

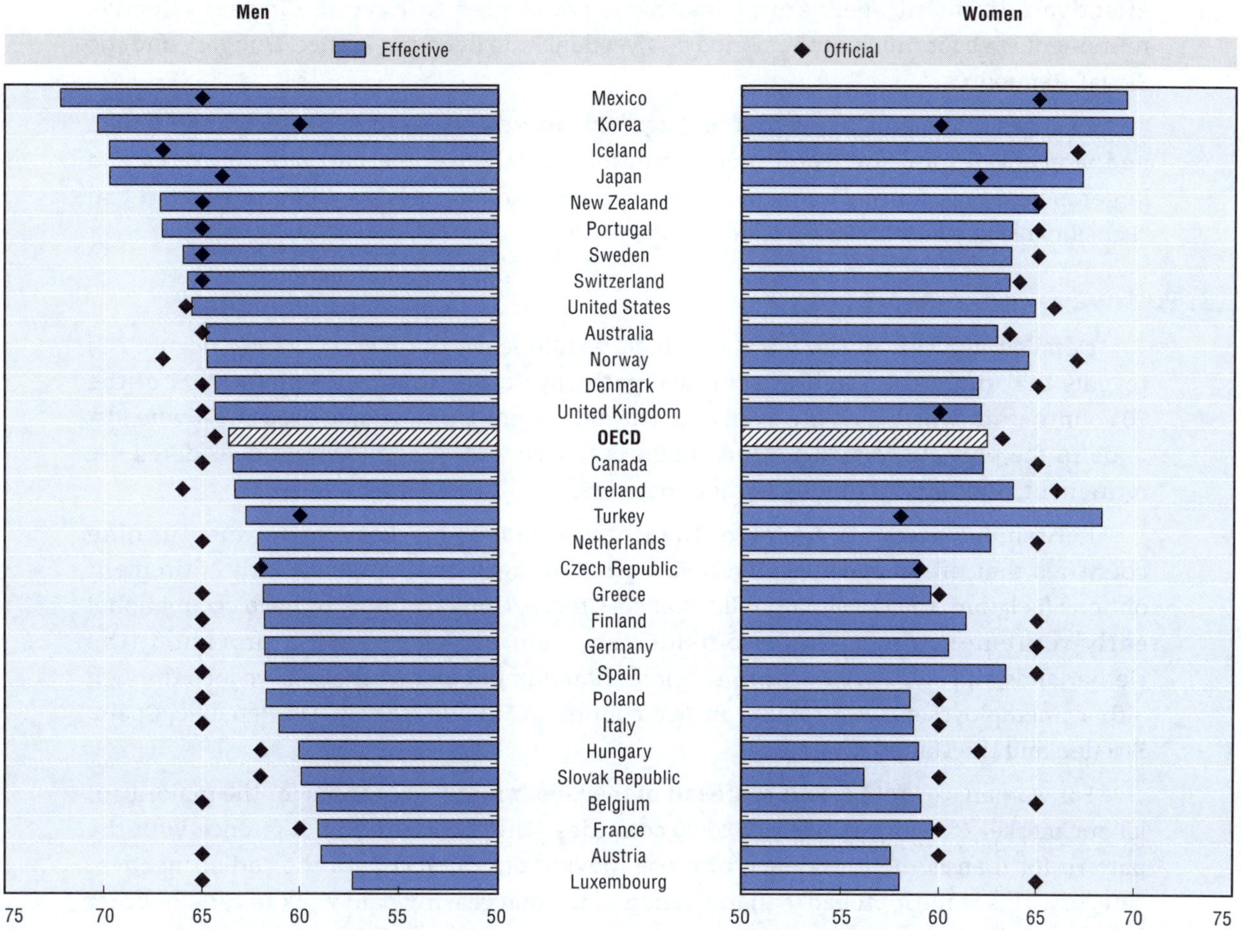

Note: Effective retirement age shown is for five-year period 2004-09; pensionable age is shown for 2010.

Source: OECD, updated from OECD (2006).

StatLink http://dx.doi.org/10.1787/888932370341

Figure 2.4. **Average labour market exit age in OECD countries, 1965-2007**

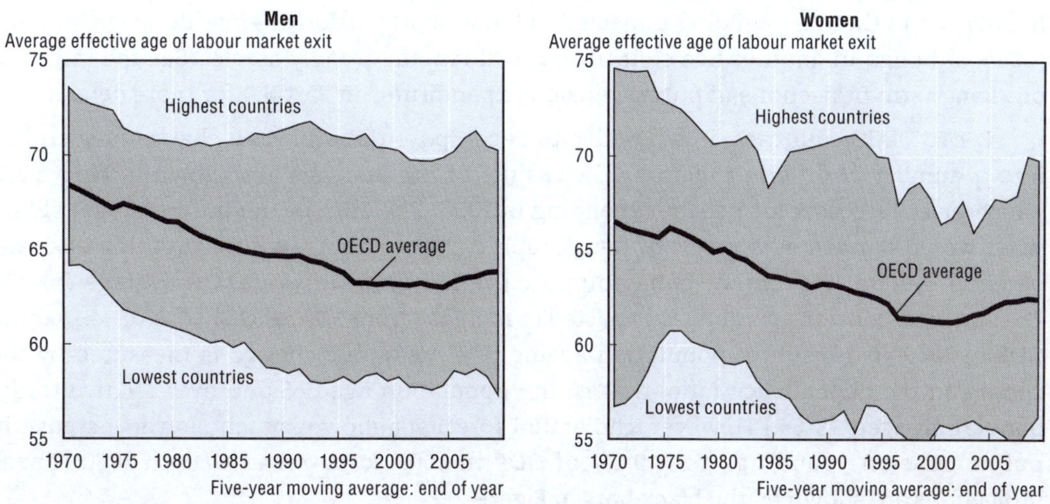

Source: OECD, updated from OECD (2006).

StatLink http://dx.doi.org/10.1787/888932370360

Iceland, Japan, Korea and Mexico have been amongst countries with the highest effective retirement ages. Countries that have tended to have the lowest effective retirement ages for much of the period analysed include Belgium, France, Hungary and the Slovak Republic.

Changes in the effective retirement age have mostly occurred in parallel for both men and women, despite the trend increase in female labour-force participation rates and larger increases in normal pension age for women than for men (see Chapter 1 in Part I on "Pensionable age and life expectancy, 1950-2050").

2.3. Pathways into retirement

Detailed analysis of the ways in which people leave the labour market (Figure 2.5) reveals that more than half of men use pathways other than retirement in 11 of the 20 countries for which data are available. The data comprise all people aged 50-64 who lost a job in the previous year. The three main pathways out of employment considered are retirement, disability or unemployment benefits.

Retirement accounts for more than half of labour-market exit for men in nine countries that either have relatively low pension ages or a range of early-retirement options (Belgium, the Czech Republic, France, Greece, Hungary, Italy) or have occupational early-retirement programmes outside the main old-age pension provision (the Netherlands and Norway). In contrast, more than half of older workers leave jobs through either unemployment or disability in five countries: Finland, the Slovak Republic, Spain, Sweden and the United Kingdom.

For women, the retirement route out of the labour market accounts for the majority of labour-market exit in just five out of 20 countries. The most striking difference with the pattern for men is the prevalence of those moving out of work into the "other inactive" category. This is most probably an indication of women ceasing paid work to care for other family members.

2.4. Fiscal imperatives and retirement in the future

Public expenditure on pensions is expected to continue growing faster than national income over the next 40 years in most of the OECD countries for which data are available. In only two of them is spending projected to fall as a proportion of gross domestic product (GDP), although in another five countries, it will remain broadly stable. (See the indicator on "Long-term projections of public pension expenditure" in Part II.4 for more details.)

For 23 OECD countries, it is possible to decompose the projected change in spending into a number of different factors. The results of the analysis are shown in Figure 2.6, which gives forecasts for pension spending in 2060. The sum of the different bars shows what would happen as a result of demographic change alone, with everything else (the pension system, retirement behaviour, etc.) remaining the same. On average for the 23 countries, pension spending is expected to increase from 9.2% of GDP in 2007 to 18.0% of GDP in 2060 as a result of population ageing. (Demographic change is measured by the change in the dependency ratio, that is, the population aged 65 and over relative to the population aged 15-64.) However, the actual forecasts show a much slower increase in public pension spending: from 9.2% of GDP in 2007 to 12.7% of GDP in 2060. These projections are shown by the black bars in Figure 2.6.

Figure 2.5. **Pathways out of employment for older workers**

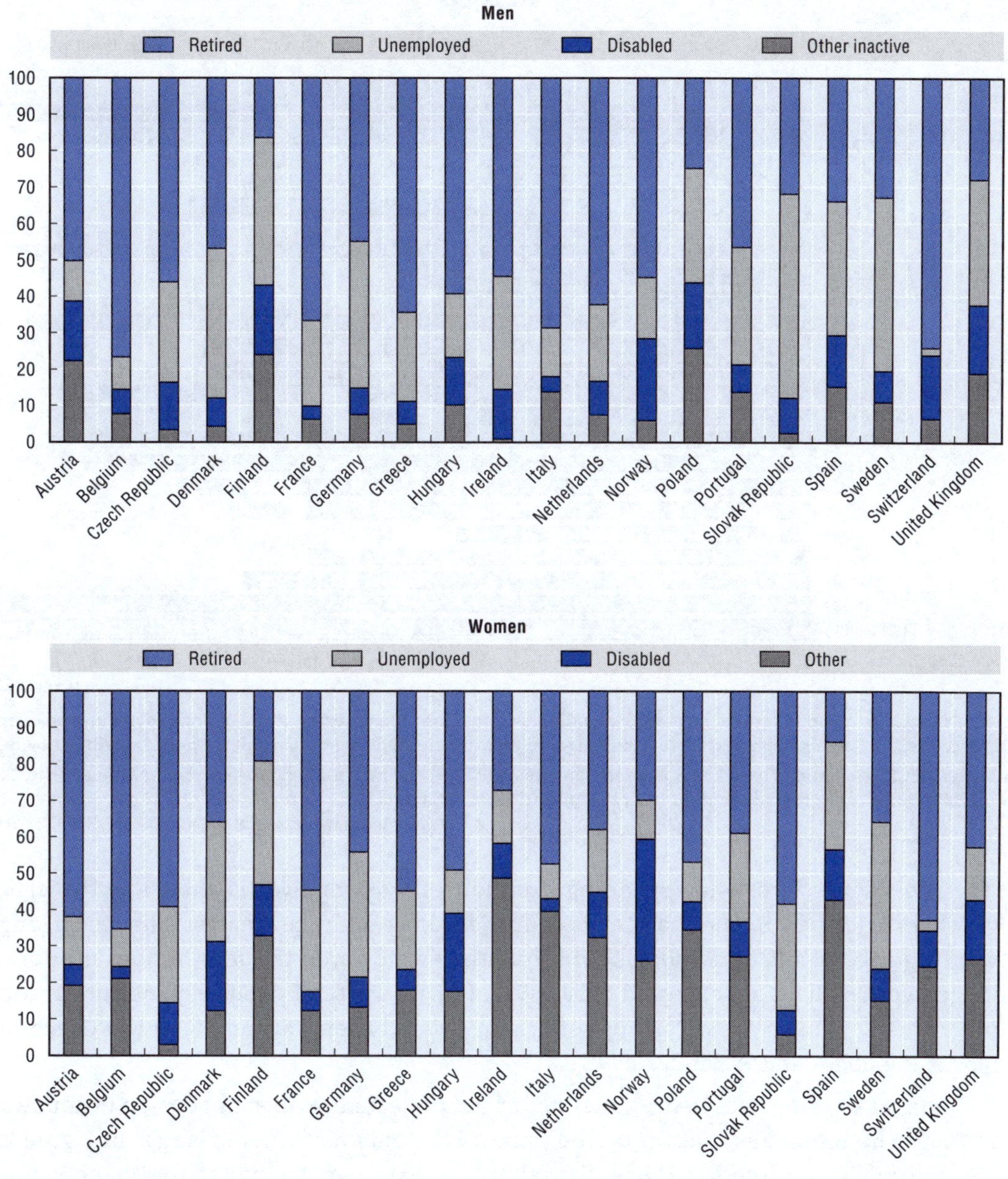

Source: OECD (2006), Figure 2.12.

StatLink http://dx.doi.org/10.1787/888932370379

The bars decompose the different factors affecting projected spending. Of greatest relevance here is the impact of assumptions of longer working lives. This combines two elements. The first of these is termed the "coverage-ratio" effect in European Commission (2009). The coverage ratio is the number of pension recipients divided by the population aged 65 and over. The second, called the "employment-rate" effect is measured by the relationship between the number of working people aged 15-64 and the population of that age. Longer working lives would improve both of these measures.

Figure 2.6. **Decomposition of different effects on projected pension expenditure in 2060**

Note: Luxembourg alone reports increased spending as a result of the coverage-ratio and employment-rate effects. Greece, Ireland, Luxembourg and the United Kingdom report increased spending result from the benefit-ratio effect.

Source: OECD calculations based on European Commission (2009) and information provided by the Office of the Chief Actuary, Office of the Superintendent of Financial Institutions, Canada.

StatLink http://dx.doi.org/10.1787/888932370398

The savings in pension spending from longer working lives is shown by the lighter grey bars in Figure 2.6. The chart ranks countries: those with the greatest reliance on longer working lives to offset demographic pressures are towards the top. In absolute terms, longer working lives are expected to save 5% of GDP's worth of public expenditure or more in Denmark, Hungary and Poland, with figures of between 4% and 5% in the Czech and Slovak Republics and Finland.

Longer working lives deliver one-half of the projected savings in pension expenditure in 2060. The remainder, shown by the darker blue bars as "other savings" in Figure 2.6, comes principally from lower benefits relative to earnings, known as the "benefit-ratio" effect. There is also a residual term reflecting the interaction between the different effects.

The changes in retirement behaviour that are assumed are, in many cases, very large. For example, labour-force participation of 55-64 year-olds is projected to increase by more than 25 percentage points between 2007 and 2060 in two countries: from 35% to 64% in Italy and 48% to 74% in Spain.[4] Large increases in participation rates – of between 15 and 20 percentage points – are also assumed in Austria, the Czech Republic, Germany and Hungary. The average assumption for the EU27 countries is a 10 point increase in economic activity among people aged 55-64.

2.5. Summary and conclusions

The long-term trend to earlier retirement came to an end for men in the mid-1990s and for women, slightly later. The average age of labour-market exit was broadly constant for a few years, but there has been a noticeable trend to later retirement in recent years. Older workers have not fared too badly during the economic downturn experienced in most OECD countries after the global financial crisis. The proportion of 55-64 year-olds in employment was constant between 2007 and 2009, compared with a decline of 1.7 percentage points in the share of 25-54 year-olds with jobs and 3.6 points for 20-24 year-olds. The proportion of 65-69 year-olds in employment in fact increased a little, from 21.1% in 2007 to 22.0% in 2009.

Governments' long-term projections for public expenditure on pensions are heavily reliant on the assumption that people will retire later in the future. But it is important to bear in mind the scale of the challenge in realising such a change. The average age of labour-market exit for men in OECD countries is 63.5 on the latest estimates and for women, it is 62.3. If life expectancy continues to increase, as most forecasts show, then significant increases in the effective retirement age are required to maintain control of the cost of pensions. In 2050, only an effective retirement age of 66.6 for men and 65.8 for women would leave the duration of retirement at the same level as it is now (based on the United Nations population projections).

The policies that governments can pursue to extend working lives are the subject of the next two special chapters of *Pensions at a Glance 2011*. The first looks at the "supply side", presenting information on incentives to work and retire embedded in pension system. The second looks at the "demand side", examining ways of ensuring that there are jobs for older workers.

Notes

1. See the indicator of "Old-age support ratios" in Part II.5.
2. See the indicator of "Long-term projections of public pension expenditure" in Part II.4.
3. The average effective age of exit from the labour market is derived from labour-force-survey data. It is the weighted average of the exit age of each five-year age cohort, starting with ages 40-44, and using absolute five-year changes in the labour force participation rate of each cohort as weights. The average exit for each cohort is assumed to be the mid-point between age groups: for example, the exit age for the cohort aged 55-59 in 2004 and 60-64 in 2009 is taken to be 60. The five-year change in participation rates is simply the difference between the rate for each age group (say, 55-59) at the beginning of the period minus the rate for the corresponding age group that is five years older (60-64) at the end of the period.
4. European Commission (2009), Table A31.

References

D'Addio, A.C., M. Keese and E. Whitehouse (2010), "Population Ageing and Labour Market", *Oxford Review of Economic Policy*, forthcoming.

European Commission (2009), "The 2009 Ageing Report: Economic and Budgetary Projections for the EU-27 Member States (2008-2060)", *European Economy*, No. 2/2009.

OECD (2006), *Ageing and Employment Policies: Live Longer, Work Longer*, OECD Publishing, Paris.

Pensions at a Glance 2011
Retirement-income Systems in OECD and G20 Countries

PART I

Chapter 3

Pensions Incentives to Retire

Individuals' decisions about work and retirement depend on the financial incentives embedded in retirement-income systems. This chapter presents measures of the pension incentive to retire, showing how the retirement income system can act as an implicit tax or subsidy on remaining in work. The analysis looks at the main retirement "window" in OECD countries, from age 60 to 65.

In addition to increases in pensionable ages (set out in Chapter 1), recent pension reforms in most countries have involved policies to reduce the incentive to retire early and increase the incentive to retire after the normal pension age.

However, the incentive to retire early remains strong in a minority of OECD countries. And there are ways in which most countries could further improve their pension system. The chapter concludes with nine policy conclusions that would reward people for working longer.

There is overwhelming evidence that the financial incentives embedded in pension systems affect retirement behaviour. This evidence base comprises both national and cross-country studies. Getting retirement incentives "right" is therefore a central concern of pension policy. Indeed, most pension-reform packages in OECD countries over the last two decades have included either increases in pension ages or other measures to encourage people to work longer.

Retirement incentives matter for reasons of both economic efficiency and equity. Of course, retirement incentives are not the be-all and end-all in explaining participation of older workers in the labour market. Health and the labour-market status of an individual's spouse also have a significant impact. "Demand-side" factors – such as macroeconomic conditions and the state of the labour market, age discrimination and industrial organisation – also matter; these are discussed in Chapter 4 in Part I on "Helping older workers find and retain jobs". Thus, appropriate incentives to keep working are rarely a *sufficient* solution to the problem of early retirement, but they are almost certainly a *necessary* part of the solution.

Retirement incentives also matter for reasons of equity. People who work more and contribute more *should* have higher pensions. Equally, those who are forced to drop out of employment early, perhaps through no fault of their own, need to have a reasonable standard of living. The aim should be to have a pension system which neither subsidises, nor excessively penalises, early retirement.

This special chapter uses an extension of the OECD pension models to look at pension entitlements of workers who retire at different ages. Section 3.1 discusses how the pension incentive to retire can be measured. It describes the impact a longer working life and a shorter retirement duration can have on entitlements in different kinds of pension scheme. Section 3.2 briefly reviews the research that shows that pension incentives have a significant effect on retirement behaviour. Sections 3.3 to 3.7 set out the empirical results of the paper. This begins with analysis of the change in pension wealth from working longer as a measure of incentives to retire, then looks at how this varies with individual earnings (Section 3.4). Sections 3.5 and 3.6 extend the analysis to bring in, first, the role of taxes and social security contributions and then the level of pension wealth as a second measure of incentives. Section 3.7 summarises these empirical results while Section 3.8 draws out some policy conclusions.

3.1. Measuring pension incentives to retire

Most studies of incentives to work use a simple indicator – the replacement rate – which measures the relationship between incomes in and out of work. This has been widely used to look at the effects of unemployment benefits and social assistance on people's labour-market behaviour.[1]

Figure 3.1 shows this measure for pensions using the example of Canada. (Illustrations for all 34 OECD countries are presented in D'Addio and Whitehouse, 2011.) Across the horizontal axis, the chart shows the age at which the individual exits the labour market,

Figure 3.1. **Gross pension replacement rates by age of labour-market exit: Canada**

Proportion of individual gross earnings

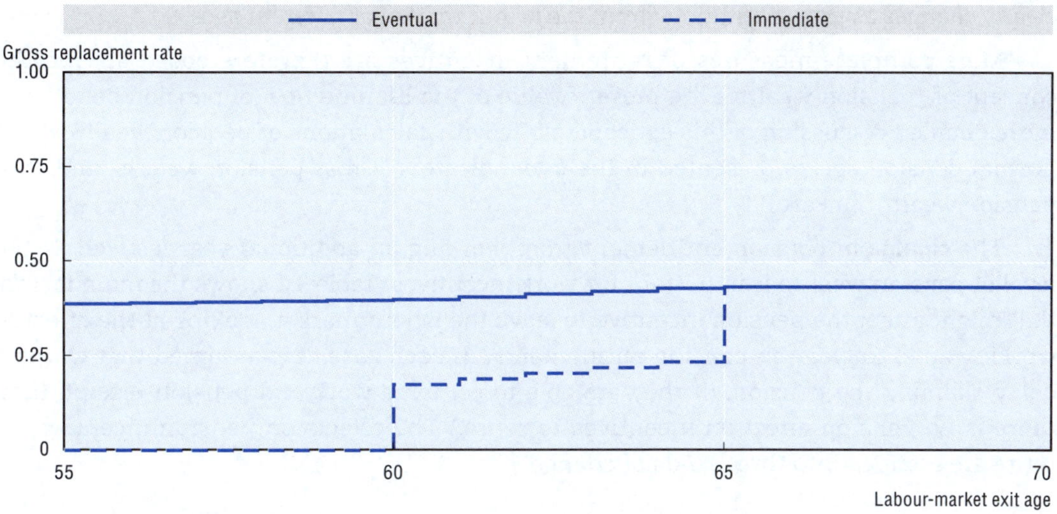

Source: OECD pension models.

StatLink http://dx.doi.org/10.1787/888932370417

covering a broad range from age 55 to 70. On the vertical axis is the pension replacement rate. These results are for an average earner. The example individual is assumed to have worked and contributed in each year from age 20 until the age of labour-market exit indicated on the chart.

The dotted line shows the replacement rate from the public pension system that is immediately available when the individual leaves the labour market. It is not possible to claim any public pension until age 60, so the immediate replacement rate is zero before that point. At age 60, it is possible to claim the public, earnings-related pension. The replacement rate at this age is low: around 20%. This is because the benefit level is automatically reduced to compensate for the longer period over which the pension is paid (see the indicator of "Normal, early and late retirement" in Part II.1 below). Between age 60 and 65, the replacement rate increases because the benefit decrement is smaller for each extra year spent in work. At age 65, there is a big jump in the replacement rate because the individual then becomes eligible for the basic and means-tested retirement benefits.

However, the immediate replacement rate does not tell the whole story of how pension systems affect people's work decisions. Although there is no immediate pension benefit available between age 55 and 60 in Canada, an extra year's work adds to the final pension benefit. This is shown by the solid line in Figure 3.1. This line shows the total benefit that be claimed from age 65, conditional on withdrawal from the labour market at different ages.

It should be clear that a simple analysis of replacement rates at different ages fails to capture the full impact of the pension system on incentives to retire or to remain in work. The comparison between incomes in and out of work presented above is a static one. But work decisions made at one point affect future pension entitlements: the analysis needs to be "dynamic". Unlike an analysis of unemployment and social-assistance benefits on incentives to work, account has to be taken of the impact of work decisions on pension entitlements in the future. More formally, the retirement-income system affects the individual's "inter-temporal budget constraint". Furthermore, the period over which pensions are paid also clearly changes as people withdraw from the labour market at different ages.

More complete measures of retirement incentives are therefore based around the concept of "pension wealth": the present value of the lifetime flow of pension benefits. A more detailed discussion of this concept, along with calculations of pension wealth at the normal pension age, is presented in the two indicators "Gross pension wealth" and "Net pension wealth" in Part II.2.

The ***change*** in pension entitlement from working an additional year (as well as the level of pension wealth) is important for work incentives. Table 3.1 shows the main factors that might affect the pension incentive to leave the labour market, looking at the effect of working an extra year on pension entitlements. In each case, it is assumed that workers delay claiming the pension. (If they are able to combine work and pension receipt, then there is no pension effect on incentives to retire.) The effects on pension incentives to retire are grouped into three kinds of change.

Table 3.1. **Pension incentives to retire in different kinds of pension plan**

	Defined benefit	Points	Notional accounts	Defined contribution
Longer working period	Extra year's entitlement.	Extra year's entitlement.	Extra year's entitlement.	Extra year's contributions.
	Extra year towards qualifying conditions.	Extra year towards qualifying conditions.	Extra year towards qualifying conditions.	–
	Valorisation of earlier years' earnings.	Uprating of pension-point value.	Notional interest on accumulated notional capital.	Investment returns on accumulated balance.
	Higher earnings replace earlier, perhaps lower, earnings in benefit formula.	Higher earnings replace earlier, perhaps lower, earnings in benefit formula.	–	–
Shorter retirement duration	Forgo a year's benefits.	Forgo a year's benefits.	Forgo a year's benefits.	Forgo a year's benefits.
	"Actuarial" adjustment.	"Actuarial" adjustment.	Lower annuity factor.	Lower annuity factor.
Delay in claiming	Probability of dying.	Probability of dying.	Probability of dying	Probability of dying.
	Discounting.	Discounting.	Discounting	Discounting.

StatLink http://dx.doi.org/10.1787/888932372165

The impact is shown for the four most common types of pension plan designed to provide income replacement rate in retirement, the second tier of the taxonomy used in *Pensions at a Glance*: see the indicator of "Architecture of national pension systems" in Part II.1. Briefly, pension entitlements in a defined-benefit (DB) scheme depend on the number of years of contributions and some measure of individual earnings. In points schemes, pension contributions "buy" a certain number of pension points. At the time of retirement, the accumulated number of points is multiplied by a pension-point value to determine the entitlement. Notional accounts – "notional" in the sense that there is no money in them – receive contributions each year and the balance earns a notional interest rate, typically linked to a macroeconomic variable such as GDP or wage growth. The accumulated notional capital at the time of retirement is then converted into a pension entitlement using an annuity calculation. In defined-contribution (DC) schemes, the process is similar to notional accounts, except that there is real money in the accounts and the interest rate depends on the financial performance of the underlying assets.[2]

The first pair of effects in Table 3.1 arises from the ***longer working period***. This changes pension rights in many different ways. In all kinds of pension schemes, the extra year's contribution usually brings some extra pension entitlement. In most DB and points schemes (and occasionally with notional accounts), the right to retire depends on the number of years of contributions. So the extra year's contributions may help the individual meet these qualifying conditions. These first two factors – shown in the first two rows of Table 3.1 – relate to the additional pension entitlement earned during the year.

In contrast, the next two factors, although again affected by a longer working period, result from changes to the value of pension entitlements already accrued. In DB plans, earlier years' earnings are typically "valorised" to allow for changes in costs and standards of living from the time that entitlements were earned to the time that pensions are claimed.[3] The parallel effect in a DC scheme is that the balance in the individual account that had built up at the beginning of the year earns investment returns during the year. In notional accounts, the same thing happens but using the notional interest rate. In point schemes, the corollary is the uprating of the value of the pension point, which increases previously accrued entitlements. These factors are shown in the third row of Table 3.1.

Finally, some DB and points schemes calculate the entitlement on a subset of years of earnings ("best" or "final" pay, for example[4]). In these cases, individual earnings might (even after valorisation or uprating of the point cost) be higher than in an earlier year. Similarly, some countries have a maximum number of years of accrual. So an extra year of work might not bring any extra entitlement, but an earlier year with lower earnings might drop out of the pension formula. These effects are shown in the fourth row of Table 3.1.

The second type of change to pensions from working a year longer stems from the ***shorter duration of retirement***. In every kind of pension scheme, individuals must, of course, forgo a year's benefits if they retire a year later. However, there are often adjustments to the value of benefits to reflect this. In DB and points schemes, this comes through "actuarial" adjustments for early or late retirement. In DC schemes and notional accounts, the route is through the annuity calculation whereby the accumulated balance is converted into a retirement-income stream.[5] This calculation reflects the expected duration of retirement. Some illustrated numbers are provided in Figure 3.2, Panel A. Based on projections for mortality rates at different ages in 2050, the chart shows additional life expectancy at age 55 will average nearly 30 years, falling to about 17 extra years at age 70. The way that is reflected in benefit calculation is shown by the "annuity factor": the present value of a pension of one unit payable each year until death. In a defined-contribution pension, for example, the value of an annuity will be the accumulated balance in the plan divided by the annuity factor.

The final elements of the pension incentive to retire reflect further costs to the worker of ***delaying the pension claim***. The worker might die during the year, and so receive nothing from the pension system. This is not taken into account in DC and most notional-accounts schemes, because annuity calculations are made at retirement and so implicitly assume the worker is still alive to claim the pension. Mortality rates increase with age, as shown in the projections for 2050 mortality rates for OECD countries in Figure 3.2, Panel B. At age 55, the probability of dying in the next year is less than 0.3%, compared with over 1.3% at age 70.

Figure 3.2. **Life expectancy, annuity factors and mortality rates by age**

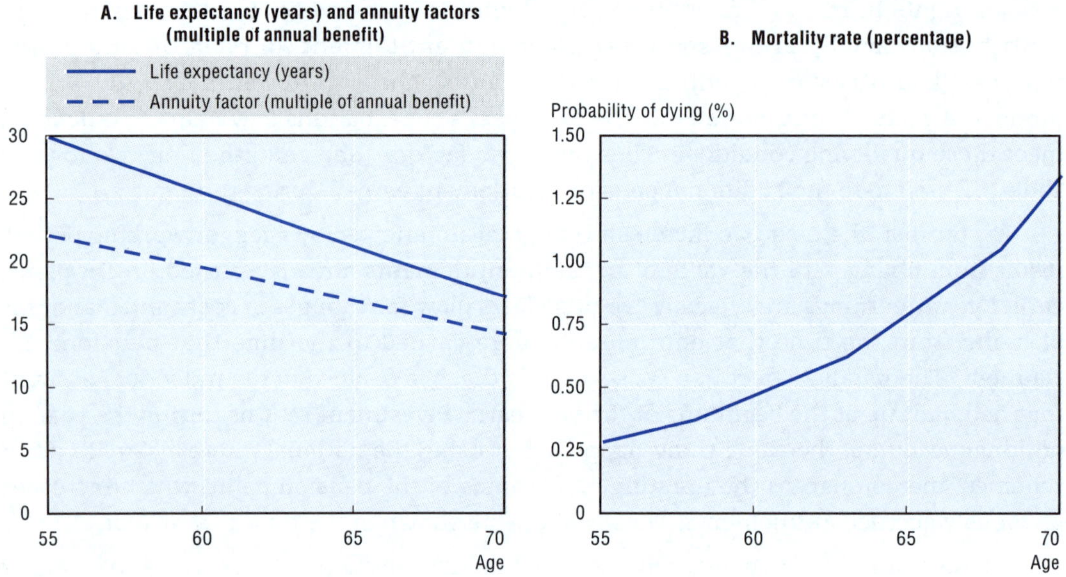

Note: Annuity factor calculated using a real discount rate of 2% and assuming a price-indexed benefit.

Source: OECD pension models based on data from United Nations, *World Population Prospects – The 2008 Revision*.

StatLink http://dx.doi.org/10.1787/888932370436

Pension entitlements must also be discounted; money in the future is worth less than money now because of the opportunity cost of forgoing consumption. The impact of discounting can be seen from the difference between life expectancy and the annuity factor in Figure 3.2, Panel A.

Taking into account all the multiple factors affecting pension entitlements outlined in Table 3.1, the change in pension wealth is then normalised to individual gross earnings. This is used to illustrate pension incentives to retire. The change in pension wealth from working an additional year can be interpreted as an implicit tax or subsidy on continuing in work. This measure compares directly two flows of income: one from retiring immediately, the other from working an additional year and then claiming the pension. The difference between the two income flows is earnings during the year plus the implicit tax or subsidy in the pension system, since this is measured relative to individual earnings.[6]

3.2. Incentives matter

A group of national experts from 11 OECD countries, co-ordinated by Gruber and Wise (1998, 1999), compared labour-force withdrawal rates between age 60 and 64 with the "implicit tax" from remaining in work exerted by the pension system. They also looked at alternative pathways out of work, such as unemployment and disability benefits. They found an elasticity of labour-force withdrawal with the implicit tax of 0.41. Japan had both the lowest withdrawal rate – with 75% of 60-64 year-olds in work – and the lowest implicit tax on continuing in work. In contrast, Belgium, Italy and the Netherlands had the highest withdrawal rates – with only around 20% of 60-64 year-olds in work – and among the highest implicit taxes on continuing to work at those ages. These general findings were confirmed by later OECD studies (Blöndal and Scarpetta, 1999; and Duval, 2003).[7, 8]

3.3. Changes in pension wealth from working longer

Changes in pension wealth from working an additional year have been calculated using the OECD pension models, as described elsewhere in *Pensions at a Glance*.

The analysis here differs from the previous studies cited above (Gruber and Wise, 1998, 1999; Blöndal and Scarpetta, 1999; and Duval, 2003) – in that it is *prospective*. It does *not* look at incentives faced by older workers today, which depend on past as well as current pension policies. Rather, it aims to evaluate the current pension-policy stance as it affects workers retiring in the future. As in the indicators of pension entitlements in Part II.2, benefits are calculated for workers who enter work at age 20 and contribute to the pension system each year until the varying age of exit from the labour market. Changes in rules that have already been legislated, but are being phased-in gradually – increases in pension age, for example – are therefore taken into account. Parameter values are those for 2008.[9]

Figure 3.3 shows the first set of results. These look at the age range of 60 to 65 (as in previous studies) because this is the main retirement "window" in OECD countries. Between the ages of 55 and 59, around 77% of people participate in the labour market, compared with 23% of people age 65-69. In the age range 60-64, labour-force participation rates are around 50%. (See Chapter 2 in Part I on "Trends in retirement and in working at older ages".) The aggregate change over the age range of 60-65 is calculated and then annualised.

Figure 3.3. **Changes in gross pension wealth for working age 60-65, men with average earnings**

Percentage of annual gross earnings

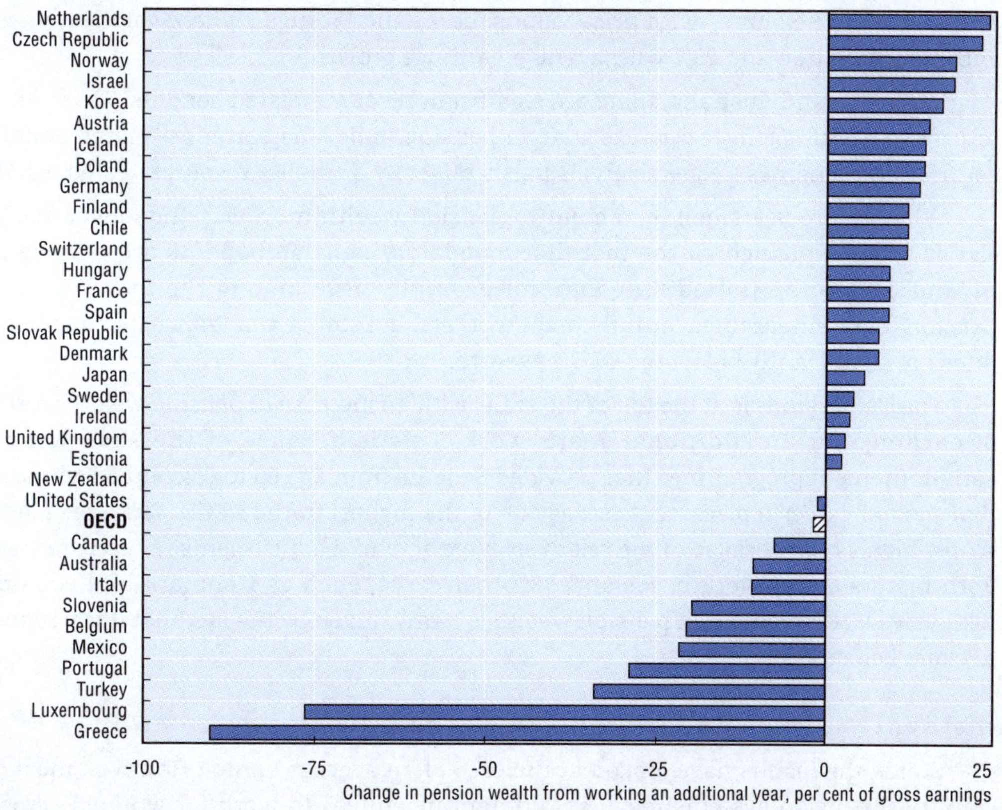

Source: OECD pension models.

StatLink http://dx.doi.org/10.1787/888932370455

The results presented in this special chapter are for men for reasons of space. Because the measures are based on pension wealth, retirement incentives for women – with lower mortality rates and higher life expectancy are different. Calculations for women will be published in D'Addio and Whitehouse (2011).

The change in pension wealth is positive in 22 countries, negative in 11 and zero in New Zealand. The very large negative values in Greece and Luxembourg dominate the picture. This arises because of the ability to retire before age 65 without actuarial reduction in benefits. Similar effects are at work in Belgium, while in Slovenia and Portugal the actuarial adjustments for retirement at different ages can be relatively small.

Other cases of negative changes in pension wealth arise because of limits on the number of years that accrue a pension entitlement: this is 35 years in the United States and 40 years in Canada. In this example of a full-career working from age 20, the full benefit is already reached at or before age 60, which limits the return to continuing in work relative to other countries.

The rules for valorisation of earnings in calculating benefits also have an effect. (Valorisation is the procedure under which earlier years' earnings are adjusted to the time of retirement to reflect changes in costs or standards of living.) Most OECD countries valorise in line with average-earnings growth. But a few do not. In the United States, for example, valorisation is with average earnings until age 60, with no adjustment from age 60 to 62, and with prices thereafter. Since the calculations are based on an assumption that earnings grow faster than prices, accrued pension rights grow more slowly than earnings after age 62 in the United States than in countries with earnings valorisation. This effect is also at work in Belgium – with price valorisation – and Portugal, where valorisation is 75% with price inflation and 25% with average-earnings growth.

In Canada and Australia, there are significant resource-tested benefits. These limit the returns to working longer because a larger pension under the earnings-related or defined-contribution schemes (respectively) is partly offset by a smaller resource-tested benefit.

Where there is a small increment to pension wealth from working longer, the small size is often explained by the fact that mandatory pension benefits are relatively low. Ireland, Japan, the United Kingdom, for example, have among the four lowest gross pension replacement rates for full-career workers. In Estonia and France, too, replacement rates are significantly below the OECD average.

The Netherlands is at the top of the scale, with an increase in pension wealth worth 24% of earnings for an additional year's work. This is because of the abolition of the early-retirement programmes that provided benefits from age 60 to 65 coupled with the fact that the full-career replacement rate is one of the highest in the OECD. The Czech Republic scores highly here because of the relatively large actuarial adjustments for early retirement. Both factors are at work in Iceland. In other cases, such as Denmark and Poland, the relatively large increment in pension wealth is partly driven by the fact that it is not possible to claim benefits before 65.

3.4. Individual earnings and changes in pension wealth

So far, the results have looked at the case of an average earner. However, most OECD countries' pension systems result in different incentives to work for workers across the earnings range. The evidence is set out in Table 3.2, which shows the change in pension

Table 3.2. **Changes in gross pension wealth for working age 60-65, men at different earnings levels**

	Individual earnings (% of average)				Individual earnings (% of average)		
	Low (50%)	Average (100%)	High (150%)		Low (50%)	Average (100%)	High (150%)
Better incentives for lower or middle earners to stay in work				**Retirement incentives strictly constant with earnings**			
Czech Republic	30.3	22.9	18.3	Australia	–10.6	–10.6	–10.6
France	8.3	9.5	–0.1	Greece	–90.2	–90.2	–90.2
Korea	26.2	17.2	13.1	Hungary	9.5	9.5	9.5
Iceland	47.7	14.7	12.2	Italy	–10.8	–10.8	–10.8
Ireland	7.3	3.6	2.4	New Zealand	0	0	0
Israel	23.1	18.9	12.6	Poland	14.6	14.6	14.6
Slovak Republic	24.1	7.9	7.9	Spain	9.4	9.4	9.4
Switzerland	13.4	12.1	8.5				
Worse incentives for lower or middle earners to stay in work				**Retirement incentives broadly constant with earnings**			
Belgium	–25.2	–20.5	–16.5	Austria	14.9	15.3	14.2
Chile	12.2	12.2	17.3	Canada	–7	–7.5	–6.4
Finland	0.8	12.2	12.2	Denmark	8.7	7.9	7.6
Germany	–16.3	13.9	13.9	Estonia	2.3	2.4	2.4
Luxembourg	–88.1	–76.4	–72.5	Japan	5.2	5.8	6
Mexico	–56.5	–21.6	0.4	United Kingdom	3.5	2.9	1.9
Netherlands	14.1	24	27.3	United States	–1.2	–1.2	0.4
Norway	–26.9	19.1	14.5				
Portugal	–61.8	–29	–28.6				
Slovenia	–59.4	–19.7	–19.7				
Sweden	–10.5	4.2	4.3				
Turkey	–78.9	–34.1	–34.1				

Source: OECD pension models.

StatLink http://dx.doi.org/10.1787/888932372184

wealth from working an additional year for people with 50%, 100% and 150% of economy-wide average earnings.

At the left-hand side of the table are 20 OECD countries where there is significant variation in retirement incentives with individual earnings. In the 14 countries on the right-hand side, retirement incentives are exactly the same for different workers in half of them, and broadly the same in the other half.

In the strictly-constant group, Greece, Hungary, Italy, Poland and Spain have pension systems with a strong link between individual earnings and pension benefits.[10] In New Zealand, the universal basic pension scheme means that the change in pension wealth is zero for everyone.

The seven countries in the broadly-constant group (at the bottom right-hand side of Table 3.2) mainly have progressive pension systems, in contrast to retirement-income provision in most of the strictly-constant group. The incentive to remain in work is a little better, the lower are individual earnings, in Austria, Denmark and the United Kingdom. The reverse – work incentives are slightly stronger for higher earners – in Canada, Estonia, Japan and the United States.

The countries where the link between individual earnings and retirement incentives are strongest (left-hand side of Table 3.2) also divide into two groups. Progressivity of pension benefits is the main reason why the eight countries in the upper part of the table have stronger work incentives for lower or middle earners. The progressivity results from quite different features of the national scheme: the basic pension in Iceland and Ireland, minimum credits for low earners in the Slovak Republic and progressive benefit formulae for earnings-related pensions in the Czech Republic and Korea.

Incentives to retire are stronger for low earners than middle or high earners in the 12 OECD countries in the lower-left part of Table 3.2. In nearly all cases, this is driven by safety-net provisions in the retirement-income system. In Belgium, Luxembourg and Portugal, for example, progressivity accentuates the negative rather than the positive (compared with the countries in the upper left-hand side of Table 3.2). In Finland, Germany, Norway and Sweden, low-income workers who will be entitled to minimum pensions or resource-tested benefits have incentives to retire early that are not shared by average and high earners. In Mexico, the minimum pension means that incentives to retire early are especially strong for low earners.

3.5. The role of taxes: Changes in net pension wealth from working longer

Pensions in payment are taxable in virtually all OECD countries' personal income tax systems. In 15 OECD countries, pensions are subject to social security contributions (usually for health or long-term care), albeit at a lower rate than levied on earnings. Taking account of these taxes and contributions – set out in the indicator of the "Tax treatment of pensions and pensioners" in Part II.2 – gives the net change in pension wealth from working longer.

To illustrate the impact of taxes and contributions on pensions in payment, Figure 3.4 plots changes in gross pension wealth on the horizontal axis and the net measure on the vertical. To make the chart easier to read, the outliers of Greece and Luxembourg are not shown. A 45°-line has been added to the chart to show cases where changes in gross and net pension wealth are equal. This occurs in two countries that do not tax pensions in payment – the Slovak Republic and Turkey – and in a number where pensions form part of

Figure 3.4. **Changes in gross pension wealth for working age 60-65, men with average earnings, gross and net terms**

Percentage of annual gross earnings

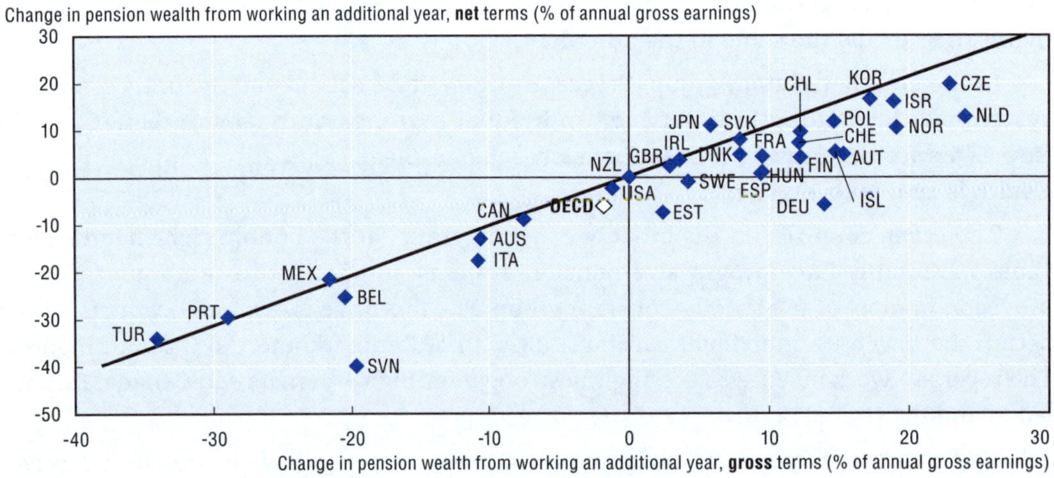

Note: Two outliers – Greece and Luxembourg – not shown for reasons of clarity.

Source: OECD pension models.

StatLink http://dx.doi.org/10.1787/888932370474

taxable income but an average earner's pension entitlement would be below the level at which income tax starts to be paid. This latter group comprises Australia, Hungary, Ireland, Mexico and Portugal.

Taxes and contributions on pensions in payment make a significant difference in other cases. For example, the Netherlands has the highest change in gross pension wealth from working longer in gross terms, but falls behind the Czech Republic, Israel and Korea in net terms. Positive changes in gross pension wealth in Estonia, Germany, Japan, Spain and Sweden turn negative when measured in net terms. On average for all OECD countries, the change in net pension wealth for working from age 60 to 65 is –7.9%, compared with –1.8% in gross terms.

3.6. Adding a dimension to the analysis: Levels of pension wealth

The previous studies of retirement incentives (Gruber and Wise, 1998, 1999; Blöndal and Scarpetta, 1999; and Duval, 2003) – have all emphasised the *change* in pension wealth as the key measure of retirement incentives. But this misses the rather obvious point that the *level* of pension wealth also matters. The change in pension wealth can be thought of as a "substitution effect": leisure becomes more attractive as the implicit subsidy to continuing on work declines or turns into an implicit tax. The level of pension wealth is akin to an "income effect". If people have a high level of pension wealth already at age 60, they may not wish to add to this by working an additional year, even if this results in a large increment in their pension entitlements. Put another way, if two individuals in different countries have the same *change* in pension wealth from working longer, but one has a higher *level* of pension wealth already earned than the other, then the pension incentive to retire will be greater in the country with the higher pension.

This section looks at levels of pension wealth, using again the baseline retirement window of age 60-65. Pension wealth is calculated at age 60. Normal pension ages for men are above age 60 in all OECD countries, and so pension wealth shown here is lower than in the indicator of "Gross pension wealth" in Part II.2 for full-career workers. This is due to the pension system. People might not have a full contribution history by age 60: pension wealth depends on the replacement rate, pension eligibility age and indexation rules. There are also actuarial effects: pension wealth depends on national life expectancy. Furthermore, people are unable to claim the pension at age 60 in most countries. The computations in these cases allow for the probability that people die between age 60 and the age at which the pension can first be drawn.

Figure 3.5 shows the level of pension wealth to which a man is entitled for working from age 20 until age 60 at different earning levels. The OECD average for a person with average earnings is just over eight times annual pay. Pension wealth is larger for low earners (with 50% of average pay) in the 26 countries in the top panel of Figure 3.5. Because pension wealth is normalised to annual individual gross earnings, then retirement-income systems that are redistributive deliver a higher replacement rate to lower earners and so higher pension wealth. Pension wealth is broadly constant with earnings in the eight countries in the lower panel.

The levels of pension wealth already earned at age 60 shown are highest in Luxembourg and Greece, irrespective of the earnings level. In both cases, replacement rates are relatively high and a full-career worker contributing from age 20 will already have a full pension entitlement by age 60. Pension wealth also exceeds ten times annual earnings for average earners in Iceland, the Netherlands, Slovenia and Spain.

Figure 3.5. **Level of gross pension wealth already accrued at age 60 by earnings level, men**

Multiple of annual gross earnings

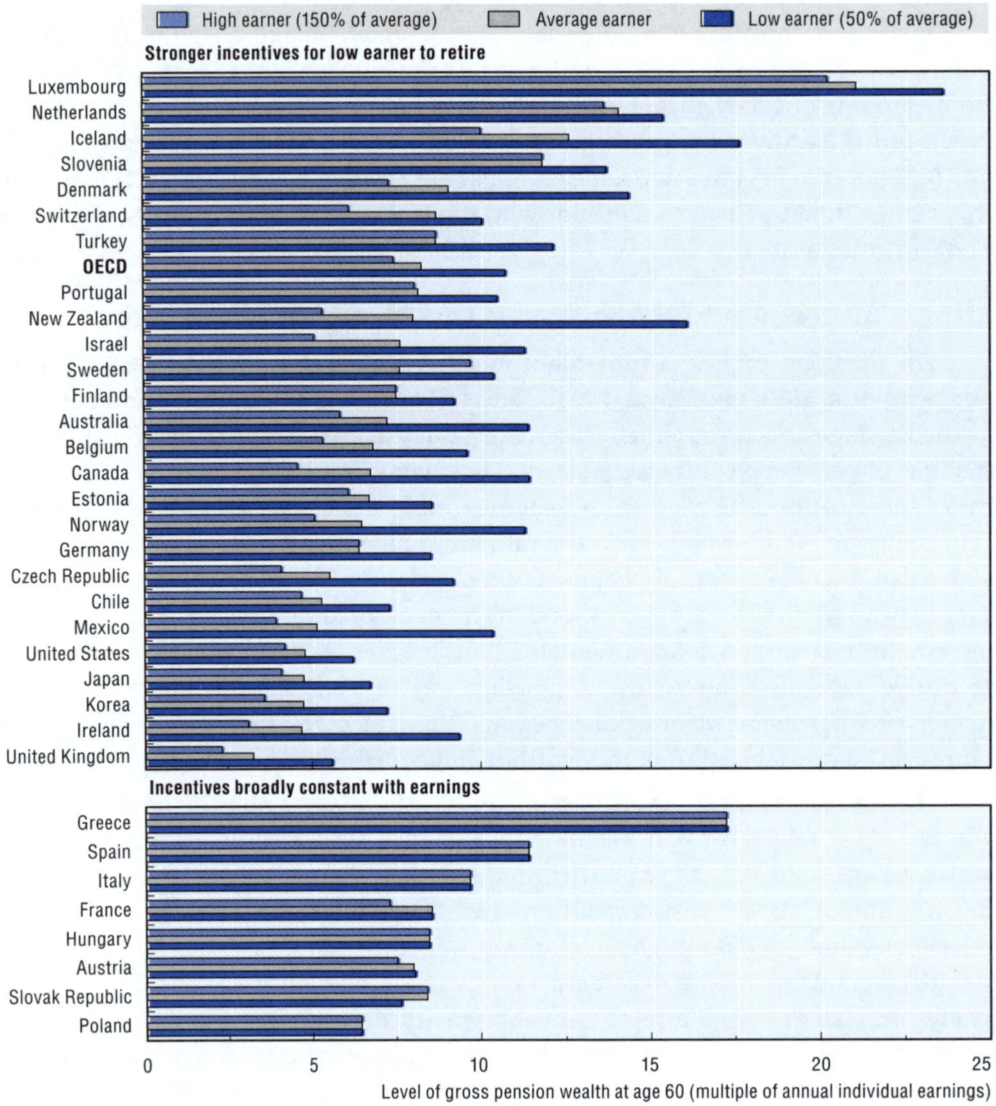

Source: OECD pension models.

StatLink http://dx.doi.org/10.1787/888932370493

On average, pension wealth for low earners is 10.4 times annual earnings, significantly higher than the 8.1 figure for average earners. The differences between the results at low and average earnings are especially large in the countries with the most redistributive pensions: the basic schemes in Ireland and New Zealand, for example.

Pension wealth is generally lower for high earners (with 150% of average pay), again because of redistributive elements but also in some cases as a result of ceilings on pensionable earnings. The OECD average pension wealth for high earners is 7.3 times their annual earnings.

3.7. Summary of the results for age 60-64

Pension incentives to retire, based on levels of and changes in pension wealth discussed above, are summarised in Tables 3.3 and 3.4. Both of them consider the main retirement window, between age 60 and 65. On each measure, the 34 OECD countries are divided into three groups: low, middle and high. Both changes and levels are presented in net terms, after allowing for taxes and contributions levied on pension income. The three columns of the tables show the change in pension wealth from continuing on work between 60 and 65. The three rows present the levels of pension wealth already achieved at 65. There are substantial differences between the groups. The level of pension wealth is more than twice as large in the "high" countries as in the group with the lowest results. Similarly, the change in pension wealth averages about –32% in the low group, +1% in the middle and +11% in the high group.

Table 3.3. **Levels of and changes in net pension wealth at ages 60-65, men with average earnings**

		Change in pension wealth from working age 60-65		
		Lowest third	Middle third	Highest third
Level of pension wealth at age 60	Lowest third	Mexico	Germany, Ireland, Sweden, United Kingdom, United States	Chile, Czech Republic, Japan, Korea, Poland
	Middle third	Australia, Belgium, Canada, Estonia	Denmark, Finland, New Zealand	Austria, Israel, Norway, Switzerland
	Highest third	Greece, Italy, Luxembourg, Portugal, Slovenia, Turkey	France, Hungary, Spain	Iceland, Netherlands, Slovak Republic

Note: Countries grouped into thirds of the distribution of both change and level of pension wealth. Mean level of pension wealth is 4.9 times individual annual earnings for the low group, 6.6 for the middle and 10.2 for the high. Mean change in pension wealth for working from age 60-64 is –31.7% of annual earnings for the low group, +1.0% for the middle group and +11.0% for the high group.
Source: OECD pension models: see D'Addio and Whitehouse (2011) for complete results.

StatLink http://dx.doi.org/10.1787/888932372203

Table 3.4. **Levels of and changes in net pension wealth at ages 60-65, men with low earnings (50% of mean)**

		Change in pension wealth from working age 60-65		
		Lowest third	Middle third	Highest third
Level of pension wealth at age 60	Lowest third	Germany	France, Sweden, United Kingdom, United States	Austria, Chile, Japan, Korea, Poland, Slovak Republic
	Middle third	Belgium, Italy, Mexico, Portugal	Denmark, Estonia, Finland, Hungary	Czech Republic, Ireland, Switzerland
	Highest third	Australia, Greece, Luxembourg, Norway, Slovenia, Turkey	Canada, New Zealand, Spain	Iceland, Israel, Netherlands

Note: Countries grouped into thirds of the distribution of both change and level of gross pension wealth. Mean level of pension wealth is 7 times earnings for the low group, 9 for the middle and 13 for the high. Mean change in pension wealth for working from age 60-64 is –49.8% for the low group, –0.9% for the middle group and +16.5% for the high group.
Source: OECD pension models: see D'Addio and Whitehouse (2011) for complete results.

StatLink http://dx.doi.org/10.1787/888932372222

The pension incentive to retire is therefore strongest at the bottom left, where levels of pension wealth are already high at age 60 and the change in pension wealth from continuing in work to age 65 is low or negative. In contrast, at the top right, levels of pension wealth are low but the increment to pension wealth from working to age 65 is high.

Starting with the case of average earners, in Table 3.3, Chile, the Czech Republic, Japan Korea and Poland have the combination of low level of and high change in pension wealth likely to keep people working. However, incentives are also pretty good in Germany, Ireland, Sweden, the United Kingdom and the United States. Although the increment to pension wealth is not as high, the low levels of pension wealth make early retirement unattractive from a financial viewpoint. In Austria, Israel, Norway and Switzerland, the level of pension wealth at 60 is towards the middle of the range in OECD countries. But large increments to pension wealth might encourage people to keep working until 65.

In Greece, Italy, Luxembourg, Portugal, Slovenia and Turkey, both the "income effect" from a high level of pension wealth and the "substitution effect" from reductions in pension wealth from working until age 65 are likely to drive people to leave the labour market well before age 65.

The picture is less clear-cut in the 16 countries not already discussed. In Iceland, the Netherlands and the Slovak Republic, for example, both levels of and changes in pension wealth are high. The impact of pension systems on retirement will therefore depend on the relative forces exerted by the income and substitution effects. In Mexico, the level of pension wealth is low but the change in pension wealth is negative. Again, it is ambiguous which effect will win out.

Table 3.4 shows the same analysis for low earners, with pay of half the average. The level of pension wealth is generally higher for low earners. The average in the group with "high" pension wealth is nearly double that in the "low" group. Changes in pension wealth average around –50% in the low group, zero in the middle and +17% in the high.

Greece, Luxembourg, Portugal, Slovenia and Turkey again have among the highest levels of pension wealth at age 60 and negative changes in pension wealth for working between 60 and 65. However, low earners in Norway are also in this group, whereas average earners had strong incentives to work on both measures. This is because of the guarantee pension in the reformed retirement-income system. Italy moves up one cell looking at low rather than average earners. This is because levels of pension wealth for a low earner are in the middle of the range in OECD countries: other pension systems have redistributive elements that push pension wealth higher for low earners, while Italy's has a strong link between pension and earnings.

Chile, Japan, Korea and Poland feature at the top right of both tables. For low earners, the level of pension wealth is also relatively low and the change in pension wealth relatively high in Austria and the Slovak Republic.

3.8. Policy implications

If older workers can retire early on high incomes relative to their earnings then they can hardly be blamed for doing so. Thus, improving incentives to work longer has been a motif of most OECD countries' pension reforms over the last two decades.

The most obvious element of pension reforms has been increases in normal pensionable ages, already underway or planned for the future, as set out in Part II.1 of this volume.[11] Since average pension ages reached a low point in the early 1990s, 14 OECD countries have already increased or plan to increase in the future pension ages for men and 18 for women.

In addition, around half of OECD countries have taken other measures to encourage people to work longer.[12] Firstly, a range of countries – Austria, Belgium, Denmark, France, Greece, Hungary, Italy and Poland (for some types of worker) – have tightened the qualifying conditions for early retirement. These conditions cover the number of years of contributions required, or the eligibility age for early retirement, or both. The Netherlands has removed tax incentives for private, occupational early-retirement schemes. Austria, Germany, Italy and Portugal either introduced or raised the level of reductions in benefits for early retirees. Increments to benefits for late retirement were introduced or enhanced in Belgium, Spain and the United Kingdom. Five countries – Canada, the Czech Republic, Finland, France and the United States – adjusted incentives for both early and late retirement. Australia has made it easier to combine work and pension receipt.

It is also important to note that many pension reforms will mean that benefits for workers entering the labour market today will be significantly lower than for workers with the same career history retiring today. Earlier analysis showed that 14 out of 20 major pension reforms in OECD countries will cut benefits for average earners, by an average of around 20%.[13] This chapter has stressed that both the *level* of and *change* in pension wealth affect incentives. Therefore, these more general cuts in benefits provide an incentive for people to remain in work longer and make retirement less financially attractive.

This chapter has assessed incentives to retire in pension systems *after* these reforms are fully in place. It is clear that most OECD countries have fixed any major problems of incentives to retire early. The retirement-income regime is relatively neutral over age of retirement. Nevertheless, pension systems sometimes still provide a powerful incentive to leave work at the earliest possible opportunity. This is most obvious in Greece and Luxembourg, although Italy, Portugal, Slovenia and Turkey also provide fairly strong incentives to retire early. Even some countries with a relatively small change in pension wealth from remaining in work could do better.

The OECD pension models allow the measures of pension wealth to be decomposed into the different parts of the retirement-income system.[14] This makes it possible to identify the particular features of pension systems which reduce work incentives.

- In Belgium, France, Greece and Luxembourg, it is possible to retire at age 60 (or earlier in some cases) without reduction in benefits to reflect the longer duration of payment. The average reduction in benefits in earnings-related schemes for each year of early retirement is around 4.5%. This is well below the actuarially neutral level of around 6-8%.[15] These actuarial reductions are low in Austria, Hungary, Italy, Norway and Slovenia. However, they are close to the actuarially neutral level in Canada, the Czech and Slovak Republics, Finland, Iceland, Japan, Korea and Spain.
- During the early-retirement window, valorisation of accrued pension rights with price inflation or a mix of price and earnings growth reduces incentives to remain in work. This applies to Belgium, Finland, France, Portugal and the United States. However, in Finland and France, other elements of the treatment of early retirees compensate for this effect.
- Estonia, the Slovak Republic and Slovenia are the only OECD countries that are not increasing normal pension age for men to at least 65. Indeed, eight countries are going beyond 65 to either 67 or 68. Earlier pension ages for women than men in Chile, Italy, Poland (all age 60) and Switzerland (age 64) look anachronistic.

- Increments in pension benefits for people who defer claiming the pension after normal pension age are close to 5% on average, still below actuarial neutrality. There are no increases payable in Belgium and Italy and the increments are small in Austria, Poland, Spain and the Swiss occupational pensions. However, a range of countries – such as Canada, the Czech Republic, Japan, the United Kingdom and the United States – offer attractive terms for deferring pensions.
- In many cases, the absence of an increment for late retirement does not particularly matter because people can combine work and pension receipt. Some countries, however, still operate earnings tests that mean that this is not possible: Belgium, Ireland and Greece, for example.
- Resource-tested schemes can have negative effects on work incentives for low earners. However, such schemes target benefits on those most in need and so reduce the need for higher taxes and contributions throughout the economy. Still, some countries have managed to combine redistributive pension systems with incentives to stay in work – Chile, the Czech Republic, Iceland, Ireland, New Zealand and Switzerland, for example – while others – such as Portugal and Slovenia – have not.
- Spain's public, earnings-related scheme has higher accrual rates at younger ages: 3.33% for the first years of contributions compared with 2% later on. A uniform accrual structure would improve incentives for older workers.
- Many OECD countries used to calculate pension benefits based on a limited subset of "best" or "final" earnings. This encourages people to retire once earnings have peaked: indeed, in some cases, continuing to work but in a lower-paid job could reduce benefits. Most countries – Austria, Finland, Italy, the Netherlands, Poland, the Slovak Republic, Sweden and the United Kingdom – have fixed this problem and will base benefits on earnings across the career. However, Greece still bases benefits on the final five years' pay and Spain on the final 15 years.
- A small number of OECD countries have limits on the number of years that can accrue pension benefits in earnings-related schemes. In Greece, for example, the maximum pension replacement rate is achieved after 35 years' contribution: only working after age 65 accrues any additional benefit. The pension entitlement in Greece may increase with additional work, but only if higher earnings replace lower earnings in the benefit formula. Similarly, the public pension scheme in the United States pays a full benefit with 35 years of contributions. There is a penalty if the pension is claimed early, but, as in Greece, extra years' contributions increase benefits solely through the mechanism of lower earnings dropping out of the benefit formula. The maximum accrual is also reached after 35 years in Spain. These policies discourage work once the maximum number of years has been achieved: they are economically inefficient. Also, they are in a sense "unfair": contributions are levied but no additional benefit is earned. Two OECD countries – Belgium and Sweden – have fixed this type of problem in pension reforms.

These nine policy conclusions are undoubtedly technical. But they are unashamedly so: the details really do matter. In the big picture, they determine whether the pension system fairly treats individuals who retire at different ages and how much or how little individual decisions over work and retirement are distorted by the pension system.

This special chapter has focused on the retirement-income system. As shown in Chapter 2 in Part I on "Trends in retirement and in working at older ages", however, many workers take alternative routes into early retirement, such as disability or unemployment benefits. Disability and unemployment are not just about financial incentives, and so are difficult to assess using the framework adopted here. Particularly important is the way benefits are policed through analysis of health status and job-search requirements. These policies are addressed in the OECD's disability reviews (see OECD, 2010) and "Ageing and employment policies" reports (OECD, 2006).

Notes

1. See the OECD's (2007), *Benefits and Wages* report for an example.
2. A more detailed analysis of these different types of scheme can be found in Whitehouse (2010).
3. The issue of valorisation is discussed in detail in the indicator of "Income-replacement pensions" in Part II.1.
4. See the indicator of "Income-replacement pensions" in Part II.1. Whitehouse (2010) and Whitehouse *et al.* (2009) provide a more detailed discussion.
5. See the indicator of "Normal, early and late retirement" in Part II.1 for information on these adjustments and an analysis of their importance. Queisser and Whitehouse (2006) provide a more detailed discussion.
6. This measure is closely linked to the concept of "actuarial neutrality", which requires that the present value of accrued pension benefits for working an additional year is the same as in the year before. See Queisser and Whitehouse (2006), for a rigorous discussion of the concept and its application to different types of pension scheme). This means that benefits increase only by the additional entitlement earned in that year. Conversely, retiring a year earlier should reduce the pension benefit both by the entitlement that would have been earned during the year and by an amount to reflect the longer duration for which the pension must be paid. For present purposes, an "actuarially neutral" pension system does not mean that the change in pension wealth (or implicit tax/subsidy) should be zero.
7. Blöndal and Scarpetta (1999) found a smaller elasticity than Gruber wand Wise (1998, 1999) of 0.28 in their study of 20 countries. (The calculations of elasticities to enable a direct comparison between these two studies was carried out by Burtless, 2004.) The different size of the effect does not reflect differences in the countries included in the two studies Rather, the cause is that estimates of the "implicit tax on remaining in work" vary between the two studies, in part because they look at different years. Nevertheless, there was still a strong and statistically significant relationship between retirement incentives and retirement behaviour.
8. Regular updates of this work have been published in the OECD's *Economic Policy Reforms: Going for Growth* report (2005-10).
9. Earlier results, using 2006 parameters and rules, were published in D'Addio, Keese and Whitehouse (2010).
10. See the indicators of "Progressivity of pension-benefit formulae" and the "Pension-earnings link" in Part II.2.
11. See also Chomik and Whitehouse (2010) for more details.
12. Whitehouse *et al.* (2010) provide a description of these changes: see also the chapters on pension reforms in OECD (2007, 2009).
13. See OECD (2009), Chapter I.2, especially Table 2.3 and the surrounding discussion, and Whitehouse *et al.* (2010), particularly Figure 3 and the discussion thereof.
14. These detailed calculations will be published in D'Addio and Whitehouse (2011).
15. The indicator of "Normal, early and late retirement" in Part II.1 and Whitehouse (2010) present and discuss these adjustments. Queisser and Whitehouse (2006) discuss the concept of actuarial neutrality and present calculations for OECD countries of neutral adjustments.

References

Blöndal, S and S. Scarpetta (1999), "The Retirement Decision in OECD Countries", *Economics Department Working Paper*, No. 202, OECD Publishing, Paris.

Burtless, G. (2004), "Pension Reform and Labour-Force Exit: Cross-National Evidence", mimeo, Brookings Institution, Washington DC.

Chomik, R. and E.R. Whitehouse (2010), "Trends in Pension Eligibility Ages and Life Expectancy, 1950-2050", *Social, Employment and Migration Working Paper*, No. 105, OECD Publishing, Paris.

D'Addio, A.C. and E.R. Whitehouse (2011), "Financial Incentives to Retire", *Social, Employment and Migration Working Paper*, OECD Publishing, forthcoming.

D'Addio, A.C., M. Keese and E.R. Whitehouse (2010), "Population Ageing and Labour Markets", *Oxford Review of Economic Policy*, forthcoming.

Duval, R. (2003), "The Retirement Effects of Old-Age Pension and Early Retirement Schemes in OECD Countries", *Economics Department Working Paper*, No. 370, OECD Publishing, Paris.

European Commission (2009), "The 2009 Ageing Report: Economic and Budgetary Projections for the EU-27 Member States (2008-2060)", *European Economy*, No. 2/2009.

Gruber, J. and D.A. Wise (1998) "Social Security and Retirement: An International Comparison", *American Economic Review*, Vol. 88, No. 2.

Gruber, J. and D.A. Wise (1999), *Social Security and Retirement around the World*, University of Chicago Press for National Bureau of Economic Research.

OECD (2006), *Ageing and Employment Policies: Live Longer, Work Longer*, OECD Publishing, Paris.

OECD (2005-10), *Economic Policy Reforms: Going for Growth*, OECD Publishing, Paris.

OECD (2007a), *Pensions at a Glance 2007: Public Policies across OECD Countries*, OECD Publishing, Paris.

OECD (2007b), *Benefits and Wages*, OECD Publishing, Paris.

OECD (2009), *Pensions at a Glance 2009: Retirement-Income Systems in OECD Countries*, OECD Publishing, Paris.

OECD (2010), *Sickness, Disability and Work: Breaking the Barriers*, OECD Publishing, Paris.

Queisser, M. and E. Whitehouse (2006), "Neutral or Fair? Actuarial Concepts and Pension-System Design", *Social, Employment and Migration Working Paper*, No. 40, OECD Publishing, Paris.

Whitehouse, E.R. (2010), "Decomposing Notional Defined-Contribution Pensions: Experience of OECD Countries' Reforms", *Social, Employment and Migration Working Paper*, No. 109, OECD Publishing, Paris.

Whitehouse, E.R., A.C. D'Addio, R. Chomik and A. Reilly (2009), "Two Decades of Pension Reform: What Has Been Achieved and What Remains To Be Done?", *Geneva Papers on Risk and Insurance*, Vol. 34, pp. 515-535.

Pensions at a Glance 2011
Retirement-income Systems in OECD and G20 Countries

PART I

Chapter 4

Helping Older Workers Find and Retain Jobs

The financial incentives in pension systems, explored in Chapter 3, undoubtedly play an important role in retirement decisions. But if there are barriers to working longer on the demand side, pension reforms designed to improve work incentives may be less effective.

This chapter describes various barriers affecting employers and employees and what might be done to tackle them. There are still ageist attitudes among employers, particularly over the ability of older workers to adapt to change. Legislation against age discrimination and public-information campaigns have been effective in some, but by no means all, countries that have adopted these policies. In some countries, older workers cost too much and early retirement provides an all-too convenient way of adjusting the size of the workforce. Strict employment-protection legislation can make it costly to hire older workers.

Employment opportunities of older workers may be limited because their skills have become devalued or they receive little help in finding new jobs. Available employment opportunities may be unattractive because of poor working conditions or unsuitable and inflexible working-time arrangements.

Finally, this chapter discusses the issue of jobs for younger and older workers. It finds that there is no evidence that older workers deprive youths of jobs. In fact, the reverse is true.

The size of the working-age population – aged 20-64 – will reach a peak in OECD countries around 2015. It will then decline by a little over 10% by 2050.[1] This prospect raises the question of where workers will be found to maintain economic growth and finance rising public-pension and healthcare costs. More needs to be done to increase productivity and mobilise all available resources in labour markets, including older workers.

The debate about increasing pension ages – the policies examined in Chapter 1 in Part I on "Pensionable age and life expectancy 1950-2050" – has often revolved around the question of whether there are jobs for older people. A similar concern applies to pension reforms that have improved incentives for older workers: they may be less effective in encouraging later retirement if there are still substantial barriers to work on the demand-side.

On the side of employers, the demand for older workers may be restricted by ageist attitudes, because older workers cost too much or because early retirement provides a convenient way of reducing the size of their workforce. On the side of older workers, their employment opportunities may be limited or unattractive because their skills have become devalued, they receive little help in finding new jobs or they face undesirable working conditions and unsuitable working-time arrangements.

4.1. A greyer workforce

The workforce has been getting older for some time. In 1966, half of employees were aged under 35; today, that figure is only just over one-third (Figure 4.1). If current patterns of employment at different ages were to continue, the median age of employees will increase from just over 40 now to 42 in 2050. In the mid-1960s, the median age was 34.

However, the age-pattern of employment is unlikely to remain the same: ageing would mean that the number of employees would decline even more rapidly than the working age population. Simply to maintain the size of the workforce in employment in OECD countries would require employment rates for 50-64 year-olds to increase substantially: to the same level as for 40- to 49-year-olds. And employment rates for 65- to 69-year-olds would need to increase from just over 20% now to 40%. The median age of employees in such a scenario would rise to 45 from just over 40 today.

The rest of this special chapter sets out how this necessarily radical change in the labour market might be achieved. It sets out the barriers that older workers face and assesses the measures that countries have taken to tackle them.

4.2. Ageism

There is no doubt that at least some employers discriminate against older workers. Almost all of the 21 country reviews in the OECD's series on *Ageing and Employment Policies* found evidence to show that employers often have negative perceptions about older workers, especially about their ability to adapt to technological and organisational change.[2] Around 6% of the adult population in the European Union reported that in the past 12 months they have personally felt discriminated against or harassed as a result of their age. This goes

Figure 4.1. **Age-structure of employment, 1966, 2009 and 2050**

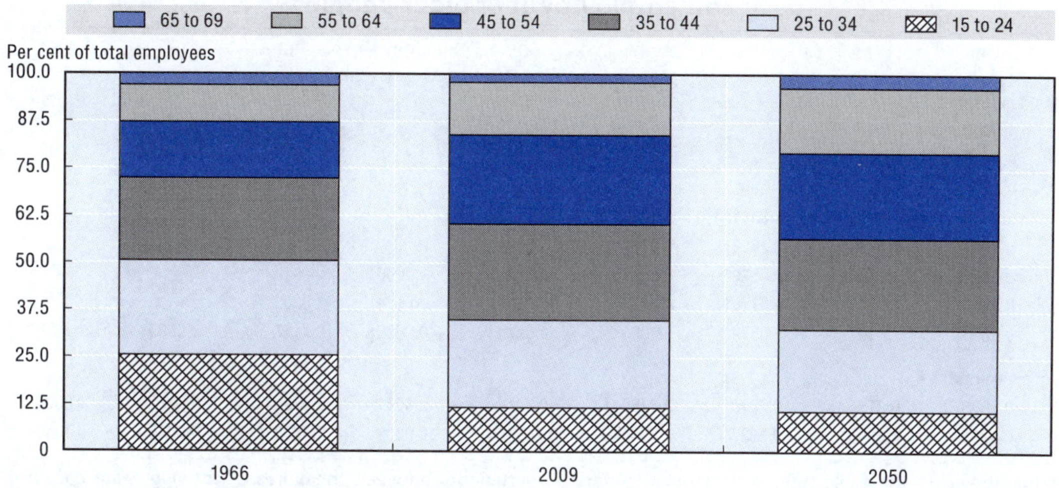

Note: The age structure calculated for 2050 assumes that employment rates by age remain the same as they were in 2009.

Source: OECD *Employment Database*; OECD calculations using United Nations, *World Population Prospects – The 2008 Revision*.

StatLink http://dx.doi.org/10.1787/888932370512

to 11% in the Czech Republic.[3] However, a detailed examination of these survey data (Table 4.1) reveals a very weak correlation between different aspects of attitudes to ageism. The different measures look at general perceptions of its prevalence, personal experience of seeing or being subject to ageism and efforts to combat age discrimination. Most importantly, attitudes to and perceptions of ageism are, at best, *positively* rather than *negatively* correlated with the employment rate of older people.

More direct evidence of age discrimination in employment has been obtained in a number of experimental field studies in which "matched" CVs are sent to employers. The invented candidates' characteristics and qualifications are the same: the only differences are in their stated age or length of work experience. The results of these studies show that, in general, older candidates were less likely to receive offers of a job interview.[4]

Virtually all OECD countries now have in place some form of ***legislation*** banning age discrimination in employment. Japan is a notable exception: more emphasis there has been placed on administrative guidelines. The United States was one of the earliest to legislate (in 1967). Many European countries took steps much more recently, in many cases prompted by a European Union directive in 2000 requiring them to do so by 2006.

Several countries have had ***public-information*** campaigns to tackle ageism in the workplace. Examples include Australia, Finland, France, the Netherlands, Norway and the United Kingdom. Employers are not just being told that they cannot discriminate against older workers through the law. They are also provided with tools and information for managing an older workforce. In some instances, there has been a strong emphasis on managing age diversity in the workplace to avoid stigmatising older workers.

The important question is, of course, are these legislative and public-information measures effective? Economic analysis demonstrates that the impact of anti-discrimination legislation need not be positive. It encourages retention of workers in the protected group, because it makes it more costly to fire them. However, there can be unintended consequences: employers might be discouraged from hiring protected employees precisely

Table 4.1. Correlation between subjective measures of age discrimination and employment of older people[1]

	D1	D2	D3	D4	D5	D6	D7	D8	e5064	c5064
Discrimination measures[2]										
D1	1.0000									
D2	**0.7930*****	1.0000								
D3	**0.4701****	**0.6858*****	1.0000							
D4	**0.3633***	**0.5500*****	**0.8891*****	1.0000						
D5	0.1841	**0.3235***	0.2856	**0.3732***	1.0000					
D6	0.2671	**0.3396***	**0.3572***	0.2647	0.2075	1.0000				
D7	**0.4798****	**0.5195*****	**0.3733****	**0.4805****	**0.6024*****	0.104	1.0000			
D8	0.2611	0.161	–0.0573***	0.1003	0.097	0.0625	0.2177	1.0000		
Employment measures[3]										
e5064	0.0533	0.0156	0.2679	**0.4165****	0.201	0.0061	**0.4722****	–0.0867	1.0000	
c5064	0.0724	**0.3359***	0.2837	**0.3706***	0.2483	–0.0808	**0.4673****	0.0855	0.1349	1.0000

1. The value shown in the table refer to Pearson correlation coefficients between measures at the aggregate country level for the EU27 countries. Statistically significant correlations are shown in bold and the level of significance is shown as: *, **, *** = significant at 10%, 5% and 1% levels, respectively.
2. Each discrimination measure refers to the (weighted) proportion of respondents in each country in a 2009 Eurobarometer survey who reported that:
   D1. Discrimination on the basis of age is very widespread or fairly widespread.
   D2. Compared with the situation five years ago, age discrimination is more common.
   D3. In the past 12 months they have personally felt discriminated against or harassed on the basis of age.
   D4. In the past 12 months they have witnessed someone being discriminated against or harassed on the basis of age.
   D5. Age may be a disadvantage for a candidate when a company wants to hire someone and has the choice between two candidates with equal skills and qualifications.
   D6. Not enough effort is made nationally to fight all forms of discrimination.
   D7. The economic crisis will contribute to an increase of discrimination on the basis of age in the labour market.
   D8. Not enough is being done to increase diversity in their workplace as far as age is concerned.
3. The employment measures refer to:
   e50-64 = Employment rate in 2008 for the population aged 50-64 years-old.
   C50-64 = Change in the employment rate between 2003 and 2008 for the population aged 50-64 years-old.

Source: D'Addio *et al.* (2010) based on Eurobarometer (2009) for the discrimination measures; and on the European Union Labour Force Survey.

StatLink http://dx.doi.org/10.1787/888932372241

because of this cost.[5] There is some evidence, most of it from the United States, that this latter effect is significant. The overall impact on employment rates for older people is less clear cut (see, for example, Adams, 2006; Lahey, 2006; and Neumark, 2008).

The prevalence of perceived age discrimination has declined in only around half of the countries for which complete data between 1995 and 2005 are available (Table 4.2). Among the countries that have taken a strong public stance against age discrimination (through legislation or public-information campaigns or both), there were fewer reports of ageism at work in Finland and the United Kingdom in 2005 than earlier, but the Netherlands recorded an increase. Similarly, there have been significant declines in perceived age discrimination in Spain and Portugal despite the fact that government action in the period in question was limited.

4.3. Labour costs and older workers

Negative attitudes may partly explain employer reluctance to hire or retain older workers, a number of more objective factors also drive employer behaviour. One of the most significant is the cost of employing older workers. If this cost rises more steeply with age than productivity does, then both retention and hiring of older workers will be affected negatively.

Table 4.2. **Proportion of workers reporting age discrimination over the previous 12 months**[1]

Percentage

	1995	2000	2005
Austria	6.9	4.3	2.4
Belgium	1.3	2.5	3.2
Czech Republic	..	5.5	5.4
Denmark	2.4	1.4	2.0
Finland	4.0	4.3	3.3
France	4.8	3.4	2.6
Germany	1.9	3.3	3.0
Greece	3.6	2.8	4.7
Hungary	..	4.8	3.3
Ireland	2.1	3.2	4.2
Italy	2.0	2.2	3.8
Luxembourg	2.1	1.2	4.1
Netherlands	2.6	3.0	3.7
Poland	..	2.1	2.4
Portugal	3.2	1.1	1.9
Slovak Republic	..	5.1	3.8
Spain	1.9	1.6	0.4
Sweden	3.0	3.9	4.0
United Kingdom	4.7	3.9	2.7
Weighted average	**3.1**	**3.2**	**3.2**
Unweighted average	**3.1**	**3.2**	**3.2**

1. The data refer to the proportion of all wage and salary earners in each country who reported that over the past 12 months they had been subjected at work to age discrimination.

Source: D'Addio *et al.* (2010) based on European Working Conditions Survey.

StatLink http://dx.doi.org/10.1787/888932372260

The most important element in labour costs is, of course, the earnings of the employee. Figure 4.2 shows how earnings vary with age. Of the 12 countries shown, the age-earnings profile is continually increasing in Belgium, France and the Netherlands. In many of the others, the pattern is an inverted U-shape; this is most pronounced in Ireland, Japan and the United Kingdom. Analysis of earlier data for a broader range of countries shows a strong age-earnings link in a few other countries, such as Austria and Germany.[6]

Figure 4.3 explores how such "seniority wages" affect the labour market for older workers. The degree to which earnings are linked with age is measured by the ratio of earnings of 55-59 year-olds to those of 25-29 year-olds. This has the expected negative correlation with the employment rate for 50-64 year-olds. However, the link is weak – the fitted regression line is only mildly downward sloping – and statistically insignificant. However, the relationship between seniority wages and hiring rates of 50-64 year-olds is strongly negative and significant at the 1% level. This finding is confirmed by firm-level data: companies with stronger seniority wages are less likely to hire older workers (Daniel and Heywood, 2007).

Economists have long sought to rationalise the existence of seniority wages. Higher pay for older workers than would be justified on productivity grounds is seen as a way of bonding employees to their jobs. If the firm invests in training workers, by "back-loading" their financial rewards, it can ensure that it reaps the rewards (see Lazear, 1981 for example). However, seniority-pay arrangements probably make less economic sense for employers today than they did in the past.[7] Workers are more mobile and the concept of

Figure 4.2. **Average earnings by age**

Index: Age 25-29 = 100

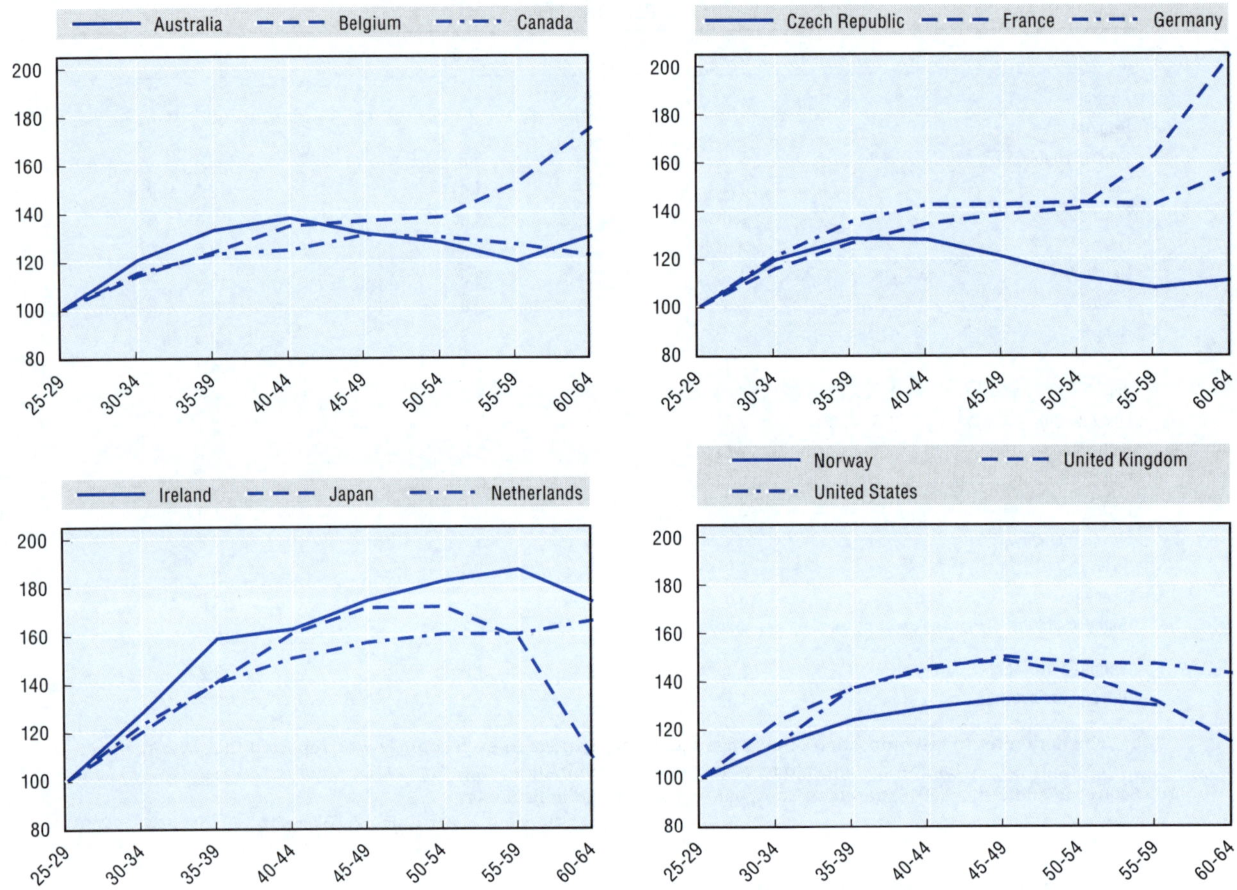

Note: The data refer to full-time workers. They cover various years over the period 2005-08.

Source: D'Addio *et al.* (2010) based on *OECD Earnings Database*.

StatLink http://dx.doi.org/10.1787/888932370531

lifetime employment with the same employer is increasingly obsolete. Furthermore, an ageing workforce, discussed in Section 4.1 of this chapter, means that seniority wages are increasingly unsustainable. It is not possible for employers to pay a growing number of older workers more than their worth in productivity terms when there is a declining number of younger workers who are paid less than their productivity. And growing competition for the diminishing pool of younger workers is likely to drive their wages up.

There is some evidence that seniority-based wage setting is indeed on the wane. In Sweden, for example, seniority clauses in public-sector pay arrangements have been replaced by performance clauses. Similarly in Japan, there is increasing emphasis in the private sector on performance-related pay, although seniority pay remains well entrenched for male "regular" workers until their mid-50s.

A number of countries have taken direct action to reduce the cost of employing older workers through wage subsidies or a reduction in social security contributions. Some of these schemes are simply targeted on age alone, while others also take account of additional characteristics of older workers. But caution is required in adopting these

Figure 4.3. **Seniority wages and labour-market outcomes for older male workers**

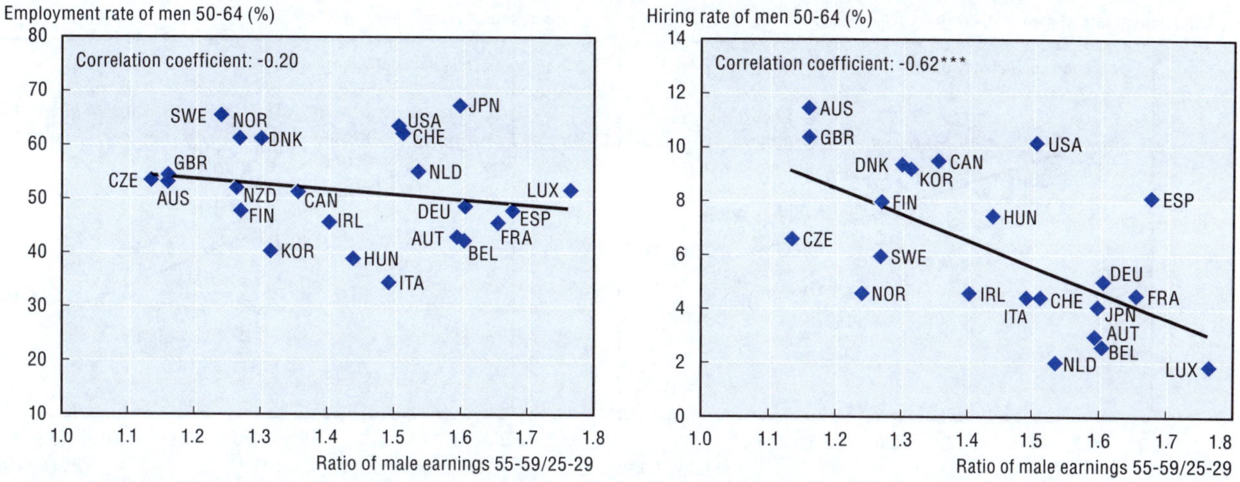

Note: The employment rate is the ratio of employees to the population in 2004. The hiring rate is the number of employees with less than one year of tenure relative to total employees. The data are from 2004, except for Korea (2000). The earnings data cover full-time workers only for various years over the period 1998-2003.

Source: D'Addio *et al.* (2010) based on *OECD Earnings Database* for the earnings data and OECD estimates based on the European Union Labour Force Survey and other national labour force surveys for the other indicators.

StatLink http://dx.doi.org/10.1787/888932370550

policies. Clearly, not all older workers have low productivity and require wage subsidies to keep their jobs. There is therefore likely to be a large "deadweight" cost to the public finances. There is also a risk of stigmatising older workers more generally.

4.4. Labour-market regulation

Employment-protection regulations – like anti-discrimination legislation – can have both positive and negative effects on older workers.[8] On the one hand, strict employment-protection legislation protects incumbent workers – who tend to be older – at the expense of "outsiders", such as women and youths. On the other hand, such protection may encourage employers to use early-retirement pathways to adjust their workforce. Often, this takes place in collusion with trade unions and the government. While this might be the optimum human-resources policy for a particular employer, it is unlikely to be best for the wider economy and society.

Figure 4.4 uses the OECD's index of the strictness of employment-protection legislation, as set out in OECD (2004b). Along the lines of Figure 4.3, it then compares this with labour-market outcomes for men aged 50-64. There is a strong negative relationship between employment protection and both the employment rates of older people and hiring rates for older workers. The correlations are statistically significant at 1% and 5% levels respectively. However, more rigorous empirical studies, controlling for other factors affecting employment rates of older workers, have mixed results, with some showing a much weaker relationship between employment protection and labour-market outcomes for older workers (see, *inter alia*, OECD, 2006b; and Dorn and Sousa-Poza, 2007).

Figure 4.4. **Employment protection and labour-market outcomes for older male workers**

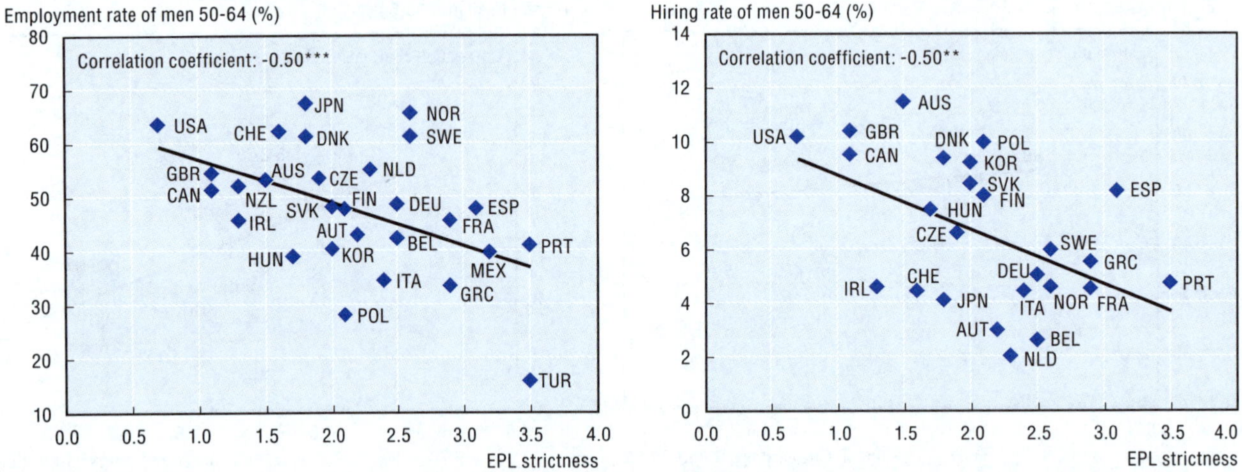

Note: The employment rate is the ratio of employees to the population in 2004. The hiring rate is the number of employees with less than one year of tenure relative to total employees. The data are from 2004, except for Korea (2000). The strictness of the employment protection legislation (EPL) is an index covering individual and collective dismissals and temporary employment: see OECD (2004b) for details.

Source: OECD (2004b); OECD calculations based on the European Union Labour Force Survey and other national labour force surveys.

StatLink http://dx.doi.org/10.1787/888932370569

4.5. Skills and training

The demands for different skills are constantly changing in response to globalisation, and changes in technology, work organisation and consumption patterns. Older workers are especially likely to see their human capital depreciate in the face of such flux. Renewing their human capital requires continued investment: through training, for example.

Unfortunately, older workers are less likely to take part in training than their younger colleagues in the 21 OECD countries for which data are available (Figure 4.5). The age gap in training is particularly large in Austria and the Netherlands in relative terms and in Australia, Finland and the United Kingdom in absolute terms (see Chapter 5 of OECD, 2003). This finding is confirmed by other studies; and the gap remains significant even when other factors are taken into account. However, it should also be noted that there are also large country differences in the overall incidence of training. For instance, whether young or old, a much smaller proportion of workers in Hungary, Italy and Portugal participate in training than is the case in Switzerland and the Nordic countries.[9]

The decline in participation with training in age could arise on the supply-side – employers and public employment services are less likely to offer training to older workers – or on the demand side: older workers are less willing to take up training opportunities. The OECD's (2003) detailed study suggests that the demand-side matters more. Older workers may be less willing to participate in training because the expected pay-back period on their investment in training activities is shorter than for younger workers.

The age gap in training incidence is negative related with both the average age of labour market and the retention of older workers relative to younger workers.[10] There is also evidence of a negative relationship between the training participation of older workers and the implicit tax on continuing to work at older ages.[11] There is a strong, positive link between training and educational attainment (see OECD, 2003; and Bassanini *et al.*, 2007).

Figure 4.5. **Training of older and younger workers**

Percentage of employees participating in education or training during the previous 12 months

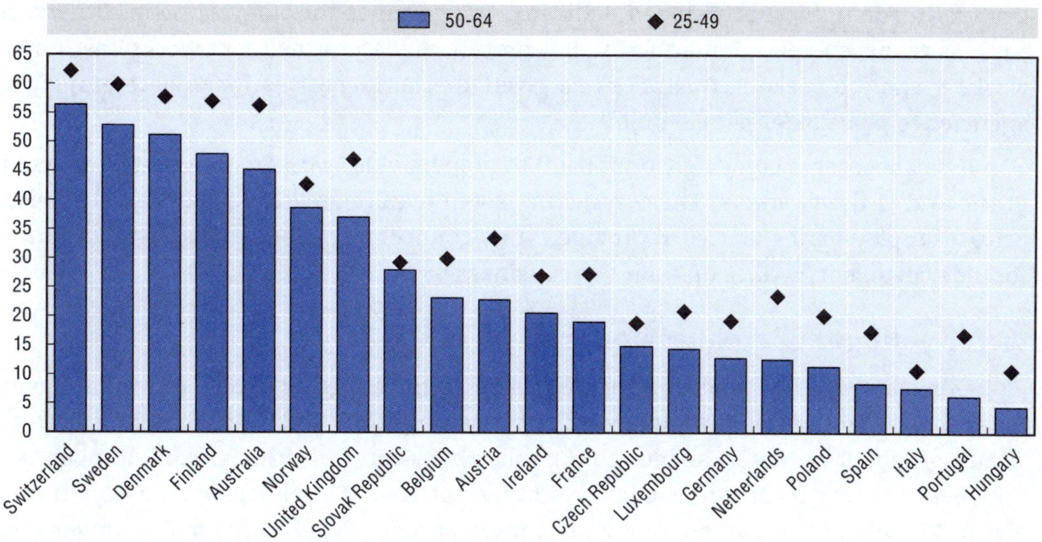

Note: The data are from 2003, except for Australia (2001).

Source: D'Addio *et al.* (2010) based on European Union Labour Force Survey lifelong learning module and Australian Survey of Education and Training.

StatLink http://dx.doi.org/10.1787/888932370588

Since educational attainment of successive cohorts is greater, this should lead to a narrowing of the age gap in training. Furthermore, longer working lives are likely to generate increased investment in training because of the longer pay-back period.

4.6. Working conditions

The health of older workers, working conditions and working-time arrangements also play an important role in retirement decisions. Several studies report that blue-collar workers and less-qualified workers are more likely to retire earlier than white-collar workers and more highly-qualified workers. Constraints on reducing working hours may also be "pushing" workers into retirement.

A number of measures have been taken by OECD countries to improve working conditions for older workers. Finland is a leader in the range of programmes to increase the "work ability" of older workers: through rehabilitation, training, improvements in occupational health and raising awareness of the work needs of older workers (OECD, 2004a, 2006). Similarly, Germany's "New Quality of Work Initiative" (INQA) promotes employability at all ages with its campaign "30, 40, 50 plus – Working healthily as you get older" (OECD, 2005).

4.7. Help in finding jobs

Long-term unemployment is a greater problem for older than younger workers. Older people find it more difficult to get new jobs. But there is often a lack of both help and pressure for them to seek work. For example, job-search requirements for receipt of benefits are weak or non-existent for the older unemployed in some countries, such as Belgium and France.

Providing employment assistance to older people is often not a priority for private and public employment agencies. But this is changing. Some countries, such as the United Kingdom, have introduced dedicated programmes for older workers. Others, such as Canada, have experimented with pilot projects to determine what works best for older workers and job seekers. Australia has given special incentives for private employment agencies to place older people in jobs.

It will become increasingly important to prepare older workers for greater job mobility at the end of their careers. These transitions will require greater resources for public and private employment agencies to provide career counselling, job-search assistance and help for older people in setting up their own businesses.

4.8. Jobs for younger and older workers

One concern often voiced in the debate about encouraging people to work longer and defer their retirement is that this will deprive youngsters of jobs. Economists call this the "lump-of-labour fallacy". The idea that public policy can re-shuffle a fixed number of jobs between workers of different ages is simply not true. This is clearly demonstrated in Figure 4.6, which compares employment rates of older (aged 55-59) and younger people (aged 20-24). The relationship between the two is positive and highly significant in statistical terms. The lump-of labour hypothesis is indeed a fallacy.

Figure 4.6. **Employment rates: Younger and older workers**

Percentage of 55-59 year-olds and 20-24 year-olds in employment, 2009

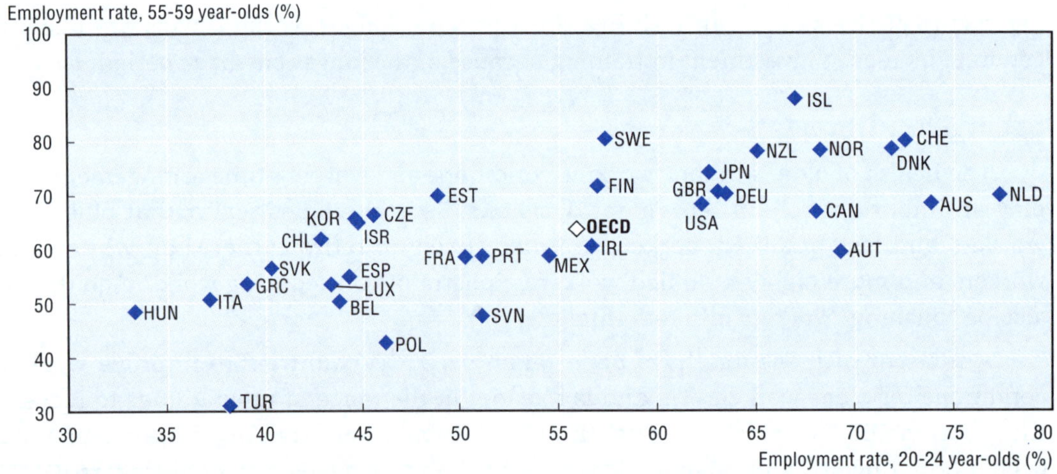

Note: Regression line shown (heteroskedasticity-adjusted standard errors in parentheses) is employment rate of 55-59 year-olds = 36.84 (6.671) + 0.4565 (0.1402) × employment rate of 20-24 years. R^2 of the regression is 0.2381.

Source: OECD calculations using Eurostat data.

StatLink http://dx.doi.org/10.1787/888932370607

However, public perceptions of the trade-off between employment of younger and older workers are significant, especially when these influence the minds of policy makers. Figure 4.7 explores views on the hypothesis: "As older people work until a later age, fewer jobs will be available for younger people". It is based on Eurobarometer data, and so only covers member states of the European Union that are also in the OECD.

Figure 4.7. **"As older people work until a later age, fewer jobs will be available for younger people": Impact of different factors on responses**

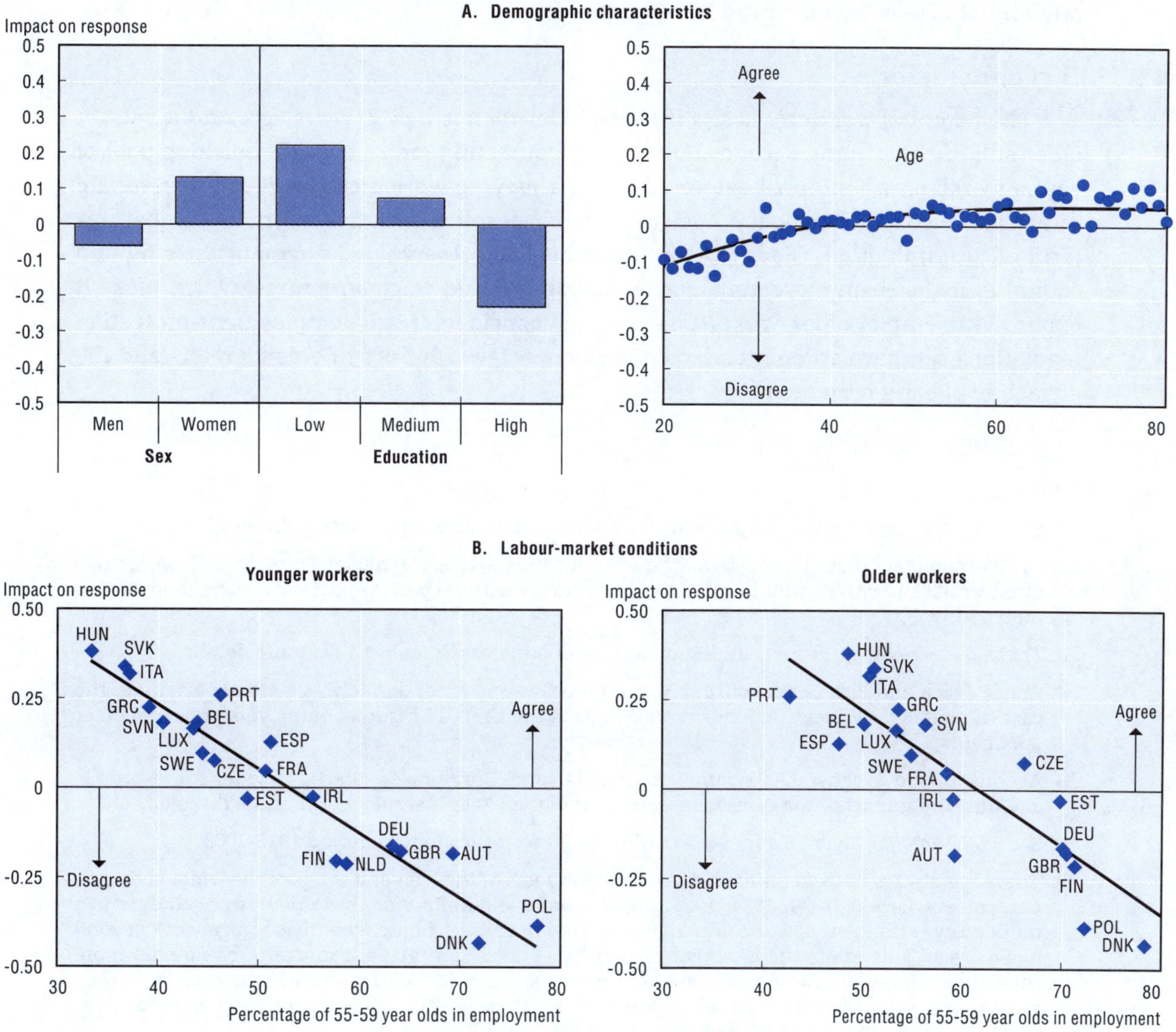

Note: Estimation based on an index with answers of strongly disagree rated as –2, somewhat disagree as –1, somewhat agree as 1 and strongly agree 2. In addition to the variables shown, the analysis controlled for region (metropolitan, other urban and rural) and economic activity (retired, other not working, employed, self-employed). The results shown are predicted values taking all these factors into account at once. All variables included in the econometric model were significant at the 1% level.

Source: OECD analysis of Eurobarometer survey of 27 113 people in the European Union, of which 21 133 are in OECD member countries; OECD *Employment Database* for employment rates.

StatLink http://dx.doi.org/10.1787/888932370626

The results are instructive. Women are significantly more likely than men to believe that older workers deny younger people jobs. Older people and those with a shorter time in education are also more likely to agree that as people work longer there will be fewer jobs for youngsters.

However, the most powerful effect on people's perceptions derives from the state of different countries' labour markets, as demonstrated in the lower two charts in Figure 4.7. Citizens of Hungary, Italy and the Slovak Republic are more likely to agree with the lump-of-labour hypothesis, yet these are countries in which employment rate for both young and older people are low. In contrast, Danes and Poles, for example, are less likely to believe that older workers deny jobs for younger workers. And they have high employment rate for both 20-24 year-olds and 55-59 year-olds.

4.9. Policy conclusions

The potential workforce is significantly older than it was 30 years ago. And it will get older still in the coming decades. Employers, competing for an ever diminishing pool of young workers, will simply have to adjust to a greying workforce. There is, however, an important role for public policy. Ageism remains, despite legislative efforts to combat this form of discrimination. Older workers need help to preserve and augment their human capital to make them more employable. Seniority-based wage structures, which make it expensive to employ older workers, need to be reconsidered. Strict employment-protection regulations can have an unintended consequence: fewer hirings of older workers and the attraction of early retirement.

Notes

1. Based on the medium variant projections of the United Nations population division.
2. For a summary of these findings for different countries, see OECD (2006a). Employers, however also often express positive attitudes about older workers with respect to attributes such as loyalty or punctuality.
3. These data are drawn from a 2009 Eurobarometer survey: see Table 4.1 for more details.
4. *Source:* Riach and Rich (2006, 2007a, 2007b).There was one exception to this general pattern: in the case of matched CVs sent for jobs in retail sales in the United Kingdom, employers preferred older applicants.
5. Acemoglu and Angrist (2001) and Houtenville and Burkhauser (2004) provide, for example, examine the impact of the Americans with Disabilities Act on employment of the disabled.
6. See OECD (2006a), Figure 3.4 for information on 20 countries for the period 1998-2003.
7. There has always been a conflict between the interests of the firm and those of the wider economy and society. Lazear (1979, 1981, 1986) argues that the corollary of these pay arrangements is a mandatory retirement age or company-sponsored pension schemes that discourage work beyond a given age. This limits the periods over which workers can take advantage of being paid more than their marginal productivity. But this may lead to older workers retiring earlier than they would otherwise. Even if they find jobs elsewhere, these jobs may be less productive (and lower paying) because of the loss of firm-specific skills.
8. For a review of the theory and empirical findings on the impact of labour-market regulations on employment, see Addison and Teixeira (2003).
9. The volume, as well as incidence, of training also matters. Training spells in the United Kingdom, for example, tend to be short relative to other European countries. Nevertheless, comparisons of training volume still point to large country differences and a substantial age gap (OECD, 2003, Chapter 5).
10. Chapter 2 in Part I on "Trends in retirement and in working at older ages" discusses the measurement of the average age of labour-market exit. The retention rate is the estimated proportion of all employees who were still with the same employer five years later. See OECD (2006a).
11. Bassanini *et al.* (2007). The implicit tax on continuing in work is analysed in detail in Chapter 3 of Part I above.

References

Adams, S. (2004), "Age Discrimination Legislation and the Employment of Older Workers", *Labour Economics*, Vol. 11, No. 2, pp. 219-241.

Addison, J. and P. Teixeira (2003), "The Economics of Employment Protection", *Journal of Labor Research*, Vol. 24, No. 1, pp. 85-129.

Acemoglu, D. and J.D. Angrist (2001), "Consequences of Employment Protection? The Case of the Americans with Disabilities Act", *Journal of Political Economy*, Vol. 109, No. 5, pp. 915-957.

Bassanini, A., A.L. Booth, G. Brunello, M. De Paola and E. Leuven (2007), "Workplace Training in Europe", in G. Brunello, P. Garibaldi and E. Wasmer (eds.), *Education and Training in Europe*, Oxford University Press.

D'Addio, A.C., M. Keese and E. Whitehouse (2010), "Population Ageing and Labour Market", *Oxford Review of Economic Policy*, forthcoming.

Daniel, K. and J. Heywood (2007), "The Determinants of Hiring Older Workers: UK Evidence", *Labour Economics*, Vol. 14, pp. 35-51.

Dorn, D. and A. Sousa-Poza (2007), "'Voluntary' and 'Involuntary' Early Retirement: An International Analysis", *IZA Discussion Paper*, No. 2714, Bonn.

Houtenville, A.J. and R.V. Burkhauser (2004), "Did the Employment of People with Disabilities Decline in the 1990s, and was the ADA Responsible? A Replication and Robustness Check of Acemoglu and Angrist", Research Brief, Rehabilitation Research and Training Center for Economic Research on Employment Policy for Persons with Disabilities, Cornell University.

Lahey, J. (2006), "State Age Protection Laws and the Age Discrimination in Employment Act", *Working Paper*, No. 12 048, NBER, Cambridge, Massachusetts.

Lazear, E.P. (1979), "Why Is There Mandatory Retirement?", *Journal of Political Economy*, Vol. 87, No. 6, pp. 1261-1284.

Lazear, E.P. (1981), "Agency, Earnings Profiles, Productivity, and Hours Restrictions", *American Economic Review*, Vol. 71, No. 4, pp. 606-620.

Lazear, E.P. (1986), "Retirement From the Labour Force", in O. Ashenfelter and R. Layard (eds.), *Handbook of Labour Economics*, North Holland, Amsterdam, pp. 305-355.

Neumark, D. (2008), "The Age Discrimination in Employment Act and the Challenge of Population Aging", *Working Paper*, No. 14 317, NBER, Cambridge, Massachusetts.

OECD (2003), *OECD Employment Outlook*, OECD Publishing, Paris.

OECD (2004-06), *Ageing and Employment Policies*, a series of 21 country reviews, OECD Publishing, Paris.

OECD (2004a), *Ageing and Employment Policies: Finland*, OECD Publishing, Paris.

OECD (2004b), *OECD Employment Outlook*, OECD Publishing, Paris.

OECD (2005), *Ageing and Employment Policies: Germany*, OECD Publishing, Paris.

OECD (2006a), *Live Longer, Work Longer*, OECD Publishing, Paris.

OECD (2006b), *OECD Employment Outlook*, OECD Publishing, Paris.

Riach, P. and J. Rich (2006), "An Experimental Investigation of Age Discrimination in the French Labour Market", *IZA Discussion Paper*, No. 2522, Bonn.

Riach, P. and J. Rich (2007a), "An Experimental Investigation of Age Discrimination in the Spanish Labour Market", *IZA Discussion Paper*, No. 2654, Bonn.

Riach, P. and J. Rich (2007b), "An Experimental Investigation of Age Discrimination in the English Labor Market", *IZA Discussion Paper*, No. 3029, Bonn.

Pensions at a Glance 2011
Retirement-income Systems in OECD and G20 Countries

PART I

Chapter 5

Linking Pensions to Life Expectancy

Increases in pensionable age, described in Chapter 1 above, are only one policy response to the fact that people are living longer. Around half of OECD countries have elements in their mandatory retirement-income provision that provide an automatic link between pensions and a change in life expectancy. This is a result of: i) mandatory defined-contribution schemes substituting for or adding to public pension provision; ii) transformation of public, earnings-related plans into notional-accounts schemes; and iii) a link between benefit levels or qualifying conditions for pensions and life expectancy. Furthermore, there has been a marked shift from defined-benefit to defined-contribution provision in voluntary, private pensions.

These changes have important implications for the way the cost of providing for pensions as life expectancy increases is shared. Increasingly, this will be borne by individual retirees in the form of lower benefits. This chapter measures the degree of uncertainty inherent in projections of life expectancy. Pension entitlements for example individuals in all 34 OECD countries are calculated under different scenarios – from slow to rapid increments in longevity. These calculations are then used to assess the degree to which the additional cost of longer lives has been shifted onto future generations of retirees with longer life expectancy.

Older people today live longer and healthier lives than previous generations did. When public pension systems were first established, people could typically look forward to only a few years of life in retirement (even if they were lucky enough to reach pension age). But in 2010, life expectancy at age 65 averaged nearly 17 years for men and 21 years for women in OECD countries. The probability that a newborn boy survives until age 65 is over 80%; the figure is over 90% for a girl.

The impressive increase in life expectancy in the course of the last century should surely be celebrated. Ageing populations are "a high-class" problem, said Bill Clinton, President of the United States, in his 1999 State of the Union address. "It's the result of something wonderful: the fact that we are living a lot longer".

Nevertheless, ageing populations pose huge challenges for economic, social and health policies in general, and for pension systems in particular. It has been obvious for some time that many pension systems needed or still need reforming to ensure long-term affordability. It is much less clear how the burden of such adjustments should be divided between today's taxpayers, contributors and retirees and future retirees. Furthermore, the estimates of life-expectancy increases on which pension decisions have been based have, regrettably, often turned out to be wrong. The growth of life expectancy, especially at retirement age, has consistently been underestimated (see Box 5.1).

The disconcerting effect on pension policymaking has been the need for repeated reforms, as changes to parameters and rules succeeded in stabilising the financial situation only for short periods. However, many of the reforms of the past 10-15 years mean that pensions will, in future, take *automatic* account of both projected increases in life expectancy and the uncertainty surrounding the estimates. Indeed, the rapid spread of such life-expectancy adjustments has a strong claim to be the most important innovation of pension policy in recent years.[1]

This policy has both economic and political attractions. The automaticity of adjustments means that governments no longer face nasty surprises in pension financing when life-expectancy projections change. Increasing life expectancy provides a neat and logical justification for cutting future benefits that may be politically more palatable than alternative reforms that would also reduce pensions.

This special chapter investigates reforms to mandatory retirement-income provision that have introduced some kind of automatic adjustment to increases in life expectancy. It explores how they have changed the way in which the financial risk of increasing life expectancy is distributed. The aim is to measure the degree to which individual retirees shoulder the extra burden of greater life expectancy on the pension system – or whether the cost is borne solely by pension providers (and, hence, by younger taxpayers and contributors).

5.1. Life expectancy and recent pension reforms

The pension landscape was dominated for much of the 20th century by ***defined-benefit*** schemes where pension benefits typically depend on the number of years of contribution

Box 5.1. **How population projections for the United Kingdom have changed over time**

Past projections of life expectancy have turned out to be wrong. Given the difficulties of any kind of forecast – particularly over long time horizons – this is unsurprising. However, life-expectancy projections have consistently *under*-predicted mortality improvements, often to a substantial degree.

The Government Actuary's Department is responsible for projecting the population of the United Kingdom, which, among many other things, provides the basis for forecasts of future public spending on pensions. The future number of people aged 65 and over is an easy-to-understand part of these projections that is directly linked to life expectancy.

Figure 5.1 shows the number of older people predicted in the future from 2011 to 2061. The different lines show the different years in which the projections were published. In 1981, for example, the number aged 65+ was expected to be just over 9 million in 2011, rising to a peak of just over 12 million in 2036 and declining thereafter. The 1985 and 1989 forecasts had a similar pattern, albeit with half a million extra pensioners in 2011 and a million more in 2036 than predicted earlier.

Figure 5.1. **Official projections of population aged 65+ for the years 2011-61, United Kingdom, by year of publication**

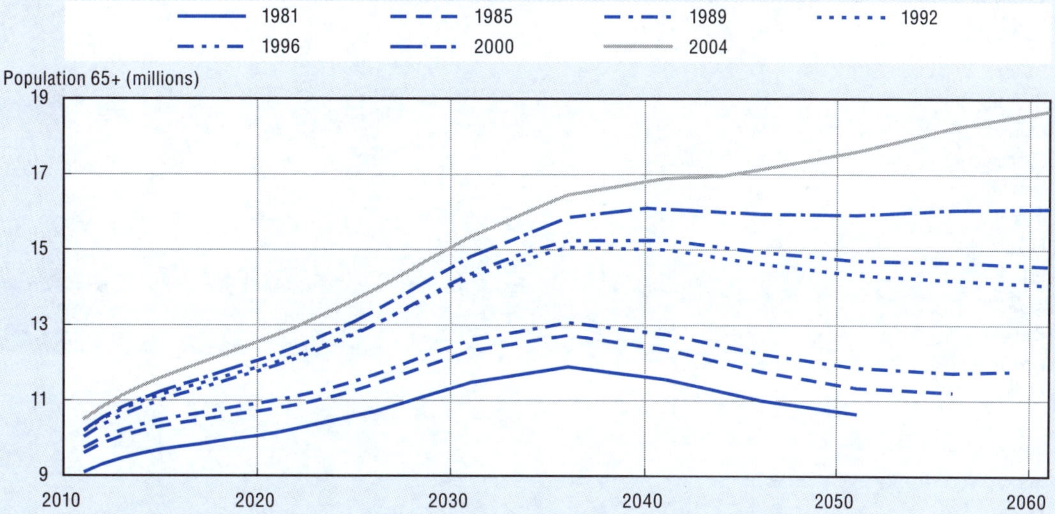

Source: Government Actuary's Department, United Kingdom.

StatLink http://dx.doi.org/10.1787/888932370645

The 1992 and 1996 projections involved a substantial revision: the peak population aged over 65 was 15 million in the latter, compared with the 12 million that had been expected in 1981. In contrast, the later forecasts alter the pattern over time of the number of older people. In the 2000 forecast, instead of a decline in the number of 65+ year-olds, this was expected to remain constant after 2036. The 2004 projection, in yet another contrast, showed a continued increase in the population aged over 65 from 2011 to 2061.

The scale of these changes in forecasts is huge. For 2036, for example, the earliest forecast (when the future pensioners were aged 10 and above) has increased by 36%: from around 12 million to 16.5 million. For 2051, the increase in projections over time has been greater still: 65%.

It is perhaps a little unfair to pick on the United Kingdom: undoubtedly, other OECD countries have seen similar underestimates. For example, the National Academy of Sciences, in a study of UN population projections, showed under-predictions of the population at older ages in Europe and North America of around 10% just 15 years forward (National Research Council, 2000). One problem has been the repeated assumption that humankind is reaching some "biological" limit to life expectancy only for mortality improvements to surpass their projections, sometimes within five years or fewer. This effect is illustrated vividly in Oeppen and Vaupel (2002).

and a measure of individual earnings. This was true of both public retirement-income provision and employer-provided private pension plans. Over the past two decades, however, this defined-benefit paradigm has been diluted. Pension systems around the world have become much more diverse. Table 5.1 sets out the main changes relevant to this special chapter: those that involve an *automatic* link between pensions and life expectancy.

Table 5.1. **Different ways of linking pensions to life expectancy**

	Mandatory defined-contribution plan	Notional accounts scheme	Benefits linked to life expectancy	Qualifying conditions linked to life expectancy	DB-to-DC shift in voluntary private provision
Australia	●				
Austria					
Belgium					
Canada					●
Chile	●				
Czech Republic					
Denmark				●	
Estonia	●				
Finland			●		
France				●	
Germany			●		●
Greece					
Hungary	●				
Iceland					
Ireland					●
Israel	●				
Italy		●			
Japan					
Korea					
Luxembourg					
Mexico	●				
Netherlands					
New Zealand					
Norway	●	●			
Poland	●	●			
Portugal			●		
Slovak Republic	●				
Slovenia					
Spain					
Sweden	●	●			●
Switzerland					
Turkey					
United Kingdom					●
United States					●

Note: See country profiles in Part III for more details on national schemes.
DB = Defined benefit; DC = Defined contribution.

StatLink http://dx.doi.org/10.1787/888932372279

The most significant reform has been the expansion of private, defined-contribution pension schemes. In some countries – such as Chile, Estonia, Hungary, Mexico, Poland, the Slovak Republic and Sweden – these have replaced all or part of the public, defined-benefit pension scheme.[2] In others, a requirement to contribute to a defined-contribution plan was added on top of existing state pensions: examples are Australia, Israel and Norway.

Thus, 10 OECD countries have mandatory defined-contribution schemes at present. Also, Denmark has very broad coverage of quasi-mandatory occupational plans that are of the defined-contribution type.

In countries with widespread, voluntary occupational pensions, employers have tended to shift these from defined benefit to defined contribution (or a mix of the two). This trend began as early as the 1970s in the United States, with Canada, Ireland and the United Kingdom following a similar pattern.[3] The two quasi-mandatory occupational schemes for private-sector workers in Sweden have also been fully defined-contribution since 2006. One motivation for these changes has been the increase in cost of defined-benefit plans as retirees live longer compared with the stable and relatively predictable cost to the employer of a particular contribution rate to a defined-contribution scheme. In Germany, the new "Riester" pensions mean that defined-contribution schemes have become more prominent in voluntary private provision of retirement income.

In ***defined-contribution*** schemes, the burden of changes in life expectancy is borne by individual retirees in the form of lower pensions. When people retire in a defined-contribution plan, the accumulated contributions and investment returns must is converted from a lump sum into a regular pension payment, known as an "annuity". The calculation of the annuity will be based on projected life expectancy of retirees at the time of retirement. So, pension replacement rates will automatically be lower as people live longer.

People do not always convert their lump sums at retirement into annuities. But even if they periodically withdraw money from their pension accounts, the amount that they can sustainably take out each period is smaller the longer is life expectancy. The lump sum accumulation at retirement is the same: it must be spread over a longer period whether it is withdrawn as an annuity or in any other way.

Notional-accounts schemes also include an annuity calculation. At the time of retirement, the accumulated contributions and notional interest is converted into a periodic payment. The rate of conversion, like the annuity rate, depends on life expectancy. This similarity between defined-contribution and notional-accounts schemes is why notional accounts have attracted the moniker of "notional-defined contribution" schemes.[4] Four OECD countries have adopted notional accounts: Italy, Poland, Norway and Sweden.

A shift from defined-benefit plans to defined-contribution or notional accounts schemes is often called a "systemic" reform because it alters the architecture of the national pension system. In contrast, some countries have carried out "***parametric***" ***reforms*** that have introduced a link to life expectancy. For example, Finland and Portugal have retained their defined-benefit, public plans. In the future, benefits will be reduced by a factor directly related to life expectancy.

In Germany, the link to life expectancy is more complex. Germany has a points scheme, where a year's contributions at average earnings covered by the pension system earns one point. The accumulated points at the time of retirement are then converted into a stream of pension payments based on a pension-point value. The adjustment of the pension point value over time now reflects the financial sustainability of the scheme. This is measured principally by the system dependency ratio: the number of people of pensioners relative to the number of workers.

To help define the kinds of pension reform analysed in this special chapter, it is useful to contrast these *automatic* adjustments of benefits to life expectancy with alternative reform strategies. The 2004 reform in Japan introduced an adjustment to benefits related to life expectancy. Public-pension benefits have been cut by 0.9% a year for new retirees; this process will continue until 2023. These adjustments, designed to stabilise the finances of the pension system in the face of rapid population ageing. They are based on the assumption of constant increase in life expectancy of 0.3% per year. But there is no mechanism by which these adjustments vary should life expectancy increase at a different rate than that anticipated. There is no *automatic* link between pensions and life expectancy.

It is, perhaps, surprising that few OECD countries have formally adopted the most obvious form of link between pensions and life expectancy: to increase the ***pensionable age*** as people live longer. There will be such a link in Denmark once the pension age completes its increase from 65 to 67 in 2027. Italy and Greece will link pension age to life expectancy from 2015 and 2020 (respectively). However it will still be possible to claim the pension at any age with 40 years of contribution in both cases.

The Pensions Commission in the United Kingdom, headed by Lord Turner, proposed an increase in the pension eligibility age from 2020 that would leave life expectancy at pension age constant. The Commission also suggested that some catch-up for past increases in life expectancy that have not been taken into account, with an additional increase in pension age by 2050 of up to two years. However, the previous government proposed instead a *pre-announced* schedule of increases in pension age, with an increase from 65 to 66 starting in 2024, to 67 from 2034 and to 68 starting in 2044 (phased in over a two-year period in each case).[5] As shown in the Part I, Chapter 1 on "Trends in pensionable ages and life expectancy, 1950-2050", this will broadly stabilise the expected time in retirement in the United Kingdom. Again, however, there is no *automatic* link with life expectancy.

France has adopted a policy of linking the number of contribution years required for a full pension to changes in life expectancy.[6] As a result, this condition is increasing from 40 years' contribution (2003-08) gradually to 41.5 years from 2013. The link is not quite as strong as that implicit in many other arrangements, such as defined-contribution plans, notional accounts or benefit links. The aim is to maintain the ratio of the expected duration of retirement to the expected length of career. Thus, extra years of life expectancy partially increase the length of retirement.

To summarise, governments commonly use increases in life expectancy to justify pension reforms, such as increasing pension ages or reducing benefits. What distinguishes the reforms analysed in this special chapter is the *automatic* link to life expectancy. Table 5.1 shows that there have been five important developments producing such an automatic link. The majority of OECD countries – 20 out of 34 – have seen one or more of these changes in the past two decades and, arguably, the effects go somewhat wider than this.[7]

5.2. How uncertain is life expectancy?

The unwelcome experience of errors in projections of life expectancy (as outlined in Box 5.1) has encouraged the development of new techniques. A fundamental objective of this endeavour has been to improve the information on which pension-policy decisions are made. Lee and Carter (1992) both formalised and popularised "extrapolative methods", illustrating their technique by projecting past mortality trends to future mortality rates in the United States until 2065.[8] The argument for extrapolating from the past is that forecasts implicitly assuming a slowdown in mortality improvements have repeatedly proved wrong. This technique has been widely applied and adopted by many official forecasters.

The baseline for the projections is mortality rates by sex and age in 2010. What these mean for life expectancy at age 65 – the most relevant age for pension policy – is shown at the left-hand side of Table 5.2. The second column shows the projections from the database of the United Nations for 2050 for the same variable. Between 2010 and 2050, life expectancy for men at age 65 is forecast to increase by about three years to 20 years (that is a total life of 85 years of age, conditional on having survived until age 65). For women the increase is projected to be 3.5 years to reach 24 years in 2050.

Table 5.2. **Life expectancy and annuity factors: Baseline data for 2010 and alternative projections for 2050**

	Baseline	UN projection	OECD projection for 2050 by percentile of the distribution of projected mortality rates				
	2010	2050	1st	25th	50th	75th	99th
Life expectancy at age 65 (years)							
Men	16.9	20.0	23.2	21.6	21.0	20.4	18.9
Women	20.5	24.0	26.9	25.5	24.9	24.3	22.9
Change from 2010 baseline (years)							
Men	*0.0*	*+3.1*	*+6.3*	*+4.7*	*+4.1*	*+3.5*	*+2.0*
Women	*0.0*	*+3.5*	*+6.4*	*+5.0*	*+4.4*	*+3.8*	*+2.4*
Annuity factor at age 65							
Men	13.7	15.7	17.7	16.8	16.4	16.0	15.1
Women	16.1	18.3	20.0	19.2	18.8	18.5	17.7
Unisex	14.8	16.9	18.8	17.9	17.5	17.1	16.2
Change from 2010 baseline (per cent)							
Men	*0.0*	*+14.6*	*+29.4*	*+22.4*	*+19.4*	*+16.6*	*+9.9*
Women	*0.0*	*+13.7*	*+24.4*	*+19.3*	*+17.0*	*+14.9*	*+9.7*
Unisex	*0.0*	*+14.2*	*+27.0*	*+20.9*	*+18.2*	*+15.7*	*+9.7*

Note: All projections based on unweighted average mortality rates for the 34 OECD member countries. Annuity factors are based on a price-indexed payment using a real discount rate of 2% per year.

Source: United Nations, *World Population Prospects – The 2008 Revision*; OECD projections based on these data: see Whitehouse (2007) for the detailed methodology.

StatLink http://dx.doi.org/10.1787/888932372298

The five columns at the right show a series of different projections made by the OECD. (These use a type of extrapolative method as discussed above; see Whitehouse (2007) for a detailed presentation of the techniques employed.) These show different scenarios for changes in mortality rates, represented here by the percentiles of the distribution resulting from 2 000 simulations.[9] At the optimistic end of the range, 1% of the time life expectancy increases by nearly 6.5 years between 2010 and 2050 (the 1st percentile column). Again, 1% of the time, life expectancy is expected to increase by 2.4 years for women and 2.0 years for men (the 99th percentile column). The median increase in these forecasts is over four years for both men and women, about one year greater than in the United Nations projections.

The degree of uncertainty in the projections is central to this special chapter. Life expectancy at age 65 differs by 4-4.5 years between the best and the worst scenarios for changes in mortality rates over the next 40 years.

The lower panel of Table 5.2 explores the financial implications of these changes. The analysis makes use of "annuity factors": the lifetime value of the flow of a pension of one unit per period.[10] For example, the baseline 2010 unisex annuity factor is 14.8. This means that the lifetime value of a USD 10 000 pension, indexed to prices, would be USD 148 000.

(Note that this calculation is a "present value": future payments are discounted at a rate of 2% a year.) Looking at the OECD projections for 2050, the unisex annuity factor is 17.9 under the median mortality rate projection. That is about 20% higher than the level in 2010: a measure of the additional cost of providing a pension for a longer period as life expectancy increases. The span of costs under different life-expectancy scenarios is also instructive: 1% of the time the annuity factor is at least 18.8 and, again 1% of the time, at most 16.2. This range is equivalent to a cost increase of providing pensions between 2010 and 2050 of 10% to 27%.

5.3. Two benchmark pension plans

In more than half of OECD countries, there have been shifts in policy and practice that link pension benefits automatically to life expectancy (Section 5.1). To explore the impact of these changes, it is useful to begin with two measures of pension entitlements. The first is the pension ***replacement rate***: the annual value of the benefit relative to individual earnings when working. The second is ***pension wealth***: the present value (or "stock") of the lifetime flow of pension benefits. Pension wealth is calculated by multiplying the replacement rate by the annuity factors discussed in Section 5.2 above. (Both replacement rates and pension wealth are discussed in greater detail in the indicators of pension entitlements in Part II.2 of this report.)

Two generic types of pension scheme are the second element of this illustration, providing a benchmark against which the features of real-world pension systems can be assessed.

- Under a pure ***defined-benefit*** pension scheme, a particular level of benefits is provided regardless of what happens to life expectancy. This means that the replacement rate is constant in different scenarios for mortality rates. However, pension wealth varies with life expectancy: a longer retirement duration means that lifetime benefits are higher and *vice versa*.
- Under a pure ***defined-contribution*** plan, the accumulation of contributions and investment returns at the time of retirement is pension wealth: it is the same whatever happens to life expectancy. However, as people live longer, pension wealth must be spread over a longer retirement duration. This is clearest in the cases where individuals buy an annuity at the point of retirement. The annuity provider will offer a lower proportion of the lump sum in pension as life expectancy increases. But it is also true when people do not buy an annuity: they cannot spend as much per period of their pension accumulation as people live longer over time. Notional-accounts schemes have similar effects: it is just that they attract notional interest and it is notional capital that is converted at retirement into a periodic payment.

It is important to remember that these are theoretical benchmarks. As with all benchmarks, it is necessary to impose a rule of *ceteris paribus*: holding other things equal. In the real world, outcomes can vary. First, the defined benefit often turns out to be not so well defined. The additional cost of longer life expectancy is initially borne by the pension provider. But this must be passed on: to contributors and taxpayers in the case of public schemes and contributors and shareholders in the case of employer-sponsored plans. Some of the extra cost has often been offset by changes in the parameters and rules of pension systems: higher pension ages, lower benefits or changed indexation of pensions in payment, for example.[11] The precise outcome, however, depends on the political process and not on some automatic rule.

Secondly, the political process can also intervene in schemes that are closer to the pure defined-contribution benchmark. Governments, for example, may fail to implement changes in benefits that are specified by the rules. This can lead to an additional burden – temporary or permanent – on contributors and taxpayers.

Individual behaviour also responds to the pension system. For example, people may choose to work longer as replacement rates fall because of longer life expectancy in the pure defined-contribution case (see also the discussion in Section 5.7). This will augment benefits through additional contributions, returns on accumulated capital and a shorter expected duration of retirement. But the increment to replacement rates from working an additional year also falls as life expectancy increases in schemes with a link to life expectancy. (These different effects are discussed in "Pension incentives to retire": Part I, Chapter 4 of this report.) The behavioural response is therefore not clear cut. Moreover, any behavioural effect will apply equally to cuts in benefits that are not a result of life-expectancy links in the pension system.

5.4. Pension entitlements and uncertain life expectancy

Pension entitlements have been calculated for all OECD countries under five different scenarios for the development of national mortality rates between 2010 and 2050. The five scenarios are the median of the distribution of outcomes, the upper and lower quartiles and the 1st and 99th percentiles. (The implications of these scenarios for mortality rates for life expectancy were illustrated in Table 5.2 above.) The two key measures of entitlements are replacement rates and pension wealth.

Four example countries, representing different types of retirement-income provision, are used to illustrate the results. Chile has a mandatory defined-contribution scheme and Italy has notional accounts. The other two countries have public defined-benefit schemes: with adjustments for life expectancy in Finland and without in Slovenia.

The left-hand chart in Figure 5.2 shows the replacement rate under the different mortality scenarios. All the results are for a man on average earnings. With Slovenia's defined-benefit plan, the replacement rate is constant at 62%. But in the other three cases, replacement rates are lowest at the highest life expectancy (1st percentile of the distribution) than they are with low life expectancy (99th percentile). In Finland, for example, the replacement rate is 56% with the lowest mortality rates and 66% with the highest.

Pension wealth is shown in the right-hand chart of Figure 5.2. In Slovenia, pension wealth is nearly 13 times annual earnings in the high life expectancy scenario but just over ten times with low life expectancy. In Chile, pension wealth is constant under the different scenarios for mortality rates. There is a slight decline in pension wealth as mortality rates increase in Finland and Italy, but this is substantially shallower than for Slovenia. For example, pension wealth is higher in Slovenia than Italy in most cases, but if mortality improvements were especially slow, Italy would show higher pension wealth than Slovenia.

Recall the two benchmarks from Section 5.3. Under a pure defined-benefit plan, replacement rates are constant while pension wealth varies with life expectancy. This is illustrated by the Slovenia case. Under a pure defined-contribution plan, the reverse is true: pension wealth is constant but the replacement rate varies with life expectancy. This is illustrated exactly by the Chile case and is close to the picture for Finland and Italy.

Figure 5.2. **Pension entitlements under different life-expectancy scenarios: Man with average earnings**

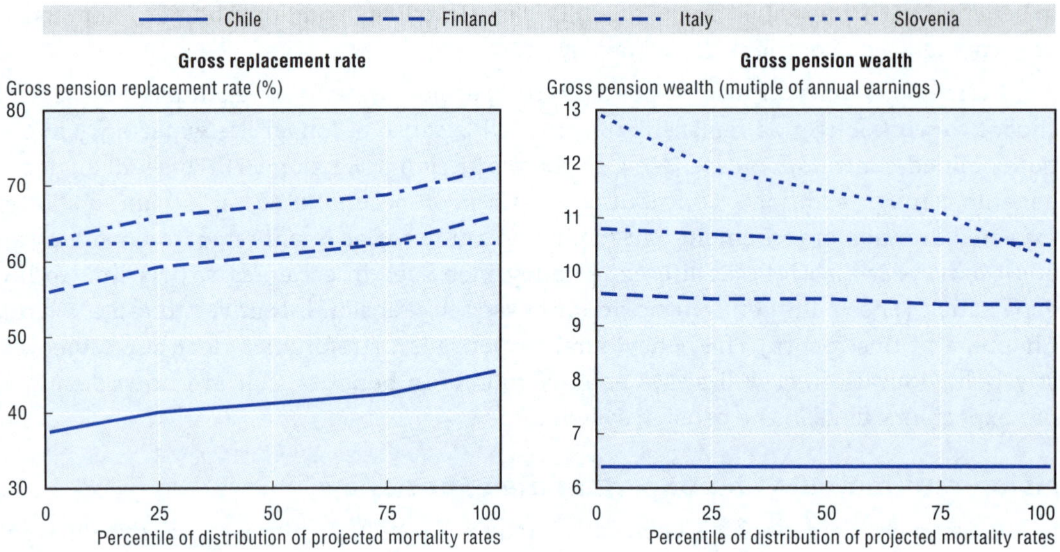

Source: OECD pension models.

StatLink http://dx.doi.org/10.1787/888932370664

Space constraints preclude illustrating the pension systems of all 34 OECD countries in this manner. Instead, Figures 5.3 and 5.4 combine the information on replacement rates and pension wealth under different scenarios for future mortality rates. The charts show the replacement rate on the vertical axis and pension wealth on the horizontal. Thus, in the first benchmark case of a pure defined-benefit scheme, the curve linking the results for the different mortality scenarios would be horizontal: a constant replacement rate and varying pension wealth. A vertical curve would be the result for the second, pure defined-contribution benchmark: varying replacement rate and constant pension wealth.

Figure 5.3 looks at four sets of countries, grouped by the linkage to life expectancy in mandatory or quasi-mandatory parts of the pension system. At the top left of the figure are countries with mandatory defined-contribution schemes (including Denmark's quasi-mandatory plans). These countries differ markedly in the size of the mandate to provide retirement incomes. Denmark, Hungary and Israel have high replacement rates and pension wealth, while Australia, Chile and Mexico have much smaller mandatory systems.

These countries also differ in the structure of the retirement-income package. In Estonia, Hungary and the Slovak Republic, public earnings-related schemes provide a significant part of retirement incomes. And none of these plans has a link to life expectancy. In Australia and Denmark, the majority of retirees receive resource-tested public benefits. Thus, as increases in life expectancy reduce the payout from defined-contribution plans, the government makes up part of the difference in higher public benefits. In Chile and Mexico, by contrast, minimum pensions do not affect the retirement income of an average earner.

These differences in the retirement-income package show up clearly in the results. Chile and Mexico are very close to the pure defined-contribution benchmark: a vertical line indicating that replacement rates vary with life expectancy but pension wealth is constant. Israel's curve is close to vertical: most of retirement-income comes from the mandatory

Figure 5.3. **Pension entitlements under different life-expectancy scenarios: Man with average earnings**

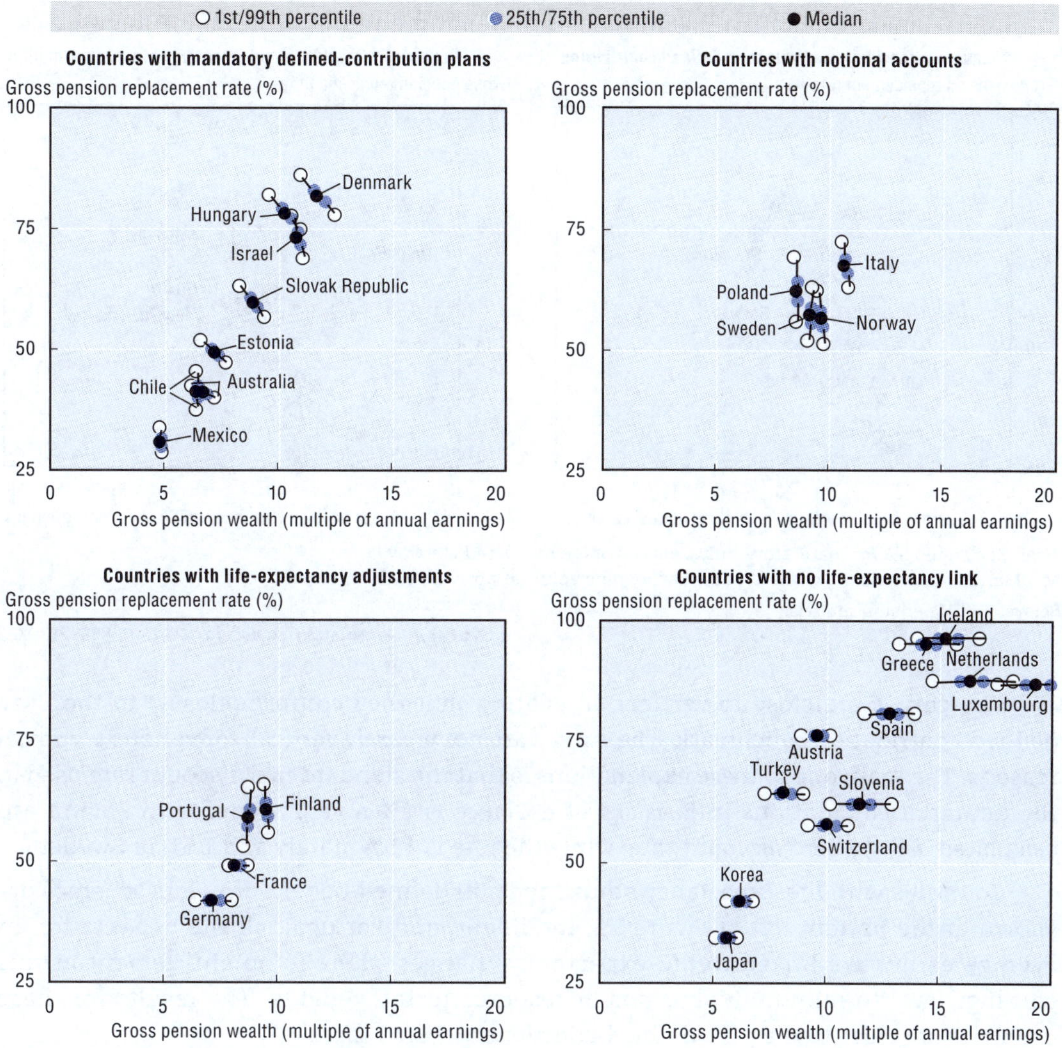

Note: The impact of the sustainability adjustment for Germany is too complex be modelled. In fact, replacement rates will vary under different life-expectancy scenarios. The calculations for Norway in this figure include the minimum ("guarantee") pension, notional accounts and the mandatory defined-contribution plan. See Figure 5.4 for information including voluntary defined-contribution plans in addition.

Source: OECD pension models.

StatLink http://dx.doi.org/10.1787/888932370683

defined-contribution scheme but there is a basic pension in addition. But the other five countries have sloping curves. High life expectancy means somewhat lower replacement rates but also, somewhat higher pension wealth due to public benefits.

The four countries with notional accounts are shown in the upper right panel of Figure 5.3. Three of them – Norway, Poland and Sweden – also have mandatory defined-contribution pensions. In addition, the calculations for Sweden include quasi-mandatory, defined-contribution, occupational benefits. In all four cases, an average earner would not be eligible for minimum pensions or resource-tested benefits and so all of their pension entitlements are linked to life expectancy.

Figure 5.4. **Pension entitlements under different life-expectancy scenarios: Man on average earnings**

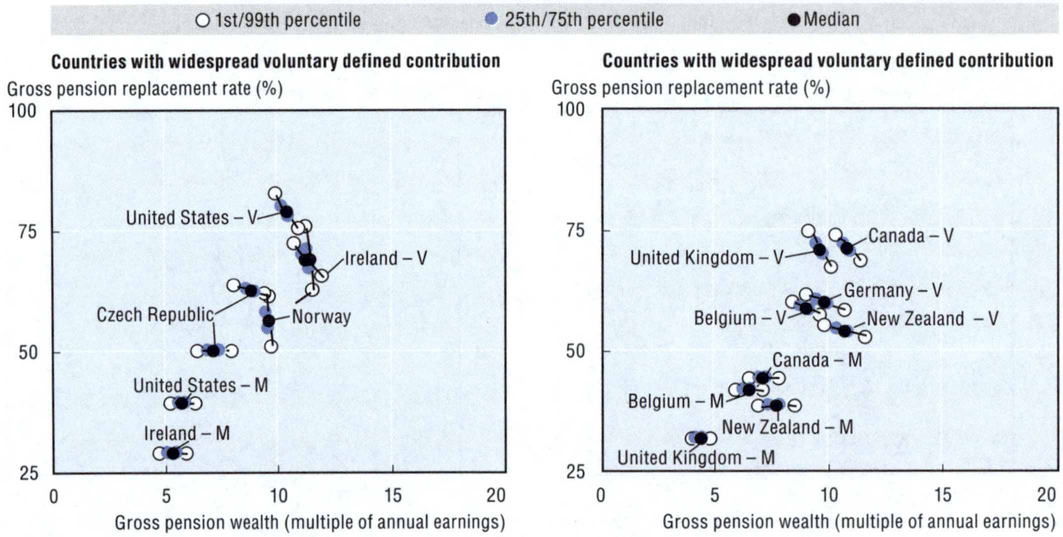

Note: See Figure 5.3 for mandatory-only analysis of Germany and Norway.
M = Mandatory provision; while V = Mandatory plus voluntary private entitlements.
Source: OECD pension models.

StatLink http://dx.doi.org/10.1787/888932370702

The curves are close to vertical, indicating that they conform closely to the pure defined-contribution benchmark. The curves are not *precisely* vertical, for various technical reasons. The main one of these explanations is that the standard real discount rate used in the actuarial calculations in *Pensions at a Glance* is 2% a year. Benefits in Poland are calculated using a zero discount rate, while the rate is 1.5% in Italy and 1.6% in Sweden.

Countries with life-expectancy adjustments in defined-benefit or points schemes are shown at the bottom left of Figure 5.3. In Finland and Portugal, all the benefits for an average earner are linked to life-expectancy changes: there is no entitlement at this earnings level to minimum pensions or resource-tested benefits. The results for these countries are close to the pure defined-contribution benchmark.

The French case poses some modelling difficulties. To recapitulate, the policy is designed to keep the ratio between the number of contribution years and the duration of retirement constant. From the current plan to increase the contribution requirement to 41 years from 2012, the median scenario for mortality rates implies an increase to 43.75 years in 2050.[12] At the highest percentile of mortality improvements, the number of years required would be 44.5 and at the lowest, 42.5. The replacement is pretty much constant across the mortality scenarios. Pension wealth is larger, the lower the mortality rates. This appears to conform to the pure defined-benefit model. However, the age at which the pension can be drawn increases with the number of contribution years as life expectancy gets longer. The implication is that about a third of the difference in lifetime pension between the scenarios is borne by retirees by having to claim their pension later while the remainder feeds through into pension wealth.[13]

There are also some difficulties in the modelling for Germany. The sustainability adjustment depends on the system dependency ratio. But it is not possible for the OECD to model this ratio under different scenarios for mortality rates. The data for Germany therefore take account of the sustainability only at the central demographic projection of the German authorities: in practice, the replacement rate will vary as life expectancy changes.

The results for countries without a link to life-expectancy are presented in the final chart in Figure 5.3. Among this group are the five OECD countries with the highest replacement rates for full-career workers on average earnings: Greece, Iceland, Luxembourg, the Netherlands and Spain. But it also includes countries – Japan and Korea – with relatively low replacement rate. Pension entitlements derive mainly from public earnings-related plans in eight countries. However, Iceland and Switzerland have mandatory private defined-benefit plans and in the Netherlands, quasi-mandatory occupational schemes are overwhelmingly of the defined-benefit type. Naturally, these countries show the characteristic pattern of the pure defined-benefit benchmark: replacement rates are constant between different scenarios for mortality rates, but pension wealth increases as life expectancy gets longer.

The final pair of charts (Figure 5.4) covers nine countries where this is widespread coverage of voluntary private pensions (40% or more of the workforce). A defined-contribution plan is modelled. Even though there remains some defined-benefit provision in some of these countries, generally this is concentrated among public-sector workers and in the private-sector is being phased out as defined-benefit plans are closed to new members. *Pensions at a Glance* deals with private-sector workers and new labour-market entrants, among whom defined-benefit coverage is low in most cases.

In all the countries shown in Figure 5.4, the mandatory part of the pension system (generally marked "M") delivers entitlements in line with the pure defined-benefit model: a constant replacement rate but varying pension wealth under different mortality scenarios, the same pattern as in the bottom right-hand panel of Figure 5.3. (Results for just mandatory schemes in Germany and Norway were show in Figure 5.3 and are not repeated here.)

Once account is taken of additional voluntary defined-contribution provision (mainly marked "V"), replacement rates do vary with pension age. However, only in Norway – with a mix of notional accounts, mandatory defined-contribution plans and voluntary defined-contribution provision – is the curve close to vertical. In other cases, replacement rates are somewhat lower with higher life expectancy. But public pension benefits mean that pension wealth increases somewhat with life expectancy. When voluntary schemes are taken into account, the pattern is similar to many of the countries with voluntary private pensions in the top right-hand chart of Figure 5.3 (Chile and Mexico apart).

5.5. An indicator of automatic life-expectancy links in pension systems

Retirement-income systems are generally made up of more than one scheme. There are the different schemes that provide an automatic link to life expectancy and those that do not. There are also means-tested retirement-income programmes that can offset some or all of the cuts in the life-expectancy-linked scheme. The is apparent from the illustrations in Figures 5.3 and 5.4, but these are complex. This section summarises these results, by calculating a simple summary index of the degree to which pension benefits from all components of the national scheme are linked to life expectancy.

The index is calibrated so that the pure defined-contribution benchmark (introduced in Section 5.3) would show a figure of 100%: all retirement benefits are linked to life expectancy and the link is complete.[14] The second benchmark – a pure defined-benefit scheme – would register zero.

Figure 5.5 presents the results. The left-hand panel shows countries with a link to life-expectancy among the mandatory or quasi-mandatory parts of their retirement-income systems. Fully 100% of the pension rights of an average earner are linked to life expectancy in three countries. But this is achieved through different means: an adjustment in the defined-benefit scheme in Portugal, a defined-contribution plan in Chile and a mix of notional accounts and two defined-contribution plans in Sweden. The link to life expectancy is also strong (75%-100%) in Finland, Italy, Mexico and Norway.

Figure 5.5. **Percentage of pension entitlements linked to life expectancy: Man on average earnings**

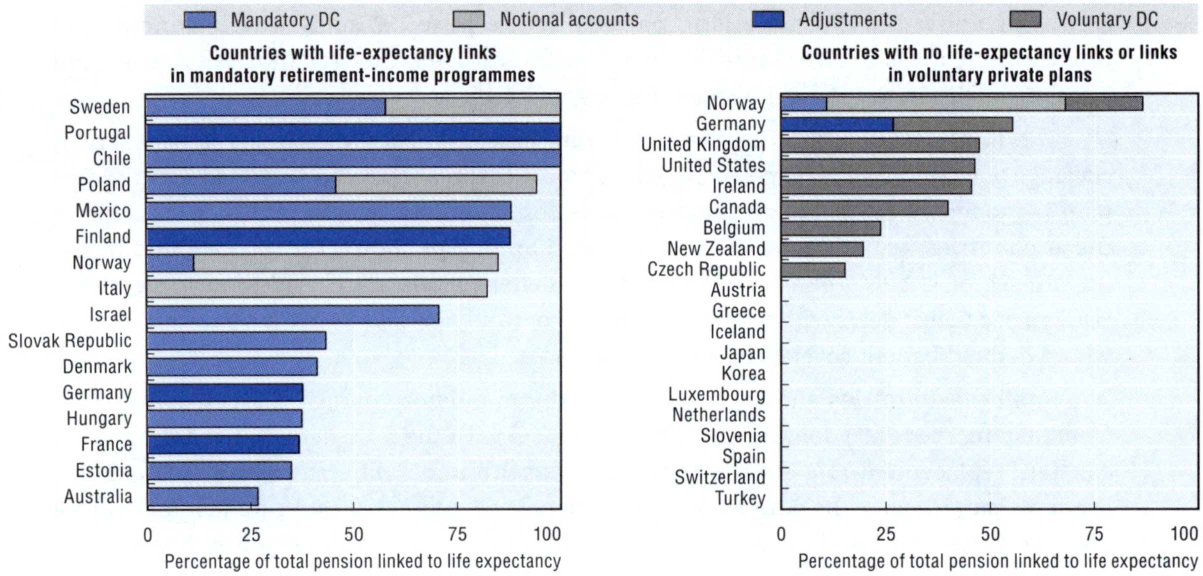

Source: OECD pension models.

StatLink http://dx.doi.org/10.1787/888932370721

At the other end of the spectrum, the proportion of earnings going into defined-contribution plans is relatively small in Estonia and Hungary. In Australia and Denmark, the majority of retirees receive means-tested retirement payments. Lower benefits from defined-contribution plans are partially made up by higher entitlements to means-tested benefits, significantly reducing the effective link between pensions and life expectancy. In Germany, the formula underlying the sustainability adjustment means that only some of the cost of longer life expectancy is borne in the form of lower benefits.

Most of the countries in the right-hand panel of Figure 5.5 have no link to life expectancy in the mandatory parts of their pension system: hence, countries from Austria down to Turkey are shown as zero. The same is true of the mandatory schemes in Belgium, Canada, the Czech Republic, Ireland, New Zealand, the United Kingdom and the United States. However, for these countries the bars show the degree of life-expectancy link for people covered by a voluntary defined-contribution plan, which amounts to between 40% and 60% of the workforce. The key difference between countries here is the size of the typical or average contribution to the private pension. Also, with the United Kingdom increasing pension age to 68 and the United States to 67, people are assumed to contribute for longer in these countries and accumulate investment returns over a longer period. Still, in none of these cases are more than 50% of overall retirement benefits linked to life expectancy because public schemes (without links) are an important source of income in old age.

For completeness, the calculations in this chart also show the effect of adding voluntary defined-contribution plans to the links to life expectancy in Germany and Norway. The overall proportion of pensions – mandatory plus voluntary – linked to life expectancy is about 55% and 85% respectively.

5.6. The impact of taxes

Most OECD counties tax pensions in payment. All OECD countries have "progressive" income taxes, meaning that the proportion of income paid in tax increases with income. In turn, this means that the *marginal* tax rate (the extra tax on an additional unit of income) is higher than the *average* tax rate (the proportion of income paid in tax). If a longer life expectancy cuts the value of pension entitlements, then the income tax liability falls at the marginal rate and the average tax rate falls. Thus, pension entitlements net of taxes are less sensitive to changes in life expectancy (where there is a link with pensions) than the gross benefit.

Figure 5.6 shows the results. Again, at the left-hand side, are countries with mandatory defined-contribution or notional accounts schemes, as well as those with life-expectancy links in public defined-benefit plans. At the right-hand side are countries that do not have such links. But the calculations have been performed on the same basis for typical voluntary private schemes in seven countries where these have broad coverage. Taxes make a difference in most cases: it is particularly large in Finland, Ireland, Israel, Italy and Norway.[15] The Slovak Republic does not tax pensions in payment, while entitlements in Canada, the Czech Republic, Hungary, Mexico and New Zealand are below the basic income-tax relief (see "Tax treatment of pensions and pensioners" in Part II.2).

Figure 5.6. **Percentage of pension entitlements linked to life expectancy: Before and after taxes and contributions**

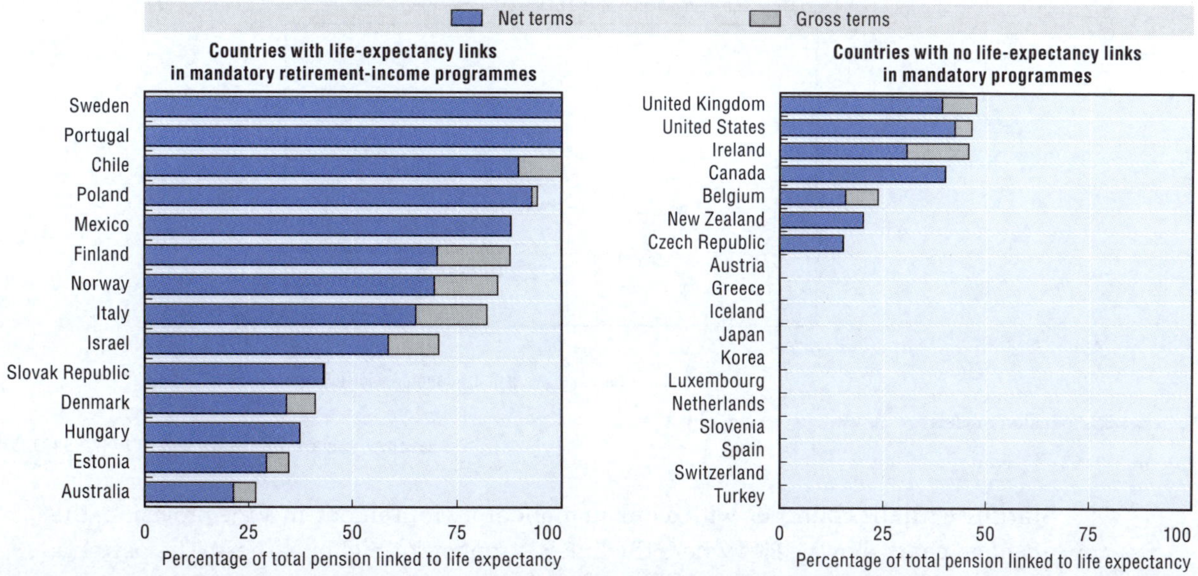

Note: Because of the complex nature of the link between pensions and life expectancy in France and Germany, it has not been possible to calculate net data for these countries.

Source: OECD pension models.

StatLink http://dx.doi.org/10.1787/888932370740

5.7. The impact of individual earnings

The results shown so far have looked at the case of an average earner. But the structure of retirement-income packages varies in many countries between individuals with different levels of earnings. Low earners, for example, are much more reliant on basic, means-tested or minimum pensions. Figure 5.7 shows how the index of the strength of the link between pensions and life expectancy varies with individual earnings.

Figure 5.7. **Percentage of pension entitlements linked to life expectancy: Impact of individual earnings**

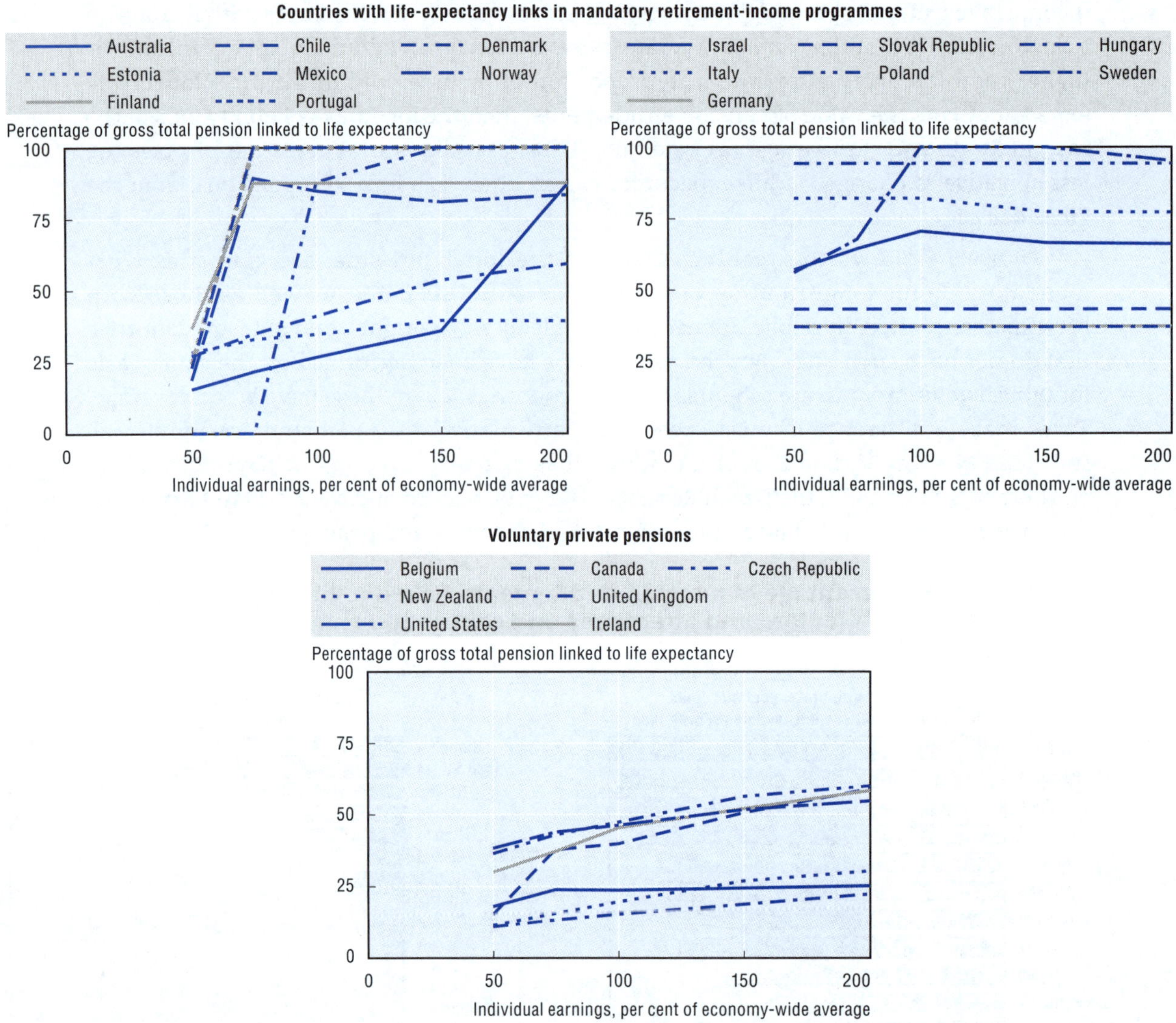

Source: OECD pension models.

StatLink http://dx.doi.org/10.1787/888932370759

Starting with the countries with a link in mandatory retirement-income provision, the top left-hand chart shows cases where the link is stronger for higher earners. The patterns in Chile, Finland, Norway and Portugal are very similar. People earning 50% of the average have pensions relatively invariant to changes in life expectancy, because as benefits from defined-contribution or earnings-related schemes are adjusted, some or all of the loss is made up with a larger entitlement to safety-net benefits. Mexico shows a similar picture, although the minimum pension affects workers on 75% as well as those on 50% of average earnings. The other three countries show a much more gradual shift to stronger links between pensions and life expectancy as earnings rise. This is because the resource-tested schemes in Australia and Denmark cover a majority of retirees from the lowest incomes upward. However, high-income retires in Australia will not be entitled to their benefit, and so there is a large jump in the curve between 150% and 200% of average earnings. Denmark and Estonia have basic pensions. Both mean that public benefits, not linked to life expectancy, provide a greater share of income in old age for low earners. For high earners, the defined-contribution scheme plays a much greater role.

In most of the countries in the right-hand chart, the share of total pensions linked to life expectancy is roughly constant with earnings. The basic pension in Israel and the guarantee pension in Sweden affect the pattern in a similar way as the countries in the left-hand chart. The slight decline in Italy at higher earnings reflects the policy of "progressive indexation", whereby smaller pensions are price indexed while larger benefits are uprated by only 75% of price inflation.

Countries with widespread voluntary private pension coverage are shown at the bottom of Figure 5.7. Most of them – Canada, the Czech Republic, Ireland, New Zealand and the United Kingdom – have basic schemes. In Belgium, the minimum pension provides a significant part of retirement incomes for low earners. The Czech Republic, the United Kingdom and the United States have progressive formulae in their public, defined-benefit schemes. As a result, low earners receive a much higher replacement rate from mandatory public programmes than high earners do. The pattern in the chart is therefore very similar to Denmark and Estonia in the chart above.

5.8. Living longer, working longer?

A link between *benefit levels* and life expectancy predominate in the pension reforms analysed in this chapter. Advocates of these reforms have argued that individuals will respond by working longer as successive cohorts live longer and benefits for a given retirement age are consequently lower.[16]

Table 5.3 gives some indication of the extra length of work required for selected countries[17] with a link to life expectancy in their mandatory retirement-income provision. It shows the current normal pension age and, using different projections for life expectancy in 2050, the age of claiming the pension that would deliver the same benefits.

In Chile, for example, the current normal pension age is 65. Under the median mortality scenario, an individual would have to work to age 66.4 years. The extra work adds to annual benefits in three ways: additional contributions, extra investment returns on accrued pension capital and a shorter duration of retirement. In the low-mortality scenario, however, work until age 68.0 would be needed to maintain benefits, while a pension age of 65.9 would be sufficient in the high-mortality scenario. This pattern is broadly replicated in other countries, such as Finland, Italy, Mexico, Poland and Sweden. The extra years needed between 2010 and 2050 from Norway's current normal pension age of 67 are also similar. Typically, just under one extra year's work will deliver the same benefit as 2010 under the high-mortality scenario, 1.5 years' in the median case and around three years with the most rapid mortality improvements.

Table 5.3. **Pension ages needed to equalise benefits in 2010 and 2050 under different mortality scenarios: Man on average earnings, selected countries**

	Current normal pension age	Pension age delivering equal replacement rate in 2050		
		Low mortality	Median mortality	High mortality
Chile	65	68.0	66.4	65.9
Estonia	63	64.0	63.5	63.3
Finland	65	68.0	66.3	65.9
Italy	65	67.7	66.2	65.9
Mexico	65	67.9	66.2	65.9
Norway	67	69.8	68.3	67.9
Poland	65	67.9	66.3	65.9
Portugal	65	66.8	65.5	65.5
Slovak Republic	62	63.4	62.7	62.4
Sweden	65	68.2	66.4	66.0

Source: OECD pension models.

StatLink http://dx.doi.org/10.1787/888932372317

In Estonia and the Slovak Republic, the extra years of work are smaller, reflecting the significance of elements of the pension package not linked to life expectancy, as illustrated in Figure 5.5 above. In Portugal, the extra years of work needed to offset life-expectancy related reductions in benefits are also small. This reflects the large increments to accrued benefits for people working after normal pension age. This can be as high as 12.0%, well above the OECD average of 4.8%.[18]

5.9. Conclusions and policy implications

Retirement used to be a luxury enjoyed only by the few; now it is an expectation for the many. The huge increase in life expectancy in the 20th century is a wonderful achievement. The first decade of the 21st century has seen continued longevity gains in most of the world. However, when added to the decline in the birth rate, the result is rapid population ageing and a rapidly growing cost of paying for pensions. As a result, pension expenditures grew 15% faster than national income between 1990 and 2007. And population ageing in OECD countries will accelerate between 2010 and 2030.

This chapter has explored *automatic* links between pensions and life expectancy, which are now in place in at least 20 of the 34 OECD countries. These can act as a mechanism for spreading the pension cost of longer lives between generations and helping the long-term financial sustainability of the retirement-income system.

It is hard to see why people approaching retirement should not bear at least some of the cost of their generation living longer than previous generations. After all, living longer is desirable. A longer life and a larger lifetime pension payout due to increased life expectancy confers a double advantage. Some link between pensions and life expectancy is therefore optimal.

The question then is: should all of the cost of longer lives be shifted onto new retirees, in the form of lower benefits or a requirement to work longer for the same benefit? The issue is complex because each individual has a lifecycle that includes periods as a contributor and as a beneficiary. There is a trade-off: greater certainty over retirement age and/or benefits *versus* greater certainty over the amount of contributions or taxes paid when working. The optimum is therefore unlikely to be a 100% link between pensions and life expectancy. In five countries with life-expectancy links in their mandatory pension system, there are also benefits without such links. In Australia, Denmark, Estonia, Hungary and the Slovak Republic, less than half of the retirement-income package is linked to life expectancy for the majority of workers.

This issue is particularly relevant for low-income workers. Cutting their already low benefits as life expectancy increases might risk a resurgence of old-age poverty. The analysis has shown that low earners in Chile, Finland, Mexico, Norway, Portugal and Sweden are protected by safety-net benefits. However, life-expectancy links are constant across the earnings range in Germany, Hungary, Italy, Poland and the Slovak Republic, although only in Italy and Poland are the links very strong.

This demonstrates that linking benefit *levels* to life expectancy must have limits. If benefit cuts push low earners onto social-assistance and other safety-net programmes in their retirement, this will offset some or all of the savings from the life-expectancy link in public earnings-related benefits (notional accounts, defined-benefit or points). It will mean additional public expenditure with private defined-contribution plans. Financial stability may be improved for parts of the pension system, but not for retirement-income provision as whole.

It is worth returning to the question raised in Section 5.1: why have countries overwhelmingly chosen to link benefit levels to life expectancy rather than pension age? If people simply continue to retire at the same age as present, then benefits will fall as life expectancy grows. The idea is that people will work longer to make up the shortfall. (The implications of this were explored in Section 5.8.) However, there is no mechanism in place to ensure that they do so.

A link of pension age to life expectancy should surely make at least as much or more intuitive sense to voters as a benefit link. It is also much better suited to countries with redistributive public pension programmes, such as Belgium, the Czech Republic, Canada, Ireland, Korea, Switzerland and the United Kingdom. The OECD's periodic *Economic Surveys* of member countries recommended a link between pension ages and life expectancy in ten of the 17 that addressed retirement-income policy (including Belgium, the Czech Republic, Hungary, the Netherlands, Slovenia and the United States). Reflecting the concerns expressed above, Poland and Sweden – with notional accounts and defined-contribution schemes – were advised in addition to increase pension ages in line with life expectancy. Only in the Slovak Republic and Slovenia was it proposed to have either pension ages or benefit levels linked to life expectancy.

On balance, a link between pension ages and life expectancy, rather than benefit levels, is the preferred policy. This, can, however, act in concert with benefit links in notional accounts, defined-contribution plans and through adjustments in other earnings-related schemes. The policy is most pressingly needed in countries with relatively high public pensions, where benefit levels are not linked to life expectancy and there are no plans to increase pension ages at present. This applies particularly to Austria, Greece, Luxembourg, Slovenia and Spain. In other cases – such as the Czech Republic, Hungary and the United States – this might be adopted once planned increases in pension age are in place.

Notes

1. This special chapter is based on earlier work, published as Whitehouse (2007, 2010). The analysis here has been updated with new information on mortality rates for 2010, to reflect systemic pension reforms – such as the introduction of notional accounts in Norway – and changes in parameters and rules in other countries between 2004 and 2008. The analysis has also been substantially extended. First, it includes the four new OECD member countries, three of which have mandatory defined-contribution plans of relevance to this chapter. Secondly, it now covers voluntary private schemes in seven OECD countries with widespread coverage of such plans. Thirdly, the impact of taxes and contributions on the results has been measured.

2. The reforms in Central and Eastern Europe have faced considerable pressure for reversal in the last two years. This is primarily for fiscal reasons, as the financial and economic crisis has significantly worsened public finances.

   Estonia diverted contributions from defined-contribution plans to the government budget for part of 2009 and all of 2010. The current plan is that contributions will be resumed at some point in 2011 and that compensation will be paid into individual accounts for the diverted contributions in the period 2014-17.

   Hungary has enacted a 14-month suspension of contributions to individual accounts for late 2010 and the whole of 2011. However, the government has recently proposed to appropriate the balances in individual accounts and permanently move contributions to the public sector (with the option to retain an individual account only available on extremely unfavourable terms.

   The previous government of the Slovak Republic attempted in 2008 and 2009 to encourage people to switch back voluntarily to the public scheme, but few chose to do so. The new administration is less keen on reversing the reform. There have been a number of proposals for reversal in Poland, including a temporary diversion of contributions from individual accounts to the government. However, there has been no action as yet.

   The calculations in this chapter assume that reforms are not reversed and temporary diversion of contributions to the government are reversed.

3. See Box 1.1 in OECD (2009) for detailed data on this trend.

4. See Whitehouse (2010) for a detailed analysis of notional accounts compared with other forms of public, earnings-related pension provision (that is, defined-benefit and points schemes).

5. See Department for Work and Pensions (2006). Note that the new government elected in May 2010 is conducting a review of this policy and has floated the idea of bringing forward the pension age increases. But there has been no mention of an automatic link between pension age and life expectancy.

6. Note that this was legislated in 2003 and does not form part of the recent pension reform.

7. For example, both the Czech Republic and New Zealand have seen a significant expansion of voluntary defined-contribution plans: see the indicator of "Coverage of private pensions" in Part II.6. The policy of conditional indexation and valorisation in the quasi-mandatory occupational plans in the Netherlands introduces a significant "defined-contribution element" into these predominantly defined-benefit schemes. Adjustments to accrued pension rights and pensions in payment are now dependent on the financial performance of the pension funds' investments. See the discussion in Box 1.1 of OECD (2009), Bikker and Vlaar (2006) and Dutch Central Bank (2007, 2010).

8. However, stochastic methods in demography are not really that new: they have been used since the late 1960s (Sykes, 1969, for example). Also, at the same time as Lee and Carter were developing their approach, McNown and Rogers (1989) devised a different stochastic technique.

9. The simulations were carried out using the standard "Monte-Carlo" method, which provides approximate solutions to a variety of mathematical problems by performing statistical sampling experiments. It uses pre-defined probability distributions of risk variables and sampling from a random number sequence to perform modelling over many simulations or trials. In this case, the underlying data are mortality rates in five-year age bands for the G7 countries from 1950 to 2002. After 2 000 draws, the results had converged.

10. See Box 3 in Whitehouse (2007) or Box 2 in Queisser and Whitehouse (2006) for a detailed explanation of how to calculate annuity factors.

11. See Whitehouse (2009) on the differences between indexation policy and practice. Parts I.2 and I.3 of OECD (2009) and Whitehouse *et al.* (2009) look at the impact of recent pension reforms on benefits for future retirees.

12. The contribution requirement is expressed in the number of quarters (trimesters) of contributions, so 43.75 years is possible within the current set-up. The exact nature of the calculation is unclear: these estimates are based on the standard *Pensions at a Glance* assumption of a full career starting at age 20. The Expected duration of retirement would increase by over four years without the adjustment: with the adjustments, the increase varies between approximately 0.5 and 2.0 years in the different mortality scenarios.

    Note also that the OECD pension models are designed to calculate pension entitlements only on an annual basis. Therefore, the calculations for partial-year values are an approximation.
13. The one-third figure makes intuitive sense, since life expectancy at pensionable age is roughly half of the 41-year contribution requirement at present. Three extra years' life expectancy are therefore (roughly) divided into two extra contribution years and one additional year in retirement.
14. Note that values have been capped at 100%. The results for Portugal and Sweden would be greater than 100% on the index formula. The curves for these two countries in Figure 5.3 go beyond the vertical of the pure defined-contribution model. They have a slight upward slope moving from left to right, indicating that pension wealth is slightly higher with lower life expectancy (rather than the same, as in the pure defined-contribution benchmark). The reasons for this are highly technical. The main one is due to the discount rate used in the calculation of benefits. Portugal's adjustment is based on life expectancy alone, which implies a discount rate of zero in the annuity-factor calculation. Sweden uses a discount rate of 1.6%. This means that there is slight over-compensation for changes in life expectancy compared with the OECD standard discount rate of 2% (which is by no means meant to imply that 2% is the "correct" rate).
15. As explained in the previous note, the true index for Portugal and Sweden in gross terms exceeds 100%, while the net terms index is exactly 100% for Sweden and a little above 100% for Portugal.
16. The phrase "live longer, work longer" is borrowed from the title of OECD (2006).
17. There is no legislation for increases in pension ages for men in the countries illustrated in Table 5.2. Other countries with links to life expectancy in mandatory retirement income programmes plan to increase pension ages. Australia, Denmark and Germany will move normal pension age from 65 to 67 and Hungary from 62 to 65. (See "Trends in pensionable ages and life expectancy, 1950-2050" in Part I, Chapter 1; "Normal, early and late retirement" in Part II.2; and Chomik and Whitehouse, 2010.) The analysis presented in Table 5.2 only makes sense in cases where there are no plans to increase normal pension ages. It is also not relevant where benefit levels rather than qualifying conditions are linked to life expectancy (Denmark and France).
18. See "Normal, early and late retirement" in Part II.2.

References

Bikker, J.A. and P.J.G. Vlaar (2006), "Conditional Indexation in Defined Benefit Pension Plans", *Working Paper*, No. 86, De Nederlandsche Bank, Amsterdam.

Chomik, R. and E.R. Whitehouse (2010), "Trends in Pension Eligibility Ages and Life Expectancy, 1950-2050", *Social, Employment and Migration Working Paper*, No. 105, OECD Publishing, Paris.

Department for Work and Pensions, United Kingdom (2006), *Security in Retirement: Towards a New Pensions System*, Cm 6841, The Stationery Office, London.

Dutch Central Bank (De Nederlandsche Bank) (2007), "Pension Contributions Stabilised, Indexation of Pensions Resumed", *Statistical Bulletin*, pp. 19-22, March.

Dutch Central Bank (De Nederlandsche Bank) (2010), "Pension Indexation Lags Behind Rising Wages and Prices", *Statistical Bulletin*, pp. 24-29, March.

Lee, R.D. and L. Carter (1992), "Modeling and Forecasting the Time Series of US Mortality", *Journal of the American Statistical Association*, Vol. 87, No. 419, pp. 659-671.

McNown, R. and A. Rogers (1989), "Forecasting Mortality: A Parameterized Time Series Approach", *Demography*, Vol. 26, No. 4, pp. 645-660.

National Research Council (2000), *Beyond Six Billion: Forecasting the World's Population*, Panel on Population Projections, in John Bongaarts and Rodolfo A. Butatao (eds.), *Committee on Population, Commission on Behavioural and Social Sciences and Education*, National Academy Press, Washington DC.

OECD (2006), *Ageing and Employment Policies: Live Longer, Work Longer*, OECD Publishing, Paris.

OECD (2009), *Pensions at a Glance: Retirement-Income Systems in OECD Countries*, OECD Publishing, Paris.

Oeppen, J. and J.W. Vaupel (2002), "Enhanced: Broken Limits to Life Expectancy", *Science*, Vol. 296, pp. 1029-1031.

Queisser, M. and E. Whitehouse (2006), "Neutral or Fair? Actuarial Concepts and Pension-System Design", *Social, Employment and Migration Working Paper*, No.40, OECD Publishing, Paris.

Sykes, Z.M. (1969), "Some Stochastic Versions of the Matrix Model for Population Dynamics", *Journal of the American Statistical Association*, Vol. 44, pp. 111-130.

Whitehouse, E.R. (2007), "Life-Expectancy Risk and Pensions: Who Bears the Burden?", *Social, Employment and Migration Working Paper*, No. 60, OECD Publishing, Paris.

Whitehouse, E.R. (2009), "Pensions, Purchasing-Power Risk, Inflation and Indexation", *Social, Employment and Migration Working Paper*, No. 70, OECD Publishing, Paris.

Whitehouse, E.R. (2010), "Decomposing Notional Defined-Contribution Pensions: Experience of OECD Countries' Reforms", *Social, Employment and Migration Working Paper*, No. 109, OECD Publishing, Paris.

Whitehouse, E.R., A.C. D'Addio, R. Chomik and A. Reilly (2009), "Two Decades of Pension Reform: What Has Been Achieved and What Remains To Be Done?", *Geneva Papers on Risk and Insurance*, Vol. 34, pp. 515-535.

PART II

Pension-policy Indicators

Part II updates the important indicators of retirement-income systems developed for the first three editions of Pensions at a Glance. *It also offers an expanded range of indicators: an additional 18 compared with the previous edition. This information – presented in a clear, "at a glance" style – provides a comprehensive and consistent framework for evaluating pension provision and pension policies.*

The 35 indicators are divided into six categories. The first of these looks at the design of retirement-income systems, presenting the main parameters and rules in a way that enables easy cross-country comparisons. The second group comprises indicators of individual pension entitlements under the pension regimes of all OECD member countries and those of other major economies that are members of the G20. Along with the familiar measure of pension replacement rates, there are indicators of pension wealth, the progressivity of retirement-income systems and the balance between public and private provision.

The analysis of pension entitlements is forward looking, in the sense that it considers the value of benefits for workers entering the labour market today. The third type of indicators look at the financial position of people of pension age currently: at average incomes, sources of incomes and risk of poverty.

Having analysed the position of individuals, the fourth group of indicators look at the finances of retirement-income systems as a whole. These comprise data on public and private expenditure on pensions, contribution rates for mandatory pensions and aggregate contribution revenues for public pension schemes. The fifth category of indicators relates to the background and context in which retirement-incomes systems must operate. These include key demographic measures – such as life expectancy and fertility – and average earnings. The sixth and final indicators set offer information specifically about private pensions and public-pension reserve funds.

Pensions at a Glance 2011
Retirement-income Systems in OECD and G20 Countries

PART II

Chapter 1

Design of Pension Systems

The four indicators in this section look in detail at the design of national retirement-income systems in OECD countries and other major economies. The first indicator sets out a taxonomy of the different kinds of retirement-income programmes found around the world. It uses this framework to describe the architecture of 42 countries' pension systems.

The other three indicators set out the parameters and rules of pension systems. The description begins with basic, targeted and minimum pensions, showing the value of these benefits and the proportion of older people covered by these programmes. The next looks at income-replacement pensions: earnings-related and defined-contribution schemes. It shows how benefits are determined in these schemes and the range of earnings that is covered by the pension system. The final indicator shows pension eligibility ages for both "normal" and "early" retirement. It also sets out the treatment of early and late retirees by the pension system.

Key results

Retirement-income regimes are diverse and often involve a number of different programmes. Classifying pension systems and different retirement-income schemes is consequently difficult. The taxonomy of pensions used here consists of two mandatory "tiers": a redistributive part and a savings part. Voluntary provision, be it individual or employer-provided, makes up a third tier.

The framework, shown in the chart, is based on the role and objective of each part of the system. The redistributive, first tier comprises programmes designed to ensure pensioners achieve some absolute, minimum standard of living. The second-tier, savings components are designed to achieve some target standard of living in retirement compared with that when working. Within these tiers, schemes are classified further by provider (public or private) and the way benefits are determined. *Pensions at a Glance* focuses mainly on these mandatory parts of the pension system, although much information is also provided on voluntary, private schemes.

Using this framework, the architecture of national schemes is shown in the table. Programmes aimed to prevent poverty in old age – first-tier, redistributive schemes – are provided by the public sector and of three main types.

Resource-tested or targeted plans pay a higher benefit to poorer pensioners and reduced benefits to better-off retirees. In these plans, the value of benefits depends either on income from other sources or on both income and assets. All countries have general social safety-nets of this type, but in some cases they only cover a few older people who had many career interruptions. Rather than mark every country in the table, only 12 OECD countries are marked in this column. Full-career workers with low earnings (30% of the average) would be entitled to resource-tested benefits in these countries.

Basic schemes pay either flat rate benefits (the same amount to every retiree) or their value depends only on years of work, not on past earnings. Additional retirement income does not change the entitlement. Some 13 OECD countries have a basic pension scheme or other provisions with a similar effect.

Minimum pensions, which share many features with resource-tested plans, are found in 18 OECD countries. The value of entitlements takes account only of pension income: unlike resource-tested schemes, it is not affected by income from savings, etc. Minimum credits in earnings-related schemes, such as those in Belgium and the United Kingdom, have a similar effect: benefits for workers with very low earnings are calculated as if the worker had earned at a higher level.

Only Ireland and New Zealand of the OECD countries do not have mandatory, second-tier provision. In the other 32 countries, there are four kinds of scheme.

Defined-benefit (DB) plans are provided by the public sector in 18 OECD countries. Private (occupational) schemes are mandatory or quasi-mandatory in three OECD countries (Iceland, the Netherlands and Switzerland). Retirement income depends on the number of years of contributions and individual earnings

There are ***points*** schemes in four OECD countries: French occupational plans (operated by the public sector) and the Estonian, German and Slovak public schemes. Workers earn pension points based on their earnings each year. At retirement, the sum of pension points is multiplied by a pension-point value to convert them into a regular pension payment.

Defined-contribution (DC) plans are compulsory in 11 OECD countries. In these schemes, contributions flow into an individual account. The accumulation of contributions and investment returns is usually converted into a pension-income stream at retirement. In Denmark and Sweden, there are quasi-mandatory, occupational DC schemes in addition to smaller compulsory plans.

There are ***notional-accounts*** schemes in four OECD countries (Italy, Norway, Poland and Sweden). These record contributions in an individual account and apply a rate of return to the balances. The accounts are "notional" in that the balances exist only on the books of the managing institution. At retirement, the accumulated notional capital is converted into a stream of pension payments using a formula based on life expectancy. Since this is designed to mimic DC schemes, they are often called notional defined-contribution plans (NDC).

Taxonomy: Different types of retirement-income provision

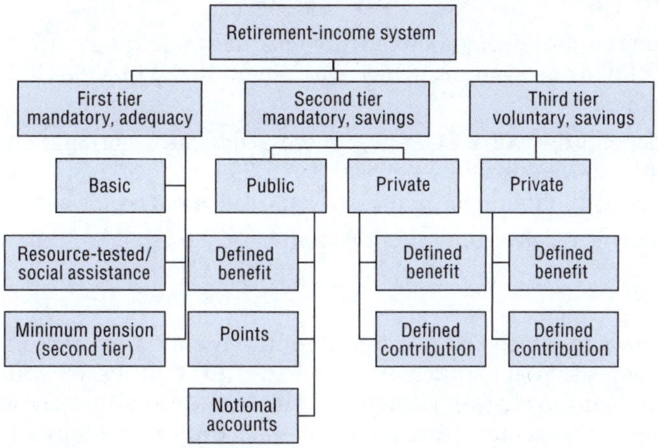

Note: See Chapter 1 of OECD (2005), *Pensions at a Glance: Public Policies across OECD Countries* and OECD (2004), *OECD Classification and Glossary of Private Pensions* for a more detailed discussion of classification issues.

StatLink http://dx.doi.org/10.1787/888932370778

Structure of retirement-income provision

	Public			Public	Private		Public			Public	Private
	Resource-tested	Basic	Minimum	Type	Type		Resource-tested	Basic	Minimum	Type	Type
OECD countries						**OECD countries** *(cont.)*					
Australia	✓				DC	New Zealand		✓			
Austria				DB		Norway			✓	NDC	DC
Belgium	✓		✓	DB		Poland			✓	NDC	DC
Canada	✓	✓		DB		Portugal			✓	DB	
Chile	✓		✓		DC	Slovak Republic			✓	Points	DC
Czech Republic		✓	✓	DB		Slovenia			✓	DB	
Denmark	✓	✓			DC	Spain			✓	DB	
Estonia		✓		Points	DC	Sweden			✓	NDC	DC
Finland			✓	DB		Switzerland	✓		✓	DB	DB
France			✓	DB + points		Turkey			✓	DB	
Germany	✓			Points		United Kingdom	✓	✓	✓	DB	
Greece			✓	DB		United States				DB	
Hungary				DB	DC						
Iceland	✓	✓			DB	**Other major economies**					
Ireland		✓				Argentina		✓		DB	
Israel		✓			DC	Brazil				DB	
Italy	✓			NDC		China		✓		NDC/DC	
Japan		✓		DB		India				DB + DC	
Korea	✓	✓		DB		Indonesia				DC	
Luxembourg	✓	✓	✓	DB		Russian Federation		✓		NDC	DC
Mexico			✓		DC	Saudi Arabia			✓	DB	
Netherlands		✓			DB	South Africa	✓				

Note: In Iceland and Switzerland, the government sets contribution rates, minimum rates of return and the annuity rate at which the accumulation is converted into a pension for mandatory occupational plans. These schemes are therefore implicitly defined benefit.
DB = Defined benefit; DC = Defined contribution; NDC = Notional accounts.
Source: See "Country profiles" in Part III of this report.

StatLink http://dx.doi.org/10.1787/888932370778

Key results

Retirement-income programmes designed to ensure adequacy of old-age incomes make up the first tier of the OECD's taxonomy of pension systems, which was set out in the previous indicator of the architecture of national pension schemes.

Safety-net retirement benefits are worth 21.6% of economy-wide mean earnings on average. Eleven countries provide a minimum pension above this safety-net level. For full-career workers, the average retirement income – including these contributory minimum pensions – is 24.4% of economy-wide average earnings.

About a third of older people receive some support from basic, targeted or minimum pensions on average.

There are three main ways in which OECD countries provide retirement incomes that are sufficient to meet a minimum standard of living in old age. The left-hand part of the table shows the value of benefits provided under these different types of scheme. Values are presented in *absolute* terms – national currency units – to allow a direct link with the detailed information in the country profiles in Part III of this report. They are also given in *relative* terms – as a percentage of economy-wide average earnings – to facilitate comparisons between countries. (See the indicator of "Earnings: averages and distribution" in Part II.5.)

Benefit values shown are for a single person. In some cases – usually with minimum contributory pensions – each partner in a couple receives an individual entitlement. In other cases – especially under targeted schemes – the couple is treated as the unit of assessment and couple receives less than twice the entitlement of a single person. (See the indicator of "Pension replacement rates: couples" in Part II.2.)

The analysis of benefit values is complicated by the existence of multiple programmes in many countries. In some cases, benefits under these schemes are additive. In others, there is a degree of substation between them. Benefit values are therefore summarised in the left-hand chart for two cases. The dark bars show the overall value of non-contributory benefits. This can be seen as the absolute minimum, safety-net income. The lighter bars show minimum contributory benefits. The entitlements shown are the maximum for a worker contributing for each year from age 20 until the standard national pension age. These can be seen as the minimum income of a low-earning, full-career worker.

In 20 countries, only non-contributory benefits are relevant. This group includes cases where basic pensions are residency-tested, such as the Netherlands and New Zealand. In Canada, Denmark and Iceland, entitlements are a mix of basic and resource-tested benefits. Finally, in countries including Austria, Finland, Germany, Italy and the United States, this refers only to resource-tested schemes, including social assistance.

In 11 countries, the picture is more complex: there is a safety-net income at a lower level and a contributory minimum at a higher level. In Ireland and Korea, for example, contributory basic pensions are worth more than resource-tested schemes. In Greece, Portugal, Spain, Sweden and Turkey, contributory minimum pensions are set at a significantly higher level than the safety-net income.

Overall, the average non-contributory benefit is worth 21.6% of economy-wide average earnings, while contributory benefits average 24.5%.

Coverage

The percentage of over 65s receiving first-tier benefits is shown in the final two columns of the table and the right-hand chart. Data are presented just for non-contributory safety-net benefits and contributory minimum pensions. The importance of these benefits varies enormously. In Greece, for example, some 60% of older people are on the contributory minimum pension and a further 19% on safety-net benefits, with slightly lower proportions for both kinds of scheme in Portugal. Nearly 80% of Australians receive at least some payment from the resource-tested scheme and nearly 70% in Denmark. In Finland, France and Sweden, it is minimum contributory benefits that are the most significant, covering 35-55% of retirees.

At the other end of the spectrum, 2% or fewer of pensioners receive safety-net benefits in Germany and Japan. The same is true of the Czech and Slovak Republics, but many of today's pensioners receive contributory minimum pensions for which data are not available on coverage.

Basic, targeted and minimum pensions

	Relative benefit value (% of average earnings)			Absolute value (units of national currency per year)			Coverage (% of over 65s receiving)	
	Basic	Targeted	Minimum	Basic	Targeted	Minimum	Targeted	Minimum
Australia		23.7			14 313		78	
Austria		26.9			10 458		11	
Belgium		26.5	28.5		10 533	11 331	5	11
Canada	14.2	17.9		6 082	7 677		34	
Chile		15.4	14.4		900 000	840 000	– 40 –	
Czech Republic	8.3	13.7	11.7	22 750	37 512	31 990	1	n.a.
Denmark	17.0	17.1		61 152	61 560		68	
Estonia	12.4	14.2		19 150	21 938		6	
Finland		18.0			6 702		2	53
France		23.1	23.3		7 537	7 624	5	36
Germany		20.3			8 424		2	
Greece		11.5	28.6		2 760	6 843	19	60
Hungary			14.6			342 000	< 1	2
Iceland	7.6	23.9		308 400	973 200		n.a.	
Ireland	29.0	27.5		11 835	11 236		28	
Israel	13.0	22.6		14 557	25 409		n.a.	
Italy		20.2	19.9		5 311	5 234	5	32

	Relative benefit value (% of average earnings)			Absolute value (units of national currency per year)			Coverage (% of over 65s receiving)	
	Basic	Targeted	Minimum	Basic	Targeted	Minimum	Targeted	Minimum
Japan	15.8	19.4		792 100	969 810		2	
Korea	7.1	3.0		2 363 760	1 008 000		60	
Luxembourg	9.3	28.5	35.6	4 500	13 764	17 232	1	29
Mexico			28.7			21 836		n.a.
Netherlands	29.2			12 718				
New Zealand	38.7			18 084				
Norway			31.4			138 216		29
Poland		17.0	22.6		5 724	7 635	12	n.a.
Portugal		13.6	27.1		2 183	4 366	17	59
Slovak Republic		24.7			65 293		1	
Slovenia		32.1	13.8		5 066	2 173	22	3
Spain		17.0	27.4		3 941	6 368	7	28
Sweden		16.3	24.8		57 432	87 330	1	55
Switzerland		24.4	17.8		18 140	13 260	12	n.a.
Turkey		5.9	38.2		1 113	7 194	– 22 –	
United Kingdom	14.0	19.2	10.5	4 716	6 451	3 528	23	n.a.
United States		19.0			7 644		7	

Note: Coverage data are for the most recent year available.
n.a.: Data are not available.
Blank cells indicate not applicable.
The coverage data for Chile and Turkey comprise different programmes.
Source: Value of benefits from country profiles in Part III. Data on coverage of benefits from national officials; European Union, Social Policy Committee (2006), "Minimum Income Provision for Older People and their Contribution to Adequacy in Retirement", *Special Pensions Study*, Brussels; Pearson and Whitehouse (2009), "Social Pensions in High-Income Countries", in R. Holzmann and N. Takayama (eds.), *Closing the Coverage Gap: The Role of Social Pensions*, World Bank, Washington DC.

StatLink http://dx.doi.org/10.1787/888932370797

Value of basic, targeted and minimum pensions

% of economy-wide average earnings

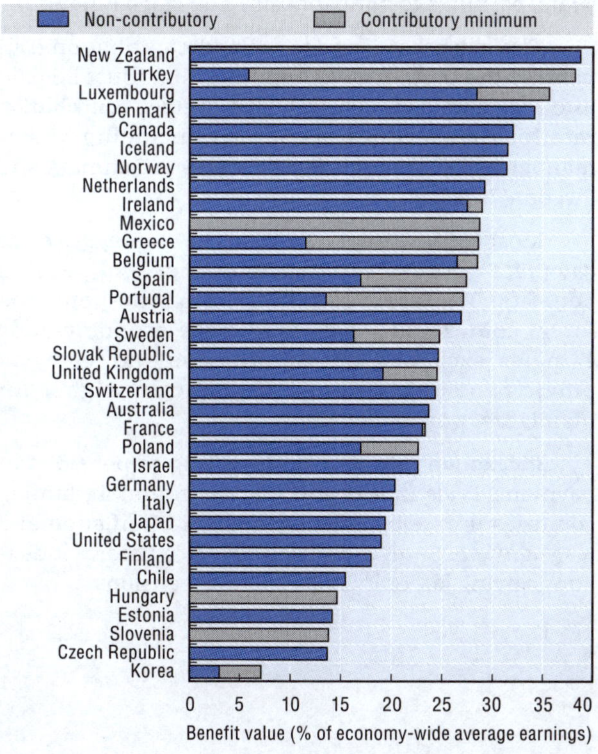

StatLink http://dx.doi.org/10.1787/888932370797

Coverage of targeted and minimum pensions

% of over 65s

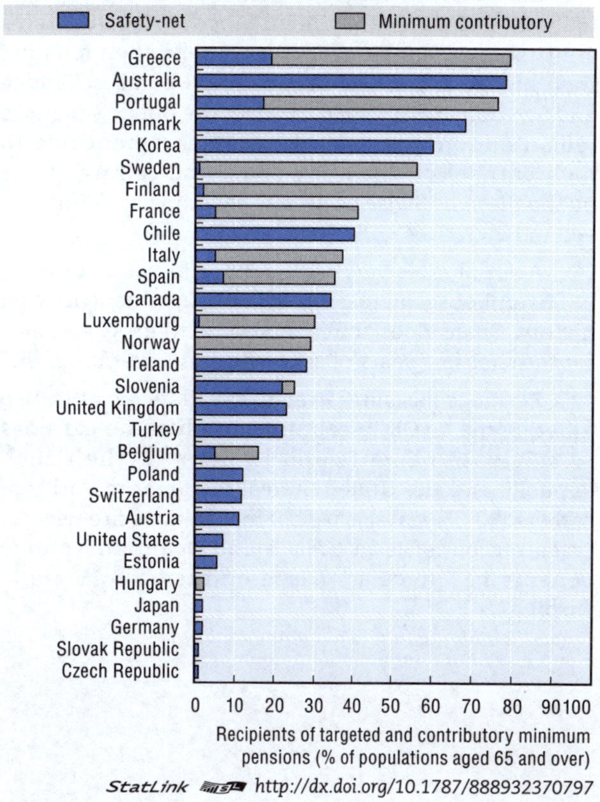

StatLink http://dx.doi.org/10.1787/888932370797

Key results

The second tier of the OECD's taxonomy of retirement-income provision comprises income-replacement pensions. The summary here shows the key parameters and rules of these schemes that determine the value of entitlements, including the long-term effect of pension reforms that have already been legislated.

Earnings-related schemes can be of three different types: defined benefit (DB), points or notional accounts (NDC). The ***accrual rate*** shows the rate at which benefit entitlements build up for each year of coverage. The accrual rate is expressed as a percentage of the earnings that are "covered" by the pension scheme.

For points systems, the effective accrual rate is calculated as the ratio of the cost of a pension point to the pension-point value. In notional-accounts schemes, the effective accrual rate is calculated in a similar way; it depends on the contribution rate, notional interest rate and annuity factors.

In a little under half of the countries with earnings-related plans (of all three types), accrual rates are "linear". Elsewhere, the benefit earned for each year of coverage varies, either with individual earnings, age or years of contributions.

Among the seven cases where accrual rates vary with earnings, the public schemes of the Czech Republic, Portugal, Switzerland and the United States are "progressive". They pay higher replacement rates to lower earners. In the United Kingdom, accrual rates are U-shaped: highest for low earners, then smaller, then higher again. The occupational plans of France and Sweden are designed to offset the public scheme's redistribution, paying a higher replacement rate to high earners on their pay above the ceiling of the public plan. In Swiss occupational plans and Finland, accrual increases with age.

Accrual rates vary with service in two countries; in Luxembourg, increasing with a longer contribution history. Spain does the reverse: the highest accruals for the first few years of coverage and lower later on.

Earnings measures used to calculate benefits also differ. Some 20 OECD countries use lifetime earnings to calculate benefits and in Canada, the Czech Republic and the United States, the great majority of careers (30-35 years) is used. Final salaries are used to calculate benefits in Greece and Spain and public benefits in France are based on the best 25 years' earnings.

Closely linked with the earnings measure is ***valorisation***, whereby past earnings are adjusted to take account of changes in living standards between the time pension rights accrued and the time they are claimed (sometimes called pre-retirement indexation). If benefits are based on the final year's salary, there is no need for valorisation. But it is necessary to protect the value of pension entitlements when benefits are based on earnings over a longer period. The uprating of the pension-point value and the notional interest rate in points and notional-accounts systems, respectively are the exact corollaries of valorisation in DB plans.

The most common practice is to revalue earlier years' pay with the growth of average earnings. Belgium, France and Spain, however, revalue earnings only with price inflation, although the effect in Spain is relatively small because only the final 15 years' salary enters the benefit formula, compared with 25 years in the French public scheme and the lifetime average in Belgium and the French occupational plans. Finland, Portugal and Turkey revalue earlier years' earnings to a mix of price and wage inflation.

The key parameter for defined-contribution (DC) plans is the proportion of earnings that must be paid into the individual account. The average ***contribution rate*** for the 11 countries shown, including quasi-mandatory DC occupational schemes in Denmark and Sweden, is 8.3%.

Most countries set a limit on the earnings used to calculate both contribution liabilities and pension benefits. The average ***ceiling*** on public pensions for 21 countries is 185% of average economy-wide earnings, excluding four countries with no ceiling on public pensions. Ceilings are typically higher for mandatory private pensions.

Indexation refers to the uprating of pensions in payment. Price indexation is most common, but six countries uprate benefits with a mix of inflation and wage growth. Some countries have progressive indexation, giving larger increases to low pensions.

Parameters and rules of income-replacement pensions

	Earnings-related schemes					DC schemes	Ceilings on pensionable earnings (% of ave. earnings)	
	Type	Accrual rate (%)	Earnings measure	Valorisation	Indexation	Contribution rate (%)	Public	Private
Australia	None					9.0		244
Austria	DB	1.78	40	w[1]	d		142	
Belgium	DB	1.33	L	p	p		118	
Canada	DB	0.63	b34	w	p [c]		104	
Chile	None					10.0		291
Czech Republic	DB	0.45 [w][2]	f30	w	33w/67p		None	
Denmark	None					10.8[3]		
Estonia	Points	1.0	L	w	50w/50p	6.0	None	None
Finland	DB	1.5 [a][4]	L	80w/20p	20w/80p		None	
France	DB/points	1.75 [w][5, 6]	b25/L	p/p	p/p		102/305[7]	
Germany	Points	1.00	L	w [c]	w [c]		154	
Greece	DB	2.57[5]	f5	w[8]	d		309[9]	
Hungary	DB	1.22	L	w	50w/50p	8.0	217	217
Iceland	DB	1.40	L	fr	p			None
Ireland	None							
Israel	None					15.0		100
Italy	NDC	1.75	L	GDP	p[10]		337	
Japan	DB	0.55	L	w	p		149	
Korea	DB	0.89	L	w	p		129	
Luxembourg	DB	1.85 [y][11]	L	w	w		195	
Mexico	None					6.5[12]		623
Netherlands	DB	1.75[13]	L[14]	w [c]	w [c]			None
New Zealand	None							
Norway	NDC	1.35	L	w	w-0.75	2.0	111	188
Poland	NDC	0.67	L	w[15]	p[15]	7.3	250	
Portugal	DB	2.25 [w][2]	L	25w/75p	p/GDP[16]		None	
Slovak Republic	Points	1.25	L	w	50w/50p	9.0	300	
Slovenia	DB	1.81	b18	w (d)	w		157	
Spain	DB	3.0 [y][17]	f15	p	p		159	
Sweden	NDC	1.21 [w]	L	w	w-1.6 [c]	2.5 + 4.5[18]	110	110/none[18]
Switzerland	DB	[w/a]	L	fr	50w/50p		104	104
Turkey	DB	2.00	L	p + 30%GDP	p		288	
United Kingdom	DB	0.89 [w][19]	L	w	p		119	
United States	DB	0.91 [w][2]	b35	w[20]	p		253	

Note: Parameters are for 2008 but include all legislated changes that take effect in the future: for example, some countries are extending the period of earnings covered for calculating benefits. Empty cells indicate that the parameter is not relevant.

[a] = Varies with age; b = Number of best years; [c] = Valorisation/indexation conditional on financial sustainability; d = Discretionary indexation; DB = Defined benefit; DC = Defined contribution; f = Number of final years; fr = Fixed rate valorisation; GDP = Growth of gross domestic product; L = Lifetime average; NDC = Notional accounts; p = Valorisation/indexation with prices; w = Valorisation/indexation with average earnings; [w] = Varies with earnings; [y] = Varies with years of service.

1. Austria: valorisation assumed to move to earnings as the averaging period for the earnings measure is extended.
2. Czech Republic, Portugal, United States: higher accrual rates on lower earnings, lower accruals on higher earnings.
3. Denmark: typical contribution rate for quasi-mandatory occupational plans.
4. Finland: higher accrual rates at older ages.
5. France and Greece: data shown combines two different programmes.
6. France: higher accrual rate on higher earnings under occupational plans.
7. France: the first ceiling relates to the national pension scheme, the second to the mandatory occupational plan modelled here (ARRCO).
8. Greece: valorisation in line with pension increases for public-sector workers.
9. Greece: effective ceiling calculated from maximum pension.
10. Italy: indexation is fully to prices for low pensions, 90% of prices or 75% of prices for higher pensions.
11. Luxembourg: higher accrual rate for longer contribution periods.
12. Mexico: additional contribution of 5.5% of minimum wage is shown previously as a basic pension.
13. Netherlands: accrual rate varies between occupational schemes.
14. Netherlands: earnings measure is average salary for around two thirds of occupational plans and final salary for one third.
15. Poland: valorisation to real wage bill growth but at least price inflation.
16. Portugal: indexation will be higher relative to prices for low pensions and *vice versa*. Indexation will be more generous the higher is GDP growth.
17. Spain: higher accrual rate on early years of service and lower on later years.
18. Sweden: the contribution rate is 2.5% for personal plans up to the ceiling for the public scheme. For quasi-mandatory occupational plans the contribution rates are 4.5% on a lower slice of earnings and 30% on an upper slice with no ceiling (in the largest scheme for private-sector workers).
19. United Kingdom: accrual rate highest for low earnings, then lower then higher again.
20. United States: earnings valorisation to age 60; no adjustment from 60 to 62; prices valorisation from 62 to 67.

StatLink http://dx.doi.org/10.1787/888932372336

Key results

The rules for eligibility to retire and draw a pension are very complex, often reflecting conflicting government objectives. On the one hand, encouraging people to work longer as the population ages has been a major feature of many pension reforms. On the other hand, government have often been concerned to protect workers perceived as vulnerable and unable to continue their jobs to an older age.

The table opposite shows the rules for normal, early and late retirement under the long-term parameters of the pension system, including changes that have been legislated but are not yet in effect. These parameters underpin the modelling of pension entitlements in Part II.2 of this report and also the detailed analysis of "Pension incentives to retire", the special chapter in Part I.3. In 15 of the 34 countries, different rules apply to different components of the overall retirement-income package and so these are shown separately.

Normal pension age

Two-thirds of OECD countries already have a normal pension age of 65 or plan to reach that level in the future. In four of these, normal pension age for women will be lower: 60 in Chile, Italy and Poland and 64 in Switzerland. Only three countries plan to have men's pension ages below 65: Estonia, the Slovak Republic and Slovenia.

Normal pension ages by sex: Long-term rules

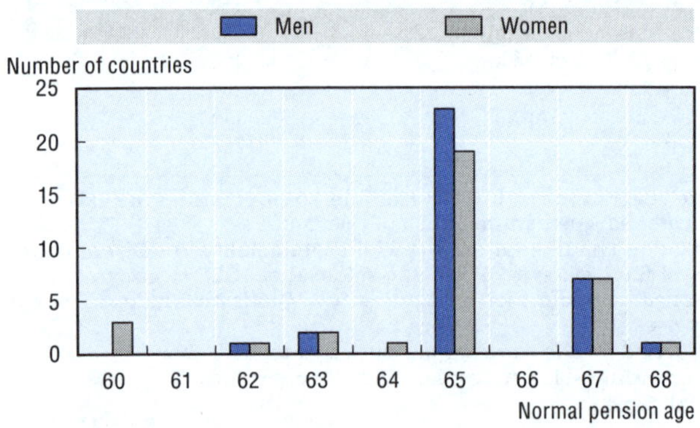

Source: Country profiles in Part III.

StatLink http://dx.doi.org/10.1787/888932370816

Eight countries will have normal pension ages for men and women above age 65. Only Iceland and Norway are currently at 67, but Australia, Denmark, Germany and the United States plan to reach that level in the future, with the United Kingdom going further to 68.

Early retirement

Seven countries will not allow early retirement in any mandatory part of the pension system: Denmark, Ireland, Netherlands, New Zealand, Poland, Turkey and the United Kingdom. In other cases, early retirement is restricted to certain schemes: in Australia, Chile and Iceland to mandatory private pensions; and in Canada and Sweden, there is no early retirement under basic or targeted programmes.

Benefits for early retirees are usually cut to reflect the longer period over which the pension is paid. In only three cases is there no reduction in benefits for early retirees (provided that certain qualifying conditions are met). In a further three, early retirement without reduction is possible.

In most defined-benefit and points schemes, the adjustment is simply a parameter of the pension system: the benefit is permanently reduced by *x*% for each year of early retirement. The adjustment for early and late retirement in the notional-accounts schemes of Italy and Sweden is not directly observed. (Poland does not allow early retirement.) However, it can be calculated from the different annuity rates or factors used to convert accumulated notional capital, which in turn are based on projections of mortality rates at different ages and the discount rates employed in the annuity calculation.

The size of the adjustments varies significantly. The largest standard decrements are in Canada – which is increasing the rate from 6.0 to 7.2% – and Finland. However, larger adjustments are possible in the Czech Republic (for people who retire at the earliest possible ages) and in Spain (for people with a smaller number of contribution years). In some cases – Belgium, France, Germany, Greece and Luxembourg – there is no benefit reduction provided a certain number of years of contributions were paid. The average decrement is 4.4% for each year of early retirement (averaging national figures, where appropriate, over different circumstances).

Late retirement

It is possible to defer claiming a pension until after the normal age in nearly all countries. Typically, an increase in accrued benefits is provided, at an average of 4.8% per year of deferral. However, the ability to combine work and pension receipt after normal pension age is common and so the size of the increment will have little influence on people's financial incentives to remain in work.

References

Queisser, M. and E.R. Whitehouse (2006), "Neutral or Fair? Actuarial Concepts and Pension-System Design", *Social, Employment and Migration Working Paper*, No. 40, OECD Publishing, Paris.

Whitehouse, E.R. (2010), "Decomposing Notional Defined-Contribution Pensions: Experience of OECD Countries' Reforms", *Social, Employment and Migration Working Paper*, No. 109, OECD Publishing, Paris.

Pension ages and treatment of early and late retirees, long-term rules, all mandatory and quasi mandatory schemes, by type of scheme

	Scheme	Early age	Reduction (%)	Normal age	Increase (%)
Australia	T	n.a.		67	0.6-3.6[1]
	DC	60	–	67	–
Austria	DB	62M/60F	4.2	65	4.2
Belgium	DB	60[2]	0.0	65	0.0
Canada	Basic/T	n.a.		65	
	DB	60	7.2	65	8.4
Chile	Basic/T	n.a.		65	
	DC	Any age[3]	–	65/60	–
Czech Republic	DB	60M/59-60F[4]	5.3/8.9[5]	65M/62-65F[4]	8.9[5]
Denmark	Basic/T	n.a.		67	5.6[6]
	DC	n.a.		67	–
Estonia	Points	60[7]	4.8	63	10.8
	DC	60	–	63	–
Finland	T	62	4.8	65	7.2
	DB	62	7.2/0.0[7]	65	0.0/4.8[8]
France	DB	56-60[9]	0.0/5.0	65	5.0
	DB (Occ)	55	4.0-7.0[10]	60	0.0
Germany	P	63	3.6/0.0[11]	67	6.0
Greece	DB	Any age/55/60[12]	0.0/6.0[13]	65	0.0[13]
Hungary	DB	63	3.6/4.8[14]	65	6.0
	DC	63	–	65	–
Iceland	Basic/T	n.a.		67	
	DB (Occ)	62	7.0[15]	67	6.0[15]
Ireland	Basic/T	n.a.		66/65	n.a.
Israel	Basic/T	62[16]		67	
	DC			67	–
Italy	NDC	Any age/61[17]	2.3-2.9[18]	65M/60F	0.0/2.6-2.9[18]
Japan	Basic/DB	60	6.0	65	8.4
Korea	DB	60	6.0	65	6.0
Luxembourg	DB	57/60[19]	0.0	65	n.a.
Mexico	Min	60[20]	0.0	65	0.0
	DC	Any age/60[20]	–	65	–
Netherlands	Basic	n.a.		65	n.a.
New Zealand	Basic	n.a.		65	n.a.
Norway	DB	62	3.8-4.7[21]	67	4.9-5.4[21]
	DC	n.a.[22]		67	–
Poland	NDC	n.a.		65M/60F	4.3-4.8M/3.7-4.2F[23]
	DC	n.a.		65M/60F	–
Portugal	DB	55	4.0-6.0[24]	65	4.0-12.0[25]
Slovak Republic	P	60[26]	6.5	62	6.5
	DC	60	–	62	–
Slovenia	DB	58[27, 29]	1.2-3.6	63[28]	0.0[29]
Spain	DB	61	6.0-7.5[30]	65	2.0/3.0[31]
Sweden	T	n.a.		65	
	NDC	61	4.1-4.7[32]	65	4.9-6.1[32]
	DC	55/61[33]	–	65	–
Switzerland	DB	63M/62F	4.5[34]	65M/64F	5.2-6.5
	DB (Occ)	60M/59F[35]	2.9[36]	65/64	2.9[36]
Turkey	DB	n.a.		65	0.0
United Kingdom	Basic/DB	n.a.		68	10.4[37]
United States	DB	62	5.0/6.7[38]	67	8.0

Pension ages and treatment of early and late retirees, long-term rules, all mandatory and quasi mandatory schemes, by type of scheme *(cont.)*

Note: Data rounded to one decimal place. Calculations for late retirement assume a maximum retirement age of 70.
DB = Defined benefit; DC = Defined contribution; n.a. = Early retirement or deferral of pension is not available; Occ = Occupational; T = Targeted. Where pension ages for men and women differ they are shown as M/F. – = Benefits automatically adjusted for early and late retirement in DC schemes.

1. Pension bonus is a single lump sum of 9.4% of age-pension entitlement multiplied by number of years' deferral squared. For comparison with other countries, it is expressed as a percentage of the age-pension benefit stream. Values shown are annualised for one and five years' deferral respectively. Recent reforms replaced this with a "work bonus" making it easier for people to combine work and pension receipt.
2. Early retirement with no actuarial reduction is possible once 35 years contributions have been made.
3. Requires a DC benefit of at least 80% of the maximum targeted benefit and a replacement rate of at least 70%.
4. Pension age for women varies with number of children they have had.
5. A 3.6% reduction in total accrual total accrual factor for first 2 years' early retirement and 6% thereafter. Increment of 6% in total accrual factor per year of late retirement. Figures shown calculated for a full-career worker, who would have a total accrual factor of 67.5% at age 65.
6. The adjustment is based on the reciprocal of life expectancy at the age at which the pension is drawn. Projected life expectancy at age 68 for 2040 is 17.9 years.
7. The public pension can be claimed up to three years before the standard age (*i.e.* from age 60 in the long term) provided that people retire and meet the 15-year qualification requirement.
8. Adjustment applies from age 62 to 63. Instead of adjustments, there is accelerated accrual in the earnings-related scheme of 4.5% of earnings per year of contributions between ages 63 and 68 compared with 1.5% at most ages. For late retirement, the adjustment shown applies from age 68 onwards.
9. Full pension will require 41 years' contributions. Retirement from age 60 without benefit reduction is subject to this contribution condition. Retirement before age 60 without reduction for long careers ranges from retirement at 56 for people with 42 years' contributions and labour-market entry before age 16 to retirement at 59 with 40 years' contributions and labour-market entry before age 17.
10. Full benefit requires 40 years' contributions. Benefit reduced by 4% for first three missing years and 5% for next two. Benefit reductions for retirement before age 60 subject depend on years of contributions.
11. Retirement from 63 requires 35 years' contributions subject to 3.6% reduction. Early retirement at age 65 (rather than 67) without actuarial reduction with 45 years' contributions.
12. Retirement at 60 with 15 years' contribution and 55 with 35 years' contributions subject to 6% reduction per year earlier than 65. Retirement with no reduction at any age requires 37 years' contributions. The recently announced reform will restrict early retirement to age 60.
13. Accelerated accrual (3.3% per year compared with 2% at younger ages) during deferral but no increment to accrued benefits.
14. Early retirement requires 37 years' contributions.
15. Adjustment varies between schemes: typical rates shown.
16. Early retirement pension up to five years before the normal rage if the number of years' contributions exceeds the minimum qualifying period by at least ten years. A partial early pension is payable from up to five years before the normal retirement age if the number of years' contributions exceeds the requirement for a full pension by less than ten years.
17. Retirement at any age is possible with 40 years' contributions and from age 61 with 36 years' contributions.
18. Adjustment for early retirement calculated from government-provided transformation coefficients projected for 2048. After age 65, the transformation coefficient is constant and so benefits do not increase for men retiring late.
19. Retirement at age 57 requires 40 years' actual (compulsory or voluntary) contributions. With 40 years' actual or credited contribution years, early retirement is possible at age 60.
20. Early retirement at age 60 conditional on 1 250 weekly contributions (approximately 25 years). DC pension available at any age if pension is at least 30% above the minimum.
21. Calculated from government-provided figures for life-expectancy divisors. This calculation results in higher increments after age 70.
22. A debate is underway as to whether access should be allowed from age 62.
23. Calculated from projected (unisex) life expectancy at ages 66-70 for men and 60-65 for women.
24. Adjustment for early retirement is 6% per year, but with more than 30 years' contributions, the number of years over which the pension is adjusted is cut by one year for each complete three years' contributions beyond 30 years. The 4% rate is an average over three years for a person with at least 30 years' contributions.
25. Increment depends on number of contributions years, ranging from 4% with 15-24 years' and 12% with more than 40 years' contributions.
26. Early retirement is also conditional on pension entitlement exceeding 1.2 times the subsistence minimum.
27. The age for early retirement is 58 years conditional on having contributed for at least 40 years. For retirement before the full pension age, reductions are of 3.6% (a year) at age 58, 3% at 59, 2.4% at 60, 1.8% at age 61 and 1.2% at 62.
28. Men with at least at least 20 years' contributions can retire at 63. With 15 years' contributions, the pension age is 65. For women, the full pension age will be 61 in 2023 conditional on 20 years' contributions.
29. Additional years of contributions up to and after the full pension age attract a higher accrual rate. From the early to normal pension age, the annual accrual rate is 3% in the first year, 2.6% the second, 2.2% in the third, 1.8% in the fourth year and 1.5% thereafter. For deferring retirement after the full pension age the accrual rate is 3.6% for the first year, 2.4% in the second and 1.2% in the third.
30. The size of the reduction depends on the number of years of contributions made: 7.5% (30-34 years), 7% (35-37 years), 6.5% (38-39 years), and 6% (more than 40 years).
31. Increment depends on the number of years of contributions: 2% for fewer than 40 years and 3% with 40 years or more contributions.
32. The implicit adjustments are calculated from the annuity calculations using projected mortality rates for 2040, the 1.6% discount rate specified in legislation and indexation of pensions in payment to wage growth minus 1.6%. They also take account of the distribution of the account balances of people who die before claiming the pension using the same mortality rates.
33. Early retirement at 61 under the mandatory DC scheme (premium pension) and from 55 under quasi-mandatory DC occupational plans.
34. A full pension requires 44 years' contributions for men and 43 years' for women. For a full-career worker, approximately 2.3 percentage points of the 6.8% reduction for early retirement reflects a missing contribution year; the actuarial adjustment is the residual.
35. Early-retirement provisions vary between schemes: these are the legal minimum.
36. Individuals' accumulated rights are converted into an annuity at the time of retirement. The annuity rate at age 65 will fall to 6.8%. Each year of early retirement results in a reduction in the annuity rate of 0.2 percentage points. For late retirement, schemes are free to set their own rules but the government's guidance is to have the same 0.2 percentage point change in benefits for each year of late retirement.
37. A lump-sum payment of deferred pension plus interest can now also be claimed instead of a pension increment.
38. The reduction is 6.67% for the first 3 years of early retirement and 5% thereafter.

Source: Country profiles in Part III of this report.

StatLink http://dx.doi.org/10.1787/888932370816

Pensions at a Glance 2011
Retirement-income Systems in OECD and G20 Countries

PART II

Chapter 2

Pension Entitlements

Pension entitlements are calculated using the OECD pension models. The calculations are based on national parameters and rules applying in 2008. They relate to workers entering the labour market in that year, and so include the full impact of pension reforms that have already been legislated but are currently being phased in. A note on methodology and assumptions precedes the indicators. This report includes five new indicators of pension entitlements in addition to the nine presented in the last edition of Pensions at a Glance.

The indicators begin with the familiar replacement rate: the ratio of pension to individual earnings. The first looks at gross (before tax) replacement rates from all mandatory sources, including compulsory private pensions, for a single person. The second shows public and private schemes separately, including data on voluntary private pensions where these have broad coverage. There follows an analysis of the tax treatment of pensions and pensioners. The fourth and fifth indicators are replacement rates in net terms, taking account of taxes and contributions paid on earnings and pensions. The next indicator, new to this edition, shows benefits for married couples in both gross and net terms. The final element in this group is an exploration of investment risk, showing how different rates of return on private pension investments affect overall retirement incomes. Again, this indicator is new to this edition.

There follows two indicators of "pension wealth": the lifetime value of the flow of retirement benefits. This is a more comprehensive measure than replacement rates because it takes account of pension ages, indexation of pensions to changes in wages or prices and life expectancy.

The balance between two policy goals – providing adequate old-age incomes and replacing a target share of earnings – is explored in the next pair of indicators. They summarise the progressivity of pension benefit formulae and the link between pensions and earnings.

The final two indicators of entitlements average across individuals with different earnings levels, showing pension levels, pension wealth and the role of each part of the retirement-income system.

Introduction

The indicators of pension entitlements that follow here in Part II.2 and the analysis of pension "savings gaps" in Part II.6 use the OECD pension models. The methodology and assumptions are common to the analysis of all countries, allowing the design of pension systems to be compared directly. Future entitlements under today's parameter and rules.

The pension entitlements that are presented are those that are currently legislated in OECD countries. Changes in rules that have already been legislated, but are being phased-in gradually, are assumed to be fully in place from the start. Reforms that have been legislated since 2008 are included where sufficient information is available.

The values of all pension-system parameters reflect the situation in the year 2008. Where reforms have taken place more recently, parameters have been re-calculated for 2008 values assuming that the changed rules were already in place.

The calculations show the pension entitlements of a worker who enters the system today and retires after a full career. The main results are shown for a single person. However, replacement rates for married couples are also presented, though they are based on 2006 rules.

Career length

A full career is defined here as entering the labour market at age 20 and working until the standard pension-eligibility age, which, of course, varies between countries. The implication is that the length of career varies with the statutory retirement age: 40 years for retirement at 60, 45 with retirement age at 65, 47 with retirement at 67, etc. Age 20 is approximately the average age of labour-market entry in OECD countries, although obviously some countries lie above and below this average. (Sensitivity analysis for situations where workers entered the labour market at age 25 rather than age 20, and so had a five-year shorter career, were presented in the 2007 edition of *Pensions at a Glance*.)

Although the main indicators show people working until the normal pension age, Chapter 3 in Part I on "Pension incentives to retire" shows calculations for people retiring both before and after the normal pension age.

People often spend periods out of paid work in unemployment, full-time education, caring for children, disabled or elderly relatives, etc. However, most OECD countries have mechanisms in place to protect the pension entitlements for such periods. Rules for periods of unemployment and caring for children, which are often very complex, are set out in the country profiles in Part III of this report. The OECD pension models include these rules. For reasons of space, the results are not presented here.

Coverage

The pension models presented here include all mandatory pension schemes for private-sector workers, regardless of whether they are public (*i.e.* they involve payments from government or from social security institutions, as defined in the System of National Accounts) or private. For each country, the main national scheme for private-sector employees is modelled. Schemes for civil servants, public-sector workers and special professional groups are excluded.

Schemes with near-universal coverage are also included, provided that they cover at least 85% of employees. Such plans are called "quasi-mandatory" in this report. They are particularly significant in Denmark, the Netherlands and in Sweden.

An increasing number of OECD countries have broad coverage of voluntary, occupational pensions and these play an important role in providing retirement incomes. For these countries, a second set of results for replacement rates is shown with entitlements from these voluntary pension plans. There is also an analysis of pension "savings gaps": how much people in countries with relatively small public pensions would need to save for old age.

Resource-tested benefits for which retired people may be eligible are also modelled. These can be means-tested, where both assets and income are taken into account, purely income-tested or withdrawn only against pension income. The calculations assume that all entitled pensioners take up these benefits. Where there are broader means tests, taking account also of assets, the income test is taken as binding. It is assumed that the whole of income during retirement comes from the mandatory pension scheme (or from the mandatory plus voluntary pension schemes in those countries where the latter are modelled).

Pension entitlements are compared for workers with a range of different earnings levels: between 0.5 times and twice the economy-wide average. This range permits an analysis of future retirement benefits of both the poorest and richer workers.

Economic variables

The comparisons are based on a single set of economic assumptions for all the OECD countries and other major economies analysed. In practice, the level of pensions will be affected by economic growth, wage growth and inflation, and these will vary across countries. A single set of assumptions, however, ensures that the outcomes of the different pension regimes are not affected by different economic conditions. In this way, differences across countries in pension levels reflect differences in pension systems and policies alone. The baseline assumptions are set out below.

Price inflation is assumed to be 2.5% per year. In practice, this assumption has little effect on the results because of indexation.

Real earnings growth of 2% per year (given the assumption for price inflation, this implies nominal wage growth of 4.55%). ***Individual earnings*** are assumed to grow in line with the economy-wide average. This means that the individual is assumed to remain at the same point in the earnings distribution, earning the same percentage of average earnings in every year of the working life. ***Earnings distribution*** data from the *OECD Database* are used in some composite indicators: see the indicator of "Average earnings" in Part II.5).

The ***real rate of return*** after administrative charges on funded, defined-contribution pensions is assumed to be 3.5% per year.

The ***discount rate*** (for actuarial calculations) is assumed to be 2% per year. The discount rate is set at the same rate as real earnings growth, which is a common finding of growth models and other dynamic economic models (See Queisser and Whitehouse, 2006 for a discussion of the discount rate.)

The baseline modelling uses country-specific projections of ***mortality rate*** from the *United Nations Population Database for the Year 2050*.

Changes in these baseline assumptions will obviously affect the resulting pension entitlements. The impact of variations in economy-wide earnings growth, and for individual earnings growing faster or slower than the average, was shown in the first edition of *Pensions at a Glance* (OECD, 2005). The impact of different rates of return is assessed in the indicator on "Investment risk and replacement rates").

The calculations assume that benefits from defined-contribution plans are paid in the form of a price-indexed life annuity at an actuarially fair price. This is calculated from the mortality projections. If people withdraw the money in alternative ways, the capital sum at the time of retirement is the same: it is only the way that the benefits are spread that is changed. Similarly, the notional annuity rate in notional accounts schemes is (in most cases) calculated from mortality data using the indexation rules and discounting assumptions employed by the respective country.

Taxes and social security contributions

Information on personal income tax and social security contributions paid by pensioners, which were used to calculate pension entitlements, are available in the online country profiles from the website: *www.oecd.org/els/social/pensions/PAG*.

The modelling assumes that tax systems and social-security contributions remain unchanged in the future. This implicitly means that "value" parameters, such as tax allowances or contribution ceilings, are adjusted annually in line with average earnings, while "rate" parameters, such as the personal income tax schedule and social security contribution rates, remain unchanged.

General provisions and the tax treatment of workers for 2008 can be found in the OECD's *Taxing Wages* report. The conventions used in that report, such as which payments are considered taxes, are followed here.

References

D'Addio, A., J. Seisdedos and E.R. Whitehouse (2009), "Investment Risk and Pensions: Measuring Uncertainty in Returns", *Social, Employment and Migration Working Paper*, No. 70, OECD Publishing, Paris.

OECD (2009), *Taxing Wages*, OECD Publishing, Paris.

Queisser, M. and E.R. Whitehouse (2006), "Neutral or Fair? Actuarial Concepts and Pension-System Design", *OECD Social, Employment and Migration Working Paper*, No. 40, OECD Publishing, Paris.

Whitehouse, E.R., A.C. D'Addio and A.P. Reilly (2009), "Investment Risk and Pensions: Impact on Individual Retirement Incomes and Government Budgets", *Social, Employment and Migration Working Paper*, No. 87, OECD Publishing, Paris.

Key results

The gross replacement rate shows the level of pensions in retirement relative to earnings when working. For workers with average earnings, the gross replacement rate averages 57% in the 34 OECD countries. But there is significant cross-country variation. At the bottom of the range, Ireland, Japan, Mexico and the United Kingdom offer future replacement rates of less than 35% to people starting work today. Iceland and Greece, at the top of the range, offer replacement rates of more than 95%. Other countries with high projected replacement rates (between 70% and 90%) are Austria, Denmark, Hungary, Luxembourg, the Netherlands and Spain.

Most OECD countries protect low-income workers from old-age poverty by providing higher replacement rates for them than for average earners. For example, workers earning only half the average receive replacement rates averaging more than 72%, compared with 57% for average earners. However, replacement rates in seven countries are the same at average and half-average pay: Austria, Germany, Greece, Hungary, Italy, Poland, the Slovak Republic and Spain.

At the top of the range, there are three countries that provide low earners with pensions higher than their earnings when working: Iceland (replacement rate of 145%), Denmark (121%) and Israel (100%). At the other end of the scale, Germany and Japan offer replacement rates of 42% and 48%, respectively. Some countries, such as Canada and New Zealand, pay relatively small benefits to average earners, but are towards the middle of the range for low-income workers.

On average in the 34 OECD countries, the gross replacement rate at 1.5 times average earnings (here called "high earnings") is 52%, somewhat below the 57% figure for average earners. For high earners, country variations are again wide. Replacement rates exceed 80% in five countries: Greece, Iceland, Luxembourg, the Netherlands and Spain. At the other end of the spectrum, Ireland and New Zealand (which have flat-rate public pensions) and the United Kingdom offer replacement rates of less than 26%.

At median earnings – the level which half of workers lie above and half below – the average gross replacement for the 34 OECD countries is 60.6%. In general, it is little different from the gross replacement at average (mean) pay. (Median earnings are between 75% and 90% of the mean; see in Part II.5 the indicator on "Earnings: averages and distribution".)

Gross pension replacement rates for women differ (due to a lower pension eligibility age for women than for men) in five countries: Chile, Israel, Italy, Poland and Switzerland. Differences between the sexes are substantial in Chile, Italy and Poland, with replacement rates around one third smaller for women than they are for men. In Israel and Switzerland, replacement rates for women are also lower than they are for men, but much less than in three countries mentioned previously. The value for women is also lower in Australia and Mexico, but this is due to higher annuity rates rather than a difference in retirement age.

For the non-OECD countries there is a wide range in the replacement rate calculations, with South Africa and Indonesia below 15% and Saudi Arabia at 100% for average earners. The average for the EU27 is considerably higher than that of the OECD34 for average and high earners.

Definition and measurement

The old-age pension replacement rate measures how effectively a pension system provides a retirement income to replace earnings, the main source of income before retirement. The gross replacement rate is defined as gross pension entitlement divided by gross pre-retirement earnings.

Often, the replacement rate is expressed as the ratio of the pension to final earnings (just before retirement). Here, however, pension benefits are shown as a share of individual lifetime average earnings (revalued in line with economy-wide earnings growth). Under the baseline assumptions, workers earn the same percentage of economy-wide average earnings throughout their career. In this case, lifetime average revalued earnings and individual final earnings are identical. If people move up the earnings distribution as they get older, then their earnings just before retirement will be higher than they were on average over their lifetime and replacement rates calculated on individual final earnings would be lower.

Gross pension replacement rates by earnings

	Individual earnings, multiple of mean for men (women where different)			
	Median earner	0.5	1	1.5
OECD members				
Australia	52.6 (50.1)	73.3 (70.8)	47.3 (44.8)	38.6 (36.1)
Austria	76.6	76.6	76.6	72.3
Belgium	42.6	60.1	42.0	32.7
Canada	48.5	76.6	44.4	29.6
Chile	48.4 (37.5)	60.0 (49.2)	44.9 (34)	41.8 (28.9)
Czech Republic	57.3	80.2	50.2	37.4
Denmark	84.7	120.6	79.7	66.1
Estonia	50.9	60.2	48.0	44.0
Finland	57.8	66.4	57.8	57.8
France	49.1	55.9	49.1	41.3
Germany	42.0	42.0	42.0	42.0
Greece	95.7	95.7	95.7	95.7
Hungary	75.8	75.8	75.8	75.8
Iceland	109.1	144.9	96.9	87.0
Ireland	34.9	57.9	29.0	19.3
Israel	85.3 (75)	100.1 (89.9)	69.6 (61.2)	46.4 (40.8)
Italy	64.5 (50.6)	64.5 (50.6)	64.5 (50.6)	64.5 (50.6)
Japan	36.3	47.9	34.5	30.0
Korea	46.9	64.1	42.1	31.9
Luxembourg	90.3	97.9	87.4	83.8
Mexico	46.3 (46.3)	57.5 (57.5)	30.9 (28.7)	29.6 (26.4)
Netherlands	89.1	93.0	88.1	86.5
New Zealand	47.8	77.5	38.7	25.8
OECD members *(cont.)*				
Norway	52.9	63.4	53.1	41.7
Poland	59.0 (43.2)	59.0 (45.3)	59.0 (43.2)	59.0 (43.2)
Portugal	54.4	63.3	53.9	53.1
Slovak Republic	57.5	57.5	57.5	57.5
Slovenia	62.4	64.3	62.4	62.4
Spain	81.2	81.2	81.2	81.2
Sweden	53.8	68.3	53.8	68.7
Switzerland	59.3 (58.5)	65.2 (64.7)	57.9 (57.1)	40.9 (40.3)
Turkey	69.5	76.4	64.5	64.5
United Kingdom	37.0	53.8	31.9	22.6
United States	42.3	51.7	39.4	35.3
OECD34	**60.6**	**72.1**	**57.3**	**52.0**
Other major economies				
Argentina	81.1 (73.8)	90.7 (83.4)	78.1 (70.8)	73.9 (66.6)
Brazil	85.9	85.9	85.9	85.9
China	82.5 (65.1)	97.9 (78.5)	77.9 (61.0)	71.2 (55.2)
India	72.4 (68.4)	95.2 (90.9)	65.2 (61.4)	55.0 (51.4)
Indonesia	14.1 (12.4)	14.1 (12.4)	14.1 (12.4)	14.1 (12.4)
Russian Federation	65.1 (57.9)	73.0 (65.9)	62.7 (55.5)	59.2 (52.1)
Saudi Arabia	100.0 (87.5)	100.0 (87.5)	100.0 (87.5)	100.0 (87.5)
South Africa	13.1	21.2	10.6	7.1
EU27	62.9 (61.0)	70.1 (68.2)	61.6 (59.7)	58.3 (56.4)

Source: OECD pension models.

StatLink http://dx.doi.org/10.1787/888932370835

Gross pension replacement rates: Average earners

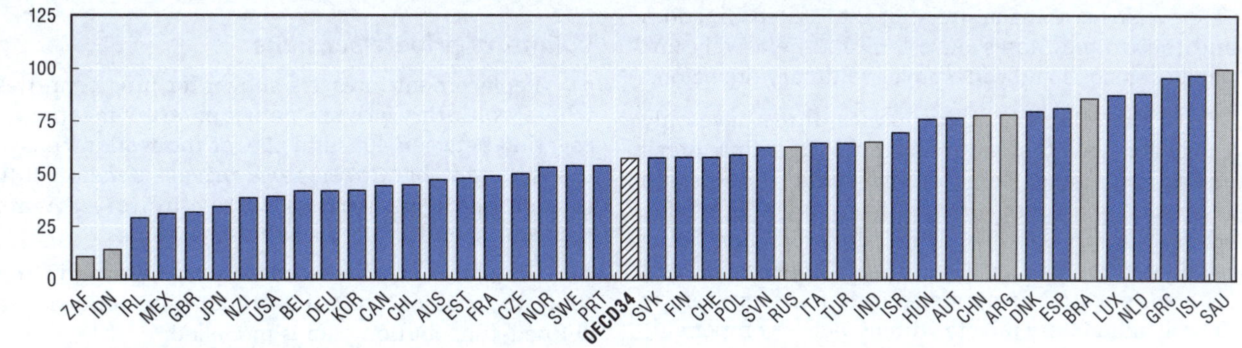

Source: OECD pension models.

StatLink http://dx.doi.org/10.1787/888932370835

Gross pension replacement rates: Low and high earners

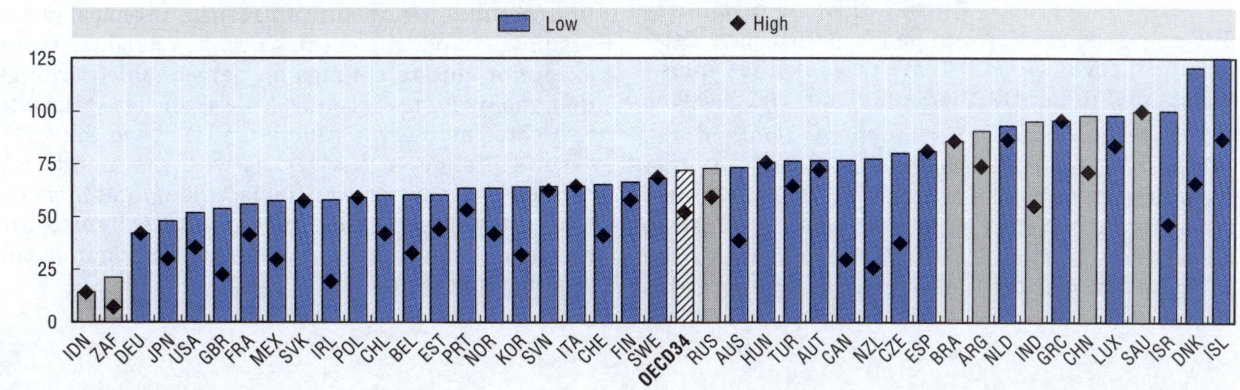

Source: OECD pension models.

StatLink http://dx.doi.org/10.1787/888932370835

Key results

Private pensions play a large and growing role in providing for old age. This is illustrated with calculations of gross pension replacement rates that have been separated out between public and private sectors. The OECD average for replacement rates of an average earner from public schemes alone is 42%, compared with 57% with mandatory private pensions included. When voluntary private pensions, under typical rules, are added, the average replacement rate is 64% for an average earner.

For the 12 OECD countries where the calculations of mandatory entitlements cover only public pensions, the replacement rate for an average earner is 64% on average. For the 14 OECD countries with data for public and mandatory private provision, the average replacement rate is 62%. For all 34 OECD countries, including public, mandatory private and voluntary private pensions, the average replacement rate is again 64%.

This shows substitution between different scheme types. Australia, Denmark, Iceland and Israel have highly targeted public programmes, so very low public replacement rates for middle and high earners are topped up with mandatory private pensions. In Chile, Hungary, Mexico, Poland, the Slovak Republic and Sweden, the substitution was direct: reforms replaced part of public provision with mandatory private pensions. Canada, Ireland, the United Kingdom and the United States have long had relatively low public pensions and widespread voluntary provision.

Of the other major economies, three have only public pensions that are mandatory: Argentina, Brazil and Saudi Arabia. Three others, India, the Russian Federation and South Africa all have voluntary private schemes, with South Africa's public pension being eliminated for average earners and above, because of its means-tested component. Indonesia's system is entirely mandatory private with no public component.

Mandatory private pensions

The first group of 14 countries has mandatory private pensions or private pensions that have near-universal coverage and so are described as "quasi-mandatory" (Denmark, the Netherlands and Sweden).

In Iceland, the Netherlands and Switzerland, private pensions are defined benefit while in other countries, they are defined contribution. Replacement rates from mandatory private schemes for average earners range from 22% to 32% in seven of the 14 countries. But they are significantly above this range in Denmark, Iceland, Israel and the Netherlands and much lower in Norway.

In seven countries, replacement rates are the same for workers earning between 50% and 150% of the economy-wide average. However, some countries have private pensions designed to cover earnings above the ceiling of the public scheme. This is the reason that replacement rates from private plans increase with earnings across the range in Chile, the Netherlands and Norway. It also explains why replacement rates for workers on 150% of average earnings are much higher in Sweden.

The pattern in Switzerland is complex. Again, low earners have a lower replacement rate to take account of public benefits. But the ceiling on earnings that must be covered by the occupational plans is relatively low.

Voluntary private pensions

Replacement rates are shown for nine countries where voluntary private pensions are widespread: covering between 40% and 65% of the workforce (see the indicator of "Coverage of private pension"). It is assumed that workers with voluntary private pensions spend a full career in the scheme.

The rules that have been modelled are in the "Country profiles" in Part III. In all nine countries, a defined-contribution plan is modelled.

In general, the defined-contribution schemes pay a constant replacement rate with earnings. (Data on actual contribution rates by earnings are not available for most countries, and so an average or typical rate is assumed across the earnings range.) Belgium is the exception due to ceilings on pensionable earnings that qualify for tax incentives. Germany also falls into this category but the ceiling is just above the 150% earnings range. In Norway, as with the mandatory defined-contribution plan, replacement rates increase with earnings because the private schemes are designed to offset some of the redistribution in public retirement benefits.

Gross pension replacement rates from public, mandatory private and voluntary private pension schemes

Percentage of individual earnings

	Public			Mandatory private			Voluntary DC			Total mandatory			Total with voluntary		
	0.5	1	1.5	0.5	1	1.5	0.5	1	1.5	0.5	1	1.5	0.5	1	1.5
OECD members															
Australia	37.9	11.8	3.2	35.4	35.4	35.4				73.3	47.3	38.6			
Austria	76.6	76.6	72.3							76.6	76.6	72.3			
Belgium	60.1	42.0	32.7				15.6	15.6	12.3	60.1	42.0	32.7	75.7	57.6	45.0
Canada	61.2	38.9	25.9				30.8	30.8	30.8	61.2	38.9	25.9	92.0	69.7	56.7
Chile	18.8	3.2	0.0	41.3	41.7	41.8				60.0	44.9	41.8			
Czech Republic	80.2	50.2	37.4				11.3	11.3	11.3	80.2	50.2	37.4	91.5	61.5	48.6
Denmark	64.7	28.9	17.0	55.9	50.7	49.0				120.6	79.7	66.1			
Estonia	37.7	25.5	21.5	22.5	22.5	22.5				60.2	48.0	44.0			
Finland	66.4	57.8	57.8							66.4	57.8	57.8			
France	55.9	49.1	41.3							55.9	49.1	41.3			
Germany	42.0	42.0	42.0				16.9	16.9	16.9	42.0	42.0	42.0	59.0	59.0	59.0
Greece	95.7	95.7	95.7							95.7	95.7	95.7			
Hungary	44.4	44.4	44.4	31.4	31.4	31.4				75.8	75.8	75.8			
Iceland	63.0	15.0	5.1	81.9	81.9	81.9				144.9	96.9	87.0			
Ireland	57.9	29.0	19.3				37.6	37.6	37.6	57.9	29.0	19.3	95.5	66.5	56.9
Israel	38.9	19.4	13.0	61.3	50.2	33.4				100.1	69.6	46.4			
Italy	64.5	64.5	64.5							64.5	64.5	64.5			
Japan	47.9	34.5	30.0							47.9	34.5	30.0			
Korea	64.1	42.1	31.9							64.1	42.1	31.9			
Luxembourg	97.9	87.4	83.8							97.9	87.4	83.8			
Mexico	30.5	4.0	2.7	26.9	26.9	26.9				57.5	30.9	29.6			
Netherlands	58.5	29.2	19.5	34.6	58.9	67.0				93.0	88.1	86.5			
New Zealand	77.5	38.7	25.8				14.6	14.6	14.6	77.5	38.7	25.8	92.1	53.4	40.5
Norway	57.7	46.1	34.2	5.7	7.0	7.5	8.6	12.0	17.1	63.4	53.1	41.7	72.0	65.0	58.8
Poland	28.7	28.7	28.7	30.2	30.2	30.2				59.0	59.0	59.0			
Portugal	63.3	53.9	53.1							63.3	53.9	53.1			
Slovak Republic	26.0	26.0	26.0	31.6	31.6	31.6				57.5	57.5	57.5			
Slovenia	64.3	62.4	62.4							64.3	62.4	62.4			
Spain	81.2	81.2	81.2							81.2	81.2	81.2			
Sweden	45.6	31.1	22.8	22.7	22.7	45.9				68.3	53.8	68.7			
Switzerland	52.3	34.5	23.7	12.8	23.4	17.1				65.2	57.9	40.9			
Turkey	76.4	64.5	64.5							76.4	64.5	64.5			
United Kingdom	53.8	31.9	22.6				36.7	36.7	36.7	53.8	31.9	22.6	90.5	68.6	59.3
United States	51.7	39.4	35.3				38.8	38.8	38.8	51.7	39.4	35.3	90.5	78.2	74.1
OECD34	**57.2**	**42.1**	**36.5**							**71.7**	**57.2**	**51.9**	**84.3**	**64.4**	**55.4**
Other major economies															
Argentina	90.7	78.1	73.9							90.7	78.1	73.9			
Brazil	85.9	85.9	85.9							85.9	85.9	85.9			
China	97.9	77.9	71.2							97.9	77.9	71.2			
India	95.2	65.2	55.0							95.2	65.2	55.0	95.2	65.2	55.0
Indonesia	14.1	14.1	14.1							14.1	14.1	14.1			
Russian Federation	35.0	35.0	35.0	17.3	17.3	17.3				52.3	52.3	52.3	35.0	35.0	35.0
Saudi Arabia	100.0	100.0	100.0							100.0	100.0	100.0			
South Africa	15.1	0.0	0.0				33.1	33.1	33.1	15.1	0.0	0.0	48.2	33.1	33.1
EU27	58.3	49.0	44.6							70.1	61.6	58.3			

DC = Defined contribution.

Source: OECD pension models.

StatLink http://dx.doi.org/10.1787/888932372355

Key results

The personal tax system plays an important role in old-age support. Pensioners often do not pay social security contributions. Personal income taxes are progressive and pension entitlements are usually lower than earnings before retirement, so the average tax rate on pension income is typically less than the tax rate on earned income. In addition, most income tax systems give preferential treatment either to pension incomes or to pensioners, by giving additional allowances or credits to older people.

Slightly more than half (18 out of 34) OECD countries provide older people with additional basic relief under the personal income tax. Generally, this takes the form of an extra tax allowance or tax credit. In many cases – Canada and the United Kingdom, for example – this additional relief is phased out for older people with higher incomes.

A significant number of countries offer tax relief for particular source of retirement income. Relief from income tax for public pensions, either full or partial, is available in 12 OECD countries. For example, between 15% and 50% of income from public pensions (social security) in the United States is not taxed, depending on the total income of the pensioner. Another four countries offer reliefs for private-pension income. In Australia, for example, benefits derived from pension contributions and investment returns that have been taxed are not taxable in payment for over 60s. (This therefore applies to the mandatory defined-contribution scheme and voluntary contributions to such plans.)

Overall, 24 OECD countries have some concession for older people or pension income under their personal income taxes. In only ten is the tax treatment of pensions and pensioners the same as it is for people of working age.

Virtually all OECD countries levy employee social security contributions on workers: Australia and New Zealand are the only exceptions. In addition to these two countries, a further 17 do not levy social security contributions on pensioners. The rate of contributions in the 15 countries that *do* levy social security contributions on retirees is always lower than the rate charged on workers. Typically, older people do not pay contributions for pensions or unemployment (for obvious reasons). However, pensioners can be subject to levies to pay for health or long-term care and, in some cases, are liable for "solidarity" contributions to finance a broad range of benefits.

Empirical results

The charts show the percentage of income paid in taxes and contribution by workers and pensioners.

Starting with pensioners, countries have been ranked by the proportion of income paid in tax at the replacement rate that an average earner would see in retirement (as set out in the indicator of "Gross pension replacement rates" above). In five OECD countries and five other major economies, such a pensioner would not pay an income tax in retirement. In some cases, such as the Slovak Republic and Turkey, this is because pensions are not taxable. In others, such as Ireland, it is because the pension income would be less than the basic income-tax reliefs offered to older people. Pensioners with the gross replacement rate for an average earner would pay 11.8% of their income in taxes and contributions.

The other two bars in the charts aim to show directly the impact of different tax and contribution treatment of earnings and pensions. The longer bar shows the amount of taxes and contributions paid by a worker with average earnings. This averages 26.4% in OECD countries and 12.8% in other major economies.

The middle bar shows how much a pensioner would pay with the same income: that is, a pension worth the same as average earnings. This averages 18.2% in OECD countries, some 8.2 percentage points less than workers pay with the same level of income.

The difference between this 18.2% rate for pensioners with an income equal to average earnings and the 11.8% paid in taxes and contributions paid on incomes equal to the gross replacement rate for an average earner illustrates the impact of progressivity in income-tax systems.

Reference

Keenay, G. and E.R. Whitehouse (2003), "The Role of the Personal Tax System in Old-age Support: A Survey of 15 Countries", *Fiscal Studies*, Vol. 24, No. 1, pp. 1-21.

Treatment of pensions and pensioners under personal income tax and social security contributions

	Extra tax	Full or partial relief for pension income		Social security contributions
	Allowance/ credit	Public scheme	Private scheme	Pensions
OECD members				
Australia	✓	✓	✓	*None*
Austria				*Low*
Belgium		✓		*Low*
Canada	✓	✓	✓	*None*
Chile	✓			*None*
Czech Republic	✓	✓		*None*
Denmark				*None*
Estonia	✓			*None*
Finland		✓		*Low*
France				*Low*
Germany		✓	✓	*Low*
Greece				*Low*
Hungary				*None*
Iceland				*None*
Ireland	✓			*Low*
Israel	✓			*Low*
Italy	✓		✓	*None*
Japan	✓			*Low*
Korea	✓	✓		*None*
Luxembourg	✓			*Low*
Mexico	✓			*None*
Netherlands	✓			*Low*
OECD members *(cont.)*				
New Zealand				*None*
Norway	✓	✓		*Low*
Poland				*Low*
Portugal	✓			*None*
Slovak Republic		✓		*None*
Slovenia	✓			*Low*
Spain		✓		*None*
Sweden				*None*
Switzerland				*Low*
Turkey		✓		*None*
United Kingdom	✓			*None*
United States	✓	✓		*None*
Other major economies				
Argentina		✓		*None*
Brazil		✓		*None*
China				
India	✓			*None*
Indonesia				*None*
Russian Federation				*Low*
Saudi Arabia				*Low*
South Africa	✓			*None*

Source: Online country profiles available at *www.oecd.org/els/social/pensions/PAG*.

StatLink http://dx.doi.org/10.1787/888932370854

Personal income taxes and social security contributions paid by pensioners and workers

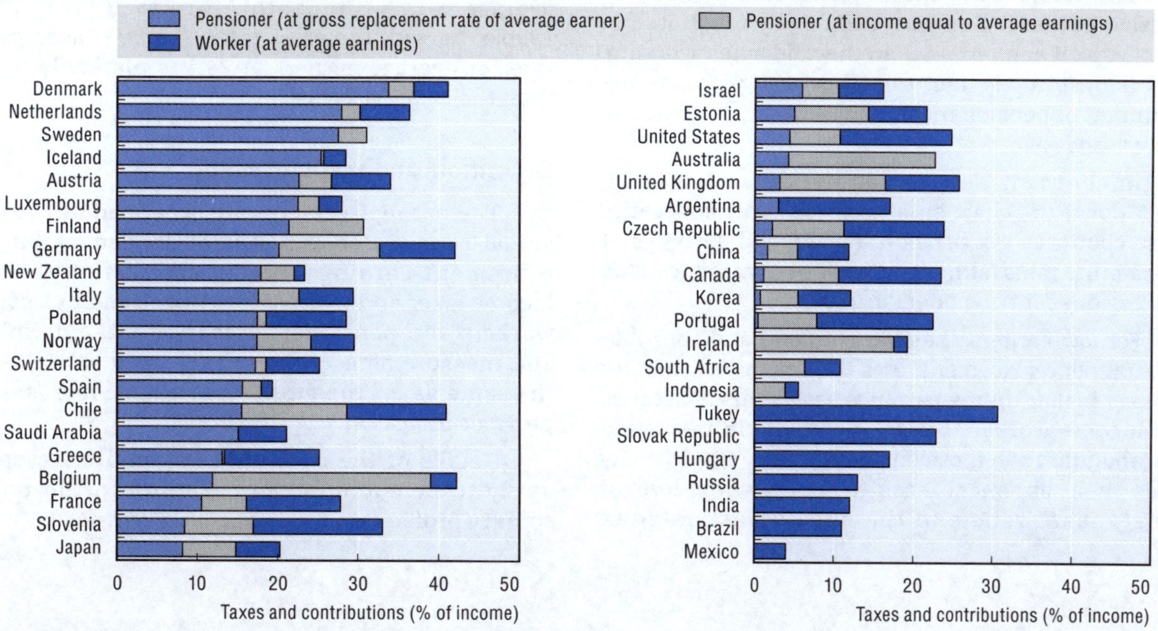

Source: OECD pension models; OECD tax and benefit models.

StatLink http://dx.doi.org/10.1787/888932370854

Key results

For average earners, the net replacement rate across OECD averages 69%, which is 12 percentage points higher than the gross replacement rate. This reflects the higher taxes and contributions that people paid on their earnings when working than they pay on their pensions in retirement. Net replacement rates again vary across a large range, from under 40% in Mexico, Ireland and Japan to well over 100% in Greece for average earners.

For low earners (with half of mean earnings), the average net replacement rate across OECD countries is 83%. For high earners (150% of mean earnings) the average net replacement rate is 63%, lower than for low earners. As with gross replacement rates, the differences with earnings reflect progressive features of pension systems, such as minimum benefits and ceilings on pensionable earnings.

The previous indicator of the "Tax treatment of pensions and pensioners" showed the important role that the personal tax and social security contribution systems play in old-age income support. Pensioners often do not pay social security contributions and receive preferential treatment under the income tax. Progressivity of income taxes coupled with gross replacement rates of less than 100% also mean that pensioners pay less in income tax than workers. As a result, net replacement rates are usually higher than gross replacement rates.

For average earners, the pattern of replacement rates across countries is different on a net rather than a gross basis. For example, the Belgian and German pension systems have considerably higher net replacement rates than gross. This is due, first, to favourable treatment of pension income under social security contributions. Secondly, because replacement rates are relatively low compared with OECD countries and personal income taxes are strongly progressive in these countries, people pay much less in income tax when retired than they did when working. This is despite the fact that the very generous tax treatment of pension income in Germany is gradually being withdrawn.

In contrast, New Zealand and Sweden move lower down the chart on a net basis. This is because these countries tax pension income and earnings at very similar rates (although Sweden re-introduced tax concessions for pensioners in 2009).

For low-earners, the effect of taxes and contributions on net replacement rates is more muted than for workers higher up the earnings scale. This is because low-income workers typically pay less in taxes and contributions than those on average earnings. In many cases, their retirement incomes are below the level of the standard reliefs in the personal income tax (allowances, credits, etc.). Thus, they are often unable to benefit fully from additional concessions granted to pensions or pensioners under the personal income tax.

The difference between gross and net replacement rates for low earners is 10 percentage points on average. Belgium and Slovenia have much higher replacement rates for low earners measure on a net basis than in gross terms.

The net replacement rate for workers earning 150% of the average is highest in Greece. Not surprisingly, the lowest replacement rates are found in the flat-rate pension systems of New Zealand and Ireland. In both countries, workers earning 150% of the average will receive pensions that amount to less than a third of their net earnings when working.

For non-OECD countries, there is very little variation in net replacement rates within countries across the earnings range. However, there is considerable difference between countries, ranging from 12% for average earners in South Africa to 108% in Saudi Arabia. As with the gross rates, the EU27 average net rate for average earners at 74% is markedly higher than the OECD34 figure.

Definition and measurement

The net replacement rate is defined as the individual net pension entitlement divided by net pre-retirement earnings, taking account of personal income taxes and social security contributions paid by workers and pensioners. Otherwise, the definition and measurement of the net replacement rates are the same as for the gross replacement rate (see the previous indicator).

Details of the rules that national tax systems apply to pensioners can be found in the online country profiles at *www.oecd.org/els/pensions/PAG*.

Net pension replacement rates by earnings

	Individual earnings, multiple of mean for men (women where different)					Individual earnings, multiple of mean for men (women where different)			
	Median earner	0.5	1	1.5		Median earner	0.5	1	1.5
OECD members					**OECD members** *(cont.)*				
Australia	65.9 (63.2)	82.5 (79.7)	58.9 (56.9)	47.1 (45.3)	Norway	62.3	81.7	62.2	51.4
Austria	89.9	91.3	89.9	84.6	Poland	68.2 (50.7)	68.1 (53.4)	68.2 (50.6)	68.3 (50.4)
Belgium	66.0	81.8	64.1	52.0	Portugal	65.5	73.4	69.2	70.5
Canada	61.5	88.7	57.3	39.7	Slovak Republic	72.9	68.3	74.5	76.7
Chile	66.0 (52.4)	74.4 (61.7)	64.3 (49.9)	62.7 (46.3)	Slovenia	90.2	82.5	85.4	86.2
Czech Republic	72.5	94.0	64.4	48.9	Spain	84.5	82.3	84.9	85.4
Denmark	94.5	131.9	89.8	80.8	Sweden	53.3	67.0	53.6	72.6
Estonia	63.1	73.4	58.3	51.4	Switzerland	66.4 (65.5)	78.6 (78.1)	64.1 (63.2)	46.2 (45.5)
Finland	64.8	72.0	65.2	64.4	Turkey	98.0	107.3	93.1	96.0
France	60.8	69.4	60.4	53.1	United Kingdom	48.0	67.5	41.5	30.5
Germany	58.4	55.6	57.9	57.2	United States	53.4	63.8	50.0	46.6
Greece	110.3	113.6	111.2	106.8	**OECD34**	**72.0**	**82.8**	**68.8**	**63.4**
Hungary	99.5	96.3	106.0	103.2					
Iceland	111.7	139.0	101.1	91.7	**Other major economies**				
Ireland	40.8	60.8	35.8	26.8	Argentina	94.7 (86.2)	106.0 (97.5)	91.3 (82.8)	87.8 (79.1)
Israel	92.2 (82.3)	103.0 (93.6)	78.2 (69.8)	56.7 (50.6)	Brazil	96.6	96.6	96.6	98.9
Italy	76.2 (63)	78.2 (63.4)	75.3 (62.1)	76.7 (62.1)	China	90.6 (71.5)	106.4 (85.3)	86.8 (69.2)	80.1 (64.7)
Japan	41.4	52.7	39.7	34.9	India	82.3 (77.8)	108.2 (103.3)	74.1 (69.8)	63.9 (58.8)
Korea	51.8	69.8	47.5	37.3	Indonesia	14.8 (13.1)	14.7 (13)	14.9 (13.2)	14.9 (13.2)
Luxembourg	96.2	103.1	94.0	90.9	Russian Federation	74.8 (66.6)	83.9 (75.7)	72.0 (63.8)	68.0 (59.8)
Mexico	46.9 (46.9)	58.2 (58.2)	32.2 (29.9)	33.3 (29.7)	Saudi Arabia	107.4 (95.1)	107.2 (94.8)	107.6 (95.2)	108.0 (95.7)
Netherlands	103.3	104.5	99.8	96.4	South Africa	14.4	22.0	11.9	8.3
New Zealand	49.6	79.4	41.5	29.4	EU27	75.7 (73.6)	81.8 (79.7)	74.2 (72.1)	70.6 (68.4)

Source: OECD pension models.

StatLink http://dx.doi.org/10.1787/888932370873

Net pension replacement rates: Average earners

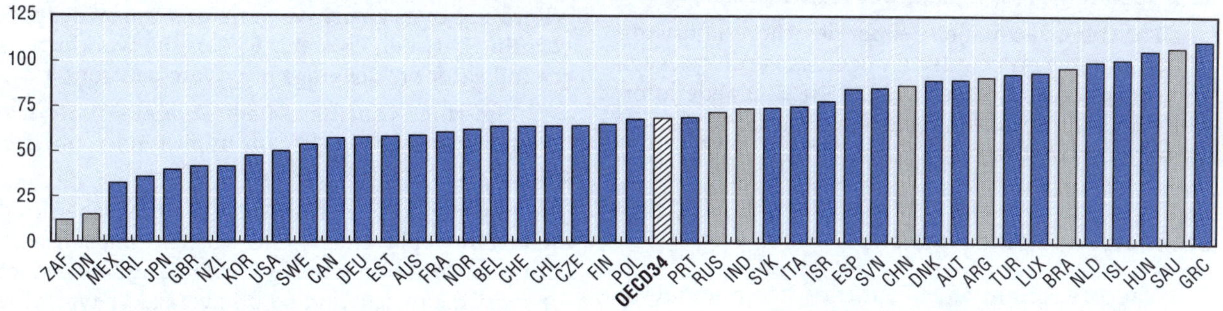

Source: OECD pension models.

StatLink http://dx.doi.org/10.1787/888932370873

Net pension replacement rates: Low and high earners

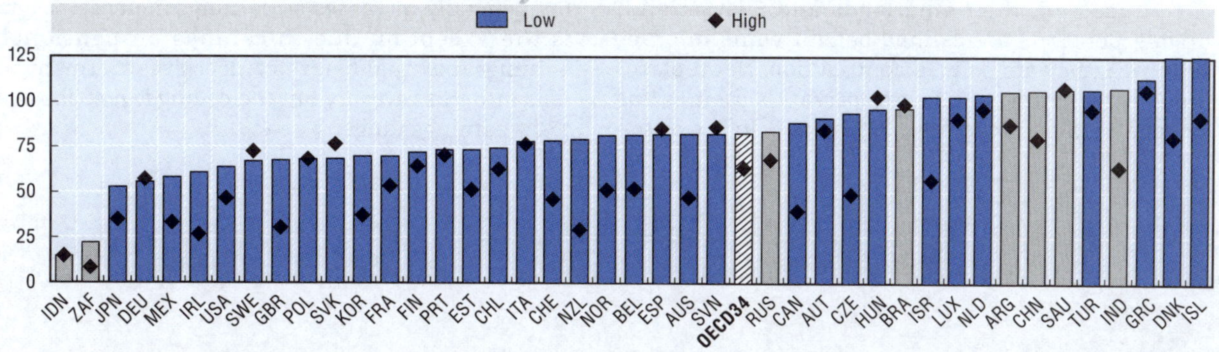

Source: OECD pension models.

StatLink http://dx.doi.org/10.1787/888932370873

Key results

The OECD average for net replacement rates of an average earner from public schemes alone is 50%, compared with 68% with mandatory private pensions included. When voluntary private pensions, under typical rules, are added, the average net replacement rate is 77% for an average earner.

The personal tax system plays an important role in old-age support. Pensioners often do not pay social security contributions and, as personal income taxes are progressive and pension entitlements are usually lower than earnings before retirement, the average tax rate on pension income is typically less than the tax rate on earned income. In addition, most income tax systems give preferential treatment either to pension incomes or to pensioners, by giving additional allowances or credits to older people. Therefore, net replacement rates are usually higher than gross replacement rates.

For the 12 OECD countries where the calculations cover only public pensions, the replacement rate for an average earner is 76% on average. For the 14 OECD countries with data for public and mandatory private provision, the average replacement rate is 72%. For all 34 OECD countries, including public, mandatory private and voluntary private pensions, the average replacement rate is 75%. Overall net replacement rates are between 10% and 12% higher than the corresponding gross replacement rate figures.

For the other major economies there is a wide variation between country and across earnings level. The exception to the latter is the Russian Federation which has identical net replacement rates across all the earnings ranges.

Mandatory private pensions

The first group of 14 countries has mandatory private pensions or private pensions that have near-universal coverage and so are described as "quasi-mandatory" (Denmark, the Netherlands and Sweden).

In Iceland, the Netherlands and Switzerland, private pensions are defined benefit while in other countries, they are defined contribution. Net replacement rates from mandatory private schemes for average earners range from 23% to 41% in six of the 14 countries. But they are significantly above this range in Chile, Denmark, Iceland, Israel and the Netherlands and much lower in Norway.

Between the combination of some countries having private pensions designed to cover earnings above the ceiling of the public scheme and the tax system in place no country has the same replacement rate across the earnings levels. This is the reason that replacement rates from private plans increase with earnings across the range in Chile, Iceland, Mexico, the Netherlands, Norway and the Slovak Republic. It also explains why replacement rates for workers on 150% of average earnings are much higher in Sweden.

The pattern in Switzerland is complex. Again, low earners have a lower replacement rate to take account of public benefits. But the ceiling on earnings that must be covered by the occupational plans is relatively low.

Voluntary private pensions

Replacement rates are shown for nine countries where voluntary private pensions are widespread: covering between 40% and 65% of the workforce (see the indicator of "Coverage of private pensions").

The rules that have been modelled are in the "Country profiles" in Part III. In all nine countries, a defined-contribution plan is modelled.

In general, the defined-contribution schemes pay a constant replacement rate with earnings. (Data on actual contribution rates by earnings are not available for most countries, and so an average or typical rate is assumed across the earnings range.) However the difference in taxation rules means that the net replacement rate differs across the earnings range, but generally increases as earnings increase. Belgium is the exception due to ceilings on pensionable earnings that qualify for tax incentives. Germany also falls into this category but the ceiling is just above the 150% earnings range.

Net pension replacement rates from public, mandatory private and voluntary private pension schemes

Percentage of individual earnings

	Public			Mandatory private			Voluntary DC			Total mandatory			Total with voluntary		
	0.5	1	1.5	0.5	1	1.5	0.5	1	1.5	0.5	1	1.5	0.5	1	1.5
OECD members															
Australia	42.6	14.8	3.9	39.9	44.1	43.2				82.5	58.9	47.1			
Austria	91.3	89.9	84.6							91.3	89.9	84.6			
Belgium	74.9	52.1	42.5				19.4	19.3	15.9	74.9	52.1	42.5	94.3	71.4	58.4
Canada	70.9	50.4	35.0				35.7	39.9	41.5	70.9	50.4	35.0	106.6	90.3	76.5
Chile	23.2	4.6	0.0	51.1	59.7	62.7				74.4	64.3	62.7			
Czech Republic	93.5	62.2	47.0				13.1	13.9	14.2	93.5	62.2	47.0	106.7	76.1	61.1
Denmark	70.8	32.6	20.8	61.1	57.2	60.0				131.9	89.8	80.8			
Estonia	46.0	31.0	25.1	27.5	27.3	26.3				73.4	58.3	51.4			
Finland	72.0	65.2	64.4							72.0	65.2	64.4			
France	69.4	60.4	53.1							69.4	60.4	53.1			
Germany	54.8	56.0	55.6				22.1	22.6	22.4	54.8	56.0	55.6	76.9	78.6	78.0
Greece	113.6	111.2	106.8							113.6	111.2	106.8			
Hungary	56.4	62.1	60.5	39.9	43.9	42.8				96.3	106.0	103.2			
Iceland	60.5	15.7	5.3	78.6	85.4	86.3				139.0	101.1	91.7			
Ireland	60.8	31.3	22.5				39.5	40.7	43.8	60.8	31.3	22.5	100.3	72.0	66.4
Israel	40.0	21.9	15.8	63.0	56.4	40.9				103.0	78.2	56.7			
Italy	72.0	71.7	71.8							72.0	71.7	71.8			
Japan	52.7	39.7	34.9							52.7	39.7	34.9			
Korea	69.8	47.5	37.3							69.8	47.5	37.3			
Luxembourg	103.1	94.0	90.9							103.1	94.0	90.9			
Mexico	30.9	4.2	3.0	27.3	28.0	30.3				58.2	32.2	33.3			
Netherlands	65.6	33.1	21.7	38.8	66.7	74.7				104.5	99.8	96.4			
New Zealand	78.9	41.1	29.0				14.9	15.5	16.4	78.9	41.1	29.0	93.9	56.6	45.4
Norway	66.3	52.4	40.4	6.6	8.0	8.8	9.8	13.6	20.2	72.9	60.3	49.2	82.7	74.0	69.5
Poland	33.2	33.2	33.3	34.9	35.0	35.0				68.1	68.2	68.3			
Portugal	73.4	69.2	70.5							73.4	69.2	70.5			
Slovak Republic	30.8	33.6	34.6	37.4	40.9	42.1				68.3	74.5	76.7			
Slovenia	82.5	85.4	86.2							82.5	85.4	86.2			
Spain	82.3	84.9	85.4							82.3	84.9	85.4			
Sweden	44.8	31.0	24.1	22.3	22.6	48.5				67.0	53.6	72.6			
Switzerland	63.2	38.2	26.8	15.5	25.9	19.4				78.6	64.1	46.2			
Turkey	107.3	93.1	96.0							107.3	93.1	96.0			
United Kingdom	62.0	37.4	26.8				42.3	43.1	43.6	62.0	37.4	26.8	104.3	80.5	70.3
United States	61.0	47.3	44.1				45.8	46.6	48.4	61.0	47.3	44.1	106.8	93.9	92.5
OECD34	**65.3**	**50.0**	**44.1**							**81.3**	**67.6**	**62.4**	**96.9**	**77.0**	**68.7**
Other major economies															
Argentina	106.0	91.3	87.8							106.0	91.3	87.8			
Brazil	96.6	96.6	98.9							96.6	96.6	98.9			
China	106.4	86.8	80.1							106.4	86.8	80.1			
India	108.2	74.1	63.9							108.2	74.1	63.9	108.2	74.1	63.9
Indonesia	14.7	14.9	14.9							14.7	14.9	14.9			
Russian Federation	40.2	40.2	40.2	19.9	19.9	19.9				60.1	60.1	60.1	40.2	40.2	40.2
Saudi Arabia	107.2	107.6	108.0							107.2	107.6	108.0			
South Africa	15.7	0.0	0.0				34.3	37.1	39.0	15.7	0.0	0.0	50.0	37.1	39.0
EU27	67.2	58.1	53.2							81.1	73.2	69.6			

DC: Defined contribution.

Source: OECD pension models.

StatLink http://dx.doi.org/10.1787/888932372374

Key results

Most of the indicators of pension entitlements in this report are based on analysis of a single person. In many countries, pension systems are effectively "individualised": the position of a married couples is the same as that of two single people with the same level of earnings. In others, however, marriage has an effect on pension entitlements.

There are two ways in which marital status affects pension entitlements. First, some systems offer "derived" rights: these are benefits for the couple that derive from the working experience and contributions of one spouse. Secondly, some retirement benefits, especially resource-tested and basic ones, are assessed using the couple as a "pension unit" rather than treating each individual separately.

The table shows calculations of pension entitlements for five different family types. In the first three, total earnings are held constant at 100% of the economy-wide average. A single person with these earnings is compared, first, with a single-earner couple and, secondly, a two-earner couple where both partners have the same level of earnings. The other two cases compare a single person with earnings of 150% of the average with a couple consisting of two earners, with pay of 100% and 50% of average earnings.

The calculations are shown using 2006 parameters and rules of pensions systems. This is because it has not been possible yet for national officials to validate the results for couples using 2008 parameters and rules (as used in the rest of this report).

Most OECD countries provide a higher gross replacement rate for one-earner couples as opposed to a single earner. The exceptions are Austria, Germany, Italy, Luxembourg, Spain and Turkey.

There is significant variation between countries in terms of the policy adopted for non-workers within a couple. In some countries, benefits are higher for couples than single people because of basic schemes that pay a higher rate to a couple than a single person (although less than the entitlement of two single people) In the Netherlands, for example, entitlement to the basic pension is effectively dependent only on residence in the country.

In Ireland and the United Kingdom, there are spousal benefits in the basic pension for partners in a couple who do not earn a full basic pension entitlement in their own right. In France there are spousal supplements for the public pension.

In Japan and the United States, there are spousal benefits in the public, earnings-related schemes. Again, these higher benefits are paid to couples where one partner has not earned a large entitlement in his or her own right.

Resource-tested schemes explain why Denmark has higher benefits for one-earner couples than for single people with average earnings. Even at average earnings, both would be eligible for resource-tested benefits. Similarly, in Belgium, Finland and Sweden, a single person on average earnings would not be entitled to a minimum pension. However, a couple with one partner earning the economy-wide average would receive a top-up from minimum pensions.

For those countries with higher replacement rates the difference is lowest in Korea and France at 3.1% and 3.2% respectively, whereas in Ireland and the Netherlands the increase is over 30 percentage points.

Pension entitlements for one-earner couples in Mexico, Poland and the Slovak Republic are *lower* than for single people with the same level of earnings. One-earner couples. This is because the annuity calculation for private pensions results in a lower benefit for couples due to longer life expectancy of a couple compared with a single person.

At higher levels of pay – namely a single person with 150% of average earnings in comparison to a couple with the principal at average earnings and the spouse at 50% average earnings – the results can be affected by ceilings on pensionable earnings. For example in Germany the ceiling on contributions is just under the 150% level, explaining the lower gross replacement rate for the single scenario. The same applies for Austria, which like Germany, has a constant gross replacement rate at all earnings levels below the contribution ceiling.

Definition and measurement

Details of parameters and rules of the treatment of couples will be published in 2011 in an OECD report on "Women and pensions".

Pension replacement rates by earnings, single people and couples, 2006 parameters and rules

	Gross replacement rate (percentage of total gross earnings)					Net replacement rate (percentage of total net earnings)				
Principal's earnings (percentage of average earnings)	100	100	50	100	150	100	100	50	100	150
Partner's earnings (percentage of average earnings)	n.a.	0	50	50	n.a.	n.a.	0	50	50	n.a.
Australia	41.6	57.5	57.5	43.3	33.1	53.1	74.5	68.9	50.8	41.8
Austria	80.1	80.1	80.1	80.1	76.4	90.3	90.3	90.5	90.3	86.3
Belgium	42.0	52.1	58.1	47.4	32.5	63.7	66.9	78.7	63.7	51.7
Canada	44.5	53.7	53.8	44.1	29.7	57.9	70.0	62.6	51.1	40.0
Czech Republic	49.7	57.3	79.2	59.6	36.4	64.1	73.8	95.3	64.1	49.4
Denmark	80.3	97.4	100.9	78.1	67.5	91.3	116.8	114.2	80.8	82.7
Finland	56.2	61.3	61.3	56.2	56.2	62.4	77.0	73.1	62.4	63.8
France	53.1	56.3	60.8	56.5	48.2	65.4	74.9	75.0	66.7	59.9
Germany	43.0	43.0	43.0	43.0	42.6	61.3	75.5	59.2	61.3	60.3
Greece	95.7	115.7	115.7	115.7	95.7	110.8	127.7	133.6	127.7	106.7
Hungary	76.9	80.2	80.4	80.2	76.9	105.5	108.0	97.8	108.0	99.2
Iceland	90.2	114.0	108.3	96.3	87.5	95.1	128.8	110.1	95.1	92.1
Ireland	34.2	64.4	68.4	45.6	22.8	40.1	75.5	68.4	40.1	30.3
Italy	67.9	67.9	64.2	65.4	67.9	74.8	73.7	74.8	74.8	77.1
Japan	33.9	52.1	47.1	38.3	29.4	38.7	57.9	51.4	38.7	33.9
Korea	42.1	45.2	66.6	51.9	33.6	46.6	50.0	71.4	49.3	38.7
Luxembourg	88.1	88.1	99.4	91.9	84.3	96.5	110.4	107.1	96.5	93.5
Mexico	36.1	29.3	55.3	37.9	34.5	38.0	30.8	56.0	30.8	39.6
Netherlands	88.3	118.6	93.4	90.0	86.6	103.2	146.7	105.0	103.2	98.6
New Zealand	38.7	58.8	58.8	39.2	25.8	41.1	63.2	61.0	31.6	29.0
Norway	59.3	62.9	55.4	51.5	49.8	69.3	88.7	71.3	59.8	60.6
Poland	61.2	60.4	60.4	60.4	61.2	74.9	73.9	73.5	73.9	75.0
Portugal	53.9	53.9	54.8	54.2	53.1	69.6	69.6	63.7	69.6	72.0
Slovak Republic	56.4	55.7	55.7	55.7	56.4	72.7	71.8	65.5	71.8	74.9
Spain	81.2	81.2	81.2	81.2	81.2	84.7	91.7	82.1	84.7	85.3
Sweden	61.5	82.1	70.3	62.6	75.6	64.1	88.0	73.4	61.6	81.2
Switzerland	58.3	76.1	67.8	59.7	40.5	64.5	101.0	79.9	64.5	44.3
Turkey	86.9	86.9	86.9	86.9	86.9	124.7	124.7	124.7	124.7	127.1
United Kingdom	30.8	39.1	50.0	37.2	21.3	40.9	52.3	62.7	40.9	29.2
United States	38.7	57.3	49.8	42.1	34.1	44.8	73.9	57.3	44.2	39.5
OECD30	**59.0**	**68.3**	**69.5**	**61.7**	**54.3**	**70.3**	**84.3**	**80.3**	**69.4**	**65.5**

Source: OECD pension models.

StatLink http://dx.doi.org/10.1787/888932372393

Key results

The financial and economic crisis of 2008 has meant that investment risk has been at the forefront of policy makers minds when thinking about pensions. Private pension funds in OECD countries lost 24% of their value on average, worth USD 5.4 trillion. However, it is important to bear in mind that private pensions are only a part of the overall retirement-income package: a major part of retirement income is generally not affected by investment risk. In some countries, means-tested pensions protect low-income workers from much investment risk and the tax system can also act as an "automatic stabiliser" of retirement incomes.

Measuring investment risk

The scale of investment risk has been analysed using historical data for eight OECD countries: Canada, France, Germany, Italy, Japan, Sweden, the United Kingdom and the United States. Detailed econometric results were then used to simulate a distribution of outcomes and probabilities for a 40-year investment horizon. The two main assets in pension-fund portfolios were analysed: equities and government bonds. The results for a portfolio split equally between these two assets are shown in the table below.

The raw results of the exercise give higher returns than those shown in the table. These were adjusted downwards to reflect, among other things, administrative charges (on which see Part II.6 the indicator of "Pension fund operating costs and fees").

The degree of investment risk: Implications for pensions

Distribution of returns, percentile point (%)	10	25	50	75	90
Annual real return (%)	2.5	3.3	4.3	5.3	6.0
Replacement rate (%)	26.9	31.9	39.9	50.5	60.0

Note: Portfolio of 50% domestic equities and 50% domestic government bonds. Replacement-rate calculation assumes 10% contribution rate and OECD average mortality rates.

Source: OECD pension models; D'Addio, A.C., J. Seisdedos and E.R. Whitehouse (2009), "Investment Risk and Pensions: Measuring Uncertainty in Returns", *Social, Employment and Migration Working Paper*, No. 70, OECD Publishing, Paris.

The table above shows that 50% of the time, investment returns will be higher or lower than 4.3% a year in real terms. This is higher than the baseline assumption of 3.5% of this report. Some 10% of the time, the real return is expected to be less than 2.5% or more than 6.0%. The table shows that these returns generate a large range of replacement rates, ranging from 27% in the worst cases to 60% in the best.

Investment risk in practice

The table opposite shows gross and net replacement rates with low, middle and high returns: the 10th, 50th and 90th percentile of the distribution of returns respectively. On the left-hand side of the table there are 10 countries where defined-contribution plans are mandatory. The nine countries on the right-hand side have broad coverage of voluntary private plans (see the indicator of "Coverage of private pensions").

The way investment risk affects retirement incomes depends crucially on the structure of the retirement-income package. First, many benefits – from public earnings-related schemes or basic pensions – are unaffected by investment returns. In Hungary, for example, the defined-contribution pension in the best scenario is worth 2.6 times its value in the worst (also see chart). However, the overall benefit varies only by a factor of 1.5 times.

Secondly, means-tested benefits can offset some of the investment risk: a smaller defined-contribution pension results in higher benefits from targeted programmes. In Australia, for example, the defined-contribution pension is 2.4 times higher in the best rather than worst scenario for returns. Overall income, including means-tested benefit, varies by a factor of just 1.6. Means-tested benefits also play an important role in Denmark.

The final stabiliser of retirement incomes in the face of investment risk is the tax system. Because marginal tax rates are generally higher than average rates (*i.e.* personal income taxes are progressive), a fall in income from defined-contribution pensions results in a more than proportionate reduction in tax liability. The effect is strongest in Denmark. Before taxes, the ratio of total pension in the best and worst cases is 1.8 compared with 1.5 after taxes are taken into account. The impact of taxes is also noticeable in Poland, but pensions in Hungary are not taxed and so there is no automatic stabiliser of retirement incomes.

Gross and net pension replacement rates with different rates of investment return

Mandatory or quasi-mandatory defined-contribution plans

		Gross replacement rate (%)			Net replacement rate (%)		
Percentile of rate of return		10	50	90	10	50	90
Annual real return (%)		2.5	4.3	6.0	2.5	4.3	6.0
Australia	DC	28.2	43.0	67.0	36.4	51.6	72.4
	Other	14.7	8.8	0.0	19.0	10.6	0.0
	Total	43.0	51.8	67.0	55.4	62.2	72.4
Chile	DC	32.6	51.2	82.2	47.4	71.6	104.1
	Other	5.9	0.4	0.0	8.5	0.5	0.0
	Total	38.5	51.6	82.2	55.9	72.1	104.1
Denmark	DC	39.4	63.0	103.2	45.0	69.6	102.8
	Other	30.6	27.1	21.1	35.0	29.9	21.0
	Total	70.0	90.1	124.3	80.0	99.5	123.7
Estonia	DC	17.9	27.4	42.7	22.2	32.6	48.9
	Other	25.5	25.5	25.5	31.6	30.4	29.2
	Total	43.4	52.9	68.3	53.8	63.1	78.1
Hungary	DC	24.7	38.6	61.7	35.3	52.2	77.3
	Other	44.4	44.4	44.4	63.6	60.2	55.7
	Total	69.1	83.0	106.1	99.0	112.4	133.0
Israel	DC	38.9	62.2	102.0	44.7	68.8	105.5
	Other	19.4	19.4	19.4	22.3	21.5	20.1
	Total	58.4	81.7	121.5	67.0	90.3	125.6
Mexico	DC	24.4	37.9	60.2	25.4	39.4	62.7
	Other	4.3	0.0	0.0	4.5	0.0	0.0
	Total	28.7	37.9	60.2	29.9	39.4	62.7
Poland	DC	23.8	37.1	59.4	27.6	42.8	67.9
	Other	28.7	28.7	28.7	33.4	33.1	32.8
	Total	52.5	65.9	88.2	61.0	75.9	100.8
Slovak Republic	DC	25.2	38.2	58.9	32.7	49.4	76.2
	Other	26.0	26.0	26.0	33.6	33.6	33.6
	Total	51.2	64.1	84.8	66.3	83.1	109.9
Sweden	DC	18.1	27.4	42.2	18.2	27.1	40.9
	Other	31.1	31.1	31.1	31.3	30.8	30.2
	Total	49.3	58.5	73.4	49.5	57.8	71.1

Voluntary or mainly voluntary defined-contribution

		Gross replacement rate (%)			Net replacement rate (%)		
Percentile of rate of return		10	50	90	10	50	90
Annual real return (%)		2.5	4.3	6.0	2.5	4.3	6.0
Belgium	DC	12.2	19.1	30.6	15.5	23.3	35.2
	Other	42.0	42.0	42.0	53.3	51.2	48.3
	Total	54.3	61.2	72.6	68.8	74.5	83.5
Canada	DC	24.2	37.8	60.5	31.3	49.0	78.5
	Other	38.9	38.9	38.9	50.3	50.4	50.5
	Total	63.0	76.7	99.3	81.6	99.4	129.0
Czech Republic	DC	8.8	13.8	22.1	11.0	17.0	26.8
	Other	50.2	50.2	50.2	62.6	61.8	60.7
	Total	59.1	64.1	72.4	73.6	78.8	87.5
Germany	DC	13.1	21.0	34.5	17.6	27.8	44.7
	Other	42.0	42.0	42.0	56.4	55.7	54.5
	Total	55.2	63.0	76.5	74.0	83.5	99.2
Ireland	DC	29.5	46.1	73.8	34.1	48.5	72.9
	Other	29.0	29.0	29.0	33.5	30.5	28.6
	Total	58.5	75.1	102.8	67.6	79.0	101.5
New Zealand	DC	11.5	18.0	28.8	12.2	19.0	30.3
	Other	38.7	38.7	38.7	41.1	41.0	40.8
	Total	50.2	56.7	67.5	53.3	60.0	71.1
Norway	DC	9.3	14.8	24.3	10.7	16.7	26.8
	Other	51.5	54.8	60.3	59.1	61.7	66.4
	Total	60.8	69.6	84.7	69.8	78.4	93.2
United Kingdom	DC	28.3	45.8	76.0	33.9	52.5	85.2
	Other	31.9	31.9	31.9	38.1	36.6	35.7
	Total	60.3	77.7	107.9	72.0	89.1	120.9
United States	DC	30.1	48.1	78.9	36.4	57.4	91.4
	Other	39.4	39.4	39.4	47.7	47.0	45.7
	Total	69.5	87.5	118.3	84.1	104.4	137.1

Source: OECD pension models; see also Whitehouse, D'Addio and Reilly (2009).

StatLink http://dx.doi.org/10.1787/888932370892

Gross pension replacement rate and taxes and contributions paid on pensions with different rates of investment return

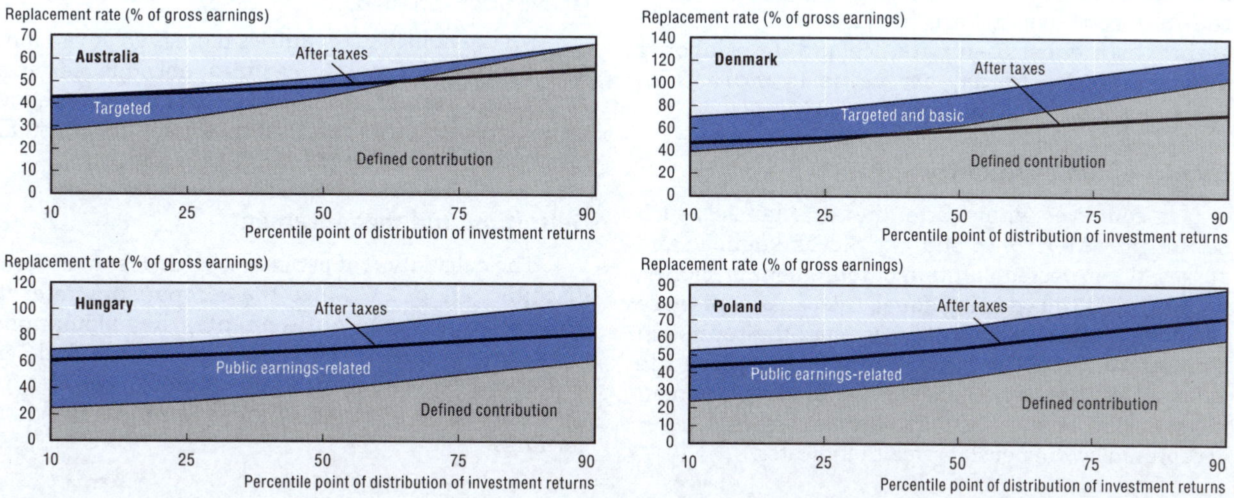

Source: OECD pension models; see also Whitehouse, D'Addio and Reilly (2009).

StatLink http://dx.doi.org/10.1787/888932370892

Key results

Pension wealth measures the total value of the lifetime flow of retirement incomes. For average earners, pension wealth is 9.6 times annual earnings on average in OECD countries. The figure is higher for women – 11.1 times individual earnings – because of their longer life expectancy.

Replacement rates give an indication of the pension promise, but they are not comprehensive measures; they look only at benefit level at the point of retirement. For a full picture, life expectancy, retirement age and indexation of pensions must also be taken into account. Together, these determine for how long the pension benefit is paid, and how its value evolves over time. Pension wealth – a measure of the stock of future flows of pension benefits – takes account of these factors. It can be thought of as the lump sum needed to buy an annuity giving the same flow of pension payments as that promised by mandatory retirement-income schemes.

Gross pension wealth for men is highest in Luxembourg at each earnings level, followed by the Netherlands, Iceland and Greece. Pension wealth in these countries averages 17.5 times earnings for average earners, about 80% higher than the OECD34 figure of 9.6 times. Pension wealth for average earners is lowest in the United Kingdom, due to relatively low replacement rates and the long-term pension age of 68.

Higher replacement rates mean that pension wealth tends to be higher for low than for average earners. For men with half- average earnings, pension wealth is 12.2 times individual earnings on average, compared with 9.6 times for people with average earnings. Similarly, for women with low earnings, pension wealth of 14.1 compares with 11.1 times individual earnings for average earners. For men, in the four countries where pension wealth for low earners is highest (Denmark, Iceland, Luxembourg and the Netherlands), its value is more than 21.0 times individual earnings.

Impact of life expectancy

In countries with shorter life expectancies, such as Hungary, Mexico, Poland, the Slovak Republic and Turkey, the expected duration of retirement is shorter, and so, other things being equal, the pension promise becomes more affordable. The effect is the reverse in Switzerland and the Nordic countries, where life expectancies are high. Unlike measures of replacement rates, the link between affordability and life expectancy is captured by the pension-wealth indicator.

Similarly, since women's life expectancy is longer than men's, pension wealth for women is relatively higher in all countries. This is simply because pension benefits can be expected to be paid over a longer retirement period. Also, some countries still have lower retirement ages for women; this extends the payment period even further.

Pension wealth is also affected by pension ages. Denmark, Germany, Iceland, Norway, the United Kingdom and the United States, for example, all have or plan to have pension ages above age 65, which reduces pension wealth.

Impact of indexation

Pension wealth is also affected by indexation rules. Although most OECD countries now index pensions in payment to prices, there are exceptions: Luxembourg, for example links pensions to average earnings, while five countries, comprising the Czech Republic, Finland, Hungary, the Slovak Republic and Switzerland, index to a mix of price inflation and earnings growth. In normal times, at least, earnings tend to grow faster than prices, so that pension wealth is higher with these more generous indexation procedures than with price indexation.

Different indexation policies also affect the pension wealth of women relative to men. Women's longer life expectancy means that they tend to benefit more from more generous indexation procedures (above price inflation, for example).

For the non-OECD countries there is great variation with South Africa at only 1.4 times individual earnings for average earners and Brazil at 22.2 times. The low value for South Africa results from a combination of the low replacement rate and low life expectancy.

Definition and measurement

The calculation of pension wealth uses a uniform discount rate of 2%. Since the comparisons refer to prospective pension entitlements, the calculations use country-specific mortality rates by age and sex projected for the year 2050. Pension wealth is expressed as a multiple of gross annual individual earnings.

Gross pension wealth by earnings

	Individual earnings, multiple of mean					
	Men			Women		
	0.5	1.0	1.5	0.5	1.0	1.5
OECD members						
Australia	13.1	8.0	6.3	14.7	8.7	6.8
Austria	10.2	10.1	9.5	11.1	11.1	10.4
Belgium	9.8	6.8	5.3	11.5	8.0	6.2
Canada	12.9	7.5	5.0	14.4	8.4	5.6
Chile	9.2	6.9	6.4	10.2	7.0	6.0
Czech Republic	12.6	7.9	5.9	15.1	9.5	7.0
Denmark	18.8	12.1	9.8	22.3	14.3	11.6
Estonia	9.2	7.3	6.7	11.9	9.4	8.5
Finland	10.9	9.5	9.5	13.0	11.4	11.4
France	10.6	9.3	7.9	12.1	10.6	8.9
Germany	7.7	7.7	7.7	9.2	9.2	9.2
Greece	15.2	15.2	15.2	17.4	17.4	17.4
Hungary	10.6	10.6	10.6	13.3	13.3	13.3
Iceland	25.5	16.1	14.1	28.8	18.0	15.8
Ireland	11.4	5.7	3.8	13.7	6.9	4.6
Israel	15.9	11.0	7.4	17.4	11.8	7.9
Italy	10.6	10.6	10.6	11.1	11.1	11.1
Japan	8.1	5.8	5.1	9.7	7.0	6.1
Korea	9.9	6.5	4.9	12.0	7.8	6.0
Luxembourg	23.6	21.1	20.2	27.4	24.5	23.5
Mexico	8.9	4.8	4.6	10.0	5.0	4.6
Netherlands	18.7	17.7	17.4	21.4	20.3	19.9
New Zealand	16.1	8.0	5.4	18.3	9.2	6.1
OECD members *(cont.)*						
Norway	11.7	9.7	7.6	13.8	11.4	8.9
Poland	8.4	8.4	8.4	9.3	8.9	8.9
Portugal	8.9	8.1	8.0	10.3	9.1	8.9
Slovak Republic	9.2	9.2	9.2	11.3	11.3	11.3
Slovenia	13.0	12.6	12.6	17.4	16.9	16.9
Spain	13.7	13.7	13.7	15.5	15.5	15.5
Sweden	11.5	9.1	11.5	12.9	10.2	12.9
Switzerland	12.4	10.8	7.6	14.2	12.2	8.6
Turkey	10.1	8.5	8.5	12.0	10.2	10.2
United Kingdom	7.6	4.5	3.2	9.0	5.3	3.8
United States	7.6	5.8	5.2	8.9	6.8	6.0
OECD34	**12.2**	**9.6**	**8.7**	**14.1**	**11.1**	**10.0**
Other major economies						
Argentina	13.2	11.4	10.8	17.0	14.5	13.6
Brazil	22.2	22.2	22.2	22.2	22.2	22.2
China	18.7	14.9	13.6	18.5	14.1	12.7
India	16.1	11.2	9.5	17.1	11.7	9.8
Indonesia	2.6	2.6	2.6	2.6	2.6	2.6
Russian Federation	10.5	9.0	8.5	13.5	11.4	10.7
Saudi Arabia	16.4	16.4	16.4	18.8	18.8	18.8
South Africa	2.9	1.4	1.0	3.5	1.8	1.2
EU27	11.7	10.2	9.6	13.9	12.2	11.4

Source: OECD pension models.

StatLink http://dx.doi.org/10.1787/888932370911

Gross pension wealth by earnings and sex

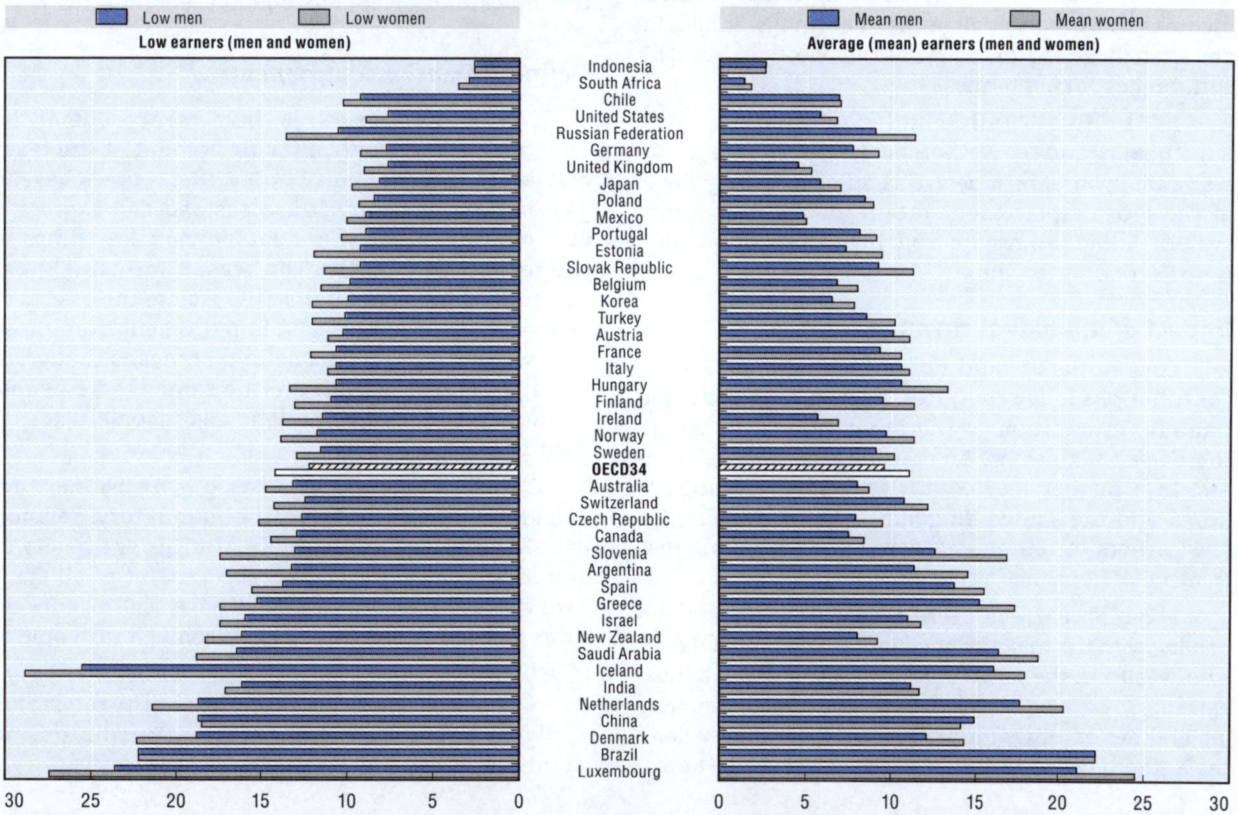

Note: Countries are ranked in order of gross pension replacement rates (GRR) of average earners, *i.e.* mean GRR in the chart.
Source: OECD pension models.

StatLink http://dx.doi.org/10.1787/888932370911

Key results

Net pension wealth, like the equivalent indicator in gross terms, shows the present value of the lifetime flow of pension benefits. But it also takes account of taxes and contribution paid on retirement incomes. Both figures for pension wealth are expressed as a multiple of individual *gross* earnings.

For average earners, net pension wealth for OECD countries averages 8.2 times gross individual earnings for men and 9.6 for women. Values are higher for women than men, due mainly to differences in life expectancy between the sexes.

Because net pension wealth is expressed as a multiple of individual gross earnings, it is less than gross pension wealth (if there is some tax liability during retirement) or the same (if pensions are not taxed or pension income is below tax thresholds). This is clear in the two charts opposite. For example, pension wealth is the same, in both net and gross terms, in the Slovak Republic and Turkey because pensions are not taxable.

The rankings of pension wealth change significantly when measured on a net rather than a gross basis. For example, the Slovak Republic has the eigth highest net pension wealth for an average earner compared with the 16th highest measured on a gross basis. The situation in Denmark is the reverse, because it levies the highest taxes on the retirement incomes of workers at all levels of earnings. It has the seventh highest gross pension wealth but the 14th highest in net terms.

In the five Nordic countries, Austria, Italy, Luxembourg and the Netherlands, retirees face a substantial tax burden. In part, this reflects the high level of the gross replacement rate from the mandatory system. But it also results from high levels of taxation in the economy as whole.

Impact of individual earnings

Low earners would not be liable for taxes and contributions in ten countries: Australia, Belgium and Canada, in addition to the seven countries where there is no tax liability on pensions for average earners. In a further four countries – Greece, Hungary, Korea and the United Kingdom – the tax liability for low earners in retirement would be very small: less than 1% of pension.

For high earners there is less variation in the results, with the majority of countries showing net pension wealth in the range of four to seven times annual earnings. The main exceptions to this are Luxembourg (at 14 times earnings for men), followed by Greece and the Netherlands at 12.3 and 11.6 respectively. The lowest figure is for the United Kingdom: 3.1 times earnings for men and 3.6 for women.

For the non-OECD economies, net and gross pension wealth are the same in Brazil, China, India, Indonesia, the Russian Federation and South Africa. As with the gross pension wealth calculation, there is a wide range among these countries, with South Africa at 1.4 times average earnings and Brazil with the highest of any country at 22.2 times average earnings.

It is important to note that these calculations look at the benefit side of the pension system only. The impact of taxes and contributions paid by people of working age on living standards during retirement relative to when working work are discussed above in the indicator of "Net pension replacement rates".

Definition and measurement

Net pension wealth is the present value of the flow of pension benefits, taking account of the taxes and social security contributions that retirees have to pay on their pensions. It is measured and expressed as a multiple of gross annual individual earnings in the respective country. The reason for using gross earnings as the comparator is to isolate the effects of taxes and contribution paid in retirement from those paid when working. This definition means that gross and net pension wealth are the same where people are not liable for contributions and income taxes on their pensions.

Taxes and contributions paid by pensioners are calculated conditional on the mandatory pension benefit to which individuals at different levels of earnings. They calculations take account of all standard tax allowances and tax reliefs as well as concessions granted either to pension income or to people of pension age.

Details of the rules that national tax systems apply to pensioners can be found in the online country profiles at *www.oecd.org/els/pensions/PAG*.

Net pension wealth by earnings

	Multiple of individual annual gross earnings					
	Men			Women		
	0.5	1.0	1.5	0.5	1.0	1.5
OECD members						
Australia	13.1	7.7	5.6	14.7	8.6	6.2
Austria	9.4	7.8	6.9	10.3	8.6	7.5
Belgium	9.8	6.0	4.4	11.5	7.1	5.2
Canada	12.9	7.4	4.9	14.4	8.3	5.5
Chile	8.1	5.8	5.1	9.0	6.1	5.1
Czech Republic	12.6	7.7	5.6	15.1	9.3	6.8
Denmark	12.8	8.0	6.2	15.3	9.5	7.4
Estonia	9.2	7.0	6.0	11.9	8.9	7.7
Finland	9.5	7.5	6.8	11.3	8.9	8.1
France	10.0	8.3	6.8	11.4	9.4	7.8
Germany	6.9	6.1	5.7	8.3	7.4	6.8
Greece	15.1	13.2	12.3	17.4	15.2	14.1
Hungary	10.3	9.2	8.0	12.9	11.4	10.1
Iceland	20.0	12.0	10.2	22.5	13.4	11.3
Ireland	11.4	5.7	3.8	13.7	6.9	4.6
Israel	15.6	10.4	6.9	17.3	11.3	7.5
Italy	10.3	8.8	8.3	11.1	9.6	8.9
Japan	7.3	5.4	4.5	8.8	6.4	5.4
Korea	9.9	6.5	4.9	11.9	7.8	5.9
Luxembourg	20.7	16.3	14.4	24.1	19.0	16.7
Mexico	8.9	4.8	4.6	10.0	5.0	4.6
Netherlands	15.3	12.8	11.6	17.5	14.6	13.3
New Zealand	13.2	6.6	4.4	15.1	7.5	5.0
OECD members *(cont.)*						
Norway	11.7	8.0	6.1	13.8	9.5	7.2
Poland	7.2	7.0	6.9	8.1	7.4	7.3
Portugal	8.9	8.0	7.6	10.3	9.1	8.6
Slovak Republic	9.2	9.2	9.2	11.3	11.3	11.3
Slovenia	13.0	11.5	10.9	17.4	15.5	14.7
Spain	12.8	11.6	11.0	14.5	13.1	12.5
Sweden	8.9	6.6	7.9	9.9	7.5	8.8
Switzerland	11.8	8.9	6.3	13.5	10.1	7.1
Turkey	10.1	8.5	8.5	12.0	10.2	10.2
United Kingdom	7.6	4.4	3.1	9.0	5.1	3.6
United States	7.6	5.6	4.9	8.8	6.5	5.6
OECD34	**11.2**	**8.2**	**7.1**	**13.1**	**9.6**	**8.2**
Other major economies						
Argentina	12.8	11.0	10.4	16.5	14.0	13.2
Brazil	22.2	22.2	22.2	22.2	22.2	22.2
China	18.7	14.6	12.7	20.0	15.5	13.7
India	16.1	11.2	9.5	17.1	11.7	9.8
Indonesia	2.6	2.6	2.6	2.6	2.6	2.6
Russian Federation	10.5	9.0	8.5	13.5	11.4	10.7
Saudi Arabia	14.7	13.9	13.3	17.0	16.2	15.5
South Africa	2.9	1.4	1.0	3.5	1.8	1.2
EU27	10.9	8.9	7.9	13.0	10.6	9.4

Source: OECD pension models.

StatLink http://dx.doi.org/10.1787/888932370930

Gross *versus* net pension wealth by sex, average earner

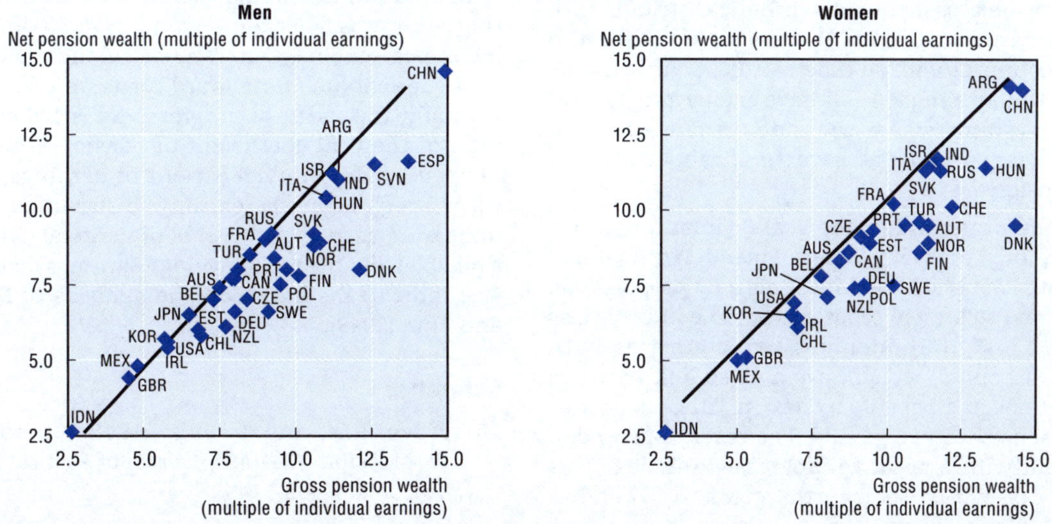

Note: The scales of both charts have been capped at pension wealth of 15 times individual earnings, which excludes Luxembourg and the Netherlands from both charts and Greece and Hungary from the chart for women.

Source: OECD pension models.

StatLink http://dx.doi.org/10.1787/888932370930

Key results

The progressivity index is designed to summarise the relationship between pension in retirement and earnings when working in a single number. The results show variation from 100 in pure basic schemes (such as Ireland and New Zealand), through zero in Hungary to a negative result in Sweden, indicating that the retirement-income system overall is regressive. The average index across OECD countries is 37. Regional differences are striking, with the index averaging 80 in the Anglophone countries: public pensions are strongly progressive. In southern European countries, by contrast, it averages just 8, indicating a very strong link between earnings and pension benefits.

"Pure-basic" pension systems pay the same benefit regardless both of their earnings history and their other sources of income. The relative pension level is independent of earnings and the replacement rate falls with earnings. "Pure-insurance" schemes, in contrast, aim to pay the same replacement rate to all workers when they retire. Defined-contribution plans generally conform to this pure-insurance model as do earnings-related schemes that offer the same accrual rate regardless of earnings, years of service or age.

These two benchmarks underpin the "index of progressivity" used for cross-country comparison of pension benefit formulae of mandatory schemes. The index is designed so that pure-basic systems score 100 and a pure-insurance schemes, zero. The former is maximally progressive; the latter is not progressive because the replacement rate is constant. A high score is not necessarily "better" than a low score or *vice versa*. Countries with a high score simply have different objectives than countries with a low score.

The table shows the Gini coefficient for gross pension benefits and the index of progressivity of the benefit formula assuming a synthetic distribution of earnings based on the OECD average. In addition to the two countries with an index of 100, Canada, Israel and the United Kingdom all have highly progressive pension systems where the index is close to 70 or higher. These countries all have significant targeted or basic pensions.

At the other end of the scale, Finland, Greece, Hungary, Italy, the Netherlands, Poland, Portugal and the Slovak Republic have almost entirely proportional systems and so limited progressivity. The index is less than 10. This group includes two countries with notional accounts, which have a close link between contributions and benefits by design. Other countries lie between these two groups. The result for Sweden stands out with a negative progressivity index. This regressivity can be seen in the gross replacement chart in the "Country profile" in Part III, which shows both low and high earners have higher replacement rates than average earners.

The final two columns explore whether inequality in pension entitlements is explained by inequality in the national earnings distribution or by differences in benefit formulae. In fact, the index of progressivity averages around 37 on both measures for the 29 countries with complete data.

It is important to note that the index of progressivity of pension benefit formulae measures only the mandatory parts of the pension systems. Some countries have extensive private occupational and personal pension provision (see the indicator of "Coverage of private pensions"). Taking these into account would make the distribution of pensioners' incomes wider.

Definition and measurement

OECD countries' retirement-income systems place differing emphasis on the roles of insurance and redistribution. The progressivity index is designed so that a pure basic scheme would give 100 and a pure insurance scheme, zero. The calculation is based on Gini coefficients, a standard measure of inequality. Formally, the index of progressivity is 100 minus the ratio of the Gini coefficient of pension entitlements divided by the Gini coefficient of earnings, on both cases weighted by the earnings distribution. Calculations were carried out with both national data (where available) and the OECD average earnings distribution. The indicator is based on the analysis of Musgrave and Thin (1948).

Reference

Musgrave, R.A. and T. Thin (1948), "Income Tax Progression 1924-48", *Journal of Political Economy*, Vol. 56, pp. 498-514.

Gini coefficients on pension entitlements and earnings

OECD average and national earnings-distribution data

	OECD average distribution		National earnings distribution		
	Pension Gini	Progressivity index	Pension Gini	Progressivity index	Gini wage
OECD members					
Australia	10.9	62.2	10.8	61.8	28.3
Austria	21.5	25.4	21.0	25.5	28.2
Belgium	11.4	60.5	10.9	55.9	24.8
Canada	3.5	88.0	3.5	87.9	29.0
Chile	21.0	27.2			
Czech Republic	9.1	68.4	9.1	68.4	28.8
Denmark	12.6	56.1	10.8	55.1	24.0
Estonia	21.0	27.0			
Finland	26.5	7.9	22.6	4.6	23.7
France	20.4	29.3	19.2	28.0	26.6
Germany	21.8	24.3	21.5	25.1	28.7
Greece	27.8	3.4	29.7	3.1	30.6
Hungary	28.8	0.0	33.0	0.0	33.0
Iceland	15.8	45.1			
Ireland	0.0	100.0	0.0	100.0	29.6
Israel	7.3	74.5			
Italy	28.5	1.1	25.6	1.2	25.9
Japan	15.3	46.9	14.6	46	27.1
Korea	8.9	69.3	9.9	69.1	32.1
Luxembourg	23.5	18.6	23.9	18.6	29.3
Mexico	14.1	51.2	18.0	51.8	37.3
Netherlands	27.2	5.7	25.4	5.6	26.9
New Zealand	0.0	100.0	0.0	100.0	28.8
Norway	15.5	46.3	13.0	44.5	23.5
OECD members *(cont.)*					
Poland	27.9	3.0	30.1	3.7	31.3
Portugal	26.7	7.4	28.9	13.6	33.5
Slovak Republic	28.6	0.8	28.6	0.8	28.8
Slovenia	21.7	24.7			
Spain	23.2	19.6	22.6	20.4	28.4
Sweden	31.7	−10.1	28.4	−16.7	24.3
Switzerland	13.5	53.0	11.6	54.4	25.5
Turkey	25.6	11.1	30.4	16.7	36.5
United Kingdom	5.0	82.8	5.0	82.8	28.8
United States	17.1	40.6	17.1	40.6	28.8
OECD34 average	**18.0**	**37.4**			
OECD29	**18.2**	**37.0**	**18.1**	**36.8**	**28.7**
Other major economies					
Argentina	24.1	16.4			
Brazil	26.7	7.4			
China	21.3	26.1			
India	16.9	41.5			
Indonesia	28.8	0.0			
Russian Federation	23.9	16.9			
Saudi Arabia	28.8	0.0			
South Africa	0.0	100.0			
EU27	21.6	25.0			

Note: OECD29 refers to the countries for which national earnings-distribution data are available.
Source: OECD pension models; *OECD Earnings Distribution Database.*

StatLink http://dx.doi.org/10.1787/888932370949

Distribution of earnings: OECD average and selected countries

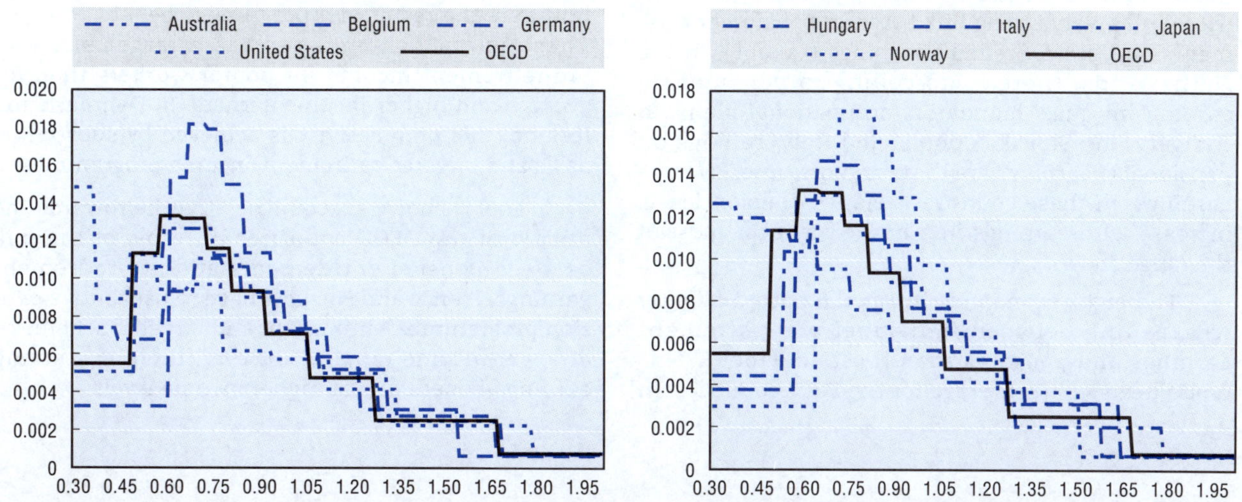

Source: *OECD Earnings Distribution Database.*

StatLink http://dx.doi.org/10.1787/888932370949

Key results

In some countries, such as Hungary, Italy and the Slovak Republic, there is a very strong link between pension entitlements and pre-retirement earnings. In contrast, flat-rate benefits in Ireland and New Zealand mean that there is no link between pension and earnings.

The charts show relative pension levels on the vertical axis and individual pre-retirement earnings on the horizontal. A flat curve in the charts shows no relationship between pension and earnings, while a linear increasing function means the link is strong.

Countries have been grouped by the degree to which pension benefits are related (or not) to individual pre-retirement earnings. The grouping is based on the distribution of pension benefits relative to the distribution of earnings, set out in the previous indicator of "Progressivity of pension benefit formulae".

Panel A shows seven countries where there is little or no link between pension entitlements and pre-retirement earnings. In addition to the flat-rate systems in Ireland, New Zealand and South Africa, the relative pension level varies little in Canada: from 38% for low earners to 44% for those on average earnings and above. Although Canada has an earnings-related pension scheme, its target replacement rate is very low, its ceiling is approximately equal to average economy-wide earnings and a resource-tested benefit is withdrawn against income from this scheme. In the United Kingdom, the earnings-related scheme has a strongly progressive formula and there is also a basic pension programme. In Australia, the relatively flat curve results mainly from the means-tested public programme. There is also a limit to the earnings for which employers must contribute to the DC scheme.

At the other end of the spectrum lie eight countries with a very strong link between pension entitlements and pre-retirement earnings (Panel F). In the Netherlands, there is no ceiling to pensionable earnings in quasi-mandatory occupational plans. In Hungary, the Slovak Republic and Italy, ceilings on pensionable earnings are three or more times average earnings. In these countries, relative pension levels increase with earnings in a linear way over most of the range shown.

The eight economies in Panel E have a slightly weaker link between individual pre-retirement earnings and pensions than those in Panel F. This group includes the average for the EU27 countries. In Estonia and Poland, there is a strong pension-earnings link from the defined-contribution and public, earnings-related pensions. But minimum benefits are expected to play a greater role than in the countries in Panel F.

It is noteworthy that most of the non-OECD countries analysed lie in these last two groups, with a relatively strong pension-earnings link: Argentina, Brazil, China, India, the Russian Federation and Saudi Arabia. Moreover, many of these countries have large informal sectors with workers not covered by the formal pension system.

One explanation is that Luxembourg and Sweden have redistributive programmes targeting a relatively high minimum retirement income worth 38% of average earnings. Secondly, Sweden has a relatively low ceiling for pensionable earnings in its public scheme of 110% of economy-wide average earnings) that weakens the link between pay and pensions compared with the countries shown in Panel F.

The remaining countries are intermediate cases. The thirteen countries in Panels B and C exhibit stronger links between pensions and pre-retirement earnings than the first group of countries (Panel A), but their pension systems have much more progressive formulae than those of the eight countries shown in Panel F. In the Czech Republic, Korea, Norway and the United States this redistribution to low earners is primarily the result of a progressive benefit formula. These public schemes replace a larger share of pre-retirement income for poorer workers than for average and higher-income earners. In Denmark and Iceland, this progressivity is achieved by substantial basic and targeted retirement-income programmes.

Panel D shows six countries that lie towards the middle of the OECD countries in terms of the link between pension entitlements and pre-retirement earnings. France and Portugal have redistributive pension programmes – minimum and targeted schemes – at lower-income ranges. However, there is a strong earnings-benefit link at higher income levels.

The link between pre-retirement earnings and pension entitlements

Gross pension entitlements as a proportion of economy-wide average earnings

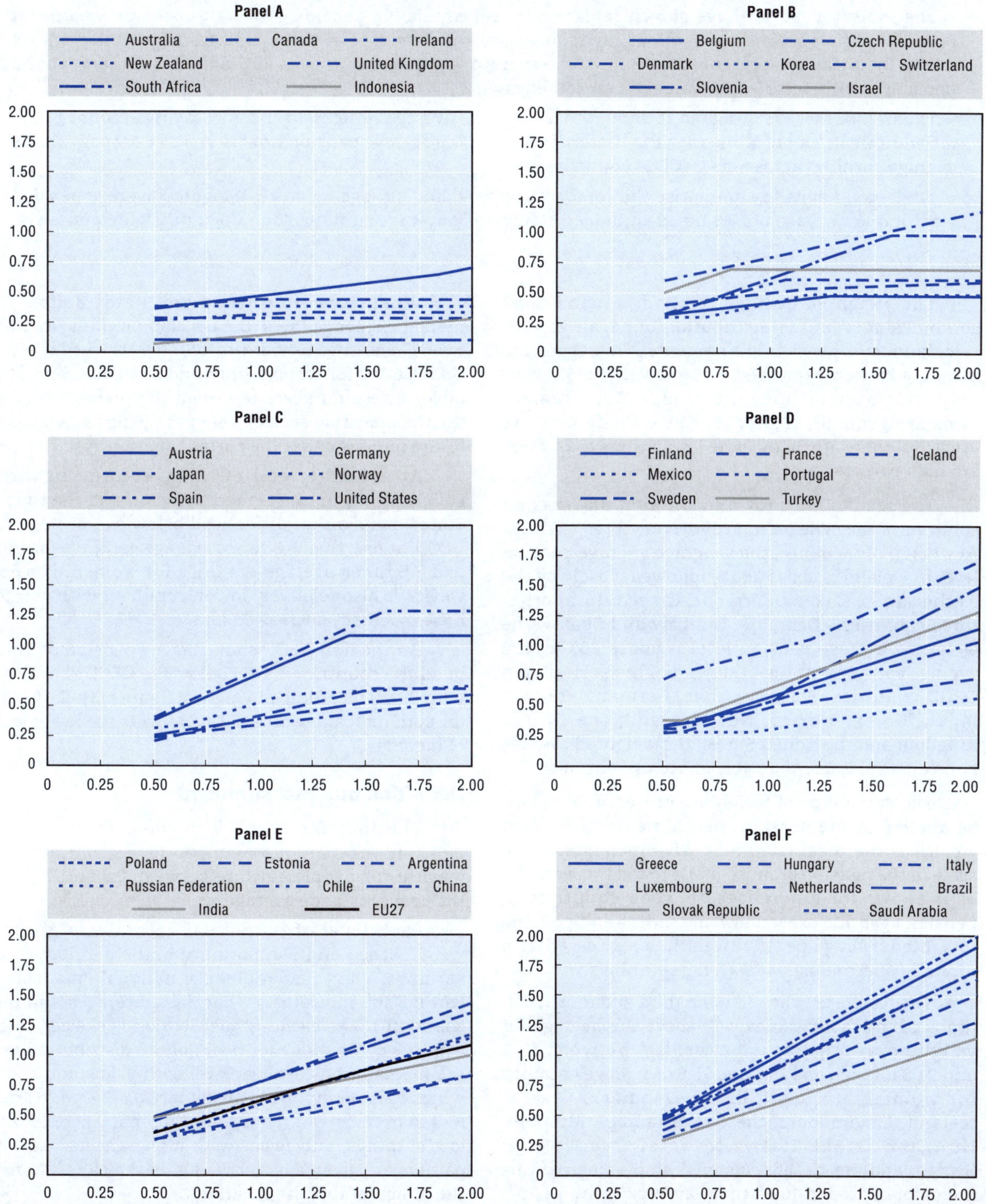

Source: OECD pension models.

StatLink http://dx.doi.org/10.1787/888932370968

Key results

The indicators so far have shown replacement rates, relative pension levels and pension wealth for people at different levels of earnings. By taking a weighted average of these indicators over the earnings range, the measures presented here show the average for the pension level at the time of retirement and pension wealth, the lifetime value of pension payments.

The first of these is designed to show the level of the average retirement income, taking account of the different treatment of workers with different incomes. The average pension level is 55.3% of economy-wide average earnings across the OECD34 countries.

The second aims to summarise the total cost of providing old-age incomes. Weighted average pension wealth is an average of 10.3 times annual economy-wide average earnings for men and 12.0 for women.

The weighted average relative pension level combines data on the distribution of earnings with calculations of pension entitlements. This aggregate measure is then expressed as a percentage of economy-wide average (mean) earnings. Replacement rates are generally higher for low earners and *vice versa*. But there are many more low earners than there are high earners.

The results are shown in the first and second columns of the table for men and women respectively. At the top of the range, the weighted average pension level in Iceland is above 100%, followed closely by the Netherlands, Luxembourg and Greece. In another three countries – Denmark, Hungary and Spain – the weighted average pension level is above 70% of the average earnings. At the other end of the scale, in ten OECD countries (Belgium, Chile, Germany, Ireland, Japan, Korea, Mexico, New Zealand, the United Kingdom and the United States) the weighted average pension level is less than 40% of average earnings

The same type of weighting procedure can also be applied to the pension wealth measure. Pension wealth is the most comprehensive measure of the scale of the pension promise made to today's workers, as it allows for differences between countries in pension ages, life expectancy and indexation policies. Weighted average pension wealth is expressed as a multiple of economy-wide average earnings.

The results are shown in the third and fourth columns of the table. Values well above the average for weighted average pension wealth, between 13.3 and 21.8 for men and 15.1 and 25.8 of average earnings for women, are found in the Denmark, Greece, Iceland, Luxembourg, the Netherlands and Spain. Hungary, Israel, Italy, Slovenia, Sweden and Switzerland are closely clustered with values of this indicator of around 10-12 times average earnings.

When converted to United States dollars (at market exchange rates) the pension promises in these twelve countries amount to USD 667 000 for men and USD 766 000 for women (fifth and sixth column of the table). These numbers represent the present value of the transfers that societies are promising on average to future retirees under the current pension system rules.

At the other end of the spectrum, in three countries (Japan, the United Kingdom and the United States) pension wealth is well below the average for OECD, at less than 6.3 times average earnings for men and 7.6 times average earnings for women. Pension wealth is also relatively low in countries with shorter life expectancy such as Poland.

For the non-OECD countries the pension promise in all the countries is well below the OECD34 average, with Brazil recording the highest figure of USD 198 000 for both men and women. This reflects the lower level of incomes.

Definition and measurement

The indicators build on the calculations of pension entitlements (pension levels and pension wealth) for people earning between 0.3 and 3 times the economy-wide average.

Each level of individual earnings is given a weight based on its importance in the distribution of earnings. The calculations use national data: see in Part II.5 the indicator of "Earnings: averages and distribution"). The earnings distribution is skewed in all countries. The mode (or peak) of the distribution and the median (the earnings level both below and above which half of employees are situated) are significantly less than the mean. Thus, there are many people with low earnings, and fewer with high earnings, so low earners are given a larger weight in the calculation of the indicator than high earners.

Weighted averages: Pension levels and pension wealth

Percentage of economy-wide average earnings

	Weighted average pension level		Weighted average pension wealth		Average pension wealth (USD)			Weighted average pension level		Weighted average pension wealth		Average pension wealth (USD)	
	Men	Women	Men	Women	Men	Women		Men	Women	Men	Women	Men	Women
OECD members							**OECD members** *(cont.)*						
Australia	47.4	44.7	9.5	10.4	479 000	524 000	Norway	48.3	48.3	9.4	11.1	732 000	865 000
Austria	67.9	67.9	9.8	10.7	557 000	608 000	Poland	56.2	42.1	8.5	9.5	119 000	133 000
Belgium	38.2	38.2	7.0	8.2	407 000	476 000	Portugal	52.1	52.1	8.7	10.0	205 000	235 000
Canada	42.0	42.0	8.7	9.8	350 000	394 000	Slovak Republic	56.3	56.3	9.2	11.3	82 000	101 000
Chile	45.6	33.7	7.7	8.0	86 000	89 000	Slovenia	57.0	57.0	12.7	17.0	293 000	392 000
Czech Republic	47.5	47.5	9.0	10.9	145 000	175 000	Spain	73.4	73.4	13.4	15.1	455 000	513 000
Denmark	80.4	80.4	13.3	15.7	937 000	1 106 000	Sweden	64.3	64.3	10.4	11.7	556 000	625 000
Estonia	47.2	47.2	7.9	10.1	114 000	146 000	Switzerland	49.6	49.0	10.4	11.9	715 000	818 000
Finland	59.6	59.6	9.7	11.6	529 000	632 000	Turkey	68.4	68.4	9.8	11.7	142 000	170 000
France	44.4	44.4	9.3	10.5	444 000	501 000	United Kingdom	30.3	30.3	5.4	6.4	332 000	394 000
Germany	39.3	39.3	7.7	9.3	466 000	563 000	United States	37.5	37.5	6.3	7.3	254 000	294 000
Greece	81.8	81.8	15.1	17.4	528 000	609 000	**OECD34**	**55.3**	**53.8**	**10.3**	**12.0**	**436 000**	**504 000**
Hungary	71.0	71.0	10.6	13.3	144 000	180 000							
Iceland	100.4	100.4	19.4	21.8	897 000	1 008 000	**Other major economies**						
Ireland	29.0	29.0	7.5	9.1	448 000	544 000	Argentina	76.6	65.5	12.0	15.3	128 000	164 000
Israel	62.7	55.4	12.2	13.2	382 000	413 000	Brazil	81.4	69.5	22.0	22.0	198 000	198 000
Italy	64.7	50.8	10.6	11.1	408 000	427 000	China	76.5	60.3	16.1	15.5	67 000	64 000
Japan	34.0	34.0	6.3	7.6	305 000	368 000	India	63.7	47.9	12.4	13.0	44 000	46 000
Korea	39.1	39.1	7.6	9.2	231 000	280 000	Indonesia	13.7	59.9	2.6	2.6	4 000	4 000
Luxembourg	82.7	82.7	21.8	25.3	1 542 000	1 789 000	Russian Federation	61.5	12.2	9.5	12.1	79 000	101 000
Mexico	37.3	35.3	7.4	8.1	50 000	55 000	Saudi Arabia	97.7	54.5	16.4	18.8	143 000	164 000
Netherlands	87.0	87.0	18.0	20.6	1 145 000	1 311 000	South Africa	10.6	85.5	1.9	2.3	26 000	32 000
New Zealand	38.7	38.7	10.6	12.0	347 000	393 000	EU27	58.7	54.7	10.5	11.9	380 000	428 000

Source: OECD pension models.

StatLink http://dx.doi.org/10.1787/888932370987

Weighted averages compared: Pension levels *versus* pension wealth by sex

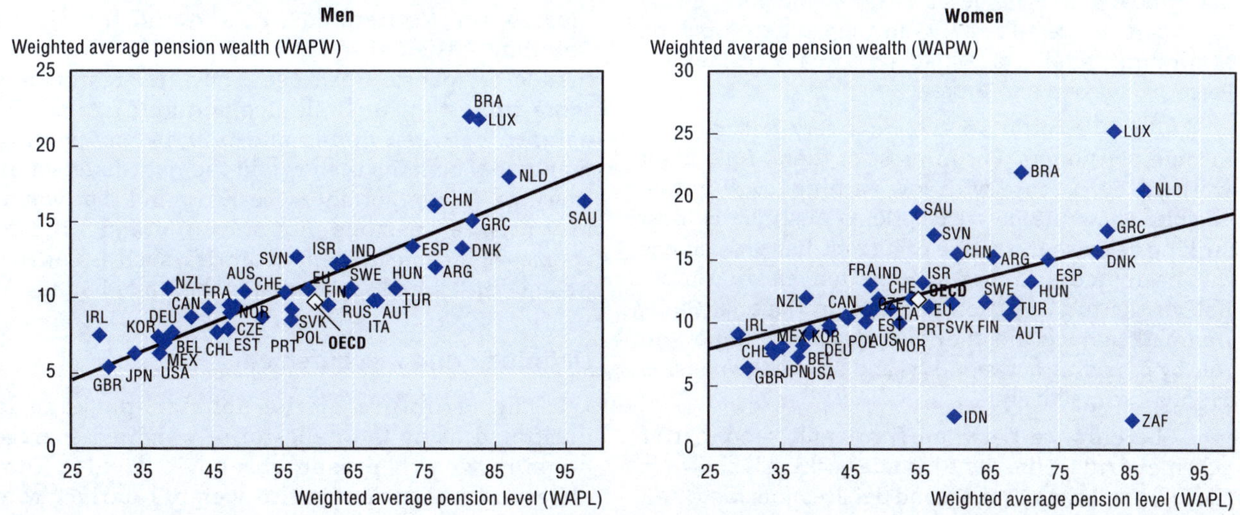

Source: OECD pension models.

StatLink http://dx.doi.org/10.1787/888932370987

Key results

The retirement-income package is divided into different components using the taxonomy from the indicator of the "Architecture of national pension systems" above. This framework divides pension systems into two mandatory tiers. The first is a redistributive part, designed to ensure pensioners achieve an absolute minimum standard of living. A savings part forms the second, with the aim of achieving a target income in retirement compared with earnings when working. This indicator, showing the division of national pension systems between these tiers and between public and private provision, again demonstrates substantial differences in national policies.

Starting with the first tier, it is important to note that the calculations cover full-career workers only. All of the first-tier programmes will be much more important for people with incomplete contribution histories. But it is hard to obtain information on the distribution of past contribution histories let alone predict them into the future.

There are basic schemes in 14 OECD countries (including Korea and Mexico, where other components of the system have the same effect). The value of these benefits does not depend on individual earnings or other pension entitlements. Mandatory pensions for full-career workers in Ireland and New Zealand are entirely from basic schemes. In Japan, Korea, the Netherlands and the United Kingdom, basic pensions contribute 41-62% of the total pension promise. They are also significant in Canada, Denmark, Estonia and Israel.

Minimum pensions are significant in 13 countries. In Belgium and the United Kingdom, minimum pension credits have a similar effect: benefits for workers with low earnings are calculated as if the worker had earned at a higher level. These credits form a very large part of overall benefits in the United Kingdom. Minimum pension are also significant in Mexico, Portugal, Sweden and Turkey.

All OECD countries have a safety-net for low-income pensioners. But in most of them, full-career workers, even those with low earnings, will not be eligible. There are nine exceptions. Australia is most striking because the whole of its first-tier provision is means-tested and this scheme makes up almost half of the total pension package. In Canada, Chile, Denmark and Iceland, they also play a very important role by providing between 17% and 23% of the pension promise, respectively.

The balance between first- and second-tier schemes in the retirement-income package is shown in the left-hand chart. The second tier accounts for 94% or more in half of OECD countries. In some – Austria, Italy, Poland, Spain and Turkey – this reflects high target replacement rates in the second tier. In others, such as Switzerland and the United States, the benefit formula of the public scheme is progressive: redistribution done by the first tier in other countries is carried out by second-tier plans. In the United Kingdom, most of the earnings-related plan goes into benefits from minimum credits.

Second-tier schemes

The second tier of mandatory benefits is divided in the table between public and private providers and between defined-contribution (DC) and defined-benefit (DB) or earnings-related provision. There are public, earnings-related schemes in 25 OECD countries. They provide almost all of benefits for full-career workers in nine: Austria, Finland, France, Germany, Greece, Italy, Slovenia, Spain and the United States.

In 14 OECD countries, private pensions are mandatory or quasi-mandatory. They are DB in Iceland, the Netherlands and Switzerland, but DC in most cases. In six countries – Australia, Denmark, Mexico, the Netherlands, Poland and the Slovak Republic – they account for 50-60% of the total, mandatory pension package. They are significantly more important in Chile, Iceland and Israel. The balance between public and private provision of mandatory benefits is shown in the right-hand chart. However, it is important to bear in mind that voluntary private pensions (not shown) are significant sources of income in many countries, such as Canada, Ireland, the United Kingdom and the United States.

Definition and measurement

The structure of the pension package is illustrated using the indicator of weighted average pension wealth presented above, divided into different components. The weights derive from earnings-distribution data.

Structure of the retirement-income package

Percentage contribution of mandatory components of the pension system to weighted average pension wealth

	First tier			Second tier				Total
	Resource-tested	Basic	Minimum	Public ER	Public DC	Private DB	Private DC	
OECD members								
Australia	40.6						59.4	100
Austria				100.0				100
Belgium			6.4	93.6				100
Canada	22.9	34.9		42.2				100
Chile	17.5						82.5	100
Czech Republic		18.9		81.1				100
Denmark	19.3	25.3					55.5	100
Estonia		32.2		26.7			41.1	100
Finland			2.3	97.7				100
France				100.0				100
Germany	3.7			96.3				100
Greece				100.0				100
Hungary				56.4			43.6	100
Iceland	22.3	10.1				67.6		100
Ireland		100.0						100
Israel		33.1					66.9	100
Italy				100.0				100
Japan		44.6		55.4				100
Korea		62.0		38.0				100
Luxembourg		15.7	0.1	84.3				100
Mexico		12.8	30.7				56.5	100
Netherlands		41.4				58.6		100
OECD members *(cont.)*								
New Zealand		100.0						100
Norway			3.7	85.4			10.9	100
Poland			1.3	49.0			49.7	100
Portugal			11.1	88.9				100
Slovak Republic			0.4	47.4			52.2	100
Slovenia	2.9		0.8	96.3				100
Spain			0.7	99.3				100
Sweden			5.6	48.0			46.4	100
Switzerland	0.2			69.3		30.5		100
Turkey			13.2	86.8				100
United Kingdom	0.3	48.2	40.8	10.8				100
United States				100.0				100
Other major economies								
Argentina		20.1		79.9				100
Brazil		100.0						100
China		55			45.0			100
India				41.1	58.9			100
Indonesia					100.0			100
Russian Federation		20.7		53.1			26.3	100
Saudi Arabia				100.0				100
South Africa		100.0						100

DB = Defined benefit; DC = Defined contribution; ER = Earnings related.

1. Belgium: includes both minimum pension and minimum credits.
2. Denmark: private DC plans include both quasi-mandatory occupational (49.0%) and the special pension (6.5%).
3. France: public pensions include both the state scheme (78.2%) and the complementary, occupational scheme (21.8%).
4. Greece: public pension is made up of the main (73.0%) and the supplementary components (27%).
5. Korea: basic component represents the part of the public pension based on average rather than individual earnings.
6. Luxembourg: basic pension also includes the end-of-the-year allowance.
7. Mexico: basic component calculated from the flat-rate government contribution to DC accounts of 5.5% the real minimum wage from 1997.
8. Sweden: private DC includes both DC schemes (12.6% and 33.8%).
9. United Kingdom: minimum pension relates to minimum credits in public, earnings-related scheme.

Source: OECD pension models.

StatLink http://dx.doi.org/10.1787/888932371006

Balance between first-tier, redistributive programmes and mandatory, second-tier, income-replacement schemes

Percentage of weighted average pension wealth

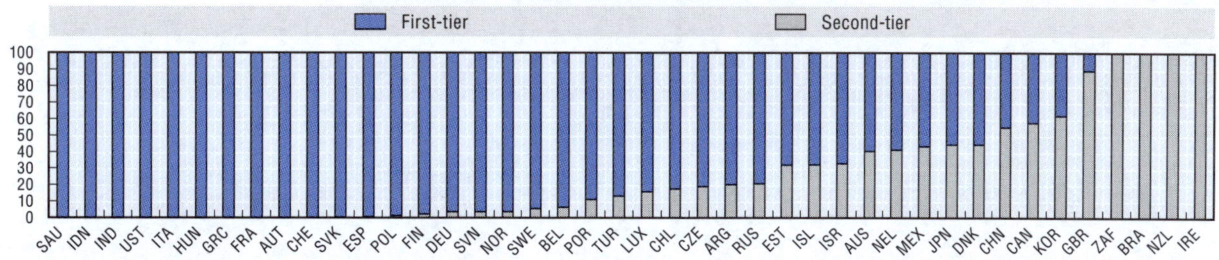

Source: OECD pension models.

StatLink http://dx.doi.org/10.1787/888932371006

Balance between public and private provision of mandatory pensions

Percentage of weighted average pension wealth

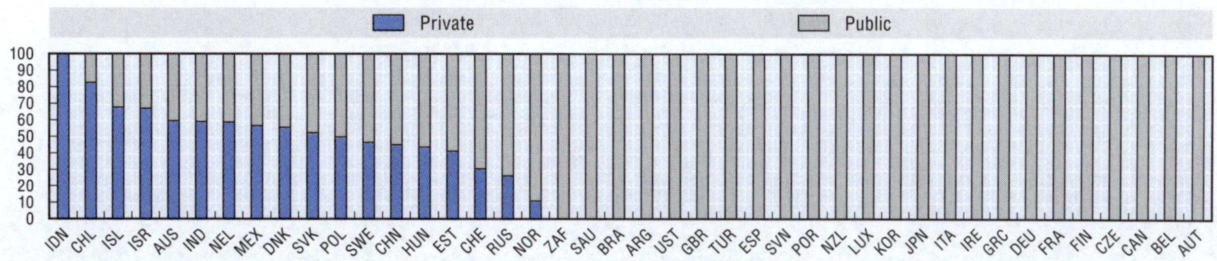

Source: OECD pension models.

StatLink http://dx.doi.org/10.1787/888932371006

Pensions at a Glance 2011
Retirement-income Systems in OECD and G20 Countries

PART II

Chapter 3

Incomes and Poverty of Older People

These two sets of indicators look at the financial position of older people in recent years. The first examines the incomes of older people, comparing them with the population as whole. It also shows how incomes vary with the age of older people and by household type and how incomes have changed over time. Data on the sources of income – from publicly provided benefits, earnings and self-employment or private pensions and on other savings – is also presented.

The second looks at poverty among older people. It shows the proportion of older people living on incomes of less than half the national average and how this varies with age, sex and household type of older people. It also compares the poverty rates of older people with those of the population as a whole.

These indicators, new to this edition of Pensions at a Glance, *are a useful complement to the analysis of pension entitlements in Part II.2. Calculations of pension entitlements provide a forward looking indicator: they look at the value of benefits for workers entering the labour market today. These indicators of income and poverty are useful in assessing the performance of national pension systems of the past in delivering adequate retirement incomes today.*

Key results

Incomes of older people are generally lower than those of the population, even when differences in household size are taken into account. On average in OECD countries, over 65s had incomes of 82% of the population as a whole in the mid-2000s. Older people's incomes grew faster than the population's between the mid-1980s and the mid-2000s in 13 out of the 25 countries where data is available. In most OECD countries, public transfers provide the bulk of income in old age.

People over 65 had incomes that were 82.4% of population incomes, on average, in the mid-2000s. Older people fared best in Austria, France, Luxembourg, Mexico and Poland, with incomes around 96% of the national average. In Ireland and Korea, by contrast, older people's incomes stood at just two-thirds of population average.

People aged 66-75 have higher relative incomes, on average, than those aged over 75: 86% and 78% of population incomes, respectively. Lower incomes for older retirees are partly explained by the fact that the 75+ group consists of people with longer-than-average life expectancy, mostly women who tend to have lower wages, shorter working hours and longer career breaks. In only three countries do the oldest old have higher incomes than younger people of pension age.

Households headed by a single person aged over 65 have incomes of only 73% of those households headed by someone of the same age group but composed of two or more adults (despite the adjustment for household size in the income measure). But single older people fare relatively well in Luxembourg, Mexico, the Netherlands and Switzerland. This is due to a mix of relatively generous survivors' benefits and benefits for non-working spouses. On the other hand, single older people fare badly in Japan, Korea, the Slovak Republic and Turkey, with incomes under 60% of those of households with two or more people.

Older people's incomes are shown in absolute (US dollar) as well as in relative terms. These averaged around USD 18 000 in the mid-2000s.

Income trends

In 13 of the 25 countries for which data are available, incomes of older people grew faster than those of the population as a whole between the mid-1980s and the mid-2000s. The largest increases were in Austria, Germany and Norway. The largest drops in older people's relative incomes over these two decades were seen in New Zealand and Turkey.

Income sources

Of the three main sources of income on which older people draw, public transfers (earnings-related pensions, resource-tested benefits, etc.) are the most important. They account for around 60% of older people's incomes on average. The over-65s most reliant on public transfers live in France and Hungary: 85% of their incomes come from that source. In Finland, occupational plans – which are publicly provided – are counted as capital income and not as public transfers. Transfers have a small share in Korea because the public pension scheme dates only from 1988.

Work and capital both account for about 20% of older people's incomes on average. Work is especially important in Japan, Korea, Mexico and Turkey, where it accounts for more than 40% of old-age income. In another seven OECD countries, work accounts for a quarter or more of old-age incomes. In some, such as Iceland and the United States, the normal pension age is higher than age 65. And in others, people keep on working to fill gaps in contribution histories. Also, incomes are measured for households; older people are assumed to draw on the earnings of younger that they live with. Work is likely to be a more important income source for older people where many of them live in multi-generational households.

Capital, mostly private pensions, represents 30% or more of old-age income in Australia, Canada, Denmark, the Netherlands, Switzerland and the United Kingdom (and Finland, see above).

Definition and measurement

Incomes from employment, self-employment, capital and public transfers. The data shown are for disposable incomes (*i.e.* net of personal income tax and social security contributions). Incomes are measured on a household basis and equivalised to adjust for differences in household size. See OECD (2008), *Growing Unequal?* for more details on definitions and data sources. The special chapter on "Incomes and poverty of older people" in OECD (2009), *Pensions at a Glance* provides a more detailed analysis.

Incomes of older people, mid-2000s

	Incomes of people aged over 65, per cent of population incomes			Incomes of single over 65s relative to other over 65s	Average incomes of over 65s (USD, PPP)		Incomes of people aged over 65, per cent of population incomes			Incomes of single over 65s relative to other over 65s	Average incomes of over 65s (USD, PPP)
	All aged over 65	Age 66-75	Aged over 75				All aged over 65	Age 66-75	Aged over 75		
Australia	69.7	71.9	66.4	78.1	17 340	Luxembourg	96.0	94.4	98.3	90.3	37 630
Austria	96.6	100.8	91.5	80.2	26 088	Mexico	97.1	98.1	95.1	90.5	6 470
Belgium	76.4	80.5	71.0	81.7	18 217	Netherlands	87.0	89.3	83.8	86.9	26 538
Canada	90.8	94.8	85.4	73.7	26 510	New Zealand	68.0	69.7	64.5	75.8	14 921
Czech Republic	79.1	80.8	76.3	66.1	11 046	Norway	78.9	88.1	69.2	64.7	23 308
Denmark	72.4	76.4	67.6	80.7	17 604	Poland	94.7	94.8	94.6	69.0	9 393
Finland	74.9	78.4	69.6	73.7	17 387	Portugal	79.5	84.1	72.7	69.0	12 507
France	94.5	97.6	91.2	84.4	21 922	Slovak Republic	78.0	83.3	68.9	56.4	7 460
Germany	91.5	96.3	85.5	79.5	22 395	Spain	79.1	81.1	76.4	78.7	15 505
Greece	80.0	83.8	74.4	68.3	15 626	Sweden	82.0	91.6	69.8	65.0	18 165
Hungary	83.8	86.8	78.8	70.0	9 597	Switzerland	80.2	82.0	76.9	88.6	24 185
Iceland	87.8	95.9	77.5	76.3	21 811	Turkey	91.9	89.5	99.7	47.9	5 829
Ireland	65.9	70.4	59.8	62.1	16 838	United Kingdom	72.9	76.7	68.2	79.0	22 053
Italy	83.4	88.4	76.0	70.2	16 687	United States	86.2	95.7	75.8	69.5	28 437
Japan	86.6	88.5	84.2	57.3	22 425	**OECD30**	**82.4**	**85.9**	**77.9**	**73.1**	**18 271**
Korea	66.7	66.3	67.4	59.7	14 238						

Note: Purchasing power parity (PPP) exchange rates are based on cross-national comparisons of actual consumption.

Source: OECD Income-Distribution Database; see OECD (2008), *Growing Unequal?*, Figure 2.4 for relative incomes by age and Table 5.A1.1 for absolute incomes.

StatLink http://dx.doi.org/10.1787/888932371025

Income trends, mid-1980s to mid-2000s

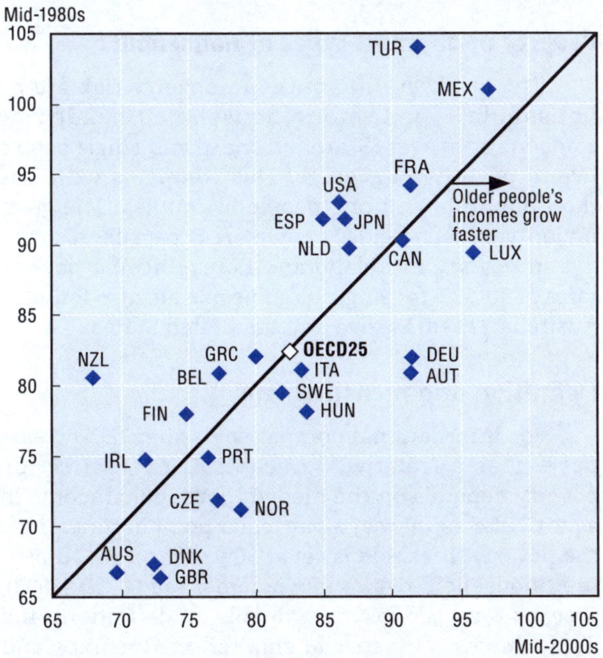

Source: OECD Income-Distribution Database; see OECD (2008), *Growing Unequal?*, Figure 2.6.

StatLink http://dx.doi.org/10.1787/888932371025

Income sources, mid-2000s

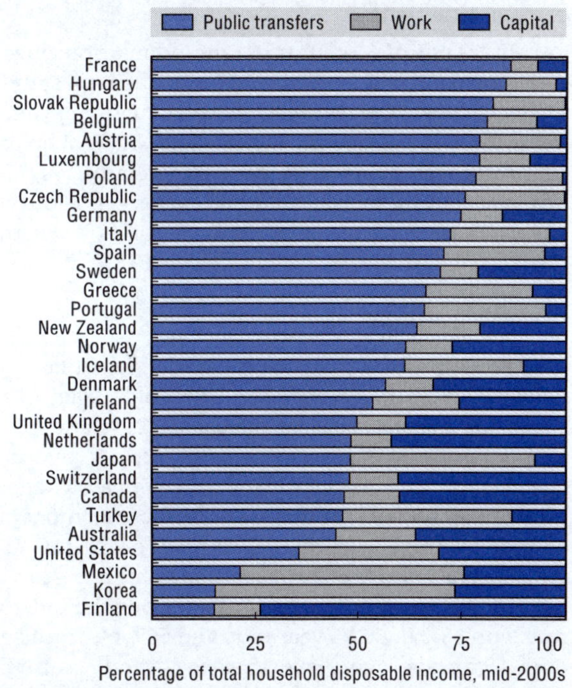

Note: Income from work includes both earnings (employment income) and income from self-employment. Capital income includes private pensions as well as income *from the returns on non-pension savings.*

Source: OECD Income-Distribution Database.

StatLink http://dx.doi.org/10.1787/888932371025

Key results

On average, 13.5% of over 65s in OECD countries live in income poverty, defined as an income below half the national median. There is large variation between countries, from two with practically no old-age poverty to four with poverty rates double the OECD average. Poverty rates are higher for older people than for the population as whole, which averages 10.6%. A greater proportion of older women live in poverty than older men and old-age poverty rates increase with age.

In the mid-2000s, poverty rates of people aged over 65 were very high in Korea (45%) and high in Australia, Ireland and Mexico (above 25%). The Czech Republic, the Netherlands and New Zealand have the fewest poor elderly: around 2%. Poverty rates are close to the OECD average of 13.5% in Belgium, Finland and Italy.

One important factor that explains the varying incidence of old-age poverty is the level at which safety-net retirement benefits are set. In Australia and Ireland, for example, these benefits were below the poverty thresholds in the mid-2000s. By contrast, the basic pension in New Zealand was much higher than the country's poverty threshold (see the indicator on "Basic, targeted and minimum pensions" in Part II.1). Korea's very high old-age poverty rate is primarily due to the fact that the public pension scheme was introduced in 1988, so retirees in the mid-2000s had little or no entitlements.

In 19 out of 30 countries, the population poverty rate is below the old-age poverty rate. The largest differences between the two are found in Australia, Greece, Ireland, Korea, Mexico and Switzerland. Older people are relatively less likely to be poor in 11 countries. Most notably among these is Poland, where the old-age poverty rate is almost 10 percentage points lower than the overall rate.

Poverty and age

Poverty among the "younger old" (aged 66-75) is generally rarer than among the "older old" (aged 75 and over); the average poverty rates are 11.7% and 16.1%, respectively. The difference between the two is in double digits in Finland, Ireland and Norway. There are many explanations for this pattern. Most significantly, as real earnings have tended to grow over time, each successive cohort of retirees has a higher starting benefit. Also, women predominate among the old: they make up 53% of 66-75 year-olds and 60% of those aged over 75 on average. Nevertheless, in four countries – Luxembourg, the Netherlands, New Zealand and Poland – the over 75s fare slightly better than their younger counterparts. And in Iceland, there is no difference in the poverty rates of the two groups.

Poverty and gender

Older women are at greater risk of poverty than older men in 27 out of 30 countries. Average poverty rates are 15% for women and 11% for men. There are three exceptions to this pattern – Iceland, Luxembourg and New Zealand – all of which have low overall poverty rates for older people. However, in five more countries – Belgium, Mexico, the Netherlands, Portugal and Turkey – older women fared relatively well, with poverty rates only a little higher than for men.

The largest gender poverty gaps are in Ireland, Finland and Norway where women's poverty rates exceed men's by more than 10 percentage points. But there are also significant differences in Austria, Italy, Japan, the Slovak Republic and the United States.

Poverty in different types of household

The starkest differences in poverty risk are by household type. Among households headed by someone aged over 65, around one in four single people live in poverty on average. This compares with less than one in ten among people in couples. The great majority of single older people are especially likely to live in poverty in Ireland and Korea. Income poverty rates of 40-50% for single older people are also found in Australia, Japan, Mexico and the United States.

Definition and measurement

For international comparisons, the OECD treats poverty as a "relative" concept. The yardstick for poverty depends on the median household income in a particular country at a particular point in time. Here, the poverty threshold is set at 50% of median, equivalised household disposable income. See OECD (2008), *Growing Unequal?* for more details on definitions and data sources. The special chapter on "Incomes and poverty of older people" in OECD (2009), *Pensions at a Glance* provides a more detailed analysis.

Income poverty rates

Percentage with incomes less than 50% of median household disposable income

	Older people (aged over 65)							Whole population (all ages)
	All 65+	By age		By sex		By household type		
		66-75	75+	Men	Women	Single	Couple	
Australia	26.9	26.1	28.3	24.6	28.9	49.9	17.7	12.4
Austria	7.5	5.3	10.2	3.6	10.1	16.4	3.9	6.6
Belgium	12.8	10.5	16.0	12.7	12.9	16.7	10.0	8.8
Canada	5.9	5.2	6.8	3.1	8.1	16.2	3.9	12.0
Czech Republic	2.3	2.0	2.6	1.4	2.9	5.6	2.0	5.8
Denmark	10.0	6.9	13.7	8.0	11.5	17.5	3.8	5.3
Finland	12.7	8.2	19.5	6.5	16.9	28.0	3.9	7.3
France	8.8	7.2	10.6	6.6	10.4	16.2	4.1	7.1
Germany	8.4	6.5	11.1	5.1	10.8	15.0	4.7	11.0
Greece	22.7	19.2	27.8	20.4	24.5	34.2	17.6	12.6
Hungary	4.6	4.2	5.5	1.8	6.6	11.1	0.8	7.1
Iceland	5.0	5.0	5.0	5.8	4.3	9.8	2.3	7.1
Ireland	30.6	25.8	37.1	24.6	35.3	65.4	9.4	14.8
Italy	12.8	11.2	15.2	8.1	16.1	25.0	9.4	11.4
Japan	22.0	19.4	25.4	18.4	24.7	47.7	16.6	14.9
Korea	45.1	43.3	49.8	41.8	47.2	76.6	40.8	14.6
Luxembourg	3.1	3.4	2.6	4.0	2.4	3.6	2.9	8.1
Mexico	28.0	26.3	31.2	27.6	28.5	44.9	20.9	18.4
Netherlands	2.1	2.2	2.0	1.7	2.4	2.6	2.3	7.7
New Zealand	1.5	1.6	1.4	2.1	0.9	3.2	1.1	10.8
Norway	9.1	3.8	14.6	3.5	13.1	20.0	1.2	6.8
Poland	4.8	5.4	3.8	2.6	6.1	6.0	5.9	14.6
Portugal	16.6	14.4	19.9	16.0	17.0	35.0	15.7	12.9
Slovak Republic	5.9	3.2	10.6	2.0	8.4	10.4	2.9	8.1
Spain	22.8	20.0	26.4	20.1	24.7	38.6	24.2	14.1
Sweden	6.2	3.4	9.8	4.2	7.7	13.0	1.1	5.3
Switzerland	17.6	16.6	19.3	15.2	19.3	24.3	14.6	8.7
Turkey	15.1	14.9	15.6	14.6	15.6	37.8	17.3	17.5
United Kingdom	10.3	8.5	12.6	7.4	12.6	17.5	6.7	8.3
United States	22.4	20.0	27.4	18.5	26.8	41.3	17.3	17.1
OECD30	**13.5**	**11.7**	**16.1**	**11.1**	**15.2**	**25.0**	**9.5**	**10.6**

Source: OECD *Income-Distribution Database*; see OECD (2008), *Growing Unequal?*, Table 5.3.

StatLink http://dx.doi.org/10.1787/888932371044

Income poverty rates by age

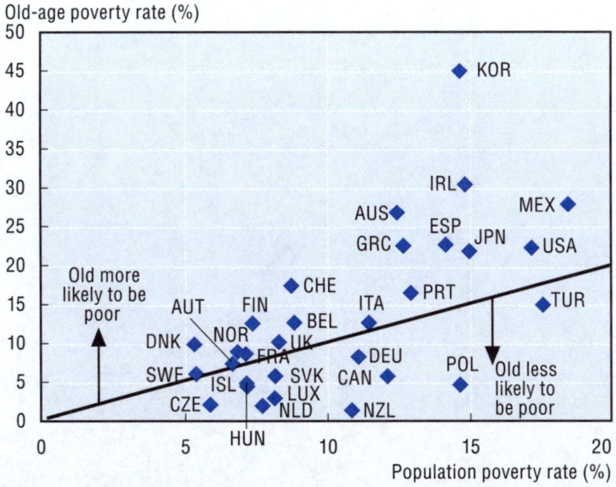

Source: OECD *Income-Distribution Database*; see OECD (2008), *Growing Unequal?*, Tables 5.1 and 5.3.

StatLink http://dx.doi.org/10.1787/888932371044

Income poverty rates of older people by sex

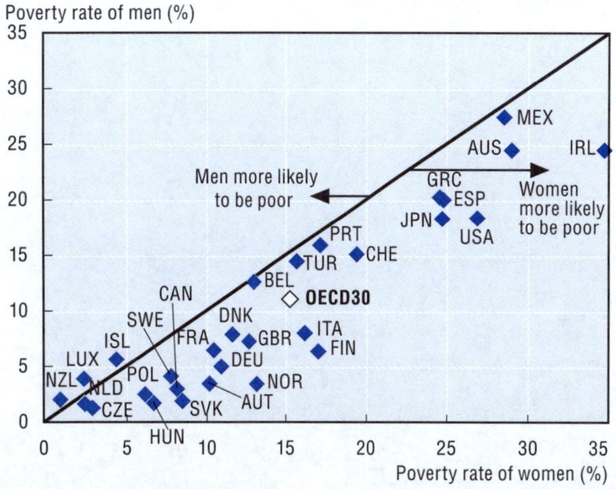

Source: OECD *Income-Distribution Database*; see OECD (2008), *Growing Unequal?*, Figure 5.6.

StatLink http://dx.doi.org/10.1787/888932371044

Pensions at a Glance 2011
Retirement-income Systems in OECD and G20 Countries

PART II

Chapter 4

Finances of Retirement-income Systems

These indicators look at the retirement-income system as a whole rather than the focus on individuals' pension entitlements and retirement incomes as in the previous two sections.

They begin with an examination of how pensions are financed. The first indicator shows contribution rates for public and mandatory private pensions for countries where these can separately be identified. It also provides data on public revenues from pension contributions.

The first of the three indicators of pension expenditures looks at public spending between 1990 and 2007. It shows how much of national income is needed to pay for public pension benefits. It also shows the importance of public pensions in the overall government budget. Data are also provided, where available, on the cost of "non-cash" benefits (for housing, for example). The second spending indicator focuses on private pension, looking at the benefit spending of mandatory, quasi-mandatory and voluntary private schemes. It also shows, where available, information on the cost of public support for private pensions through tax incentives.

The final indicator looks at long-term financial projections of pension spending, showing how public expenditures on pensions are likely to evolve in the period from 2007 to 2060. This draws on the European Union's second report on ageing for the EU27 countries plus Norway and on national sources for some further OECD countries and other major economies.

Key results

Pension contribution rates have remained broadly stable since the mid-1990s. The average contribution rate in the 25 OECD countries that levy separate public contributions increased from 19.2% in 1994 to 19.6% in 2009, reaching a high of 20.0% in 2004. This probably reflects governments' concerns over the effect on employment of high labour taxes. Indeed, these concerns seem to have taken precedence over the pressure on pension-system finances from aging populations and maturing of schemes.

In the 23 countries for which data are available, revenues from these contributions were worth an average of 5.1% of national income, representing 14.2% of total government revenues raised from taxes and contributions.

Most of the measures presented in *Pensions at a Glance* look at the benefits side of the pension system. These indicators look at the contribution side.

The left-hand side of the table looks at the evolution of contribution rates. Around two-thirds of countries with separate pension contributions saw rates unchanged between 2004 and 2009: Austria, Belgium, Canada, Chile, France, Greece, Italy, Korea, Luxembourg, the Netherlands, Poland, Slovenia, Spain, Sweden, Switzerland, Turkey and the United States. In addition, there were only very small changes in Finland, Germany and Israel. There were significant increases in contribution rates in Hungary, with a smaller increase also in Japan. In contrast, there were cuts in contribution rates in Estonia and the Slovak Republic. These were often motivated by a desire to reduce labour taxes to increase employment.

The right-hand side of the table looks at the money raised from contributions to public pension schemes. The revenue figures complement those for the contribution rate, because they illustrate the effect of other parameters of the pension system. For example, most OECD countries have ceilings on pension contributions, which range from around the level of average earnings to 3.7 times in Italy and 6.2 times in Mexico. A lower ceiling will, of course, reduce revenues for a given contribution rate. In other countries, there are floors to contributions, which can mean that low earners pay little or no contributions. Finally, some countries' revenues may be affected by the size of the informal sector or under-reporting of earnings.

Public revenues from pension contributions are highest in Finland, at 9.1% of gross domestic product (GDP). Despite the contribution rate in Turkey being around the same as the OECD average, it raises just 2.2% of national income in contributions, reflecting the size of the informal sector. Contribution revenues are also low in Canada – 2.8% of GDP – because of the low contribution rate (half the OECD average) and the low ceiling (around average earnings).

On average, employee contributions raise a total of 1.8% of GDP compared with 2.9% of GDP for employers' contributions. Employees pay 35% of the total, on average, compared with 57% of the total paid by employers. (The remainder is mainly accounted for contributions from the self-employed, although it also includes contribution from other groups, such as the unemployed.) The great bulk of contributions is levied on employers in the Czech Republic, Finland, Hungary, Italy and Spain. However, it is important to bear in mind that levies on employers have been shown in numerous economic analyses to be passed, in part or in full, onto workers. This can take the form of lower wages or fewer jobs. In many countries, the contributions are evenly balanced between employer and employee levies, including Austria, Belgium, Canada, Germany, Japan, Luxembourg, Switzerland, Turkey and the United States.

The final column of the table shows pension contributions as a percentage of total government revenues from taxes and contributions. This time, Italy does not show the highest figure. In Greece and Spain, pension contributions account for 24-25% of total revenues, compared with 19.9% in Italy. In Australia, Denmark and New Zealand, pensions are financed by general revenues. For the reasons explained above, pension contributions are a relatively small part of government revenues in Canada, Korea and Turkey.

Public pension contribution rates and revenues

	Pension contribution rate (per cent of gross earnings)							Pension contribution revenues, 2008			
								(per cent of GDP)			(per cent of total taxes)
	1994	1999	2004	2007	2009	Employee 2009	Employer 2009	Employee	Employer	Total	
Australia			Private pension contributions only					0.0	0.0	0.0	0.0
Austria	22.8	22.8	22.8	22.8	22.8	10.3	12.6	3.5	3.8	8.0	18.9
Belgium	16.4	16.4	16.4	16.4	16.4	7.5	8.9	2.3	2.0	4.7	10.7
Canada	5.2	7.0	9.9	9.9	9.9	5.0	5.0	1.3	1.3	2.8	8.3
Chile			29.8	29.8	29.8	28.8	1.0				
Czech Republic	26.9	26.0	28.0	32.5	28.0	6.5	21.5	1.8	6.0	8.3	22.2
Denmark			Private pension contributions only					0.0	0.0	0.0	0.0
Estonia			35.0	22.0	22.0	2.0	20.0				
Finland	18.6	21.5	21.4	20.9	21.6	4.5	17.1	1.6	7.1	9.1	21.2
France	21.5	16.7	16.7	16.7	16.7	6.8	9.9				
Germany	19.2	19.7	19.5	19.9	19.9	10.0	10.0	2.6	3.0	6.6	18.2
Greece	20.0	20.0	20.0	20.0	20.0	6.7	13.3	3.1	3.7	7.9	24.7
Hungary	30.5	30.0	26.5	29.5	33.5	9.5	24.0	1.1	5.8	6.8	17.3
Iceland			No separate pension contribution								
Ireland			No separate pension contribution								
Israel			6.1	6.2	6.9	3.9	3.1				
Italy	28.3	32.7	32.7	32.7	32.7	9.2	23.8	2.1	6.5	8.6	19.9
Japan	16.5	17.4	13.9	14.6	15.4	7.7	7.7	2.9	2.9	5.8	20.4
Korea	6.0	9.0	9.0	9.0	9.0	4.5	4.5	1.5	1.0	2.5	9.3
Luxembourg	16.0	16.0	16.0	16.0	16.0	8.0	8.0	2.6	2.4	6.0	16.5
Mexico			Private pension contributions only					0.0	0.0	0.0	0.0
Netherlands	17.9	17.9	17.9	17.9	17.9	17.9	0.0				
New Zealand			No contributions					0.0	0.0	0.0	0.0
Norway			Private pension contributions only								
Poland		19.5	19.5	19.5	19.5	9.8	9.8	3.6	2.7	7.7	22.1
Portugal			No separate pension contribution								
Slovak Republic	28.5	27.5	26.0	24.0	18.0	4.0	14.0	0.8	2.3	4.1	13.8
Slovenia			24.4	24.4	24.4	15.5	8.9				
Spain	29.3	28.3	28.3	28.3	28.3	4.7	23.6	1.3	6.8	9.0	24.2
Sweden	19.1	15.1	18.9	18.9	18.9	7.0	11.9	2.6	3.7	6.4	13.3
Switzerland	9.8	9.8	9.8	9.8	9.8	4.9	4.9	2.7	2.7	5.9	20.3
Turkey	20.0	20.0	20.0	20.0	20.0	9.0	11.0	1.1	1.1	2.2	9.3
United Kingdom			No separate pension contribution								
United States	12.4	12.4	12.4	12.4	12.4	6.2	6.2	2.3	2.3	4.6	16.3
OECD34	**19.2**	**19.3**	**20.0**	**19.8**	**19.6**	**8.4**	**11.2**	**1.8**	**2.9**	**5.1**	**14.2**
Other major economies											
Argentina			28.0	23.7	23.7	11.0	12.7				
Brazil			31.0	31.0	31.0	11.0	20.0				
China			28.0	28.0	28.0	8.0	20.0				
India			24.0	24.0	24.0	12.0	12.0				
Indonesia			6.0	6.0	6.0	2.0	4.0				
Russian Federation			28.0	26.0	26.0	0.0	26.0				
Saudi Arabia			18.0	18.0	18.0	9.0	9.0				
South Africa			No contributions								
EU27			23.8	23.3	22.5	7.9	14.0				

Note: All figures are rounded to one decimal place. The OECD average figure for contribution rates excludes the countries for which there are no pension contributions or they are part of contributions to wider social security programmes. The OECD average figure for contribution revenues includes zero for the countries with no contributions in the calculation.

In some cases, pension contribution revenues have been calculated assuming that the revenues are split between different social security programmes in the same proportion as the contribution rates. The total contribution includes payments from people who are not employed (principally the self-employed).

Finland: contribution rates are now higher for employees aged 53 and over. There is an additional levy on employers that varies between 0.8% and 3.9% of payroll, depending on the employer's capital. France and the Netherlands: it is not possible to separate the contribution revenues into those for pensions and for other purposes. Poland: the contribution rate for pensions was cut by 3 percentage points in July 2007; the earlier, higher figure is shown.

Source: OECD (various years), *Taxing Wages*; OECD (2008), *Revenue Statistics*; Social Security Administration, United States (various years), *Social Security Programs throughout the World*; OECD pension and tax models.

StatLink http://dx.doi.org/10.1787/888932372412

Key results

Public spending on cash old-age pensions and survivors' benefits in the OECD increased 15% faster than the growth in national income between 1990 and 2007, from an average of 6.1% of gross domestic product (GDP) to 7.0%. Public pensions are often the largest single item of government expenditure, accounting for 17% of total government spending on average.

Italy spent the largest proportion of national income on pensions among OECD countries from 2000: 14.1% (nearly one-seventh) of GDP. Other countries with high public pension spending are also found in continental Europe, with Austria, France and Greece at about 12% of GDP and Germany, Poland and Portugal at about 11%. Pensions generally account for between 25% and 30% of total public expenditure in these countries. High spending partly results from demographics: these seven countries are mostly among the oldest of OECD countries.

The left-hand chart compares pension spending in 2007 with the old-age dependency ratio for that year. (The dependency ratio is the percentage of the adult – aged 20 and over – population that is aged 65 and over. It is the inverse of the "Old-age support ratio", presented in the indicator in Part II.5.) There is a strong relationship, but it is far from deterministic. Countries such as Japan, Sweden, Switzerland and the United Kingdom face similar or worse demographics but have significantly lower pension spending than the seven countries at the top of the scale.

Iceland, Korea and Mexico spend less than 2% of GDP on public pensions. They are all relatively young countries. Also, Korea's pension system is immature: the public, earnings-related scheme was only established in 1998. In Mexico, low spending also reflects relatively narrow coverage of pensions (only around 35% of employees). In Iceland, much of retirement income is provided by compulsory occupational schemes (see the next indicator of "Pension-benefit expenditures: Public and private"), leaving less role for the public sector in providing old-age income.

Spending also tends to be low in other countries with favourable demographics, such as Australia, Canada, Ireland and New Zealand. However, this is not always the case: Turkey spends 6% of GDP on public pensions despite being the second youngest OECD country in demographic terms. This is more than Denmark, the Netherlands, the United Kingdom and the United States, despite the fact that these countries have 2-3 times as many over 65s relative to the population as Turkey does.

Trends

Pension spending was a fairly stable proportion of GDP over the period 1990-2007 in six countries: Belgium, Canada, Ireland, Spain, Sweden and the United States.

In five countries, public pension spending grew more slowly than national income. In New Zealand, the decline of over 40% reflects two policies: freezing the value of the basic pension in 1992-94 and increasing pension age from 60 to 65. There were significant falls in pension spending in Iceland, Luxembourg, the Netherlands and Norway as well.

Public pension expenditure more than doubled relative to national income in six OECD countries. In Korea, Mexico and (to a lesser degree) Turkey, this reflected the low starting point in 1990. But Poland and Portugal moved from spending below the OECD average to well above. The change in Japan results from rapid ageing.

Gross and net spending

The penultimate column of the table shows public spending in *net* terms: after taxes and contributions paid on benefits. The right-hand chart compares this with *gross* pension spending. Net spending is significantly below gross in three of the highest spending countries – Austria, France and Italy – and in the Nordic countries, where taxes are relatively high. Gross and net spending are similar where pensions are not taxable (Slovak Republic) or public benefits are generally below basic tax reliefs (Australia, the Czech Republic, Ireland and the United Kingdom).

Non-cash benefits

The final column of the table shows total gross public spending on older people, including non-cash benefits. In six countries, such benefits exceed 1% of GDP. The most important in Denmark, Finland, Norway and Sweden are housing benefits. These are defined as "non-cash benefits" because they are contingent on particular expenditure by individuals. Australia and Japan also record high figures for non-cash benefits.

Public expenditure on old-age and survivors benefits

	Public expenditure on cash benefits for old-age and survivors									Total inc. non-cash (% of GDP)
	Level (% of GDP)					Change (%)	Level (% of total government spending)		Level in net terms (% of GDP)	
	1990	1995	2000	2005	2007	1990-2007	1990	2007	2007	2007
Australia	3.0	3.6	3.8	3.3	3.4	*11.2*	8.6	10.1	3.3	4.5
Austria	11.4	12.3	12.3	12.5	12.3	*7.8*	22.1	25.3	10.6	12.7
Belgium	9.1	9.4	8.9	9.0	8.9	*–2.9*	17.4	18.3	8.0	9.0
Canada	4.2	4.7	4.3	4.2	4.2	*–1.2*	8.5	10.6	3.9	4.2
Chile		6.9	7.5	5.9	5.2					5.2
Czech Republic	6.1	6.3	7.5	7.3	7.4	*21.8*		17.5	7.4	7.7
Denmark	5.1	6.2	5.3	5.4	5.6	*8.6*	9.2	10.9	4.1	7.3
Estonia			6.0	5.3	5.2			15.2		5.3
Finland	7.3	8.8	7.7	8.4	8.3	*13.3*	15.1	17.5	6.8	9.2
France	10.6	12.0	11.8	12.3	12.5	*17.5*	21.5	23.9	11.7	12.8
Germany	9.0	10.7	11.2	11.5	10.7	*19.1*		24.5	10.4	10.7
Greece	9.9	9.6	10.7	11.7	11.9	*20.9*		26.3		12.0
Hungary			7.4	8.6	9.1			18.3		9.6
Iceland	2.2	2.4	2.2	2.0	1.9	*–14.7*		4.5	1.8	2.3
Ireland	3.9	3.5	3.1	3.4	3.6	*–7.7*	9.0	9.7	3.4	3.9
Israel		4.7	4.9	5.1	4.8			10.7		5.0
Italy	10.1	11.3	13.6	14.0	14.1	*38.9*	19.1	29.4	12.4	14.1
Japan	4.9	6.1	7.4	8.7	8.8	*80.5*		27.0	8.4	10.1
Korea	0.7	1.2	1.4	1.5	1.7	*130.5*	3.7	5.7	1.7	1.9
Luxembourg	8.2	8.8	7.5	7.2	6.5	*–19.8*	21.6	18.1	5.9	6.6
Mexico	0.5	0.7	0.9	1.2	1.4	*202.0*		7.2	1.4	1.4
Netherlands	6.7	5.8	5.0	5.0	4.7	*–29.8*	12.2	10.4	4.1	5.5
New Zealand	7.4	5.7	5.0	4.3	4.3	*–41.8*	14.0	10.9	3.5	4.3
Norway	5.6	5.5	4.8	4.8	4.7	*–16.6*		11.4	3.8	6.5
Poland	5.1	9.4	10.5	11.4	10.6	*107.0*		25.2	9.7	10.7
Portugal	4.9	7.2	7.9	10.3	10.8	*119.8*			10.2	10.8
Slovak Republic		6.3	6.3	6.2	5.8			17.0	5.8	6.2
Slovenia			10.6	9.9	9.6			22.7		9.7
Spain	7.9	9.0	8.6	8.1	8.0	*1.5*		20.5	7.4	8.5
Sweden	7.7	8.2	7.2	7.6	7.2	*–6.8*		14.1	5.3	9.5
Switzerland	5.6	6.7	6.6	6.8	6.4	*14.2*	18.6	19.9		6.7
Turkey	2.4	2.7	4.9	5.9	6.1	*159.2*				6.2
United Kingdom	4.8	5.4	5.3	5.6	5.4	*11.0*	11.6	12.0	5.1	5.9
United States	6.1	6.3	5.9	5.9	6.0	*–1.5*	16.4	16.3	5.6	6.0
OECD	**6.1**	**6.7**	**6.9**	**7.1**	**7.0**	***14.5***		**16.5**	**6.2**	**7.4**

Note: See Adema, W. and M. Ladaique (2009), "How Expensive is the Welfare State? Gross and Net Indicators in the OECD Social Expenditure Database (SOCX)", *Social, Employment and Migration Working Paper*, No. 92, OECD Publishing, Paris, for more details on the data, sources and methodology.

Source: OECD Social Expenditures Database (SOCX); OECD Main Economic Indicators Database.

StatLink http://dx.doi.org/10.1787/888932371063

Demographic pressures and public pension expenditure

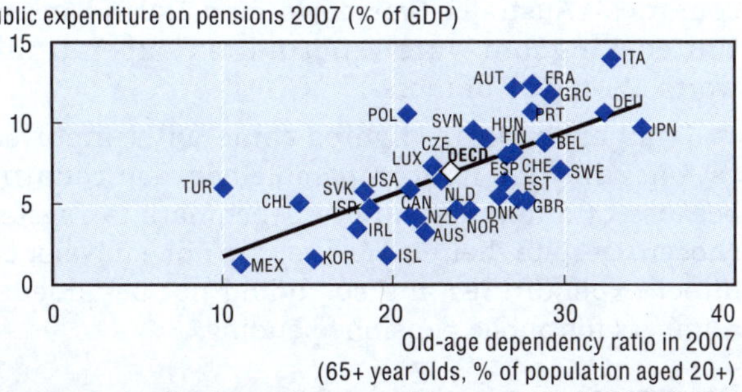

Note: Regression line is pension expenditure = –2.091 (1.908) + 0.3835 (0.07814) × dependency ratio, where heteroskedasicity adjusted standard errors are given in parentheses. The coefficient on the dependency ratio is significant at the 1% level and the R^2 of the regression is 0.4670.

Source: *OECD Social Expenditures Database (SOCX); United Nations, World Population Prospects – The 2008 Revision.*

StatLink http://dx.doi.org/10.1787/888932371063

Gross and net public pension expenditure

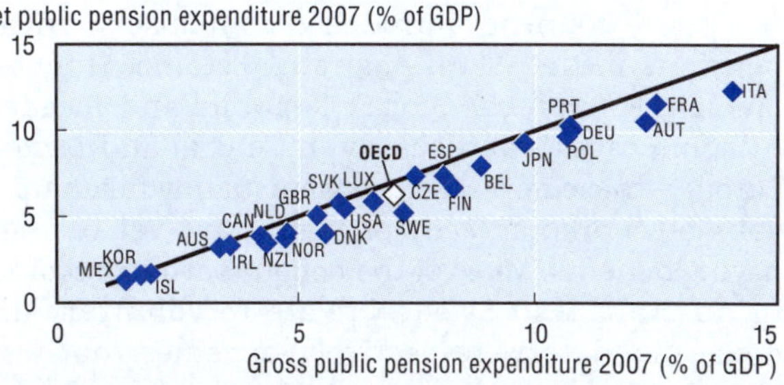

Note: The chart shows a 45° line. See Adema, W. and M. Ladaique (2009), "How Expensive is the Welfare State? Gross and Net Indicators in the OECD Social Expenditure Database (SOCX)", *Social, Employment and Migration Working Paper*, No. 92, OECD, Paris, for more details on the data, sources and methodology.

Source: *OECD Social Expenditures Database (SOCX).*

StatLink http://dx.doi.org/10.1787/888932371063

Key results

Payments from private pension schemes were worth 1.6% of gross domestic product (GDP) on average in 2007 in the 25 OECD countries for which data are available. This is equivalent to one-fifth of average public spending on retirement benefits. Private-pension payments increased 23% faster than GDP between 1990 and 2007, which is faster than public pension spending.

Private pensions are mandatory or achieve near-universal coverage through industrial relations agreements ("quasi-mandatory") in 14 out of 34 OECD countries. In others, voluntary private pensions – either individual ("personal") or employer-provided ("occupational") – have broad coverage.

The biggest flow of private-pension payments is in Switzerland: 6% of GDP in 2007. Added to public spending, total benefits are 12.4% of GDP, a similar figure to public pension expenditure in Austria, France and Greece, for example. Swiss occupational plans are compulsory, although the data on private-pension payments includes benefits above the statutory minimum level.

The Netherlands, where occupational plans are "quasi-mandatory", has the next highest figure for private-pension benefits: 5.2% of GDP. The next three countries – Canada, the United Kingdom and the United States – record private-pension payments of between 4% and 5% of GDP. Private pensions here are voluntary, but both occupational and personal plans have broad coverage. (In the United Kingdom, there is a small mandatory component related to individuals who "contract out" of the public earnings-related scheme: see the country profiles in Part III.) Iceland – with mandatory occupational schemes – and Belgium and Japan (where private pensions are voluntary) have the next highest benefit expenditures on private pensions, at around 3% or more of GDP.

Many countries introduced compulsory private pensions in the 1990s: Australia, Estonia, Hungary, Mexico, Poland, the Slovak Republic and Sweden. In some cases – particularly in Central and Eastern Europe – these new schemes were mainly taken up by younger workers. Many of them have yet to begin paying benefits. Much of the benefit payouts recorded in Australia and Sweden relate to voluntary and quasi-mandatory (respectively) schemes that were already in place before private pensions were made compulsory. In all these cases, it will be some decades before all retirees have spent a full career in compulsory private pension plans.

Trends

The fastest growth in private-pension payments has been from a relatively low base (less than 0.5% of GDP). But there are exceptions, such as Belgium, Iceland and Switzerland. Swiss occupational pensions became compulsory in 1985, which extended coverage significantly. This is now being reflected in the rapid growth in private pension entitlements as each successive generation of retirees has spent longer on average covered by private pensions.

Tax breaks

Most OECD countries offer a favourable tax treatment to retirement savings made through private pension plans. Often, individual contributions are fully or partially deductible from income-tax liabilities and investment returns are fully or partially relieved from tax. Some countries offer tax relief on pension payments (see the indicator of "Tax treatment of pensions and pensioners" in Part II.2).

The cost of these fiscal incentives is measured in many OECD countries using the concept of "tax expenditures", developed in the 1960s. This attempts to quantify the value of the preferential tax treatment relative to a benchmark tax treatment. The idea is that this is the amount the government would have to provide as a subsidy (a direct expenditure) to achieve the same effect.

Data on tax expenditures for retirement savings are available for 21 OECD countries. More than half of these figures are 0.2% of GDP or less. And in only five countries – Australia, Canada, Iceland, Ireland and the United Kingdom – are reported tax expenditures worth 1% of GDP or more.

Tax expenditure figures come with important caveats: they are not comparable between countries because of differences in the benchmark tax system chosen. Despite their name, they are not equivalent to direct expenditures and so should not be added to numbers for public pension spending.

Reference

OECD (2010), *Tax Expenditures in OECD Countries*, OECD Publishing, Paris.

Pension-benefit expenditures: Public and private

	Scheme type	Benefit expenditure of private pension schemes						Public and private benefit spending (% of GDP)	Tax breaks for private pensions (% of GDP)
		Level (% of GDP)					Change (%)		
		1990	1995	2000	2005	2007[1]	1990-2007	2007	2007[2]
Australia	v		1.8	2.9	1.9	1.9		5.3	2.7
Austria	v	0.4	0.4	0.5	0.5	0.5	*22.4*	12.8	0.1
Belgium	v	1.0	1.7	2.0	3.5	3.7	*261.2*	12.6	0.1
Canada	v	2.6	3.5	4.0	4.3	4.1	*58.4*	8.2	2.0
Chile	m		1.0	1.1	1.3	1.1		6.3	
Czech Republic	m	a	a	0.2	0.2	0.2		7.7	0.1
	v	a	0.0	0.0	0.0	0.1			
Denmark	q/m	1.5	1.8	2.0	2.3	2.2	*41.2*	7.7	
Estonia								5.2	
Finland	v	0.1	0.4	0.3	0.2	0.2	*154.3*	8.5	0.1
France	m	0.2	0.1	0.2	0.2	0.2	*10.6*	12.8	0.0
	v	0.1	0.1	0.1	0.1	0.1	*162.8*		
Germany	v	0.6	0.7	0.8	0.8	0.8	*24.1*	11.5	0.8
Greece	v	0.4	0.4	0.5	0.4	0.4	*6.9*	12.3	
Hungary								9.1	
Iceland	v	1.4	1.8	2.3	2.8	3.0	*113.5*	4.9	1.0
Ireland	v	0.9	1.1	1.0	1.0	0.9	*0.9*	4.5	1.2
Israel								4.8	
Italy	m	2.7	3.1	1.2	1.1	1.2	*–57.1*	15.5	0.0
	v	0.3	0.2	0.2	0.2	0.2	*–22.1*		
Japan	m	0.2	0.3	0.5	a	a		12.7	0.7
	v	a	a	3.0	2.3	2.9			
Korea	v	m	0.0	0.0	0.0	0.0		1.7	
Luxembourg	v	a	a	a	0.6	0.5		7.0	0.5
Mexico								1.4	0.2
Netherlands	m	a	0.0	0.0	0.0	0.0		10.0	
	q	3.9	4.7	4.8	5.2	5.2	*34.8*		
New Zealand								4.3	
Norway	v	0.6	0.6	0.6	0.6	0.6	*2.7*	5.3	0.6
Poland								10.6	0.2
Portugal	v	0.3	0.3	0.4	0.6	0.5	*58.8*	11.3	0.1
Slovak Republic	v	a	0.1	0.2	0.4	0.5		6.3	0.2
Slovenia								9.6	
Spain								8.0	0.2
Sweden	q/m	1.2	1.9	1.8	2.1	2.1	*72.8*	9.3	
Switzerland	m	3.2	4.9	5.8	6.0	6.0	*88.7*	12.4	
	v	0.0	0.0	0.0	0.0	0.0	*23.5*		
Turkey								6.1	
United Kingdom	v/m	4.3	5.2	6.1	4.8	4.5	*6.2*	9.9	1.2
United States	v	2.7	3.1	3.8	3.8	4.3	*61.0*	10.3	0.8
OECD		**1.3**	**1.4**	**1.5**	**1.6**	**1.6**	***23.3***	**8.4**	**0.6**

m = Mandatory private scheme; q = Quasi mandatory; and v = Voluntary.

1. Data for Australia, Canada and Chile are from 2005.
2. Data for Iceland, Norway, Poland and the United Kingdom are from 2005. See Adema, W. and M. Ladaique (2009), "How Expensive is the Welfare State? Gross and Net Indicators in the OECD Social Expenditure Database (SOCX)", *Social, Employment and Migration Working Paper*, No. 92, OECD Publishing, Paris, for more details on the data, sources and methodology.

Source: OECD Social Expenditures Database (SOCX); OECD Main Economic Indicators Database.

StatLink http://dx.doi.org/10.1787/888932371082

Tax incentives for private pensions

2003 parameters and rules

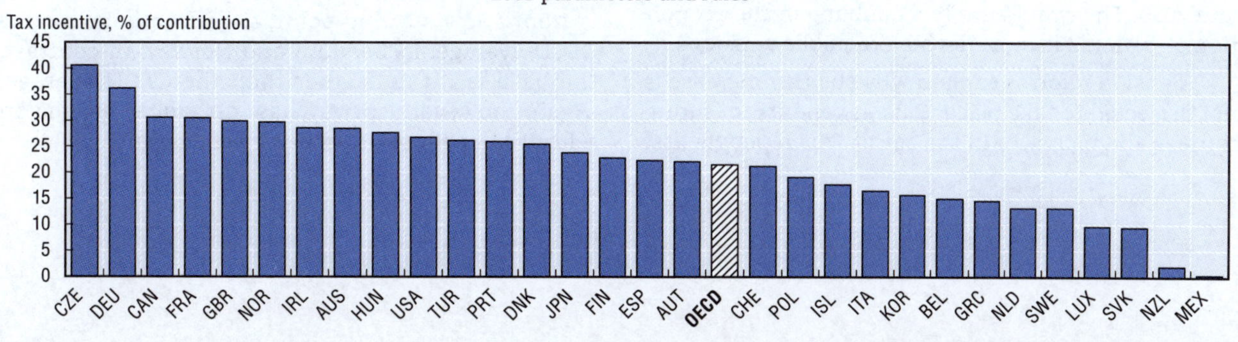

Source: Yoo, K.Y. and A. De Serres (2004), "Tax Treatment of Private Pension Savings in OECD Countries", *OECD Economic Studies*, Vol. 39, No. 2, OECD Publishing, Paris, pp. 73-110.

StatLink http://dx.doi.org/10.1787/888932371082

Key results

Public spending on pensions has been on this rise in most OECD countries for the past two decades, as shown by the previous two indicators. Long-term projections show that pension spending is expected to go on growing in 25 out of 29 OECD countries where data are available. On average pension expenditure is forecast to grow from 8.4% of gross domestic product (GDP) in 2010 to 11.4% of GDP in 2050.

The main driver of growing pension expenditures is demographic change. The projections shown opposite are derived either from the European Union's ageing report – which covers its 27 members plus Norway – or from national projections. In the main, data are presented forwards to 2060, although the horizon is 2050 for three countries. Long-term projections are a vital tool in planning pension policy: there is often a long lag time between a pension reform and the time it begins to affect public pension expenditure.

There are some differences in the range of different programmes covered in the forecasts, reflecting the complexity and diversity of national retirement-income provision. For example, data for a number of countries do not include special schemes for public-sector workers while in others they are included. Similarly, projections can either include or exclude spending on resource-tested benefits for retirees. The coverage of the data also differs from the *OECD Social Expenditures* (SOCX) *Database*, from which the data on past spending trends in the previous two indicators were drawn. The numbers for 2007 may differ between the SOCX *Database* and the sources used here because of the different range of benefits covered.

Nevertheless, the figures do reveal broad trends. Pension spending is projected to grow 40% faster than GDP over the period 2010 to 2060 on average in both the OECD29 and EU27 groupings. Although this is a significant additional piece of national income, this rate of growth is much slower than demographic change would have delivered. The indicator of the "Old-age support ratio" in Part II.5 below shows a halving of the number of people of working age to the number of people of pension age between 2010 and 2050. This would imply a doubling in the proportion of national income devoted to public pensions.

Pension reforms explain why such an increase is not projected to take place. Cuts in benefits for future retirees and increases in the age at which people first claim pensions will reduce growth in public pension expenditure. In a number of countries – Denmark, France, Italy, Sweden and the United States – pension expenditure is broadly stable over the forecast horizon. Only two countries – Estonia and Poland – expect a substantial reduction in spending over time. Both of these countries have introduced mandatory defined-contribution plans as a substitute for part of public, earnings-related benefits. However, similar reforms in Hungary and the Slovak Republic are not expected to reverse the trend growth in public pension spending.

In five countries, pension spending is expected to double or increase further between 2010 and 2060. In Greece and Luxembourg, public spending is already above the OECD average and is projected to exceed 20% of GDP by 2060. (However, these forecasts do not take account of the impact of the Greek pension reforms enacted in 2010.) Japan, which will be the demographically oldest OECD country in 2060, will also see a rapid increase, from just below the OECD average to well above. The rate of change is also very rapid in Ireland and Korea. However, the increases are in both cases from a low base, and pension spending will still be much below the OECD average in 2060. In Korea, this rapid increase reflects both the fact that it is the most rapidly ageing OECD country and that the pension scheme was only established in 1988 and so is not yet mature. In Slovenia, spending will increase nearly as rapidly, from 10.1% of GDP in 2010 to 18.6% in 2060.

The rate of growth in pension spending is expected to be close to the average in five countries. In Australia, Switzerland and the United Kingdom, this is from a low starting point, significantly below the OECD average. In Belgium and Norway, in contrast, the base is rather higher than the OECD average. (Again, however, Norway has introduced a pension reform since these projections were made.)

Projections of public expenditure on pensions, 2007-60

	2007	2010	2015	2020	2025	2030	2035	2040	2045	2050	2055	2060
OECD countries												
Australia	3.6	3.6	3.6	3.7		4.3		4.7		4.9		
Austria	12.8	12.7	12.8	13.0	13.4	13.8	13.9	13.9	14.0	14.0	13.9	13.6
Belgium	10.0	10.3	10.9	11.8	13.0	13.9	14.4	14.6	14.7	14.7	14.8	14.7
Canada	4.6	5.0	5.4	5.8	6.3	6.6	6.6	6.5	6.4	6.3	6.3	6.2
Chile												
Czech Republic	7.8	7.1	6.9	6.9	7.0	7.1	7.6	8.4	9.4	10.2	10.8	11.0
Denmark	9.1	9.4	10.2	10.6	10.5	10.6	10.5	10.4	10.0	9.6	9.3	9.2
Estonia	5.6	6.4	6.2	5.9	5.8	5.6	5.4	5.4	5.3	5.3	5.2	4.9
Finland	10.0	10.7	11.8	12.6	13.4	13.9	13.9	13.6	13.4	13.3	13.3	13.4
France	13.0	13.5	13.5	13.6	13.9	14.2	14.5	14.4	14.3	14.2	14.1	14.0
Germany	10.4	10.2	10.1	10.5	11.0	11.5	11.9	12.1	12.2	12.3	12.5	12.8
Greece	11.7	11.6	12.2	13.2	14.8	17.1	19.4	21.4	23.0	24.0	24.3	24.1
Hungary	10.9	11.3	10.9	11.0	10.9	11.0	11.4	12.2	12.7	13.2	13.7	13.8
Iceland		4.0								6.9		
Ireland	4.0	4.1	4.3	4.6	5.0	5.4	5.8	6.4	7.1	8.0	8.4	8.6
Israel												
Italy	14.0	14.0	14.0	14.1	14.3	14.8	15.2	15.6	15.4	14.7	14.2	13.6
Japan												
Korea	0.6	0.9	1.1	1.4	2.0	2.5	3.1	3.9	4.8	5.5	6.0	6.5
Luxembourg	8.7	8.6	8.9	9.9	12.1	14.2	16.6	18.4	20.7	22.1	23.7	23.9
Mexico		2.4								3.5		
Netherlands	6.6	6.5	7.2	7.8	8.4	9.3	10.0	10.3	10.3	10.3	10.4	10.5
New Zealand	4.0	4.7	4.8	5.3	5.9	6.7	7.3	7.7	7.8	8.0		
Norway	8.9	9.6	10.8	11.5	12.0	12.7	13.2	13.4	13.4	13.3	13.5	13.6
Poland	11.6	10.8	9.6	9.7	9.7	9.4	9.3	9.2	9.1	9.1	9.0	8.8
Portugal	11.4	11.9	12.1	12.4	12.6	12.6	12.3	12.5	12.8	13.3	13.1	13.4
Slovak Republic	6.8	6.6	6.3	6.3	6.9	7.3	7.8	8.3	8.8	9.4	9.9	10.2
Slovenia	9.9	10.1	10.6	11.1	12.0	13.3	14.7	16.1	17.3	18.2	18.6	18.6
Spain	8.4	8.9	9.2	9.5	10.1	10.8	11.9	13.2	14.6	15.5	15.6	15.1
Sweden	9.5	9.6	9.5	9.4	9.4	9.5	9.5	9.4	9.1	9.0	9.2	9.4
Switzerland	6.4	6.3	6.6	6.8	7.5	8.1	8.6	8.6	8.8	8.6		
Turkey		7.3								11.4		
United Kingdom	6.6	6.7	6.8	6.9	7.2	7.6	7.8	8.0	7.9	8.1	8.6	9.3
United States	4.3	4.6	4.8	4.9	4.9	4.9	4.9	4.8	4.8	4.8	4.7	4.7
OECD28		**8.4**	**8.6**	**8.9**		**10.0**		**10.8**		**11.4**		
Other major economies												
Argentina		5.9								8.6		
Brazil		8.5								15.8		
China		2.2								2.6		
India		1.7								0.9		
Indonesia		0.9								2.1		
Russian Federation	5.2	7.9		7.3		6.4		6.1		6.0		
Saudi Arabia		2.2								7.1		
South Africa	1.1	1.3	1.7	1.8	1.8	1.7	1.6	1.6	1.5	1.5	1.5	1.4
EU27	8.9	9.1	9.2	9.6	10.0	10.6	11.1	11.6	12.1	12.5	12.8	12.9

Note: OECD28 figure shows only countries for which complete data between 2010 and 2050 are available. EU27 figure is a simple average of member states (not the weighted average published by the European Commission). Pension schemes for civil servants and other public-sector workers are generally included in the calculations for EU member states: see European Commission, *op. cit.* Expenditures on these schemes are not included for Canada, Japan, South Africa and the United States. Projections are not available, in some cases, for separate resource-tested programmes for retirees. This is the case for the United States and some EU member states as set out in European Commission, *op. cit.* Similarly, data for Korea cover the earnings-related scheme but not the basic (resource-tested) pension.

Source: European Commission (2009), "The 2009 Ageing Report: Economic and Budgetary Projections for the EU-27 Member States (2008-2060)", in *European Economy*, No. 2/2009, Brussels; Commonwealth of Australia (2010), *Australia to 2050: Future Challenges*; calculations provided by the Office of the Chief Actuary, Office of the Superintendent of Financial Institutions, Canada; National Pensions Research Institute, Korea; the Russian Federation: Pension Fund of the Russian Federation (2009), "Actuarial Forecast of Developments of the Pension Fund of the Russian Federation", Department of Actuarial Valuation and Strategic Planning; South Africa, OECD Secretariat estimates assuming a universalised basic pension; Social Security Administration (2010), *Annual Report of the Board of Trustees of the Federal Old-Age and Survivors Insurance and Federal Disability Insurance Trust Funds*, Document 111-137, House of Representatives, United States; Standard and Poor's (2010), *Global Aging 2010: An Irreversible Truth for Argentina, Brazil, China, Iceland, India, Indonesia, Mexico, Saudi Arabia, Turkey*.

StatLink http://dx.doi.org/10.1787/888932372431

Pensions at a Glance 2011
Retirement-income Systems in OECD and G20 Countries

PART II

Chapter 5

Demographic and Economic Context

Population ageing has been one of the main driving forces behind pension policies and reforms in the past two decades. Ageing is the result of two demographic changes.

The first is a decline in the number of births. Fertility rates and how they have changed over time are explored in the first indicator in this section, along with a brief discussion of explanations for the trends. The second factor pushing population ageing is increasing life expectancy. Changes in life expectancy – at birth and at age 65 – over time are shown. There is also a brief discussion of how life expectancy might change in the future.

Population ageing itself is addressed by the third indicator. The degree of ageing is measured with the support ratio: the number of people of working age relative to the number of pension age. The old-age support ratio is shown for a century: historical data back to 1950 and projections forward to 2050.

The final indicator shows the economic context. It gives data on average (mean) earnings, calculating using the OECD's "average-worker" measure, for 2008. These data are used widely in the report: many values for parameters and results for pension entitlements are reported as percentages of national average earnings. There is also information on the distribution of earnings. The indicators of pension entitlements are often given at median earnings, that is, the level below and above which half the population lie. The earnings-distribution data are also included in the calculation of indicators of the structure of the pension package, pension progressivity and weighted averages of pension levels and pension wealth.

Key results

The total fertility rate is below the replacement level – the number of children needed to keep the total population constant – in 29 out of 34 OECD countries for 2005-10. The only exceptions are Israel and Mexico (with 2.8 and 2.2 children per woman, respectively) and Iceland, Turkey and the United States (at replacement level of 2.1). However in more than two-thirds of OECD countries there has been a moderate increase in fertility rates over the last decade. Fertility rates have a profound implication for pension systems because they, along with life expectancy, are the drivers of population ageing.

Fertility rates averaged 1.69 across OECD countries in the period 2005-10, well below the level that ensures population replacement. The trend to fewer children has been going on since the 1970s. The fall in fertility rates reflects changes in both individuals' lifestyle preferences and in the constraints of everyday living, such as labour-market insecurity, difficulties in finding suitable housing and unaffordable childcare.

The positive (and widening) gap between the number of children women declare that they want and the number that they actually have shows the influence of these constraints.

Another effect comes from changing marital status. The larger share of women that are unmarried may have depressed fertility rates, particularly in countries where there is a strong link between marriage and maternity, particularly Japan and Korea. The link is also significant in several European countries, such as Greece, Italy, Poland and Switzerland. However, the childbearing patterns of unmarried women have also changed. For example, half or more of births now occur outside of marriage in France, Iceland, Norway and Sweden. The average proportion of births outside marriage in OECD countries is now one-third of the total.

The recent increase in fertility rates is predicted to continue, albeit very slowly, with increases of just 0.01 during each five year period. It is forecast to average 1.80 across OECD countries by 2045-50.

Low fertility rates have wider social and economic consequences. First, the decline in population can become self-reinforcing, as the number of women of childbearing age falls. Secondly, there are fewer family carers to help people in old age. Thirdly, there is a growing tax burden on people of working age to finance pensions and health care for older people. Fourthly, the workforce will also age and so might be less adaptable to technological change, thereby reducing productivity and economic growth. Finally, ageing may result in a smaller pool of savings to finance investment in the economy as older people use their savings to support their consumption.

The trend towards lower fertility rates has been accompanied by (and is partly explained by) the gradual increase in average childbearing age: from 28 in 1995-2000, it is forecast to exceed 30 by 2045. Postponing childbearing has lasting consequences. First, it increases the probability that women remain childless or have fewer children than desired. Secondly, it raises the risk of morbidity for both mothers and their children.

Among the other major economies, Argentina, India, Indonesia, Saudi Arabia and South Africa all currently have fertility rates well above the replacement level of 2.1. Nevertheless, the trend follows that of the OECD countries, with most falling to or below replacement by 2025-30. The average age of childbearing is also considerably lower than in most OECD countries, typically by at least two years.

Definition and measurement

The total fertility rate is the number of children that would be born to each woman if she were to live to the end of her child-bearing years and if the likelihood of her giving birth to children at each age was the currently prevailing age-specific fertility rates. It is generally computed by summing up the age-specific fertility rates defined over a five-year interval. A total fertility rate of 2.1 children per women ensures broad stability of the population, on the assumptions of no migration flows and unchanged mortality rates.

References

D'Addio, A.C. and M. Mira d'Ercole (2005), "Trends and Determinants of Fertility Rates in OECD Countries: The Role of Policies", *Social, Employment and Migration Working Paper*, No. 27, OECD Publishing, Paris.

OECD (2009), *Society at a Glance*, OECD Publishing, Paris.

Total fertility rates, 1975-2050

	1975-80	1985-90	1995-2000	2005-10	2015-20	2025-30	2035-40	2045-50
OECD members								
Australia	1.99	1.86	1.78	1.83	1.85	1.85	1.85	1.85
Austria	1.65	1.44	1.37	1.38	1.46	1.56	1.66	1.76
Belgium	1.71	1.56	1.60	1.77	1.84	1.85	1.85	1.85
Canada	1.73	1.62	1.56	1.57	1.67	1.77	1.85	1.85
Chile	2.80	2.65	2.21	1.94	1.85	1.85	1.85	1.85
Czech Republic	2.31	1.92	1.17	1.41	1.57	1.67	1.77	1.85
Denmark	1.68	1.54	1.76	1.84	1.85	1.85	1.85	1.85
Estonia	2.06	2.20	1.33	1.64	1.84	1.85	1.85	1.85
Finland	1.66	1.66	1.74	1.83	1.85	1.85	1.85	1.85
France	1.86	1.81	1.76	1.89	1.85	1.85	1.85	1.85
Germany	1.52	1.43	1.34	1.32	1.39	1.49	1.59	1.69
Greece	2.32	1.53	1.30	1.38	1.46	1.56	1.66	1.76
Hungary	2.12	1.82	1.38	1.35	1.47	1.57	1.67	1.77
Iceland	2.29	2.12	2.06	2.10	1.98	1.86	1.85	1.85
Ireland	3.48	2.29	1.90	1.96	1.87	1.85	1.85	1.85
Israel	3.41	3.05	2.94	2.81	2.46	2.22	2.04	1.90
Italy	1.94	1.34	1.22	1.38	1.44	1.54	1.64	1.74
Japan	1.83	1.66	1.37	1.27	1.30	1.40	1.50	1.60
Korea	2.92	1.60	1.51	1.22	1.29	1.39	1.49	1.59
Luxembourg	1.49	1.47	1.72	1.66	1.74	1.84	1.85	1.85
Mexico	5.25	3.63	2.67	2.21	1.89	1.85	1.85	1.85
Netherlands	1.60	1.56	1.60	1.74	1.81	1.85	1.85	1.85
New Zealand	2.18	2.03	1.95	2.02	1.95	1.85	1.85	1.85
Norway	1.81	1.80	1.85	1.89	1.85	1.85	1.85	1.85
Poland	2.26	2.15	1.48	1.27	1.34	1.44	1.54	1.64
Portugal	2.41	1.62	1.46	1.38	1.44	1.54	1.64	1.74
Slovak Republic	2.47	2.15	1.40	1.28	1.40	1.50	1.60	1.70
Slovenia	2.20	1.66	1.25	1.36	1.52	1.62	1.72	1.82
Spain	2.57	1.46	1.18	1.43	1.65	1.75	1.84	1.85
Sweden	1.66	1.91	1.56	1.87	1.85	1.85	1.85	1.85
Switzerland	1.53	1.53	1.47	1.45	1.54	1.64	1.74	1.83
Turkey	4.72	3.28	2.57	2.13	1.97	1.85	1.85	1.85
United Kingdom	1.72	1.81	1.70	1.84	1.85	1.85	1.85	1.85
United States	1.79	1.92	1.99	2.09	1.95	1.85	1.85	1.85
OECD34	**2.26**	**1.91**	**1.68**	**1.69**	**1.71**	**1.73**	**1.77**	**1.80**
Other major economies								
Argentina	3.44	3.05	2.63	2.25	2.08	1.92	1.85	1.85
Brazil	4.31	3.10	2.45	1.90	1.60	1.50	1.60	1.75
China	2.93	2.63	1.80	1.77	1.84	1.85	1.85	1.85
India	4.89	4.15	3.46	2.76	2.30	1.96	1.85	1.85
Indonesia	4.73	3.40	2.55	2.19	1.88	1.85	1.85	1.85
Russian Federation	1.94	2.12	1.25	1.37	1.53	1.63	1.73	1.83
Saudi Arabia	7.28	6.22	4.62	3.17	2.56	2.15	1.86	1.85
South Africa	5.00	4.00	2.95	2.55	2.30	2.10	1.94	1.85
EU27	2.07	1.82	1.49	1.53	1.61	1.67	1.74	1.79

Source: United Nations, *World Population Prospects – The 2008 Revision.*

StatLink http://dx.doi.org/10.1787/888932371101

Mean age of childbearing

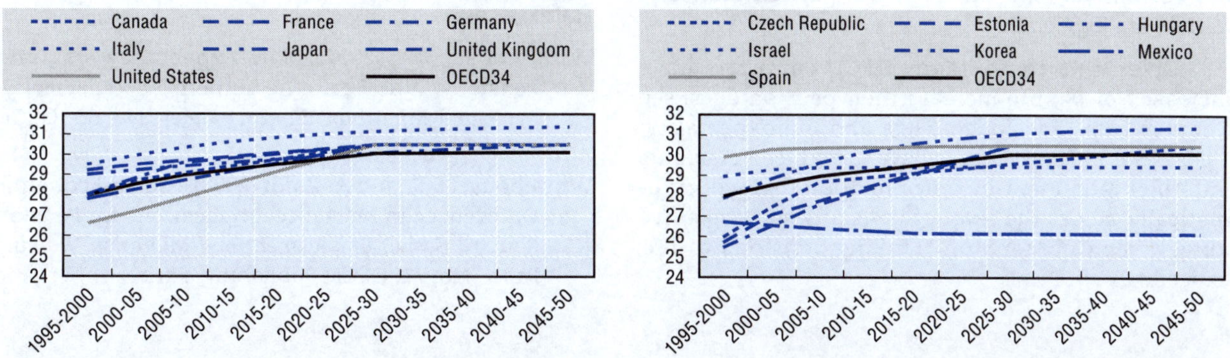

Source: United Nations, *World Population Prospects – The 2008 Revision.*

StatLink http://dx.doi.org/10.1787/888932371101

Key results

The remarkable increase in life expectancy is one of the greatest achievements of the last century. Lives continue to get longer, and this trend is predicted to continue. In 2005-10, life expectancy at birth averaged 76.1 years for men and 81.8 years for women. Among women, the figure was highest in Japan (86.2 years), followed by France, Switzerland, Italy and Spain. For men, life expectancy at birth was highest in Iceland (80.2 years) followed by Switzerland, Australia, Japan and Sweden.

Life expectancy at older ages is especially important for the finances of retirement-income systems. And older people are living ever longer. In 2005-10, on average in OECD countries, women aged 65 could expect to live an additional 19.9 years, which is forecast to increase to 23.5 years by 2045-50. Men of the same age could expect to live 16.4 more years in 2005-10, with a projected increase of 3.1 years by 2045-50 to reach 19.5 years. Gender gaps in the longevity of older people are expected to remain broadly constant in relative terms but increase in absolute terms (from 3.5 to 4.0 years on average in OECD countries). Paying a pension from age 65 will become around 20% more expensive under these forecasts.

There is considerable variation between OECD countries in life expectancy at older ages. Women in Japan are predicted to live another 27.3 years on reaching age 65 in 2045-50. In contrast, women in Turkey are expected to live an extra 19.2 years from age 65 in 2045-50. The figure for Japan is considerably higher than any other country, with France being the next highest at 25.5 years.

For men there is less variation between countries than there is for women. Switzerland has the longest life expectancy at age 65 of 22.0 years in 2045-50, followed by Iceland at 21.4 years. Again, Turkey has the shortest life expectancy for a 65-year-old: 15.4 years.

The gender life-expectancy gap at age 65 is predicted to be between three and five years in favour of women for virtually every OECD country in 2045-50. The main exception to this is Japan, with a differential of over six years, a result of the particularly long female life expectancy.

Given this trend, many OECD countries have increased or plan to increase their pension ages: see Chapter 1 on "Pensionable age and life expectancy, 1950-2050" in Part I. Others have introduced elements into their retirement-income provision that will automatically adjust the level of pensions as people live longer: see Chapter 5 on "Linking pensions to life expectancy" in Part I.

Unsurprisingly, life expectancy at birth is also highest in Japan, for women, at 86.2 years, compared to the OECD average of 81.8 years in 2005-10. For men, Japan records one of the highest values. But, at 79.0 years, it lies behind Iceland (80.2), Switzerland (79.3) and Australia (79.1).

Overall longevity gains are due to rising living standards, but also greater access to quality health services. However, gains in life expectancy have been smaller among people from lower socio-economic groups. Socio-economic differences in mortality rates are lower at pension age (above 65) than they are for people of working age.

Turning to the non-OECD major economies, life expectancy is generally lower. Life expectancy at birth is 53.2 years for women and 49.9 years for men in South Africa. Both figures are at least ten years below those of any of the other countries covered, thus reflecting the prevalence of HIV/AIDS. The Russian Federation is also an outlier in having much the greatest gender gap in life expectancy at birth of 12.9 years, compared with an OECD average of 6.7 years.

Definition and measurement

Life expectancy is defined as the average number of years that people of a particular age could expect to live if they experienced the age- and sex-specific mortality rates prevalent in a given country in a particular year: in this case, 2005-10 and 2045-50. Since the determinants of longevity change slowly, life expectancy is best analysed over a long time horizon.

References

Whitehouse, E.R. (2007), "Life-Expectancy Risk and Pensions: Who Bears the Burden?", *Social, Employment and Migration Working Paper*, No. 60, OECD Publishing, Paris.

Whitehouse, E.R. and A. Zaidi (2008), "Socio-Economic Differences in Mortality: Implications for Pension Policy", *Social, Employment and Migration Working Paper*, No. 71, OECD Publishing, Paris.

Additional life expectancy at age 65, in years, men and women, 2005-10 and 2045-50

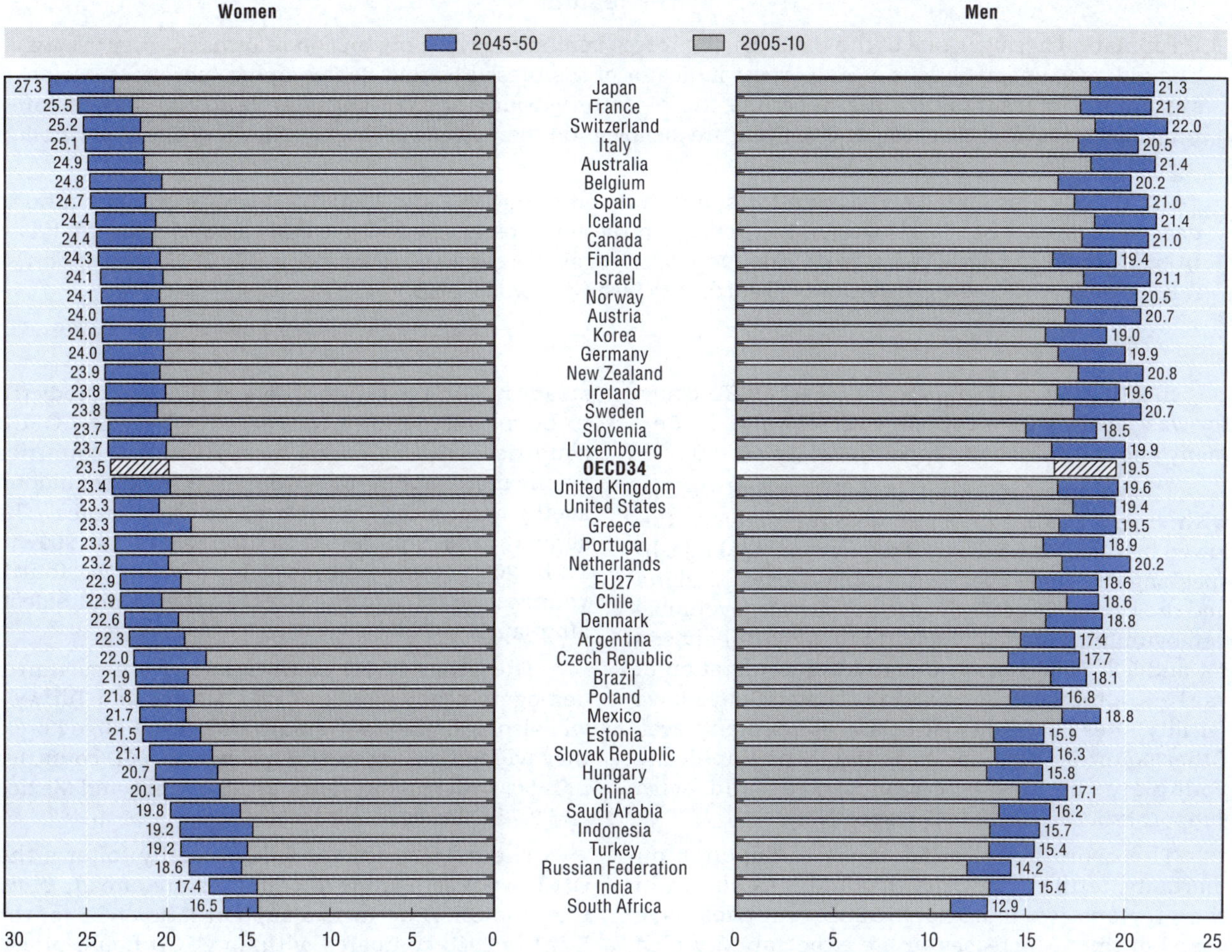

Source: United Nations, *World Population Prospects – The 2008 Revision.*

StatLink http://dx.doi.org/10.1787/888932371120

Life expectancy at birth, in years, men and women, 2005-10

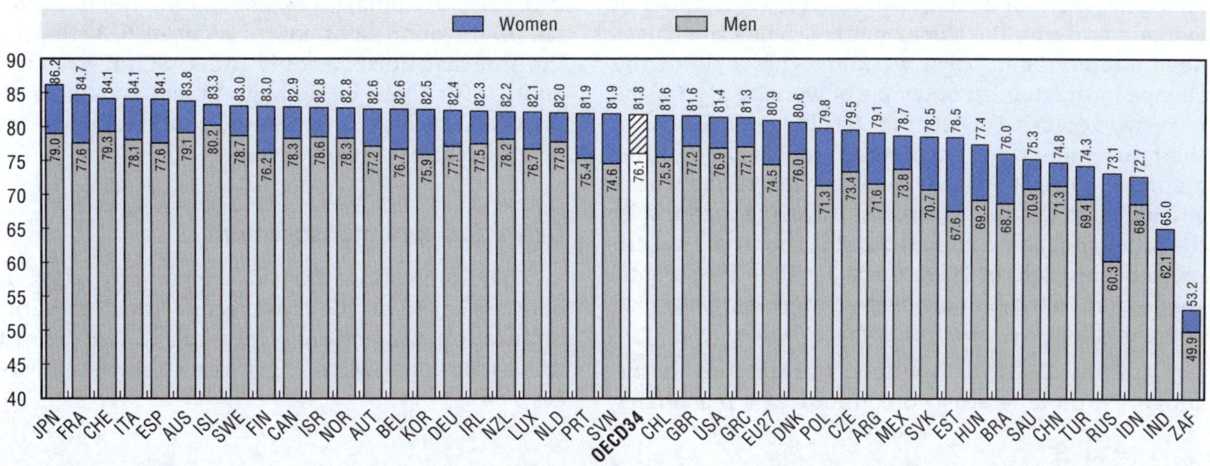

Source: United Nations, *World Population Prospects – The 2008 Revision.*

StatLink http://dx.doi.org/10.1787/888932371120

Key results

Population ageing is one of the main driving forces behind the wave of pension reforms in recent years. The old-age support ratio is an important indicator of the pressures that demographics pose for pension systems. It measures how many people there are of working age (20-64) relative to the number of retirement age (65+). At the moment, there are just over four people of working age for every one of pension age on average.

OECD countries have been ageing for some time: between 1950 and 1980, the average support ratio decreased from 7.2 to 5.1. However, the decline in the more recent period has been slower, with the fall from 5.1 to 4.1 taking 30 years. From 2010, population ageing is expected to accelerate. By 2025, the support ratio is projected to reach three and fall further to just over two in 2050.

In 2010, the demographically oldest OECD country was Japan, with a support ratio of only 2.6. Germany and Italy also had support ratios below 3.0.

The youngest countries were Turkey and Mexico, with support ratios of 9.8 and 8.6 respectively, followed by Chile, at 6.5. Four of the five mainly English-speaking OECD members – Australia, Canada, Ireland and the United States – all have a relatively favourable demographic situation. Support ratios range between 4.4 and 5.3. This is partly due to inward migration of workers, although Ireland and the United States have fertility rates currently just below replacement level. Other countries that are currently demographically young are the Slovak Republic and Poland, with support ratios of 5.4 and 4.9 respectively.

The evolution of support ratios depends on mortality, fertility rates and migration. As shown in the previous two indicators, OECD countries have seen continual increases in life expectancy, which most analysts forecast to continue in the future. This increases the number of older people and so the number of pensioners.

There have also been substantial declines in fertility, which, of course, will reduce the number of workers entering the labour market. Since the babies have already been born, we know the scale of the change in the number of people of working age for the next two decades. For example, fertility rates fell below the replacement level on average in OECD countries around 1980, meaning that each new generation will be smaller than that of its parents. By 2000, for example, the number of births implies that the cohort of "millennium babies" will be 20-25% smaller than its parents' generation. In the future, however, there is a great deal of uncertainty over how fertility rates will evolve.

For the OECD as a whole, the decline in the support ratio is forecast to continue at a reasonably steady rate in the future. There is, however, predicted to be a considerable convergence between OECD countries, with demographically younger countries ageing more rapidly. By far the most rapid population ageing among OECD countries will be in Korea. The support ratio is projected to drop from 6.1 in 2009 to 1.5 by 2050. Korea will move from being the fourth youngest country in the OECD to the second oldest, after Japan.

The other OECD countries that are currently demographically young – Chile, Mexico and Turkey – will also age relatively rapidly. However, unlike Korea, they will remain among the youngest OECD countries in 2050, with support ratios of 2.5 in Chile and Mexico and 3.2 in Turkey.

The pattern for the EU27 broadly follows the OECD average. European countries are already older than the OECD average: a support ratio of 3.5 for the EU27 in 2010 compares with an OECD figure of 4.1. By 2050, the support ratio for the EU is just 1.8.

All of the other major economies have a support ratio above that of the OECD average. However, many face rapid population ageing in the coming decades. In Brazil and China, for example, the support ratio will fall from around eight now to 2.5 in 2050. By the end of the forecast horizon, only India, Saudi Arabia and South Africa will be demographically younger than the OECD average situation today, with support ratios of 4.5, 4.6 and 6.1 respectively.

Definition and measurement

The projections for old-age support ratios used here are based on the most recent "medium-variant" population projections. They are drawn from the United Nations, *World Population Prospects – The 2008 Revision*.

Old-age support ratios: Historical and projected values, 1950-2050

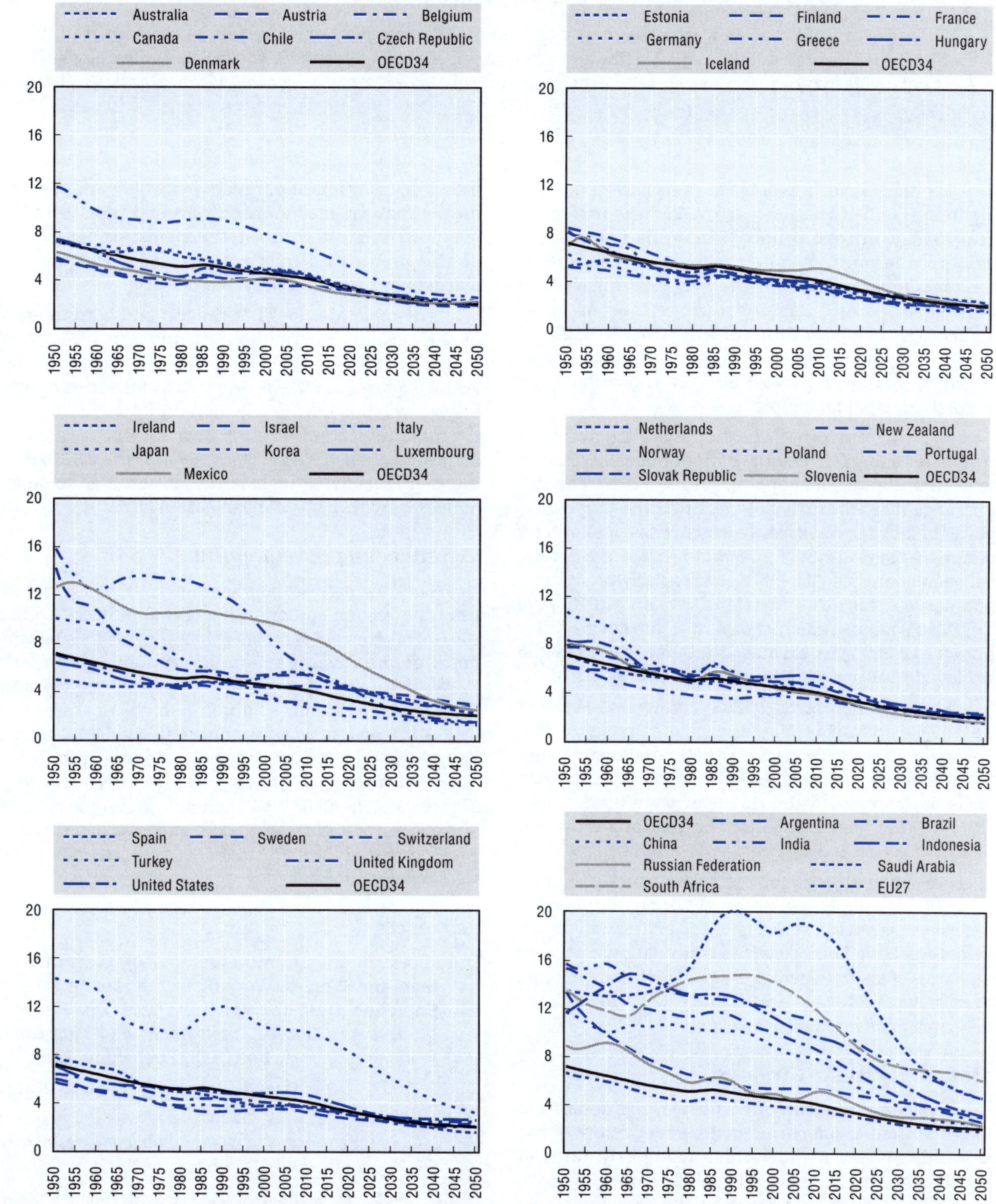

Source: United Nations, *World Population Prospects – The 2008 Revision.*

StatLink http://dx.doi.org/10.1787/888932371139

Key results

"Average earnings" are an important metric underlying the presentation of system parameters and the results of pension modelling. The distribution of earnings is used to calculate composite indicators, such as the progressivity of pension systems, the structure of the retirement-income package and weighted averages.

The table reports average earnings levels according to the OECD's average-wage (AW) measure for the year 2008. (Only one country, Turkey, is not yet able to supply earnings data on the broader basis and so the modelling is based on the old, APW measure of average earnings.) Earnings are defined as gross wages before deductions of any kind (including personal income taxes and social security contributions), but including overtime pay and other cash supplements paid to employees.

Average earnings are displayed in national currencies and in US dollars (both at market exchange rates and at purchasing power parities, PPP). The PPP exchange rate adjusts for the fact that the purchasing power of a dollar varies between countries: it allows for differences in the price of a basket of goods and services between countries. *The Economist* regularly produces a popular and easy-to-understand version of PPP – the "Big-Mac" index – which shows how currencies differ from the level that would mean the burger cost the same worldwide (see *www.economist.com/markets/bigmac/*).

Earnings across the OECD countries averaged USD 40 600 in 2008 at market exchange rates. At PPP, average earnings were USD 34 900. The lower figure for PPP earnings suggests that many OECD countries exchange rates with the US dollar were higher than the rate that would equalise the cost of a standard basket of goods and services.

Average earnings for the other major economy countries are not based on the AW or another consistent basis as such a series is unfortunately not available. Data have been collected from national sources and thus vary between average individual income, average covered wage and average wage for a particular group of workers as available.

Mean and median earnings

Most of the results presented in this report are based around mean earnings. However, many of the key indicators are shown also using estimates of "median" earnings, that is the level below and above which half of workers' earnings lie. The table also shows, from the *OECD Earnings Distribution Database*, median earnings as a percentage of mean earnings. There is significant variation between countries. The broad distribution of earnings in Turkey and Mexico means that the median is only around three-fifths of mean earnings. In contrast, the median is nearly 90% of the mean in Canada, Denmark, Finland and Sweden and as high as 95.5% in Iceland.

The table also looks at the top and bottom ends of the earnings distribution. For the lowest decile of earnings (10% of workers earn less than this), the average for the OECD29 is below 50% of mean earnings, a level which is used as the case of a "low earner" in the main indicators. The top decile – 10% of workers earn more than this – averages 166% for the OECD29. In the main results, a "high earner" is assumed to be an individual with 150% of mean earnings.

Definition and measurement

The "average-worker" series (AW) was adopted from the second edition of *Pensions at a Glance* (OECD, 2007). This concept is broader than the previous benchmark of the "average manual production worker" (APW) because it covers more economic sectors and includes both manual and non-manual workers. The new AW measure was introduced in the OECD report *Taxing Wages* and also serves as the benchmark for *Benefits and Wages*. The third edition of *Pensions at a Glance* (OECD, 2009) also included a comparison of replacement rates under the old and new measures of earnings for eight countries where the results were significantly different.

References

D'Addio, A.C. and H. Immervoll (2010), "Earnings of Men and Women Working in the Private Sector: Enriched Data for Pensions and Tax-Benefit Modelling", *Social, Employment and Migration Working Paper*, No. 108, OECD Publishing, Paris.

OECD (2007), *Benefits and Wages*, OECD Publishing, Paris.

OECD (2007), *Pensions at a Glance: Public Policies across OECD Countries*, OECD Publishing, Paris.

OECD (2009), *Pensions at a Glance: Retirement-Income Systems in OECD Countries*, OECD Publishing, Paris.

OECD (2009), *Taxing Wages 2007-2008*, OECD Publishing, Paris.

Average earnings and points of the earnings distribution, 2008

National currency and USD at market price and purchasing-power-parity exchange rates

	OECD measures of average earnings			Exchange rate with USD		Points of earnings distribution (% of mean earnings)		
	National currency (AW)	USD, market exchange rate	USD, PPP	Market rate	PPP	Lowest decile	Median	Top decile
OECD members								
Australia	60 400	50 400	40 900	1.20	1.48	49.5	83.3	167.5
Austria	38 800	56 800	45 600	0.68	0.85	48.1	82.7	164.0
Belgium	39 700	58 100	45 600	0.68	0.87	60.4	84.5	153.4
Canada	43 000	40 200	34 800	1.07	1.23	44.6	89.1	166.9
Chile	5 826 000	11 200	15 900	522.46	365.73			
Czech Republic	274 500	16 100	20 000	17.08	13.70	49.3	85.2	153.1
Denmark	359 300	70 500	43 800	5.10	8.20	60.9	89.0	150.4
Estonia	157 000	14 700	18 100	10.69	8.67			
Finland	37 300	54 500	40 400	0.68	0.92	62.3	89.5	147.9
France	32 700	47 800	37 200	0.68	0.88	55.1	81.2	159.5
Germany	41 400	60 500	50 600	0.68	0.82	43.4	87.0	165.7
Greece	23 900	35 000	34 100	0.68	0.70	42.8	68.0	147.7
Hungary	2 338 800	13 600	18 300	172.47	127.86	37.8	74.3	176.0
Iceland	4 068 000	46 200	34 100	88.00	119.34		95.5	
Ireland	40 900	59 700	43 400	0.68	0.94	45.2	82.7	169.0
Israel	112 400	31 300	31 300	3.59	3.59			
Italy	26 300	38 500	32 800	0.68	0.80	56.1	85.1	156.6
Japan	5 000 500	48 400	42 700	103.39	117.03	52.4	87.6	162.7
Korea	33 500 000	30 400	42 600	1 100.86	785.78	39.9	81.7	181.7
Luxembourg	48 400	70 700	53 300	0.68	0.91	48.9	77.9	167.3
Mexico	76 000	6 800	10 200	11.15	7.45	27.4	62.2	216.7
Netherlands	43 500	63 600	51 700	0.68	0.84	51.7	84.0	158.8
New Zealand	46 700	32 800	31 300	1.43	1.49	51.2	87.2	160.6
Norway	440 000	77 900	50 700	5.65	8.68	63.2	88.9	149.0
Poland	33 700	14 000	18 300	2.41	1.84	39.2	80.3	169.3
Portugal	16 100	23 500	25 100	0.68	0.64	40.9	69.3	189.2
Slovak Republic	8 700	12 700	16 200	0.68	0.54	45.1	78.7	163.5
Slovenia	15 800	23 100	25 100	0.68	0.63			
Spain	23 200	33 900	32 100	0.68	0.72	52.3	78.2	171.2
Sweden	352 500	53 400	39 900	6.60	8.84	56.0	89.8	150.9
Switzerland	74 500	68 700	47 500	1.08	1.57	56.6	84.9	153.4
Turkey	18 800	14 500	20 600	1.30	0.91	42.0	55.2	203.7
United Kingdom	33 600	61 500	53 100	0.55	0.63	39.6	75.5	165.9
United States	40 300	40 300	40 300	1.00	1.00	36.7	77.1	177.6
OECD34		**40 600**	**34 900**			**48.2**	**81.2**	**166.2**
Other major economies								
Argentina	33 700	10 600	18 600	3.17	1.81			
Brazil	16 500	9 000	11 300	1.83	1.46			
China	28 900	4 200	7 600	6.95	3.80			
India	154 400	3 500	9 600	43.51	16.01			
Indonesia	13 100 000	1 400	2 400	9 698.96	5 454.52			
Russian Federation	207 500	8 300	14 500	24.85	14.33			
Saudi Arabia	32 600	8 700	10 700	3.76	3.04			
South Africa	114 300	13 800	24 700	8.26	4.64			
EU27		37 300	31 100					

Note: Average earnings are not available on the AW measure for Turkey, for which the APW (average production worker) definition is used. Average earnings are rounded to the nearest 100 and exchange rates rounded to decimal places.

AW = Average wage; PPP = Purchasing power parity.

Source: OECD (2009), *Taxing Wages 2007-2008*; *OECD Main Economic Indicators*; *OECD Earnings Distribution Database*; see D'Addio, A.C. and H. Immervoll (2010), "Earnings of Men and Women Working in the Private Sector: Enriched Data for Pensions and Tax-Benefit Modelling", *Social, Employment and Migration Working Paper*, No. 108, OECD Publishing, Paris.

StatLink http://dx.doi.org/10.1787/888932372450

Pensions at a Glance 2011
Retirement-income Systems in OECD and G20 Countries

PART II

Chapter 6

Private Pensions and Public Pension Reserves

The range of indicators of private pensions and public pension reserves is greatly expanded in this edition of Pensions at a Glance.

The first of these eight indicators looks at the proportion of the working age population covered by private pensions. It distinguishes between mandatory, quasi-mandatory and voluntary schemes and between occupational provision, through an employer-provided or industry-wide scheme, and personal provision, arranged by an individual with a pension provider.

The institutional structure of private pensions is examined next. This shows the type of vehicle that is used to provide pensions, distinguishing between private pension funds, book reserves and insurance contracts. This indicator also examines pension types, split between defined-benefit, defined-contribution and mixed or hybrid schemes.

There then follows an analysis of pension gaps. This illustrates the amount that individuals would need to save in voluntary private pensions to achieve a specific level of income in retirement.

The fourth indicator reports assets in private pensions and public reserves for 2009. The way these assets are invested is explored in the fifth indicator. There then follows an analysis of the investment performance of private pensions and public pension reserves in 2008 and 2009.

The seventh indicator looks at operating expenses of private pension schemes and the fees charged to pension members in mandatory defined-contribution plans.

The final indicator focuses on defined-benefit occupational pension schemes. It examines how the assets in these schemes compare with their current and future liabilities in the form of pension payments. Funding ratios of 2 100 exchange-listed companies' schemes are presented for 2007, 2008 and 2009, disaggregated by the country of domicile of the company.

Key results

Private pension arrangements have been growing in importance in recent years as pension reforms have reduced public pension entitlements. In 17 OECD countries, private pensions are mandatory or quasi-mandatory (that is, they achieve near-universal coverage of employees through collective bargaining agreements). In a further six OECD countries, voluntary private pensions (occupational and personal) cover a significant part of the work age population: more than 40%.

Sixteen of the thirty-four OECD countries have some form of mandatory or quasi-mandatory private pension system in place, ensuring a high coverage of the working age population. In Finland, Iceland, Norway and Switzerland, occupational pensions are mandatory and cover between 70% and 80% of the working age population: employers must operate a scheme and contribution rates are set by the government. Iceland has the highest coverage rate of any OECD country at 82.5% of the working age population. Other occupational pension systems can be classified as quasi-mandatory: through industry-wide or nation-wide collective bargaining agreements, employers establish schemes that employees must join. As not all sectors may be covered by such agreements, these systems are not classified as mandatory. Examples include the occupational pension systems in Denmark, the Netherlands and Sweden. In these countries, the coverage is close to the one in countries with mandatory systems, with 60% or more of the working age population covered.

Mandatory personal accounts systems have been recently introduced in Latin America and Central and Eastern Europe to replace part of social security benefits. Such plans can be found in Estonia, Hungary, Mexico, Poland and the Slovak Republic, as well as in Denmark and Sweden. While coverage is nearly universal in Denmark and Sweden, it is still not the case in the other countries, where older workers tend not to be covered by the new systems. The coverage rate of around 30-50% will therefore increase over time as new workers join personal pensions. Some of these countries also have a high incidence of informal employment which limits coverage levels.

Coverage of voluntary occupational pension plans varies across countries. These plans are called voluntary in the sense that employers, in some countries jointly with employees, are free to set up an occupational plan. Personal pension plans are voluntary when individuals can freely decide whether to join them or not. The coverage of voluntary pension plans (both occupational and personal) is above 50% in Canada, the Czech Republic and the United Kingdom and close to 50% in Slovenia. On the other hand, the coverage of voluntary pension plans is very low (below 5%) in countries such as Greece, Luxembourg, Portugal and Turkey. In these countries the generosity of public pensions may explain the low private pension coverage. Coverage of voluntary personal pensions is also low in Mexico (1.6%) which has a mandatory private pension system.

Two countries, Italy and New Zealand, have introduced automatic enrolment (with an opt-out clause) into private pension plans at the national level. The results have been mixed. New Zealand has achieved a coverage rate of 43% in the new "KiwiSaver" scheme. In Italy, in 2007 the severance pay provision (so called *Trattamento di Fine Rapporto* – TFR) was automatically paid into an occupational pension plan if the employee did not make an explicit choice to remain in the TFR. Despite this rule, only 12.8% of the working age population is covered by a voluntary pension plan in Italy.

Coverage of voluntary private pensions has a hump-shaped relationship with age, reaching a peak at prime working ages, *i.e.* 35-44 or 45-54, depending on the country, and tends to increase with earnings.

Definition and measurement

Several measures of private pension coverage coexist. Individuals can be considered as covered by a private pension plan either if they have assets in a private pension plan, they contribute to a plan, or contributions are being made on their behalf. To be a member of a private pension plan from the perspective proposed here, an individual must have assets or have accrued benefits in a plan. Hence, an individual who does not contribute (for various reasons, including unemployment) or on behalf of whom contributions are not made during a year would still be considered as a plan member if he/she has assets or has accrued benefits in the plan. A large difference between the two measures of coverage arises in countries with large informal sectors.

Counting individuals more than once may arise when using administrative data as individuals can be members of both occupational and personal voluntary pension plans. Therefore total voluntary pension plan coverage cannot be obtained by summing occupational and personal coverage data. For example, in the case of Canada, 33.9% of the working age population are members of occupational plans and 35.1% have personal pensions, while overall voluntary pension coverage is 52.6%. This implies that 48% of people with occupational pension plans also have a personal plan.

Coverage of private pension schemes by type of plan, 2009

As a % of working age population (16-64 years)

	Mandatory/ quasi-mandatory	Voluntary		
		Occupational	Personal	Total
OECD members				
Australia[1, 2, 3]	68.5	..	..	..
Austria	n.a.	12.1	25.7	..
Belgium[2]	n.a.	38.5	..	..
Canada[2]	n.a.	33.9	35.1	52.6
Chile	74.8	..	..	..
Czech Republic	n.a.	n.a.	60.2	60.2
Denmark	ATP: ~70.0 QMO: ~59.0	n.a.	..	..
Estonia	65.0	n.a.	..	..
Finland	~100.0	7.4	21.3	28.8
France[4]	n.a.	3.5	7.0	..
Germany[5]	n.a.	32.2	29.9	..
Greece	n.a.	0.2	..	..
Hungary	43.6	n.a.	19.2	19.2
Iceland[3]	82.5	n.a.	..	..
Ireland	n.a.	28.6	10.5	37.6
Israel	35.2	..	..	..
Italy	n.a.	7.5	5.5	12.8
Japan	n.a.	..	..	..
Korea	n.a.	18.8	12.2	..
Luxembourg	n.a.	3.4	..	..
Mexico	50.2	1.5	0.1	1.6
Netherlands	69.3	n.a.	..	..
New Zealand	..	9.1	42.9	..
OECD members *(cont.)*				
Norway	..	..	22.0	..
Poland	53.0	1.2	..	..
Portugal	n.a.	4.3	..	..
Slovak Republic	36.5	n.a.	21.8	21.8
Slovenia[6]	n.a.	..	..	48.2
Spain	n.a.	7.0	28.1	..
Sweden[3]	PPM: ~76.0 QMO: ~68.0	n.a.	..	..
Switzerland[2]	70.1	n.a.	..	..
Turkey	..	0.5	4.2	4.7
United Kingdom[7]	n.a.	49.1	18.1	..
United States[3]	n.a.	32.8	24.7	41.1
Other major economies				
Argentina	..	n.a.	..	..
Brazil[8]	n.a.	2.0	6.1	..
EU27	..	..	..	..
China	..	..	..	..
India	..	..	..	..
Indonesia	..	..	..	..
Russian Federation[3]	..	5.4	..	..
Saudi Arabia	..	..	..	..
South Africa[8]	n.a.	23.4	..	..

. .: Means not available.
n.a.: Means not applicable.
1. Data refer to the total mandatory and voluntary.
2. Data refer to 2008.
3. OECD estimate based on data provided by national authorities as a % of total employment. The data provided has been adjusted by the ratio of total employment to the working age population. This implicitly assumes that individuals outside the labour force are not covered.
4. Data refer to 2006.
5. Coverage of occupational pensions refers to 2007 and includes all second pillar pensions. Coverage of personal pensions refers to 2008 and includes Riester and Rürup pension plans.
6. Data may include multiple counting as a person may be a member of more than one type of plan at any one time, particularly if the person has a number of employments in the year.
7. Data may include multiple counting between active and deferred members of occupational pension schemes, and occupational and personal pensions. The percentages are based on a working life of 16-64 for men and 16-59 for women.
8. Data refer to 2007.

Source: OECD *Global Pension Statistics* and national supervisory authorities' estimates.

StatLink http://dx.doi.org/10.1787/888932371158

Coverage of voluntary private pension plans by age and earnings

As a % of total employment

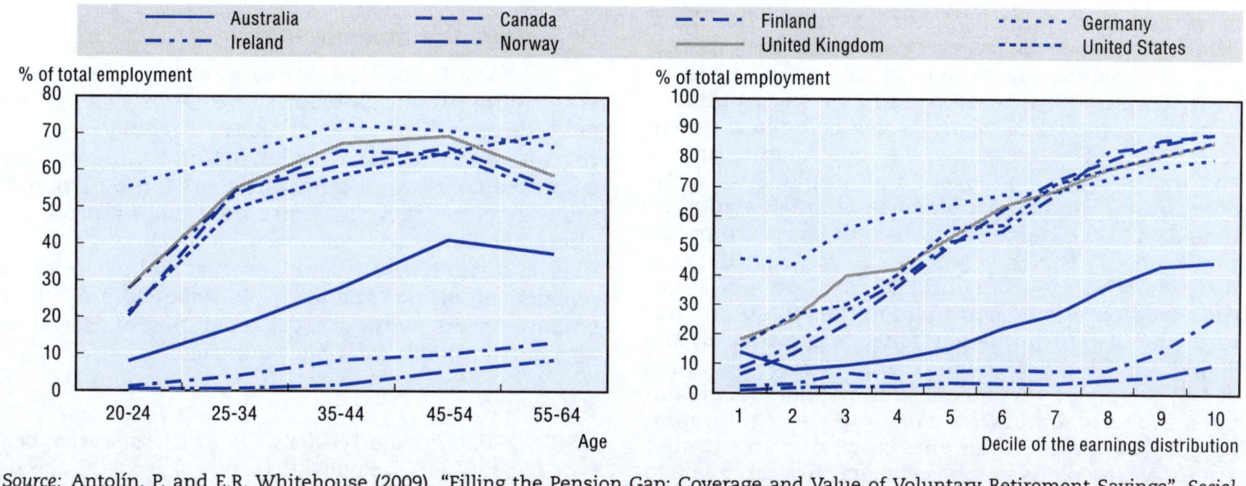

Source: Antolín, P. and E.R. Whitehouse (2009), "Filling the Pension Gap: Coverage and Value of Voluntary Retirement Savings", *Social, Employment and Migration Working Paper*, No. 69, OECD Publishing, Paris; OECD analysis of national datasets (Finland and Norway); national sources.

StatLink http://dx.doi.org/10.1787/888932371158

Key results

Private pension plans can be funded through various financing vehicles. In 2009, for OECD countries for which data were available, on average, 74% of OECD private pension assets were held by pension funds, 19% were held in pension insurance contracts run by life and pension insurance companies, 4% were held in retirement products provided by banks or investment management companies, and 3% were book reserves.

Within pension funds, DC plans are playing an increasing role, even if DB plans still dominate pension fund assets in some countries, largely due to their historical prominence as the favoured arrangement for occupational (workplace) pensions in many countries.

Occupational pensions are overwhelmingly funded through pension funds in most OECD countries, the main exception being countries such as Belgium, Denmark, France, Norway and Sweden where pension insurance contracts play a larger role, and Germany where book reserves – provisions sponsoring employers' balance sheets – are the main type of financing vehicle for occupational pension plans. Personal pension plans are often funded through pension insurance contracts or financial products provided by banks and asset managers. The main exception to this general trend are the mandatory personal pension plans established in countries such as Chile, Hungary, Mexico, Poland and the Slovak Republic. These systems can only be financed via pension funds during the asset accumulation stage (before retirement). At retirement, the accumulated assets may (or in some cases have to) be converted into an annuity, which is classified as a pension insurance product.

In 2009, for countries for which data is available, on average, 74% of OECD private pension markets were held by pension funds, 19% were held in pension insurance contracts run by life and pension insurance companies, 4% were held in retirement products provided by banks or investment management companies, and 3% were book reserves.

In broad terms, and depending on how pension benefits are calculated and who bears the inherent risk, pension plans can either be defined benefit (DB) or defined contribution (DC) in nature. In DC plans, participants bear the brunt of risk, while in traditional DB plans sponsoring employers assume most of the risks. Employers in some countries have introduced hybrid and mixed DB plans, which come in different forms, but effectively involve some degree of risk sharing between employers and employees. In the conditional indexation plans in countries such as Canada and the Netherlands, benefit levels are conditional on the fund's solvency status. Cash balance plans (another type of hybrid DB plan) provide benefits based on a fixed contribution rate and a guaranteed rate of return (the guarantee is provided by the sponsoring employer, hence these plans are classified as DB). Such plans are increasingly popular in Belgium (where by law, employers must provide a minimum return guarantee), Germany, Japan and the United States. Mixed plans are those where the plan has two separate DB and DC components which are treated as part of the same plan. For instance, the plan may calculate benefits under a DC formula up to a certain age before retirement and apply a DB formula thereafter. There are also DC plans such as those in Denmark, Iceland and Switzerland which offer guaranteed benefits or returns and in which risks are borne collectively by plan members. They are classified as DC as whenever there is no recourse to the sponsoring employer in case of underfunding. Such plans, however, provide a degree of predictability over future benefits similar to that of DB plans.

Occupational pension plans in OECD countries have traditionally been DB. However, in recent years, occupational pension plan sponsors have in many countries shown a growing interest in DC plans, as demonstrated by the number of employers that have closed DB plans to new entrants and encouraged employees to join DC plans (and in some cases also frozen benefit accruals for existing employees). DB plans, however, still play an important role, largely due to their historical prominence as the favoured arrangement for occupational (workplace) pensions in many countries. In 2009, traditional DB assets accounted for most of pension funds' assets in countries like Canada, Finland, France, Germany, Korea, Luxembourg, Norway, Portugal, the United Kingdom and the United States, where public sector pension funds remain overwhelmingly DB. At the other extreme, all pension funds are classified as DC in Chile, Czech Republic, Greece, Hungary, Poland, the Slovak Republic and Switzerland. In other OECD countries, the DB-DC split varies.

Definition and measurement

The OECD has established a set of guidelines for classifying private pensions (see OECD, 2005). The analysis uses this framework. Data is readily available for pension funds. On the other hand, not all countries collect and report information on pension insurance contracts or retirement saving products offered by banks or investment management companies. Information on book reserves, which refer to pension provisions made by plan sponsors on their balance sheets (without legal separation of assets), is also only available for a few countries.

Reference

OECD (2005), *Private Pensions: OECD Classification and Glossary*, OECD Publishing, Paris. The OECD classification is available at *www.oecd.org/dataoecd/0/49/38356329.pdf*.

Private pension assets by type of financing vehicle in selected OECD countries, 2009

As a % of total assets

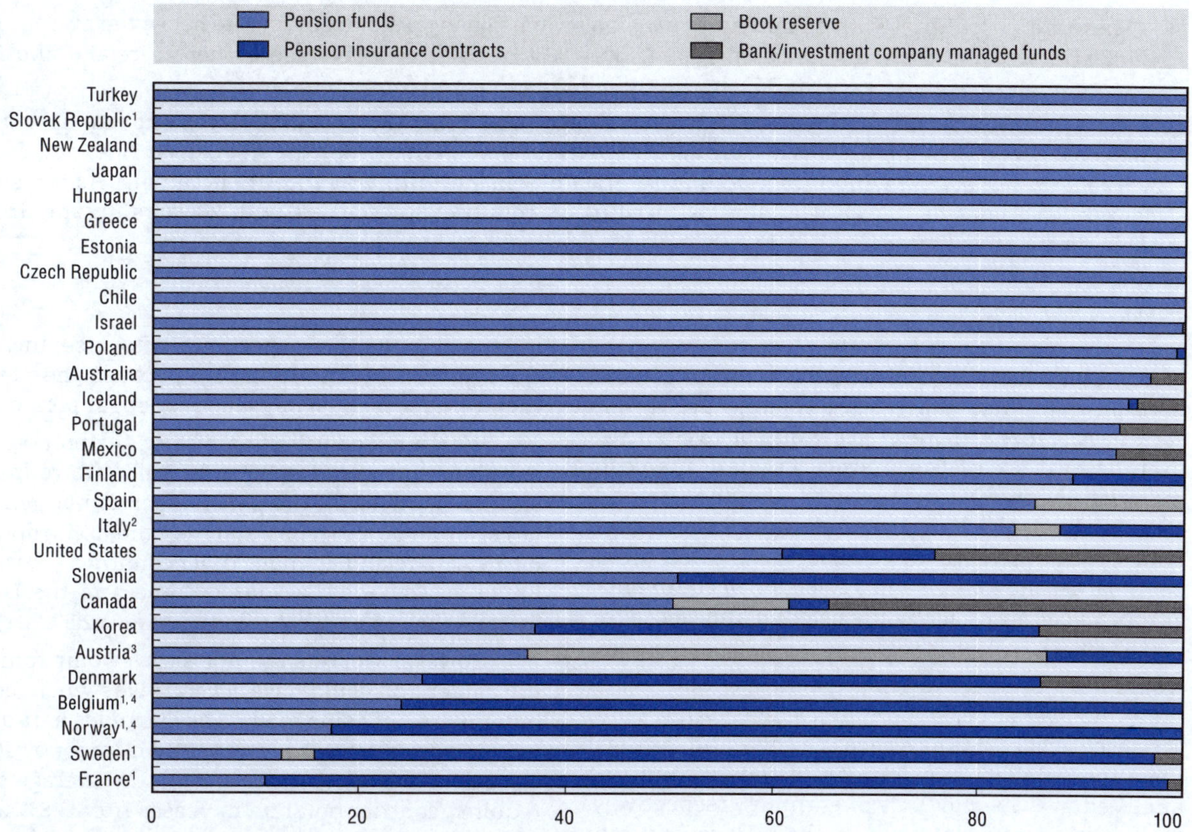

1. Data refer to 2008.
2. Data related to book reserve plans refer to the plans' net technical provisions.
3. Data related to book reserve plans and pension insurance contracts are OECD estimates.
4. Data related to pension insurance contracts are OECD estimates.

Source: OECD *Global Pension Statistics.*

StatLink http://dx.doi.org/10.1787/888932371177

Relative shares of DB, DC and hybrid pension fund assets in selected OECD countries, 2009

As a % of total assets

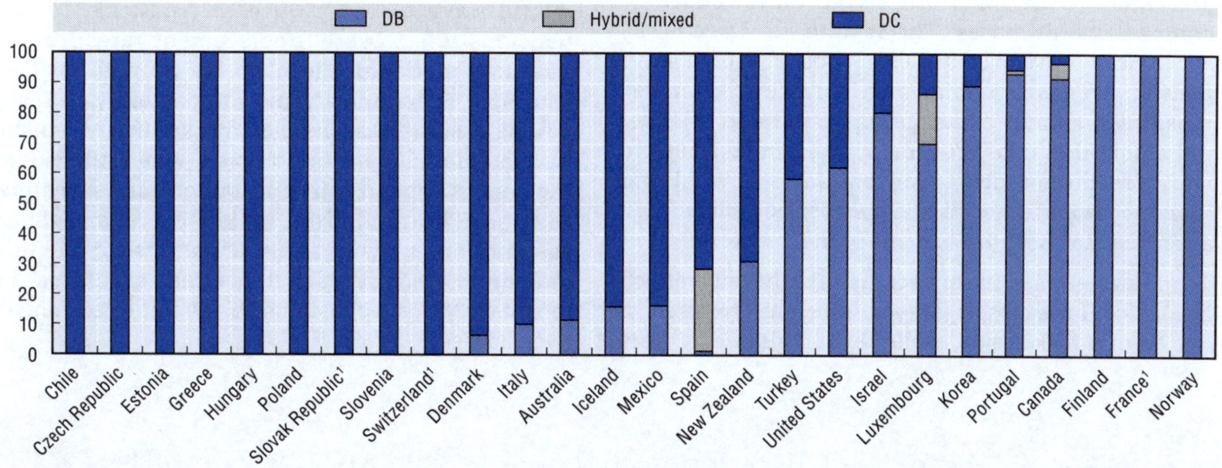

1. Data refer to 2008.

Source: OECD *Global Pension Statistics.*

StatLink http://dx.doi.org/10.1787/888932371177

Key results

There are 18 countries with a mandatory pension scheme giving a replacement rate below the average for the 34 OECD countries. This "pension gap" is over 28% of pay for an average earner in Ireland and for women in Mexico. It also exceeds 25% in the United Kingdom and for men in Mexico.

Pension contributions required to fill the pension gap and bring the overall replacement rate up to the OECD average can be up to 7.5% of earnings if contributions are made for the full career. However, most workers do not start paying into a voluntary private pension until well into their careers. As a result, contribution rates of 10-15% would be required in six countries for workers with 20 years missing from their contribution records.

The calculations include all *mandatory* programmes for providing retirement income, which can include compulsory private pensions and broad social-assistance schemes. This group of 18 countries includes all six of the mainly English speaking members of the OECD: Australia, Canada, Ireland, New Zealand, the United Kingdom and the United States. It also includes the two East Asian OECD members – Japan and Korea – and a selection of continental European countries, including Belgium and Germany.

In the United Kingdom, private pension schemes would need to deliver a replacement rate of 25.4% to bring the overall pension of an average earner up to the level of the OECD average. Sweden and Portugal have the smallest pension gap of the 18 countries analyzed at 3.5% and 3.4% of earnings, respectively. For the 18 countries as a whole, the replacement rate from mandatory pensions is 43.1% for (men) average earners. This implies a pension gap of 14.3% on average. For Mexico, the results for men and women are different because annuities are calculated on a sex-specific basis and so women must spread their accumulation over a longer retirement period.

The countries in the filling the pension gap chart are listed in the same order as the first chart for comparative purposes. The results are affected by differences between countries in pension ages: a lower pension age (as in Estonia and France, for example), meaning a shorter contribution period and a longer retirement duration. In Germany, the United Kingdom and the United States, contribution rates are lower than they would otherwise be, because normal pension ages are increasing to 67 and 68 in the long term.

Differences in life expectancy also have an effect. In Mexico, for example, 65-year-olds are projected to live an extra 20.3 years, while this figure is 25.3 years in Japan. Longer life expectancy, of course, increases the required contribution rate because the pension that it finances must be paid for a longer period.

With a full contribution history, the proportion of earnings that would need to be paid into retirement savings plans to fill the pension gap is not generally large: around 6% in Japan and the United Kingdom and over 7% in Ireland. In many other countries – Australia, Belgium, Canada, Germany, Korea and the United States – the required contribution rate is 2.5%-4.1%.

However workers are not always going to have a full career and could have several years where contributions are not being made. The examples here are for individuals delaying the start of their career by 10 and 20 years. For the countries shown, the average of the required contribution rate increases from 3.8% with a full career to 5.3% with ten missing years and to 8.0% with 20 years missing. With 20 years missing the required contribution level would be 15.6% in Ireland and 13.4% in Japan, more than double the level required for a full career.

Definition and measurement

The pension gap measures how much people would have to contribute to voluntary, private pensions to lift overall replacement rates from the national, mandatory level to the average for OECD countries. For simplicity and comparability, the calculations assume that people with voluntary pensions have a defined-contribution plan, where the value of the benefit depends on contributions and investment returns. The modelling makes the same general assumptions as with the calculations for the other indicators. In particular it assumes an annual real return of 3.5% on pension savings, net of administrative charges.

The pension gap

Gross replacement rate for an average earner from mandatory pension schemes and difference from OECD average replacement rate

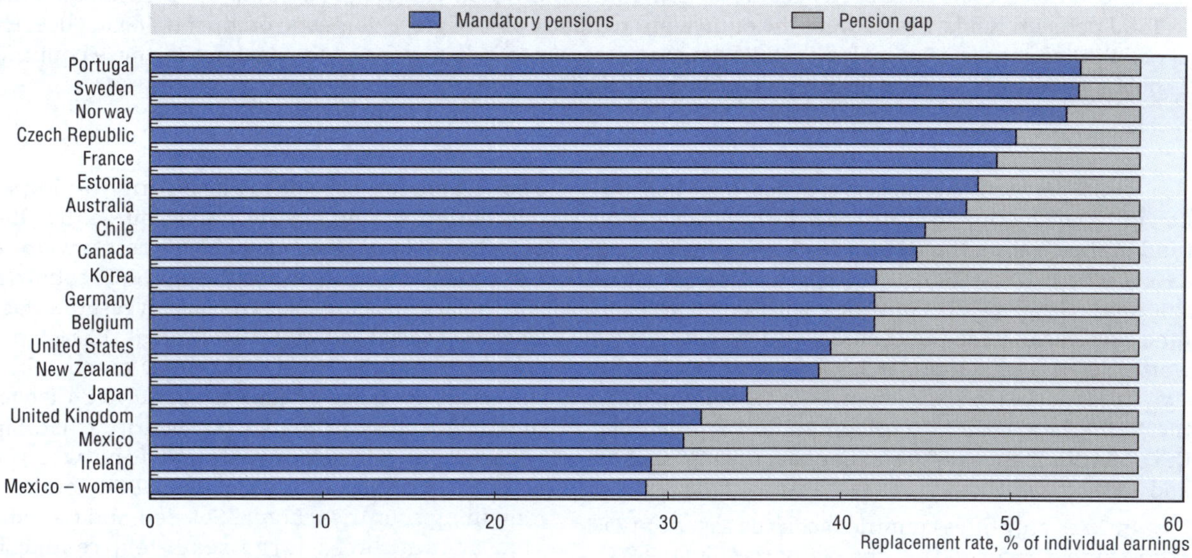

Source: OECD pension models; *OECD Earnings Distribution Database*.

StatLink http://dx.doi.org/10.1787/888932371196

Filling the pension gap

Contribution rate required for average earner to reach OECD average gross replacement rate

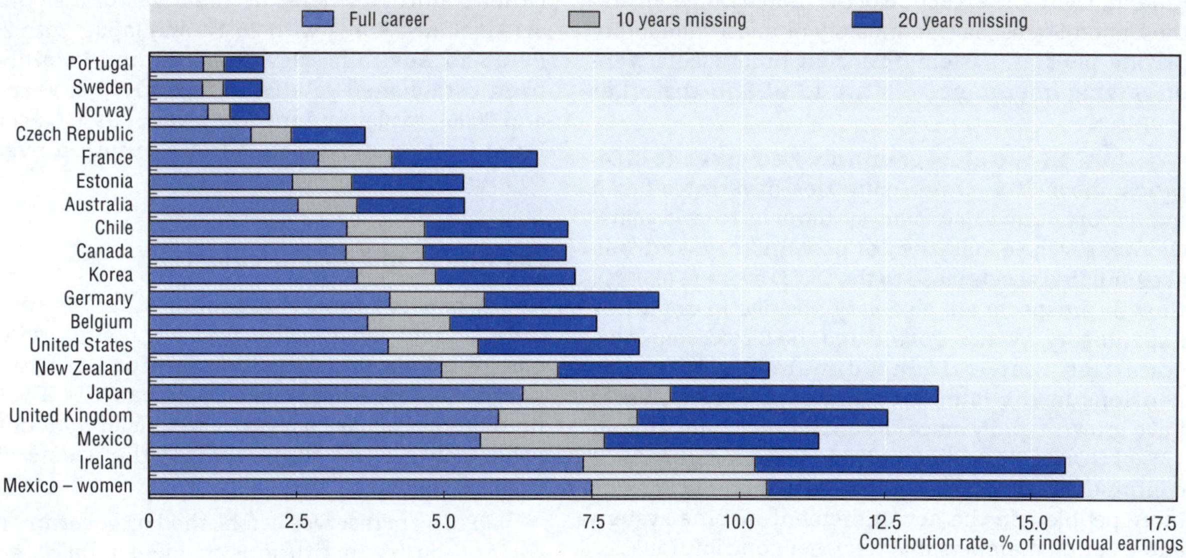

Source: *OECD Earnings Distribution Database*.

StatLink http://dx.doi.org/10.1787/888932371196

Key results

Substantial assets have been accumulated in most OECD countries to help meet future pension liabilities. Total pension funds' assets were the equivalent to nearly 68% of gross domestic product (GDP) in 2009. Half of OECD countries have built up public pension reserves to help pay for state pensions. In these countries, public pension reserves were worth nearly 20% of GDP.

OECD pension fund assets reached USD 16.8 trillion in 2009. The United States had the largest pension fund market within the OECD member countries with assets worth USD 9.6 trillion, representing 57.1% of the total. Other OECD countries with large pension fund systems include the United Kingdom with assets worth USD 1.6 trillion and a 9.5% share of OECD pension fund market in 2009; Japan, USD 1.0 trillion, 6.2%; the Netherlands, USD 1.0 trillion and 6.1%; Australia, USD 0.8 trillion and 4.8%; and Canada, USD 0.8 trillion and 4.8%.

In 2009, only three countries achieved asset-to-GDP ratios higher than 100% – the Netherlands (129.8%), Iceland (118.3%) and Switzerland (101.2%). In addition to these countries, Australia (82.3%), the United Kingdom (73.0%) and the United States (67.6%) exceeded the OECD weighted average asset-to-GDP ratio of 67.6%. In such countries, funded pensions have been in place for a long time, and with the exception of the United Kingdom and the United States, have mandatory or quasi-mandatory private pension systems. Pension fund assets were of varying importance relative to GDP in the other countries.

Only 13 out of 34 countries had asset-to-GDP ratios above 20%. Other countries have introduced mandatory funded pension systems in recent years. Of these, Chile has the longest history and has accumulated assets close to the OECD average (65.1%). Growth prospects are also very positive in countries like Hungary, Mexico, Poland and the Slovak Republic, countries that introduced mandatory private pensions in the late 1990s and early 2000s. Assets have grown rapidly since that point, reaching around 13% of GDP in Hungary and Poland. These figures will continue growing over coming years and decades as more people join the new retirement-income system and existing members make further contributions.

Public pension reserve funds (PPFRs) are expected to play a major role in the future financing of public pension systems, alleviating the impact of population ageing on the public purse. By the end of 2009, the total amounts of PPRFs assets were equivalent to USD 4.6 trillion for the 16 OECD countries for which data are available. The largest reserve was held by the US social security trust fund at USD 2.5 trillion, accounting for 54.7% of total OECD assets, although the assets consist of non-tradable IOUs issued by the US Treasury to the social security trust. Japan's government pension investment fund was second at USD 1.3 trillion – 28.2% of the OECD total. Of the remaining countries, Korea, Sweden and Canada had also accumulated large reserves, respectively accounting for 4.7%, 2.3% and 2.3% of the total.

In terms of total assets relative to the national economy, on average, PPRF assets accounted for 19.6% of GDP in the OECD area in 2009. The highest ratio was observed in the Swedish AP funds with 27.2% of GDP. Other countries where the ratio was of a significant size included Korea with 26.1% and Japan with 25.8%. PPRFs in Australia, New Zealand and Poland have been established relatively recently (between 2002 and 2006), explaining the low level of assets accumulated up to now. Assets should build up over the coming years.

Definition and measurement

A pension fund is a pool of assets forming an independent legal entity that are bought with the contributions to a pension plan for the exclusive purpose of financing pension plan benefits. The plan/fund members have a legal or beneficial right or some other contractual claim against the assets of the pension fund.

PPRFs are reserves established by governments or social security institutions to meet public pension expenditure. The assets in such reserve funds form part of the government sector, broadly defined.

Assets in pension funds and public pension reserve funds in OECD countries, 2009

As a % of GDP and in millions of USD

	Pension funds		Public pension reserve funds			Pension funds		Public pension reserve funds	
	% of GDP	USD	% of GDP	USD		% of GDP	USD	% of GDP	USD
OECD members					**OECD members** *(cont.)*				
Australia	82.3	808 224	5.9	51 629	Norway[7]	7.3	27 852	5.0	18 963
Austria	4.9	18 987	n.a.	n.a.	Poland	13.5	58 143	0.5	2 343
Belgium[1]	3.3	16 677	5.0	23 480	Portugal	13.4	30 441	5.7	13 068
Canada	62.9	806 350	8.5	108 627	Slovak Republic[1]	4.7	4 640	n.a.	n.a.
Chile	65.1	106 596	2.1	3 420.8	Slovenia	2.6	1 266	n.a.	n.a.
Czech Republic	6.0	11 332	n.a.	n.a.	Spain	8.1	118 056	5.7	83 387
Denmark[2]	43.3	133 980	n.a.	n.a.	Sweden[1, 8]	7.4	35 307	27.2	108 785
Estonia	6.9	1 371	n.a.	n.a.	Switzerland[1]	101.2	496 957	n.a.	n.a.
Finland	76.8	182 286	n.a.	n.a.	Turkey	2.3	14 017	n.a.	n.a.
France[1, 3]	0.8	21 930	4.3	118 669	United Kingdom[9]	73.0	1 589 409	n.a.	n.a.
Germany[4]	5.2	173 810	n.a.	n.a.	United States	67.6	9 583 968	17.9	2 540 348
Greece	0.0	63	n.a.	n.a.	**OECD34**	**67.6**	**16 777 792**	**19.6**	**4 642 111**
Hungary	13.1	16 886	n.a.	n.a.					
Iceland	118.3	14 351	n.a.	n.a.	**Other major economies**				
Ireland	44.1	100 278	13.7	31 049	Argentina[10]	11.5	30 105	n.a.	n.a.
Israel	46.9	95 257	n.a.	n.a.	Brazil[10]	17.1	224 218	n.a.	n.a.
Italy	4.1	86 818	n.a.	n.a.	EU27	..	..	n.a.	n.a.
Japan[5]	25.2	1 042 770	25.8	1 308 704	China[10]	0.6	19 980	n.a.	n.a.
Korea	2.2	29 632	26.1	217 768	India	5.4	61 971	n.a.	n.a.
Luxembourg	2.2	1 171	n.a.	n.a.	Indonesia	2.2	9 614	n.a.	n.a.
Mexico	7.5	107 135	0.3	3 605	Russian Federation[11]	1.5	14 987	n.a.	n.a.
Netherlands	129.8	1 028 077	n.a.	n.a.	Saudi Arabia	..	..	n.a.	n.a.
New Zealand[6]	11.8	13 755	7.1	8 265	South Africa[10]	58.4	165 630	n.a.	n.a.

Note: "Total OECD" represents the weighted average of funds' assets as a % of GDP or total funds' assets in millions of USD for countries for which data are shown.

n.a.: Means not applicable.

1. Pension funds' data refer to 2008.
2. Pension funds' data refer to autonomous occupational pension funds only. In addition to these plans, total assets managed by occupational pension insurance contracts amounted to 99.3% of GDP.
3. Public pension reserve funds' data refer to 2008.
4. Pension funds' data refer to autonomous occupational pension funds only. In addition to these plans, total assets managed by occupational pension insurance contracts amounted to 13.3% of GDP in 2008.
5. Pension funds' data are Bank of Japan's data.
6. Public pension reserve funds' data refer to June 2009.
7. The Government Pension Fund – Global, which was previously a sovereign wealth fund called the Government Petroleum Fund, draws its funding from oil revenues and has a mandate that goes beyond financing pension expenditures; so it is not classified as a sovereign pension reserve fund. The figure in this table, therefore, only refers to the Government Pension Fund – Norway, formerly the National Insurance Scheme Fund (5.0%). By contrast the total assets of the larger Government Pension Fund – Global, would amount to 109.6% of GDP.
8. Pension funds' data refer to autonomous occupational pension funds only. In addition to these plans, total assets managed by the premium pension system amounted to 8.9% of GDP and assets managed by occupational pension insurance contracts to 38.9% of GDP in 2008.
9. Pension funds' data are an OECD estimate.
10. Data refer to 2007.
11. Data refer to 2006.

Source: OECD *Global Pension Statistics.*

StatLink http://dx.doi.org/10.1787/888932372469

Key results

At the end of 2009, traditional asset classes (primarily bonds and equities) were still the most common kind of investment in pension fund and public pension reserve fund portfolios. Proportions of equities and bonds vary considerably across countries but there is, generally, a greater preference for bonds.

In most OECD countries for which 2009 data were available, bonds and equities remain the two most important asset classes, accounting for over 80% of total pension funds' portfolio at the end of 2009 in nine OECD countries. In Austria, for example, 54.9% of total pension funds' assets were invested in bonds, while 26.8% were in equities, giving Austrian pension funds an aggregate average weighting of 81.7% in equities and bonds. The combined proportion of bonds and equities relative to the total pension funds' portfolio in 2009 was 96.7% for Poland, 95.4% for Mexico, 93.8% for Chile, 89.7% for Norway, 88.4% for Denmark, 85.2% for Israel, 84.7% for the Czech Republic and 82.2% for Hungary. At the other extreme, this combined proportion was below 50% for Estonia (37.9%), Korea (36.5%) and Luxembourg (44%).

Proportions of equities and bonds vary considerably in pension funds' portfolio across countries. Although there is, in general, at the end of 2009, a greater preference for bonds, the reverse is true in some OECD countries, namely Australia, where equities outweigh bonds by 54.4% to 12.8%; Finland by 40.6% to 37.5%; and the United States by 45.4% to 31.4%. Equities and bonds were in the same range as bonds in Canada and Chile, with more than one-third of all pension funds' investments.

Within the "bonds" category, public sector bonds, as opposed to corporate bonds, comprise a significant share of the combined bond holdings of pension funds in many countries. For example, public sector bonds comprise 100% of total bond holdings in Greece and Turkey, 96.6% in Poland, 85.8% in Israel and 85.5% in Hungary, but only 30.7% in Norway, 26.7% in Chile and 8.9% in Germany.

Cash and deposits also account for a significant share of pension funds' portfolio in some OECD countries. For example, the proportion of cash and deposits in total portfolio in 2009 was as high as 20.7% for Slovenia, 27.8% for Turkey, 32.1% for Greece, 40.2% for Korea and 42.6% for Luxembourg.

In most OECD countries, loans, real estate (land and buildings), unallocated insurance contracts and private investment funds only account for relatively small amounts of pension funds' assets although some exceptions exist. Real estate, for example, is a significant component of pension fund portfolios in Switzerland, Portugal, Finland, Canada and Australia (in the range of 5 to 10% of total assets). Anecdotal evidence shows that pressure to decreased DB funding gaps and raise returns is driving a move into alternative investments with pension funds increasingly using derivatives to hedge risks and as an alternative to direct investment in the underlying markets.

Bonds and equities were also the predominant asset classes within PPRF portfolios at the end of 2009. There was also a strong equity bias in some reserve funds, which reflects their long-term investment outlook and generally greater investment autonomy. For example, in 2009, Ireland's national pensions reserve fund invested 72.0% of its assets in equities and 5.5% in bonds, while the figures for Norway were 61.4% and 33.9%, for Sweden (AP3 fund) 50.2% and 35.6%, and 44.2% and 23.7% for Australia. On the other hand, reserve funds in Japan, Portugal, Poland and Mexico invested much more in bonds than equities in 2009.

The extreme cases are those of the Belgian, Spanish and US PPRFs, which are by law fully invested in government bonds (except 3.3% of total assets invested in cash and deposits for the Spanish fund).

Some PPRFs also started to invest in real estate and non traditional asset classes like private equity and hedge funds. For example, the funds with the highest allocation to private equity and hedge funds were New Zealand (26.7% of total in 2009), Canada (17.1%) and Australia (12.7%).

Pension funds' asset allocation for selected investment categories in selected OECD countries, 2009

As a % of total investment

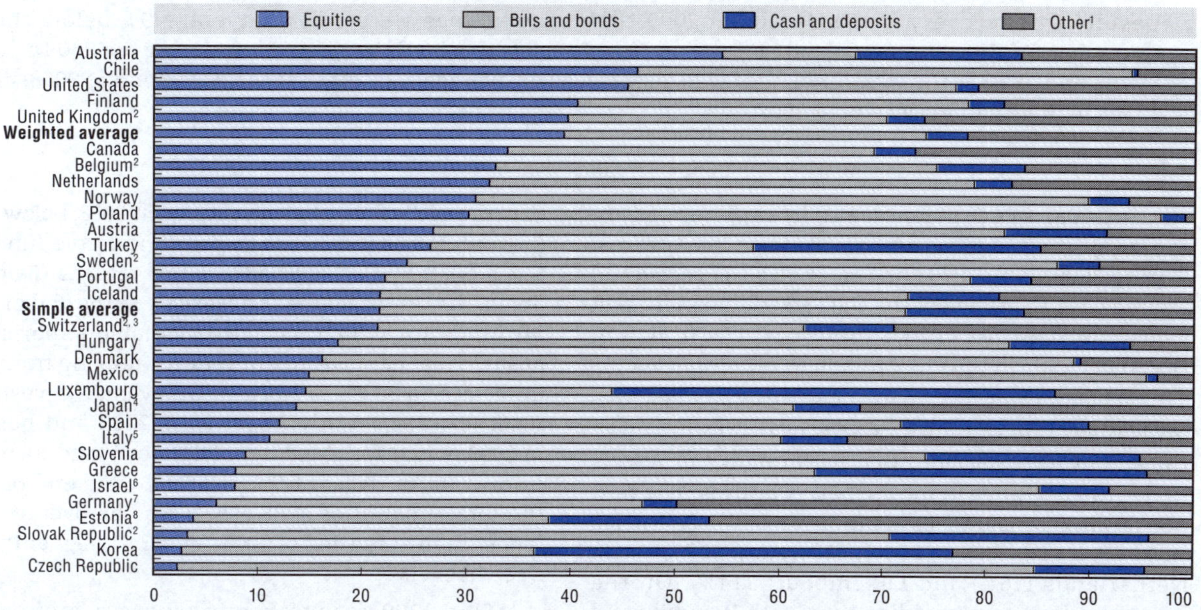

Note: The *GPS Database* provides information about investments in mutual funds and the look-through mutual fund investments in cash and deposits, bills and bonds, shares and other. When the look-through was not provided by the countries, estimates were made based on asset allocation data for open-end companies (mutual funds) from the *OECD Institutional Investors' Database*. Therefore, asset allocation data in this Figure include both direct investment in shares, bills and bonds and cash and indirect investment through mutual funds.

1. The "Other" category includes loans, land and buildings, unallocated insurance contracts, private investment funds, other mutual funds (*i.e.* not invested in cash, bills and bonds or shares) and other investments.
2. Data refer to 2008.
3. The high value for the "Other" category is mainly driven by land and buildings (11%) and other mutual funds (8%).
4. Bank of Japan's data. The high value for the "Other" category is mainly driven by outward investments in securities (26%), for which the split between various securities is not available.
5. The high value of the "Other" category is mainly driven by unallocated insurance contracts (22%).
6. The "Shares" category includes all mutual funds' investments, as the split between various securities is not available.
7. The high value for the "Other" category is mainly driven by loans (30%) and other mutual funds (16%).
8. The high value for the "Other" category is mainly driven by private investment funds (46%).

Source: OECD *Global Pension Statistics.*

StatLink http://dx.doi.org/10.1787/888932371215

Public pension reserve funds' asset allocation for selected investment categories in selected OECD countries, 2009

As a % of total investment

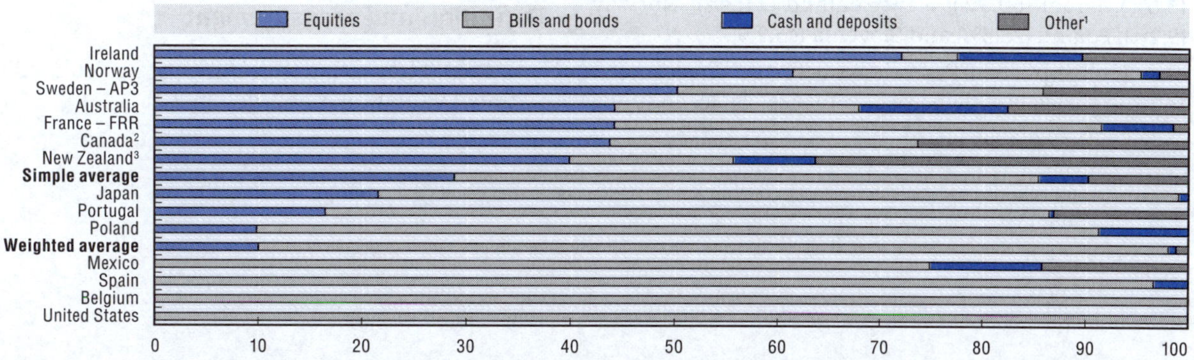

1. The "Other" category includes structured products, land and buildings, private investment funds, loans, unallocated insurance contracts, and other investments.
2. The high value for the "Other" category is mainly driven by private investment funds (17%).
3. Data refer to June 2009. The high value for the "Other" category is mainly driven by private investment funds (27%).

Source: OECD *Global Pension Statistics.*

StatLink http://dx.doi.org/10.1787/888932371215

Key results

During 2009, pension funds experienced a positive real investment rate of return of 6.5% on average. Despite this recovery, by 31 December 2009 their asset values were still on average 9% below their December 2007 levels. In 2009, public pension reserve funds regained the ground lost during the 2008 crisis. By the end of 2009, the total amount of PPRF assets was on average 7.3% higher than at the end of 2008, and 13.9% higher than in December 2007.

In 2008, OECD pension funds experienced on average a negative return of 22.5% in real terms. During 2009, pension funds in the OECD recovered around USD 1.5 trillion of the USD 3.5 trillion in market value that they lost in 2008 (from USD 18.7 trillion in December 2007 to USD 15.3 trillion in December 2008).

Pension funds experienced on average a positive investment rate of return of 6.5% in real terms up to the end of 2009. Pension fund performance in 2009 is in the 10-15% range in most OECD countries. The best performing pension funds amongst OECD countries in 2009 were Chile (23%), Hungary (17%), the Netherlands (16%) and Luxembourg (14%). On the other hand, in countries like the Czech Republic and Korea, pension funds had, on average, low positive investment rate of returns (under 5%). Pension funds in Iceland even experienced a negative performance in 2009 (–10%).

Despite this recovery, pension fund assets in most OECD countries have not climbed back above the level managed at the end of 2007 and it will be some time before the 2008 losses are fully recovered. For the countries for which information is available, on average, pension fund assets were, as of 31 December 2009, 9% below their December 2007 level. Some countries however already recovered completely from the 2008 losses. This is the case of Austria (assets at the end of 2009 were 4.0% above the December 2007 level), Chile (8.4%), Estonia (34.4%), Hungary (23.3%), Iceland (3.5%), Israel (60.9%), New Zealand (11.3%), Norway (9.2%), Poland (28.3%) and Slovenia (45.2%).

The impact of the crisis on PPRFs' investment returns varies greatly across countries, as some funds experienced strong negative returns in 2008, below –20% (Ireland, Norway, the French pension reserve fund and Sweden), while others had positive returns (Belgium, Spain, the United States and Mexico). At the end of 2009, all funds for which data are available experienced positive real net investment returns, ranking from 1.3% in Mexico to 30.7% in Norway. On average, investment returns were slightly negative in 2008 and positive in 2009 (when weighted by total assets), and increased from –2.0% in 2008 to 6.2% in 2009. By the end of 2009, the total amount of PPRF assets was on average 7.3% higher than at the end of 2008, and 13.9% higher than in December 2007.

The 2009 recovery represents a major step towards correcting the damage caused by the bursting of two major bubbles within the same decade. When measured over a longer investment period, performance looks healthier though still below long-term trends. The average yearly real rate of return over the last five years ranges from –0.6% in Ireland to 4.1% in Sweden (the 6th AP fund). For the countries that have longer data series, performance figures look somewhat brighter. For instance, over the last 10 years, the IMSS reserve in Mexico had an average real return of 3.4% annually; the Polish demographic reserve fund's return was 5.9% and the government pension fund – Norway's 4.6%.

Definition and measurement

Real (after inflation) returns are calculated using national valuation methodologies.

Pension funds' real net investment return in selected OECD countries, 2008-09 (%)

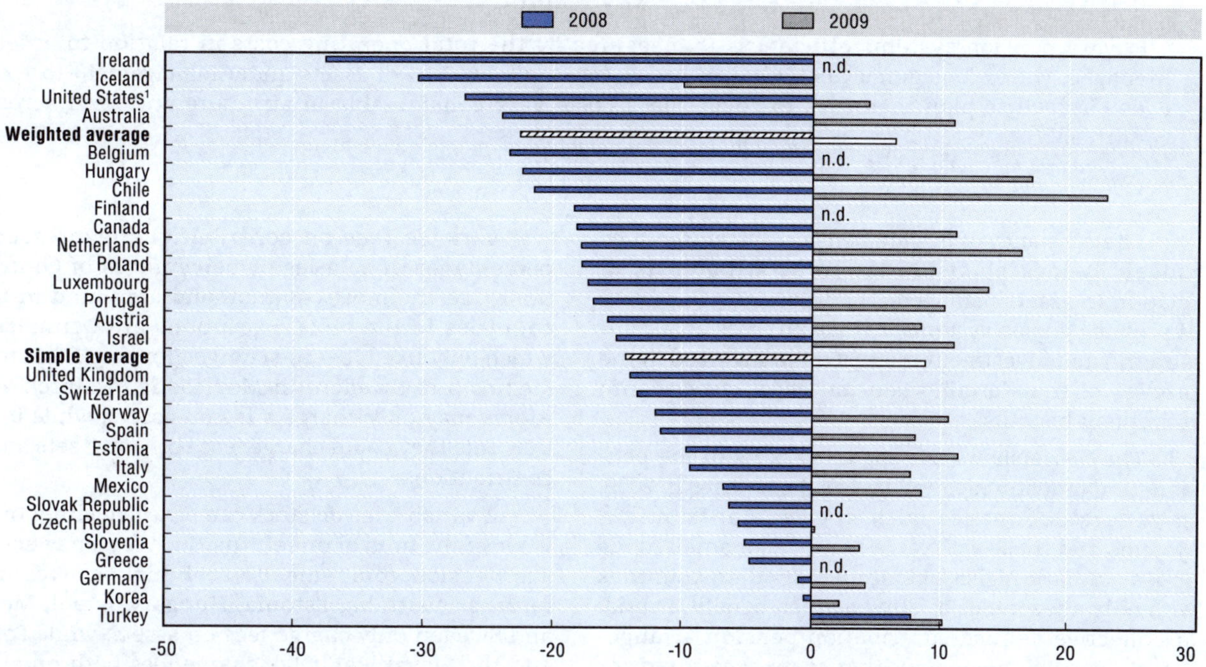

1. 2009 data refer to the period January-June 2009.

Source: OECD *Global Pension Statistics.*

StatLink http://dx.doi.org/10.1787/888932371234

PPRFs' real net investment return in selected OECD countries, 2008-09 (%)

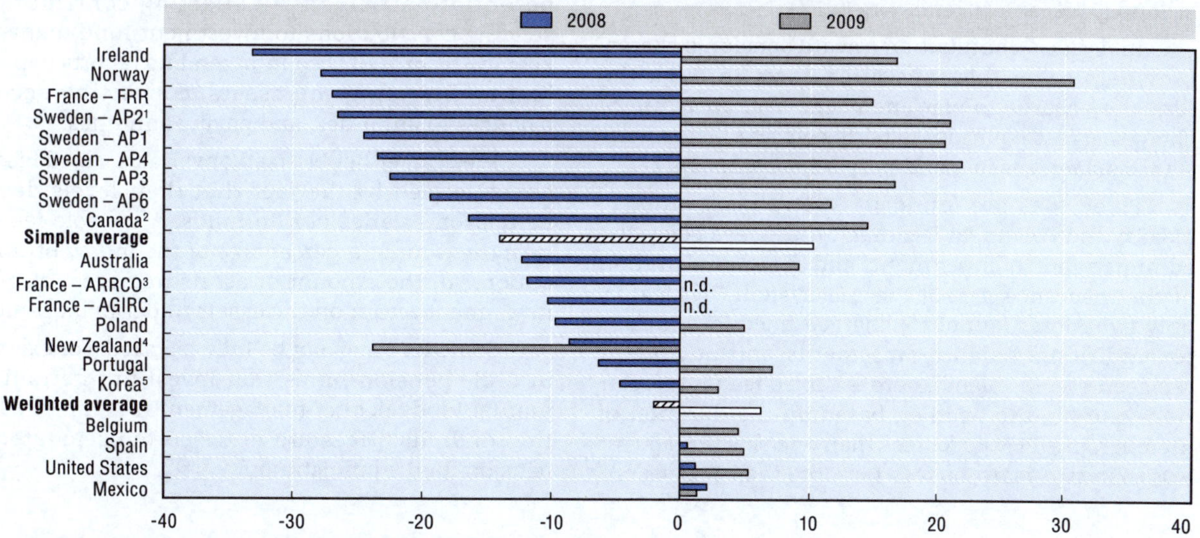

1. There are five Swedish National Pension Funds (AP1-AP4 and AP6).
2. 2009 data refer to fiscal year 2010 ending 31 March 2010.
3. AGIRC and ARRCO are unfunded mandatory supplementary plans for white-collar and blue-collar workers respectively, with reserves. More information on these plans can be found in the OECD *Private Pensions Outlook 2008.*
4. Data refer to June of each year.
5. 2009 data refer to the period January-March 2010.

Source: OECD *Global Pension Statistics.*

StatLink http://dx.doi.org/10.1787/888932371234

Key results

Private pension systems efficiency, as measured by the total operating costs in relation to assets managed, varies considerably between countries, ranking from 0.1% of assets under management to 1.2% Fees charged to plan members to cover these costs vary considerably in structure and level across countries.

The efficiency of private pension systems can be judged by looking at the total operating costs in relation to assets managed. The total operating costs of private pension systems include all costs of administration and investment management involved in the process of transforming pension contributions into retirement benefits.

The figure shows the operating costs of the pension fund industry reported by OECD countries in 2009. In general, countries with defined-contribution systems and those with large numbers of small funds appear to have higher operating costs than countries with only a few funds offering defined-benefit, hybrid, or collective defined-contribution pension arrangements. For instance, operating costs accounted for 1.2% of assets under management in Mexico, 1.1% in Spain, 0.9% in Slovenia, 0.8% in Chile and New Zealand, and 0.7% in the Slovak Republic and Hungary. On the other hand, they accounted for less than 0.3% of total assets in Austria (0.2%), Greece (0.2%), Denmark (0.1%), Iceland (0.1%) and Luxembourg (0.1%).

In defined-contribution private pension systems, providers cover their operating costs through the fees they charge to plan members. The structure of charges across countries is fairly complex. The analysis considers fees in mandatory DC systems only.

Fixed fees are found in Australia, Denmark, Mexico and Poland. In Denmark, these fees cover the administration of investments and the administration of the insurance part of the ATP system. In Mexico, only two Afores (out of 16) charged fixed fees in 2009 for additional balance statements and document replacement. In Poland, there is a fixed fee for transfer from one fund to another, based on the duration of membership (PLN 60 for less than one year, PLN 80 for less than two years, no fees for more than two years).

Variable fees on contributions (expressed as percentages of salaries or percentages of contributions) are the most common and are found in most countries in the table. Exceptions are Denmark, in which only fixed fees are charged for the ATP, Estonia, Mexico and Sweden. In Mexico, as of March 2008, Afores may only charge a fee on assets, while before that date they could charge fees both on assets and on contributions.

A variable fee on stock can be levied either on the value of the fund or on returns. Such fees may encourage pension companies to seek higher investment returns. Australia, Estonia, Hungary, Israel, Mexico and Sweden only charge fees on assets, while Poland and the Slovak Republic, charge fees both on assets and on returns.

Definition and measurement

Operating costs include marketing the plan to potential participants, collecting contributions, sending contributions to investment fund managers, keeping records of accounts, sending reports to participants, investing the assets, converting account balances to annuities, and paying annuities.

Fees can either be fixed or variable. Fixed fees are characterised by the fact that their levels depend neither on salaries nor on funds. A variable fee may take the form of a percentage of the inflow of contributions, of the amount of assets managed, or of the investment return on the assets under management.

Some fees may not be fully reported. For example, in Chile pension funds that invest in international mutual funds deduct management fees directly from the fund. Such fees are not reported separately by pension fund administrators.

Pension funds' operating expenses as a share of total investments in selected OECD countries, 2009 (%)

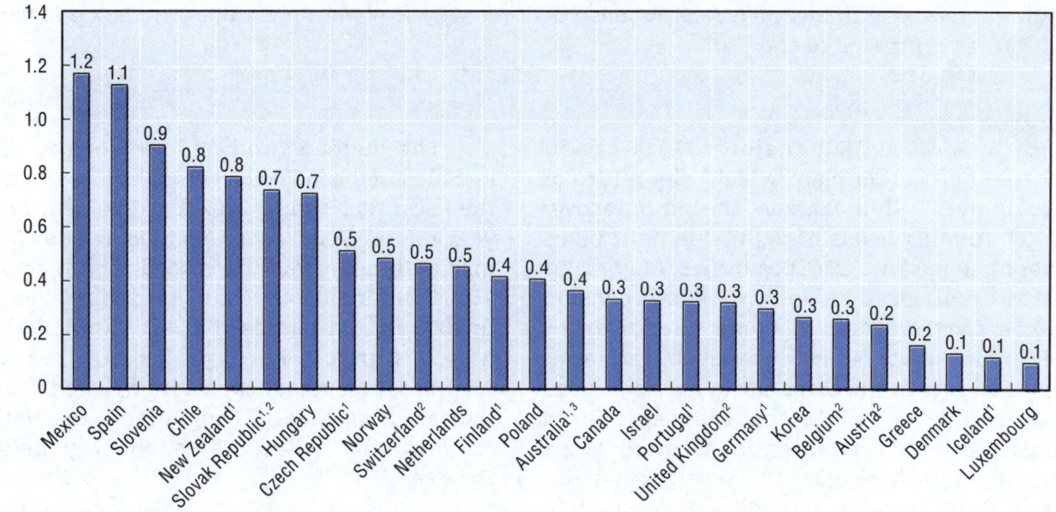

1. Data do not include investment management costs.
2. Data refer to 2008.
3. Data do not include self-managed superannuation funds.

Source: OECD *Global Pension Statistics.*

StatLink http://dx.doi.org/10.1787/888932371253

Average administration fee in mandatory DC systems in selected OECD countries, 2009

	Net fee on contributions (as a % of salary)	Fee on assets (as a % of individual account balances)	Fee on return (as a % of investment income)	Fixed fee (in local currency)
Australia	0-4.5% on contributions	0.7-2.53		38 (annual)
Chile	1.50			
Denmark				362
Estonia		1.54		
Hungary	0.44	0.57		
Israel	4.3% on contributions	0.39		
Mexico		1.70		From 13.02 to 21.70
Poland	0.44	0.41	0.023% of assets	From 80 to 160 (transfer fee)
Slovak Republic	1% on contribution (fee for maintaining of a personal pension account)	Max. 0.025% of the average net monthly value of pension fund´s assets	Max. 5.6% of one sixth of the return achieved during past six months	
Sweden		0.42-1.21		

Source: National supervisory authorities' estimates.

StatLink http://dx.doi.org/10.1787/888932371253

Key results

Funding ratios of exchange-listed companies' defined-benefit plans were still significantly lower at the end of 2009 as compared to end 2007.

About 60% of OECD pension assets are in defined-benefit and other plans which offer return or benefit guarantees. While markets started to recover during 2009, funding levels of defined-benefit plans remain very low in some OECD countries. Major 2008 asset losses experienced by defined-benefit pension funds were partly offset in some countries by decreases in the level of defined-benefit obligations as a result of increases in the corporate bond yields used for valuation purposes. In 2009, countries experienced the opposite effect, with large investment gains that were offset to some extent in several countries by increased defined-benefit obligations due to decreased in corporate bond yields. Furthermore, some countries such as Australia experienced reduced investment returns due to adverse exchange rates movements.

The figure shows estimated median funding level of the aggregate defined-benefit obligations of 2 100 publicly traded companies as published in their annual financial statements as of their fiscal years ending 2009, 2008 and 2007. Therefore, it shows the estimated median per cent by which a company's pension fund assets exceed (or do not exceed) the company's defined-benefit obligation as defined by international accounting standards. Companies are grouped by country of domicile.

Of the companies included in the index used, those that are domiciled in South Africa and Brazil had, on median, the best funded status of the companies in the study. These were the only countries whose companies had, on median, pension plan assets that exceeded the associated pension obligations on an accounting basis. The rest of the countries are on median to some extent under-funded. Companies domiciled in Norway, Belgium, Sweden and Japan had on median the lowest funded status on an accounting basis.

The median funding level for the companies included in the index decreased from a 13% deficit as of the fiscal year ending 2007 to a 23% deficit as of fiscal year ending 2008. As of fiscal year ending 2009, the median funding level decreased slightly to a deficit of 26%. The funding level worsened in 2009 as compared to 2008 in companies that are domiciled in South Africa, Canada, Portugal, the United Kingdom, Australia, Ireland and Japan. It improved in companies that are domiciled in Switzerland, the Netherlands, Finland, the United States, Norway, Belgium and Sweden.

Definition and measurement

The level of funding, that is, the ratio of pension plan assets to liabilities, is estimated using accounting data from pension plans' sponsors. Comprehensive requirements for the reporting of pension obligations exist for exchange-listed companies that sponsor defined-benefit plans.

The funding level was calculated using a sample of companies and a global index, covering 2 100 companies that reported a defined-benefit obligation due to pensions as of their fiscal year ending in 2007, 2008 and 2009. This global index is a total market equity index created by Thomson Financial Limited that covers 50 countries and all sectors.

Companies are grouped by country of domicile. Therefore, data represent pension plans' administered by headquartered companies and not the pension plans of the country of domicile. It is important to note also that the funding levels found in corporate financial statements are most often reported on a global aggregate basis and can only serve as a very broad indication of what may have happened on a plan specific level or on a country regulatory funding basis.

Estimated median percentage surplus or deficit of 2100 exchange-listed companies' aggregate defined-benefit obligations

In percentage, by country of domicile[1]

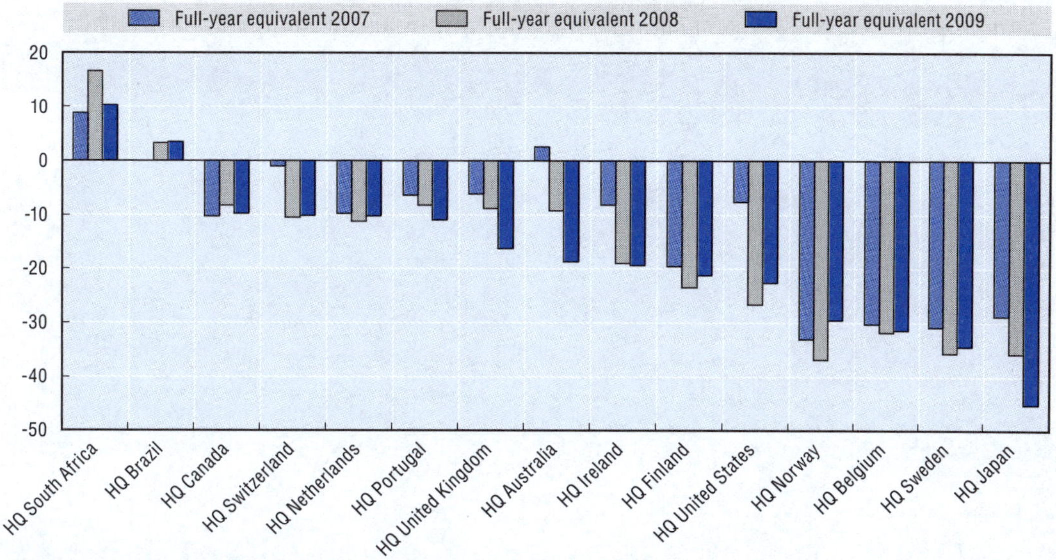

1. Only companies from the index that reported a defined-benefit obligation in 2009 were included. Fiscal year-end 2007 data is not available for Brazil.

Source: Thomson Reuters Datastream.

StatLink http://dx.doi.org/10.1787/888932371272

PART III

Country Profiles

This part of Pensions at a Glance *presents profiles of national pension systems. Each country profile summarises the architecture of national schemes and provides key indicators on demographics, public pension spending and average earnings. It then goes on to provide the detailed parameters and rules of the pension system in 2008, explains the calculation of pension entitlements and show the main results.*

First, there is a brief guide to the contents of the national profiles, which are then presented, first, for the 34 OECD countries and, second, for the eight other major economies that are members of the G20.

Guide to the Country Profiles

The country profiles use a common framework. First, there is a brief summary of the national retirement-income system and a table of key indicators. This background table comprises average earnings, public pension expenditures, life expectancy and the dependency ratio (the number of pensioners for every 100 workers). Data both for the country in question and the average for the OECD as a whole are presented.

Secondly, there is a detailed description of the rules and parameters of the pension schemes that make up each country's retirement-income system. These are structured as follows.

- Qualifying conditions: pension eligibility (or "retirement") age and years of contributions required to receive a pension.
- Benefit calculation: the rules for each schemes making up the pension system, such as basic, resource-tested and minimum pensions as well as public, earnings-related and mandatory private plans.
- Voluntary private pensions: the parameters of typical voluntary plans are provided for the countries for which replacement rates under these schemes were modelled in the indicator of "Gross replacement rates from public and private pensions" in Part II.
- Variant careers 1: the rules and conditions under which workers can retire early or continue to work beyond the standard retirement age and the impact on pension entitlements.
- Variant careers 2: rules for protecting pensions for people who are out of paid work due to caring for children or unemployment.

The treatment of pensioners under the personal income tax and social security contributions, for reasons of space, is not described in this edition (for all OECD countries, taxes and social security contributions paid by workers are those in force in the year 2008). However, the online version of the country profiles, available at *www.oecd.org/els/social/pensions/PAG*, do include this information. For details on the taxes and social security contributions paid by workers, see OECD (2009), *Taxing Wages*.

Values of all pension parameters and other relevant figures such as minimum wages are given in national currencies and as a proportion of average earnings. (See the indicator of "Earnings: Averages and distribution" in Part II.5.)

In each country profile, a table gives expected relative pension values, replacement rates and pension wealth at different individual levels of earnings for mandatory pension schemes. (See Part II.1 of this report for definition and measurement of the different indicators.) These are given in both gross and net terms (the latter taking account of taxes and contributions paid when working and when drawing the pension).

Summary charts show the breakdown of the gross relative pension value into the different components of the pension scheme (the first row of the charts). As far as possible, the same, terminology is used to describe these schemes. The particular national scheme that is described can be found in the text of the country study. Some standard abbreviations are used in the legends of the charts:

- SA: social assistance.
- Targeted: separate resource-tested schemes for older people.
- Minimum: a minimum pension within an earnings-related scheme.
- Basic: a pension based only on number of years of coverage or residency.
- Earnings related: all public earnings-related programmes, including notional accounts and points schemes as well as traditional defined-benefit plans.
- DC: defined-contribution, mandatory private plans.
- Occupational: mandatory or quasi-mandatory pensions, which can be provided by employers, industry-wide schemes (Netherlands), profession-based schemes (Sweden) or publicly (Finland, France).

The second row of country charts shows the effect of personal income taxes and social security contributions on relative pension values and replacement rates, giving the gross and net values.

The charts use a standard scale to ease comparisons between countries: the scale for replacement rates runs to 125% while that for relative pension values runs to 2.5 times average earnings. The charts show pension entitlements for people earning between 50% and 200% of economy-wide average earnings.

Australia

Australia: Pension system in 2008

Australia's retirement income system has three components: a means tested Age Pension funded through general taxation revenue; the superannuation guarantee, a compulsory employer contribution to private superannuation savings; and voluntary superannuation contributions and other private savings, which are encouraged to support self provision in retirement.

Key indicators

		Australia	OECD
Average earnings	AUD	60 400	48 600
	USD	50 400	40 600
Public pension spending	% of GDP	3.3	7.0
Life expectancy	At birth	81.5	78.9
	At age 65	84.8	83.1
Population over age 65	% of working-age population	22.1	23.6

Qualifying conditions

The Age Pension[1] is payable from age 65 for men. Women's pensionable age – currently 63.5 – will increase gradually to become 65 by 2014. Pension age will then be increased by six months every two years from 2017 until it reaches 67 by 2023. The minimum age for withdrawing superannuation guarantee benefits is currently 55, but this will increase gradually to 60 by 2025.

Benefit calculation

Defined contribution

The superannuation guarantee[2] was introduced in 1992. It consists of a mandatory employer contribution to a private pension plan. The pension plans may be operated by the employer, industry associations, and financial service companies or even by individuals themselves. The mandatory contribution rate has been 9% of employee earnings since the 2002-03 tax year.

Employers need not contribute for workers earning less than AUD 450 a month (equivalent to AUD 5 400 a year), but they can choose to contribute for these workers (Note that this minimum has not been raised in the past). There is also a limit to the earnings covered by the superannuation guarantee: employers need not contribute for employees' pay above this threshold. For each quarter of the financial year 2006-07, this amount was AUD 35 240 and for each quarter of the year 2007-08, it is AUD 36 470. This limit is worth around 2.5 times average wages and is indexed to a measure of average earnings.

The withdrawal stage of the superannuation guarantee complicates the calculations. Although there are some defined-benefit occupational plans, most employees are members of defined-contribution schemes. Members can take out the accumulated capital as a lump sum or some sort of income stream. Currently, most benefits are taken as a lump sum. For comparison with other countries (where defined-benefit plans predominate), the capital from the superannuation guarantee is assumed to be converted to a price-indexed annuity. The annuity calculation is based on mortality data for Australia.

Targeted

The Age Pension is designed to provide a safety net for those unable to save enough through their working life and to supplement the retirement savings of others. The income and assets tests (means test) are used to target payments to those in need.

The value of the Age Pension is adjusted biannually and is paid fortnightly. In September 2007, the maximum single rate of pension was AUD 538 a fortnight, increasing to AUD 547 in March 2008 and AUD 562 in September 2008. (All values have been rounded to the nearest dollar.) This gives an average for the tax year of an annual benefit of AUD 14 313.

The Age Pension's value is increased in line with price increases as measured by the consumer price index (CPI). Where necessary, a further increase is made to ensure that it does not fall below 25% of pre-tax Male Total Average Weekly Earnings on the national definition (which is slightly different from the earnings measure used in OECD analysis).

The Age Pension starts to be reduced once annual income from other sources exceeds a threshold known as the "free area". This is adjusted annually in July. The amounts for 2008 were AUD 132 in the first half and AUD 138 in the second half of the year (again calculated fortnightly). An assets test also applies. Almost 44% of all pensioners have their benefits reduced by the means test and are therefore on part-rate Age Pension. Within this group 82% are income tested and 18% are assets tested. Just over 56% of pensioners are on the maximum rate Age Pension.

Variant careers

Early retirement

Access to superannuation benefits (including superannuation guarantee benefits) is currently possible for retirement on or after age 55 (increasing to age 60). Individuals who are still working can also access their benefits from age 55, but only in the form of a non-commutable income stream. The Age Pension is not paid earlier than the qualifying age for men (age 65) and women (age 63.5, increasing to 65 by 2014).

Late retirement

It is possible to defer claiming superannuation after 65. Employers are required to make superannuation contributions under the superannuation guarantee arrangements for their eligible employees up to the age of 70.

It is also possible to defer claiming the Age Pension after 65. The pension bonus scheme pays a once-only, tax-free lump sum to eligible members who defer claiming the Age Pension and continue to work. The bonus is paid when the eligible member claims and receives the Age Pension. A person must register and work a minimum of 12 months from date of registration, and must complete at least 960 hours of gainful work each year. The bonus can be accrued for up to five years. The amount of bonus depends on the rate of the Age Pension a person qualifies for when they eventually claim and receive it. The bonus is 9.4% of the basic age pension entitlement for the first year of deferral. For two years, the bonus is four times that amount, nine times for three years, 16 times for four years and 25 times for five years. The maximum, five-year bonus is equivalent to 2.35 times one year's maximum Age Pension entitlement.

Childcare

There is no specific protection for periods out of work in the superannuation guarantee. Voluntary contributions are possible for periods out of paid work.

The means-tested structure of the Age Pension provides some protection for people with periods out of the workforce, in that it provides a safety net and supplements the retirement incomes of those unable to save enough during their working life.

Unemployment

There is no specific protection in the superannuation guarantee for periods out of work. Voluntary contributions are possible for periods out of paid work.

There are no credits in the superannuation scheme for periods of unemployment.

The means-tested structure of the Age Pension provides some protection for people with periods out of the workforce, in that it provides a safety net and supplements the retirement incomes of those unable to save enough during their working life.

Notes

1. *Note by the Australian Government:* Australia's Age Pension cannot be compared directly to benefits for the aged provided by other OECD countries, which are primarily aimed at income replacement. Australia's Age Pension is mean-tested, non-contributory and is funded from general taxation revenue. In addition to cash payments provided by the Age Pension, Australian seniors can be eligible for a comprehensive system of concessions for health and pharmaceuticals and other living expenses.
2. *Note by the Australian Government:* The Australian system also includes (government-supported) superannuation. OECD calculations include superannuation but differ from those of the national government.

Pension modelling results: Australia

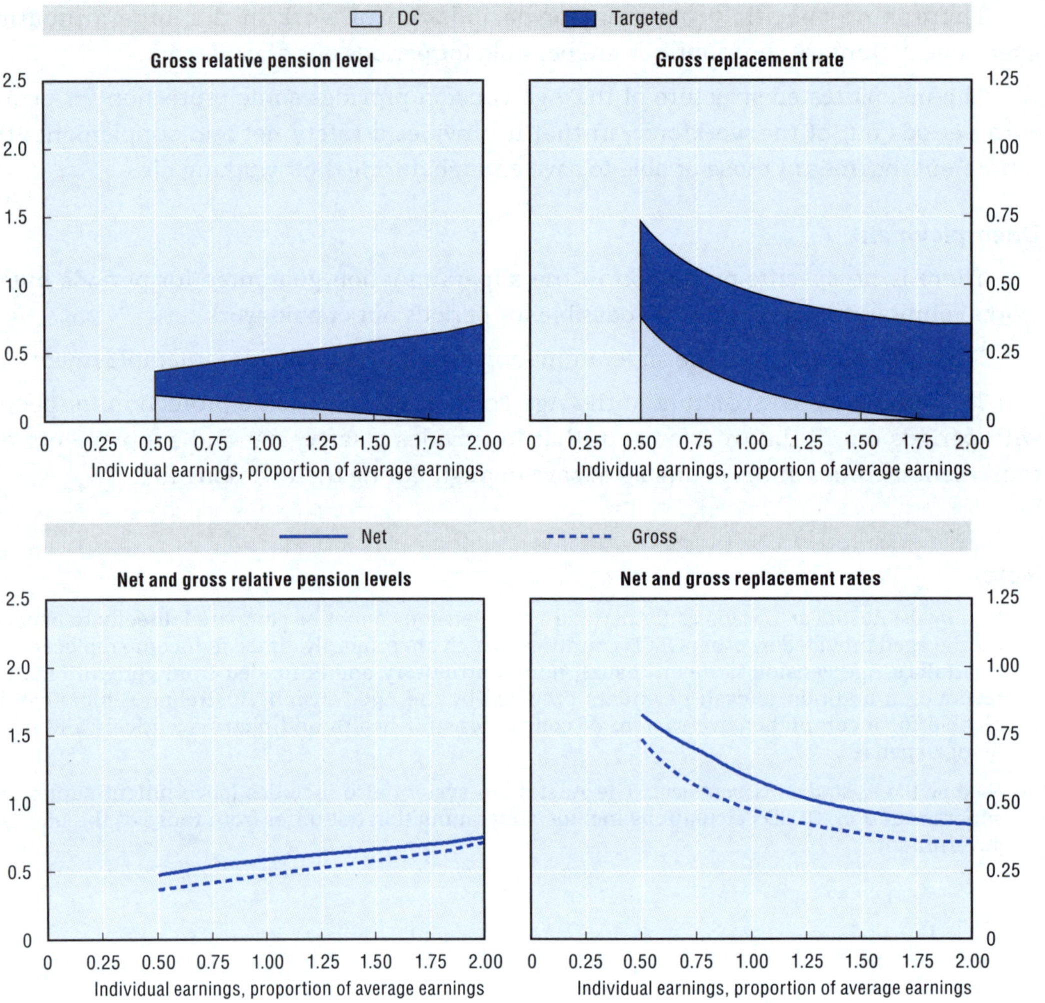

Men *Women (where different)*	Median earner	Individual earnings, multiple of average				
		0.5	0.75	1	1.5	2
Gross relative pension level	43.7	36.7	42.0	47.3	57.9	70.9
(% average gross earnings)	*41.6*	*35.4*	*40.1*	*44.8*	*54.2*	*63.6*
Net relative pension level	56.0	47.3	54.2	58.9	66.3	75.0
(% net average earnings)	*53.7*	*45.7*	*51.8*	*56.9*	*63.8*	*70.1*
Gross replacement rate	52.6	73.3	56.0	47.3	38.6	35.4
(% individual gross earnings)	*50.1*	*70.8*	*53.5*	*44.8*	*36.1*	*31.8*
Net replacement rate	65.9	82.5	69.3	58.9	47.1	42.0
(% individual net earnings)	*63.2*	*79.7*	*66.2*	*56.9*	*45.3*	*39.2*
Gross pension wealth	9.0	13.1	9.7	8.0	6.3	5.7
(multiple of individual gross earnings)	*10.0*	*14.7*	*10.7*	*8.7*	*6.8*	*5.8*
Net pension wealth	9.0	13.1	9.7	7.7	5.6	4.6
(multiple of individual gross earnings)	*10.0*	*14.7*	*10.7*	*8.6*	*6.2*	*4.9*

StatLink http://dx.doi.org/10.1787/888932371310

Austria

Austria: Pension system in 2008

The pension system consists of a defined-benefit public scheme with an income-tested top-up for low-income pensioners.

Key indicators

		Austria	OECD
Average earnings	EUR	38 800	27 800
	USD	56 800	40 600
Public pension spending	% of GDP	12.3	7.0
Life expectancy	At birth	79.9	78.9
	At age 65	83.5	83.1
Population over age 65	% of working-age population	27.6	23.6

Qualifying conditions

Normal pension age is 65 for men. For women, retirement age is currently 60 years but will be increased to 65 between 2024 and 2033. There is a coverage condition: 180 months (15 years) in the last 30 years or 300 months (25 years) during the full lifetime. Alternatively, 180 months of contributions actually paid (as opposed to coverage alone) are sufficient. Insured months are either contributory months (from employment or voluntary contributions) or supplementary (*i.e.* credited months, known as *Ersatzzeiten*) for which only limited contributions are paid. Within the 2005 pension reform the number of contribution years due to gainful employment required for old-age-pension has been reduced from 15 to seven years. The remaining minimum insurance period of eight years can be reached, *e.g.* by child raising periods.

Benefit calculation

Earnings related

The pension benefit currently accrues at 1.80% of earnings for each year of contributions but this will fall gradually, reaching 1.78% by 2009.

The earnings measure is currently the best 20 years' earnings. The valorisation procedure is complex although in practice adjustments have been closer to price inflation than to earnings growth. The averaging period is being extended; it will reach 40 years from 2028. Valorisation under this new procedure is still under discussion. The modelling takes this full-career measure and assumes that earlier years' earnings are revalued in line with earnings growth, though the final year is not adjusted.

Contributions are payable up to a ceiling of EUR 55 020 a year, corresponding to 142% of average earnings.

In 2008, pensions in payment were adjusted in four steps depending on the monthly pension amount. Pensions up to EUR 747 by 1.7%, pensions in between EUR 747 and EUR 1 050 by an amount of EUR 21, pensions in between EUR 1 050 and EUR 1 700 by 2.0%, pensions in between EUR 1 700 and EUR 2 161.50 digressive from 2.0% to 1.7% and pensions above EUR 2 161.50 by an amount of EUR 36.75.

Targeted

There is a means-tested top-up (*Ausgleichszulage*) that ensures a minimum retirement income of EUR 747 per month for single people and EUR 1 120 for a couple. There are 14 annual payments. Again, adjustment of the safety-net income is discretionary; the modelling implicitly assumes that it will rise in line with average earnings.

Variant careers

Early retirement

Retirement is currently possible from 62 for men and from 57 for women, subject to 37.5 years of contributions or credits. From 2017 on, the earliest retirement age for women will be 60. Pensions taken before the age of 65 are reduced by 4.2% for each year that the pension is claimed early.

Late retirement

For retirement between the ages of 65 and 68 the pension is increased by 4.2% per year and there is no such increment after 68. Workers who defer their pension continue to pay contributions thereby increasing their pension entitlements.

Combining work and pensions is possible but there is an earnings limit. If pensioners below the age of 65 earn more than EUR 349.01, the pension is fully withdrawn. After age 65, unlimited earnings from work and pension receipt are permitted.

Childcare

Periods spent out of paid work for childcare are taken into account in two different ways. Childcare periods of up to four years per child are credited on the basis of a fictitious pensionable salary of EUR 1 350 per month. But only two years per child are covered years and count towards the qualifying period for pension entitlement.

Unemployment

Periods of receiving unemployment insurance benefits and unemployment assistance (at 70% of the assessment basis) count as contribution years.

Pension modelling results: Austria

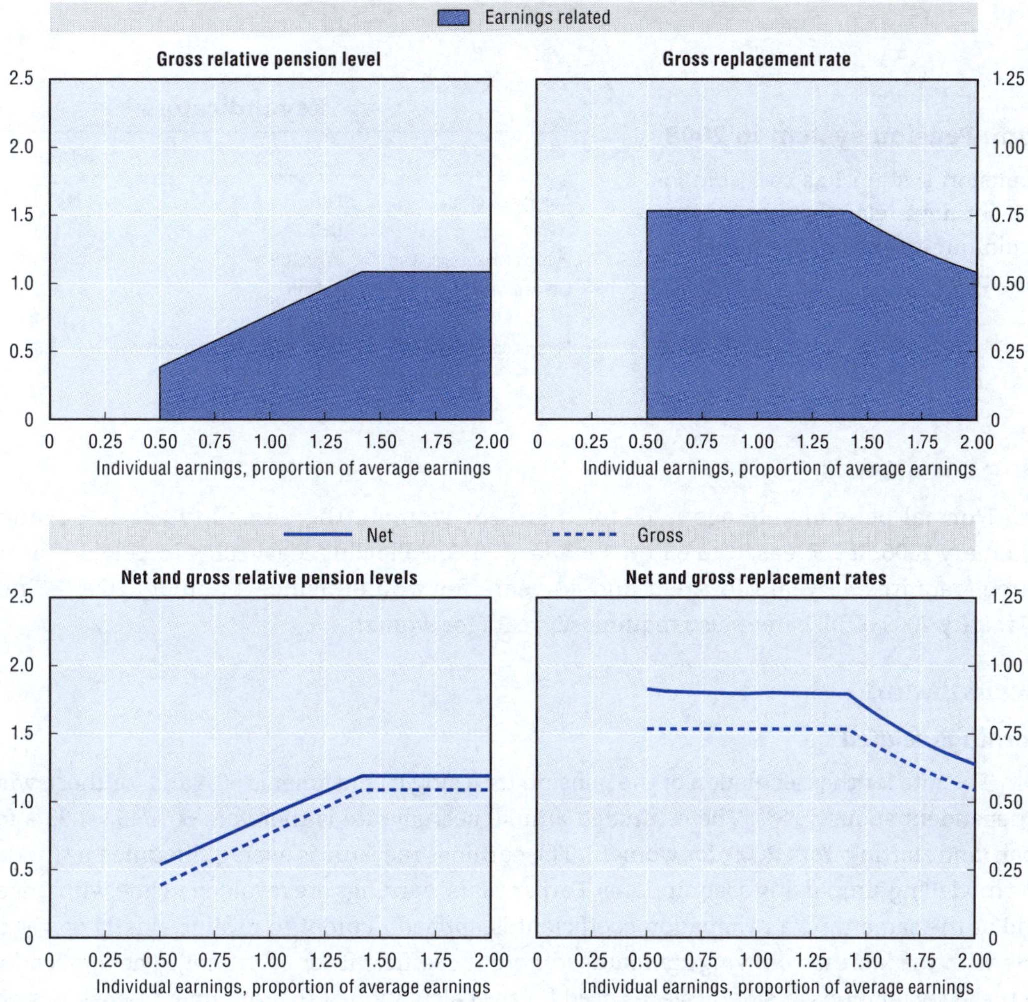

Men *Women (where different)*	Median earner	Individual earnings, multiple of average				
		0.5	0.75	1	1.5	2
Gross relative pension level	63.6	38.3	57.5	76.6	108.5	108.5
(% average gross earnings)						
Net relative pension level	77.4	53.5	71.5	89.9	118.8	118.8
(% net average earnings)						
Gross replacement rate	76.6	76.6	76.6	76.6	72.3	54.3
(% individual gross earnings)						
Net replacement rate	89.9	91.3	90.1	89.9	84.6	63.7
(% individual net earnings)						
Gross pension wealth	10.2	10.2	10.2	10.1	9.5	7.1
(multiple of individual gross earnings)	*11.2*	*11.1*	*11.1*	*11.1*	*10.4*	*7.8*
Net pension wealth	8.2	9.4	8.3	7.8	6.9	5.2
(multiple of individual gross earnings)	*9.0*	*10.3*	*9.2*	*8.6*	*7.5*	*5.7*

StatLink http://dx.doi.org/10.1787/888932371329

Belgium

Belgium: Pension system in 2008

The pension system has two components: an earnings-related public scheme with a minimum pension and a means-tested safety net.

Key indicators

		Belgium	OECD
Average earnings	EUR	39 700	27 800
	USD	58 100	40 600
Public pension spending	% of GDP	8.9	7.0
Life expectancy	At birth	79.6	78.9
	At age 65	83.4	83.1
Population over age 65	% of working-age population	28.8	23.6

Qualifying conditions

Normal pensionable age is 65 for men. For women, the eligibility age is 64 since 1 January 2006. It increased to 65 on 1 January 2009. Following legal rules in Belgium a full career requires 45 years for men and 44 years for women (since 1 January 2006). Since 1 January 2009 a full career also requires 45 years for women.

Benefit calculation

Earnings related

The rate for the calculation of the pension for a single pensioner is 60% and for those with a dependent spouse, 75%. The estimated annual accrual rate is therefore 60%/45 = 1.33% for men (and starting from 2009, for women). The earnings measure is average lifetime pay (under the modelling simplifying assumptions). Earlier years' earnings are revalued in line with prices and at the same time a revaluation coefficient is applied in order to revalue elderly wages in line with the increase of living standards (different coefficient for each year). The application of these revaluations of elderly wages used for the calculation of the retirement pension is not modelled.

The full pension is paid provided the qualifying conditions above are met. For shorter contribution histories, the pension will be provided, but calculated on the lower number of career years.

There is a ceiling to yearly pensionable earnings of EUR 46 895.18 for 2008.

Pensions in payment are uprated in line with a consumer price index (so-called "Health index" that excludes some goods). There have also been discretionary real increases (called "adaptations to well-being"). However, these increments have recently been more targeted to the lowest or the longest-running pensions. From 2008 onwards, legislation obliges the government to make decisions on uprating of pensions every two years, based on advice of the social partners.

There are additional payments ("holiday" and "supplementary" allowances), payable once a year. These are equal to the value of the monthly pension up to a ceiling of EUR 585.83 for a single person and EUR 731.92 for pensioners with a dependent spouse (amounts payable in May 2008).

Minimum annual credit

In cases of pensioners with low earnings or part-time work throughout their career, there is a minimum annual credit designed to increase the attributed pension entitlements for them. Annual earnings of less than EUR 18 389, (level applicable starting on 1 January 2008) (EUR 18 756.44 on 1 May 2008 and EUR 19 131.53 on 1 September 2008) are inflated to this level. To qualify for the minimum credits, at least 15 years' insurance is necessary, for an equivalent of at least one-third of a full-time employment. (This gives an effective minimum pension for a full-career worker for a single person with a 45 year contribution history raised to this level for each year of the career). The application of this minimum annual credit cannot lead to the attribution of a pension superior to EUR 15 864.90 (EUR 16 181.74 on 1 May 2008 and EUR 16 505.35 on 1 September 2008) for a pension at "family pension"-rate or EUR 12 691.91 (EUR 12 945.38 on 1 May 2008 and EUR 13 204.27 EUR on 1 September 2008) for a pension at "isolated person" rate. If the pension calculation should result in such a pension, the "minimum annual credit" application will not be applied for all eligible career years, until the pension passes under this ceiling.

Minimum earnings-related pension

There is also a minimum earnings-related pension which corresponds to EUR 11 032.28 for pensioners meeting the full contribution condition (45 years) (EUR 11 252.61 from 1 May 2008 and EUR 11 707.19 at 1 September 2008) for a single person or EUR 13 786.01 (EUR 14 061.33 from 1 May 2008 and EUR 14 629.39 from 1 September 2008 onwards) with a dependent spouse. The benefit will be a proportion of this minimum in the case of less-than-full careers, if the beneficiary has at least two-thirds of the full number of years. In the other case, the benefit value will simply be obtained through the application of the benefit formula (there will be no "levelling up" of the benefit in line with the minimum pensions).

The minimum pension is indexed to prices, excluding certain goods. Benefits are increased by 2% each time cumulative inflation exceeds a certain threshold (2%) since the last adjustment.

Pensioners will receive the higher of the minimum pension described here and the pension calculated (eventually with application of the "minimum annual credit" for those career years fulfilling the conditions).

Pension bonus

For pensions starting from 1 January 2007 onwards and before 2013, work after the age of 62 or beyond 44 years of contributions will be credited with a bonus (EUR 2 for each day worked, limited to EUR 624 (not indexed)for each full year of work), following the "generation pact".

Working after normal retirement age can also be used to plug career gaps to obtain a full pension or can improve the pension amount, since only the 45 last years are used in the calculation.

Safety-net income: Targeted

In the case of elderly people, who have no pension rights based on a professional activity or whose pension rights are very low, a means tested safety net income can be attributed. This so-called "GRAPA" (Garantie de revenue aux personnes âgées) is a part of the social assistance measures, which are complementary to the social security provisions (*e.g.* legal pension for workers of the private sector as modelled).

The means tested safety-net income for the elderly is EUR 10 380.47 (EUR 10 587.77 from 1 May 2008 and EUR 10 630.83 from 1 September 2008) for a pensioner living alone and EUR 7 785.49 (EUR 7 490.97 from 1 May 2008 and EUR 8 099.78 from 1 September 2008) for an older person living with others. Indexation is again to prices excluding certain goods. For the means test, "normal" pension revenue is taken into account for only 90% of its real amount.

Age limits correspond to the legal age: 65. During a transitional period (for GRAPA attributed between 1 January 2006 and 31 December 2008 it is possible to apply for GRAPA at the age of 64 (for women). Since 1 January 2009, the age limit is 65 in all cases.

Voluntary private pension

A scheme of sectoral complementary pensions was introduced in 2003 to further extend the second pillar pension system. The contribution rates are fixed through (sectoral) collective labour agreements, and can vary between economic sectors. (The modelled contribution rate is 4.25%.)

Variant careers

Early retirement

Since 2005, early retirement is possible from age 60, subject to 35 years contributions. There is no actuarial reduction in the pension calculation in the scheme of wage-earners. The pension however, can be incomplete, due to the possible incompleteness of the career (less than 45 years). There is an earnings test limiting the opportunity to combine an early retirement pension with work. This is stricter than the earnings test applied after normal pension age.

Late retirement

It is possible to defer pension after the normal retirement age. For people who continue working after normal retirement age, this can permit to plug career gaps to obtain a full(er) pension or can improve the pension amount, since only the last 45 years (44 years for women) are used in the calculation of the pension benefit.

Otherwise, it is possible to combine pensions and earnings (after normal pension age) within limits. For annual earnings under EUR 21 436.50 (single) or EUR 26 075.00 (with a dependent child), the pensions will not be reduced. Above this ceiling, the pension will be reduced by the amount that earnings surpass these limits. If actual earnings are 15% above the limits above then the pension will be completely withdrawn (for as long as the earnings surpass the ceiling).

Before the legal (normal) pension age, the limits for cumulating pensions and earnings are limited to EUR 7 421.57 or EUR 11 132.37 respectively, with the same 15% earnings restriction.

Childcare

A maximum of three years in total caring for children may count as gainful employment, if the person benefits from the so called "tijdskrediet". *Tijdskrediet* is a right for all employees in the private sector and they could benefit from a full suspension of labour activities or of a half-time reduction of labour time if they had worked more than three-quarters of full time for at least 12 months preceding the start of "tijdskrediet". They also need to have worked for the same employer for more than a year, during the 15 months before the application for the start of the "tijdskrediet" period. When a person withdraws totally from the labour market, no compensation is made. These years count in the numerator of the benefit formula. The value for earnings in the formula is the last earnings before the labour-market absence.

Unemployment

Periods on unemployment insurance benefits are credited under the pension system. The unemployment years count in the numerator of the benefit formula, and earnings prior to the period of unemployment are used in the calculation base for the entire unemployment period. There is no limit to the number of years credited. The application of this crediting however, will lead to a slightly lower pension benefit than in case of a full active career as this credit amount does not necessarily follow completely the full real wage growth over the credited period. Unemployment above the age of 62 or after 42 years of career will not allow for the application of the "pension bonus" for these years.

Pension modelling results: Belgium

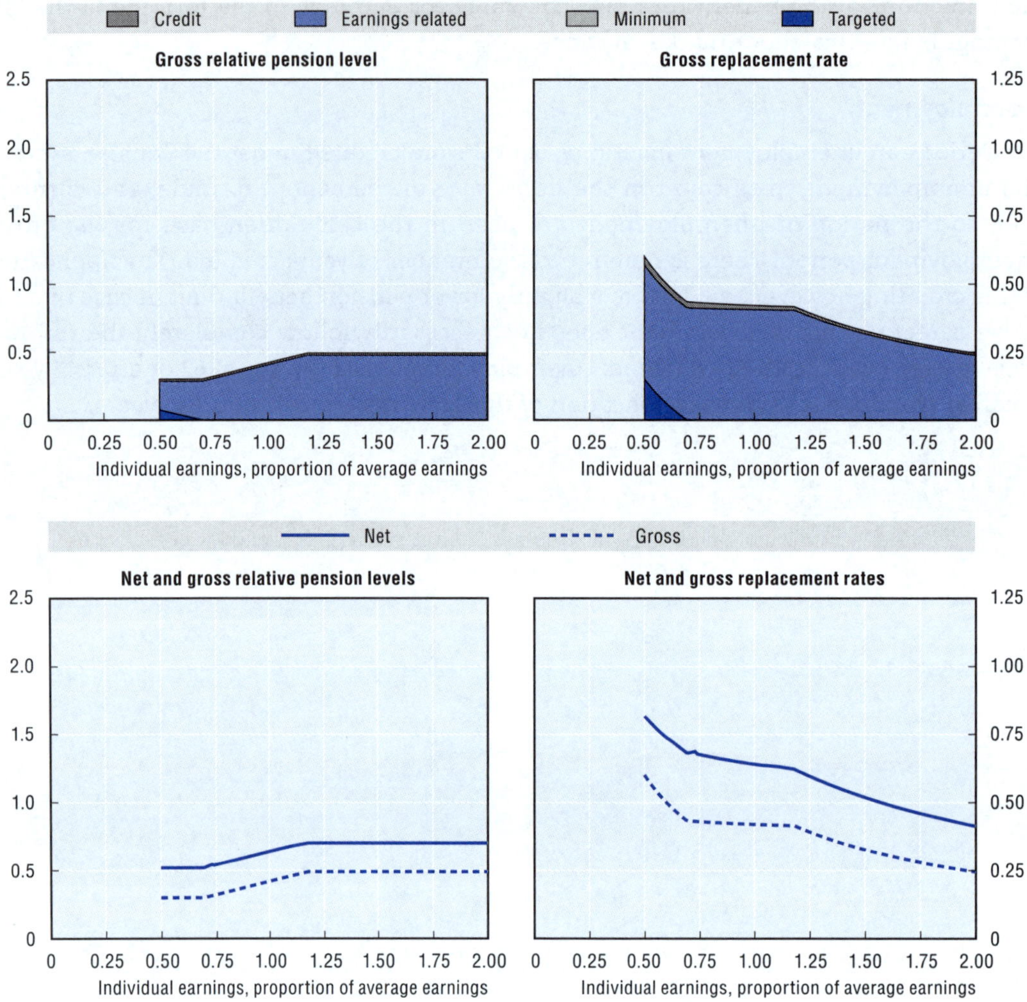

Men *Women (where different)*	Median earner	Individual earnings, multiple of average				
		0.5	0.75	1	1.5	2
Gross relative pension level	36.2	30.1	32.3	42.0	49.1	49.1
(% average gross earnings)						
Net relative pension level	58.3	52.0	54.5	64.1	70.3	70.3
(% net average earnings)						
Gross replacement rate	42.6	60.1	43.0	42.0	32.7	24.5
(% individual gross earnings)						
Net replacement rate	66.0	81.8	67.6	64.1	52.0	41.4
(% individual net earnings)						
Gross pension wealth	6.9	9.8	7.0	6.8	5.3	4.0
(multiple of individual gross earnings)	*8.1*	*11.5*	*8.2*	*8.0*	*6.2*	*4.7*
Net pension wealth	6.5	9.8	6.8	6.0	4.4	3.3
(multiple of individual gross earnings)	*7.6*	*11.5*	*8.0*	*7.1*	*5.2*	*3.9*

StatLink http://dx.doi.org/10.1787/888932371348

Canada

Canada: Pension system in 2008

The pension system offers a universal flat-rate benefit, which can be topped up with an income-tested benefit, and earnings-related public schemes.

Key indicators

		Canada	OECD
Average earnings	CAD	43 000	43 400
	USD	40 200	40 600
Public pension spending	% of GDP	4.2	7.0
Life expectancy	At birth	80.6	78.9
	At age 65	84.3	83.1
Population over age 65	% of working-age population	21.6	23.6

Qualifying conditions

The basic old age security (OAS) pension is subject to a residence test, with $^{1}/_{40}$th of the maximum pension earned for each year of residence after age 18 up to a maximum of 40 years. A minimum of ten years' residence is required to receive any benefit. It is payable from age 65.

For the earnings-related scheme, a full pension requires about 40 years' contributions but a single valid contribution is sufficient to generate an entitlement. Normal pension eligibility age is 65 but an early pension can be claimed from age 60.

Benefit calculation

Basic

The 2008 full pension level for the OAS pension was CAD 6 082.23. The value of the basic pension is price-indexed.

This pension is subject to an income test operated through the tax system (a "claw-back"). For income above CAD 64 718 a year, the basic pension in 2008 was withdrawn at a 15% rate. It is also indexed to prices.

Targeted

The guaranteed income supplement (GIS) is added to the basic OAS pension. The combination gave a maximum benefit of CAD 13 759.26 in 2008 for a single pensioner.

The GIS is reduced against income other than the basic pension at a 50% rate. The target benefit level is price-indexed.

Earnings related

Earnings-related pensions and benefits are provided by the Canada Pension Plan (CPP)/ Québec Pension Plan (QPP). The CPP and QPP offer broadly similar benefits. The scheme targets a replacement rate of 25% of earnings, based on average lifetime salary (excluding the 15% of years with the lowest earnings). Earlier years' pay is re-valued in line with economy-wide earnings. As noted previously, the full benefit requires about 40 years' contributions with proportional reductions for shorter work histories. The maximum earnings-related retirement pension for 2008 was CAD 884.58 a month.

People earning less than CAD 3 500 a year are not required to contribute. There was a ceiling to contributions of CAD 44 900 in 2008. The ceiling is indexed to increases in average earnings while the contribution floor is frozen in nominal terms.

The value of the earnings-related pension after retirement is uprated annually in line with prices.

Voluntary private pension

There is an additional voluntary pension which is assumed to be defined contribution. The contribution rate is assumed to be 8.5%.

Variant careers

Early retirement

Early retirement beginning at age 60 is possible in the state earnings-related scheme subject to a benefit reduction of 6% per year. Early retirement is not possible in the other two public schemes (basic and means-tested).

Late retirement

The earnings-related pension can be deferred, earning a 6% increment for each year after age 65 – up to a maximum of five years. The basic and income-tested benefits cannot be deferred. The income-test for the latter includes earnings, whilst for the former there is a claw-back against large incomes, again including earnings.

Childcare

Years of caring for children under the age of 7 are excluded from the averaging period in the pension calculation and these years are excluded from the contributory period under the earnings-related scheme.

Unemployment

Up to 15% of the contributory period may be excluded in calculating average earnings in the earnings-related scheme. This drop-out is intended to compensate for periods of unemployment, illness, schooling, etc. There are no credits for periods of unemployment.

Pension modelling results: Canada

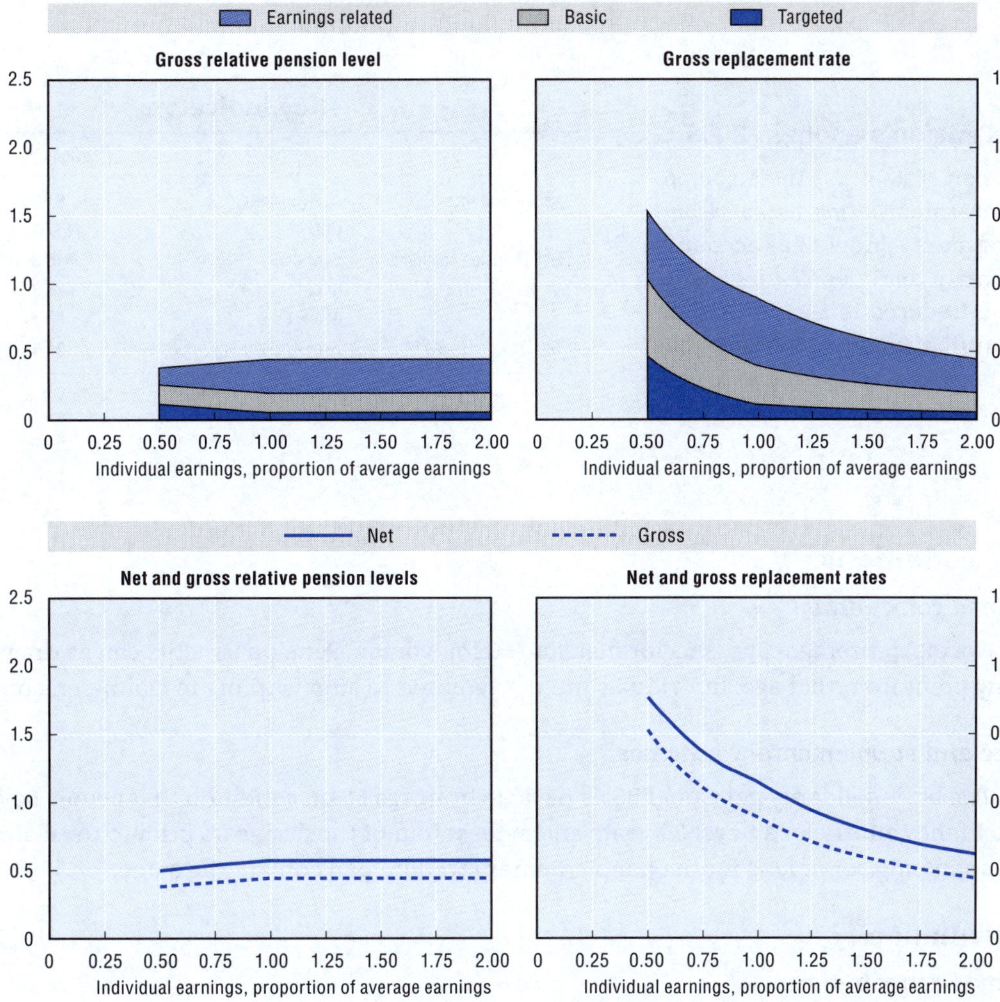

Men *Women (where different)*	Median earner	Individual earnings, multiple of average				
		0.5	0.75	1	1.5	2
Gross relative pension level	43.2	38.3	41.4	44.4	44.4	44.4
(% average gross earnings)						
Net relative pension level	55.9	50.0	54.1	57.3	57.3	57.3
(% net average earnings)						
Gross replacement rate	48.5	76.6	55.2	44.4	29.6	22.2
(% individual gross earnings)						
Net replacement rate	61.5	88.7	68.3	57.3	39.7	31.1
(% individual net earnings)						
Gross pension wealth	8.1	12.9	9.3	7.5	5.0	3.7
(multiple of individual gross earnings)	*9.1*	*14.4*	*10.4*	*8.4*	*5.6*	*4.2*
Net pension wealth	8.1	12.9	9.3	7.4	4.9	3.7
(multiple of individual gross earnings)	*9.1*	*14.4*	*10.4*	*8.3*	*5.5*	*4.1*

StatLink http://dx.doi.org/10.1787/888932371386

Chile

Chile: Pension system in 2008

The pension system has three components: a redistributive first tier, a second tier of mandatory individual accounts and a voluntary third tier. The individual accounts, introduced in 1981, are of the defined-contribution type. The redistributive first tier was substantially extended in a pension reform in 2008.

Key indicators

		Chile	OECD
Average earnings	CLP (million)	5.83	21.21
	USD	11 200	40 600
Public pension spending	% of GDP	5.2	7.0
Life expectancy	At birth	78.6	78.9
	At age 65	83.7	83.1
Population over age 65	% of working-age population	14.8	23.6

Qualifying conditions

Defined contribution

Normal retirement age is 65 for men and 60 for women. Pension benefits can be drawn at any point from that age. Individuals are not required to stop working to claim pension.

Basic and supplementary schemes

The basic solidarity pension (PBS) is payable from age 65 on condition that people have lived in the country for at least 20 years and at least four of the five years prior to the claim. The qualifying conditions for the supplementary welfare pension are the same.

Benefit calculation

Defined contribution

The contribution rate for individual accounts is 10% of earnings. Administrative charges are levied on top of this contribution (not out of the mandatory contribution).

There is a ceiling on contributions, which in 2008 was set at 60 "unidad de fomento" (real, that is inflation adjusted, units), which was CLP 1 287 283 per month, equal to eight times the minimum wage in December 2008 and 291% of average earnings. From 2009 onwards, the ceiling will be indexed to average earnings.

At retirement, the accumulated capital can be used to buy an immediate life annuity, to get a temporary income with a deferred life annuity, to take programmed withdrawals, or to buy an immediate life annuity with programmed withdrawals. A withdrawal of 15 "unidad de fomento" (UFs) is made from the individual account to cover for funeral expenses. For comparison with other countries, replacement rates have been calculated assuming an actuarially fair annuity, using sex-specific annuity rates.

Basic

The basic pension (PBS) was CLP 60 000 in 2008-09. This was increased to CLP 75 000 from 1 July 2008 as a result of the 2008 reform. The modelling uses this higher value for the basic pension and assumes it is indexed to wages.

Supplementary

The 2008 reform also introduced a pension-income-tested supplement as a replacement for the previous minimum pension. This is payable to all individuals whose defined-contribution pension is less than a specified amount: the maximum welfare pension threshold (PMaS). This threshold will increase over time as the new system is phased in:

	Maximum welfare pension (PMaS, CLP)	Target coverage of older people (%)
July 2008-June 2009	70 000	40
July-August 2009	120 000	45
September 2009-June 2010	150 000	50
July 2010-June 2001	200 000	55
July 2011 onwards	255 000	60

The supplementary benefit increases, at first, with individual income from the defined-contribution scheme. The increment is 1 – the value of the basic pension (PBS) divided by the maximum welfare pension (PMaS), *i.e.* 14.3% for the period July 2008-June 2009, when the PBS is CLP 60 000 and the PMaS is CLP 70 000. From 2011, the PBS will be CLP 75 000 and the PMaS CLP 255 000. Thus, the increment in benefits will rise to 70.6% of individual entitlements under the defined-contribution plan. For people with defined-contribution pensions above the value of the basic pension, the value of the supplement is reduced. The benefit is defined as the value of the basic pension (PBS) – the ratio of PBS to the value of the maximum welfare pension (PMaS) multiplied by the value of the defined-contribution pension. The key ratio of PBS to PMaS is 85.7% in 2008-09, falling to just 29.4% from mid-2011 onwards.

The objective of this new supplementary pension is to improve the living standards of low-income workers when they move into retirement. The table above shows that the government expects 40% of the poorest pensioners to benefit from the new programme in 2008-09, increasing to 60% from mid-2011 onwards. The modelling of pension entitlements uses the parameters that will be in place from 2011 (and so will be those applicable to a new labour-market entrant in 2008). The modelling assumes the value of the supplementary pension will be indexed in line with wages from 2011 onwards.

Variant careers

Early retirement

Early retirement is allowed at any age in the defined-contribution scheme as long as the capital accumulated in the account is sufficient to finance a pension above particular thresholds. The first condition is that the benefit must be worth 150% of the minimum pension under the old system. From July 2012 onwards, this will change to 80% of the maximum welfare pension, PMaS. The second condition is that a certain replacement rate is reached, relative to earnings in the ten years prior to drawing the pension. This replacement-rate threshold is increasing: from 64% in 2008-09 to 67% in 2009-10 and 70% from August 2010 onwards.

The normal retirement age is reduced by one or two years for each five years of work under arduous conditions in specified occupations. The maximum reduction of the normal retirement age is ten years.

Late retirement

It is possible to defer pension claiming after normal retirement age.

Childcare

A pension voucher is given to women for each child that they have had when they reach 65 years of age. The voucher is equivalent to 10% of 18 months' minimum wages at the time of birth plus the average net rate of return on defined-contribution pension plans from the birth until the pension claim. The average interest rate is calculated for "fund C" of the private pensions: the middle one in terms of the risk-return trade-off. This is transformed into a pension flow when the woman claims her pension.

Unemployment

No credits are given. A separate unemployment insurance system has existed since 2002.

Pension modelling results: Chile

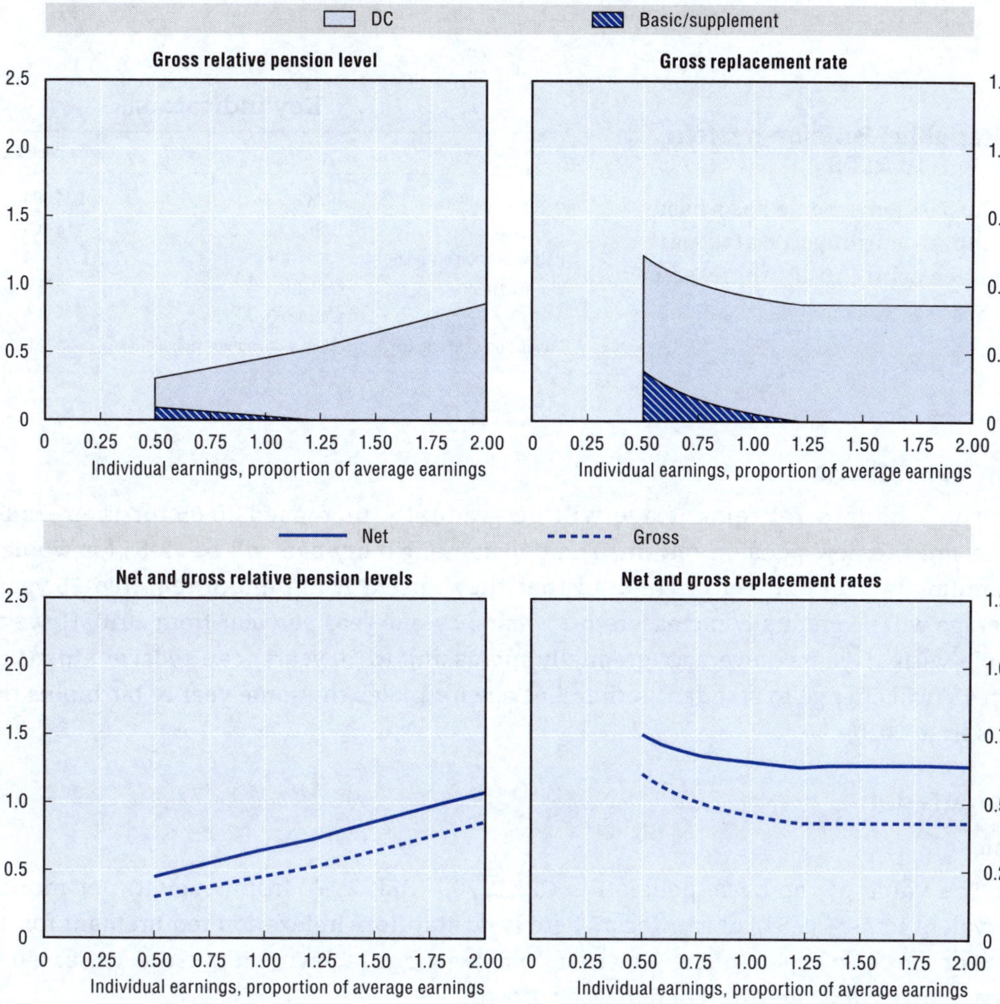

Men *Women (where different)*	Median earner	Individual earnings, multiple of average				
		0.5	0.75	1	1.5	2
Gross relative pension level	39.2	30.0	37.4	44.9	62.7	83.7
(% average gross earnings)	*30.4*	*24.6*	*29.3*	*34.0*	*43.3*	*52.7*
Net relative pension level	56.9	44.5	54.5	64.3	84.3	105.5
(% net average earnings)	*45.1*	*36.9*	*43.5*	*49.9*	*62.3*	*73.4*
Gross replacement rate	48.4	60.0	49.9	44.9	41.8	41.8
(% individual gross earnings)	*37.5*	*49.2*	*39.1*	*34.0*	*28.9*	*26.4*
Net replacement rate	66.0	74.4	66.9	64.3	62.7	62.5
(% individual net earnings)	*52.4*	*61.7*	*53.4*	*49.9*	*46.3*	*43.5*
Gross pension wealth	7.4	9.2	7.6	6.9	6.4	6.4
(multiple of individual gross earnings)	*7.8*	*10.2*	*8.1*	*7.0*	*6.0*	*5.5*
Net pension wealth	6.3	8.1	6.6	5.8	5.1	4.8
(multiple of individual gross earnings)	*6.8*	*9.0*	*7.1*	*6.1*	*5.1*	*4.5*

StatLink http://dx.doi.org/10.1787/888932371405

Czech Republic

Czech Republic: Pension system in 2008

The public pension scheme has a basic element and an earnings-related part calculated according to a progressive formula.

Key indicators

		Czech Republic	OECD
Average earnings	CZK	274 500	693 400
	USD	16 100	40 600
Public pension spending	% of GDP	7.4	7.0
Life expectancy	At birth	76.4	78.9
	At age 65	80.8	83.1
Population over age 65	% of working-age population	22.6	23.6

Qualifying conditions

The standard retirement age will be gradually increased to 65 for men under phase 1 of the new pension reform. The pension eligibility age will be 62-65 for women, depending on the number of children that they raised. A minimum required 25 years' coverage will be gradually increased to 35 years, by one year per year from 2010. However people with 15 years' coverage (gradually increasing to 20 years) can receive a pension from 65 (will change to standard retirement age for males the same year of birth plus five years from 2010).

Benefit calculation

Basic

The value of the basic pension is CZK 1 700 (CZK 2 170 from August) per month, equivalent to 7.4% (9.5%) of earnings. There is no statutory indexation requirement for the value of the basic benefit alone. However, total pensions in payment must be increased by at least prices plus one-third of real wage growth.

Earnings related

The earnings-related pension gives 1.5% of earnings for each year of contributions. The earnings measure currently averages across all years since 1985, but it will gradually reach 30 years (in 2015). Earlier years' earnings are valorised by the growth of economy-wide average earnings.

There is a progressive benefit formula, with the first CZK 10 500 per month replaced at 100%, the slice of earnings between this limit and CZK 27 000 at 30%, with a 10% replacement above this level. The first threshold, below which there is 100% replacement, is equivalent to 45.9% of average earnings, while the second threshold is 118.0% of average earnings. There is no statutory indexation requirement for these thresholds, but both these thresholds change annually.

There is no specific statutory indexation requirement for the earnings-related pension component in payment. However, the combined total pension benefit (flat-rate and earnings-related components) is adjusted to price inflation plus at least one-third of real wage growth.

Minimum

The total value of the minimum monthly newly granted pension benefit is CZK 2 470 (CZK 2 940), which is made up of a minimum earnings-related pension of CZK 770 plus the basic component of CZK 1 700 (CZK 2 170). It is worth 10.8% (12.9%) of average earnings.

Social assistance

As of 1 January 2007, the living minimum is composed of one component and created by living minimum ensuring subsistence and other basic personal needs. The living minimum of individual (and therefore also living-alone pensioner) amounted to CZK 3 126 per month. As of 1 January 2007, the part expressing the need for financial sources necessary for covering common costs of household, that is the housing costs and related services, was removed from the structure of living minimum. The social protection in housing is solved within the framework of the state social benefit system, providing housing benefits and in the system of assistance in material need by surcharge for housing.

Voluntary private pension

There is an additional voluntary pension which is assumed to be defined contribution. The contribution rate is assumed to be 2.8%.

Variant careers

Early retirement

It is possible to retire three years (increasing to five years, but no earlier than age 60) before the standard retirement ages, *i.e.* at 60 for men and 59-60 for women subject to 25 years' coverage, increasing in line with general qualification conditions to 35 years. The total accrual factor (*i.e.* number of years of contributions multiplied by the accrual rate) is permanently reduced by 0.9% for each 90 days for the first 720 day of early retirement (3.6% per year), and 1.5% for each 90 days thereafter (6% per year from 2010). For a full-career worker, this is equivalent to a decrement in the pension level (rather than the replacement rate) for early retirement of 3.6/64.5 (1.5% times 43 years) = 5.6%.

Late retirement

It is possible to defer claiming the pension beyond the normal pension age. The total accrual factor is increased by 1.5% for each 90-day period of deferral (6% per year). There is no additional pension accrual for deferred retirement. It is also possible to combine pension receipt while continuing to work (from 2010 granted pension (total accrual factor) will be increased by 0.4% for each 360 days of work while receiving full pension). The first phase of pension reform will also introduce the possibility of receiving half old-age pension. Combination of half old-age pension and work will increase total accrual factor by 1.5% for each 180 days of work.

Childcare

Women are entitled to retire earlier depending on the number of children they have had:

Number of children	1	2	3	4+
Early retirement (years)	0	1	2	3

In addition, there are credits for labour-market absences during periods caring for children up to four years old (or older in case of severe disability). These years are then ignored in the calculation of earnings for pension purposes so that these absences do not reduce the assessment base. (This approach is used for all non-contributory periods.)

Unemployment

Periods on earnings-related unemployment insurance are credited in the pension system. The duration of unemployment insurance entitlement varies with age: six months up to age 50, nine months from 50 to 55 and 12 months for over 55s. In addition, up to three years spent unemployed without entitlement to unemployment insurance are also credited (from 2009 only one year of unemployment without benefits before the age of 55 will be credited). The unemployment period used for the pension calculation is reduced to 80%, meaning that if an individual had five years' unemployment over the career, this would count as four years for pension purposes. If the unemployment period is in the decisive (reference) period (last 30 years before retirement starting 1986) for the average assessment base calculation, this period is excluded from the calculation and only the income from which the premium is paid is used.

Pension modelling results: Czech Republic

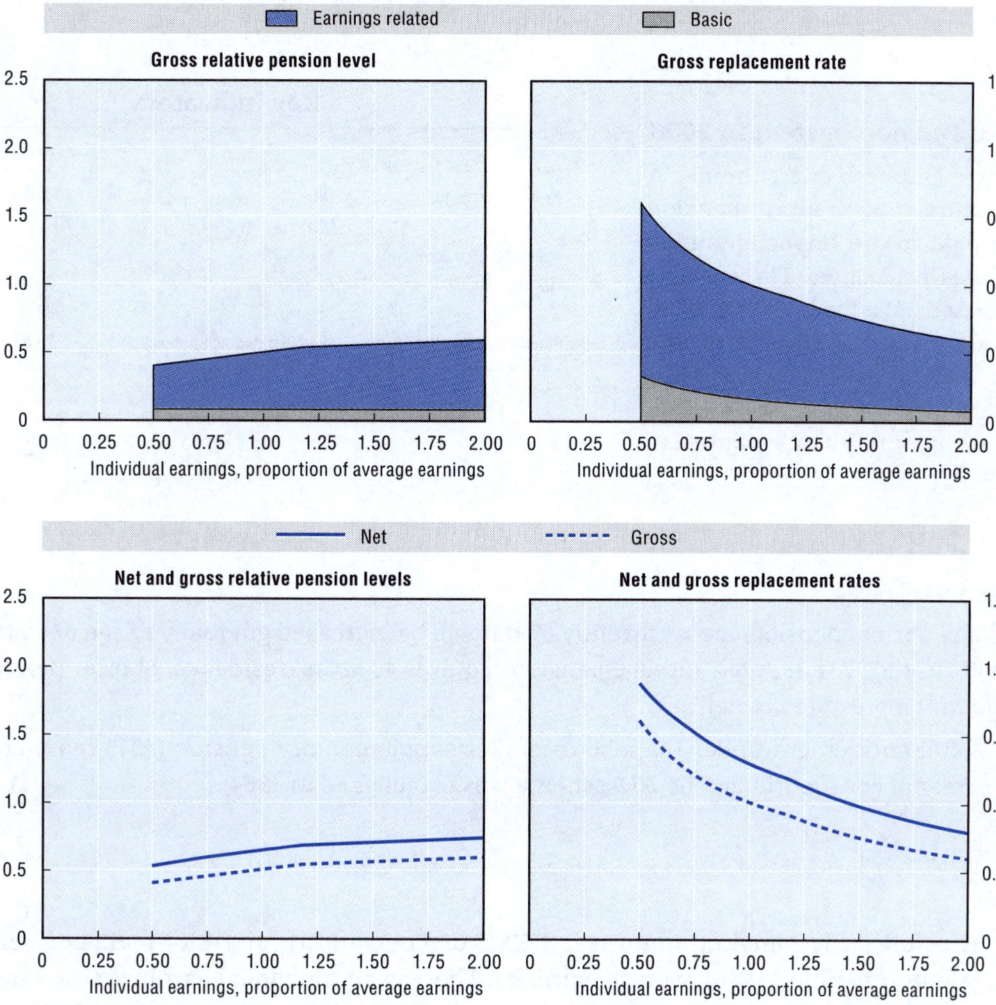

Men *Women (where different)*	Median earner	Individual earnings, multiple of average				
		0.5	0.75	1	1.5	2
Gross relative pension level *(% average gross earnings)*	46.4	40.1	45.2	50.2	56.0	59.4
Net relative pension level *(% net average earnings)*	60.3	52.6	59.1	64.4	70.4	74.0
Gross replacement rate *(% individual gross earnings)*	57.3	80.2	60.2	50.2	37.4	29.7
Net replacement rate *(% individual net earnings)*	72.5	94.0	75.8	64.4	48.9	39.3
Gross pension wealth *(multiple of individual gross earnings)*	9.0 *10.8*	12.6 *15.1*	9.4 *11.4*	7.9 *9.5*	5.9 *7.0*	4.7 *5.6*
Net pension wealth *(multiple of individual gross earnings)*	8.9 *10.7*	12.6 *15.1*	9.4 *11.3*	7.7 *9.3*	5.6 *6.8*	4.4 *5.3*

StatLink http://dx.doi.org/10.1787/888932371443

Denmark

Denmark: Pension system in 2008

There is a public basic scheme. A means-tested supplementary pension benefit is paid to the financially most disadvantaged pensioners. There is also a scheme based on individuals' contribution records, viz. the ATP. In addition, compulsory occupational schemes negotiated as part of collective agreements cover about 90% of full-time employees.

Key indicators

		Denmark	OECD
Average earnings	DKK	359 300	207 000
	USD	70 500	40 600
Public pension spending	% of GDP	5.6	7.0
Life expectancy	At birth	78.3	78.9
	At age 65	82.6	83.1
Population over age 65	% of working-age population	26.8	23.6

Qualifying conditions

The normal pension age is currently 65 but will be increased gradually to age 67 in the period 2024-27. A full public old-age pension requires 40 years' residence. Shorter periods qualify for a pro-rated benefit.

A full entitlement under the labour-market supplementary pension (ATP) requires a full career of contributions. The ATP scheme was established in 1964.

Benefit calculation

Basic

The full basic pension amount is DKK 5 096 per month or DKK 61 152 per year, equivalent to around 17% of average earnings. There is an individual earnings test which means that the basic pension will be reduced if work income exceeds DKK 259 700 (approximately three-quarters average earnings). The benefit is reduced at a rate of 30% against earned income above this level.

Targeted

The full pension supplement is DKK 5 130 per month or DKK 61 560 per year for single persons and DKK 28 752 per year for couples. The actual amounts are tested against all sources of personal income (including ATP and occupational pensions) apart from public pension. If household personal income exceeds DKK 57 300, the targeted pension supplement is reduced by 30% of the excess income for single persons. The couples household income test is calculated for income above DKK 115 000 at a rate of 15%.

Connected with the public old-age pension, a new supplementary pension benefit of DKK 7 800 was introduced in 2004. The supplementary pension benefit is taxable and paid once a year. The benefit is means-tested and targeted to the poorest pensioners without significant cash savings (maximum cash savings are DKK 59 900).

The public old-age pension (the basic and targeted amounts plus the pension supplement) is adjusted annually in line with average earnings. The adjustment is based on an index of wage increases during the two preceding years. If nominal earnings growth exceeds 2%, a maximum of 0.3% of the excess increase is allocated to a social spending reserve. Thus, indexation of pensions and other social benefits is based upon wage increases less any allocation to the reserve.

In 2008 a special tax deduction for worker-related earnings was introduced to defer full exit from labour market. From July 2008 each pensioner under the old-age pensions system can subtract work income up to DKK 30 000 yearly in calculation of basic and targeted pensions.

Occupational

These schemes are fully funded defined-contribution schemes agreed between the social partners. Coverage of these schemes is almost universal. Contributions are typically between 9% and 17% of earnings. In 2006, the percentage for the majority of Danish workers has been raised to 10.8% and this contribution rate is used for the modelling. Benefits are usually withdrawn as an annuity. The assumed interest rate is 1.5% for recent contributions or new schemes. However, the schemes operate on a "with-profit" basis, with pension increases depending on the return on assets and mortality experience of the fund. Many schemes also allow lump sum withdrawals. Since 2000, the annuity calculation must use unisex mortality tables.

Defined contribution

ATP (the Danish Labour Market Supplementary Pension) is a statutory, fully funded, collective insurance based, defined-contribution scheme. ATP provides a lifelong pension from the age of 65 and a survivors' lump sum benefit for dependents in the case of the death of the individual member. ATP covers all wage earners and almost all recipients of social security benefits. ATP membership is voluntary for the self-employed. ATP covers almost the entire population and comes close to absolute universality.

Technically, the old-age pension of ATP is a guaranteed deferred annuity. The contribution is a fixed amount – as opposed to a percentage of income – varied only against the number of hours worked. A full-time employee will pay DKK 2 927 in 2008. Contributions are split, with two-thirds paid by the employer and one-third by the worker. The contribution schedule (the sum of employer and employee contribution) against hours worked is shown in the following table (for monthly paid workers):

Monthly hours	< 39	39-77	78-116	> 116
Contribution, DKK/month as from 2008	0	81	163	244
Monthly hours	< 39	39-77	78-116	> 116
Contribution, DKK/month as from 2009	0	90	180	270

The contribution is adjusted if and when the social partners decide to do so as part of collective agreements. Over the past 20 years the contribution has been increased in steps more or less in line with average earnings. The modelling assumes that the contribution will increase in line with average earnings. An increase of approximately 10% has been agreed for 2009.

Until 2002, each DKK 396 of contributions earned DKK 100 of pension benefits paid from 65 regardless of the age at which they were made. This implied an average (across all accruing cohorts) interest rate of around 4.5%. From 2002, a nominal interest rate of 1.5% has been assumed. In the model, it is assumed that the ATP earns the same interest rate as assumed for funded defined-contribution schemes in other OECD countries.

The ATP scheme increases pensions in payment and pension rights alike if its financial condition allows. This is done in the form of bonus allowances. Increases are guaranteed as are earned rights.

The modelling assumes full indexation to price inflation.

An entirely new ATP pension accrual system has been introduced as from 2008. The model is based on swap interest rates as opposed to a fixed nominal interest rate of *e.g.* 1.5%. The new pension accrual system will abandon the age-differentiated allocation to the guarantee and bonus pools and instead adopt a uniform division, with 80% of all contributions going to the guarantee pool and 20% going to the bonus pool.

Variant careers

Early retirement

There is a partial early retirement pension for workers aged between 60 and 65 who continue to work for 12 to 30 hours a week. The scheme is being phased out. It now applies only for workers born before 1 January 1959. The beneficiary must reduce weekly hours worked by at least seven hours a week or at least one-quarter of total hours worked in an average week. The partial pension is calculated as a fixed amount for every hour that is reduced. The amount is approximately DDK 76 an hour for 2007. Since 1999 beneficiaries are subject to a pension deduction.

People covered by either early-retirement programme revert to the standard old-age pension once they reach the normal retirement age of 65 (due to their age they will not be affected by the legislated rise in the retirement age in the period 2024-27).

Late retirement

It is possible to defer the public old-age pension for up to ten years. The increment for deferring pension for a year is the ratio of the period of deferral to average life expectancy at the time the pension is drawn. For example, population projections show life expectancy for a 68-year-old to be 17.1 years. Thus, the increment for deferring for a year from age 67 would be 1/17.1 = 5.8%.

Childcare

For periods on maternity/paternity/parental benefits, double the amount of contributions is paid for ATP. The beneficiary will pay one-third of the contribution, with two-thirds being paid by the government/municipality. Maternity/paternity/parental benefits can be paid for up to 52 weeks in total. The four weeks prior to the birth and the first 14 weeks after the birth are reserved for the mother. The father is entitled to two weeks of leave during the first 14 weeks after the birth (paternity leave). The last 32 weeks can be divided or shared between the father and the mother (parental leave). Those out of the labour market caring for children beyond the maternity period typically switch to another scheme which also carries an ATP contribution. It is not common for young parents not to resume work when the leave period ends unless the child is *e.g.* ill or disabled in which cases there normally will be possibilities for drawing on some sort of public benefit with contribution to ATP. There are no credits or contributions for occupational pension schemes for periods out of paid work caring for children.

Unemployment

During unemployment, the unemployment insurance (or municipality if not insured) take over the payment obligation of the employer, and ATP contributions are paid at the double rate when receiving benefit from the unemployment insurance (normal rate if social assistance benefit). The government pays two-thirds of the payment when unemployment insurance is exhausted and the individual is on unemployment/social assistance. There are no credits or contributions for occupational pension schemes for periods of unemployment.

There is also a voluntary early retirement programme linked with unemployment insurance, which pays benefits between ages 60 (gradually increasing to age 62 between 2019 and 2022) and until the normal pension age. To qualify, individuals must have been members of the unemployment insurance fund for at least 25 years within the last 30 years and have paid voluntary early-retirement contributions during this period. They must also satisfy the conditions for entitlement to unemployment benefits in the event of unemployment at the time of transition to the voluntary early-retirement scheme. The benefit amount corresponds to the rate of unemployment benefits, subject to a limit of 91% of the maximum rate of unemployment benefit, equivalent to DKK 3 110 per week for full-time workers and DKK 2 075 for part-time workers (2006 figures). It is not possible to combine receipt of voluntary early-retirement benefits with the social pension.

People who defer the take up of voluntary early-retirement benefits for at least two years after they have become entitled to the benefit and are still working receive a higher rate of voluntary early-retirement benefit that is equivalent to the maximum rate of unemployment benefit (or DKK 3 415 per week in 2006). For three years' full-time work when an individual qualifies for voluntary early-retirement or the equivalent, a one-off lump-sum is paid up to a maximum of DKK 124 860 in 2006.

Pension modelling results: Denmark

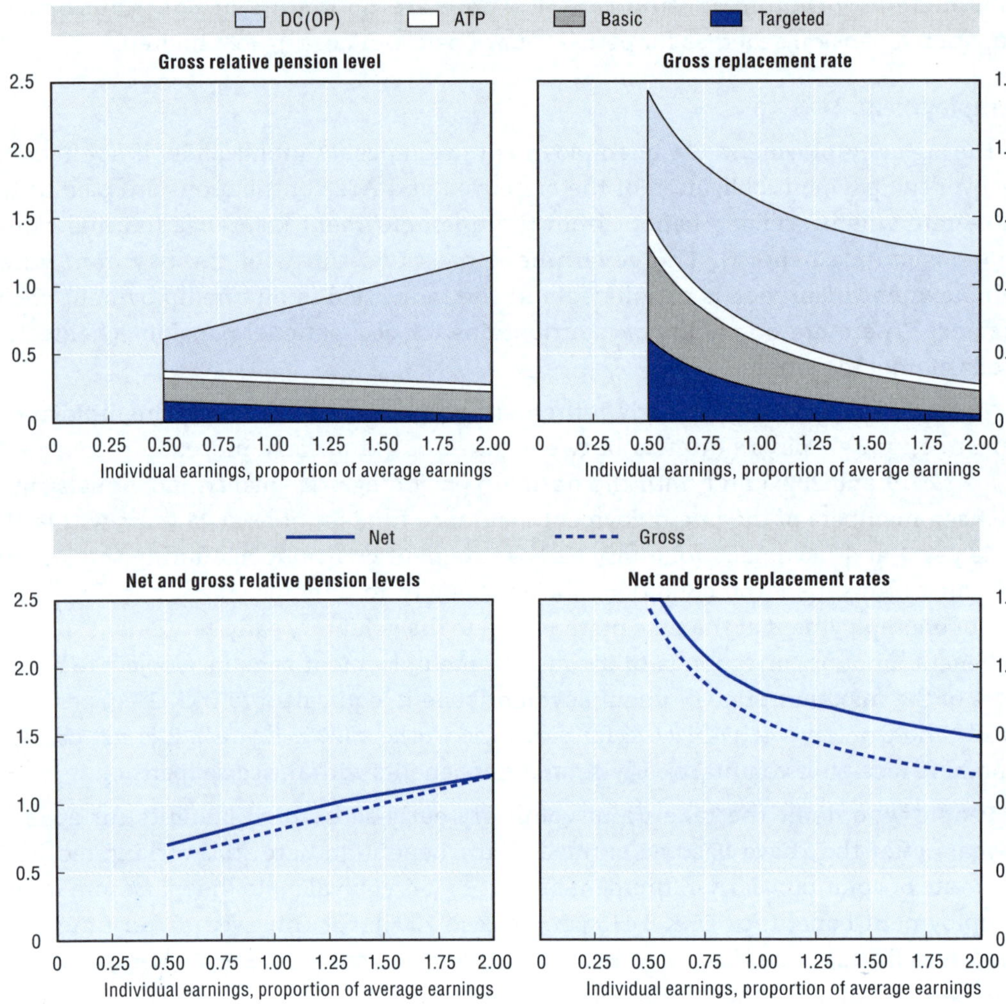

Men *Women (where different)*	Median earner	Individual earnings, multiple of average				
		0.5	0.75	1	1.5	2
Gross relative pension level	75.4	60.3	70.0	79.7	99.1	118.5
(% average gross earnings)						
Net relative pension level	85.6	69.9	80.0	89.8	106.5	119.8
(% net average earnings)						
Gross replacement rate	84.7	120.6	93.3	79.7	66.1	59.2
(% individual gross earnings)						
Net replacement rate	94.5	131.9	103.3	89.8	80.8	73.3
(% individual net earnings)						
Gross pension wealth	12.9	18.8	14.3	12.1	9.8	8.7
(multiple of individual gross earnings)	*15.3*	*22.3*	*17.0*	*14.3*	*11.6*	*10.3*
Net pension wealth	8.6	12.8	9.6	8.0	6.2	5.2
(multiple of individual gross earnings)	*10.2*	*15.3*	*11.4*	*9.5*	*7.4*	*6.1*

StatLink http://dx.doi.org/10.1787/888932371462

Estonia

Estonia: Pension system in 2008

The system combines an earnings-related public scheme with mandatory contributions to funded pensions. There is also a flat-rate, basic element and a safety-net, national pension.

Key indicators

		Estonia	OECD
Average earnings	EEK	157 000	434 200
	USD	14 700	40 600
Public pension spending	% of GDP	5.3	7.0
Life expectancy	At birth	73.0	78.9
	At age 65	80.6	83.1
Population over age 65	% of working-age population	27.6	23.6

Qualifying conditions

The pension eligibility age is 63 for men and will reach 63 for women from 2016. The qualification period is at least 15 years of pensionable service.

Benefit calculation

Basic

The flat-rate base amount was EEK 1 699.94 per month in April 2008 and EEK 1 373.58 in 2007/08 and is only payable along with an earnings-related pension.

Earnings related

Pension benefits are calculated on the amount of contributions paid on an individual's behalf relative to the average contribution paid. This is the annual pension-insurance coefficient of the person. The accumulation of those coefficients at retirement is multiplied by the value of a year of pensionable service to calculate pension entitlements. The value of a year of pensionable service was EEK 54.43 in July 2007 and EEK 65.01 in April 2008.

There is no ceiling to earnings for contribution or benefit purposes.

Pensions in payment are indexed to the arithmetic average of consumer prices and contribution revenues annually each April. This applies to the base amount, the value of a year of pensionable service in the earnings-related scheme and the value of the benefit under the targeted scheme.

Targeted

A minimum retirement-income guarantee is provided by the national pension. This was EEK 1 573.31 per month in July 2007 and EEK 1 913.14 in April 2008.

Defined contribution

Individuals choosing the funded option must make an additional contribution of 2% of earnings into their pension fund. Four per cent of the total social security contribution is then also diverted to this fund. New labour-market entrants (that is, those born in 1983 or after) are required to take the funded option. Most current workers can choose this option (that is, those born in 1942 or after, *i.e.* up to age 60). Over 580 000 people have taken out individual accounts.

Variant careers

Early retirement

The public pension can be claimed up to three years before the standard age (*i.e.* from age 60 in the long term) provided that the individual retires and if the condition of a 15-year qualification period is met. The pension is reduced by 4.8% for each year that an individual retires early.

Late retirement

The public pension can be deferred after the normal pension age. Deferring pension earns an increment of 10.8% per year. During the deferral period, the worker continues to contribute and earn extra entitlement. It is also possible to combine work and pension receipt. In this case, contributions are again paid and the pension is recalculated annually.

Childcare

The state pays the employer contribution on behalf of recipients of childcare allowance up to three years per child. This is 20% on assumed earnings of EEK 700. Individuals who receive parental benefits need to pay the contribution to the defined-contribution scheme.

Unemployment

There are no credits for periods of unemployment.

Pension modelling results: Estonia

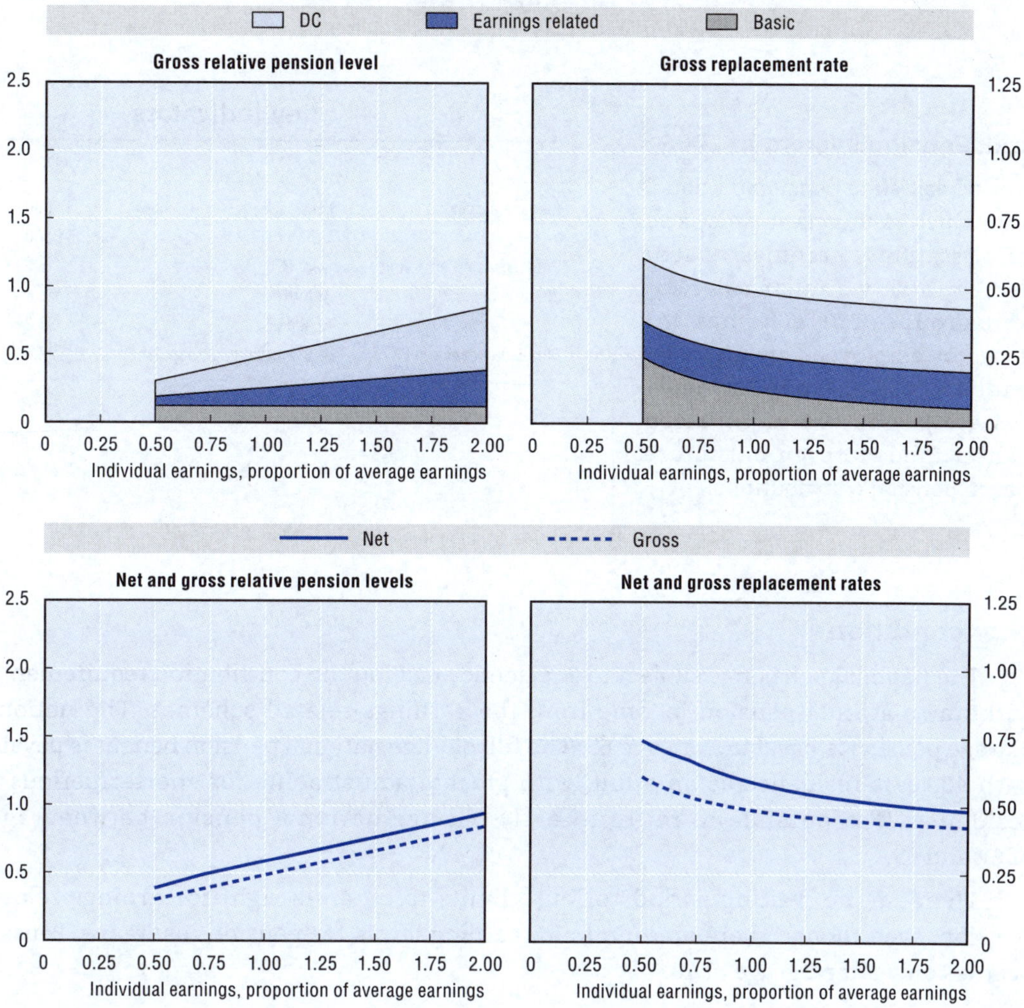

Men *Women (where different)*	Median earner	Individual earnings, multiple of average				
		0.5	0.75	1	1.5	2
Gross relative pension level *(% average gross earnings)*	41.2	30.1	39.1	48.0	66.0	83.9
Net relative pension level *(% net average earnings)*	51.6	38.4	49.5	58.3	75.9	93.5
Gross replacement rate *(% individual gross earnings)*	50.9	60.2	52.1	48.0	44.0	41.9
Net replacement rate *(% individual net earnings)*	63.1	73.4	65.1	58.3	51.4	47.8
Gross pension wealth	7.8	9.2	8.0	7.3	6.7	6.3
(multiple of individual gross earnings)	*9.9*	*11.9*	*10.2*	*9.4*	*8.5*	*8.1*
Net pension wealth	7.6	9.2	7.9	7.0	6.0	5.5
(multiple of individual gross earnings)	*9.8*	*11.9*	*10.1*	*8.9*	*7.7*	*7.1*

StatLink http://dx.doi.org/10.1787/888932371481

Finland

Finland: Pension system in 2008

There is a basic state pension (national pension), which is income-tested, and a range of statutory earnings-related schemes, with very similar rules for different groups. The schemes for private-sector employees are partially pre-funded while the public-sector schemes are pay-as-you-go financed (with buffer funds to even out future increases in pension contributions).

Key indicators

		Finland	OECD
Average earnings	EUR	37 300	27 800
	USD	54 500	40 600
Public pension spending	% of GDP	8.3	7.0
Life expectancy	At birth	79.6	78.9
	At age 65	83.3	83.1
Population over age 65	% of working-age population	27.4	23.6

Qualifying conditions

The national pension is subject to a residency test (but no contribution requirements), withdrawn against pension income from the earnings-related schemes. The national old-age pension is payable from age 65. The full old-age national pension benefit is payable with 40 years residence as an adult, with *pro rata* adjustments for shorter periods of residence. It is possible to retire to early old-age national pension between ages of 62 and 65.

There are no waiting periods or euro limits to obtain a right to earnings-related pension, even though there are minimum earning levels for pension insurance. Pension accrues only after the age of 18.

Benefit calculation

Earnings related

Among different earnings-related schemes, the scheme for private sector employees (TEL) is covered here.

From 2005, the accrual rate is 1.5% of pensionable earnings at ages 18-52, 1.9% at ages 53-62 and 4.5% at ages 63-67. For a full-career worker working from age 20 until retirement at age 65, the total lifetime accrual will be 77.5% of pensionable earnings (if pensionable earnings are assumed to remain constant for the whole career).

Pensionable earnings are, from 2005, based on average earnings of the whole career. However, as pension accrues differently in different age groups (see above), the earnings received by older workers have more weight in the total pension. When the pensionable earnings are calculated the amount corresponding to employee's pension contribution is deducted from the earnings. In 2008, the employee's pension contribution was 4.1% for employees under 53 years old and 5.2% for employees 53 years old or older. Note, however, that the replacement rates are shown relative to total gross earnings (for comparison with other countries) rather than this measure of pensionable earnings.

Earlier years' earnings are re-valued in line with a mix of economy-wide earnings and prices. From 2005, wage growth has an 80% weight and price inflation, 20%. At the baseline assumptions for prices and wages growth, this policy reduces the value of the pension to 91.5% compared with a policy of full earnings valorisation of earlier years' pay. After retirement, the earnings-related pension is uprated using a formula of 20% of earnings inflation and 80% of price inflation.

From 2010 new earnings-related pensions will be reduced according to increases in life expectancy from 2009. (The calculations use lagged mortality data: for 2010, for example, the data are the average for 2004-08 compared to base year which is based on data for 2003-07.) Between 2002 and 2040, the Statistics Finland mortality projections imply an increase in life expectancy at age 65 from 18.0 years to 24.1 (calculated from unisex mortality rates). The adjustment takes the form of an annuity calculation using a discount rate of 2% per year. The adjustment expected in the year 2040, based on the mortality projections, is to reduce benefits to 85.2% of their value under the pre-reform rules. The life expectancy coefficient is calculated for each cohort at the age of 62.

There is no contribution floor and no ceiling to contributions or pensionable earnings, which means there is no pension ceiling either. However, there are minimum earnings limit for pension insurance.

The Finnish Centre for Pensions co-ordinates the schemes, resulting in a single pension payment even for people who have been members of different plans.

Targeted (national pension)

The full basic monthly benefit for a single pensioner in 2008 was EUR 558.46 (around one-fifth of average earnings). The national pension is reduced by 50% of the difference between other pension income and a small disregard which in 2008 was EUR 591 per year. No pension is payable once other pension income exceeds EUR 1 154.30 or EUR 1 028.13 per month.

From 2005 on, earnings-related (employment) pension accrued after the age of 63 will be disregarded when national pension entitlement is calculated.

The basic pension benefit, the parameters of the means test and pension payable are uprated annually in line with prices. In practice there have been additional increases based on separate decisions.

Variant careers

For non-standard careers a salary base is used when calculating pension for unpaid periods. If the pension accrual is based on the salary on which the benefit is based there is no deduction of pension contribution (see section "Benefit calculation/earnings related" above). Usually the corresponding amount has already been deducted when the wage for the calculation of the benefit has been calculated.

Early retirement

Early national old-age pension is available from the beginning of the month following one's 62nd birthday. Its amount is permanently reduced (in comparison with the ordinary old-age pension) by 0.4% for each month the pension is to be paid before the normal pensionable age of 65 years. The pension will not rise to its regular level when the recipient reaches the age of 65. These rules operate from 2005.

Early retirement is possible at age 62 under the earnings-related scheme, subject to a 0.6% benefit reduction per month of early retirement until the age of 63. After the age of 63 there is no reduction in pension. However, there is more rapid accrual of earnings-related benefits after this age (see above).

Late retirement

From 2004 the national pension can be deferred after the age of 65 and the pension is then increased by 0.6% for each month by which retirement is postponed.

From 2005 onwards, the increment for late retirement is reduced to 0.4% for each month (4.8% per year) in the earnings-related scheme after age 68. There is no adjustment between ages 63 and 68 because of the accelerated accrual of pension at those ages.

It is possible to combine receipt of pension and earnings from work. From 2005 after taking the old-age pension, earnings accrue additional pension and the accrual rate is 1.5% per year until the age of 68.

Childcare

From 2005 onwards, during periods of maternity, paternity and parent's allowance, the pension accrues based on 1.17 times the salary, on which the family benefit is based. The maximum paid parental leave period is 11 months.

For unpaid periods of childcare by either parent during which child home-care allowance is claimed, pensions accrue as if the person received a salary of EUR 588.54 per month (2008), which is around one-fifth of average earnings. This is the case until the child reaches the age of three.

People on parental leave are not liable for pension contributions. The pension accruing for paid parental leave is paid by the earnings-related pension system. The state finances the pension for periods of unpaid childcare leave.

The part of the pension that is based on unpaid periods of child care (and studies) is not included in the income test of the national pension.

Unemployment

Following the 2005 reform, earnings-related unemployment benefits accrue pension rights based on the proportion of the salary (75%) on which the benefit is based. Only unemployment benefit received before the age of 63 generate a pension credit.

Unemployment-insurance benefits are paid for 500 days (around 23 months, with average 21.5 days per month). If an unemployed person reaches age 59 before the 500 days have accrued, earnings-related unemployment can be paid until age 65. (Due to age limits these rules will not be applied before 2009.) Individuals receiving allowance after 500 days are entitled to choose claiming old-age pension from age 62. In such cases, there is no reduction for early retirement and earnings-related unemployment benefits cease. After the period with earnings-related unemployment benefits, flat-rate or income-tested (under various conditions) unemployment assistance could be claimed but the period under these benefits are not credited for the pension entitlement.

Pension modelling results: Finland

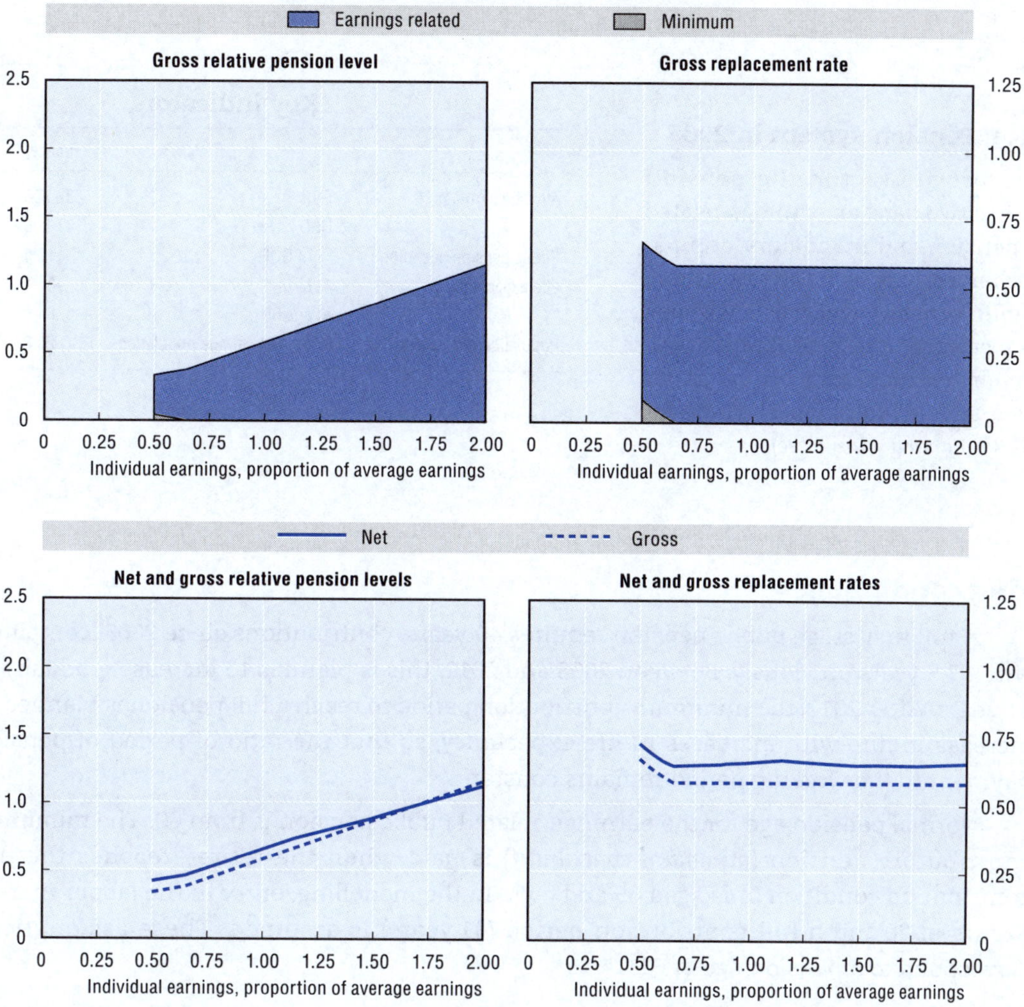

Men *Women (where different)*	Median earner	Individual earnings, multiple of average				
		0.5	0.75	1	1.5	2
Gross relative pension level	52.0	33.2	43.3	57.8	86.7	115.5
(% average gross earnings)						
Net relative pension level	59.6	41.6	51.2	65.2	88.4	112.1
(% net average earnings)						
Gross replacement rate	57.8	66.4	57.8	57.8	57.8	57.8
(% individual gross earnings)						
Net replacement rate	64.8	72.0	64.1	65.2	64.4	65.1
(% individual net earnings)						
Gross pension wealth	9.5	10.9	9.5	9.5	9.5	9.5
(multiple of individual gross earnings)	*11.4*	*13.0*	*11.4*	*11.4*	*11.4*	*11.4*
Net pension wealth	7.6	9.5	7.8	7.5	6.8	6.4
(multiple of individual gross earnings)	*9.1*	*11.3*	*9.4*	*8.9*	*8.1*	*7.7*

StatLink http://dx.doi.org/10.1787/888932371500

France

France: Pension system in 2008

In the private sector, the pension system has two tiers: an earnings-related public pension and mandatory occupational schemes, based on a points system. The public scheme also has a without means test minimum contributory pension (*minimum contributif*). In addition there is a targeted minimum income for the elderly (*minimum vieillesse*).

Key indicators

		France	OECD
Average earnings	EUR	32 700	27 800
	USD	47 800	40 600
Public pension spending	% of GDP	12.5	7.0
Life expectancy	At birth	81.1	78.9
	At age 65	84.9	83.1
Population over age 65	% of working-age population	28.2	23.6

Qualifying conditions

A full first-stage public pension requires 40 years' contributions since 2003, compared with 37.5 years previously. Between 2008 and 2012, this is planned to increase gradually to 41 years. After 2012, the minimum contribution period to reach a full pension is planned to increase in line with increases in life expectancy, so that the ratio of period of pension payment to the working period remains constant.

Normal pension age for the earnings-related public pension is from 60. The minimum contributory pension (*minimum contributif*) is paid when the retiree reaches the full contribution condition or is aged 65 and over. In the modelling, entry in the labour market occurs at 20 and a full contribution period (41 years) is assumed. These assumptions correspond to a pension age of 61.

Benefit calculation

Earnings related

The public pension targets a replacement rate of 50% after a full career (which is 40 years' contributions and then increased further as described above). For each missing quarter, the pension is reduced by two means:

- The pension rate is reduced by 1.25% (or by 5% for each missing year), these rates (*décote*) concern people born after 1952.
- In addition, the pension amount is reduced *pro rata* (0.61% – 1/164 for one missing quarter).

The earnings measure is based on a number of best years of earnings, valorised in line with price inflation. From 2008 onwards, pay will be averaged over 25 years, whereas it is over 24 years in 2007, and was over 23 years in 2006.

Because of the limited number of years included in the earnings measure for calculating pension benefits and the policy of valorisation in line with prices, the replacement rate in the French public system is very sensitive to the time profile of earnings throughout the worker's career. Given the baseline assumption of continuous real earnings growth of 2% over a worker's career, combined with the fact that the OECD calculations use the lifetime revalued average earnings as reference salary, the replacement rates calculated are lower than those calculated using the observed salary progression in France, where increases are concentrated primarily in the first half of the career. The 2003 reform introduced an objective from 2008 for people with a full career on the minimum wage to receive a pension equivalent of at least 85% of the net minimum wage.

There is a ceiling on eligible earnings, which in 2008 was EUR 33 276. This is approximately equal to average earnings on the OECD measure. Benefits in payment are indexed to prices.

Contributory minimum pension ("minimum contributif")

There is an untargeted minimum pension in the "regime general" regardless of the amount of pension received from other basic or supplementary schemes. From January to August, the annual amount was EUR 6 958.21 for those aged 65 years with at least a one-quarter registered career or EUR 7 603.41 if the recipient has at least 40 actually contributed years. From September to December 2008, the amounts were EUR 7 013.87 and EUR 7 664.23 respectively. This is worth 23.3% of average earnings on the OECD measure. To be eligible for the full benefit, 40 years (planned to be extended to 41 years in 2012) of contributions, or being aged 65 and over are needed (the minimum pension is pro-rated for shorter periods). The value of the minimum pension is indexed to prices.

Mandatory occupational

The ARRCO scheme covers the majority of private-sector employees. Different rules apply to "cadres" (those in professional or managerial positions) under the AGIRC programme; the following regulations apply to non-cadres.

Although actual contributions are higher, benefits are only earned on 6% of earnings under the ceiling of the public scheme. Between one and three times the public-scheme ceiling, benefits are earned on 16% of pay. Thus, the ARRCO ceiling is three times that of the public pension scheme: EUR 99 828. (Note that there is no ceiling for the AGIRC scheme for cadres.)

Each year, the number of points earned is the value of contributions divided by the cost of a pension point. At retirement, the accumulated number of points is converted into a pension benefit by multiplying them by the value of a pension point. The pension-point value was EUR 1.1480 from April 2007 to April 2008 and EUR 1.1648 from April 2008, giving an annual figure for calendar 2008 of EUR 1.1606. The pension-point cost was EUR 13.9684 for calendar year 2008.

Uprating of the cost and value of pension points is agreed between the social partners. The current agreement, valid until 2008, is to increase the cost of pension points in line with earnings and the value of pension points in line with prices. The modelling assumes that this differential uprating between the cost and value of a point will continue. Again, this policy of effective valorisation of earlier years' entitlements to prices results in lower benefits than valorisation to earnings. At the baseline assumptions, the reduction is to 69% of the pension entitlement under earnings valorisation.

It is important to note that the uprating policy for these two parameters affects both the path of pensions in payment (here termed "indexation") and the change in value of pension entitlements between the time they were earned and the time they are withdrawn (akin to the process of "valorisation" in earnings-related schemes).

Targeted minimum pension ("minimum vieillesse")

There is a means tested minimum income benefit for people aged 65 worth EUR 7 537.30 a year for a single person (EUR 13 521.27 for a couple) in 2008. This benefit, equivalent to 23% of average earnings (on the OECD measure) is adjusted in line with prices. Full-career workers will rarely be eligible for the old-age assistance programme (*minimum vieillesse*), since the mandatory occupational pension supplements the public pension benefit

Variant careers

Early retirement

Pre-retirement operates through a separate programme administered by the employment fund (FNE). Early retirement is possible from 57 and from 56 under certain circumstances related to working conditions. The replacement rate is around 80%. At the normal pension age (or at the age when workers become eligible for a full regular old-age pension up to 65), individuals switch to the public pension. The period on FNE benefits is fully credited for the public pension.

Early retirement, namely before 60, is allowed in the public pension scheme, in the following conditions:

- At 56 for people who have entered the labour force before 16 and have validated at least 42 years, among them at least 42 years with effective contribution.
- At 58 for people who have entered the labour force before 16 and have validated at least 42 years, among them at least 41 years with effective contribution.
- At 59 for people who have entered the labour force before 17 and have validated at least 42 years, among them at least 40 years with effective contribution.

Under the occupational pension, early retirement is also possible, often subject to reductions related either to age of retirement or years of contributions or both. Retirement is possible at age 60 with 40 years' coverage without a reduction. With fewer than 40 years' coverage, the pension is adjusted as shown in the table with the adjustment being that which is more favourable: relating to the retirement age or to the number of missing years. For retirement at age 61, for example, the pension is reduced to 83% of the full value. However, if the individual retires at 61 with 39 years' contributions, the reduction is only to 96%, because there is only one missing year.

Retirement age	55	56	57	58	59	60	61	62	63	64
Missing years						5	4	3	2	1
Coefficient	0.43	0.50	0.57	0.64	0.71	0.78	0.83	0.88	0.92	0.96

Late retirement

When people work after age 60 and have reached the qualifying conditions for a full pension (which will be 41 years' coverage), each additional year increases the benefit under the public scheme by 5%.

For the period of deferred retirement, people continue to accumulate ARRCO points.

Work and pension receipt can be combined subject to some limits, provided people leave their usual job.

Childcare

A mother raising a child for at least nine years (before the child reaches 16) is credited with two years' coverage per child in the public scheme, whether she continued to work or not during that time. Both parents can receive a 10% increase in final pension payout in the public plan if they have raised three or more children for at least nine years before age 16.

Periods out-of-work or working part time caring for a child under three are also credited in the public and occupational pension schemes (*Assurance Vieillesse des Parents au Foyer* – AVPF). Credits are awarded as if the parent had earned the minimum wage. The three-year maximum applies to the first two children: credited periods are longer for subsequent children. To qualify, parents must be entitled to family benefits and have earnings below thresholds (EUR 21 991 for the first child and EUR 5 075 more for subsequent children). This credit is cumulated with the two years credited per child in the public scheme.

Unemployment

Periods of involuntary unemployment are fully credited towards the state pension when unemployment benefits are received, including the following programmes: *allocation unique dégressive*, *allocation chômeurs âgés*, *allocation formation reclassement*, *allocation de solidarité spécifique*, *allocation spécifique d'attente* and *allocation d'insertion*. For each completed 50 days of unemployment per year, one-quarter of contributions is attributed (with a maximum of four-quarters per year). Nevertheless, these periods do not enter in the calculation of the average reference wage (*salaire annuel moyen*) based on the 25 best years of earnings and therefore in the pension calculation.

There is also a credit for the first period of unemployment without unemployment payments to a maximum of one year for the people under 55. Subsequent periods of involuntary unemployment without unemployment payments are credited to a maximum of one year only if this follows a period of unemployment with unemployment benefits. There is no credit for periods in receipt of social assistance (*revenu minimum d'insertion*).

In the mandatory occupational plans, periods of unemployment enable accumulation of pension points if the person had contributed to one of these plans before the beginning of unemployment. These points are calculated according to a "daily reference wage" (*salaire journalier de référence*) which is the last wage (on a year basis) divided by 365.

Pension modelling results: France

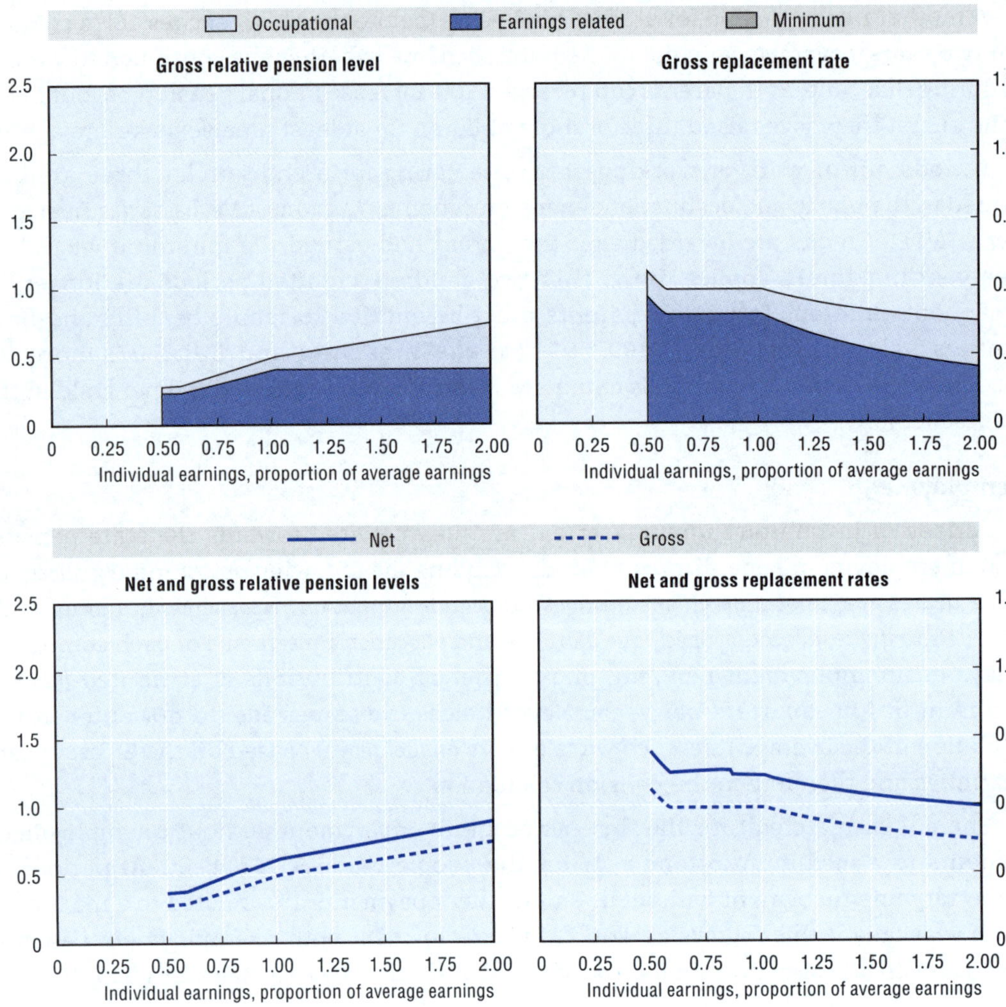

Men *Women (where different)*	Median earner	Individual earnings, multiple of average				
		0.5	0.75	1	1.5	2
Gross relative pension level	39.8	28.0	36.8	49.1	61.9	74.2
(% average gross earnings)						
Net relative pension level	49.9	36.6	46.3	60.4	74.7	88.5
(% net average earnings)						
Gross replacement rate	49.1	55.9	49.1	49.1	41.3	37.1
(% individual gross earnings)						
Net replacement rate	60.8	69.4	60.6	60.4	53.1	49.0
(% individual net earnings)						
Gross pension wealth	9.3	10.6	9.3	9.3	7.9	7.1
(multiple of individual gross earnings)	*10.6*	*12.1*	*10.6*	*10.6*	*8.9*	*8.0*
Net pension wealth	8.5	10.0	8.5	8.3	6.8	6.1
(multiple of individual gross earnings)	*9.6*	*11.4*	*9.6*	*9.4*	*7.8*	*6.9*

StatLink http://dx.doi.org/10.1787/888932371519

Germany

Germany: Pension system in 2008

The statutory public pension system has a single tier and is an earnings-related PAYG system. Calculation of pensions is based on pension points. There is a social-assistance safety net for low-income pensioners.

Key indicators

		Germany	OECD
Average earnings	EUR	41 400	27 800
	USD	60 500	40 600
Public pension spending	% of GDP	10.7	7.0
Life expectancy	At birth	79.8	78.9
	At age 65	83.4	83.1
Population over age 65	% of working-age population	32.8	23.6

Qualifying conditions

At present the regular old-age pension is payable from age 65 with at least five years' contributions. Fewer than five years' contributions earn no benefit. The statutory retirement age will be gradually increased to 67 during the next two decades. For those born 1964 or later, the statutory retirement age will be 67.

Benefit calculation

Earnings related

A year's contribution at the average earnings of contributors earns one pension point. The relevant average earning is approximately identical to the National Accounts average earnings. Contributions based on lower or higher income earn proportionately less or more pension points. Contributions are levied on annual earnings up to EUR 63 600 in 2008. The ceiling is equivalent to 208% of the relevant average earnings. The relevant earnings were EUR 30 625 in 2008. This is only equivalent to 74% of the OECD average earnings measure.

At retirement, the pension points of every year are summed up. The sum of pension points is then multiplied by a "pension-point value", which was EUR 316.98 in 2008. The pension point value is valid for newly retired and already retired pensioners. It is uprated annually in line with gross wages as a starting point but depends also on two additional factors. The first factor incorporates changes of the contribution rates to the statutory pension scheme and to the subsidised voluntary occupational and personal pension schemes. An increase of contribution rates will reduce the adjustment of pension point value. The second, so-called sustainability factor links the adjustment of the pension-point value to changes in the system dependency ratio, that is, the ratio of pensioners to contributors.

These factors were integrated into the indexation rules with the aim to limit the increase of the contribution rate from the current 19.9% to 22%. The increase of the contribution rate and of the pensioner/contributor ratio will result in indexation to less than average wages. In the long run, future adjustment of the pension-point value is expected to be 14% below the increase of average earnings.

The relevant average earnings for calculating the pension points as well as the pension-point value are slightly different in the new Länder. This difference is assumed to disappear in the long run as wages will align.

Social assistance

For people with low income there is a social assistance which is also applicable for pensioners. The social-assistance amounts, in the Western Länder, in 2008 to EUR 8 424 per year including average benefits for housing and fuel costs; this is equivalent to 26.7% of relevant average gross earnings and 20.3% of OECD average earnings.

Voluntary

There is an additional voluntary and private pension which can be provided by banks, insurance companies or investment funds (so called Riester-pension). State incentives are given for building up a Riester- pension.

Variant careers

Early retirement

Early retirement is possible from 63 with 35 years' contributions with reductions. If retiring before the age of 67, benefits are reduced by 3.6% per year of early retirement. In addition, retiring at age 63 compared to someone retiring at 67, pension entitlements are significantly lower due to working four years less and not earning additional pension points. Besides this the old-age pension for severely handicapped people can be claimed. People with an assessed degree of disability of at least 50% and at least 35 years of coverage can presently retire at age 60 with a maximum reduction of 10.8%. The retirement age of this pension will be gradually increased from age 60 to 62 years.

An exception to the increase of the statutory retirement age to 67 is as follows: people can still retire at the age 65 without reductions if they complete 45 years of insured employment, child care or from child-raising periods up to age 10.

Late retirement

Deferring the pension after 67 earns a 6% increment for each year of additional work.

Childcare

For children born in 1992 or later one parent is credited for a period of three years with one pension point per year (equal to contributions based on average earnings). For children born before 1992 only one pension point is credited. The state pays corresponding contributions for these entitlements. These entitlements can be taken by either an employed or non-employed parent or can be shared between parents. There are also credits for periods caring for children up to age of 10. These years count towards the number of years needed to qualify for a pension (*Berücksichtigungszeit*) and in addition have an effect on the pension entitlement. If people work while their children are under 10 or if at least two children under 10 are parented, they receive a bonus of up to 0.33 pension points per year. However, this cannot result in a total accrual exceeding one pension point per year.

Unemployment

The unemployment insurance contributes to the pension scheme on behalf of the unemployed. During the first period of unemployment benefits (*Arbeitslosengeld I*), contributions are paid on the basis of 80% of previous gross earnings. The first period lasts between six and 24 months depending both on age and contribution years. Thereafter, the unemployed person moves to the second type of unemployment benefit (*Arbeitslosengeld II*), which is both paid at a lower rate and is means-tested. For this period, the unemployment insurance pays contributions on the basis of EUR 205 per month, so that 0.0834 pension-points are earned for each year during the second period of unemployment.

Pension modelling results: Germany

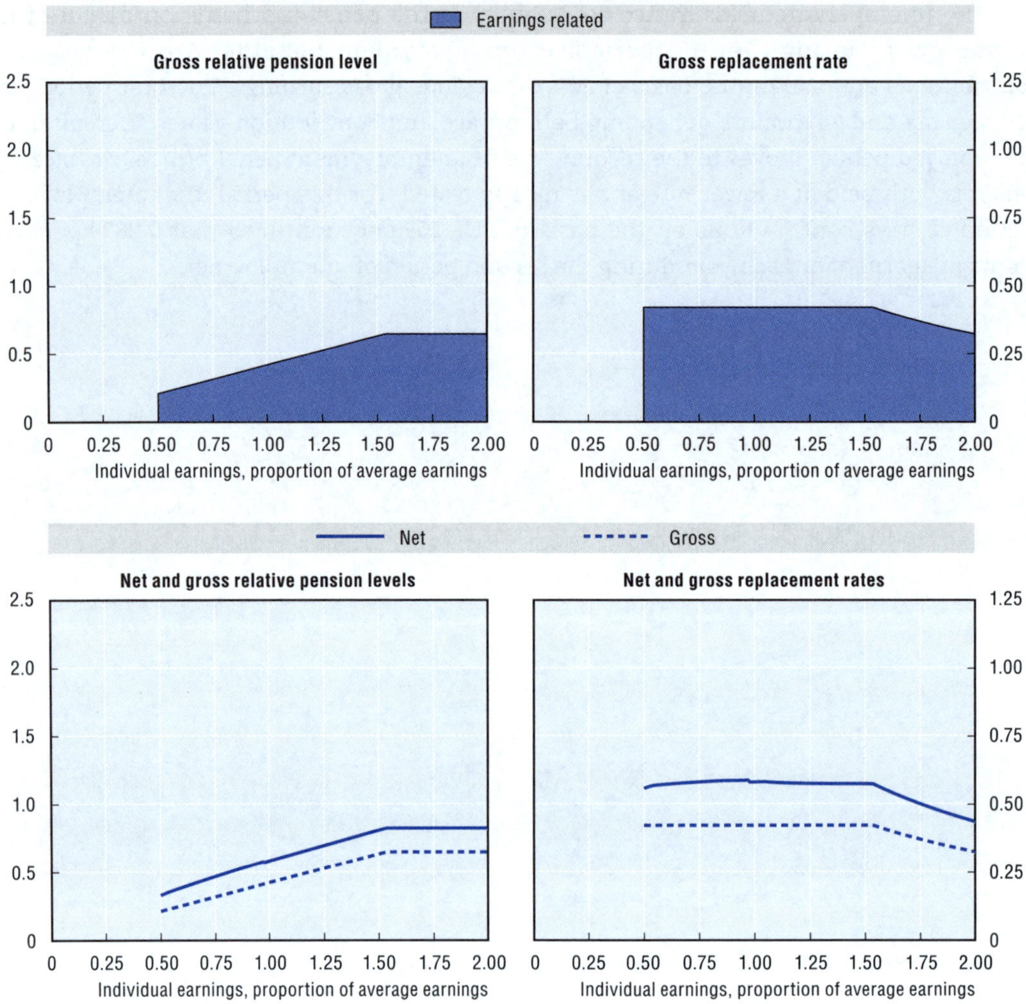

Men *Women (where different)*	Median earner	Individual earnings, multiple of average				
		0.5	0.75	1	1.5	2
Gross relative pension level	36.6	21.0	31.5	42.0	63.0	64.6
(% average gross earnings)						
Net relative pension level	52.6	32.7	46.5	57.9	80.5	82.1
(% net average earnings)						
Gross replacement rate	42.0	42.0	42.0	42.0	42.0	32.3
(% individual gross earnings)						
Net replacement rate	58.4	55.6	57.9	57.9	57.2	43.4
(% individual net earnings)						
Gross pension wealth	7.7	7.7	7.7	7.7	7.7	5.9
(multiple of individual gross earnings)	*9.2*	*9.2*	*9.2*	*9.2*	*9.2*	*7.1*
Net pension wealth	6.4	6.9	6.6	6.1	5.7	4.3
(multiple of individual gross earnings)	*7.7*	*8.3*	*7.9*	*7.4*	*6.8*	*5.2*

StatLink http://dx.doi.org/10.1787/888932371538

Greece

Greece: Pension system in 2008

Pensions are provided through an earnings-related public scheme with two components plus a series of minimum pensions/social safety nets.

Key indicators

		Greece	OECD
Average earnings	EUR	23 900	27 800
	USD	35 000	40 600
Public pension spending	% of GDP	11.9	7.0
Life expectancy	At birth	79.2	78.9
	At age 65	82.6	83.1
Population over age 65	% of working-age population	29.1	23.6

Qualifying conditions

The normal pension age is 65 for both men and women. A pension from this age requires a minimum of 4 500 days of contributions (equivalent to 15 years). Workers with a contribution record of 11 100 working days (37 years) can retire on a full benefit regardless of age. There are concessions for people who work in arduous or unhygienic occupations and for women with dependant or disabled children.

The minimum social pension requires 15 years' contributions.

Benefit calculation

Earnings-related scheme: main component

For labour-market entrants from 1993, the pension is 2% of earnings for each year of contributions up to 35 years. There is therefore a maximum replacement rate of 70% for people retiring at the normal age or earlier.

The earnings measure is the average over the last five years before retirement. These earnings (without the Christmas, Easter or vacation bonus) are adjusted, in line with increases defined in national income policy and taken into account for the calculation of the final pension amount.

There is a maximum pension, calculated as four times the GNP per capita. For 2008 the GNP per capita was formed as follows:

Between 1 January 2008 and 30 September 2008, EUR 679.75, consequently the maximum pension amounted to EUR 2 719, and from 1 October 2008 to 31 December 2008, EUR 693.35, consequently the maximum pension amounted to EUR 2 773.4.

Adjustment of pensions in payment is discretionary. Since 2005, all pensions are increased by the same proportion. Given the lack of consistent practice in recent benefit adjustments, pension wealth calculations are based on price indexation.

	2007	2008
Inflation (%)	2.9	4.2
Increases (%)	4	3% from 1/1/08 plus 2% from 1/10/08

All pensions have 14 monthly payments.

Earnings-related scheme: Supplementary component

The full supplementary pension is 20% of the earnings measure under the main component of the earnings-related scheme for workers with 35 years of contributions. The pension is proportionally reduced for shorter contribution periods, implying a linear accrual rate of 0.57%. The value is increased by 1/35th for each year of contributions (300 days) beyond 35 years.

Minimum pension

The amounts are adjusted annually as part of the income policy. For 2008, the main pensions were as follows:

a) Old-age and disability pension:
Between 1 January 2008 and 30 September 2008: EUR 486.02; and from 1 October 2008 to 31 December 2008: EUR 495.74.

b) Survivors pension:
Between 1 January 2008 and 30 September 2008: EUR 388.80; and from 1 October 2008 to 31 December 2008: EUR 396.58.

The minimum supplementary pensions for the same year were as follows:

a) Old-age and disability pension:
Between 1 January 2008 and 30 September 2008: EUR 119.17; and from 1 October 2008 to 31 December 2008: EUR 121.55.

b) Survivors pension:
Between 1 January 2008 and 30 September 2008: EUR 95.33 and from 1 October 2008 to 31 December 2008: EUR 97.24.

Income-tested scheme: Social solidarity benefit

This scheme, introduced in 1996, is a non-contributory, means-tested benefit payable to low-income pensioners eligible under most schemes (apart from the farmers' pension programme).

Eligibility for benefits under this scheme, known as EKAS, requires that total net income from all sources is less than EUR 7 750.42 (2008). Total taxable income must not exceed EUR 9 042.16 and the total taxable family income, EUR 14 070.23.

Income level, lower limit (EUR)	0	7 058.42	7 335.25	7 519.75	7 750.43
Benefit per month (EUR)	230.00	172.50	115.00	57.50	0

Variant careers

Early retirement

Early retirement is possible subject to reductions, as shown in the table below. The adjustment is 1/200 per month of early retirement, which is equivalent to 6% per year.

Number of years	Eligibility age	Conditions
15	65	No reduction
15	60	With reduction (1/200)
37	Any	No reduction

Late retirement

It is possible to retire after the normal pension age of 65 and a contribution period of 35 years. An increased accrual rate of 3.3% is applied in the main component up to 68 years of age and for a maximum of three extra years; there is no accrual rate for those working after this period (maximum replacement rate of 80%). The supplementary component also continues to accrue.

It is possible to combine work and pension receipt as long as the people are no younger than 55 years of age. In that case the part of their monthly pension income that exceeds EUR 733 is reduced by 70%; there is an increment for dependent children.

Childcare

As of 2003, there is a credit towards the pension qualifying conditions of one year for the first child (300 days of insurance) and two years (600 days of insurance) for each subsequent child to a maximum of three children. This credit can be bought off by either parent and cannot count towards the minimum required insurance period, or for the cases of 37 years, 4 500 days or 3 500 days of insurance.

Unemployment

Periods of unemployment can be credited up to 200 days during the lifetime. If the unemployment period overlaps with the final five years used as a base for the calculation of pensionable earnings, it is omitted and the period used for computing pensionable earnings is extended backwards.

Long term unemployed (*i.e.* unemployed for at least 12 consecutive months) aged at least 60 (men) or 55 (women) (or 55 and 50, respectively, when employed in arduous and unhealthy jobs) who lack up to 1 500 days for qualifying for an old-age and/or supplementary pension by IKA-ETAM, may optionally continue their insurance until they fulfil the minimum pension requirements. The corresponding social contributions are paid by a special account of the Labour Employment Office (LAEK).

Pension modelling results: Greece

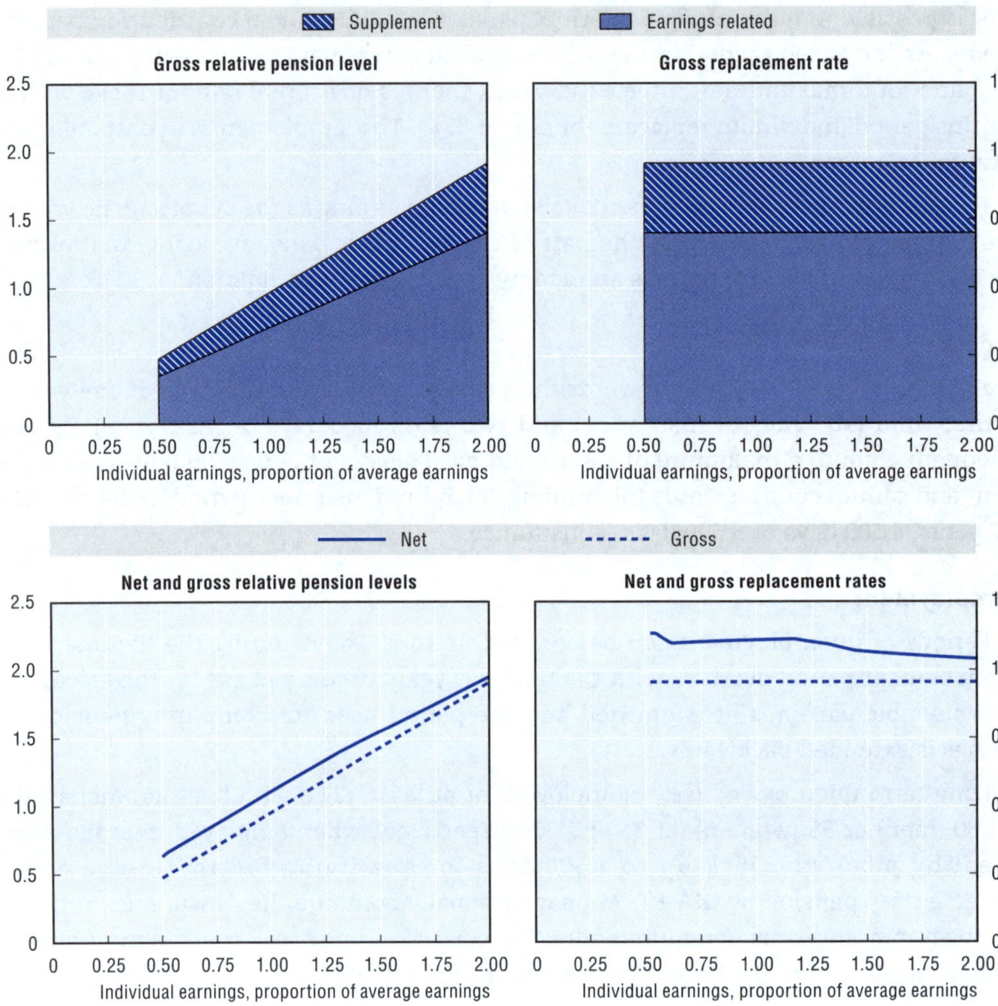

Men *Women (where different)*	Median earner	Individual earnings, multiple of average				
		0.5	0.75	1	1.5	2
Gross relative pension level	65.1	47.9	71.8	95.7	143.6	191.4
(% average gross earnings)						
Net relative pension level	81.4	63.7	87.9	111.2	155.3	195.5
(% net average earnings)						
Gross replacement rate	95.7	95.7	95.7	95.7	95.7	95.7
(% individual gross earnings)						
Net replacement rate	110.3	113.6	110.5	111.2	106.8	104.2
(% individual net earnings)						
Gross pension wealth	15.2	15.2	15.2	15.2	15.2	15.2
(multiple of individual gross earnings)	*17.4*	*17.4*	*17.4*	*17.4*	*17.4*	*17.4*
Net pension wealth	14.2	15.1	13.9	13.2	12.3	11.6
(multiple of individual gross earnings)	*16.3*	*17.4*	*16.0*	*15.2*	*14.1*	*13.3*

StatLink http://dx.doi.org/10.1787/888932371557

Hungary

Hungary: Pension system in 2008

The new system combines an earnings-related public pension with mandatory fully funded defined-contribution schemes. This applies to new labour-market entrants and people aged 4 or under at the time of reform. Older workers could choose between this mixed system or a pure pay-as-you-go, public pension. The modelling assumes that workers are covered by the mixed system.

Key indicators

		Hungary	OECD
Average earnings	HUF (million)	2.34	7.00
	USD	13 600	40 600
Public pension spending	% of GDP	9.1	7.0
Life expectancy	At birth	73.3	78.9
	At age 65	79.9	83.1
Population over age 65	% of working-age population	25.6	23.6

Qualifying conditions

A phased increase in the pension eligibility age will equalise this at 62 for both men and women (from 60 and 55 respectively). The age for men reached 62 in 2000 and will reach 62 for women from the beginning of 2009. As from 2010, the statutory unisex retirement age will be increased gradually, reaching 65 by 2022. The first affected age cohort are those persons born in 1952. In addition, 20 years' service is required for both the earnings-related pension and the minimum pension. 15 years' service is required to receive a partial pension.

The reformed system was introduced in January 1998. People who switched voluntarily to the new, mixed system were allowed to return to the pure pay-as-you-go system until the end of 2002. The switch back option is available for a few people aged 52+ (only 3% of the total number of fund members) by the end of 2009. Moreover, the obligation for new entrants to join a private pension fund was suspended in calendar year 2002 but reintroduced in 2003.

Benefit calculation

Earnings related

For those covered by the mixed system, the accrual rate is 1.22% of earnings for each year of service (subject to the contribution ceiling, see below). This compares with an accrual rate of 1.65% for those covered by the pay-as-you-go system alone.

The earnings base used to be net-gross (*i.e.* gross wage less employee's contribution) pay in all years since 1988, moving towards the full lifetime. This was changed into net pay from 2008. Earlier years' earnings were valorised with economy-wide average earnings to a point two years before retirement in 2006. The last three years' earnings prior to retirement were entirely unvalorised. This was changed from 1 January 2008, to full valorisation (to the year preceding retirement, in 2009 as well). The summary effect of the two changes will be about an 8% reduction.

A ceiling to pensionable earnings was introduced in 1992. Roughly speaking, the ceiling is about three times the gross wage since 2005 but it is set in advance. The ceiling was HUF 19 500 per day in 2008.

The pension in payment has been indexed half to wages and half to prices since 2001 but further *ad hoc* increases were applied.

As of 2010 indexation will be linked to GDP growth.

GDP growth	Consumer price (%)	Net average monthly earnings (%)
X-3%	100	–
3-4%	80	20
4-5%	60	40
5%-X	50	50

There was an additional month's pension from 2006. Before 2009 all pensioners received the 13th month pension. As of 1 January 2009 the rules on eligibility to 13th month pension has been changed according to the following. The upper limit of the amount of 13th month pension is set at HUF 80 000 and eligibility criteria has been tightened to only those persons who have reached the standard retirement age, 62 years of age. Under-age pension recipients of their own right will not receive this 13th month benefit from 2009, while under age disability pensioners and survivor's pensioners – except temporary widow's pensioners – will receive this benefit. According to the new legislation adopted in May 2009, this option has ceased (recipients will not receive second half of the benefit in November). As of 2010 the 13th month pension will be totally abolished.

Minimum

There is a minimum pension, which was worth HUF 28 500 per month in 2008 (around 15% of gross average earnings and it is around 18% of net average monthly earnings). The value is indexed in the same way as benefits under the earnings-related scheme, that is, half prices and half average earnings. Rules on minimum pension have also been modified according to the December 2008 amendments. According to the amendment the government decides upon the minimum amount of old-age, invalidity pension and orphan's allowance as of 2009. According to former rules, the amount of minimum pension was increased with the annual (January) pension increase; new rules leave the decision of the amount to the government. The amounts remain unchanged in 2009.

Defined contribution

As of 2008 the contribution rate in case of pension fund members (mixed system):

	To the 1st pillar PAYG, DB (%)	To the 2nd pillar funded, DC (%)	Total (%)
Employers' contribution rate	24	0	24
Employees' contribution rate	1.5	8	9.5
Total	**25.5**	**8**	**33.5**

Some 8% of gross pensionable earnings are diverted to the funded plan from 2004 for people covered by the mixed public-private pension option (either by choice or by mandate). This represents an increase from 6% (1998-2002) and 7% (2003). For 2008, the employer' total pension contribution rate has been raised from 21 to 24%, the employees' total part has changed from 8.5% to 9.5%. The reason for the increase is only the rearrangement of the health and pension funds; the budget of the disability pension system was transferred from the Health Insurance Fund to the Pension Insurance Fund. (The contribution rate for health insurance was decreased by the same percentage point, thus the total contribution burden of the employers and employees has not changed.)

The accumulated amount must be converted into an annuity on retirement. According to the current legislation the annuity must provide at least the same Swiss indexation of the pension in payment as the public pension scheme. Unisex life tables must be used to calculate annuity rates. Currently (end of 2009) Hungary is working on the new legislation of private pension system concerning to the annuities and those institutions. First payments from this pillar are expected to be provided from 2013.

Variant careers

Early retirement

In 2008 early retirement is possible for men at age 60 and at age 57 for women without actuarial reduction. When pension ages are equalised at 62 in 2009, early retirement (advanced pension eligibility) will be available from 59 for women and 60 for men. According to the new adopted legislation, the advanced retirement age will gradually increase to 63 years.

According to the new legislation, as of 2010 advanced pension rules are also tightened along with the increase in standard retirement age.

Men born after 31 December 1950 or women born after 31 December 1958 attaining at least 37 years of service and ceasing gainful activity can retire two years early with a reduction to the pension. The pension is reduced by 0.3% per missing month, if the claimant is one year younger than his/her relevant retirement age. If the claimant is more than one year younger than his/her relevant retirement age the amount is reduced by 3.6% plus 0.4% for every additional missing month.

Late retirement

It is possible to defer the earnings-related pension. The pension is increased by 0.5% for each month of deferral.

Childcare

The periods spent on childcare were counted as credit in the PAYG between 1988 and 1998. All earnings earned since 1988 are counted into the pension base and this credit is not counted at all, because it would decrease the average earnings of pension base. (These benefits are ignored in the calculation of pension base.)

Since 1998 pension contribution has to be paid after these benefits, and if amounts of childcare benefits are favourable for the insured, these benefits will be counted into the pension base.

People can take the following benefits: pregnancy confinement benefit, child care fee, child care allowance and child raising support.

Pregnancy confinement benefit (*terhességi gyermekágyi segély*) is for women in the pregnancy period or giving birth, for 24 weeks (168 days). The benefit is 70% of the daily average gross earnings of the previous year. Child care fee (*gyermekgondozási díj*) could be claimed by one of the parents on day after the expiry period of pregnancy confinement benefit and the entitlement runs to the second birthday of the child (maximum 24 months). The benefit amount is 70% of the daily average gross earnings of the previous year up to the maximum of twice of the minimum wage (HUF 96 600 in 2008). It's obligatory to pay individual pension contribution, which was 9.5% in 2008. Child care allowance (*gyermekgondozási segély*) is for one of the parents who cares for the child until the child's third birthday (maximum 36 months), or in case of twin children until the end of the year they reach school age, or in case of a permanently ill or seriously disabled child until they are ten years of age (maximum 120 months). The monthly amount is equal to the minimum old-age pension of HUF 28 500 as from January 2008 irrespective of the number of children in the family, and in case of twins the amount is doubled, irrespective of the number of twins in the family. After the child's first birthday, also grandparents can claim the benefit. It's obligatory to pay the individual pension contribution which was 9.5% in 2008. Child raising support (*gyermeknevelési támogatás*) for one of the parents who cares for the child and who raises three or more underage children for the period between the third and the eighth birthday of the youngest child (maximum 60 months). The monthly amount is equal to the minimum old-age pension, irrespective of the number of children.

The total amount of periods taken off work is not maximized and entitlements are not added up, though it depends on the age and number of the children and the composition of the family.

In 2008, pension contribution after child care benefits is paid by:

	Individual	Employer	Government
Pregnancy confinement benefit	–	–	–
Child care fee	X	–	X
Child care allowance	X	–	X
Child raising support	X	–	X

Unemployment

The unemployed are covered by the earnings-related pension system. Generally, the periods of unemployment are qualified as a pensionable service. The earnings measure for the period of unemployment is the most favourable of: *i)* the amount of unemployment benefits; or *ii)* the average of previous and subsequent earnings.

Older unemployed people can receive special pre-retirement benefits if they have received unemployment insurance benefits for 140 days, will reach pensionable age within five years, have exhausted their unemployment benefit entitlement within eight years of pensionable age and have contributed to the pension scheme for at least 20 years.

Pension modelling results: Hungary

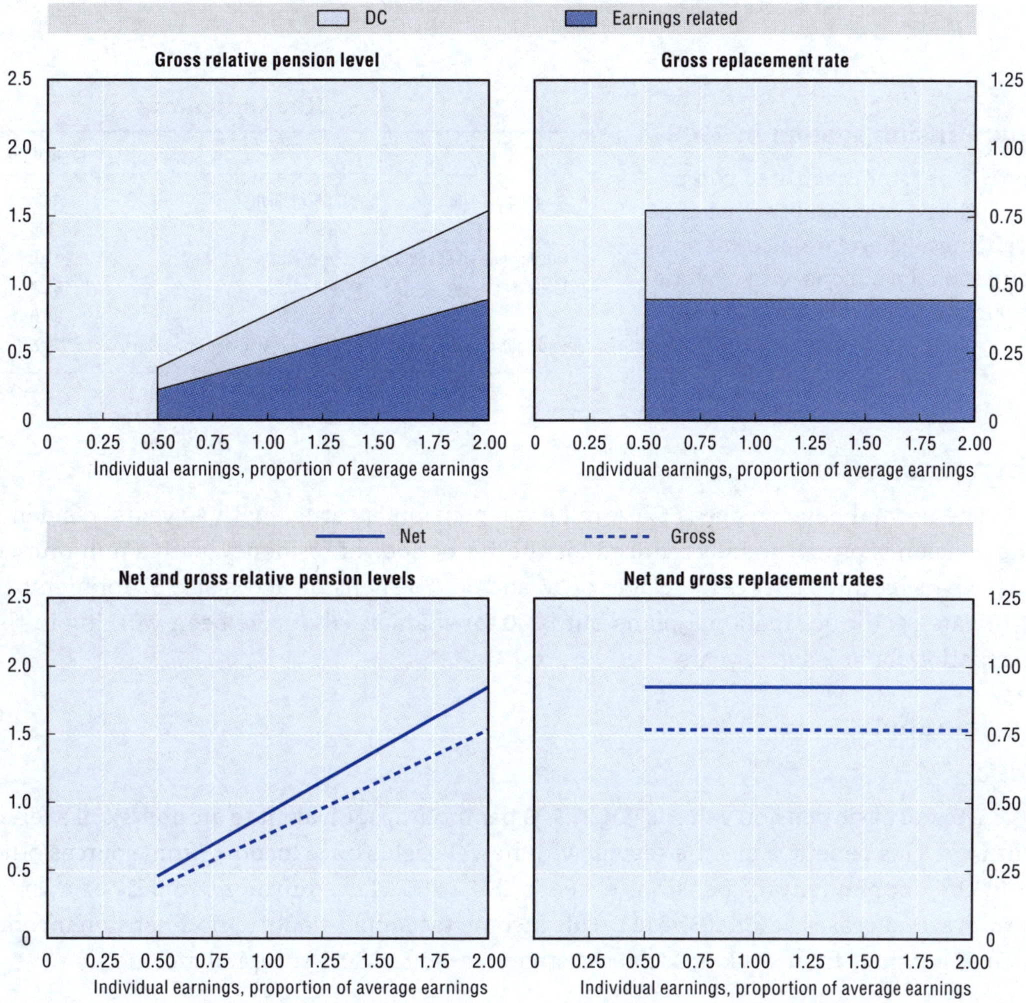

Men *Women (where different)*	Median earner	Individual earnings, multiple of average				
		0.5	0.75	1	1.5	2
Gross relative pension level *(% average gross earnings)*	56.1	37.9	56.9	75.8	113.8	151.7
Net relative pension level *(% net average earnings)*	83.6	59.8	84.5	106.0	139.8	178.5
Gross replacement rate *(% individual gross earnings)*	75.8	75.8	75.8	75.8	75.8	75.8
Net replacement rate *(% individual net earnings)*	99.5	96.3	99.9	106.0	103.2	102.9
Gross pension wealth	10.6	10.6	10.6	10.6	10.6	10.6
(multiple of individual gross earnings)	*13.3*	*13.3*	*13.3*	*13.3*	*13.3*	*13.3*
Net pension wealth	9.8	10.3	9.7	9.2	8.0	7.7
(multiple of individual gross earnings)	*12.2*	*12.9*	*12.2*	*11.4*	*10.1*	*9.6*

StatLink http://dx.doi.org/10.1787/888932371576

Iceland

Iceland: Pension system in 2008

The public pension has three components, including a basic and two income-tested schemes. There are also mandatory occupational pensions with a hybrid (albeit mainly defined-benefit) formula.

Key indicators

		Iceland	OECD
Average earnings	ISK (million)	4.07	3.57
	USD	46 200	40 600
Public pension spending	% of GDP	1.9	7.0
Life expectancy	At birth	81.7	78.9
	At age 65	84.5	83.1
Population over age 65	% of working-age population	19.5	23.6

Qualifying conditions

The normal pension age is 67. A full basic pension is earned with 40 years' residency. The pension is proportionally reduced for shorter periods of residency, with a minimum of three years required between the ages of 16 and 66. The pension age is also 67 for members of private-sector occupational plans but is 60 for seamen who have been working in this occupation for at least 25 years.

Benefit calculation

Basic

The full basic pension value is ISK 25 700 per month, equivalent to around 8% of average earnings. This benefit is income-tested: withdrawal begins once income (from sources other than the supplementary pension) exceeds ISK 2 296 111, equivalent to 56% of average earnings, and ceases at ISK 3 324 111. This income test applies only to non-pension income, such as earnings from work or social assistance as well as 50% of capital income.

Targeted

A second element is the pension supplement. The maximum value of this benefit is ISK 81 100 per month for a single person, some 24% of average earnings. This benefit is withdrawn against income above ISK 1 842 000 per year (around 45% of average earnings). The basic pension, however, does not affect the value of the pension supplement. The withdrawal rate for the income test in the pension supplement is 45%.

The benefit levels are adjusted annually in accordance with the current State Budget. Adjustments are to take account of public-sector pay (which is assumed here to be equal to the standard assumption of economy-wide earnings growth) and the price level pursuant to the cost-of-living index.

Mandatory occupational

Employer schemes are mandatory. The law requires schemes to target a replacement rate of 56% with 40 years' contributions, giving an accrual rate of 1.4% for each year of service. Coverage is mandatory for people aged 16 to 70. The earnings base in this calculation is average lifetime salary for each year of membership. There is no ceiling to pensionable earnings. Past earnings are valorised in line with price inflation plus 3.5% interest rate.

Occupational pensions in payment must by law be increased in line with consumer price inflation.

In practice, many schemes pay more than the legal minimum outlined above, typically introducing a hybrid defined-contribution/defined-benefit element into the system. There is a minimum contribution to occupational schemes of 12% of earnings. The employee pays 4% and the employer 8%. Contributions above the level needed to finance the statutory benefits described above can be used either to increase defined-benefit entitlements or diverted to individual accounts thus delivering a defined-contribution pension. However, the modelling covers only the mandatory component and not these extra-statutory benefits as they are not guaranteed.

Variant careers

Early retirement

Under the mandatory occupational scheme, early retirement rules vary between funds, depending on the structure of fund membership. In the private sector, the normal retirement age is 67 and the pension can be claimed from 65. In general, pensions are reduced by 7% for each year that pension is claimed early.

It is not possible to claim the basic or targeted pensions before the normal pension age.

Late retirement

Under the mandatory occupational scheme, workers can postpone retirement until the age of 70 with a pension increase of 9% for each year of deferral. Workers who defer their pension continue to contribute and earn extra pension entitlements. In some cases, the total contribution period is limited to 32 years.

Those who began receiving a pension after 1 January 2007 can defer receiving their pension up to the age of 72, but the amount of benefits increase by 0.5% for every month pension payments are deferred.

Childcare

The residency-tested basic pension and the targeted schemes automatically protect women who leave paid work to care for children. There are no specific credits for childcare absences. The occupational pension funds themselves make no provisions for women who must leave work to care for children. The government social assistance scheme contains benefits for parents (men or women) who must take care of children with long-term illnesses or disabilities. Such benefits are also provided in cases where people must take care of close relatives (*e.g.* adult son or daughter taking care of aged parent).

Unemployment

The contribution base, on which the minimum 10% contribution is levied, includes unemployment insurance benefits as well as earnings but excludes all other benefits.

Pension modelling results: Iceland

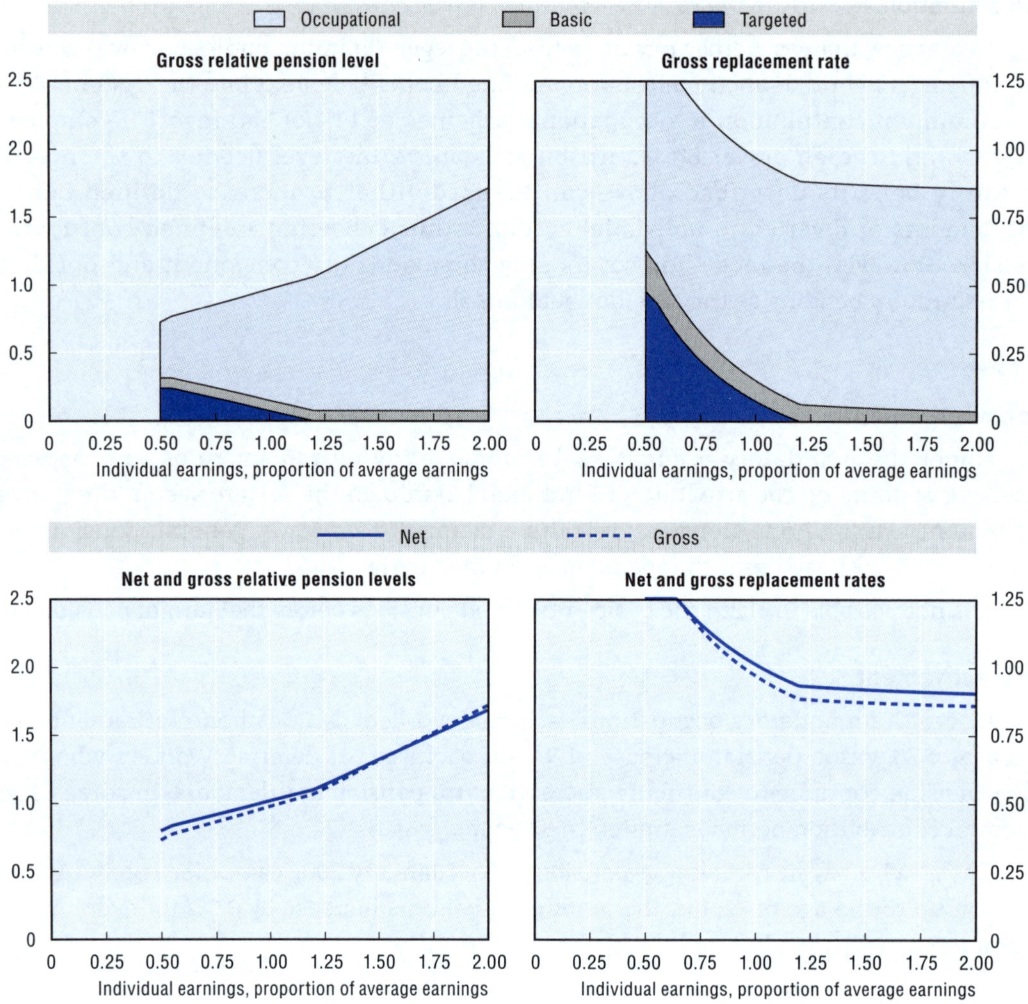

Men *Women (where different)*	Median earner	Individual earnings, multiple of average				
		0.5	0.75	1	1.5	2
Gross relative pension level *(% average gross earnings)*	88.4	72.5	85.7	96.9	130.4	171.4
Net relative pension level *(% net average earnings)*	93.4	79.1	91.0	101.1	131.2	168.0
Gross replacement rate *(% individual gross earnings)*	109.1	144.9	114.2	96.9	87.0	85.7
Net replacement rate *(% individual net earnings)*	111.7	139.0	116.0	101.1	91.7	90.2
Gross pension wealth	18.5	25.5	19.5	16.1	14.1	13.9
(multiple of individual gross earnings)	*20.7*	*28.8*	*21.9*	*18.0*	*15.8*	*15.5*
Net pension wealth	14.0	20.0	14.8	12.0	10.2	9.7
(multiple of individual gross earnings)	*15.7*	*22.5*	*16.6*	*13.4*	*11.3*	*10.9*

StatLink http://dx.doi.org/10.1787/888932371595

Ireland

Ireland: Pension system in 2008

The public pension is a basic scheme paying a flat rate to all who meet the contribution conditions. There is also a means-tested pension to provide a safety net for the low-income elderly. Voluntary occupational pension schemes have broad coverage: over half of employees.

Key indicators

		Ireland	OECD
Average earnings	EUR	40 900	27 800
	USD	59 700	40 600
Public pension spending	% of GDP	3.6	7.0
Life expectancy	At birth	79.9	78.9
	At age 65	83.3	83.1
Population over age 65	% of working-age population	18.0	23.6

Qualifying conditions

The State Pension (contributory) is payable from age 66 while the State Pension (transition) is paid from 65. Full entitlement to both benefits requires an average of 48 weeks contributions or credits per year throughout the working life. The pension value is reduced for incomplete contribution histories. However, State Pension (contributory) requires a minimum average of ten weeks' contributions per year and the State Pension (transition) requires a minimum of 24 weeks per year. There is also a minimum total period of paid (as opposed to credited) contributions of 260 weeks (equivalent to five years' full coverage).

The means-tested pension is payable from age 66.

Benefit calculation

Basic

The maximum values of the State Pension (contributory) and the State Pension (transition) are both EUR 223.30 per week (paid for 53 weeks per year) for 2008, which is 28.9% of average earnings (on the OECD measure of average earnings). There is an additional EUR 148.80 for a dependant adult of working age and EUR 200 for a dependant aged 66 or over. Pensions are usually increased on an annual basis, decided by government in the context of the annual budget. In recent years, increases have been in excess of earnings growth.

Pensioners are entitled to many benefits-in-kind. The government estimates that the price of these goods and services would be EUR 950 per year, excluding health benefits. (Note that the modelling covers only cash benefits and not benefits-in-kind.)

Targeted

The maximum value of the means-tested benefit is EUR 212 per week for a single person with an extra EUR 140.10 for an adult dependant for 2008. The single person's benefit is worth 27% of average earnings. There is a small weekly disregard of EUR 30 in the means test, and there is an additional earnings disregard of EUR 200: otherwise, the benefit is withdrawn at 100% of income. There is also an assets test, with capital of more than EUR 20 000 being converted to income using a standard formula.

Voluntary private pension

There is an additional voluntary pension which is assumed to be defined contribution. The contribution rate is assumed to be 10%.

Variant careers

Early retirement

Pensions cannot be claimed before the normal eligibility age.

Late retirement

Work and pension can be combined subject to earnings being less than EUR 38 per week under the State Pension (transition), which is payable for one year. However, the State Pension (contributory) is not subject to an earnings test. It is not possible to defer claiming the pension.

Childcare

Eventual public pension entitlement is not affected by periods out of paid work for caring purposes.

Unemployment

Eventual public pension entitlement is not affected by periods of unemployment.

Pension modelling results: Ireland

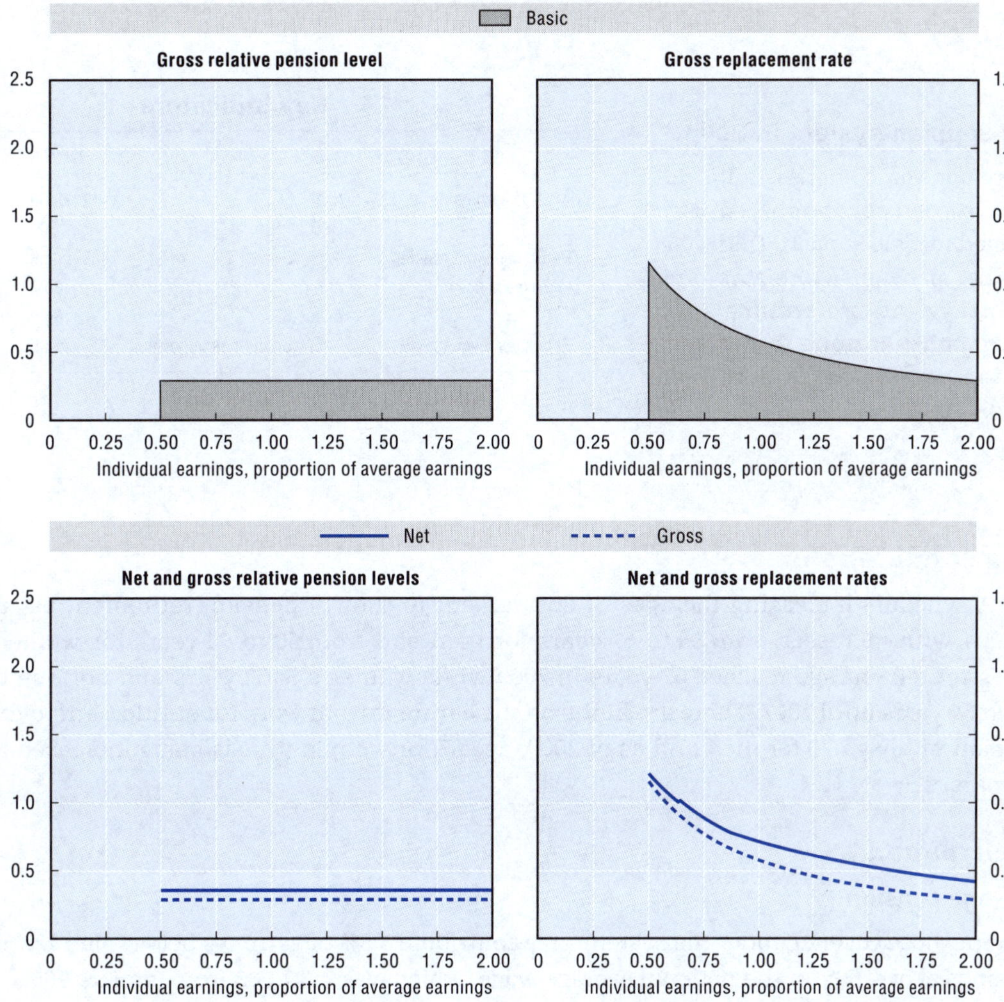

Men *Women (where different)*	Median earner	Individual earnings, multiple of average				
		0.5	0.75	1	1.5	2
Gross relative pension level	29.0	29.0	29.0	29.0	29.0	29.0
(% average gross earnings)						
Net relative pension level	35.8	35.8	35.8	35.8	35.8	35.8
(% net average earnings)						
Gross replacement rate	34.9	57.9	38.6	29.0	19.3	14.5
(% individual gross earnings)						
Net replacement rate	40.8	60.8	44.5	35.8	26.8	21.2
(% individual net earnings)						
Gross pension wealth	6.8	11.4	7.6	5.7	3.8	2.8
(multiple of individual gross earnings)	*8.3*	*13.7*	*9.1*	*6.9*	*4.6*	*3.4*
Net pension wealth	6.8	11.4	7.6	5.7	3.8	2.8
(multiple of individual gross earnings)	*8.3*	*13.7*	*9.1*	*6.9*	*4.6*	*3.4*

StatLink http://dx.doi.org/10.1787/888932371652

Israel

Israel: Pension system in 2008

The state pension comprises a universal insurance pension combined with means-tested income support. Until 2008 second-pillar pensions were common, but voluntary. As of January 2008 mandatory contributions to defined-contribution pension funds have been introduced.

Key indicators

		Israel	OECD
Average earnings	ILS	112 400	145 700
	USD	31 300	40 600
Public pension spending	% of GDP	4.8	7.0
Life expectancy	At birth	80.7	78.9
	At age 65	84.0	83.1
Population over age 65	% of working-age population	18.5	23.6

Qualifying conditions

A schedule increasing the ages of entitlement to the NII pension retirement began in 2004 with increases from 65 to 67 years for men and from 60 to 64 years for women. Men's retirement age reached 67 years in 2009 while women's is 62 years and not due to reach 64 years until 2017. There are limits on the earnings from work for entitlement to the pension until age 70 for men and as of 2009, age 67 for women (this is being increased to 70 years).

Benefit calculation

Old-age pension

For those covered under the system they contribute 3.5% of earnings below, plus 12% of earnings above, 60% of the national average wage, which was ILS 7 663 from January 2008.

The minimum earnings for contribution purposes are ILS 3 585, equal to the minimum wage. Anyone earning less than this amount pays contributions as if earning the minimum.

The maximum earnings for contribution purposes are five times the national average wage as of January 1 each year.

Social insurance

A single pensioner receives 16.5% of the old-age basic amount a month, with a couple receiving 24.8%. The old-age basic amount is ILS 7 352.

There is a seniority increment where the pension is increased by 2% for each year of insurance coverage exceeding ten years, up to a maximum equal to 50% of the pension.

The income supplement is paid if income, including the pension, is less than the minimum level for subsistence. Rates vary between 28.8% and 62.9% of the old-age basic amount a month, depending on marital status and the number of children. The resulting amount is increased by an additional 7%.

Income support is withdrawn at a rate of 60% in the presence of income from defined-contribution pensions.

Defined contribution

Mandatory contributions have applied to earnings up to the average wage for all employees since January 2008. Initially the rates were modest with a total contribution of 2.5% but are scheduled to increase to 15% (5% from employees and 10% from employers) by 2013. Half of the employers' contribution also provides severance insurance which, if utilised, diminishes the pension.

Minimum

The minimum is covered within the social insurance referenced above.

Variant careers

Early retirement

It is not possible to receive a pension prior to the normal pension age.

Late retirement

The pension is increased by 5% for each year of deferred retirement.

Pension modelling results: Israel

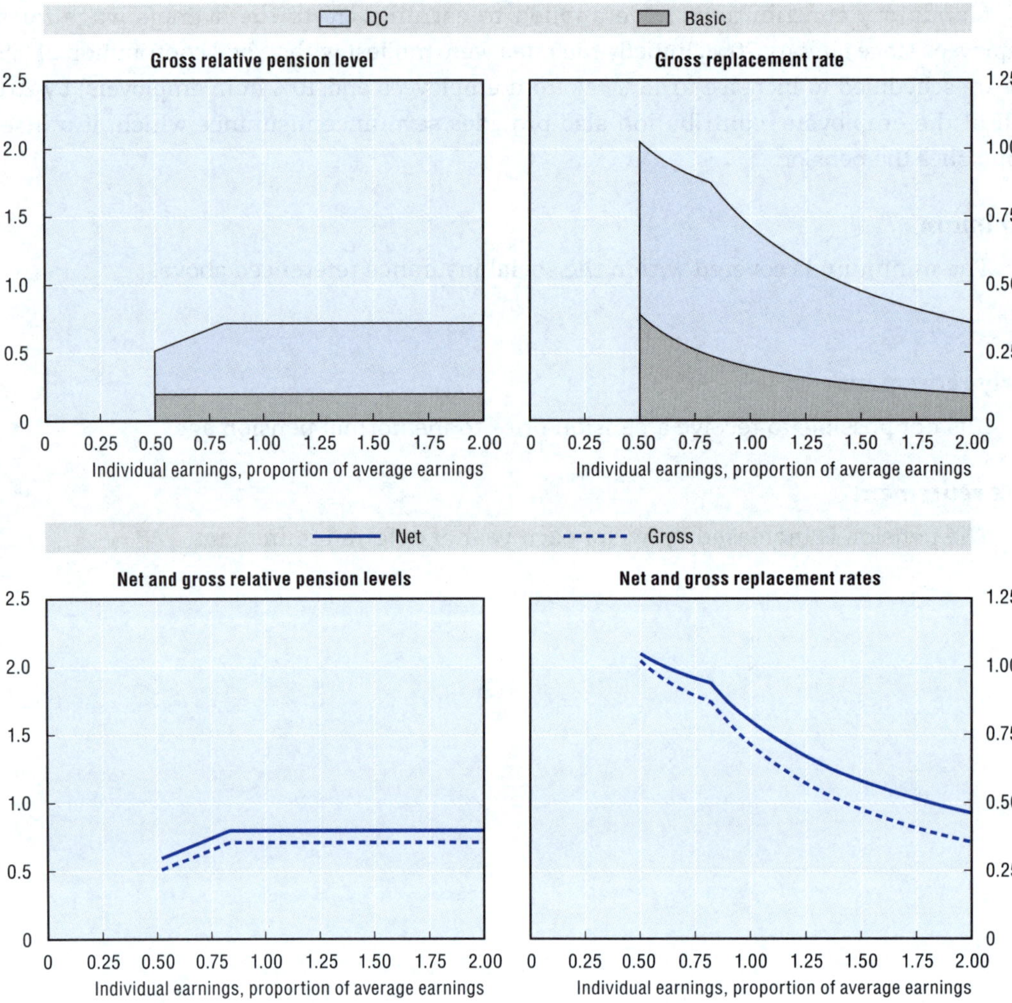

Men *Women (where different)*	Median earner	Individual earnings, multiple of average				
		0.5	0.75	1	1.5	2
Gross relative pension level	69.1	50.1	65.4	69.6	69.6	69.6
(% average gross earnings)	*60.7*	*44.9*	*57.7*	*61.2*	*61.2*	*61.2*
Net relative pension level	77.7	58.7	74.1	78.2	78.2	78.2
(% net average earnings)	*69.4*	*53.4*	*66.3*	*69.8*	*69.8*	*69.8*
Gross replacement rate	85.3	100.1	87.2	69.6	46.4	34.8
(% individual gross earnings)	*75.0*	*89.9*	*76.9*	*61.2*	*40.8*	*30.6*
Net replacement rate	92.2	103.0	93.7	78.2	56.7	45.2
(% individual net earnings)	*82.3*	*93.6*	*83.9*	*69.8*	*50.6*	*40.4*
Gross pension wealth	13.5	15.9	13.8	11.0	7.4	5.5
(multiple of individual gross earnings)	*14.5*	*17.4*	*14.9*	*11.8*	*7.9*	*5.9*
Net pension wealth	12.8	15.6	13.1	10.4	6.9	5.2
(multiple of individual gross earnings)	*13.9*	*17.3*	*14.3*	*11.3*	*7.5*	*5.7*

StatLink http://dx.doi.org/10.1787/888932371671

Italy

Italy: Pension system in 2008

The new Italian pension system is based on notional accounts. Contributions earn a rate of return related to GDP growth. At retirement, the accumulated notional capital is converted into an annuity taking account of average life expectancy at retirement. It applies in full to labour-market entrants from 1996 onwards.

Key indicators

		Italy	OECD
Average earnings	EUR	26 300	27 800
	USD	38 500	40 600
Public pension spending	% of GDP	14.1	7.0
Life expectancy	At birth	81.1	78.9
	At age 65	84.5	83.1
Population over age 65	% of working-age population	33.0	23.6

Qualifying conditions

The normal pension age under the new system will be 60 for women and 65 for men from 2008 onwards.

Benefit calculation

Under the contribution-based regime the private and public employees contribution rate is 33%, of which about one-third is paid by the employee and two-thirds by the employer; the amount of pension is calculated as a product of two factors: the total lifelong contributions, capitalised with the nominal GDP growth rate (in line with a five-year moving average) and the transformation coefficient whose calculation is mainly based on the probabilities of death, the probabilities of leaving any widow or widower and the number of years that a survivor's benefit will be withdrawn. As a consequence, benefits are strongly related to retirement age – the lower the age, the lower the pension.

The transformation coefficients are reviewed every three years. They are available for the age bracket 57-65, but workers may not retire earlier than 65 unless they have reached the eligibility requirements stated by the current legislation and an amount of pension not less than 1.2 times the old-age allowance.

The baseline assumption in modelling all countries is 2% annual real wage growth. Given the projected decline in the Italian labour force, a consistent assumption is that real GDP growth is 1.6% per year.

For employees, in 2008, minimum pay for contribution purposes is EUR 177.42 per week (35% of average earnings). Maximum earnings for benefits are EUR 88 669 per year under the new scheme, or just over 337% of average earnings.

The indexation of pensions in payment is complex, since smaller pensions are accorded a more generous treatment than larger pensions. In 2008, for benefits up to five times the minimum pension there is full price indexation of pensions in payment. This threshold is EUR 2 180.70 per month for 2007 (which is used to index pensions in 2008). For benefits between five and eight times the minimum pension, pensions in payment are uprated by 75% of price inflation. Above this threshold, there is no indexation. From

January 2009, for benefits up to five times the minimum pension there is full price indexation of pensions in payment. This threshold is EUR 2 217.80 per month for 2008 (which is used to index pensions in 2009). Above this threshold, pensions in payment are uprated by 75% of price inflation.

Voluntary

There is an additional voluntary, supplementary occupational system. It consists of both open funds and closed collectively agreed funds. The closed funds can be funded by both employers and employees as well as from the Tfr. The open funds provide an annuity based on contributions. The current Tfr contribution rate is 6.91%. The number of workers enrolled in a private pension fund is still low. For this reason, the Finance Act for 2007 has anticipated (with some changes) the pension reform recently passed which introduced further measures in order to foster the development of the second pillar: *a)* higher fiscal incentives; and *b)* silence-as-assent for the transfer of the private severance pay (Tfr). In particular, the latter means that the current severance pay accumulation is supposed to be transferred to private pension funds, unless he/she applies for communicating his/her refusal. However, enrolments in the private pension funds remain on a voluntary basis.

Social assistance

The minimum pension is abolished for people covered only under the new system; *i.e.* entrants after 1996. However, pensioners with incomes below the social-assistance level can claim a means-tested benefit from age 65. Including supplements, the 2008 value of the social-assistance benefit (*assegno sociale*) was EUR 5 310.63. There is a higher benefit of EUR 7 540 for over 70s. These are equivalent to 20% and 29% of average earnings, respectively.

Variant careers

Early retirement

Under the previous system, workers could retire at age 57 if they had contributed to the system for 35 years. From January 2008, minimum age has been increased to 58 years (59 years if self-employed). A recent reform, approved as part of the 2008 budget process, has introduced a quota system based on a combination of age and seniority, so the minimum age to request early retirement (seniority pensions) will increase from 57 to 61 years old by 2013 as shown in table.

	Employees		Self-employed	
	Quota	Age	Quota	Age
From 1 July 2009 to 31 December 2010	95	59	96	60
From 1 January 2011 to 31 December 2012	96	60	97	61
From 1 January 2013	97	61	98	62

However, it will remain possible to retire at any age with 40 years' contributions.

Late retirement

Women have the right to continue working until the normal pension age for men. Retirement is not compulsory at 65 but employers have the right to dismiss employees reaching that age. From January 2009 it is possible to totally combine employment and pension receipts. Referring to pensions under the contribution-based regime: *a)* it is possible to totally combine employment and anticipated old-age pension receipts for pensioners who have 40 or more years of seniority; *b)* it is possible to totally combine employment and old-age pension receipts for pensioners who are 65 years old or more, if male, and 60 years old or more, if female.

It is possible to defer the pension claim after age 65, however the transformation coefficient remains the same, and benefits increase only because of the accumulation of further contributions and their (notional) capitalization for one or more further years.

Childcare

The pension is increased for mothers by giving them a more generous transformation coefficient. For mothers of one or two children this is the transformation coefficient of their actual retirement age plus one year. For three or more children this is the actual retirement age plus two years. Thus, according to the projected transformation coefficients, the effect is to increase the pension by around 3% for one or two children, and 6% for three or more children.

Unemployment

All the unemployment insurance schemes – *cassa integrazione guadagni* (CIG), *indennità di mobilità* and *indennità di disoccupazione* – give rise to credited contributions for the time the benefit is received. Previous earnings are used as a base for pension calculation.

The maximum credit period is five years over the lifetime for people that entered the labour market from 1993 onwards. This affects only the right to receive a seniority pension. Furthermore, credited contributions for *indennità di disoccupazione* – the general unemployment scheme – cannot be counted towards the 35-year contribution requirement although they do count (under the five-year limit) towards the 40-year requirement.

Contributions are normally paid by the government, with the exception of *indennità di mobilità* in the first year of receipt and CIG, which are partially paid by the employee at a reduced rate of 5.54%.

Pension modelling results: Italy

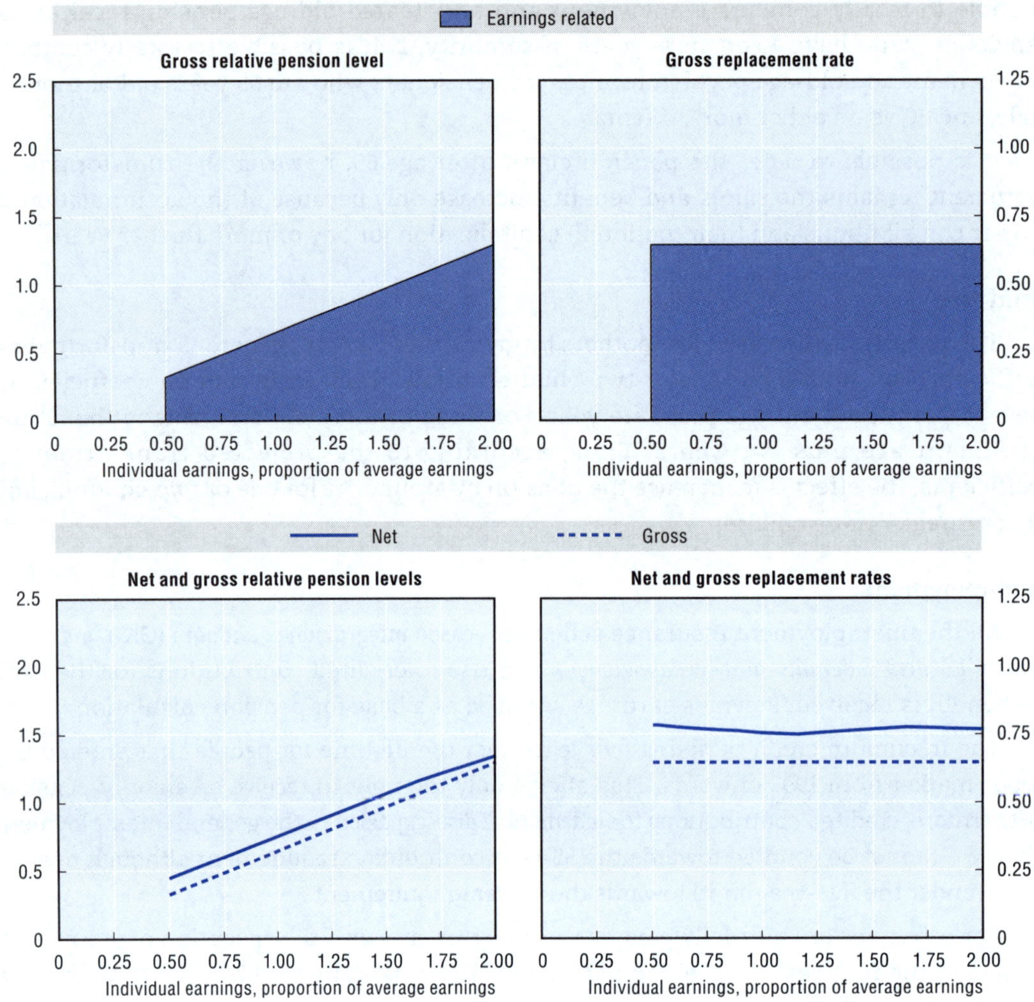

Men *Women (where different)*	Median earner	Individual earnings, multiple of average				
		0.5	0.75	1	1.5	2
Gross relative pension level	54.9	32.3	48.4	64.5	96.8	129.1
(% average gross earnings)	*43.0*	*25.3*	*37.9*	*50.6*	*75.9*	*101.2*
Net relative pension level	66.3	44.2	60.0	75.3	106.5	134.0
(% net average earnings)	*54.8*	*35.8*	*49.8*	*62.1*	*86.3*	*110.7*
Gross replacement rate	64.5	64.5	64.5	64.5	64.5	64.5
(% individual gross earnings)	*50.6*	*50.6*	*50.6*	*50.6*	*50.6*	*50.6*
Net replacement rate	76.2	78.2	76.7	75.3	76.7	76.7
(% individual net earnings)	*63.0*	*63.4*	*63.7*	*62.1*	*62.1*	*63.3*
Gross pension wealth	10.6	10.6	10.6	10.6	10.6	10.5
(multiple of individual gross earnings)	*11.1*	*11.1*	*11.1*	*11.1*	*11.1*	*11.1*
Net pension wealth	9.1	10.3	9.3	8.8	8.3	7.7
(multiple of individual gross earnings)	*9.9*	*11.1*	*10.3*	*9.6*	*8.9*	*8.5*

StatLink http://dx.doi.org/10.1787/888932371690

Japan

Japan: Pension system in 2008

The public pension system has two tiers: a basic, flat-rate scheme and an earnings-related plan (employees' pension scheme).

Key indicators

		Japan	OECD
Average earnings	JPY (million)	5.00	4.20
	USD	48 400	40 600
Public pension spending	% of GDPr	9.8	7.0
Life expectancy	At birth	82.6	78.9
	At age 65	85.7	83.1
Population over age 65	% of working-age population	35.5	23.6

Qualifying conditions

The old-age, basic pension is paid from age 65 with a minimum of 25 years' contributions. The full basic pension requires 40 years of contributions, with benefits adjusted proportionally for shorter or longer contribution periods.

The earnings-related pension is paid in addition to basic pension, with a minimum of one month contribution, provided a pensioner is entitled to the basic pension. The pension age is gradually being increased from 60 to 65 years (between 2001 and 2013 for men and between 2006 and 2018 for women) for the flat-rate component and from 60 to reach 65 years for men in 2025 and for women in 2030 for the earnings-related component. The earnings-related component of the employees' pension scheme is adjusted for shorter or longer contribution periods.

Benefit calculation

Basic

The full basic pension for 2008 was JPY 792 100 per year, corresponding to 15.8% of average earnings. The basic pension is price indexed.

Social assistance

There is social assistance as other income security system. Older people are covered by the general social assistance scheme. The social assistance amount for single household aged 60-69 in Tokyo in 2008 is JPY 969 810 (*i.e.* 19% of average earnings) per year excluding housing benefit and other relevant benefit.

Earnings related

The employees' pension scheme has a flat-rate and an earnings-related component, of which the earnings-related part is by far the most important. The accrual rate was 0.75% of earnings excluding bonuses until fiscal year 2002. From fiscal year 2003, the base for calculating pension was extended to include bonuses. With the extension of the base for calculating the pension, the accrual rate has been reduced to 0.5481% of earnings (including bonuses).

Earlier years' earnings are valorised in line with economy-wide average net earnings.

There is a ceiling on earnings subject to contributions of JPY 620 000 a month equivalent to 149% of average earnings.

The flat-rate benefit depends on year of birth. In 2008, it ranged between JPY 1 676 and JPY 3 143 per month of contributions. This is paid only to pensioners between 62 and 64 years and this benefit will be phased out by 2013 for men.

The employees' pension in payment is price indexed.

Contracting out

Employers, who have at least 1 000 employees, may "contract out" a portion of the earnings-related pension (substitution part) if they cover their employees themselves; around 15% of employees participate in these schemes. Contracting-out requires that employers offer at least 150% (before 2005: 110%) of the benefit that the public earnings-related scheme would have provided. The calculation of the pension required for contracting out is based on lifetime average nominal earnings. Indexation of pensions in payment and valorisation of past earnings is financed by the government.

The contribution rate in contracted-out schemes is determined by the government depending on the age structure of the covered employees and the actuarial assumption. Until 1996, however, the rate was uniform across plans. Since 2005, the rate ranges between 2.4% and 5% of total remuneration.

Since 2001, the government has also been promoting defined-contribution pension schemes and defined-benefit occupational pension schemes. As a consequence, several employees' pension funds have been dissolved.

Variant careers

Early retirement

Until 2001, a "specially provided" employees' pension was available at age 60. This is being phased out and retirement with a full benefit will not be possible before age 65.

Early retirement at a reduced benefit is possible in both the basic and earnings-related schemes. The benefit is reduced by 0.5% per month of early retirement, *i.e.* 6% per year. Individuals can claim the flat-rate component of the employees' pension between 60 and 65. The pension in payment is indexed to net average earnings until the pensioner reaches age 65 and price-indexed after age 65.

Late retirement

It is possible to defer receipt of the basic and earnings-related pensions. Deferral increases the pension benefit by 0.7% per month, *i.e.* 8.4% per year. Pension rights continue to accrue for each year of contributions beyond 65.

From 2006, combining work and pension after age 65 became possible provided total income (from earnings and pension) does not exceed JPY 480 000. Above this limit, half of the excess will be reduced from the full earnings-related pension payment but basic pension will be paid in full. From April 2007, the reduction has also been applied to the workers over 70 but they do not need to pay contribution.

Childcare

Periods spent out of paid work for childcare are credited in the earnings-related scheme. As of 2005, the maximum period has been extended from one to three years. If additional children are born while caring for a child, this period is extended until when the last child becomes 3 years old. During this period, contributions are considered to be made fully based on the earnings just before leave, and in calculating the benefit and qualifying conditions the entire exemption period is credited. In case parents work part time because of childcare responsibilities, the contribution will be made based on the current earnings but the pension benefits will be calculated based on their full-time previous earnings.

If people stay out of paid work after three years and income level drops, the rule under unemployment, below, also applies.

Unemployment

Workers who become unemployed or whose income is below a certain level do not need to contribute to the earnings-related scheme but they need to contribute to the basic scheme. Unemployed people may be exempted from paying all, three-quarters, a half or one-quarter of contributions, depending on the household income level. A single person with previous year's income less than JPY 570 000 is exempted from paying any contribution. People with income less than JPY 930 000 are entitled to one-quarter of contributions, those with income lower than JPY 1 410 000 pay one-half of contributions and those with income less than JPY 1 890 000 pay three-quarters of contributions.

For the periods of full exemption, people are entitled to one-third (after April 2009, one-half) of the basic pension and for the period with one-quarter of contribution, one-half (after April 2009, five-eighths) of the basic pension. For the periods with one-half contribution, people gain two-thirds (after 2009, three-quarters) of the basic pension and for the period with three-quarters of contribution, five-sixths (after April 2009, seven-eighths) of the basic pension is credited. The exempted period is counted as full contribution period in assessing the qualifying conditions.

It is possible to pay contributions later to receive higher pension after retirement.

Pension modelling results: Japan

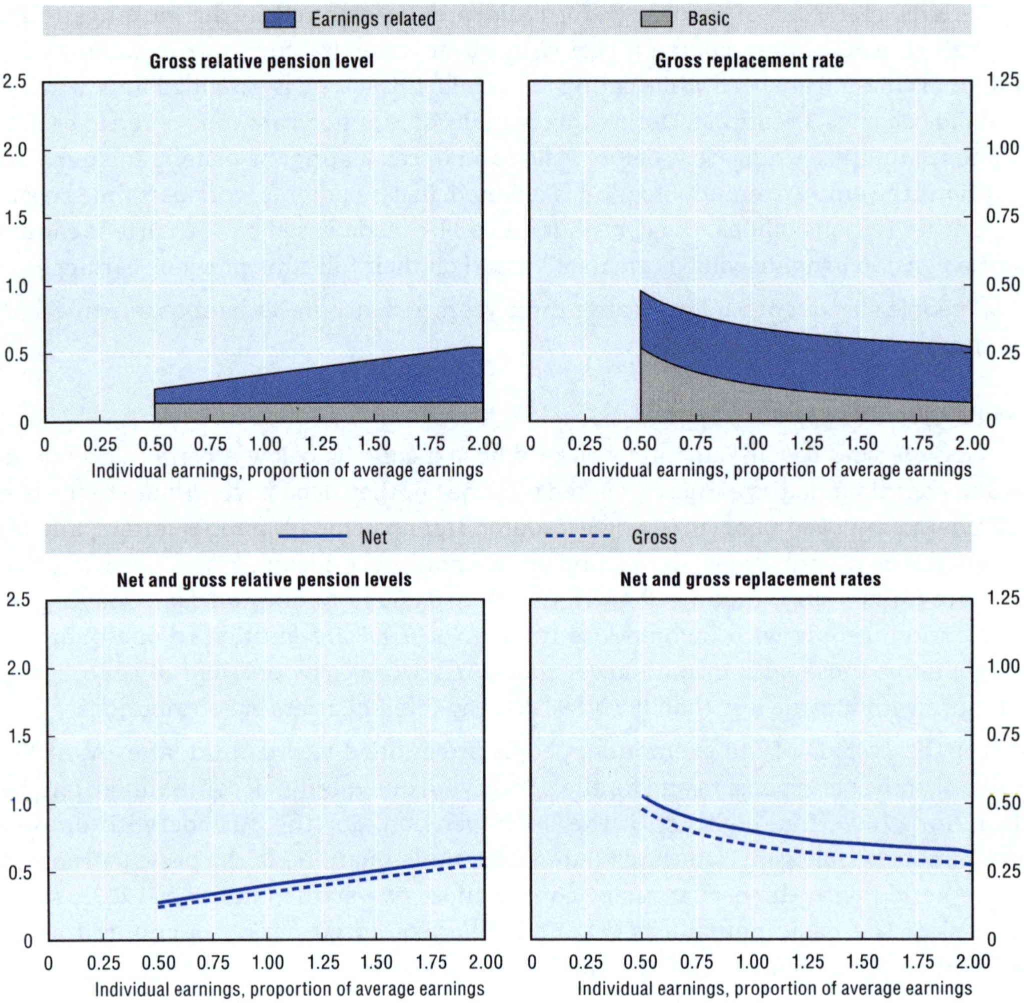

Men *Women (where different)*	Median earner	Individual earnings, multiple of average				
		0.5	0.75	1	1.5	2
Gross relative pension level	31.9	24.0	29.2	34.5	44.9	54.1
(% average gross earnings)						
Net relative pension level	36.8	27.2	33.5	39.7	50.2	59.5
(% net average earnings)						
Gross replacement rate	36.3	47.9	38.9	34.5	30.0	27.0
(% individual gross earnings)						
Net replacement rate	41.4	52.7	43.9	39.7	34.9	31.7
(% individual net earnings)						
Gross pension wealth	6.1	8.1	6.6	5.8	5.1	4.6
(multiple of individual gross earnings)	*7.4*	*9.7*	*7.9*	*7.0*	*6.1*	*5.5*
Net pension wealth	5.6	7.3	6.0	5.4	4.5	4.0
(multiple of individual gross earnings)	*6.8*	*8.8*	*7.2*	*6.4*	*5.4*	*4.8*

StatLink http://dx.doi.org/10.1787/888932371709

Korea

Korea: Pension system in 2008

The Korean public pension scheme was introduced relatively recently. It is an earnings-related scheme with a progressive formula, since benefits are based on both individual earnings and the average earnings of the insured as a whole.

Key indicators

		Korea	OECD
Average earnings	KRW (million)	33.50	44.70
	USD	30 400	40 600
Public pension spending	% of GDP	1.7	7.0
Life expectancy	At birth	79.2	78.9
	At age 65	83.0	83.1
Population over age 65	% of working-age population	15.8	23.6

Qualifying conditions

The pension is currently available from age 60 provided the individual has contributed for ten years or more. A reduced, early pension can be drawn from age 55.

The normal pension age is gradually being increased reaching 65 from 2033. The modelling assumes the long-term pension age of 65 and that the early pension age will be raised from 55 to 60.

Benefit calculation

Earnings related

The earnings replacement rate of the pension for 40 years of contributions is 50% in 2008 and will be reduced 0.5pt every year between 2009 and 2028 until reaching 40%. The model assumes that the 40% is calculated over a 45-year period. The earnings measure is the average of individual lifetime average earnings, valorised in line with wage growth, and average earnings of the insured of the national pension, measured over the previous three years and valorised in line with prices (A value). There is a ceiling on pensionable earnings of KRW 3.6 million per month, equivalent to 215% of the A value in 2008.

The maximum level of benefit is 100% of individual earnings. The benefit is indexed to prices after retirement. People aged 60 and over do not pay contributions and benefits are not accrued after this age.

Basic age pension

Some 60% of those aged 65 and over can get the means tested "basic age pension" from 2008. It was planned that the beneficiaries-to-be would be increased to 70% in 2009. This benefit is a flat rate of 5% of the three-year average earnings of the insured of the national pension every year. The benefit is reduced in phases according to income and assets of the aged. Couple rate is 80% of single rate each.

Variant careers

Early retirement

When, starting in 2013, the normal pension age increases from 60 to 65, the early pension age is assumed to increase from 55 to 60. At 60, the early old-age pension will then be 70% of the normal old-age pension. The benefit is increased by 6% every year, so a person who retires at age 64 will be entitled to 94% of the full old-age pension.

Late retirement

People can earn extra pension from retiring late. The benefit is increased by 6% every year and the maximum deferral is five years until age 70.

If the pensioners between 65 and 69 have earnings higher than the average earnings of the insured as a whole, their pension paid at 65 will be 50% of full old-age pension with the benefit increasing by 10% according to age increase, which is known as the "active old-age pension". Therefore, if the pensioner between 65 and 69 is working, they can choose either the "deferred pension" or the "active old-age pension".

Childcare

A person who is not engaged in labour market activities for childcare could apply for contribution exemption and be exempted from payment of contributions during the period requested. They are able to increase the insured period by paying the exempted contributions by themselves after resuming income-earning activities.

The insured who gives birth to a child, except for the first child, after 1 January 2008 can get pension credits. The credits given are 12 months to a maximum of 50 months according to the number of children being born after that time.

Unemployment

An unemployed person could apply for contribution exemption and be exempted from payment of contributions during the period requested. They are able to increase the insured period by paying the exempted contributions by themselves after resuming income-earning activities.

Pension modelling results: Korea

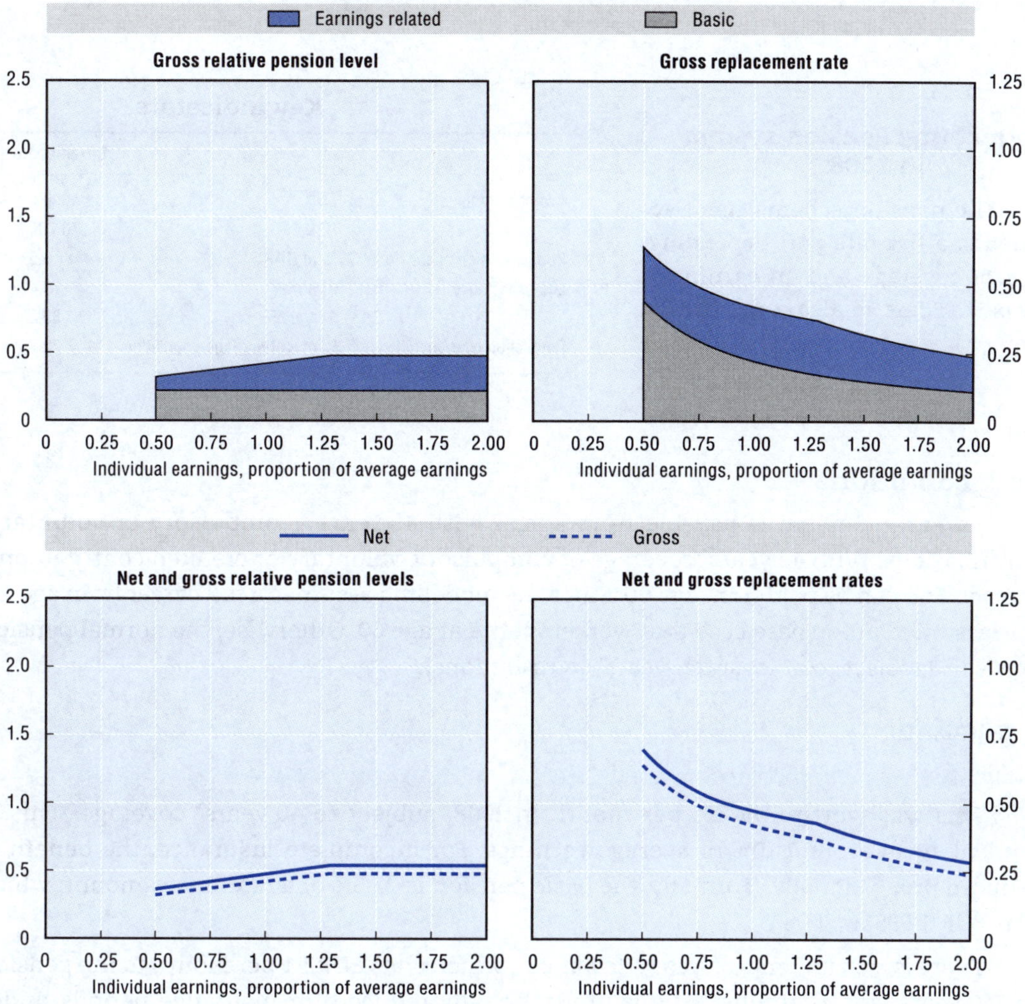

Men *Women (where different)*	Median earner	Individual earnings, multiple of average				
		0.5	0.75	1	1.5	2
Gross relative pension level	38.5	32.1	37.1	42.1	47.9	47.9
(% average gross earnings)						
Net relative pension level	43.5	36.3	41.9	47.5	53.9	53.9
(% net average earnings)						
Gross replacement rate	46.9	64.1	49.4	42.1	31.9	23.9
(% individual gross earnings)						
Net replacement rate	51.8	69.8	54.4	47.5	37.3	28.5
(% individual net earnings)						
Gross pension wealth	7.3	9.9	7.6	6.5	4.9	3.7
(multiple of individual gross earnings)	*8.7*	*12.0*	*9.2*	*7.8*	*6.0*	*4.5*
Net pension wealth	7.2	9.9	7.6	6.5	4.9	3.7
(multiple of individual gross earnings)	*8.7*	*11.9*	*9.2*	*7.8*	*5.9*	*4.4*

StatLink http://dx.doi.org/10.1787/888932371728

Luxembourg

Luxembourg: Pension system in 2008

The public pension scheme has two components: a flat-rate part depending on years of coverage and an earnings-related part. There is also a minimum pension.

Key indicators

		Luxembourg	OECD
Average earnings	EUR	48 400	27 800
	USD	70 700	40 600
Public pension spending	% of GDP	6.5	7.0
Life expectancy	At birth	79.4	78.9
	At age 65	83.2	83.1
Population over age 65	% of working-age population	22.7	23.6

Qualifying conditions

An early pension is payable from age 57 with 40 years' (compulsory or voluntary) contributions. With 40 years' coverage of compulsory, voluntary or credited contributions, the pension can be paid from age 60. Since the modelling assumes a full career from age 20, it is assumed in the base case that workers retire at age 60. Otherwise, the normal pension age is 65 (subject to at least ten years' contributions).

Benefit calculation

Basic

This was worth EUR 375 per month in 2008, subject to 40 years' coverage. This is equivalent to around 10% of average earnings. For incomplete insurance, the benefit is reduced proportionally. (Formally, the basic pension is 23.5% of a reference amount, which was EUR 1 595 in 2008.)

There is also an "end-of-year allowance", which adds EUR 51 per month to the pension for 40 years' contributions. This is proportionally reduced for insurance periods under 40 years, implying around EUR 1.28 per month for each year covered. The end-of-year allowance is indexed to nominal earnings (see below).

Earnings related

The accrual rate for the earnings-related pension is 1.85%. The earnings measure used in the formula is lifetime average pay re-valued in line with nominal earnings.

The accrual rate is higher for older workers and those with longer contribution periods. For each year of work after age 55, the accrual rate is increased by 0.01 percentage points. Furthermore, each year of contributions beyond 38 also attracts an additional accrual of 0.01 percentage points. The maximum accrual rate is 2.05% per year. Under the standard assumption of a full career starting at age 20, the accrual rate is 2.01%.

The maximum pension in 2008 was EUR 6 647 per month (formally specified as $^{25}/_{6}$ of the reference amount). This is just under 165% of average earnings.

Benefits are automatically indexed to changes in the cost of living (if cumulative inflation is at least 2.5%). In addition, adjustments to increases in real wages must be considered every two years. Recent practice has seen increases close to earnings and the modelling assumes that this practice continues.

Minimum

The minimum is EUR 1 436 per month (defined as 90% of the reference amount), conditional on 40 years' coverage, equivalent to about 36% of average earnings. This is proportionally reduced for shorter periods subject to a minimum of 20 years of service periods (compulsory, voluntary or credited contributions).

Social assistance

The social-assistance safety-net level is EUR 1 147 per month for a single person.

Variant careers

Early retirement

It is possible to retire at 57 with 40 years' paid contributions and at 60 with 40 years' paid or credited contributions. Early retirees may work periodically provided earnings do not exceed one-third of the minimum social income. There is no actuarial adjustment to benefits for early retirement.

In addition, there are a number of pre-retirement programmes. Relevant here are the pre-retirement solidarity and pre-retirement adaptation schemes. The first allows early retirement on the condition that the employer hires a job seeker assigned by the employment administration. The second allows early retirement for older workers losing their jobs due to restructuring or bankruptcy. Both schemes apply from age 57 up to age 60. The pre-retirement benefit is 85% of prior earnings in the first year, 80% in the second year, and 75% in the third. The earnings measure is pay in the preceding three months.

Late retirement

The pension has to be claimed at the retirement age of 65. After this age, it is possible to combine work and pension benefits without reductions in the pension benefit.

Childcare

"Baby years" (two years for one and four years for two children) are credited as insured time. Pensionable earnings are based on pay immediately before the baby years are claimed. The period counts as qualifying conditions and enters in the flat rate component of the pension formula.

Employees who could not claim baby-years due to an insufficient contribution period have the right to a special monthly allowance in retirement of EUR 92 per child.

Non-contributory periods bringing up children under age 6 count towards the qualifying conditions.

Unemployment

Periods of receiving unemployment benefits are credited: pension contributions from the benefits are paid by state (two-thirds) and beneficiary (one-third). The period unemployed counts towards the qualifying conditions and enters in the earnings-related component of the pension formula. For this period, unemployment benefit is used as a base for pension calculation.

Pension modelling results: Luxembourg

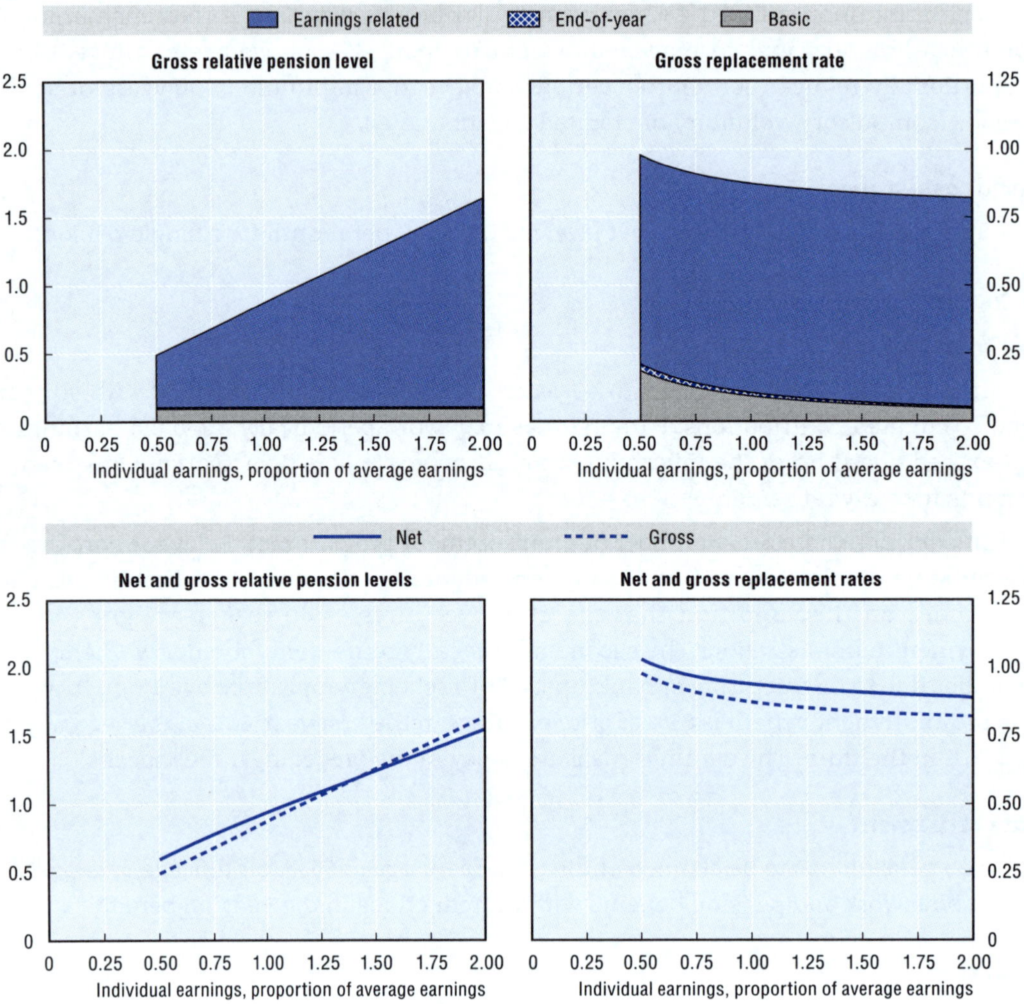

Men *Women (where different)*	Median earner	Individual earnings, multiple of average				
		0.5	0.75	1	1.5	2
Gross relative pension level *(% average gross earnings)*	70.5	49.0	68.2	87.4	125.8	164.2
Net relative pension level *(% net average earnings)*	80.1	59.6	78.1	94.0	124.4	154.8
Gross replacement rate *(% individual gross earnings)*	90.3	97.9	90.9	87.4	83.8	82.1
Net replacement rate *(% individual net earnings)*	96.2	103.1	96.7	94.0	90.9	89.0
Gross pension wealth	21.8	23.6	21.9	21.1	20.2	19.8
(multiple of individual gross earnings)	*25.3*	*27.4*	*25.5*	*24.5*	*23.5*	*23.0*
Net pension wealth	17.8	20.7	18.1	16.3	14.4	13.5
(multiple of individual gross earnings)	*20.7*	*24.1*	*21.0*	*19.0*	*16.7*	*15.6*

StatLink http://dx.doi.org/10.1787/888932371747

Mexico

Mexico: Pension system in 2008

Old-age pensions are covered under a defined-contribution scheme mandatory for private sector workers, privately managed and funded. The contributions are made by workers, employers and government. There is a minimum pension for those who listed at least 24 years.

Key indicators

		Mexico	OECD
Average earnings	MXN	76 000	452 800
	USD	6 800	40 600
Public pension spending	% of GDP	1.4	7.0
Life expectancy	At birth	76.2	78.9
	At age 65	82.8	83.1
Population over age 65	% of working-age population	11.3	23.6

Qualifying conditions

Normal retirement age is 65 for men and women, subject to 1 250 weeks (around 24 years) of contribution.

Benefit calculation

Funded scheme

Workers and employers contribute a total of 6.275% of earnings to an individual account, to which is added a government contribution equivalent to 0.225% of earnings. An additional 5% contribution is made to an individual housing account (a scheme known as Infonavit) which reverts to the retirement account when it is not used. Finally, the government contributes a fixed amount indexed quarterly to inflation into all individual retirement accounts per day of contribution called *cuota social* or social fee. As of May 2009, the Social Security Law was amended in order to establish a progressive social fee, seeking to benefit workers who earn the lowest salaries. The first progressive social fees published were as follows: for workers who earn up to one minimum wage, the social fee is MXN 3.87077; for those who earn between 1.01 and four times the minimum wage, MXN 3.70949; for those in the 4.01 to seven times the minimum wage bracket, MXN 3.54820; for those in the 7.01 to ten times the minimum wage bracket, MXN 3.38692 and finally, for those who earn between 10.01 and 15 times the minimum wage, MXN 3.22564. The social fee is indexed to inflation every three months.

There is a ceiling on contributions which is 25 times the minimum wage.

The calculations assume that the individual converts the accumulated account balance (discounting a survival insurance that must be bought to cover the survivors' benefits) into a price-indexed annuity at normal pension age. Annuity rates are sex-specific.

Minimum pension

The minimum pension is equivalent to the same 1997 real minimum wage value indexed to inflation (MXN 21 836.08 in 2008). The link to the real minimum wage (minimum wage: MXN 18 932.40 in 2008) means that the minimum pension is effectively price-indexed.

Variant careers

Early retirement

Early retirement is possible from age 60 for men and women. Conditions are that the worker is not employed and that at least 1 250 weekly contributions have been made.

Members may retire at any age if the accumulated capital in their account allows them to buy an annuity that is at least 30% higher than the minimum guaranteed pension. In this case, the member does not have to complete the 1 250 weeks of contributions.

Late retirement

It is possible to defer the pension after age 65.

Childcare

There are no credits for periods spent out of paid work due to childcare responsibilities.

Unemployment

There are no credits for periods of unemployment.

However, Article 191, Fraction II, of the Mexican Social Security Law, states that when a worker is unemployed, he/she will have the right to withdraw some money from his/her old-age/retirement sub-account. Unemployed members whose individual account has been open for at least five years may withdraw the lower of the equivalent of 90 days of their salary or 11.5% of their account balance. Unemployed members whose individual account has been open for at least three years and have paid at least two years of contributions may withdraw up to 30 days of their salary with a limit of ten minimum monthly wages.

The workers can claim this amount from the forty-sixth natural day in which they were unemployed. In order for the worker to be eligible for this benefit, they must have credit in their corresponding account statements.

Pension modelling results: Mexico

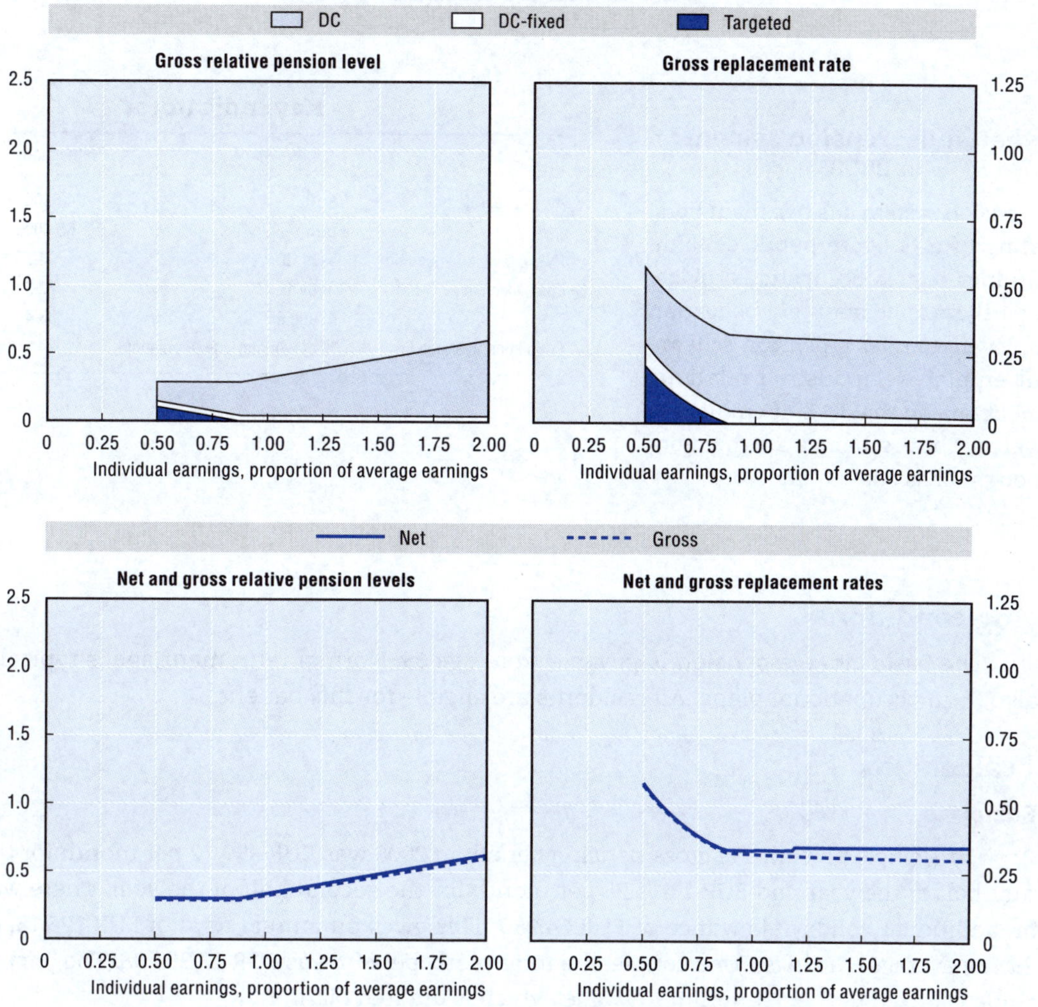

Men *Women (where different)*	Median earner	Individual earnings, multiple of average				
		0.5	0.75	1	1.5	2
Gross relative pension level	28.7	28.7	28.7	30.9	44.4	57.9
(% average gross earnings)				*28.7*	*39.6*	*51.6*
Net relative pension level	29.9	29.9	29.9	32.2	46.3	60.3
(% net average earnings)				*29.9*	*41.3*	*53.8*
Gross replacement rate	46.3	57.5	38.3	30.9	29.6	28.9
(% individual gross earnings)				*28.7*	*26.4*	*25.8*
Net replacement rate	46.9	58.2	38.8	32.2	33.3	33.5
(% individual net earnings)				*29.9*	*29.7*	*29.9*
Gross pension wealth	7.2	8.9	5.9	4.8	4.6	4.5
(multiple of individual gross earnings)	*8.1*	*10.0*	*6.7*	*5.0*	*4.6*	*4.5*
Net pension wealth	7.2	8.9	5.9	4.8	4.6	4.5
(multiple of individual gross earnings)	*8.1*	*10.0*	*6.7*	*5.0*	*4.6*	*4.5*

StatLink http://dx.doi.org/10.1787/888932371766

Netherlands

Netherlands: Pension system in 2008

The pension system has two main tiers, consisting of a flat-rate public scheme and earnings-related occupational plans. Although there is no statutory obligation for employers to offer a pension scheme to their employees, industrial-relations agreements mean that 91% of employees are covered. These schemes are therefore best thought of as quasi-mandatory.

Key indicators

		Netherlands	OECD
Average earnings	EUR	43 500	27 800
	USD	63 600	40 600
Public pension spending	% of GDP	4.7	7.0
Life expectancy	At birth	79.9	78.9
	At age 65	83.4	83.1
Population over age 65	% of working-age population	24.1	23.6

Qualifying conditions

The basic old-age pension is payable from age 65. Normal retirement age is typically also 65 in occupational plans. All residents are eligible for this benefit.

Benefit calculation

Basic

For a single person, the gross pension benefit in 2008 was EUR 999.72 per month for the first half of the year and EUR 1 011.98 per month for the second half of the year. There was an additional holiday allowance of EUR 647.80. This gives an annual total of EUR 12 718, or 29% of average earnings. For a couple, the total yearly benefit was EUR 17 380.08. The benefit value is linked to the net minimum wage, which is uprated biannually.

The basic benefit accrues at 2% of the full value for each year a worker lives or works in the country. There is also a social-assistance scheme for older people. Its value is equal to the net basic pension.

Occupational schemes

The Netherlands also has a private pension system with broad coverage. The system consists of 656 pension funds (end of 2008); 95 of these funds concern industry-wide schemes. Under certain conditions, Dutch companies may opt out of these plans if they offer their own scheme with equivalent benefits. Furthermore there are around 550 single-employer plans. Another 46 000 (in 2005) mainly smaller employers offer schemes operated by insurance companies.

Approximately 90% of the employees in pension funds are covered by a defined-benefit scheme. The remaining employees in pension funds are covered by a defined-contribution scheme.

For about 97% of participants in defined-benefit schemes (about 87% of all employees in pension funds), the earnings measure is based on lifetime average earnings, and for about 1.3% on the final salary. For the remainder it is either a combination of the two (1%) or a fixed amount (less than 1%).

Most final-salary schemes give 1.75% of those earnings for each year of service, implying a replacement rate of 70% after a complete 40-year career. In most average-salary schemes the accrual rate varies from 1.75% to 2% per year of service.

There are no legal requirements for valorisation of earlier years' pay and practice varies between schemes according to rules agreed upon by the social partners. For approximately 85% of the participants in average wage schemes, past earnings are valorised in line with growth of average earnings while for 15% the rate of inflation is used. The modelling assumes an average-salary scheme with valorisation to average earnings.

Although there is no legal uprating requirement, most pensions in payment are raised on an annual basis as well. Nearly 60% of the pensions in payment are indexed to wage growth in the respective industry, while some 35% of the pensions are indexed to prices.

Pension rights are fully transferable when people change jobs. There is a legal requirement to index pension rights of people leaving a scheme before retirement in exactly the same way as pensions in payment are indexed. Vesting periods are very short.

There is no ceiling to pensionable earnings.

Occupational pensions are integrated with the public pension system. The current tax rules allow a maximum benefit of 100% of final pay at 65 from both public and private systems. Most schemes have a target total replacement rate of 70% of final pay, so private benefits are reduced by a franchise amount.

Variant careers

Early retirement

The basic pension is not payable before age 65.

In 2005, the tax-favoured status of separate early retirement programmes (called "VUT") and which led to pre-pension benefits between ages 60 and 65 was abolished to stimulate labour-market participation of older workers.

Late retirement

It is not possible to defer the basic old-age pension scheme after 65. It is possible to combine the basic pension receipt with work.

The rules on pension deferral vary between occupational plans. It is possible to combine the occupational pension scheme with work. Indeed, some schemes allow a member to draw a pension and continue to work with the same employer. There is no legislation regarding this issue.

Childcare

In the basic old-age pension scheme, periods out of paid work are automatically covered. In the occupational schemes, there are no credits for childcare periods during which people are out of paid work but the accrual of pension rights continues over remaining working years. However, many schemes allow voluntary contributions to cover the aforementioned periods of absence.

Unemployment

There are no credits in the occupational plans for periods of unemployment. Again, the basic old-age scheme covers such periods automatically. In addition, the social partners administer a fund (FVP) which makes it possible for older workers to extend their pension accrual for a certain period during unemployment. The government has no formal relationship with this fund.

Pension modelling results: Netherlands

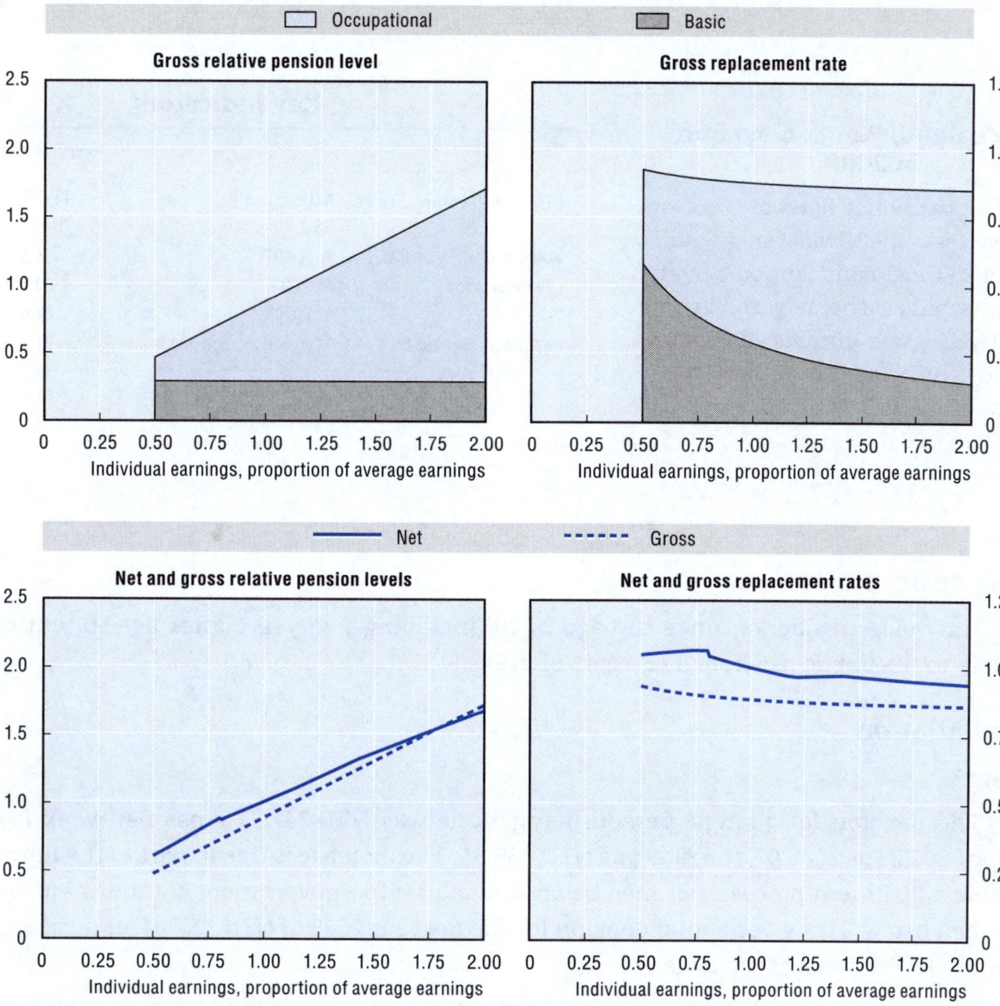

Men *Women (where different)*	Median earner	Individual earnings, multiple of average				
		0.5	0.75	1	1.5	2
Gross relative pension level *(% average gross earnings)*	74.8	46.5	67.3	88.1	129.8	171.4
Net relative pension level *(% net average earnings)*	88.8	59.6	82.8	99.8	135.8	167.2
Gross replacement rate *(% individual gross earnings)*	89.1	93.0	89.8	88.1	86.5	85.7
Net replacement rate *(% individual net earnings)*	103.3	104.5	106.1	99.8	96.4	93.6
Gross pension wealth *(multiple of individual gross earnings)*	17.9 *20.5*	18.7 *21.4*	18.1 *20.7*	17.7 *20.3*	17.4 *19.9*	17.2 *19.7*
Net pension wealth *(multiple of individual gross earnings)*	13.5 *15.5*	15.3 *17.5*	14.1 *16.2*	12.8 *14.6*	11.6 *13.3*	10.7 *12.3*

StatLink http://dx.doi.org/10.1787/888932371785

New Zealand

New Zealand: Pension system in 2008

The public pension is flat rate based on a residency test. The KiwiSaver, an auto-enrolment defined-contribution private retirement savings scheme with capped public subsidies was introduced in 2007. Employed KiwiSaver members were estimated to be over 30% of the workforce by the end of 2008.

Key indicators

		New Zealand	OECD
Average earnings	NZD	46 700	57 900
	USD	70 700	40 600
Public pension spending	% of GDP	4.3	7.0
Life expectancy	At birth	80.2	78.9
	At age 65	84.0	83.1
Population over age 65	% of working-age population	21.2	23.6

Qualifying conditions

Ten years' residency since the age of 20 (including five years after age 50) entitles people to the public pension at 65 years of age.

Benefit calculation

Basic

The pension for a single person living alone was NZD 347.77 gross per week from 1 April 2008. For 2006/07, the rate was NZD 336.65. The increase is due in part to the normal annual adjustment process, outlined below and in part to a government commitment, also outlined below. This gives a total pension for the tax year 2008 of NZD 18 084, equivalent to around 39% of average earnings.

State pension entitlements from other countries are taken into account in calculating the total payable.

The rate of public pension is indexed to prices, but is subject to a floor and ceiling linked to movement in wages. For a couple, the governing legislation requires that the net-of-tax rate at each 1st April must be not less than 65% and not more than 72.5% of a net-of-tax surveyed weekly earnings measure. The net-of-tax rates for single people are set at 65% (living alone) and 60% (sharing accommodation) of the net-of-tax couple rate. If movements in prices remain consistently below movements in the net-of-tax surveyed weekly earnings, effectively the latter becomes the index.

The current government has made a commitment that the net-of-tax rate at each 1st April is to be a minimum of 66% rather than 65% of the net-of-tax earnings measure.

Voluntary private pensions

Coverage of occupational pension plans has been falling for some time, and is currently around 9%. The new KiwiSaver scheme, however, achieved coverage of 44% within its first year of operation (from July 2007). The default contribution rate for this scheme is 4% of earnings, divided equally between employees and employers.

Variant careers

Early retirement

It is not possible to claim the pension before the normal eligibility age of 65.

Late retirement

Receipt of the public pension is not dependent on retirement. It is therefore possible to combine pension and employment.

While people are not obliged to claim the public pension on reaching the qualifying age, there is no advantage in deferring a claim.

Childcare

Eventual public pension entitlement is not affected by periods out of paid work for caring purposes.

Unemployment

Eventual public pension entitlement is not affected by periods of unemployment.

Pension modelling results: New Zealand

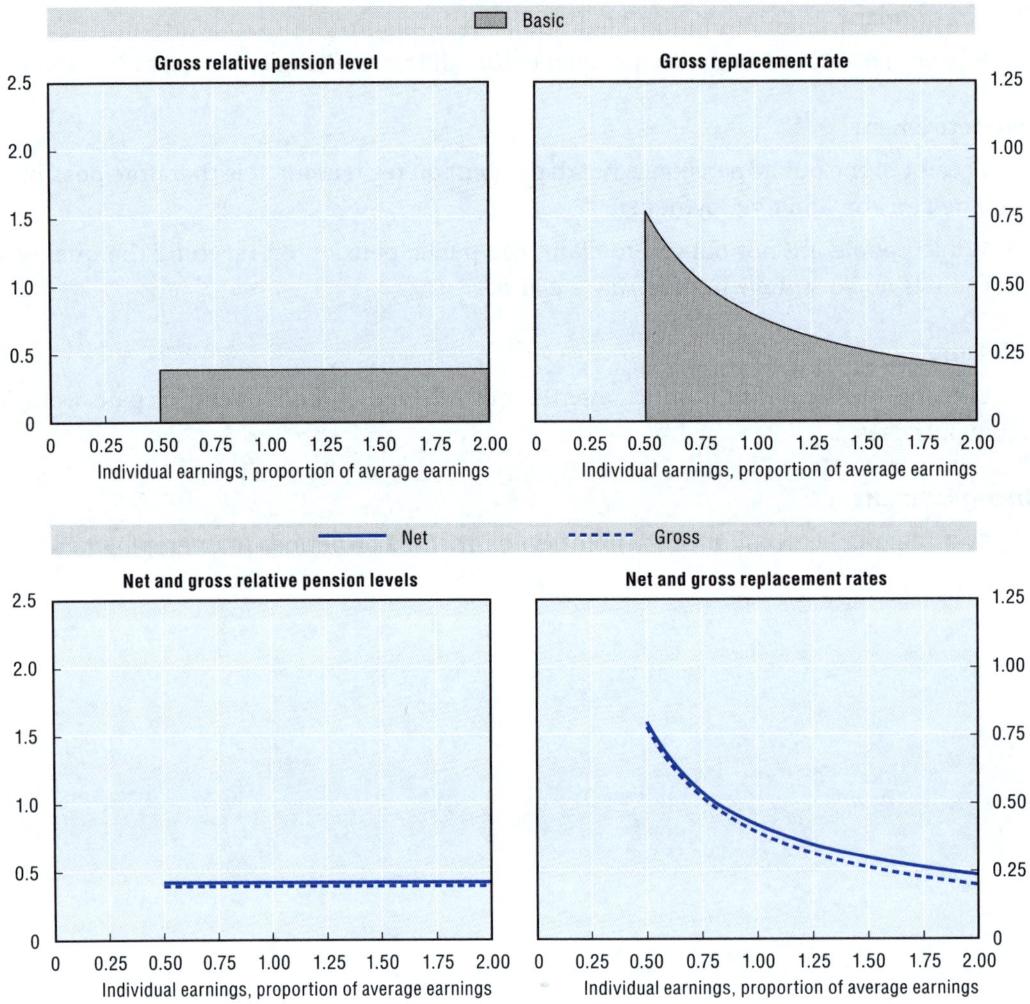

Men *Women (where different)*	Median earner	Individual earnings, multiple of average				
		0.5	0.75	1	1.5	2
Gross relative pension level	38.7	38.7	38.7	38.7	38.7	38.7
(% average gross earnings)						
Net relative pension level	41.5	41.5	41.5	41.5	41.5	41.5
(% net average earnings)						
Gross replacement rate	47.8	77.5	51.7	38.7	25.8	19.4
(% individual gross earnings)						
Net replacement rate	49.6	79.4	53.5	41.5	29.4	23.0
(% individual net earnings)						
Gross pension wealth	9.9	16.1	10.7	8.0	5.4	4.0
(multiple of individual gross earnings)	*11.3*	*18.3*	*12.2*	*9.2*	*6.1*	*4.6*
Net pension wealth	8.2	13.2	8.8	6.6	4.4	3.3
(multiple of individual gross earnings)	*9.3*	*15.1*	*10.0*	*7.5*	*5.0*	*3.8*

StatLink http://dx.doi.org/10.1787/888932371804

Norway

Norway: Pension system in 2008

The new public pension system, beginning in 2011, will consist of an income pension, and a guarantee pension for people with no or only a small income pension. The guarantee pension is income-tested against the income pension. In 2006, a mandatory occupational pension was introduced in the private sector.

Key indicators

		Norway	OECD
Average earnings	NOK	440 000	229 300
	USD	77 900	40 600
Public pension spending	% of GDP	4.7	7.0
Life expectancy	At birth	80.6	78.9
	At age 65	83.8	83.1
Population over age 65	% of working-age population	24.6	23.6

Qualifying conditions

Persons with a residence period in Norway of at least three years between the ages of 17 and 67 (inclusive) are entitled to the guarantee pension in the new system. A full guarantee pension is granted after a forty year long residence period, and it is reduced proportionally for shorter residence periods.

Benefit calculation

Income pension

In the new system pension entitlements are accumulated through income from work or through other types of pension earning, between the age of 13 and 75 years. The individual will each year increase their pension entitlements corresponding to 18.1% of their pensionable income, up to a ceiling. The pension entitlements are each year increased in line with wage growth.

Many benefits under the National Insurance Scheme are determined in relation to the basic amount (G) that was NOK 69 108 as an average for 2008. The ceiling in the new income pension is 7.1 basic amounts. The average wage for a full-time employee in Norway in 2008, based on OECD estimates, was about NOK 440 000 or 6.4 basic amounts. The ceiling on pension earnings is thus about 112% of the average wage.

Currently the retirement age is fixed at 67 years in the public pension scheme. From 2011 it is decided to introduce flexible retirement for the age group 62-75 years based on actuarial neutrality. It will then be possible to combine work and pension fully or partly from the age of 62 without an earnings test. From 2011 it is also decided to introduce a life expectancy adjustment of the pension for new old-age pensioners. The life expectancy adjustment will be determined for each cohort, based mainly on remaining life expectancy. The factors will be determined when the cohorts are 61 years, and will not be adjusted later. Each cohort will receive a separate life expectancy factor from the age of 62 until the age of 75. At the time of retirement the annual pension is calculated by dividing the accumulated pension entitlements by a life expectancy divisor.

The income pension will after retirement be indexed to wages, but then subtracted a fixed factor of 0.75% a year.

Guarantee pension

The guarantee pension will replace the minimum pension in our current pension system and will be at the same level.

The minimum pension for single pensioners in 2010 will be equivalent to two basic amounts, or about 31% of average earnings. The guarantee pension is income tested by 80% against the income pension.

The guarantee pension will be indexed in line with wages, but adjusted for the effect of the life expectancy factor at 67 years. In the long term projections of Statistics Norway life expectancy at 67 is assumed to increase by about 0.5% a year. According to the projections the guarantee pension will be adjusted to wages, but then subtracted a factor of about 0.5% a year due to the life expectancy adjustment.

Defined-contribution scheme

From 2006, employers must make a minimum contribution of 2% of the earnings of their employees to a defined-contribution pension plan. (If employers offer a defined-benefit scheme instead, then the benefits must be at least the same level as the expected benefits under the mandatory 2% contribution.) Contributions are only required on earnings between the basic amount (G) and 12 times the basic amount.

Benefits can currently only be taken at age 67, but it is discussed as part of the pension reform to introduce flexible retirement from the age of 62 from 2011. They must be withdrawn over a minimum period of ten years. For comparison with the results for other countries, it is assumed that the benefit is taken as a price-indexed annuity calculated using unisex mortality tables.

Voluntary private pension

There is an additional voluntary pension which is assumed to be defined contribution. The contribution rate is assumed to be 3% between 1G and 6G and 6% of earnings between 6G and 12G.

Variant careers

Early retirement

About two-thirds of employees work in businesses participating in early retirement programmes under the Contractual Early Retirement Scheme (AFP). This scheme, which was introduced in 1989, allows retirement from age 62. The pension level under this scheme is about the same as the ordinary old-age pension from 67 years of age, *i.e.* if the person had continued until that age in the job he/she was holding at the time he/she actually retired.

The calculation of AFP pensions differs somewhat between sectors, but the basic principle is that AFP pensions are calculated in the same manner as the permanent disability pension (granting pension points for the remaining years until 67). In addition AFP-pensioners receive a so-called AFP-supplement.

There are some qualifying conditions (the listing is not complete). First, the pensioner must be employed in the same firm for the last three years (alternatively covered in an AFP scheme for the last five years). Second, the annual earnings must be at least the basic amount (G) at the time of retirement. The annual wage must also exceed one basic amount (G) during at least ten years after age 50. Earnings in the ten best years in the period from 1967 until the year prior to retirement have exceeded at least twice the basic amount.

From 2011 the AFP-scheme in the private sector will be made a supplement to the public old-age pension scheme. The supplement will be equivalent to about 4.2% of pensionable income, and can be accumulated up to the age of 62. Also this supplement will be based on actuarial neutrality and can be withdrawn between the age of 62 and 70. In the private sector it will be possible to combine the public old-age pension, the AFP-supplement and work without an earnings test.

In the public sector it is determined to continue with the present system of a special AFP-scheme for the age group 62-66 years also after introducing flexible retirement from 62 years in the public pension scheme. In the public sector it will then not be possible to combine work and pension without an earnings test.

Late retirement

People can defer their pension after age 67 and continue to work and people can combine working with receiving a pension. There is no additional increment earned by deferring pension after 67.

Childcare

Caregivers are credited with pension earning equivalent to 4.5 basic amounts a year or about NOK 311 000 in the income pension. This corresponds to about 71% of an average full-time wage. Caregivers comprise parents caring for children below 6 years of age and individuals taking unpaid care of disabled, sick or elderly persons in the home.

Parents with lower annual earnings than 4.5 basic amounts have these earnings topped up. Parents with annual earnings exceeding 4.5 basic amounts do not get any top up. The family may apply for having the points granted to the father instead of the mother, but only one of the parents may receive this kind of pension earnings in any given year. For the other group, pension earnings are granted on the basis of individual applications.

Unemployment

The unemployed will be credited pension earnings based on the income they had before becoming unemployed up to a ceiling of 7.1 basic amounts.

Pension modelling results: Norway

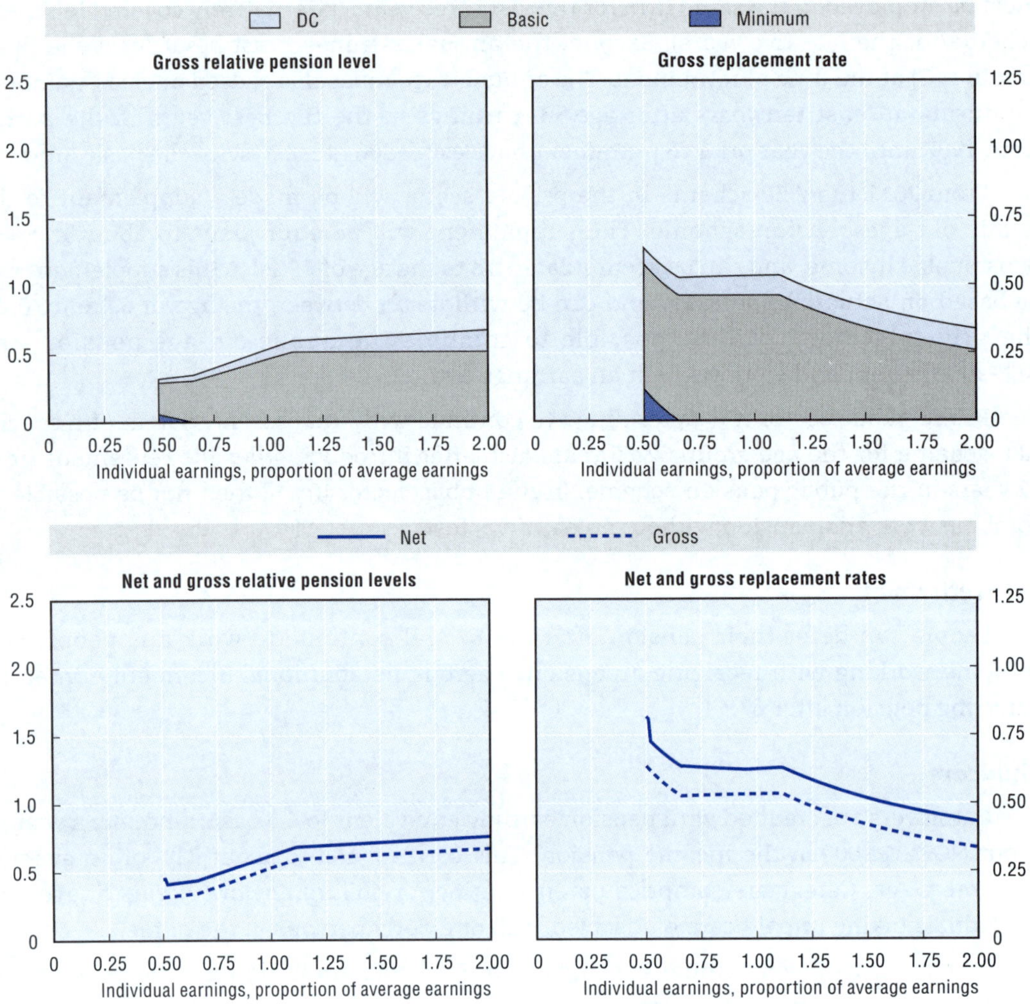

Men *Women (where different)*	Median earner	Individual earnings, multiple of average				
		0.5	0.75	1	1.5	2
Gross relative pension level	47.1	31.7	39.5	53.1	62.5	66.7
(% average gross earnings)						
Net relative pension level	56.4	45.0	48.9	62.2	71.5	75.6
(% net average earnings)						
Gross replacement rate	52.9	63.4	52.6	53.1	41.7	33.4
(% individual gross earnings)						
Net replacement rate	62.3	81.7	62.9	62.2	51.4	42.9
(% individual net earnings)						
Gross pension wealth	9.7	11.7	9.7	9.7	7.6	6.0
(multiple of individual gross earnings)	*11.4*	*13.8*	*11.4*	*11.4*	*8.9*	*7.0*
Net pension wealth	8.2	11.7	8.4	8.0	6.1	4.8
(multiple of individual gross earnings)	*9.6*	*13.8*	*9.9*	*9.5*	*7.2*	*5.6*

StatLink http://dx.doi.org/10.1787/888932371823

Poland

Poland: Pension system in 2008

The scheme is based on a system of notional accounts. People under 30 (born in 1969 and after) at the time of the reform must also participate in the funded scheme; people aged 30-50 (born between 1949 and 1968) could choose the funded option. However, the choice had to be made in 1999 and it was irrevocable, with the exception of those who could retire early.

Key indicators

		Poland	OECD
Average earnings	PLN	33 700	97 800
	USD	14 000	40 600
Public pension spending	% of GDP	10.6	7.0
Life expectancy	At birth	75.5	78.9
	At age 65	81.2	83.1
Population over age 65	% of working-age population	20.6	23.6

Qualifying conditions

The minimum pension age in the new system will be 65 for men and 60 for women. For the minimum pension, 25 and 20 years' contributions are required from men and women, respectively.

Benefit calculation

Earnings related

A contribution of 12.22% of earnings (or 19.52% for workers born between 1949 and 1968 who do not choose funded tier) will be credited to individuals' notional accounts. The notional interest rate has been defined as 100% of the growth of the real covered wage bill, and no less than price inflation. This notional interest rate is applied retrospectively to accounts from the year 2000.

At retirement, accumulated notional capital is divided by the "g-value" to arrive at the pension benefit. The g-value is average life expectancy at retirement age: this process is equivalent to the process of annuitisation in funded pension systems. The g-value is calculated using life tables published by the Central Statistical Office. In the modelling, actuarial data from the *United Nations Population Database* is used.

The ceiling to contributions and pensionable earnings is set at 2.5 times average earnings projected for a given year in the state budget law. It is PLN 85 290 in 2008 and PLN 95 790 in 2009.

Between 1999 and 2004 pensions in payment were uprated in line with 80% of prices and 20% of average earnings, projected for a given year. Note, however, that from 2005 the minimum indexation is to prices from past years, in years when compounded inflation from the year preceding previous indexation is above 5%. From 2008 pensions in payment were uprated in line with at least 80% of prices and 20% of average earnings for a given year. The actual indexation factor is negotiated with the Tripartite Committee. Until 2009, the Committee did not reach the agreement and minimum indexation was applied.

Minimum pension

There is a minimum pension under the pay-as-you-go scheme, which is about 25% of average earnings. From 1 March 2008 it was PLN 636.29 and from1 March 2009, PLN 675.10.

Indexation is the same as with pensions from the pay-as-you-go system. Additional lump-sum payments for those receiving low pensions were paid in those years where there was no regular indexation of benefits (2005 and 2007). From 2008 the minimum pension is adjusted to 80% inflation plus 20% of wage growth, as with other pensions in payment.

In the new pension scheme, the minimum retirement guarantee shall be financed by state budget and paid when total mandatory old-age pension is lower than the minimum.

Defined contribution

Some 7.3 percentage points of the total contribution are diverted to the funded scheme for those compulsorily covered or choosing this option.

The law on annuities, adopted by the Parliament at the beginning of 2009 assumes that pension savings will be converted into the single annuity using unisex life tables at retirement age, but not before age of 65. Women, who retire before that year will receive payments (temporary capital pensions) based on programmed withdrawal from their individual accounts until they reach age of 65, which are managed by Open Pension Funds. Upon reaching age 65, the balance in their individual accounts is used to purchase life annuities. The temporary pension will be calculated and indexed such as pension from the earnings-related tier (used in the model calculation).

There is still no regulation on institutions paying annuities.

Variant careers

Early retirement

There are no provisions for early retirement in the general pension system.

The old pension system (applicable to persons born before 1949) allowed various forms of early retirement for specific groups, such as miners, railway workers, teachers, people working in special conditions and women. Eligibility to early retirement has been postponed until the end of 2008. Additionally, from 2005 the miners had their early retirement pension system reinstated according to the pre-1999 rules.

The bridging pensions system that comes into force from 2009 covers people working in special conditions, based on the new list (medically verified), c.a. 270 000. Workers will receive a bridging pension for up to five years (ten years for some occupations such as: pilot, steel workers, etc.) before retirement age. This benefit is financed from state budget (since 2010 also from contributions paid by employers). Bridging pension is, as with the pension formula in the earnings-related system, based on unisex life expectancy for age 60.

Moreover under the new law, workers who are not entitled to receive the bridging pension and have reached 15 years in special conditions or with special characteristics before 1 January 2009 are entitled to compensation. This compensation will be calculated at the moment of retirement (women – at least 60 years; men – at least 65 years) and added to the initial capital.

Late retirement

It is possible to defer both the notional and the funded, defined-contribution pension component without any age limits. People who defer claiming pension after normal pension age contribute and earn extra pension.

It is possible to combine work and pension receipt. For old-age pensioners below legal retirement age (in the old pension system), there are limits to income. If the work income is above 70% of average wage, the pension is reduced, if it is above 130% of average wage, the pension payment is suspended.

Childcare

During periods of maternity leave, contributions to the pension system are paid from the state budget based on the maternity benefit, which is the average wage over the past six months, net of social security contributions. From 2004, the averaging period has been extended to 12 months. 1 January 2009 maternity leave period will be 20 weeks for one child, while it will last 31 weeks for two children, 33 weeks for three children, 35 weeks for four children and 37 weeks for five or more children, depending on the number of children at one delivery.

Parental leave is possible for a period up to 36 months per child. During this time, pension contributions are paid for the schemes in which a person is a member and the amount of social welfare benefit was used as a base (420 PLN) for the pension, disability and health contributions. For 2009-11 the base for contribution payment is minimum wage (c.a. 40% of average wage) and from 2012 60% of average wage. In both cases, the government pays the contributions on behalf of the parent on leave.

All periods for which contributions are paid qualify for the minimum pension guarantee.

Unemployment

There is a scheme of pre-retirement allowances, available to unemployed people who were laid off (for example, due to liquidation, bankruptcy or restructuring). Pre-retirement allowances are paid from the state budget to women from 55 and men from 60 until reaching pension age. These rules are in force from May 2004. Earlier pre-retirement benefits were granted to women from 50 and men from 55. Pre-retirement benefits are not subject to contributions to the pension scheme.

During periods of unemployment benefit receipt, the government pays the contributions to the pension system based on the size of the unemployment benefit (12.22% of the benefit to notional account and 7.3% to defined-contribution scheme). All the periods for which contributions are paid qualify for the minimum pension guarantee.

Pension modelling results: Poland

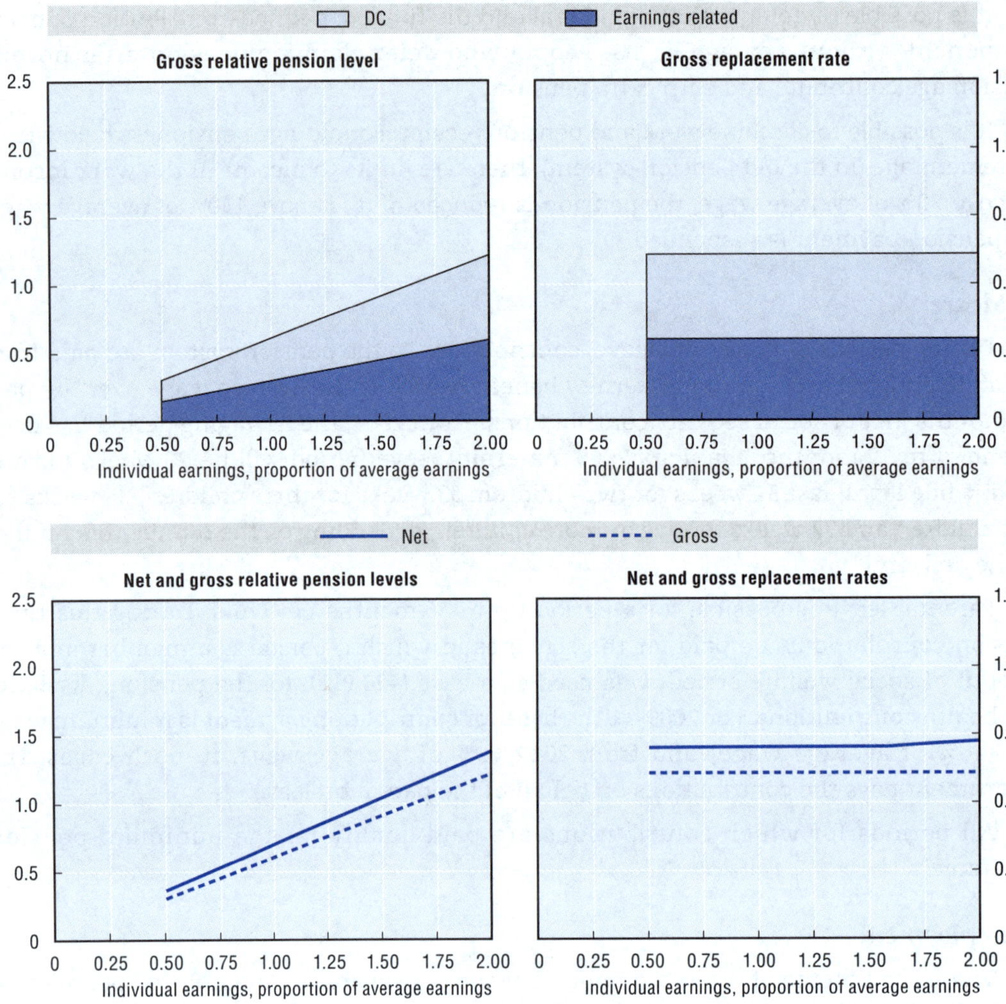

Men *Women (where different)*	Median earner	Individual earnings, multiple of average				
		0.5	0.75	1	1.5	2
Gross relative pension level	47.2	29.5	44.2	59.0	88.5	118.0
(% average gross earnings)	*34.6*	*22.6*	*32.4*	*43.2*	*64.8*	*86.4*
Net relative pension level	55.1	35.3	51.8	68.2	101.1	134.0
(% net average earnings)	*41.0*	*27.7*	*38.6*	*50.6*	*74.7*	*98.8*
Gross replacement rate	59.0	59.0	59.0	59.0	59.0	59.0
(% individual gross earnings)	*43.2*	*45.3*	*43.2*	*43.2*	*43.2*	*43.2*
Net replacement rate	68.2	68.1	68.2	68.2	68.3	70.3
(% individual net earnings)	*50.7*	*53.4*	*50.8*	*50.6*	*50.4*	*51.8*
Gross pension wealth	8.4	8.4	8.4	8.4	8.4	8.4
(multiple of individual gross earnings)	*8.9*	*9.3*	*8.9*	*8.9*	*8.9*	*8.9*
Net pension wealth	7.0	7.2	7.1	7.0	6.9	6.9
(multiple of individual gross earnings)	*7.5*	*8.1*	*7.6*	*7.4*	*7.3*	*7.3*

StatLink http://dx.doi.org/10.1787/888932371842

Portugal

Portugal: Pension system in 2008

Portugal has an earnings-related public pension scheme with a means-tested safety net.

Key indicators

		Portugal	OECD
Average earnings	EUR	16 100	27 800
	USD	23 500	40 600
Public pension spending	% of GDP	10.8	7.0
Life expectancy	At birth	78.7	78.9
	At age 65	82.8	83.1
Population over age 65	% of working-age population	28.3	23.6

Qualifying conditions

The standard pension age is 65 although early retirement is possible from age 55. A minimum of 15 relevant years of contributions are required for retirement at 65. Early retirement is possible with 30 years of contributions.

The social pension is payable from age 65. Every year, in July and December, the pensioners receive an additional amount equal to their monthly pension.

Benefit calculation

Earnings related

The pension amounts are calculated according to the following formula:

Pension amount = Reference earnings × Accrual rate × Sustainability factor

The annual earnings registered in the social security and taken into account to the Reference Earnings calculation (RE) are adjusted according to the consumer price index (CPI), without considering the home factor.

For the purpose of calculating the pension according to the whole insurance career, the earnings amounts registered between 1 January 2002 and 31 December 2011 are adjusted by applying an index resulting from the weighting of 75% of the CPI, and of 25% of the average evolution of the earnings which underlie the contributions stated to the social security, whenever this evolution is higher than the CPI. The annual adjustment index cannot be higher than the CPI, plus 0.5%.

The adjustment is made by applying the coefficient, corresponding to each one of the years considered, to the annual earnings taken into account for the reference earnings calculation. The indexes for the calculation basis adjustment will be reassessed after 31 December 2011.

For the reference earnings calculation purpose, whenever the number of calendar years with earnings registration is higher than 40, it will take into account the best 40 annual earnings, after they have been adjusted.

The pension accrues at 2% of the earnings base for each year of contributions for 20 or fewer years' contributions, with a lower limit of 30%. For beneficiaries with 21 or more years of contributions, the accrual rate ranges between 2% and 2.3% depending on earnings. The schedule for the accrual rate depends on individual earnings relative to the value of the IAS (*Indexante dos Apoios Sociais* – Social Support Index; EUR 407.41 in 2008). Each slice of earnings accrues pension at a different rate. Pension accrues for a maximum of 40 years.

Reference earnings/IAS	≤ 1.1	> 1.1-2.0	> 2.0-4.0	> 4.0-8.0	> 8.0
Accrual rate (%)	2.3	2.25	2.2	2.1	2

The earnings measure is presently the best ten of the final 15 years. However, this base is currently being extended, such that it will reach lifetime average earnings from 2017. Those already paying contributions by 31 December 2001 and who met the eligibility conditions for old-age pension at that date will have their pension calculated from the most favourable of three possible formulas: 1) applying the previous rules (2% accrual for each year of contributions and earnings being those of the best ten years of the final 15 years); 2) applying the new rules above described to the entire contributory career; and 3) or *pro rata* application of both rules according to the contributory career. Those already paying contributions by 31 December 2001, but who have not met the eligibility conditions for old-age pension at that date, will have their pension calculated from the most favourable of the above three possible formulas, if they retire between 2002 and 2016; or by the most favourable of formulas No. 2 and 3, if they retire after 31 December 2016. People who joined the system after 2002 will be fully covered by the new rules. For people with more than 40 years' contributions, only the best 40 count in the benefit formula.

The sustainability factor is an adequacy factor of the pensions system to the demographic changes; this factor results from the relation between the average life expectancy at age 65 in 2006 and the one that will occur in the year before the pension claim. The sustainability factor considered is the one verified in the year of the old-age pension beginning or at the date of the invalidity pension conversion into an old-age pension; this factor applies to old-age pensions beginning from 1 January 2008 and to old-age pensions resulting from the conversion of invalidity pensions (it is applied at the date of conversion, when the pensioner completes 65 years of age).

This sustainability factor does not apply to the old-age pensions resulting from the conversion of invalidity pensions beginning up to 31 December 2007 or total invalidity pensions, if the insured person:

- At the date when he/she completes 65 years of age, had received this pension for more than 20 years.
- Was registered in the social security on 1 June 2007 and had received this pension for a longer period than half of the time that elapsed between that date and the one on which he/she completes 65 years of age.

The sustainability factor for 2008 was 0.56%.

Pensions in payment are indexed to prices, with larger increases on smaller pensions. In January 2008 the increases of pensions already in payment are: 2.4% for pensions not higher than EUR 611.12; 1.9% for those between EUR 611.12 and EUR 2 444.46; 1.65% for those between EUR 2 444.46 and EUR 4 888.92; and 0% for those equal or higher than EUR 4 888.92.

As the law which established the IAS determined that the pensions are to be adjusted annually from 1st January of each year, in 2008 the pensions will have an additional increase amounting to 2/14 of the regular increase, as a compensation for the postponement of the December 2007 adjustment to January 2008. This extra increase was not included in the values presented above.

In case of accumulation of earnings with an old-age pension the monthly amount of pension is increased by 1/14 of 2% of the total earnings registered; this increase is effective from 1 January of each year and it refers to the earnings registered in the previous year.

Minimum

There is a monthly minimum pension for the contributory scheme with values varying according to the length of contributory career, as shown in the table below. There are 14 monthly payments.

Years of contribution	Increase (EUR)
< 15	236.47
15 to 20	236.76
21 to 30	291.05
31 and over	363.81

When the pension amount calculated according to the general rules is lower than the guaranteed minimum amount, it will be increased by the so called social supplement whose value is equal to the difference between the guaranteed minimum amount and the statutory or legal pension amount.

The social supplement granting is not subject to assets or residence test.

Targeted

For people aged 65 or more who do not qualify for the earnings-related scheme, the monthly social pension was EUR 181.91 in 2008.

This is only paid if total income for a single person does not exceed 30% of the IAS or 50% of the IAS in case of couples. Again, there are 14 monthly payments.

Pensioners of the social pension are entitled to receive the Solidarity Extra Supplement on top of their pension. The monthly amount of this benefit is EUR 16.83 for those under 70 years old and EUR 33.65 for those with at least 70 years of age.

The Solidarity Supplement for the Elderly (SSE), the main targeted benefit aimed at fighting poverty among the elderly, came into full effect in 2008 by extending eligibility to people aged 65 or older. Additional eligibility conditions for this benefit are: receiving old-age or survivors' pension (national citizens not entitled to the social pension because they do not fulfil its means test may also be eligible); and fulfilling the SSE means test.

The SSE resembles the Social Insertion Income as it is a supplement equal to the difference between the beneficiary's income and a given threshold, which is at the same time the means test condition. The SSE is therefore equal to the difference between the beneficiary's income and the following Reference Amounts (RA):

- EUR 4 800 per year for singles.
- EUR 8 400 per year for couples.

The beneficiary's income is composed of: his/her own income; the spouse's income; part of the income of their sons' households, denominated "family solidarity". The "family solidarity" component is added to the beneficiary's income to determine entitlement and the amount of the SSE.

To calculate the "family solidarity", for each son/daughter the total yearly income of his/her household is taken and divided by the number of adult equivalents in that household (scale of equivalence: 1 to the first adult; 0.7 for each subsequent adult and 0.5 for each minor) and then, according to the table below, the family solidarity is determined as a percentage of the equivalent income of the household. Those whose sons or daughters households' equivalent income is placed in the 4th tier are not eligible for the SSE.

Tier	Equivalent income of the household	Family solidarity (% of the equivalent income)
1st	2.5 × RA	0
2nd	> 2.5 × RA and ≤ 3.5 × RA	5
3rd	> 3.5 × RA and ≤ 5 × RA	10
4th	> 5 × RA	Exclusion from SSE

Variant careers

Early retirement

Early retirement is possible if the insured person has at least 55 years of age and 30 calendar years with earnings registration.

When the insured person claims the pension before 65 years of age under the scheme for rendering pensionable age flexible, it is applied a reduction rate of 0.5% for each month of anticipation until that age. Nevertheless, the number of anticipation months will be reduced by 12 months for each period of three years that exceeds those 30 calendar years

The number of anticipation months is determined between the date of anticipated pension claim and the date when the insured person completes 65 years of age. The insured persons that receive a reduced anticipated pension and have ceased their activity may continue to pay contributions voluntarily in order to increase the pension amount.

If the insured person meets the conditions required to claim anticipated old-age pension without being applied any reduction factor and if he/she does not claim it, the pension will be increased by applying a rate of 0.65% to the number of months completed between the month when those requirements were met and the date when he/she reaches 65 years of age, or the date of pension beginning if this occurs before that age.

Late retirement

If the insured person claims the old-age pension when he/she is older than 65 years and has at least 15 calendar years with earnings registration relevant to the pension calculation, the pension amount will be increased by applying the respective monthly rate multiplied by the number of months completed between the month of pension beginning and the month when he/she has reached 65 years of age. The working age limit is 70.

The monthly increase rate varies according to the number of calendar years with earnings registration completed by the insured person until the date of pension beginning, as follows:

Age	Contributory career (years)	Monthly increase rates
More than 65 years old	15 to 24	0.33
	25 to 34	0.5
	35 to 39	0.65
	More than 40	1

When calculating the global increase rate, it will be taken into account the months with earnings registration due to effective work. The increased pension amount cannot be higher than 92% of the best reference earnings out of the reference earnings on which the statutory pension calculation was based.

Childcare

Maternity periods (both full leave and part-time work) count in calculating the pension entitlement. These are credited towards the qualifying conditions. Pensionable earnings for these periods are based on pay in the six months before the second month of the start of the leave.

From 2002, periods of up to three years caring for children under 12 working part time can be treated as if these are periods of full-time work.

Unemployment

Periods on unemployment benefits count in calculating pension benefits. Pensionable earnings for these periods are based on pay in the six months before the second month of the start of the unemployment period. This applies both to unemployment and to social unemployment benefits.

There are special rules applying to people in long-term unemployment. People aged 57 or over who are long-term unemployed can retire at age 62 with full pension without decrement. It is required that the minimum contribution conditions are met and unemployment-benefit entitlement is exhausted.

Early retirement is also possible from age 57 with 22 years' contributions for individuals who become unemployed at age 52 or more. In these cases, the pension is reduced with a 6.0% annual decrement, with a maximum of five years' reduction applied. The table below shows the rules applicable to unemployment benefits claimed after 1 January 2007.

Whenever unemployment is due to an agreed work contract cessation, the pension amount will be subject to an additional reduction rate which will last until the pensioner is 65 years old.

Means-tested unemployment assistance subsidy is provided if registered contribution is more than 180 days in the 12 months prior to unemployment and monthly earnings before unemployment is less than 80% of the minimum wage. This allowance can be extended until beneficiaries meet the conditions for early retirement provided that they are 50 years of age.

Pension modelling results: Portugal

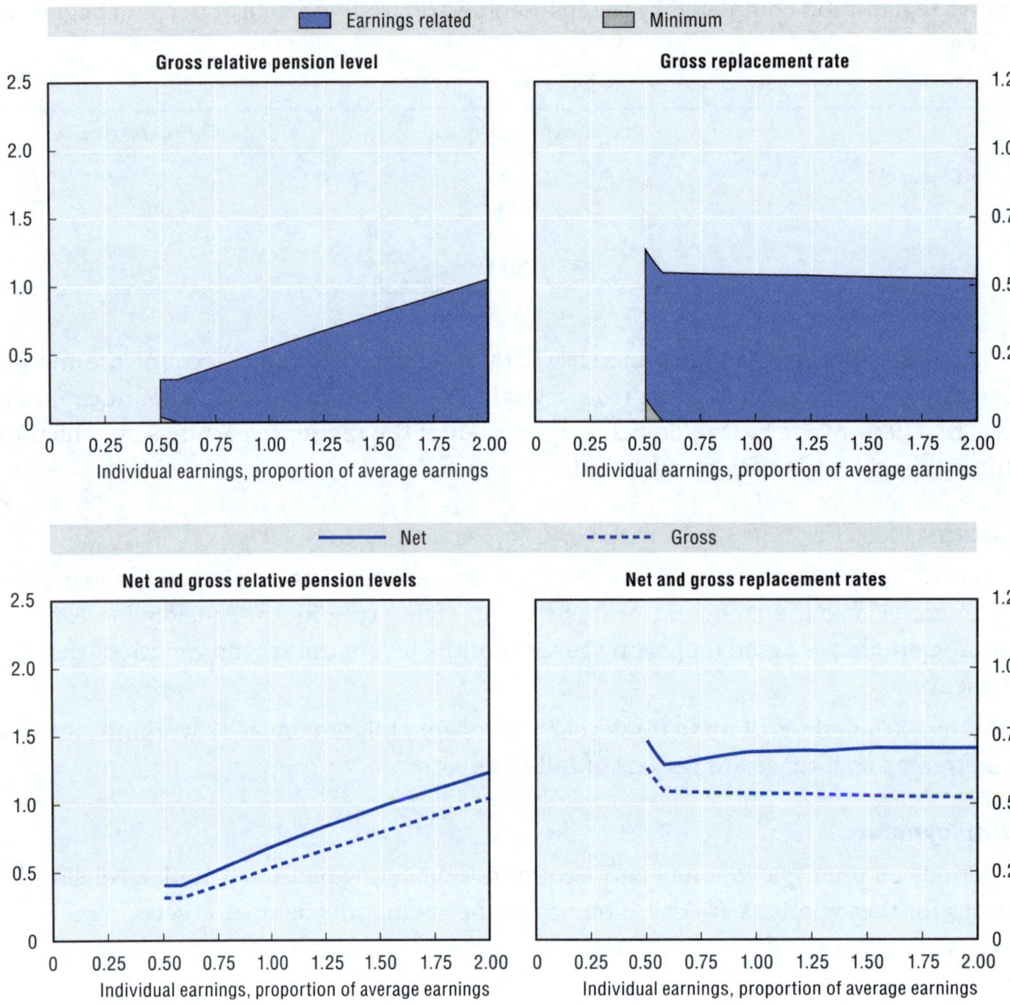

Men *Women (where different)*	Median earner	Individual earnings, multiple of average				
		0.5	0.75	1	1.5	2
Gross relative pension level	37.6	31.6	40.7	53.9	79.7	104.9
(% average gross earnings)						
Net relative pension level	48.4	40.8	52.5	69.2	98.4	123.5
(% net average earnings)						
Gross replacement rate	54.4	63.3	54.3	53.9	53.1	52.4
(% individual gross earnings)						
Net replacement rate	65.5	73.4	66.5	69.2	70.5	70.6
(% individual net earnings)						
Gross pension wealth	7.5	8.9	7.5	8.1	8.0	7.9
(multiple of individual gross earnings)	*8.7*	*10.3*	*8.7*	*9.1*	*8.9*	*8.8*
Net pension wealth	7.5	8.9	7.5	8.0	7.6	7.2
(multiple of individual gross earnings)	*8.7*	*10.3*	*8.7*	*9.1*	*8.6*	*8.1*

StatLink http://dx.doi.org/10.1787/888932371861

Slovak Republic

Slovak Republic: Pension system in 2008

The earnings-related, public scheme is similar to a points system, with benefits that depend on individual earnings relative to the average. Low-income workers are protected by a minimum amount of earnings on which pension is calculated. All pensioners are eligible for social assistance benefits. Defined-contribution plans were introduced at the beginning of 2005.

Key indicators

		Slovak Republic	OECD
Average earnings	EUR	8 700	27 800
	USD	12 700	40 600
Public pension spending	% of GDP	5.8	7.0
Life expectancy	At birth	74.6	78.9
	At age 65	80.3	83.1
Population over age 65	% of working-age population	18.3	23.6

Qualifying conditions

Since January 2008, 15 years of pension insurance are needed to be eligible for a benefit. Pension ages are being increased gradually, to be equalised between the sexes at age 62. For men, pension age of 62 was reached in 2006. For women, the increase in pension age is being spread over the period 2004-14. All women will reach the single pension age of 62 years in reality in 2024, 2015 is the date for legal rising of the pension age. For instance it means that women who will be 53 years old in 2014 and have reared five or more children will have their retirement age of 53 years increased by 99 months.

In the old-age saving scheme one needs fifteen years of savings period in addition to reaching the pension age.

Benefit calculation

Earnings related

Contributors to the pension scheme earn annual pension points. These are calculated as the ratio of individual earnings to economy-wide average earnings. The pension entitlement is the sum of pension points over the career multiplied by the pension-point value.

This was EUR 8.9955 for 2009. The pension-point value is indexed to average earnings (according growth in the third quarter of calendar year). National average earnings in 2008 were EUR 723.03 per month. Dividing the point value by the earnings figure gives the equivalent to the accrual rate in a defined-benefit scheme, which is just 1.25%.

There is a ceiling to earnings for contributions, which is set at four times average earnings. For benefit calculation the ceiling is set by maximum Pension Points at level 3 (three times of average earnings). The earnings data are lagged, so the ceiling for the first half of 2009 was four times average earnings in 2007 (EUR 668.72 per month). In the second half, the ceiling was based on 2008 data for average earnings (EUR 723.03 per month). At the baseline assumptions for earnings growth and price inflation, the lagging means that the ceiling for paying contributions is slightly less than four times contemporaneous average earnings.

Pensions in payment are indexed to the arithmetic average of earnings growth and price inflation.

For workers joining defined-contribution plans, the benefits under the public, earnings-related scheme are aliquot part of those of workers who remain only in the public plan. These workers are supposed to get the second half of their pension from life insurance or combined from life insurance and an old-age pension company.

Minimum

There is no minimum pension. However, there is a minimum assessment base for pension purposes that is equal to the minimum wage. The minimum wage was EUR 295.50 from the beginning of January 2009. The minimum wage is worth just under 40% of average earnings.

Defined contribution

The contribution rate for the defined-contribution scheme is 9% of earnings. Participation was mandatory for workers entering the labour market for the first time from January 2005; all others had the possibility to choose by June 2006 to remain solely under the public scheme or join the mixed system. However, since 1 January 2008 participation in the mixed system is voluntary for people joining the labour market for the first time. The last amendment of Act No. 43/2005 Coll. on the old-age pension saving system, that has been approved by the Parliament of the Slovak Republic, has changed the conditions that specify the beginning of the period for deciding whether to join the second pillar or not. This measure is focused only on new entrants and is effective from 1 January 2009. New entrants have six months to make their decision when their pension insurance lasts at least 150 days. When their pension insurance lasts less than 150 days this period does not count towards the period of 6 months. The aim is to secure young people (for instance students) that work during their studies only for a certain period. New entrants do not have to wait until they reach 150 days of pension insurance, they can make their decision whenever they want after they have started to pay premiums. The defined-contribution pension can be taken as an annuity or as a combination of scheduled withdrawal and annuity. The modelling assumes withdrawal in the form of a price-indexed annuity using unisex annuity rates.

Variant careers

Early retirement

Early retirement is possible. Benefits are reduced by 0.5% for each 30 days, or part thereof, that the pension is claimed early (equivalent to 6.5% per year). Early retirement also requires that the resulting pension has to be higher than 1.2 times the adult subsistence income level. The subsistence income level was and still is EUR 185.19 in 2009. The subsistence minimum for the calendar year 2008 was worth 24.7% of average earnings, meaning that the minimum pension required for early retirement has to be higher than EUR 222.30 which is 30% of average earnings. Average early retirement pension was EUR 327.60 in 2008, which is 45.3% of average earnings.

Currently there are three conditions which are necessary to be met on early retirement: maximum two years before reaching retirement age, acquired the fifteen-year contribution and the requirement for the level of the benefit.

Late retirement

It is possible to defer claiming the pension after the normal pension age. The benefit is increased by 0.5% for each month of deferral (6.5% per year). For people who claim the pension and continue to work, the pension will be recalculated when the individual eventually retires adding one half of the points earned during that period.

Childcare

There are pension credits for people caring for children up to the age of 6 with the state paying the relevant contributions. The assessment base for pensions is 60% of average earnings prior to the period spent caring for children. In the first half of each calendar year, it is based on average earnings two years before the absence started. In the second half, the calculation uses earnings in the calendar year immediately before the absence. There is more generous provision for carers of disabled children (pension credits for people caring for disabled children up to the age of 18). The carer and also the child have to have permanent address in the Slovak Republic and the carer has to register for pension insurance by reason of this care.

These rules also apply for the defined-contribution scheme (old-age pension scheme).

Unemployment

Unemployed people are not credited in the pension system. However, they can make use of provisions for voluntary pension insurance.

Pension modelling results: Slovak Republic

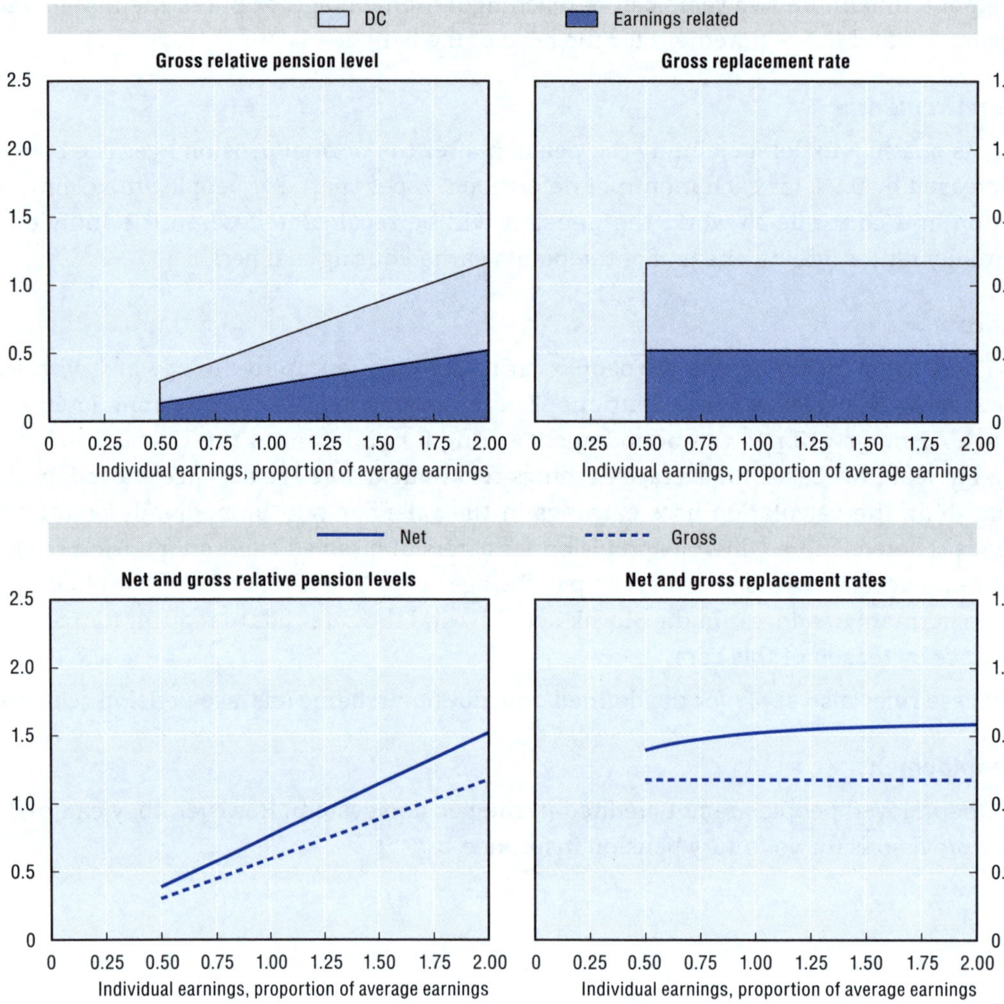

Men *Women (where different)*	Median earner	Individual earnings, multiple of average				
		0.5	0.75	1	1.5	2
Gross relative pension level *(% average gross earnings)*	46.6	28.8	43.1	57.5	86.3	115.1
Net relative pension level *(% net average earnings)*	60.4	37.3	55.9	74.5	111.8	149.0
Gross replacement rate *(% individual gross earnings)*	57.5	57.5	57.5	57.5	57.5	57.5
Net replacement rate *(% individual net earnings)*	72.9	68.3	72.3	74.5	76.7	77.7
Gross pension wealth *(multiple of individual gross earnings)*	9.2 *11.3*	9.2 *11.3*	9.2 *11.3*	9.2 *11.3*	9.2 *11.3*	9.2 *11.3*
Net pension wealth *(multiple of individual gross earnings)*	9.2 *11.3*	9.2 *11.3*	9.2 *11.3*	9.2 *11.3*	9.2 *11.3*	9.2 *11.3*

StatLink http://dx.doi.org/10.1787/888932371918

Slovenia

Slovenia: Pension system in 2008

There is an earnings-related pension with a minimum pension. There is a social-assistance scheme for low-income pensioners.

Key indicators

		Slovenia	OECD
Average earnings	EUR	15 800	27 800
	USD	23 100	40 600
Public pension spending	% of GDP	9.6	7.0
Life expectancy	At birth	78.3	78.9
	At age 65	82.3	83.1
Population over age 65	% of working-age population	24.8	23.6

Qualifying conditions

The main qualifying conditions are shown in the table. For women, the number of years' contributions needed to retire at the minimum age is increasing at three months per year to reach 38 years from 2013. At the same time, the minimum pension age is increasing by four months per year to reach 58 from 2014. The pension ages for women with shorter contribution histories are also increasing.

Men	Contribution years	15	20	40
	Pension age	65 years	63 years	58 years
Women (2008)	Contribution years	15	20	36 years 9 months
	Pension age	63 years	61 years	56 years
Women (2014)	Contribution years	15	20	38
	Pension age	63 years	61 years	58 years

A "full pension age" has recently been introduced, and this will reach 63 for men from 2009 and 61 for women from 2023.

Benefit calculation

Earnings related

The earnings-related scheme pays 35% of earnings for men and 38% for women once the minimum qualifying condition (15 years' contributions) has been met. Thereafter, the accrual rate is 1.5% per year. This means that the replacement rate with the full contribution condition (40 years for men, 38 for women) is 72.5% for both sexes.

The earnings measure is based on a period of best consecutive years since 1970. The period of assessment has been extended since 2000 and reached 18 years from 2008. The pension is calculated on the basis of individual net earnings.

The adjustment of earlier years' earnings to reflect changes in costs and standards of living is currently very complex. First, earlier years' earnings are valorised in line with the growth in economy-wide average earnings. Then, to equalise the value of pensions between retirees in different years, benefits of new retirees are reduced by a factor relating to earnings growth in the last few years. For example, valorised earnings for an individual retiring in 2007 were cut to 76.3% of their full value. For an individual retiring in 2008, the reduction factor was 74.9%.

There is a minimum pension rating base that applies to pensionable earnings. The minimum base had three different values during calendar 2008, averaging EUR 517.40 per month.

There is also a maximum to pensionable earnings, set at four times the minimum pension rating base. This averaged EUR 2 069.60 per month in 2008.

Pensions in payment are increased broadly in line with the growth in average gross earnings two times per year (February and November). The measure of pension increase is the growth of the minimum pension rating base, which must not exceed (with indexations in February and November) the estimated growth of average gross earnings in that year. The increase of average pension is lower according to the adjustment of a majority of pensions each February than to changes in the value of each qualifying year since 2000.

Minimum

The minimum pension is defined as 35% of the minimum pension rating base.

Targeted

There is a means-tested social-security allowance for low-income pensioners. Its value depends on the number of years of contributions. People with 15 years' contributions receive 60% of the difference between the limit amount for the assessment of social-security allowance (the target minimum level of income) and their pension entitlement. Those with 20 years' contribution receive 70% and those with a full career receive 100%.

The limit amount for the assessment of social-security allowance was EUR 422.20 from 1 February 2008 and is the same for all regardless of contribution years. The indexation rule for targeted pension is the same as for other pensions.

From 1 February 2008, a pensioner on a pension lower than the social-security allowance limit amount was entitled to this allowance if his/her income, together with income of his/her family members who he/she was living with in the same household, in 2007, did not exceed EUR 388.86 per member per month, and if the property of all family members did not exceed EUR 22 407.55.

Variant careers

Early retirement

For retirement before the full pension age, the pension is reduced as follows:

Age (lower limit)	58	59	60	61	62
Reduction (monthly) (%)	0.3	0.25	0.2	0.15	0.1
Reduction (annual) (%)	3.6	3	2.4	1.8	1.2

The maximum possible reduction of old-age pension for men amounts to 18.0% and for women to 10.8%.

Late retirement

If a person postpones claiming old-age pension at the minimum pension age (currently – in 2008 – 58 for men and 56 for women, equalised at 58 from 2014), additional years of insurance up until full pension age attract a higher accrual rate.

	Contribution years (lower limit)				
Men	41	42	43	44	After
Women	39	40	41	42	After
Accrual rate (%)	3	2.6	2.2	1.8	1.5

There is also an adjustment to benefits for people who defer their pension claim after the full pension age. In the first year (age 63 to 64 for men and age 61 to 62 for women), the increment is 0.3% per month. It falls to 0.2% per month in the second year and 0.1% in the third. The maximum possible increment is therefore 7.2%.

Childcare

Maternity periods of up to a year are covered by the pension system. Contributions based on the value of the minimum wage are paid by the state. The benefits for this period are calculated on the basis of earnings when the mother was working.

In addition, one of the parents who switch to part-time work when the child is 3 or under is treated as if he or she worked full time.

There is also the possibility of paying voluntary contributions for periods out of the labour market caring for children up to age 7.

Unemployment

Recipients of unemployment insurance benefits are covered by the pension system, with the Employment Agency paying the contributions. People over 50 with 25 years' insurance can receive unemployment benefits for 18 months and older workers (over 55) with 25 years' insurance can receive unemployment benefits for 24 months. For people with longer periods of unemployment who have exhausted their entitlement to unemployment insurance, the state pays the contribution and credits up to three years required to meet the qualifying conditions.

The value of unemployment benefits (both insurance and assistance payments) is taken into account when calculating pension benefits.

Pension modelling results: Slovenia

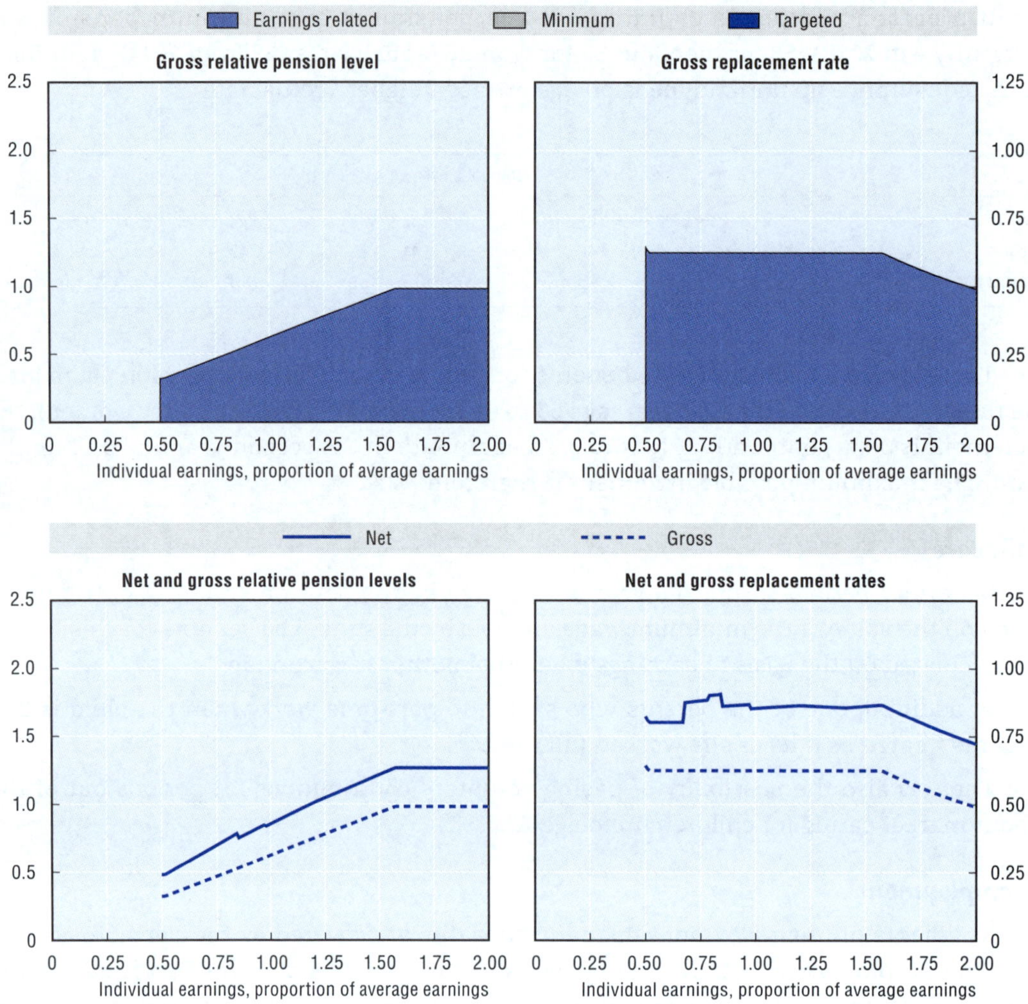

Men *Women (where different)*	Median earner	Individual earnings, multiple of average				
		0.5	0.75	1	1.5	2
Gross relative pension level	50.5	32.1	46.8	62.4	93.6	98.3
(% average gross earnings)						
Net relative pension level	75.5	48.0	69.9	85.4	121.5	126.6
(% net average earnings)						
Gross replacement rate	62.4	64.3	62.4	62.4	62.4	49.1
(% individual gross earnings)						
Net replacement rate	90.2	82.5	88.1	85.4	86.2	72.2
(% individual net earnings)						
Gross pension wealth	12.6	13.0	12.6	12.6	12.6	9.9
(multiple of individual gross earnings)	*16.9*	*17.4*	*16.9*	*16.9*	*16.9*	*13.3*
Net pension wealth	12.6	13.0	12.6	11.5	10.9	8.5
(multiple of individual gross earnings)	*16.9*	*17.4*	*16.9*	*15.5*	*14.7*	*11.5*

StatLink http://dx.doi.org/10.1787/888932371937

Spain

Spain: Pension system in 2008

The Spanish public pension system consists of a single, earnings-related benefit in the contribution level, with a means-tested minimum pension. There is also a non-contribution means-tested level, which replaces the previous special social assistance scheme.

Key indicators

		Spain	OECD
Average earnings	EUR	23 200	27 800
	USD	33 900	40 600
Public pension spending	% of GDP	8.0	7.0
Life expectancy	At birth	80.8	78.9
	At age 65	84.3	83.1
Population over age 65	% of working-age population	26.8	23.6

Qualifying conditions

The retirement age for a full benefit is 65 years for men and women. 15 years of contributions are necessary to qualify for a pension benefit.

Benefit calculation

Earnings related

The benefit accrues according to a schedule. After 15 years' contributions, it is 50% of the earnings base. Over the next ten years, an extra 3% is accrued per year, followed by 2% per year thereafter. The maximum accrual is 100%, reached after 35 years' contributions.

The earnings base is pay over the last 15 years, uprated in line with prices, apart from the last two years. This means that the replacement rate relative to final salary is less than 100%. On the standard assumptions for earnings growth and price inflation, this is calculated to be 81%.

There is a ceiling to earnings for contributions and benefit purposes of EUR 36 889.2 corresponding to 159% of average earnings.

Benefits are price-indexed.

Minimum and maximum

There is a minimum pension payable from age 65 amounting to EUR 530.63 per month, or 32.0% of average earnings, for pensioners without a dependent spouse, and EUR 661.34 per month, or 39.9% of average earnings, for pensioners with a dependent spouse. There are 14 payments per year. There is also a new minimum pension payable to widows amounting EUR 651.63 per month for widows with children in charge.

Due to specific policy from 2004, minimum pensions have increased above the price index in the last years. From 2004 to 2008 price index has increased 13.1% and minimum pensions have increased in a range between 34.4% and 27.0% depending on the type of pension.

The maximum pension is EUR 2 393.87 per month in 2008 (14 payments per year).

Variant careers

Early retirement

Early retirement is available from age 61 for people entering the system in 1967 or later who are unemployed, provided they have contributed for at least 30 years. The actuarial reduction depends on the number of years of contributions: 7.5% (30-34 years), 7% (35-37 years), 6.5% (38-39 years), and 6% for more than 40 years of contributions.

For people who entered the system before 1967, early retirement is possible from age 60. If retirement is voluntary the reduction is 8% per year. If it is not voluntary reductions are the same as in the case of people aged 61 or more who entered the system in 1967 or later.

The minimum pension for early retirees is EUR 494.44 or 30% of average earnings for pensioners without a dependent spouse, and EUR 618.08 per month, or 37% of average earnings for pensioners with a dependent spouse, and after 65 they move to the higher level.

Between 61 and 64, it is possible to combine partial pension receipt and a part-time job, if working hours are reduced between 25% and 75%. Another employee must replace the remaining working hours left by the partial pensioner. 15 years of contributions are required. Partially retired workers must have been with the last employer for at least six years and contributed 30 years or more in total. For people entering the system after 1967, the possibility for partial pensions starts from 60.

Late retirement

It is possible to defer the pension after normal retirement age. For workers who have contributed 15 years or more and continue working after 65 years old, the pension will increase their benefit by 2% of the base of calculation per additional year. The increase is 3% with 40 years of contributions. Pensioners entitled of a maximum pension entering retirement with 66 years or more will receive an annual lump sum (2% of the maximum pension per additional year after 65, 3% with 40 years of contributions).

From 65 there is also the possibility of combining partial pension and part-time job. In this case, there is no obligation to replace the remaining working hours.

Childcare

There is coverage for the maternity and paternity period. Two years out of the labour market looking after children count towards eligibility for a pension benefit.

Unemployment

During periods of unemployment-benefit receipt, the government pays all of the employers' contribution and 35% of the employee's contribution to the pension insurance scheme. The remaining 65% of the employee's contribution is paid by the worker. The base salary for contributions is the average salary in the six months prior to unemployment. The duration of the benefits depends on the number of contribution days during the prior six years, varying between four months and two years. The unemployment assistance which is paid thereafter does not create any pension credits, except for people 52 or more. For these people, contributions for old-age pension are paid by the government up to retirement age. These contributions are levied on the minimum base of EUR 699.9 per month.

Pension modelling results: Spain

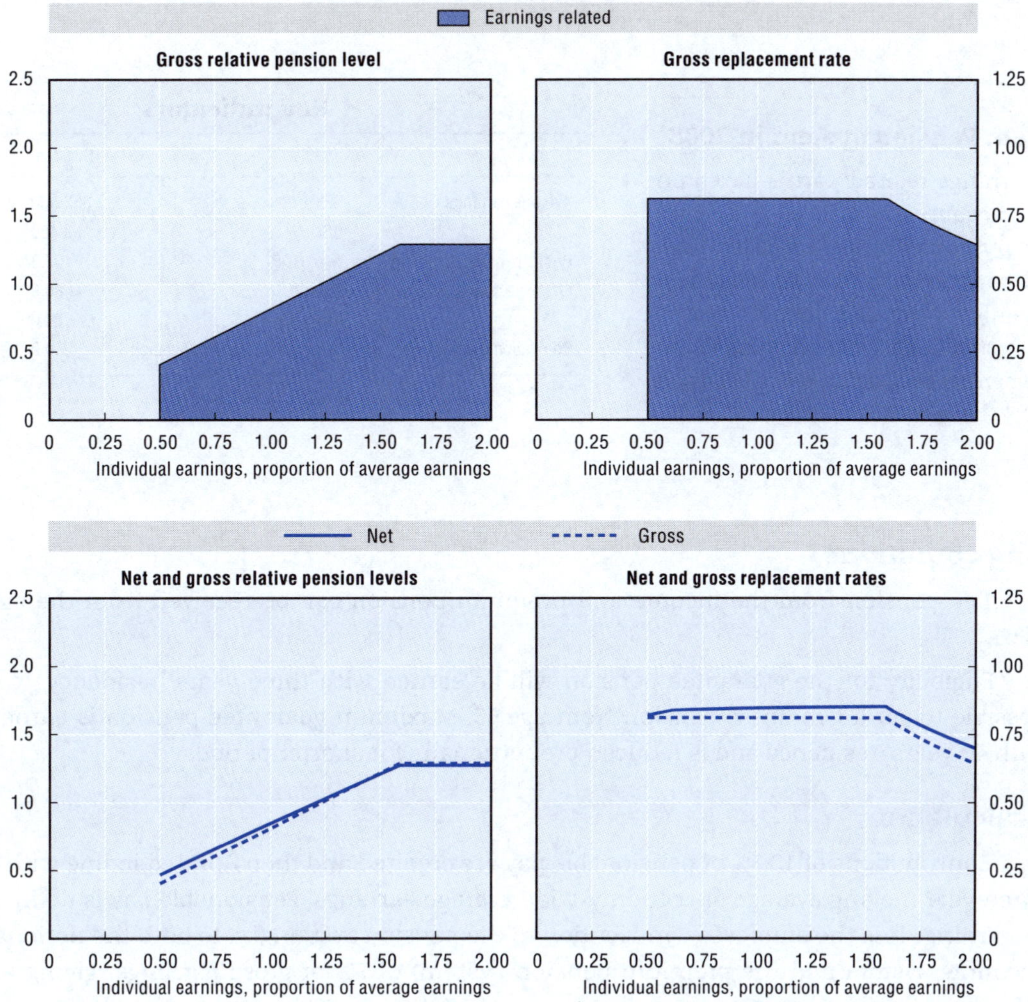

Men *Women (where different)*	Median earner	Individual earnings, multiple of average				
		0.5	0.75	1	1.5	2
Gross relative pension level	63.3	40.6	60.9	81.2	121.8	129.0
(% average gross earnings)						
Net relative pension level	68.3	46.9	66.1	84.9	121.1	127.6
(% net average earnings)						
Gross replacement rate	81.2	81.2	81.2	81.2	81.2	64.5
(% individual gross earnings)						
Net replacement rate	84.5	82.3	84.4	84.9	85.4	70.2
(% individual net earnings)						
Gross pension wealth	13.7	13.7	13.7	13.7	13.7	10.9
(multiple of individual gross earnings)	*15.5*	*15.5*	*15.5*	*15.5*	*15.5*	*12.3*
Net pension wealth	11.9	12.8	12.0	11.6	11.0	8.7
(multiple of individual gross earnings)	*13.5*	*14.5*	*13.6*	*13.1*	*12.5*	*9.8*

StatLink http://dx.doi.org/10.1787/888932371975

Sweden

Sweden: Pension system in 2008

The earnings-related part is based on notional accounts and there is a small mandatory contribution to individual, defined-contribution funded pensions. There is also a pension-income-tested top-up. Occupational pension plans – with defined-benefit and defined-contribution elements – have broad coverage.

Key indicators

		Sweden	OECD
Average earnings	SEK	352 500	267 800
	USD	53 400	40 600
Public pension spending	% of GDP	7.2	7.0
Life expectancy	At birth	80.9	78.9
	At age 65	84.0	83.1
Population over age 65	% of working-age population	30.2	23.6

Qualifying conditions

The pension from the income and premium pension can be received from the age of 61.

Eligibility for the guarantee pension will be earned with three years' residency. It is possible to get a guarantee pension from age 65. Maximum guarantee pension is earned with 40 years' residency and is reduced proportionally for shorter periods.

Benefit calculation

Contributions of 18.5% of pensionable pay are credited and then uprated in line with a three-year moving average of economy-wide average earnings. Pensionable pay is defined as earnings less the employee contribution to the pension system (*i.e.* to both the notional accounts system and the premium pension system) of 7% of gross earnings, giving an effective contribution rate on gross earnings of 17.21%, 14.88% to the notional-accounts system and 2.33% to the defined-contribution funded pensions. Contributions are only levied when annual earnings exceed a small floor of SEK 17 343 in 2008, just under 5.0% of average earnings, although they are due on the whole of earnings for all people earning above the floor. There is a ceiling to benefits calculated in terms of pensionable earnings of SEK 360 000 in 2008. However, this again relates to pensionable earnings, giving an effective ceiling relative to gross earnings of SEK 387 360 in 2008 (around 110% of average earnings). Employer contributions are also paid only to the ceiling, but there is an additional tax on earnings above the ceiling. This tax has the same percentage as the pension contribution but goes directly to the central government budget. It does not accrue any pension rights.

Earnings related

The new earnings-related scheme uses notional accounts. The notional accounts are increased every year by the distribution of the pension balances of deceased persons of the same age as the survivors (inheritance gains). The inheritance gains from people who die before the earliest possible retirement age (61 years) are relevant. After this age the inheritance gains factor is estimated on the basis of the mortality observed for an earlier period (computed from five year unisex mortality tables).

At retirement, the accumulated notional capital will be converted into an annuity. This calculation will use a coefficient depending on individual retirement age and contemporaneous life expectancy (based on the previous five year unisex mortality tables). A real discount rate of 1.6% a year will be assumed in this calculation. Illustrative values for the annuity coefficient at age 65 are 15.4 for 2000 rising to 16.8 by 2020 and 17.4 by 2040. The annuity coefficient is currently 18.0 for retirement at 61 and 12.8 at age 70 for people born in 1940.

After retirement, pensions are uprated with the increase in nominal average earnings less the imputed interest rate in the annuity divisor of 1.6%.

There is also a "balance mechanism": if assets (the buffer fund plus the estimated value of assets in the form of contribution revenues) fall below liabilities (accrued notional pension capital and capital value of outgoing pensions), then indexation of pensions in payment and returns credited to notional accounts are reduced by the ratio of assets to liabilities. The balancing ratio is now 0.9826. The balance ratio for year t is used to calculate the balance number or the need for activating the balancing mechanism in year t + 2. An activated balancing mechanism would mean lower replacement rates from the national system but will produce higher results when the pension system recovers and the balance figure increases (the balance index can exceed the income index during the recovery period).

For modelling purposes, the annuity coefficients are calculated using the above rules and the relevant mortality data from the *United Nations Population Database*. It is assumed that the balance mechanism does not affect the uprating of benefits.

Minimum

The "guarantee pension" is an income-tested top-up for people with low levels of benefit from notional accounts. For a single person, the full guaranteed benefit in 2008 was SEK 87 330 for a single pensioner born after 1938 or 25% of gross average earnings.

The guarantee pension is withdrawn at 100% against the first SEK 51 660 (2008) of income, for a single person, from the earnings-related pension, thereafter at 48%. This threshold is equivalent to 15% of average earnings. Only when earnings-related pension exceeds SEK 125 870 – nearly 36% of average earnings – is entitlement to the guarantee exhausted.

The guarantee level is price indexed under current legislation. However, the baseline assumption in the modelling for all countries is that the value of safety-net retirement benefits will tend, over time, to track average earnings rather than decline relative to general living standards.

There is also a housing benefit that covers 93% of housing costs up to a maximum of SEK 5 000 per month for a single pensioner. The benefit is an important part of the minimum living standard for Swedish pensioners. This means-tested benefit is not included in the modelled calculations.

Defined contribution

A further 2.5% of pensionable income (giving an effective contribution rate against gross earnings of 2.33%) will be paid into personal pension accounts: the premium pension. People have a broad choice of where these funds are invested.

At retirement, people have a choice over the way benefits are withdrawn. First, people can convert the pension into an annuity to avoid investment risk. Alternatively, people will be able to choose a variable annuity, where their funds continue to be invested by their chosen fund manager. These annuities do not have a guaranteed value. The principle of the pension calculation in this case is that the value of the account is divided by an annuity divisor (based on estimated average life expectancy) and the pension benefit is credited with an estimated future interest rate of 3% minus administrative costs. If returns exceed 3%, then either an additional payment is made or the balance of the account is higher and so, therefore, is the base for calculating the annual pension.

Quasi-mandatory occupational

The occupational schemes together are estimated to cover almost 90% of employees. There are only four major occupational schemes. The modelling has used the ITP scheme for white-collar workers, which mixes defined-benefit and defined-contribution elements. This plan has now been renegotiated. The old plan is current for those born in 1978 or earlier with some minor changes and the new plan covers those born in 1979 or later.

ITP1

From 1 January 2007, salaried employees born in or after 1979 began to accrue a retirement pension under the new ITP1 plan from the age of 25. It is a complete defined-contribution plan. The contribution is 4.5% of salary portions up to 7.5 income base amounts (SEK 360 000 for 2008). For salary portions in excess of 7.5 income base amounts (divided by 12 for one month) the contribution is 30%. The pensionable salary becomes the gross salary paid out in cash, excluding reimbursement of expenses. Premiums are paid from the first SEK of salary.

The employee can choose the form of the savings and the fund manager. However, at least half the contribution is invested in traditional pension insurance. The employee can also choose repayment cover and family cover of one, two, three or four price base amounts per year over 5, 10, 15 or 20 years. The contributions of those who do not specify a choice are invested in traditional pension insurance with no repayment cover or family cover. This default choice is the one that is modelled.

Employees whose yearly salary exceeds ten income base amounts (SEK 480 000 in 2008) may choose to be covered under the new plan upon agreement with their employer. This applies regardless of whether the employee has a traditional ITP2 plan or has taken out an alternative ITP.

Variant careers

Early retirement

Retirement is possible from age 61 in the public pension scheme (both the income pension and the premium pension). There is no fixed retirement age. The notional-accounts and annuity calculations provide an automatic actuarial reduction depending on the age of retirement.

The income-tested guarantee pension cannot be claimed before 65. If the notional-accounts pension is withdrawn before or after age 65, the guarantee pension is still calculated as if the pension had been withdrawn at age 65.

In the new ITP1 plan, pensions are normally paid from the age of 65, but may be taken out from the age of 55. Pensions are life-long but can be paid in full or in part for a limited period of at least five years. The annuity is modelled as one that gives lifelong payments. The size of the pension is determined by the amount of premiums paid, the return, fees and taxes, and for how long the pension is to be disbursed.

Late retirement

It is possible to defer the notional accounts and premium pension with no upper age limit, again with automatic actuarial adjustments. It is also possible to combine work and pension receipt. Finally, pensions can be withdrawn partially (at 25, 50 or 75% of the full pension). The guarantee pension is adjusted against other pensions from the Swedish old-age pension system and from comparable foreign national pensions, but is not reduced by wage income, capital income, occupational pension or private pension insurance. Thus, it is also possible to combine work with receipt of the guarantee pension.

It is possible to defer the ITP1 occupational pension after age 65. No additional pension rights can be accrued after age 65.

Childcare

Years are credited under the public pension scheme for any period when you have and live with children aged four or under. In a household with two parents the credits go to the parent with the lowest income if an active choice is not made. Individuals receive the best of three different ways of calculating the credit. First, if income is zero or lower than previous earnings, then the credits are based on the earnings the year before the child was born. Secondly, for low-income workers or people who were not working before childcare responsibilities started, the credits are based on 75% of economy-wide average earnings. Thirdly, if income actually rises or does not decrease to a great extent as childcare responsibilities begin, then the credit is set at one income base amount. In all three cases, the government makes the total contributions to the pension system (covering both the income pension and the premium pension). This is, however, up to the earnings ceiling in the pension system defined under the section "contributions".

Furthermore, parental benefits paid to people on parental leave from work are also considered pensionable income. The beneficiary pays the employee pension contribution of 7% on benefit income. The government makes all the "employer contributions" of 10.21% for incomes from social security including parental benefits.

The parental benefit is payable for a period of 480 days as follows:

- 390 days at 80% of the parent's annual income up to a ceiling of ten price base amounts (equivalent to a monthly salary of SEK 34 175 in 2008).
- 90 days at a universally applicable flat rate of SEK 180/day.

The parental benefit is computed daily. Parents on low income or no income at all receive a minimum guaranteed benefit of SEK 180/day. The 480 cash benefit days are divided equally between the parents (*i.e.* 240 days to each parent). A parent may also transfer up to 180 of her or his days to the other parent.

Under the ITP occupational plan, there is a recommendation that the employer contributes to an employee's pension during periods of up to 11 months for parental leave (and most do so).

Unemployment

Unemployment benefits and training allowances paid to unemployed people taking up labour-market programmes are pensionable income, with the government making the "employer" contribution. Income-related unemployment benefits are 80% of previous earnings for the first two hundred days. From day 201 up to day 300 the benefit is 70% of previous earnings. Thereafter the benefit period is ended unless one is the parent of a child below the age of 18 for whom the benefit remains at a level of 70% of previous earnings for an extended period of 150 days. The unemployment benefits are disbursed up to a ceiling of SEK 680 per day and subject to a minimum payment of SEK 320 per day (applies only if the unemployed person has worked full time during 12 months preceding unemployment).

After the receipt of days in unemployment the beneficiary is entitled to be enrolled within the job and development guarantee programme. A participant in the job and development guarantee programme is entitled to activity support or development benefits. If the jobseeker has had an unemployment benefit before enrolment in the jobs and development guarantee then this benefit will equal 65% of earnings from the time before unemployment (max SEK 680 per day). If the jobseeker has not previously been entitled to unemployment benefits he or she will receive the daily benefit of SEK 223 per day.

Pension modelling results: Sweden

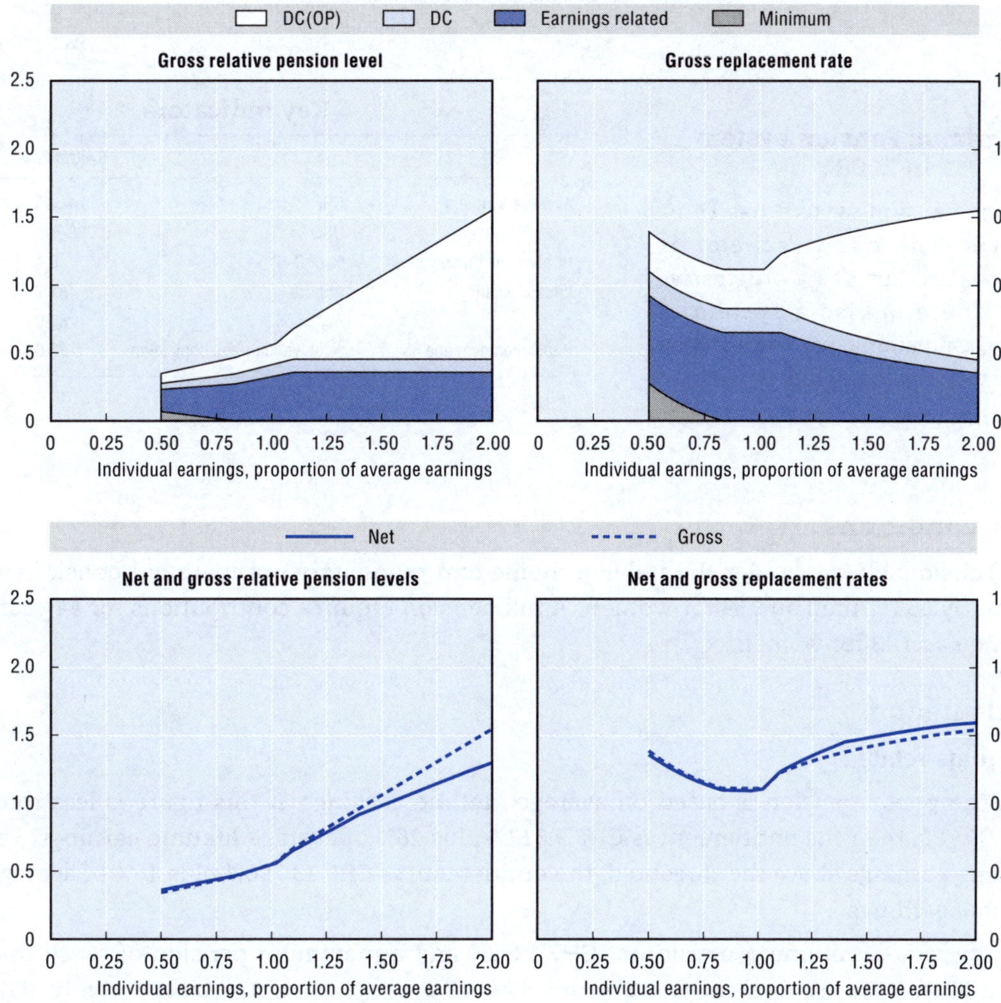

Men *Women (where different)*	Median earner	Individual earnings, multiple of average				
		0.5	0.75	1	1.5	2
Gross relative pension level	48.4	34.1	42.6	53.8	103.0	150.1
(% average gross earnings)						
Net relative pension level	48.8	35.9	43.6	53.6	96.4	127.3
(% net average earnings)						
Gross replacement rate	53.8	68.3	56.8	53.8	68.7	75.0
(% individual gross earnings)						
Net replacement rate	53.3	67.0	56.3	53.6	72.6	78.3
(% individual net earnings)						
Gross pension wealth	9.1	11.5	9.6	9.1	11.5	12.5
(multiple of individual gross earnings)	*10.2*	*12.9*	*10.8*	*10.2*	*12.9*	*14.1*
Net pension wealth	6.7	8.9	7.2	6.6	7.9	7.8
(multiple of individual gross earnings)	*7.5*	*9.9*	*8.1*	*7.5*	*8.8*	*8.7*

StatLink http://dx.doi.org/10.1787/888932371994

Switzerland

Switzerland: Pension system in 2008

The Swiss pension system has three main parts. The public scheme is earnings related, but has a progressive formula. There is also a system of mandatory occupational pensions and an income-tested supplementary benefit.

Key indicators

		Switzerland	OECD
Average earnings	CHF	74 500	44 000
	USD	68 700	40 600
Public pension spending	% of GDP	6.4	7.0
Life expectancy	At birth	81.7	78.9
	At age 65	85.0	83.1
Population over age 65	% of working-age population	27.0	23.6

Qualifying conditions

Pensionable age under the public scheme and mandatory occupational pensions is currently 65 for men and 64 for women. A full pension requires contributions for 44 years for men and 43 for women.

Benefit calculation

Earnings related

The public pension is based on average lifetime earnings. If this figure is less than CHF 39 780, then the entitlement is CHF 9 812.4 plus 26% of average lifetime earnings. For lifetime earnings above the threshold, the entitlement is CHF 13 790.4 plus 16% of average lifetime earnings.

There is a minimum pension of CHF 13 260 and a maximum pension of twice that level. These are equivalent to 18% and 36% of average earnings, respectively. The maximum benefit is reached when average lifetime earnings are CHF 79 560, equivalent to 107% of economy-wide average earnings.

Pensions in payment are indexed 50% to prices and 50% to nominal earnings.

Mandatory occupational

The system of mandatory occupational pensions was introduced in 1985. It is built around "defined credits" to an individual's pension account. These vary by sex and age:

Men, of age + women from 2005	25-34	35-44	45-54	55-64
Women, of age (1987-2004)	25-31	32-41	42-51	52-62/63
Credit (% of co-ordinated earnings)	7	10	15	18

The value of accumulated credits at retirement naturally depends on the required interest rate applied to earlier years' contributions. This was, for a long period until the end of 2002, 4%, but was cut to 3.25% in 2003 and to 2.25% in 2004. The interest rate was raised to 2.5% in 2005 and to 2.75% in 2008. If the interest rate is broadly equivalent to the growth rate of earnings, then a full career in the system will give a man at age 65 accumulated credits of 500% of earnings. However, higher (or lower) outcomes are possible if the interest rate exceeds (is less than) growth in earnings. The modelling assumes that the interest rate applied to the credits will be equivalent to earnings over the long term.

The system has a minimum annuity rate of 7.05% for men (65) and 7.1% for women (64) that is applied to this notional capital sum. This gives a full career replacement rate of (500 × 7.05 =) 35.25% (subject to the interest rate being equal to earnings growth). From 2005, the minimum annuity rate is being reduced from 7.20% over a ten-year period, eventually reaching 6.8%.

The defined credits (and hence the replacement rate) apply only to "co-ordinated" earnings. This is pay between three-quarters of the maximum pension of the public scheme (CHF 19 890) and three times the maximum pension of the public scheme (CHF 79 560). These thresholds are equivalent to 27% and 107% of average earnings. The co-ordination deduction is 7/8 of the maximum pension of public scheme (CHF 23 205). Note that the ceiling for pensionable pay is the same in the public scheme and in the mandatory occupational pension sector. There is a minimum for co-ordinated earnings of one eighth of the maximum value. Credits accrue at this minimum level for people with co-ordinated earnings below this level.

Targeted

The amount of the annual benefit is the share of expenditure recognized that exceeds the income determinants. The expenditure on basic needs are provided by law and amounts to CHF 18 140 for single people (CHF 27 210 for couples), equivalent to 24% and 36% respectively of average earnings. The supplementary benefit is indexed in the same way as the public old-age pensions, *i.e.* to a mixed index of 50% prices and 50% wages. There are discretionary cantonal additions for low-income pensioners; these are disregarded in the model.

Variant careers

Early retirement

Early retirement in the public scheme is possible two years before the standard retirement age, *i.e.* from age 63 for men and 62 for women as of 2005. In case of early retirement, the full value is reduced by 6.8% for each year of early claiming. This is equivalent to an actuarial adjustment, of 4.5% because it is claimed early and $^{1}/_{44}$ = 2.3% of the adjustment reflects the additional year that the member has not contributed.

For women born in 1947 or before, the reduction in pension benefits from their full value is 3.4% per year of early retirement.

Early retirement is permitted in occupational schemes. In practice, schemes may allow retirement up to five years before the normal age, although schemes can decide on their own policy. Generally, the statutory annuity rate is reduced from 7.05% at age 65 (from the 7.1% at age 64 for women), by 0.2 percentage points per year of early retirement. (Note that this conversion rate will fall gradually to 6.8% over the ten years starting in 2005.) The 0.2 point reduction is equivalent to an actuarial adjustment, as conventionally measured, of 2.8-2.95% per year of early retirement (increasing with the extent of early retirement). Including also the loss of contributions and credits as a result of early retirement, the theoretical benefit is 7.6% (one year) – 6.6% (five years) lower per year of early retirement. The loss increases the earlier the retirement is taken. (The range given is from age 64 to age 60.)

Late retirement

Both public and occupational pensions can be deferred after normal pension age. Pensions are adjusted in the same way as for early retirement. The pension can be deferred for up to five years after the normal pension age. The pension is increased according to the following schedule:

Deferral	1 year	2 years	3 years	4 years	5 years
Adjustment (%)	5.2	10.8	17.1	24.0	31.5

It is also possible to claim the public pension at 65 and continue working.

Contributions are not levied on people working after age 65 if earnings are below CHF 16 800 per year. For earnings above that level, contributions are levied when people defer the pension or claim the pension while continuing their work but no additional pension entitlement can be earned.

In the occupational plans, the annuity rate is increased by 0.2 percentage points for each year that retirement is deferred according a recommendation of the Federal Social Insurance Office (pension funds decide freely on the percentage points). The authorities, in practice, allow deferral for up to five years.

In principle, it is possible to combine receipt of the occupational pension with continuing to work. In practice, these are mainly cases of people with incomplete careers or people who have retired early rather than late. Therefore, the modelling assumes that people defer their occupational pension if they continue to work after the normal pension age. People do not continue to contribute after 65 under the public pension scheme.

Childcare

Years of childcare (for children under age 16) are credited in the public scheme as if earnings had amounted to three times the minimum pension of the year in which the caring parent retires. For 2008, this was CHF 39 780, corresponding to 52% of economy-wide average earnings. If the caring parent is married during the caring period, the credits are split equally between the spouses.

Credits for childcare are not required in occupational schemes.

Unemployment

Unemployment benefits are subject to social security contributions and so count towards the public pension just as if they were earnings. Unemployment insurance pays 80% of previous earnings. Persons with no child maintenance, who receive a full daily allowance of more than CHF 140 or who are not disabled receive 70% of the insured salary. The duration of unemployment insurance varies between 260 and 520 days. Once unemployment insurance is exhausted and a former worker is on social assistance, they do not pay contribution. If income is very low, then municipal authorities often pay the minimum contribution.

There are no credits for unemployment periods in occupational schemes.

Pension modelling results: Switzerland

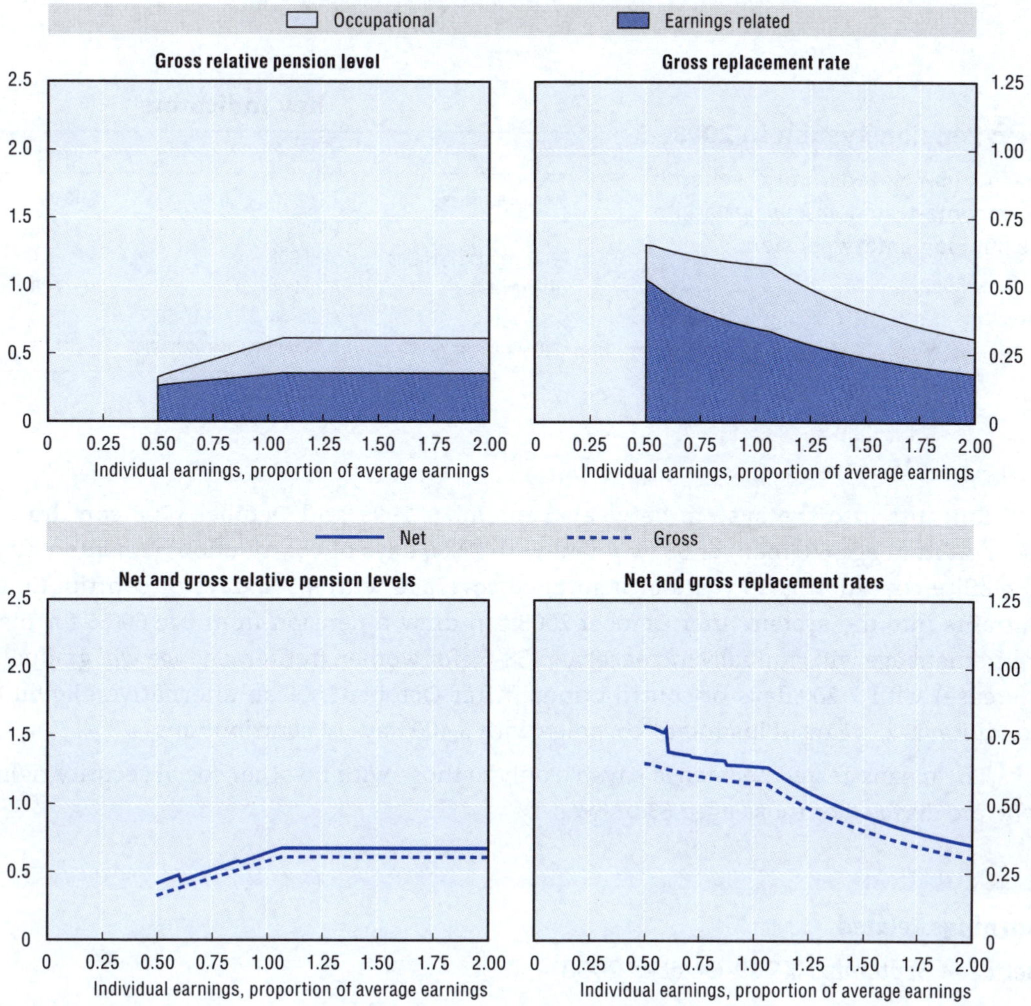

Men *Women (where different)*	Median earner	Individual earnings, multiple of average				
		0.5	0.75	1	1.5	2
Gross relative pension level	50.4	32.6	45.4	57.9	61.3	61.3
(% average gross earnings)	*49.8*	*32.4*	*44.9*	*57.1*	*60.4*	*60.4*
Net relative pension level	57.0	41.4	51.2	64.1	67.9	67.9
(% net average earnings)	*56.2*	*41.2*	*50.6*	*63.2*	*66.9*	*66.9*
Gross replacement rate	59.3	65.2	60.6	57.9	40.9	30.7
(% individual gross earnings)	*58.5*	*64.7*	*59.8*	*57.1*	*40.3*	*30.2*
Net replacement rate	66.4	78.6	67.3	64.1	46.2	35.5
(% individual net earnings)	*65.5*	*78.1*	*66.5*	*63.2*	*45.5*	*35.0*
Gross pension wealth	11.1	12.4	11.3	10.8	7.6	5.7
(multiple of individual gross earnings)	*12.6*	*14.2*	*13.0*	*12.2*	*8.6*	*6.5*
Net pension wealth	9.3	11.8	9.6	8.9	6.3	4.7
(multiple of individual gross earnings)	*10.7*	*13.5*	*10.9*	*10.1*	*7.1*	*5.4*

StatLink http://dx.doi.org/10.1787/888932372013

Turkey

Turkey: Pension system in 2008

An earnings-related public scheme with an income-tested safety net and a flat-rate supplementary pension.

Key indicators

		Turkey	OECD
Average earnings	TRY	18 800	52 700
	USD	14 500	40 600
Public pension spending	% of GDP	6.1	7.0
Life expectancy	At birth	71.8	78.9
	At age 65	79.0	83.1
Population over age 65	% of working-age population	10.1	23.6

Qualifying conditions

Entrants into the system between September 1999 and October 2008 can draw a pension from age 60 (men) or 58 (women) with 7 000 days of contributions. An alternative eligibility condition is 25 years of insurance coverage with 4 500 days of contributions. Entrants into the system after October 2008 can draw a pension from age 60-65 for men (retirement age will gradually increase) and 58-65 for women (retirement age will gradually increase) with 7 200 days of contributions. After October 2008 an alternative eligibility condition is 25 years of insurance coverage with 5 400 days of contributions.

The means-tested pension is payable only to those with no other social security rights who are disabled or those aged 65 or over.

Benefit calculation

Earnings related

Between September 1999-October 2008

The pension under the scheme is based on average lifetime earnings revalued in line with nominal GDP growth and the change of CPI [(1 + GDP) × (1 + CPI)]. The pension has a non-linear formula with years of coverage. The first ten years earn a pension of 35% of pay, with 2% per year extra for the next 15 years and 1.5% per year thereafter.

After October

The pension under the new scheme is based on average lifetime earnings revalued in line with nominal GDP growth and the change of CPI [(1 + CPI + %30 GDP)]. The pension's formula is a pension of 2% for one year coverage and it cannot exceed 90% of pension.

There is a floor above which contributions are required. This is TRY 693 for the second half of 2009.

There is a ceiling to pensionable earnings; its value was TRY 4 504.50.

According to the law acted in 1999 pensions are monthly indexed by consumer price index. But since 2003 indexation of pensions in payment is determined once or twice a year, either by Budget Laws/Other Laws or by Board of Cabinet. For 2009 pensions are increased 3.84% in January and 1.83% in July.

Minimum

There is a minimum pension, which in 2009 varied between TRY 590.7 and TRY 608.3.

Targeted

The means-tested pension is paid quarterly. For the first half of 2009 the pension was TRY 90.7 per month, for the second, pension is TRY 94.8 per month.

Variant careers

Early retirement

Workers in specific industries (*e.g.* mining) and people with disability can retire early but other workers cannot claim pensions before the eligibility ages.

Late retirement

It is possible to defer the pension beyond the normal pension age.

Childcare

There is no credit for periods spent out of paid work caring for children.

Unemployment

There is no credit for periods of unemployment.

Pension modelling results: Turkey

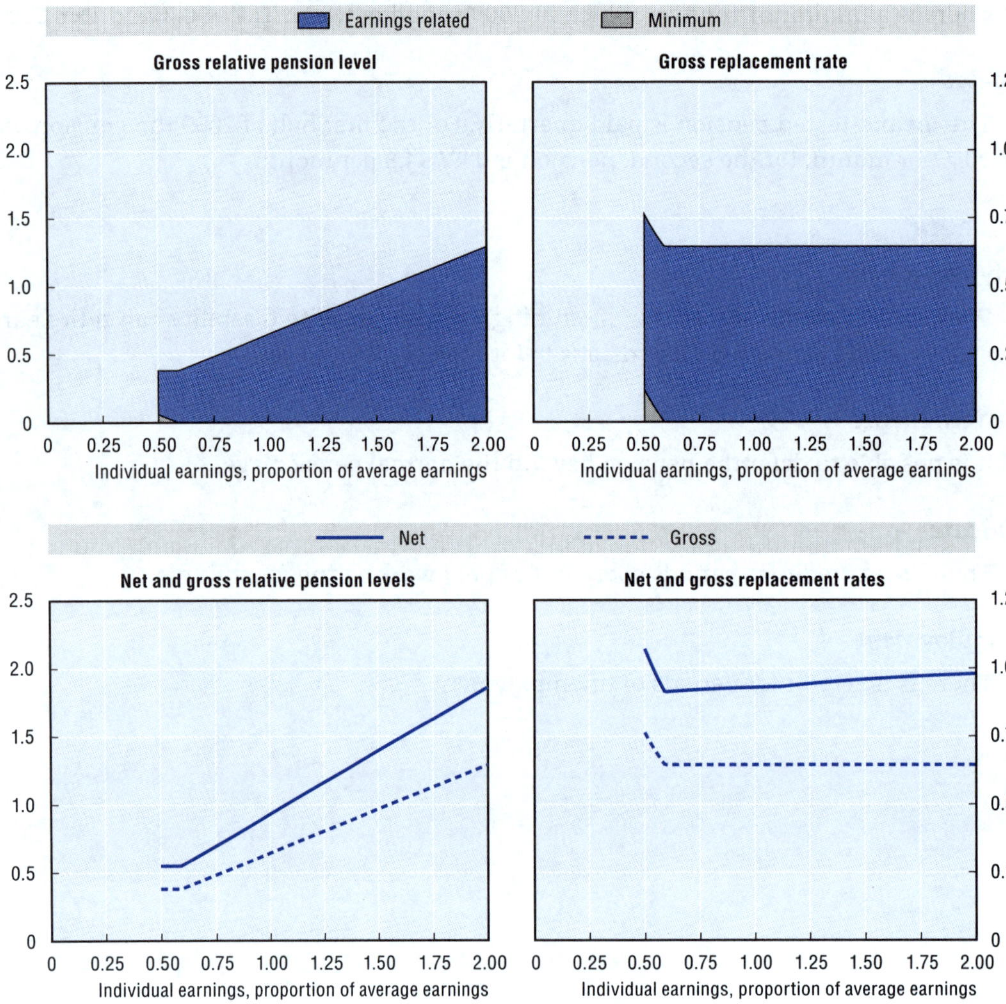

Men *Women (where different)*	Median earner	Individual earnings, multiple of average				
		0.5	0.75	1	1.5	2
Gross relative pension level	38.2	38.2	48.4	64.5	96.8	129.1
(% average gross earnings)						
Net relative pension level	55.1	55.1	69.8	93.1	139.6	186.1
(% net average earnings)						
Gross replacement rate	69.5	76.4	64.5	64.5	64.5	64.5
(% individual gross earnings)						
Net replacement rate	98.0	107.3	92.2	93.1	96.0	98.1
(% individual net earnings)						
Gross pension wealth	9.2	10.1	8.5	8.5	8.5	8.5
(multiple of individual gross earnings)	*10.9*	*12.0*	*10.2*	*10.2*	*10.2*	*10.2*
Net pension wealth	9.2	10.1	8.5	8.5	8.5	8.5
(multiple of individual gross earnings)	*10.9*	*12.0*	*10.2*	*10.2*	*10.2*	*10.2*

StatLink http://dx.doi.org/10.1787/888932372032

United Kingdom

United Kingdom: Pension system in 2008

The public scheme has two tiers, (a flat-rate basic pension and an earnings-related additional pension), which are complemented by a large voluntary private pension sector. Most employee contributors "contract out" of the state second tier into private pensions of different sorts. An income-related benefit (pension credit) targets extra spending on the poorest pensioners.

Key indicators

		United Kingdom	OECD
Average earnings	GBP	33 600	22 200
	USD	61 500	40 600
Public pension spending	% of GDP	5.4	7.0
Life expectancy	At birth	79.4	78.9
	At age 65	83.2	83.1
Population over age 65	% of working-age population	27.3	23.6

Qualifying conditions

State pension age, currently 60 for women born on or before 5 April 1950 and 65 for men, will gradually be equalised from 2010 reaching 65 in 2020. As a result of the Pensions Act 2007, state pension age will increase to 66 between 2024 and 2028; to 67 between 2034 and 2036 and 68 between 2044 and 2046. The eligibility age for the guarantee credit element of the pension credit is 60, and will increase in line with the women's state pension age. The new savings credit element of pension credit is only available from 65 for both men and women.

To qualify for the basic state pension, people need: *i)* to pay; or *ii)* have been treated as having paid social security contributions; or *iii)* have credits for around nine-tenths of their potential working lives (39 years for women with a state pension age of 60; 44 years for men and women with a state pension age of 65). A proportionally reduced state pension is available for people who do not meet the full condition, but only to a minimum of 25% (*i.e.* ten years for women with a state pension age of 60; 11 years for men and women with a state pension age of 65). As a result of the Pension Act 2007, the number of years of contributions or credits required for entitlement to a full basic state pension will be reduced to 30 with proportionally reduced state pensions available where a person has a minimum of one year's contribution or credits for people reaching state pension age on or after 6 April 2010.

Benefit calculation

Basic

The full basic state pension for a single person is GBP 90.70 per week in 2008/09, equivalent to nearly 14% of average earnings.

Earnings related

For earnings between the lower earnings limit (GBP 4 680 per year in 2008/09) and the low earnings threshold (GBP 13 500), the replacement rate is 40% of the difference. The lower earnings limit is worth nearly 14% of average earnings while the low earnings threshold is 40%. This also applies to people covered by credits. This is equivalent to treating people earning below the low earnings threshold as if they had earned at this level. Over the next range, the replacement rate is 10%, ending at GBP 31 100 in 2008/09. Between this threshold and the ceiling, the replacement rate is 20%. The ceiling is GBP 40 040 in 2008/09. The upper threshold is worth around 93% of average earnings and the ceiling is 119% of average earnings.

The benefit value is calculated on average lifetime salary, with earlier years' pay uprated in line with average economy-wide earnings. The benefit is then price-indexed after retirement.

As a result of the Pensions Act 2007, from 2010 the income bands will reduce to two. Between the lower earnings limit and the low earnings threshold, the replacement rate will be 40% of the difference. Between the lower earnings threshold and the ceiling, the replacement rate will be 10%. From a date to be set, Band 1 income will provide a flat-rate entitlement of GBP 1.60 a week for each qualifying year (in 2008/09 earnings terms). Furthermore, from April 2009 the cap on accruals (the ceiling) is frozen through the introduction of an upper accrual point at GBP 770 a week (GBP 40 040 per year).

Contracting out

Some 35% of employees are "contracted-out" of the state second pension (the additional pension element of the State scheme), into an occupational pension scheme (provided by an employer), a personal pension or a stakeholder plan (both provided by financial-services companies). Occupational schemes are mainly defined benefit and whilst there was a rapid growth in defined-contribution occupational plans, numbers have since fallen. In broad terms, for employees who leave the state system (contract out) into a private pension arrangement, both they and their employer pay a lower rate of National Insurance contributions. For a contracted-out defined-contribution pension plan, the employer and employee continue to pay the full rate of National Insurance contributions (although there is a small reduction in the case of defined-contribution occupational plans), but the State makes a contribution to the plan, related to the employee's age, referred to as the rebate. Schemes which are contracted-out on defined-benefit basis must meet a minimum benefit standard as set out in the Reference Scheme Test. The Pensions Act 2007 includes measures to abolish contracting-out on a defined-contribution basis, expected to happen from 2012.

The government sets the social security rebates, reviewed every five years, on the advice of the Government Actuary. The rebates are designed to broadly reflect the value of the state pension rights forgone as a result of being contracted-out.

Targeted

The Pension Credit, introduced in 2003, is a tax free weekly benefit for people aged 60 or over who are living on low incomes and guarantees all pensioners an income above a certain level. The Pension Credit is an income-related benefit and is not based on National Insurance contributions. There are two elements to the Pension Credit, the guarantee credit and the savings credit. The guarantee credit ensures a minimum level of income by providing financial help for people aged 60 and over whose income is below the standard minimum guarantee amount. In 2008/09 this was GBP 124.05 for individuals and GBP 189.35 for couples (these amounts may be higher for people with severe disabilities, caring responsibilities or certain housing costs).

The savings credit is an extra amount for people aged 65 or over who have made modest provision for their retirement. It is designed to reduce the effective withdrawal rate of benefits from 100% under its predecessors to 40%. People, whose income (excluding any guarantee credit) is below their guarantee credit minimum guarantee and above the savings credit threshold, GBP 91.20 for individuals and GBP 145.80 for couples respectively in 2008/09, receive 60% of the difference between their income and the threshold up to a maximum of GBP 19.71 for individuals and GBP 26.13 for couples, respectively. For people with incomes above their guarantee credit minimum guarantee (that is they are not entitled to the guarantee credit), the maximum savings credit is reduced by 40% of their income over their guarantee level.

The qualifying age for Pension Credit will increase in line with the rise in state pension age between 2010 and 2020.

Voluntary private pension

The government will also introduce a new national pension savings scheme. Using the same principles as New Zealand's KiwiSaver, this will have a default contribution rate of 8%, which is a little below the 9% average contribution rate to existing defined-contribution occupational schemes. The modelling assumes a contribution of 8% of earnings.

Variant careers

Early retirement

A state pension will not be paid before state pension age.

Late retirement

Until April 2005, deferral of the state pension was possible for up to five years after state pension age. This earned an increment of about 7.4% for each year. From April 2005, the time limit for deferral was removed and the increment increased to about 10.4% for each full year of deferral. Also, it is possible instead to take a taxable lump sum provided the deferral has been for a minimum of 12 consecutive months. The lump sum is made up of the state pension foregone during the deferral period, plus interest which is guaranteed to be at least two percentage points above the repo rate (the Bank of England base rate). The choice has to be made when the state pension is eventually claimed.

Childcare

Both tiers of the public pension scheme (basic state pension and state second pension) provide protection for periods of child care. This covers both people not in paid work and those working but earning below the lower earnings limit who therefore do not contribute to the system. For the basic state pension, this is called Home Responsibilities Protection (HRP), and covers years spent caring for at least one child under 16. HRP reduces the number of years required for a full pension so that, with sufficient HRP, only 20 years' work (including periods when national insurance contributions may be credited) is required to receive the full basic state pension. For the state second pension, years caring for a child under age six are credited; caring parents are deemed to have earnings at the low earnings threshold: GBP 13 500 per year in 2008/09.

As a result of the Pensions Act 2007, people attaining state pension age after 2010 will able to build up entitlement to state second pension if they are caring for children up to the age of 12.

Unemployment

Periods of unemployment on insurance or assistance benefits are credited for the basic state pension. There are no credits for periods on these benefits for the state second pension.

Pension modelling results: United Kingdom

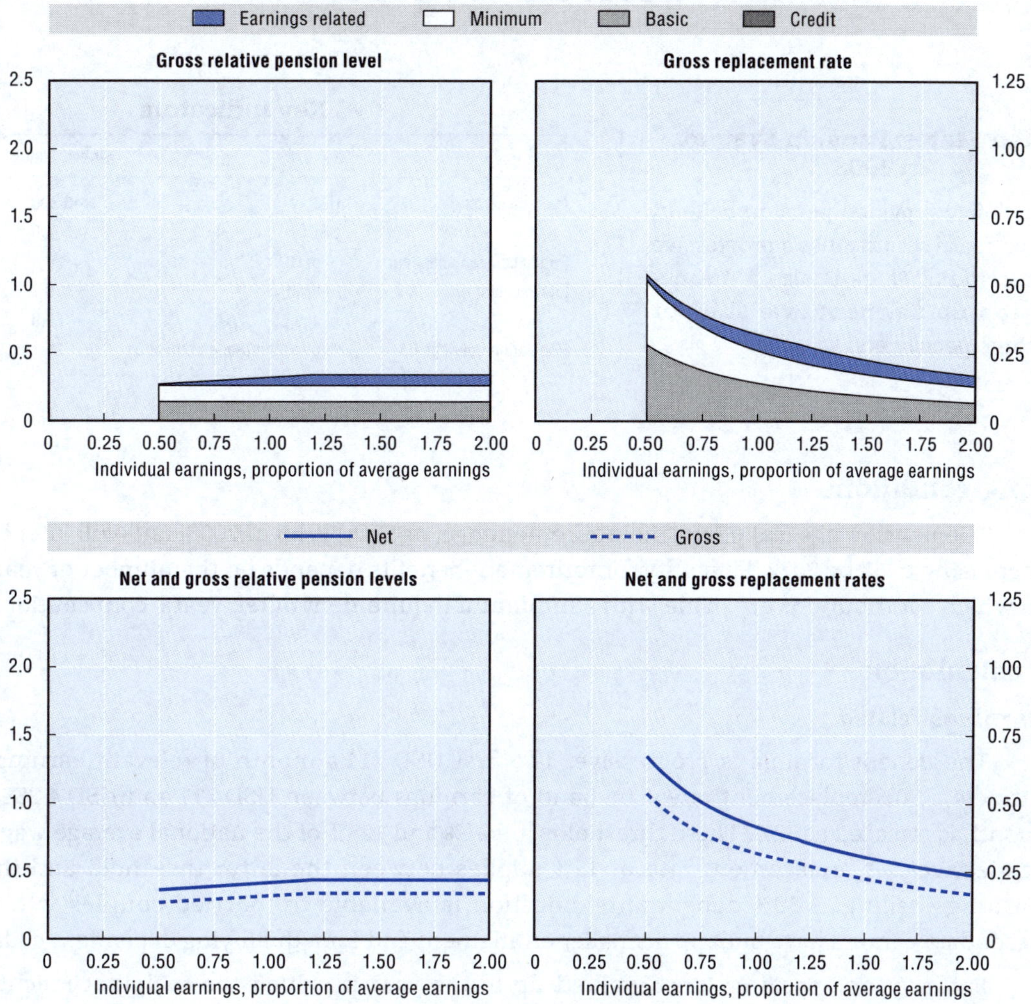

Men *Women (where different)*	Median earner	Individual earnings, multiple of average				
		0.5	0.75	1	1.5	2
Gross relative pension level	30.0	26.9	29.4	31.9	33.8	33.8
(% average gross earnings)						
Net relative pension level	39.5	36.2	38.9	41.5	43.6	43.6
(% net average earnings)						
Gross replacement rate	37.0	53.8	39.2	31.9	22.6	16.9
(% individual gross earnings)						
Net replacement rate	48.0	67.5	50.6	41.5	30.5	23.9
(% individual net earnings)						
Gross pension wealth	5.3	7.6	5.6	4.5	3.2	2.4
(multiple of individual gross earnings)	*6.2*	*9.0*	*6.5*	*5.3*	*3.8*	*2.8*
Net pension wealth	5.2	7.6	5.5	4.4	3.1	2.3
(multiple of individual gross earnings)	*6.0*	*9.0*	*6.4*	*5.1*	*3.6*	*2.7*

StatLink http://dx.doi.org/10.1787/888932372051

United States

United States: Pension system in 2008

The publicly provided pension benefit, known as social security, has a progressive benefit formula. There is also a means-tested top-up payment available for low-income pensioners.

Key indicators

		United States	OECD
Average earnings	USD	40 300	40 600
	USD	40 300	40 600
Public pension spending	% of GDP	6.0	7.0
Life expectancy	At birth	79.1	78.9
	At age 65	83.9	83.1
Population over age 65	% of working-age population	21.1	23.6

Qualifying conditions

The pension age (called normal retirement age, or NRA) is 66 in 2008, and will later be increasing to 67 by 2022. Eligibility for retirement benefits depends on the number of years in which contributions are made with a minimum requirement of ten years' contributions.

Benefit calculation

Earnings related

The benefit formula is progressive. The first USD 711 a month of relevant earnings attracts a 90% replacement rate. The band of earnings between USD 711 and USD 4 288 a month is replaced at 32%. These thresholds are 21% and 128% of the national average wage, respectively. A replacement rate of 15% applies between the latter threshold and the earnings ceiling. A 50% dependants' addition is available to married couples where secondary earners have built up a smaller entitlement and for a qualifying dependent child.

Earlier years' earnings are revalued up to the year in which the recipient reaches age 60 in line with growth in economy-wide average earnings. There is no adjustment of earnings for years after age 60. The basic benefit is computed for payment at age 62. Thereafter, the basic benefit is adjusted in line with prices. The benefit is based on the career average earnings for the 35 highest years of earnings, after revaluing, including years with zero earnings if needed to total 35 years.

The earnings ceiling for both contributions and benefits is USD 102 000 a year, corresponding to 253% of the national average wage updated annually in line with growth in economy-wide earnings.

Pensions in payment are adjusted in line with price increases.

Minimum

There is a minimum pension under social security. People earning less than a special minimum primary insurance amount are given a minimum pension that depends on their lifetime total years of coverage, varying between USD 35 for 11 years' coverage and USD 721 for 30 years' coverage. The threshold for this minimum pension was USD 11 385 in 2008, or 28% of the national average wage. (The threshold is defined formally as 15% of the "old law" contribution and benefit base.) The minimum pension does not affect the modelling results because the earnings range affected is below that presented.

Targeted

The United States provide a means-tested benefit for the elderly, known as supplemental security income. Individuals without an eligible spouse over the age of 65 can be eligible for up to USD 7 644 a year depending on assets and other income. The benefit rate for cases where both members of a couple are eligible is USD 11 482 (50% higher than the rate for singles). These benefit rates are equivalent to around 19% and 28% of the national average wage, respectively. The benefit is indexed to price increases.

The asset tests are strict: individuals without an eligible spouse are limited to USD 2 000 worth of assets and eligible couples to USD 3 000, excluding personal belongings, a home, a car, funeral insurance and life insurance (the last two up to USD 1 500 in value). There is a small (USD 20 a month) "disregard" in calculating the entitlement. The benefit is then withdrawn at a 100% rate against income above this level.

The analysis is complicated by the fact that states can supplement the federally determined minimum. While eight states pay only the federal minimum, 29 administer their own system, nine offer supplements that are operated solely by the federal Social Security Administration (SSA), and six offer supplements administered by both the state and SSA. The average supplemental payment in the 15 states with SSA administration is 29% of the maximum federal benefit for single pensioners and 50% for couples. Note that the modelling does not include these additional payments.

Voluntary private pension

There is an additional voluntary pension which is assumed to be defined contribution. The contribution rate is assumed to be 9%.

Variant careers

Early retirement

Early retirement is possible from 62, subject to an actuarial reduction. For each year of retirement before the normal age, the benefit is reduced by 6.75%. However, after three years, the reduction falls to 5%. This applies to retirees with a NRA of over 65.

Late retirement

Initial receipt of the pension may be deferred until after NRA, and credit is given for deferment up to age 70. The actuarial increment for those attaining age 62 in 2008 and later is 8% for each year deferred.

It is also possible to combine work and pension receipt subject to an earnings test. For beneficiaries who are receiving benefits in a year before the year they reach their NRA, the pension is reduced by 50% of earnings in excess of USD 13 560. For workers who have reached their NRA, there is no benefit reduction based on earnings.

Childcare

There are no provisions for credits during periods of childcare (except for workers who become disabled at younger ages, who may drop years of child care from their benefit computation).

Unemployment

There are no provisions for credits during periods of unemployment. However periods of unemployment may be omitted from the calculation of earnings for benefit purposes in many cases as only the highest 35 years of earnings are considered. Periods of disability are omitted from the 35 years of earnings considered.

Pension modelling results: United States

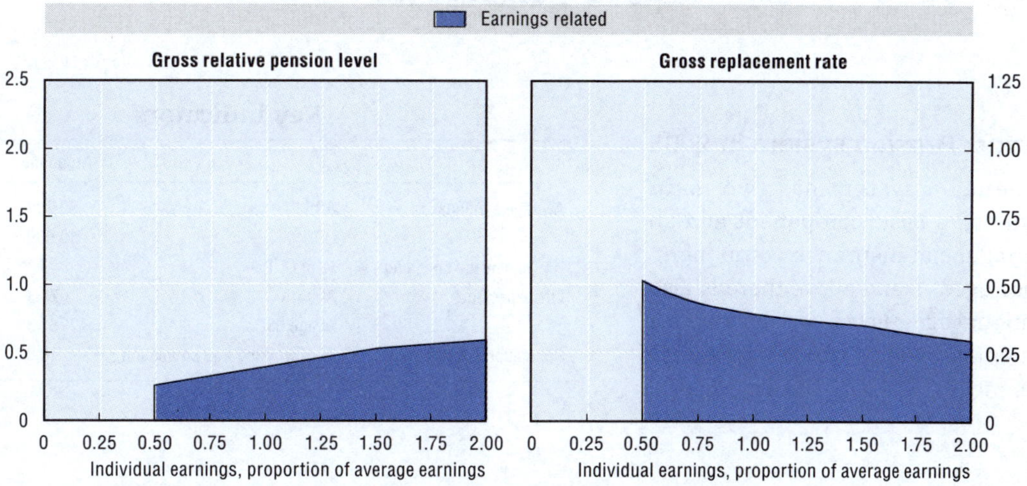

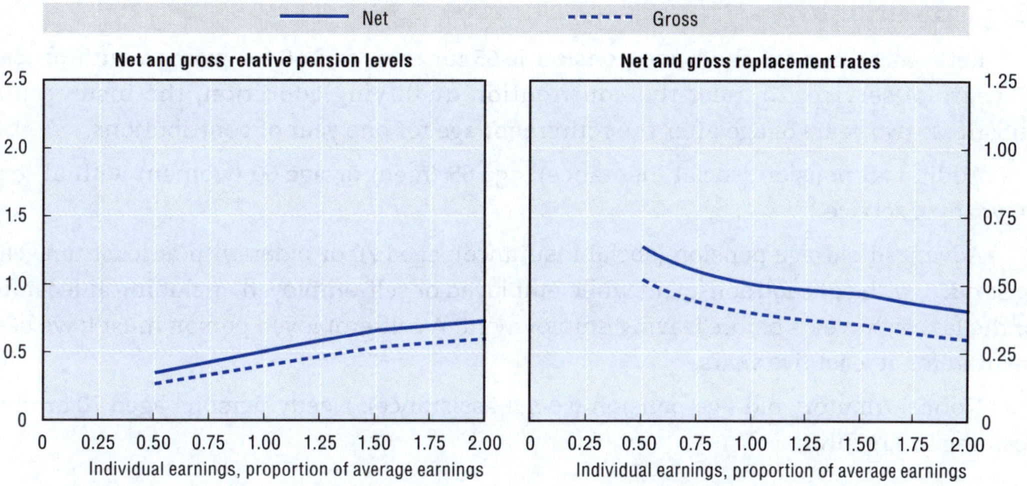

Men *Women (where different)*	Median earner	Individual earnings, multiple of average				
		0.5	0.75	1	1.5	2
Gross relative pension level	34.3	25.9	32.6	39.4	53.0	59.5
(% average gross earnings)						
Net relative pension level	43.9	33.9	41.9	50.0	65.5	72.8
(% net average earnings)						
Gross replacement rate	42.3	51.7	43.5	39.4	35.3	29.7
(% individual gross earnings)						
Net replacement rate	53.4	63.8	54.7	50.0	46.6	40.3
(% individual net earnings)						
Gross pension wealth	6.3	7.6	6.4	5.8	5.2	4.4
(multiple of individual gross earnings)	*7.2*	*8.9*	*7.5*	*6.8*	*6.0*	*5.1*
Net pension wealth	6.0	7.6	6.2	5.6	4.9	4.1
(multiple of individual gross earnings)	*7.0*	*8.8*	*7.2*	*6.5*	*5.6*	*4.7*

StatLink http://dx.doi.org/10.1787/888932372070

Argentina

Argentina: Pension system in 2008

The pension system has two main components: a basic component and an additional social insurance component. For those aged 70 and above there is also an additional age-related social insurance component, as well as a social assistance component.

Key indicators

		Argentina	OECD
Average earnings	ARS	33 700	128 700
	USD	10 600	40 600
Public pension spending	% of GDP		7.0
Life expectancy	At birth	75.3	78.9
	At age 65	81.8	83.1
Population over age 65	% of working-age population	18.9	23.6

Qualifying conditions

Retirement age for the basic pension is 65 for men and 60 for women with at least 30 years of service. To meet the contribution qualifying condition, the insured may substitute two years of age after the retirement age for one year of contributions.

Additional pension (social insurance): age 65 (men) or age 60 (women) with at least 30 years of service.

Advanced old-age pension (social insurance): aged 70 or older with at least ten years of service, with contributions paid while employed or self-employed, including at least five of the last eight years before leaving employment. A self-employed person must have been insured for at least five years.

Noncontributory old-age pension (social assistance): Needy persons aged 70 or older residing in Argentina.

Benefit calculation

Old-age pension

The monthly pension is ARS 326.

Additional pension (social insurance)

The monthly pension is 1.5% of the insured's average adjusted monthly earnings in the last ten years (weighted average adjusted amounts for all periods for self-employed persons) for each year of lifetime service.

Advanced-age old-age pension

The monthly pension is 70% of the basic old-age pension, plus the additional pension.

The minimum monthly advanced-age old-age pension is ARS 770.

The combined minimum monthly old-age pension (the sum of all contributory pensions) is ARS 770.

The maximum monthly old-age pension (sum of the basic and social insurance pensions) is ARS 5 646.

Pensions are paid monthly with a 13th payment equal to the regular monthly payment divided in half and paid in June and December. Benefits are adjusted automatically in March and September based on changes in tax revenue, wage indexes, and revenue of the National Social Security Administration.

Noncontributory old-age pension (social assistance)

The monthly pension is ARS 539 (70% of the minimum pension of ARS 770). Additional benefits may be paid for dependents under Family Allowances, below.

Pension modelling results: Argentina

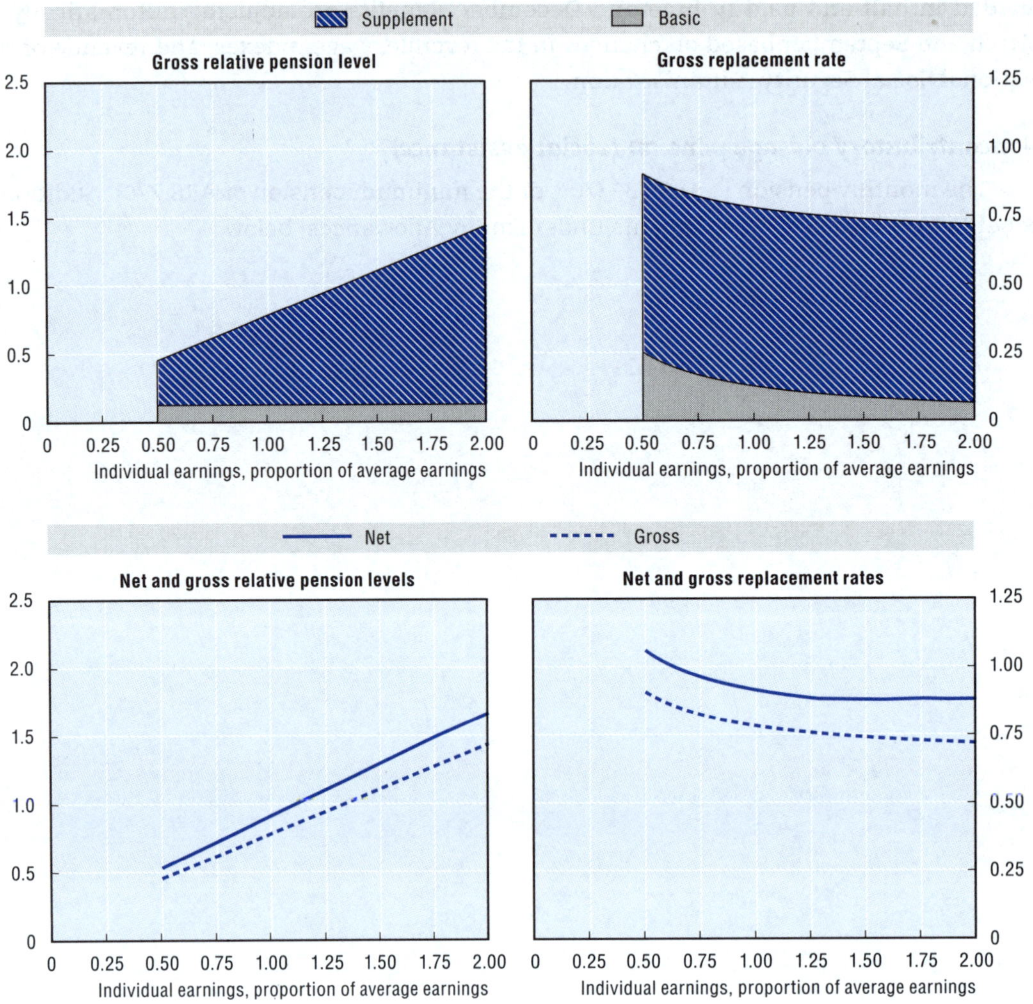

Men *Women (where different)*	Median earner	Individual earnings, multiple of average				
		0.5	0.75	1	1.5	2
Gross relative pension level	65.7	45.3	61.7	78.1	110.9	143.7
(% average gross earnings)	*59.8*	*41.7*	*56.3*	*70.8*	*100.0*	*129.1*
Net relative pension level	76.7	53.0	72.1	91.3	129.6	166.2
(% net average earnings)	*69.8*	*48.7*	*65.8*	*82.8*	*116.8*	*150.8*
Gross replacement rate	81.1	90.7	82.3	78.1	73.9	71.8
(% individual gross earnings)	*73.8*	*83.4*	*75.0*	*70.8*	*66.6*	*64.5*
Net replacement rate	94.7	106.0	96.2	91.3	87.8	88.0
(% individual net earnings)	*86.2*	*97.5*	*87.7*	*82.8*	*79.1*	*79.8*
Gross pension wealth	11.8	13.2	12.0	11.4	10.8	10.5
(multiple of individual gross earnings)	*15.1*	*17.0*	*15.3*	*14.5*	*13.6*	*13.2*
Net pension wealth	11.5	12.8	11.6	11.0	10.4	10.0
(multiple of individual gross earnings)	*14.6*	*16.5*	*14.9*	*14.0*	*13.2*	*12.8*

StatLink http://dx.doi.org/10.1787/888932371291

Brazil

Brazil: Pension system in 2008

The *Regime Geral de Previdência Social* (RGPS), covers the private sector workforce. It is financed through payroll taxes, shared by the employer and the employee, revenues from sales taxes and federal transfers that cover shortfalls of the system. It is a mandatory, pay-as-you-go financed single-pillar scheme, which is operated by the National Social Security Institute.

Key indicators

		Brazil	OECD
Average earnings	BRL	16 500	74 500
	USD	9 000	40 600
Public pension spending	% of GDP		7.0
Life expectancy	At birth	72.4	78.9
	At age 65	82.5	83.1
Population over age 65	% of working-age population	11.3	23.6

Qualifying conditions

Private-sector employees are entitled to retire with a full pension at age 65 for men and 60 for women if they have a contribution record of at least 15 years. Alternatively, it is possible to retire after having contributed to social security for 35 years for men and 30 years for women, irrespective of the retiree's age. For the models we assume retirement for men at 55 and at 50 for women.

Benefit calculation

Old-age pension

For persons first insured after 28 November 1999, average earnings for benefit calculation purposes are based on the best 80% of total monthly earnings, multiplied by the *Factor Previdenciario*. The *Factor Previdenciario* is not applied to arduous work with 15, 20, or 25 years contributions. The *Factor Previdenciario* is an actuarial coefficient based on the insured's contribution rate, contribution period, age, and life expectancy. The minimum monthly earnings for benefit calculation purposes are equal to the legal monthly minimum wage (BRL 465). The maximum monthly earnings for benefit calculation purposes are BRL 2 894.28. The minimum pension for minimum monthly contributions is equal to the legal monthly minimum wage.

Contributions vary by earnings level at 8% for monthly earnings up to BRL 965.67, 9% for earnings from BRL 965.68 to BRL 1 609.45 and 11% for earnings from BRL 1 609.46 to BRL 3 218.90.

There are thirteen payments a year with benefits adjusted annually according to changes in the consumer price index.

Variant careers

Early retirement

Early retirement is allowed at age 53 with at least 30 years of contributions (men) or age 48 with at least 25 years of contributions (women).

Late retirement

Pensions can be claimed along with employment, and there is therefore no incentive to delay payment.

Pension modelling results: Brazil

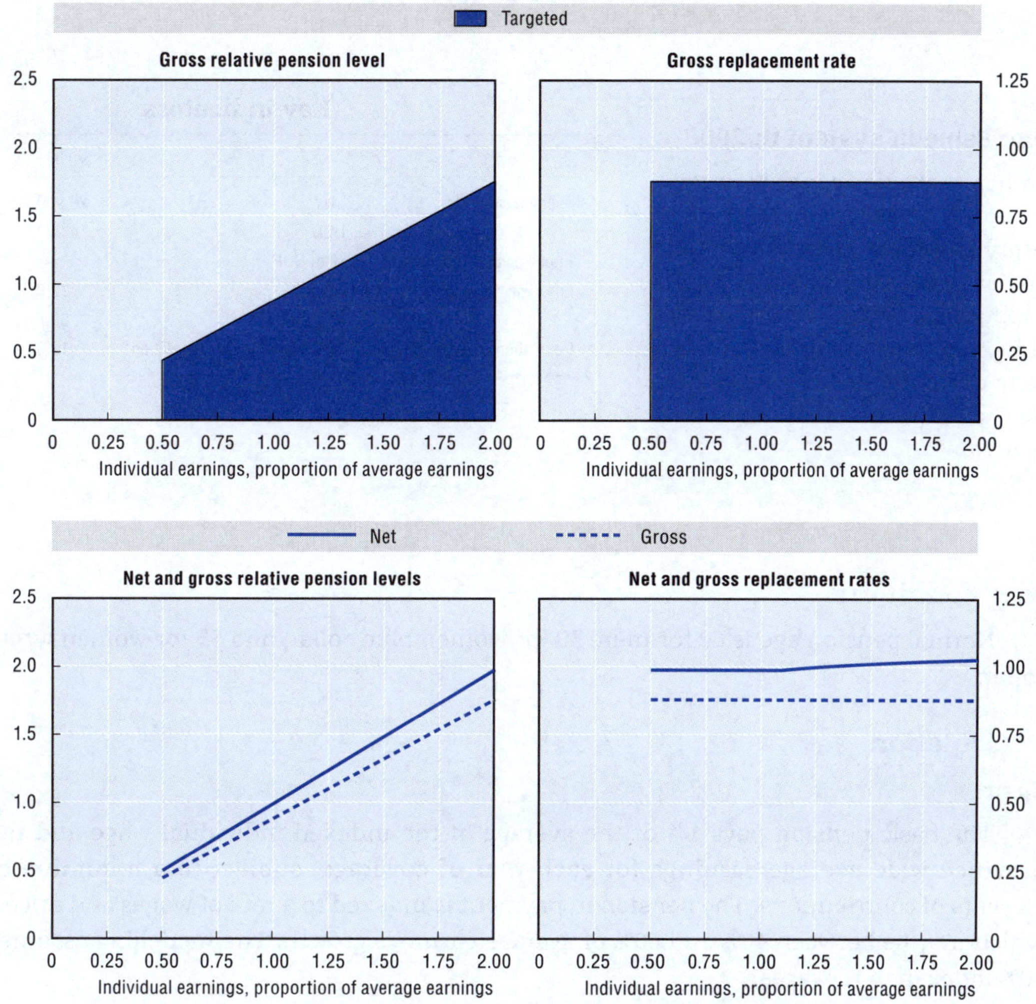

Men *Women (where different)*	Median earner	Individual earnings, multiple of average				
		0.5	0.75	1	1.5	2
Gross relative pension level	69.6	43.0	64.5	85.9	128.9	171.9
(% average gross earnings)	*51.6*	*31.9*	*47.8*	*63.7*	*95.6*	*127.5*
Net relative pension level	78.2	48.3	72.4	96.6	144.9	193.1
(% net average earnings)	*58.0*	*35.8*	*53.7*	*71.6*	*107.4*	*143.2*
Gross replacement rate	85.9	85.9	85.9	85.9	85.9	85.9
(% individual gross earnings)	*63.7*	*63.7*	*63.7*	*63.7*	*63.7*	*63.7*
Net replacement rate	96.6	96.6	96.6	96.6	98.9	100.4
(% individual net earnings)	*71.6*	*71.6*	*71.6*	*71.6*	*73.3*	*74.5*
Gross pension wealth	22.2	22.2	22.2	22.2	22.2	22.2
(multiple of individual gross earnings)	*22.2*	*22.2*	*22.2*	*22.2*	*22.2*	*22.2*
Net pension wealth	22.2	22.2	22.2	22.2	22.2	22.2
(multiple of individual gross earnings)	*22.2*	*22.2*	*22.2*	*22.2*	*22.2*	*22.2*

StatLink http://dx.doi.org/10.1787/888932371367

China

China: Pension system in 2008

China has a two-tier pension system, consisting of a basic pension and a mandatory employee contribution to a second-tier plan. This system, which was introduced in 1998, was significantly revised in 2006. It covers urban workers and many of the parameters depend on province-wide (rather than national) average earnings.

Key indicators

		China	OECD
Average earnings	CNY	28 900	282 100
	USD	4 200	40 600
Public pension spending	% of GDP		7.0
Life expectancy	At birth	73.0	78.9
	At age 65	80.7	83.1
Population over age 65	% of working-age population	12.6	23.6

Qualifying conditions

Normal pension age is 60 for men, 50 for women blue collar, and 55 for women white collar.

Benefit calculation

Basic

The basic pension pays 1% of the average of the indexed individual wage and the province-wide average earnings for each year of coverage, subject to a minimum of 15 years of contributions. The pension in payment is indexed to a mix of wages and prices, which may be between 40% and 60% of average earnings growth. The modelling assumes 50% indexation to wages.

Defined contribution (funded or notional accounts)

The second-tier system comprises individual accounts. In addition to the north-eastern provinces (Liaoning, Jilin and Heilongjiang), a further 8 have funded individual account systems. In other cases, the accounts are largely notional and are credited with a notional interest rate.

Employees pay 8% of wages to the individual account system. The accumulated balance in the fund or the notional account is converted into a stream of pension payments at the time of retirement by dividing the balance by a government-determined annuity factor, depending on individual retirement age and average national life expectancy. In all provinces, these annuity factors for both males and females (for monthly benefits) are:

Age	40	45	50	55	60	65	70
Factor	233	216	195	170	139	101	56

Pensions in payment are indexed to a mix of wages and prices (see the description of the basic pension above).

Variant careers

Early retirement

It is possible to claim pensions at 55 for men and 50 for women if the individual is engaged in physical work. If the individual is totally disabled, pensions will commence at 50 for men and 45 for women subject to 15 years of contributions.

Late retirement

It is possible to defer pension payments until after normal pension age, but the pension benefit is not valorised.

Pension modelling results: China

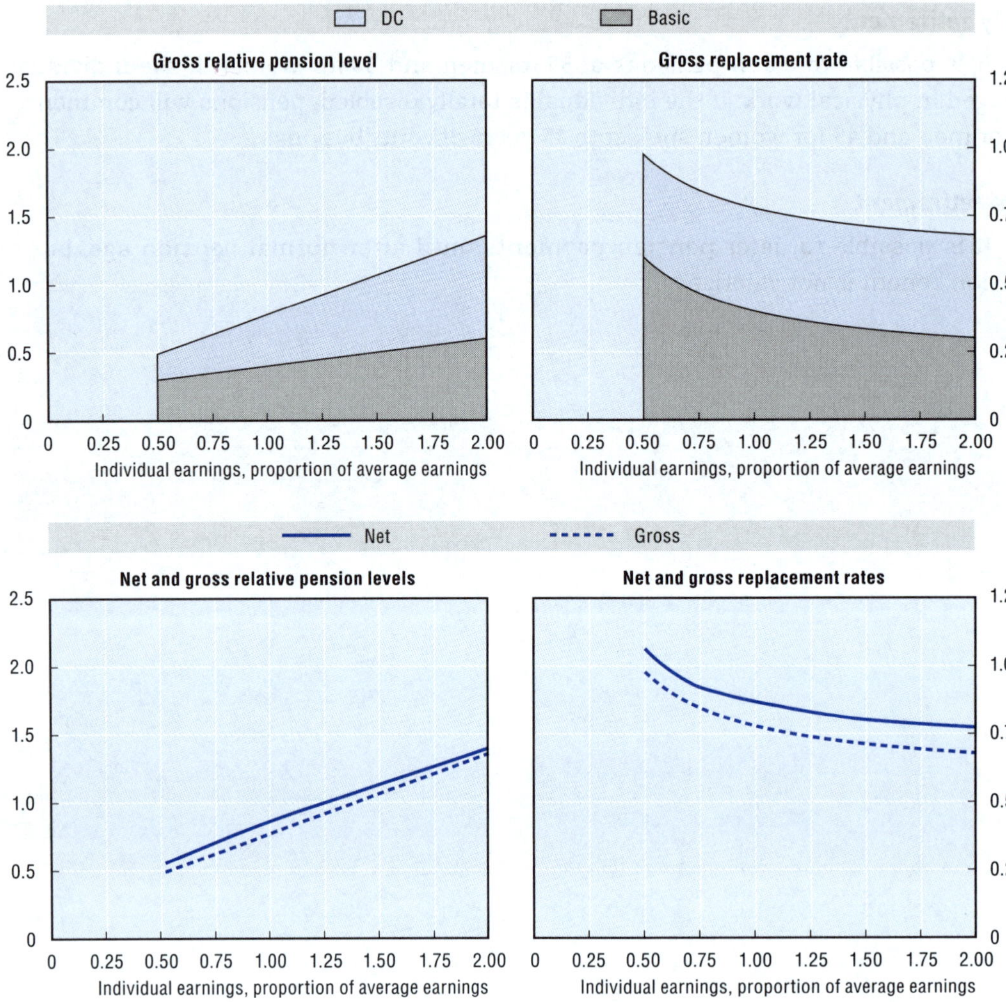

Men *Women (where different)*	Median earner	Individual earnings, multiple of average				
		0.5	0.75	1	1.5	2
Gross relative pension level	66.9	48.9	63.4	77.9	106.8	135.7
(% average gross earnings)	*52.7*	*39.2*	*50.1*	*61.0*	*82.7*	*104.5*
Net relative pension level	75.8	55.5	71.9	86.8	113.4	139.6
(% net average earnings)	*59.8*	*44.5*	*56.8*	*69.2*	*91.5*	*111.3*
Gross replacement rate	82.5	97.9	84.5	77.9	71.2	67.9
(% individual gross earnings)	*65.1*	*78.5*	*66.8*	*61.0*	*55.2*	*52.2*
Net replacement rate	90.6	106.4	92.1	86.8	80.1	77.3
(% individual net earnings)	*71.5*	*85.3*	*72.8*	*69.2*	*64.7*	*61.6*
Gross pension wealth	15.8	18.7	16.1	14.9	13.6	13.0
(multiple of individual gross earnings)	*16.6*	*20.0*	*17.0*	*15.5*	*14.0*	*13.3*
Net pension wealth	15.8	18.7	16.1	14.6	12.7	11.8
(multiple of individual gross earnings)	*16.6*	*20.0*	*17.0*	*15.5*	*13.7*	*12.5*

StatLink http://dx.doi.org/10.1787/888932371424

India

India: Pension system in 2008

Workers are covered under the earnings-related employee pension scheme and defined-contribution employee provident fund administered by the Employees Provident Fund Organisation (EPFO) and other employer managed funds.

Key indicators

		India	OECD
Average earnings	INR	154 400	1 766 300
	USD	3 500	40 600
Public pension spending	% of GDP		7.0
Life expectancy	at birth	63.6	78.9
	at age 65	78.7	83.1
Population over age 65	% of working-age population	9.0	23.6

Qualifying conditions

Normal pension age for earnings-related pension scheme is 58 with minimum of ten years of contribution and for earnings-related provident fund schemes, it is 55 years.

The average annual earnings of covered workers were estimated to be INR 154 418 in 2007.

Benefit calculation

Employees Provident Fund Scheme (EPF)

The employee contributes 12% of his monthly salary towards this fund and the employer matches this contribution. 3.67% of the employer's share goes towards the EPF. This combined 15.67% accumulates as a lump sum.

There is no annuity and full accumulations are paid on retirement from service after attaining 55 years of age. For comparison with other countries, for replacement rate purposes the pension is shown as a price-indexed annuity based on sex-specific mortality rates.

Employees Pension Scheme (EPS)

Of the 12% contribution payable by the employer as mentioned above, 8.33% is diverted to EPS and the Central Government contributes a subsidy of 1.17% of the salary into the EPS. This accumulation is used to pay various pension benefits on retirement or early termination. The kind of pension a member gets under the scheme depends upon the age at which they retire and the number of years of eligible service.

Monthly pension = (pensionable salary × pensionable service)/70

The maximum possible replacement rate is roughly 50%. To obtain the maximum benefit, a member would not only need to be in the scheme for 35 years, but would also need to opt for contributions at higher salary at the time of joining the scheme. This option cannot be exercised retrospectively. Otherwise, there is a ceiling to contributions of INR 6 500.

Variant careers

Early retirement

The EPS can be claimed from age 50 with ten years of contribution and the benefits are reduced by 3% per year of early retirement. If a member leaves his job before rendering at least ten years of service, he is entitled to a withdrawal benefit. The amount he can withdraw is a proportion of his monthly salary at the date of exit from employment. This proportion depends on the number of years of eligible services he has rendered. No pension is payable in cases where there is a break in service before ten years.

In case of EPF, there are multiple scenarios which allow for early access to the accumulation. Partial withdrawals relate to marriage, housing advance, financing life insurance policy, illness of members/family members, withdrawals are also permitted one year before retirement, etc. In addition to various permitted partial withdrawals, employees can close their account and withdraw the full corpus in case they move from one employer to another or decide to retire early.

No gratuity can be claimed before five years of service.

Late retirement

It is not possible to delay claiming pension after normal pension age.

Pension modelling results: India

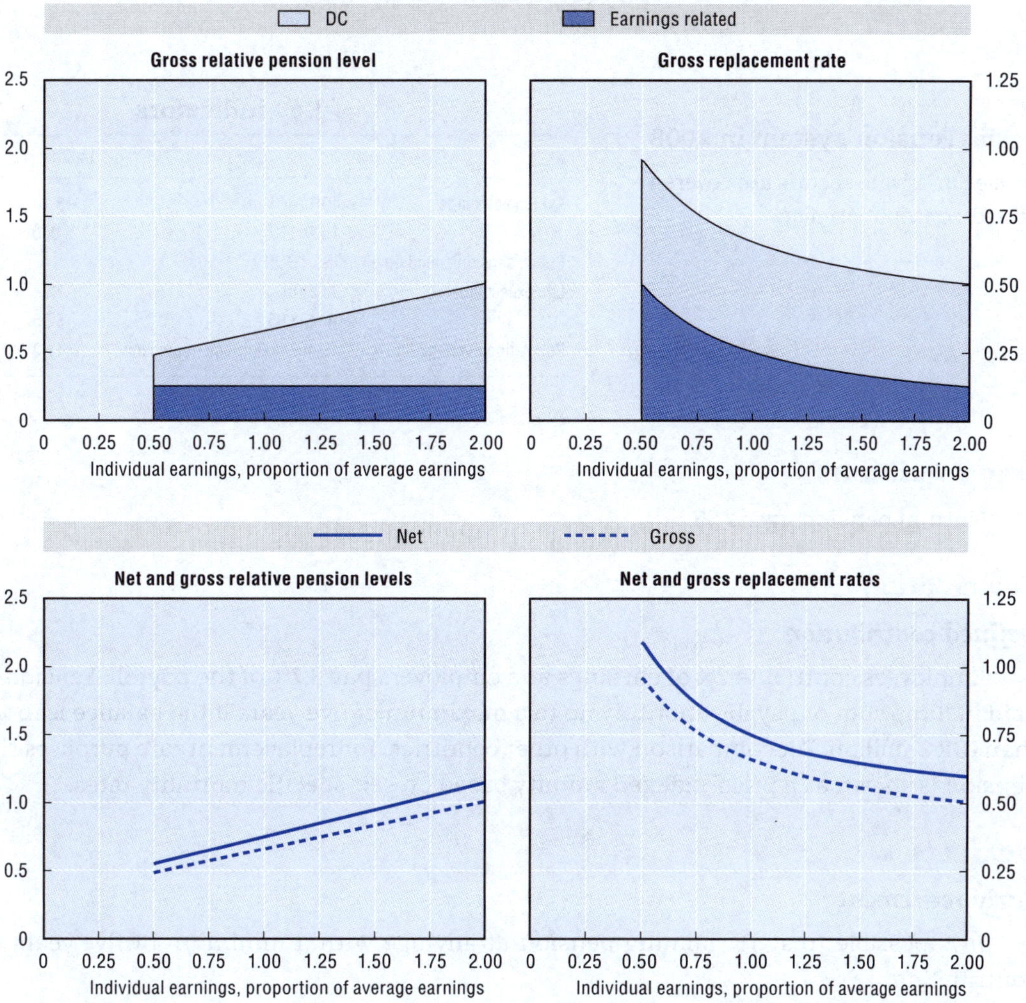

Men *Women (where different)*	Median earner	Individual earnings, multiple of average				
		0.5	0.75	1	1.5	2
Gross relative pension level	58.7	47.6	56.6	65.2	82.6	99.9
(% average gross earnings)	*55.4*	*45.4*	*53.6*	*61.4*	*77.0*	*92.7*
Net relative pension level	66.7	54.1	64.3	74.1	93.8	113.5
(% net average earnings)	*63.0*	*51.6*	*60.9*	*69.8*	*87.5*	*105.3*
Gross replacement rate	72.4	95.2	75.4	65.2	55.0	49.9
(% individual gross earnings)	*68.4*	*90.9*	*71.4*	*61.4*	*51.4*	*46.3*
Net replacement rate	82.3	108.2	85.7	74.1	63.9	59.2
(% individual net earnings)	*77.8*	*103.3*	*81.1*	*69.8*	*58.8*	*54.3*
Gross pension wealth	12.4	16.1	12.9	11.2	9.5	8.7
(multiple of individual gross earnings)	*13.0*	*17.1*	*13.5*	*11.7*	*9.8*	*8.9*
Net pension wealth	12.4	16.1	12.9	11.2	9.5	8.7
(multiple of individual gross earnings)	*13.0*	*17.1*	*13.5*	*11.7*	*9.8*	*8.9*

StatLink http://dx.doi.org/10.1787/888932371614

Indonesia

Indonesia: Pension system in 2008

Employees in private sectors are covered by a defined-contribution plan.

Key indicators

		Indonesia	OECD
Average earnings	IDR (million)	13.10	393.78
	USD	9 000	40 600
Public pension spending	% of GDP		7.0
Life expectancy	At birth	72.4	78.9
	At age 65	82.5	83.1
Population over age 65	% of working-age population	11.3	23.6

Qualifying conditions

Normal pension age is 55.

Benefit calculation

Defined contribution

Employees contribute 2% of earnings and employers pay 3.7% of the payroll. Pension is paid in lump sum or payable monthly up to a maximum of five years if the balance is more than IDR 3 million. For comparison with other countries, for replacement rate purposes the pension is shown as a price-indexed annuity based on sex-specific mortality rates.

Variant careers

Early retirement

It is possible to start claiming pension at any age with a minimum of five years of contribution.

Late retirement

It is not possible to start claiming pension after normal pension age.

Pension modelling results: Indonesia

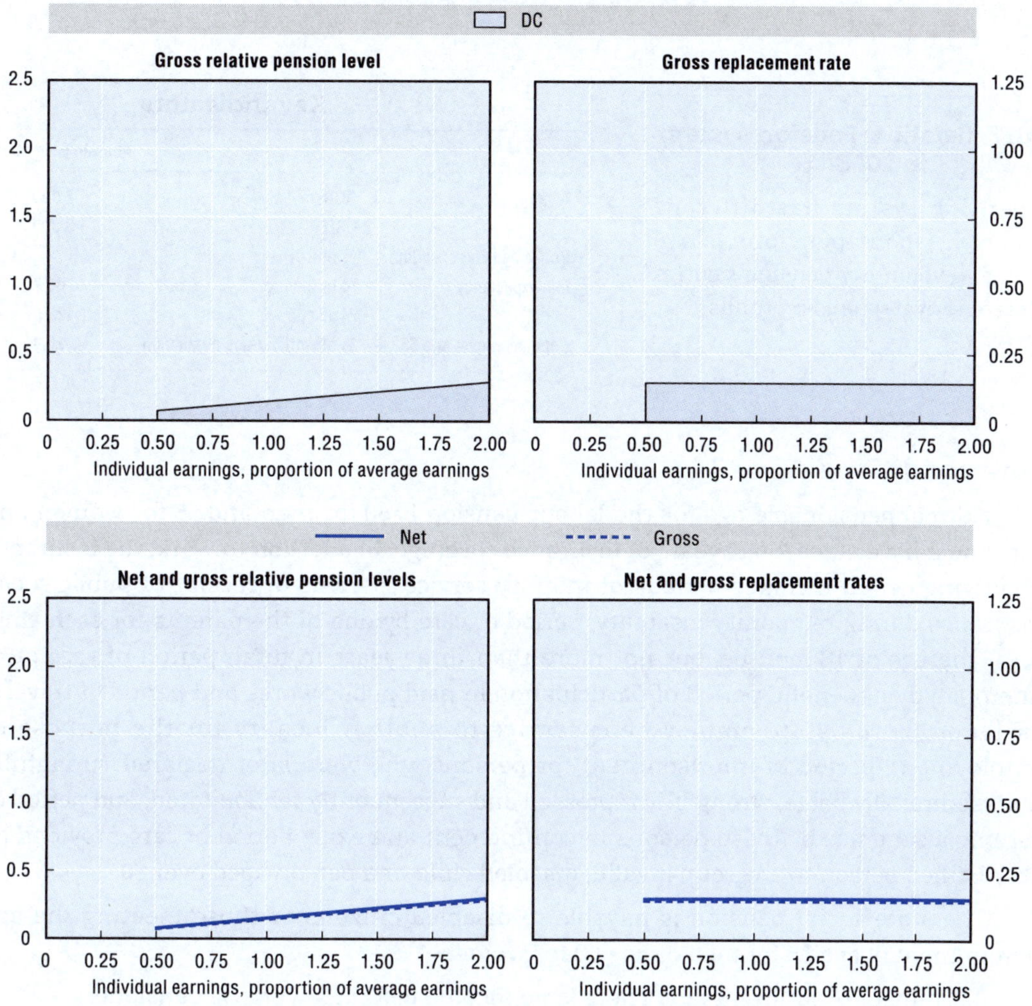

Men *Women (where different)*	Median earner	Individual earnings, multiple of average				
		0.5	0.75	1	1.5	2
Gross relative pension level	11.4	7.0	10.5	14.1	21.1	28.1
(% average gross earnings)	*10.1*	*6.2*	*9.3*	*12.4*	*18.7*	*24.9*
Net relative pension level	12.1	7.4	11.2	14.9	22.3	29.4
(% net average earnings)	*10.7*	*6.6*	*9.9*	*13.2*	*19.8*	*26.2*
Gross replacement rate	14.1	14.1	14.1	14.1	14.1	14.1
(% individual gross earnings)	*12.4*	*12.4*	*12.4*	*12.4*	*12.4*	*12.4*
Net replacement rate	14.8	14.7	14.8	14.9	14.9	14.8
(% individual net earnings)	*13.1*	*13.0*	*13.1*	*13.2*	*13.2*	*13.2*
Gross pension wealth	2.6	2.6	2.6	2.6	2.6	2.6
(multiple of individual gross earnings)	*2.6*	*2.6*	*2.6*	*2.6*	*2.6*	*2.6*
Net pension wealth	2.6	2.6	2.6	2.6	2.6	2.6
(multiple of individual gross earnings)	*2.6*	*2.6*	*2.6*	*2.6*	*2.6*	*2.6*

StatLink http://dx.doi.org/10.1787/888932371633

Russian Federation

Russian Federation: Pension system in 2008

The pension system has different components: labour pensions, state pensions, and voluntary pension savings at non-state (private) pension funds.

Key indicators

		Russian Federation	OECD
Average earnings	RUB	207 500	1 009 000
	USD	8 300	40 600
Public pension spending	% of GDP		7.0
Life expectancy	At birth	66.7	78.9
	At age 65	78.6	83.1
Population over age 65	% of working-age population	20.4	23.6

Qualifying conditions

Normal pensionable age for the labour pension is 60 for men and 55 for women and they must have at least five years of insurance coverage. In addition to work, the insurance qualifying period includes periods of military service, periods of receipt of public social insurance during temporary disability, period of care by one of the parents for each child until the age of 18 months, but not more than three years in total, period of receipt of unemployment benefit, period of participation in paid public works and period of travel if assigned by the state employment service to another locality for the purpose of employment, period of imprisonment for persons who were later declared wrongfully made criminally liable, wrongfully repressed and subsequently rehabilitated, and period of serving a sentence by these persons in confinement and exile, period of care provided by able-bodied person to a I group invalid, disabled child or a person aged over 80.

The state social pension is payable to disabled citizens or those meeting the age requirement of age 65 for men or age 60 for women.

Retirement is not necessary. There is no income test for a working pensioner.

Benefit calculation

Pensions are financed out of the contributions to mandatory pension insurance (for basic and insured parts of labour pension) in accordance with the Federal Law on Mandatory Pension Insurance and also from transfers from the federal budget to the budget of the Pension Fund of the Russian Federation, allocated for financing of the basic part of labour pensions, state pensions and social pensions. About 60% of such transfers are funded by revenue from the Unified Social Tax, as regards the amounts posted to the federal budget.

Labour pension

The benefit is calculated as the sum of three components:

- a basic flat-rate benefit (basic part of the labour pension, BPLP);
- a benefit based on the notional account (IPLP); and
- a benefit based on the value of the individual account (contributions plus interest, FPLP) to be paid in general beginning in 2013.

The old-age BPLPs in 2008 was RUB 1 794 for a pensioner aged 80 and younger with no dependant.

In accordance with the Law on Labour Pensions in the Russian Federation, IPLP is calculated based on the amount of the so-called pension capital accumulated as of the date application for pension at a notional funded account subject to annual indexation as prescribed by the RF Government. Starting from 1 April 2003, the annual coefficient for indexation of pension capital is 1.204.

The amount of a monthly pension is determined as quotient of the amount of pension capital on account divided by the expected period of pension payment in months. At present it is 228 months (19 years). The assigned IPLP is also subject to indexation in the order prescribed by the government.

As of today, there is no formula for the calculation of the FPLP yet.

There is no officially stated minimum or maximum monthly pension.

Variant careers

Early retirement

It is not possible to claim the pension before the normal eligibility.

Late retirement

The old-age labour pension can be deferred. If so, for calculation of the IPLP every full year of retirement deferral decreases the expected period of pension payment by one year (12 months). The minimum expected period of pension payment is 14 years (168 months). So it is inexpedient to defer application for labour pension for more than five years.

Childcare

Periods of childcare are included in the insurance coverage (qualifying period).

Unemployment

Unemployment benefits are subject to UST or mandatory pension contributions.

Pension modelling results: Russian Federation

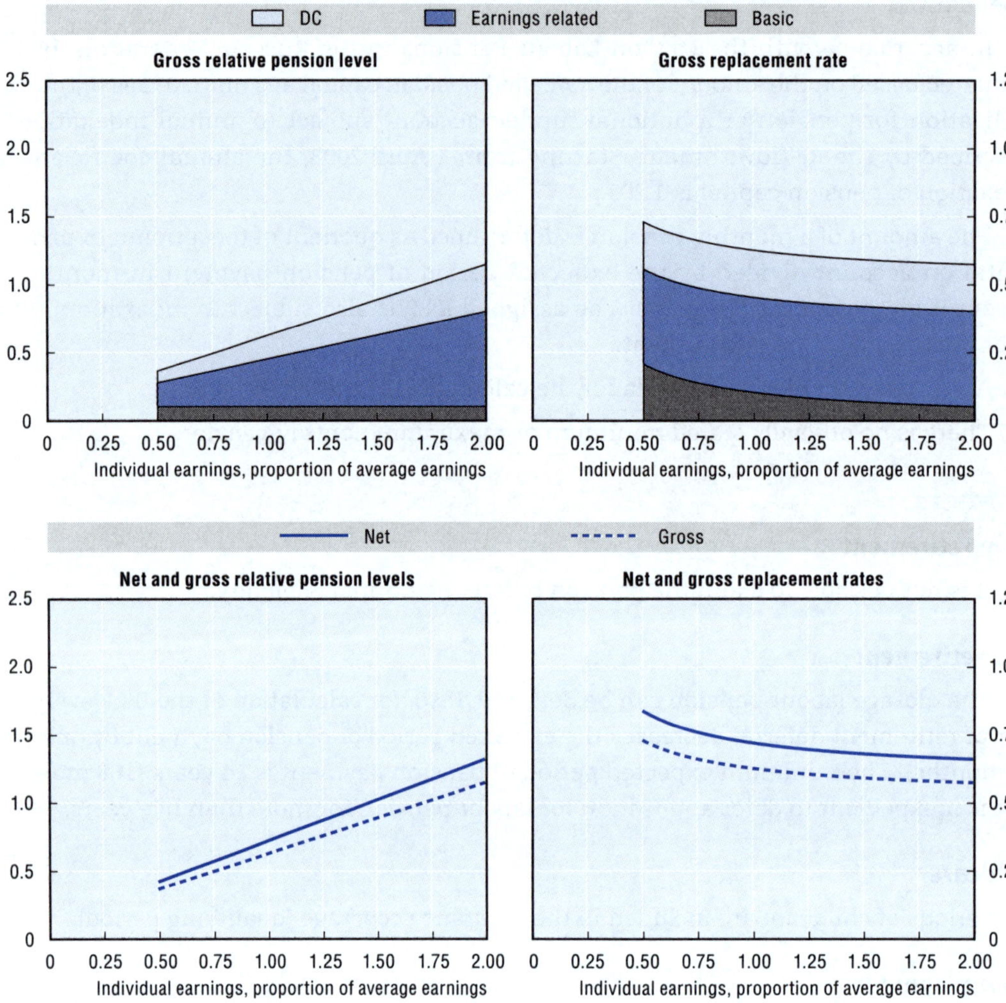

Men *Women (where different)*	Median earner	Individual earnings, multiple of average				
		0.5	0.75	1	1.5	2
Gross relative pension level	52.7	36.5	49.6	62.7	88.8	114.9
(% average gross earnings)	*46.9*	*32.9*	*44.2*	*55.5*	*78.1*	*100.6*
Net relative pension level	60.6	42.0	57.0	72.0	102.1	132.1
(% net average earnings)	*53.9*	*37.9*	*50.8*	*63.8*	*89.7*	*115.7*
Gross replacement rate	65.1	73.0	66.1	62.7	59.2	57.5
(% individual gross earnings)	*57.9*	*65.9*	*59.0*	*55.5*	*52.1*	*50.3*
Net replacement rate	74.8	83.9	76.0	72.0	68.0	66.1
(% individual net earnings)	*66.6*	*75.7*	*67.8*	*63.8*	*59.8*	*57.8*
Gross pension wealth	9.4	10.5	9.5	9.0	8.5	8.3
(multiple of individual gross earnings)	*11.9*	*13.5*	*12.1*	*11.4*	*10.7*	*10.3*
Net pension wealth	9.4	10.5	9.5	9.0	8.5	8.3
(multiple of individual gross earnings)	*11.9*	*13.5*	*12.1*	*11.4*	*10.7*	*10.3*

StatLink http://dx.doi.org/10.1787/888932371880

Saudi Arabia

Saudi Arabia: Pension system in 2008

Employees in the public and private sectors. Voluntary coverage for persons who are self-employed, are working abroad, or no longer satisfy the conditions for compulsory coverage.

Key indicators

		Saudi Arabia	OECD
Average earnings	SAR	32 600	152 500
	USD	8 700	40 600
Public pension spending	% of GDP		7.0
Life expectancy	At birth	73.1	78.9
	At age 65	79.5	83.1
Population over age 65	% of working-age population	5.3	23.6

Qualifying conditions

Age 60 (men) or age 55 (women) with at least 120 months of paid or credited contributions (credited contributions must not exceed 60 months).

Age 55 (men) with at least 120 months of contributions if engaged in arduous or unhealthy work.

Benefit calculation

Old-age pension

The pension is based on 2.5% of the insured's average monthly earnings during the last two years for each year of contributions, up to 100%.

The minimum monthly earnings for benefit calculation purposes are SAR 1 500 (SAR 1 200 for self-employed persons). The maximum monthly earnings for benefit calculation purposes are SAR 45 000.

The average monthly earnings for benefit calculation purposes must not exceed 150% of the insured's monthly earnings at the beginning of the last five-year contribution period.

If the insured's monthly earnings decrease during the last two years before retirement, special provisions apply to adjust the average monthly earnings used for benefit calculation purposes.

The minimum pension is SAR 1 725.

Old-age settlement

A lump sum is paid equal to 10% of the insured's average monthly earnings during the last two years before retirement for each month of the first five years of contributions plus 12% for each additional month.

Variant careers

Early retirement

At any age with at least 300 months of contributions and if no longer covered by the programme; at least 120 months of contribution if sentenced to prison for one or more years.

Late retirement

It is not possible to defer the pension.

Pension modelling results: Saudi Arabia

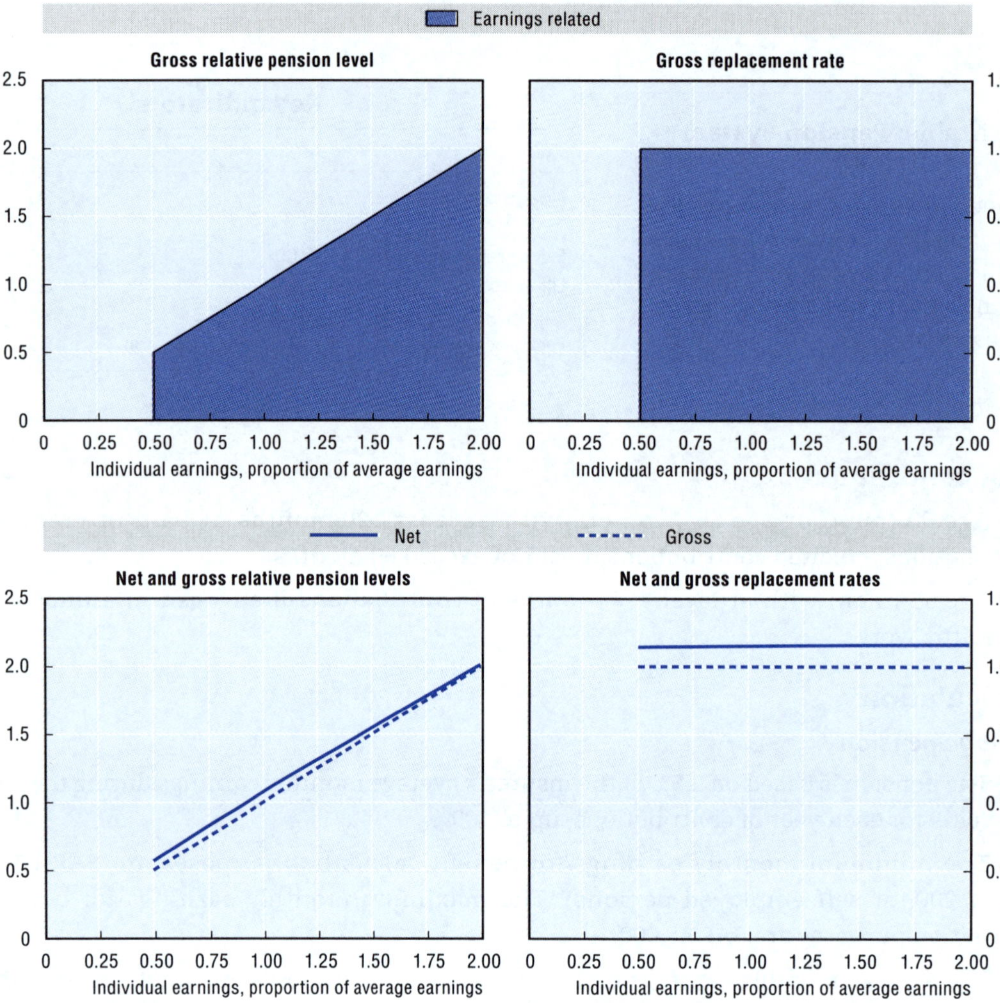

Men *Women (where different)*	Median earner	Individual earnings, multiple of average				
		0.5	0.75	1	1.5	2
Gross relative pension level	81.0	50.0	75.0	100.0	150.0	200.0
(% average gross earnings)	*70.9*	*43.8*	*65.6*	*87.5*	*131.3*	*175.0*
Net relative pension level	88.8	56.7	82.9	107.6	154.7	201.4
(% net average earnings)	*78.6*	*50.1*	*73.1*	*95.2*	*137.1*	*178.1*
Gross replacement rate	100.0	100.0	100.0	100.0	100.0	100.0
(% individual gross earnings)	*87.5*	*87.5*	*87.5*	*87.5*	*87.5*	*87.5*
Net replacement rate	107.4	107.2	107.4	107.6	108.0	108.2
(% individual net earnings)	*95.1*	*94.8*	*94.7*	*95.2*	*95.7*	*95.7*
Gross pension wealth	16.4	16.4	16.4	16.4	16.4	16.4
(multiple of individual gross earnings)	*18.8*	*18.8*	*18.8*	*18.8*	*18.8*	*18.8*
Net pension wealth	14.2	14.7	14.3	13.9	13.3	13.0
(multiple of individual gross earnings)	*16.5*	*17.0*	*16.5*	*16.2*	*15.5*	*15.1*

StatLink http://dx.doi.org/10.1787/888932371899

South Africa

South Africa: Pension system in 2008

The public pension is flat rate based on a residency test. There are also voluntary occupational schemes but coverage for these is not high.

Key indicators

		South Africa	OECD
Average earnings	ZAR	114 300	335 400
	USD	13 800	40 600
Public pension spending	% of GDP		7.0
Life expectancy	At birth	51.5	78.9
	At age 65	77.7	83.1
Population over age 65	% of working-age population	8.0	23.6

Qualifying conditions

The pension age in 2008 is 61 for men and 60 for women. However the age requirement for men has been lowered to 60 from April 2010.

Benefit calculation

Old-age pension

The pension is means-tested with individuals having an income of under ZAR 27 522 for singles and ZAR 58 224 for couples. The benefit amount is up to ZAR 1 010 per month for singles and ZAR 2 020 for couples. The average wage used for 2008 was ZAR 114 324.

Voluntary private pension

The default contribution rate for this scheme is 9% of earnings, divided equally between employees and employers.

Variant careers

Early retirement

It is not possible to claim the pension before the normal eligibility age of 60.

Late retirement

Receipt of the old-age pension is not dependent on retirement. It is therefore possible to combine pension and employment.

While people are not obliged to claim the public pension on reaching the qualifying age, there is no advantage in deferring a claim.

Childcare

Eventual public pension entitlement is not affected by periods out of paid work for caring purposes.

Unemployment

Eventual public pension entitlement is not affected by periods of unemployment.

Pension modelling results: South Africa

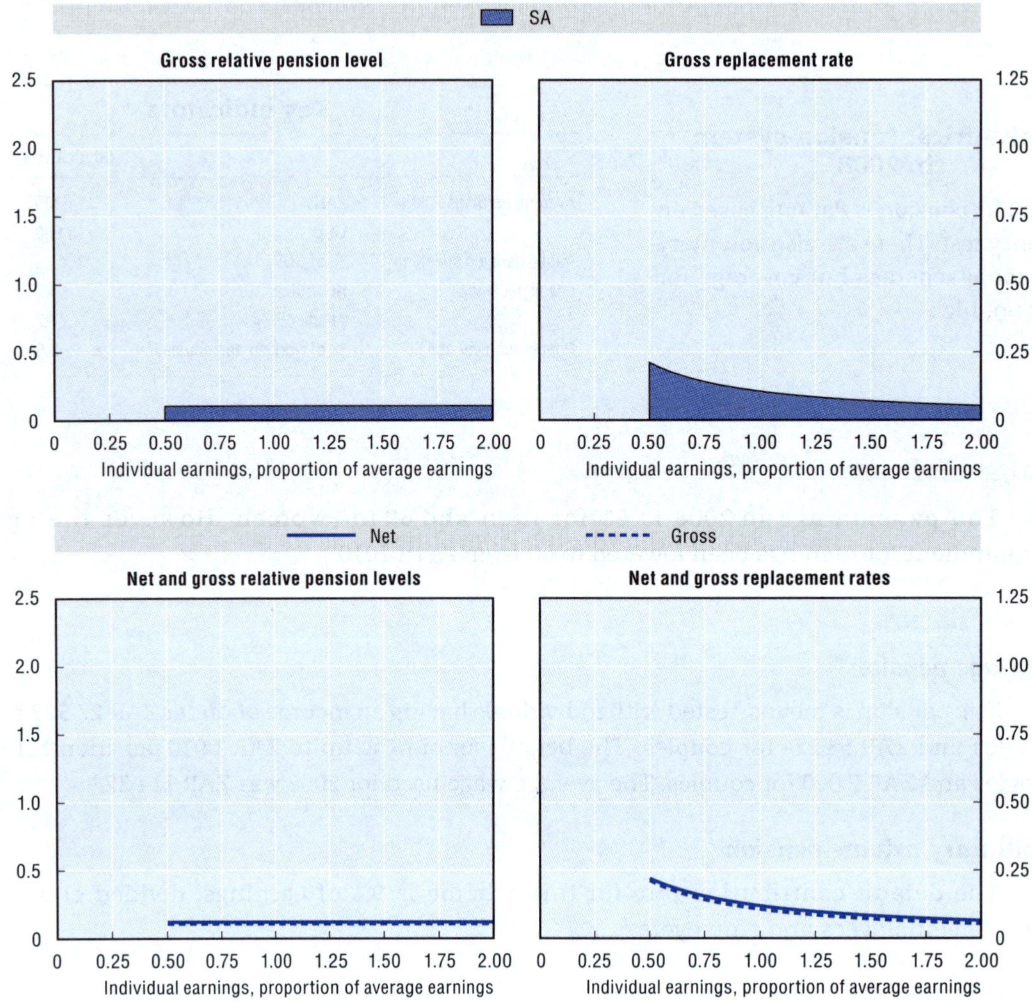

Men *Women (where different)*	Median earner	Individual earnings, multiple of average				
		0.5	0.75	1	1.5	2
Gross relative pension level	10.6	10.6	10.6	10.6	10.6	10.6
(% average gross earnings)						
Net relative pension level	11.9	11.9	11.9	11.9	11.9	11.9
(% net average earnings)						
Gross replacement rate	13.1	21.2	14.1	10.6	7.1	5.3
(% individual gross earnings)						
Net replacement rate	14.4	22.0	15.4	11.9	8.3	6.5
(% individual net earnings)						
Gross pension wealth	1.8	2.9	1.9	1.4	1.0	0.7
(multiple of individual gross earnings)	*2.2*	*3.5*	*2.4*	*1.8*	*1.2*	*0.9*
Net pension wealth	1.8	2.9	1.9	1.4	1.0	0.7
(multiple of individual gross earnings)	*2.2*	*3.5*	*2.4*	*1.8*	*1.2*	*0.9*

StatLink http://dx.doi.org/10.1787/888932371956

ORGANISATION FOR ECONOMIC CO-OPERATION AND DEVELOPMENT

The OECD is a unique forum where governments work together to address the economic, social and environmental challenges of globalisation. The OECD is also at the forefront of efforts to understand and to help governments respond to new developments and concerns, such as corporate governance, the information economy and the challenges of an ageing population. The Organisation provides a setting where governments can compare policy experiences, seek answers to common problems, identify good practice and work to co-ordinate domestic and international policies.

The OECD member countries are: Australia, Austria, Belgium, Canada, Chile, the Czech Republic, Denmark, Estonia, Finland, France, Germany, Greece, Hungary, Iceland, Ireland, Israel, Italy, Japan, Korea, Luxembourg, Mexico, the Netherlands, New Zealand, Norway, Poland, Portugal, the Slovak Republic, Slovenia, Spain, Sweden, Switzerland, Turkey, the United Kingdom and the United States. The European Commission takes part in the work of the OECD.

OECD Publishing disseminates widely the results of the Organisation's statistics gathering and research on economic, social and environmental issues, as well as the conventions, guidelines and standards agreed by its members.

OECD PUBLISHING, 2, rue André-Pascal, 75775 PARIS CEDEX 16
(81 2011 01 1 P) ISBN 978-92-64-09523-6 – No. 57749 2011